Argumentation and Debate

Critical Thinking for Reasoned Decision Making

TWELFTH EDITION

AUSTIN J. FREELEY
Late, John Carroll University

DAVID L. STEINBERG
University of Miami

WADSWORTH
CENGAGE Learning™

Australia • Brazil • Japan • Korea • Mexico • Singapore • Spain • United Kingdom • United States

Argumentation and Debate: Critical Thinking for Reasoned Decision Making, Twelfth Edition
Austin J. Freeley, Late
David L. Steinberg

Publisher: Lyn Uhl

Executive Editor: Monica Eckman

Assistant Editor: Kimberly Gengler

Editorial Assistant: Kimberly
  Apfelbaum

Associate Technology Project
  Manager: Jessica Badiner

Marketing Manager: Erin Mitchell

Marketing Assistant: Mary Anne
  Payumo

Associate Content Project Manager:
  Jessica Rasile

Art Director: Linda Helcher

Production Technology Analyst:
  Jamison MacLachlan

Print Buyer: Susan Carroll

Permissions Editor: Mardell
  Glinski-Schultz

Production Service: Newgen

Cover Designer: Ke Design

Cover Image: © Imagemore Co., Ltd.

Library of Congress Control Number: 2007941012

ISBN-13: 978-0-495-09590-3
ISBN-10: 0-495-09590-7

Wadsworth Cengage Learning
25 Thomson Place
Boston, MA 02210
USA

Cengage Learning products are represented in Canada by Nelson Education, Ltd.

For your course and learning solutions,
visit **academic.cengage.com**

Purchase any of our products at your local college store or at our preferred online store **www.ichapters.com**

Printed in the United States of America
1 2 3 4 5 6 7 12 11 10 09 08

To Dr. Austin J. Freeley and Trudy.
David L. Steinberg

Brief Contents

Contents

Preface

Now more than ever, debate is popular. During the 2008 election cycle, more than 40 televised debates involving the candidates for president and vice president will help to inform the voting public about the policies and personalities of the competing debaters. Election campaigns at every level, from local to national offices, routinely involve formal debates. The Urban Debate League movement has expanded local public school participation in competitive debate, and international efforts have encouraged the growth of debate around the globe. Academic debate on campuses is vibrant, and students get in line to take debate courses.

The twelfth edition of *Argumentation and Debate* continues the features that have led to its wide use by "generations" of students for over 50 years, while reflecting the newest trends and knowledge in the practice and study of argumentation and debate. To that end, David L. Steinberg continues to build upon the groundbreaking work of Austin J. Freeley, the author of the first nine editions. Dr. Freeley passed away on January 14, 2005. His words form the foundation of this book and the inspiration for its evolution. Although the fundamental nature of educational debate was established in classical times by Aristotle, Protagoras, and the scholars who followed them through the ages, contemporary debate continues to change and evolve at an ever-increasing rate. Along with many updates and revisions, this edition provides timely material on:

- Concept Boxes (key concepts set aside in boxes in bulleted lists or key word format)
- Updated examples
- References to new research about debate and argumentation
- Addition of new and tested classroom exercises
- Expanded discussion of ethical decision making
- Description of the research process in the wired era

- Explanation of performance as argumentation
- Updated presidential debate (2004) and expanded discussion of political debates through the "YouTube" debates of 2007
- Expanded links to debate resources
- Expanded bibliography
- "Flowcharts" identifying Speaker duties in Policy and Value Debate Formats

Most chapters provide a miniglossary of terms and conclude with a set of suggested exercises designed to provide experiential learning of the chapter's concepts. Throughout the text many important materials are presented in insets that we hope will prove helpful to the student.

This book is designed for all who seek to improve their critical thinking, reasoned decision making, and advocacy skills. In particular this text is designed for the undergraduate course in argumentation and debate. It is appropriate for any course that empowers students as active citizens participating in the societal demands of democracy.

Austin J. Freeley recorded his thanks to his professors, mentors, and friends in the first edition of this book. The memory of their contributions is luminous across the years.

David L. Steinberg would like to record his thanks to his debate mentors, David Thomas, Norma Cook, Jim Brooks, Warren Decker, and Brenda Logue, and his terrific assistant coaches for teaching him far more than he could teach them. His sincere thanks go to each of them, including Dan Leyton, Dale Reed, Ernie Quierido, David Cram-Helwich, Christopher Cooper, Nicole Colston, Gavin Williams, Matt Grindy, Nicole Richter, Kenny McCaffrey, and Johnny Prieur. Johnny's work inspired and informed the updates on research and evidence organization in Chapter 5.

He would also like to acknowledge his boys, Adam and John, who make him very proud, and his supportive and caring wife, Victoria, with much love.

Steinberg is grateful to Dr. Freeley for giving him the opportunity to contribute to this project and, thus, to be a small part of his tremendous legacy.

Thanks to all the wonderful people at Cengage who work hard to make this book a reality, including Kimberly Gengler, Monica Eckman, Jessica Rasile, and Smitha Pillai, who are exceptionally patient, professional, and understanding.

Finally, thanks to the many students we have taught and judged over the years, and those who will carry the tradition into the future. They are our inspiration, helping us refine our thinking and develop more cogent statements on many matters, and have provided many of the examples found throughout this text.

David L. Steinberg

1

Critical Thinking

After several days of intense debate, first the United States House of Representatives and then the U.S. Senate voted to authorize President George W. Bush to attack Iraq if Saddam Hussein refused to give up weapons of mass destruction as required by United Nations's resolutions. Debate about a possible military action against Iraq continued in various governmental bodies and in the public for six months, until President Bush ordered an attack on Baghdad, beginning Operation Iraqi Freedom, the military campaign against the Iraqi regime of Saddam Hussein. He did so despite the unwillingness of the U.N. Security Council to support the military action, and in the face of significant international opposition.

Meanwhile, and perhaps equally difficult for the parties involved, a young couple deliberated over whether they should purchase a large home to accommodate their growing family or should sacrifice living space to reside in an area with better public schools; elsewhere a college sophomore reconsidered his major and a senior her choice of law school, graduate school, or a job. Each of these situations called for decisions to be made. Each decision maker worked hard to make well-reasoned decisions.

Decision making is a thoughtful process of choosing among a variety of options for acting or thinking. It requires that the decider make a choice. Life demands decision making. We make countless individual decisions every day. To make some of those decisions, we work hard to employ care and consideration; others seem to just happen. Couples, families, groups of friends, and coworkers come together to make choices, and decision-making bodies from committees to juries to the U.S. Congress and the United Nations make decisions that impact us all. Every profession requires effective and ethical decision making, as do our school, community, and social organizations.

We all make many decisions every day. To refinance or sell one's home, to buy a high-performance SUV or an economical hybrid car, what major to select, what to have for dinner, what candidate to vote for, paper or plastic, all present us with choices. Should the president deal with an international crisis through military invasion or diplomacy? How should the U.S. Congress act to address illegal immigration?

Miniglossary

Argumentation   Reason giving in communicative situations by people whose purpose is the justification of acts, beliefs, attitudes, and values.

Coercion   The threat or use of force.

Critical thinking   The ability to analyze, criticize, and advocate ideas; to reason inductively and deductively; and to reach factual or judgmental conclusions based on sound inferences drawn from unambiguous statements of knowledge or belief.

Debate   The process of inquiry and advocacy; the seeking of a reasoned judgment on a proposition.

Deontological ethics   An ethical approach that is process- or act-oriented, and is based on the notion that actions have moral value.

Ethics   A set of constructs that guide our decision making by providing standards of behavior telling us how we ought to act.

Good reasons   Reasons that are psychologically compelling for a given audience, that make further inquiry both unnecessary and redundant—hence justifying a decision to affirm or reject a proposition.

Persuasion   Communication intended to influence the acts, beliefs, attitudes, and values of others.

Propaganda   The use of persuasion by a group (often a closely knit organization) in a sustained, organized campaign using multiple media for the purpose of influencing a mass audience.

Teleological ethics   An ethical approach that is results oriented, and would focus on the good or bad consequences of an action or a decision.

Is the defendant guilty as accused? *The Daily Show* or the ball game? And upon what information should I rely to make my decision?

Certainly some of these decisions are more consequential than others. Which amendment to vote for, what television program to watch, what course to take, which phone plan to purchase, and which diet to pursue all present unique challenges. At our best, we seek out research and data to inform our decisions. Yet even the choice of which information to attend to requires decision making. In 2006, *TIME* magazine named YOU its "Person of the Year." Congratulations! Its selection was based on the participation not of "great men" in the creation of history, but rather on the contributions of a community of anonymous participants in the evolution of information. Through blogs, online networking, YouTube, Facebook, MySpace, Wikipedia, and many other "wikis," knowledge and "truth" are created from the bottom up, bypassing the authoritarian control of newspeople, academics, and publishers. We have access to infinite quantities of information, but how do we sort through it and select the best information for our needs?

The ability of every decision maker to make good, reasoned, and ethical decisions relies heavily upon their ability to think critically. Critical thinking enables one to break argumentation down to its component parts in order to evaluate its relative validity and strength. Critical thinkers are better users of information, as well as better advocates.

Colleges and universities expect their students to develop their **critical thinking** skills and may require students to take designated courses to that end. The importance and value of such study is widely recognized.

The executive order establishing California's requirement states:

> Instruction in *critical thinking* is designed to achieve an understanding of the relationship of language to logic, which would lead to *the ability to analyze, criticize, and advocate ideas, to reason inductively and deductively, and to reach factual or judgmental conclusions based on sound inferences drawn from unambiguous statements of knowledge or belief.* The minimal competence to be expected at the successful conclusion of instruction in critical thinking should be the ability to distinguish fact from judgment, belief from knowledge, and skills in elementary inductive and deductive processes, including an understanding of the formal and informal fallacies of language and thought.

Competency in critical thinking is a prerequisite to participating effectively in human affairs, pursuing higher education, and succeeding in the highly competitive world of business and the professions. Michael Scriven and Richard Paul for the National Council for Excellence in Critical Thinking Instruction argued that the effective critical thinker:

- raises vital questions and problems, formulating them clearly and precisely;

- gathers and assesses relevant information, using abstract ideas to interpret it effectively; comes to well-reasoned conclusions and solutions, testing them against relevant criteria and standards;

- thinks open-mindedly within alternative systems of thought, recognizing and assessing, as need be, their assumptions, implications, and practical consequences; and

- communicates effectively with others in figuring out solutions to complex problems.

They also observed that critical thinking "entails effective communication and problem solving abilities and a commitment to overcome our native egocentrism and sociocentrism."[1] Debate as a classroom exercise and as a mode of thinking and behaving uniquely promotes development of each of these skill sets. Since classical times, debate has been one of the best methods of learning and applying the

---

1. Michael Scriven and Richard Paul, "Defining Critical Thinking," The Critical
Thinking Community, http://www.criticalthinking.org/aboutCT/definingCT.shtml.

Critical Thinking

- Life demands decision making
- The ability to make reasoned decisions relies on critical thinking
- Critical thinking enables analysis and evaluation of arguments
- Critical thinking improves the use of information as well as advocacy
- Teaching and learning critical thinking are important roles of education
- Debate teaches critical thinking

---

principles of critical thinking. Contemporary research confirms the value of debate. One study concluded:

> The impact of public communication training on the critical thinking ability of the participants is demonstrably positive. This summary of existing research reaffirms what many ex-debaters and others in forensics, public speaking, mock trial, or argumentation would support: participation improves the thinking of those involved.[2]

In particular, debate education improves the ability to think critically. In a comprehensive review of the relevant research, Kent Colbert concluded, "The debate–critical thinking literature provides presumptive proof favoring a positive debate–critical thinking relationship."[3]

Much of the most significant communication of our lives is conducted in the form of debates. These may take place in intrapersonal communications, in which we weigh the pros and cons of an important decision in our own minds, or they may take place in interpersonal communications, in which we listen to arguments intended to influence our decision or participate in exchanges to influence the decisions of others.

Our success or failure in life is largely determined by our ability to make wise decisions for ourselves and to influence the decisions of others in ways that are beneficial to us. Much of our significant, purposeful activity is concerned with making decisions. Whether to join a campus organization, go to graduate school, accept a job offer, buy a car or house, move to another city, invest in a certain stock, or vote for Garcia—these are just a few of the thousands of decisions we may have to make. Often, intelligent self-interest or a sense of responsibility will require us to win the support of others. We may want a scholarship or a particular job for ourselves, a customer for our product, or a vote for our favored political candidate.

---

2. Mike Allen, Sandra Berkowitz, Steve Hunt, and Allan Louden, "A Meta-Analysis of the Impact of Forensics and Communication Education on Critical Thinking," *Communication Education,* vol. 48, no. 1 (Jan. 1999), p. 28.
3. Kent Colbert, "Enhancing Critical Thinking Ability Through Academic Debate," *Contemporary Argumentation and Debate: The Journal of the Cross Examination Debate Association,* vol. 16 (1995), p. 69.

Good Reasons

- Argumentation relies on good reasons
- Good reasons are audience-based justifications for or against propositions
- Good reasons differ by audience and are therefore, impacted by culture
- Argumentation guides decision making

Some people make decisions by flipping a coin. Others act on a whim or respond unconsciously to "hidden persuaders." If the problem is trivial—such as whether to go to a concert or a film—the particular method used is unimportant. For more crucial matters, however, mature adults require a reasoned means of decision making. Decisions should be justified by good reasons based on accurate evidence and valid reasoning.

Argumentation is reason giving in communicative situations by people whose purpose is the justification of acts, beliefs, attitudes, and values—a definition based on language adopted at the National Developmental Conference on Forensics.[4] British philosopher Stephen Toulmin makes a similar point when he asks, "What kind of *justificatory activities* must we engage in to convince our fellows that these beliefs are based on 'good reasons'?"[5] **Good reasons** may be defined as "reasons which are psychologically compelling for a given audience, which make further inquiry both unnecessary and redundant—hence justifying a decision to affirm or reject a proposition."[6]

Note that what constitutes good reasons for one audience may not be good reasons for another. When Taslina Nasrin wrote her novella *Lajja (Shame)*, she became a target of Muslim fundamentalists. Their fury mounted when she was quoted—or misquoted, she insists—as saying that the Koran should be "revised thoroughly" to give equal rights to women. After all, Islam's central article of faith is that the Koran is the literal word of God and is thus above revision. Nasrin's challenge thus was seen as blasphemy and prompted legal charges and Muslim *fatwas,* or religious decrees, calling for her death:

> A crowd of 100,000 demonstrators gathered outside the Parliament building in Dhaka to bay for her blood.... One particularly militant faction threatened to loose thousands of poisonous snakes in the capital unless she was executed.[7]

---

4. James H. McBath, ed., *Forensics as Communication* (Skokie, Ill.: National Textbook, 1975), p. 11.
5. Stephen Toulmin, *Knowing and Acting* (New York: Macmillan, 1976), p. 138.
6. David Zarefsky, "Criteria for Evaluating Non-Policy Argument," in *Perspectives on Non-Policy Argument,* ed. Don Brownlee, sponsored by CEDA (privately published, 1980), p. 10.
7. *Time,* Aug. 15, 1994, p. 26.

This incident provides a dramatic example of cultural differences. To Muslim fundamentalists in Bangladesh, even being suspected of calling for a revision of the Koran is a "good reason" for execution.

In most of the world and for most Muslims, "blasphemy" is not perceived as a good reason for death. In America, freedom of the press, enshrined in the First Amendment to the Constitution, is perceived as a good reason for allowing an author to express just about any opinion. A debater needs to discover the justificatory activities that the decision renderers will accept and to develop the good reasons that will lead them to agree with the desired conclusion—or, of course, to reject the reasons advanced by an opponent.

First we will consider debate as a method of critical thinking and reasoned decision making. Then we will look at some other methods of decision making and see how they relate to argumentation and debate.

I. DEBATE

Debate is the process of inquiry and advocacy, a way of arriving at a reasoned judgment on a proposition. Individuals may use debate to reach a decision in their own minds; alternatively, individuals or groups may use it to bring others around to their way of thinking.

Debate provides reasoned arguments for and against a proposition. It requires two competitive sides engaging in a bipolar clash of support for and against that proposition. Because it requires that listeners and opposing advocates comparatively evaluate competing choices, debate demands critical thinking. Society, like individuals, must have an effective method of making decisions. A free society is structured in such a way that many of its decisions are arrived at through debate. For example, law courts and legislative bodies are designed to utilize debate as their means of reaching decisions. In fact, any organization that conducts its business according to parliamentary procedures has selected debate as its method. Debate pervades our society at decision-making levels.

The ancient Greeks were among the first to recognize the importance of debate for both the individual and society. Plato, whose dialogues were an early form of cross-examination debate, defined *rhetoric* as "a universal art of winning the mind by arguments, which means not merely arguments in the courts of justice, and all other sorts of public councils, but in private conference as well."[8]

Aristotle listed four functions for rhetoric.[9] First, it prevents the triumph of fraud and injustice. Aristotle argued that truth and justice are by nature more powerful than their opposites, so when poor decisions are made, speakers with right on their side have only themselves to blame. Thus, it is not enough to know the right decision ourselves; we also must be able to argue for that decision before others.

---

8. Plato, *Phaedrus*, 261. Translators Cooper and Jowett use slightly different terms in interpreting this passage. This statement draws from both translations.
9. See Aristotle, *Rhetoric*, I, 1.

Second, rhetoric is a method of instruction for the public. Aristotle pointed out that in some situations scientific arguments are useless; a speaker has to "educate" the audience by framing arguments with the help of common knowledge and commonly accepted opinions. Congressional debates on health care or tax policies are examples of this. The general public, and for that matter the majority of Congress, is unable to follow highly sophisticated technical arguments. Skilled partisans who have the expertise to understand the technical data must reformulate their reasons in ways that both Congress and the public can grasp.

Third, rhetoric makes us see both sides of a case. By arguing both sides, we become aware of all aspects of the case, and we will be prepared to refute our opponents' arguments.

Fourth, rhetoric is a means of defense. Often knowledge of argumentation and debate will be necessary to protect ourselves and our interests. As Aristotle stated: "If it is a disgrace to a man when he cannot defend himself in a bodily way, it would be odd not to think him disgraced when he cannot defend himself with reason. Reason is more distinctive of man than is bodily effort." Similarly, in the nineteenth century, John Stuart Mill placed great emphasis on the value of debate:

> If even the Newtonian philosophy were not permitted to be questioned, mankind could not feel as complete assurance of its truth as they now [in 1858] do. The beliefs which we have the most warrant for, have no safeguard to rest on, but a standing invitation to the whole world to prove them unfounded. If the challenge is not accepted, or is accepted and the attempt fails, we are far enough from certainty still; but we have done the best that the existing state of human reason admits of; we have neglected nothing that could give the truth the chance of reaching us; if the lists are kept open, we may hope that if there be a better truth, it will be found when the human mind is capable of receiving it; and in the meantime we may rely on having attained such approach to truth as is possible in our day. This is the amount of certainty attainable by a fallible being, and this is the sole way of attaining it.[10]

Half a century ago the United States Senate designated as Senate Immortals five senators who had shaped the history of the country by their ability as debaters: Henry Clay, Daniel Webster, John C. Calhoun, Robert M. La Follette, Sr., and Robert A. Taft. The triumvirate of Webster, Clay, and Calhoun especially towered over all the others and were the near-unanimous choices of senators and scholars alike. As John F. Kennedy, then a freshman senator, pointed out, "For over thirty years they dominated the Congress and the country, providing leadership and articulation on all the great issues of the growing nation."[11] For their part La Follette and Taft were selected as the outstanding representatives of,

10. John Stuart Mill, *On Liberty* (New York: Burt, n.d.), pp. 38–39.
11. John F. Kennedy, Senate speech, May 1, 1957, from a press release.

respectively, the progressive and the conservative movements in the twentieth century. In honoring these "immortals," the Senate recognized the importance of debate in determining the course of American history.

Our laws not only are made through the process of debate but are applied through debate as well. Today's trial attorneys cite the famous dictum of attorney Joseph N. Welch as a guide for contemporary legal practices:

> America believes in what lawyers call "the adversary system" in our courtrooms, including our criminal courts. It is our tradition that the District Attorney prosecutes hard. Against him is the lawyer hired by the defendant, or supplied by the court if the defendant is indigent. And the defendant's lawyer defends hard. We believe that truth is apt to emerge from this crucible. It usually does.[12]

We need debate not only in the legislature and the courtroom but in every other area of society as well. Most of our rights are directly or indirectly dependent on debate. As the influential journalist Walter Lippmann pointed out, one of our most cherished rights—freedom of speech—can be maintained only by creating and encouraging debate:

> Yet when genuine debate is lacking, freedom of speech does not work as it is meant to work. It has lost the principle which regulates and justifies it—that is to say, dialectic conducted according to logic and the rules of evidence. If there is no effective debate, the unrestricted right to speak will unloose so many propagandists, procurers, and panderers upon the public that sooner or later in self-defense the people will turn to the censors to protect them. It will be curtailed for all manner of reasons and pretexts, and serve all kinds of good, foolish, or sinister ends.
>
> For in the absence of debate unrestricted utterance leads to the degradation of opinion. By a kind of Gresham's law the more rational is overcome by the less rational, and the opinions that will prevail will be those which are held most ardently by those with the most passionate will. For that reason the freedom to speak can never be maintained by objecting to interference with the liberty of the press, of printing, of broadcasting, of the screen. It can be maintained only by promoting debate.[13]

We need debate both to maintain freedom of speech and to provide a methodology for investigation of and judgment about contemporary problems. As Chaim Perelman, the Belgian philosopher-rhetorician whose works in rhetoric and argumentation are influential in argumentation and debate, pointed out:

---

12. Joseph N. Welch, "Should a Lawyer Defend a Guilty Man?" *This Week* magazine, Dec. 6, 1959, p. 11. Copyright 1959 by the United Newspapers Magazine Corporation.
13. Walter Lippmann, *Essays in the Public Philosophy* (Boston: Little, Brown, 1955), pp. 129–130.

If we assume it to be possible without recourse to violence to reach agreement on all the problems implied in the employment of the idea of justice we are granting the possibility of formulating an ideal of man and society, valid for all beings endowed with reason and accepted by what we have called elsewhere the universal audience.[14]

I think that the only discursive methods available to us stem from techniques that are not demonstrative—that is, conclusive and *rational* in the narrow sense of the term—but from argumentative techniques which are not conclusive but which may tend to demonstrate the *reasonable* character of the conceptions put forward. It is this recourse to the rational and reasonable for the realization of the ideal of universal communion that characterizes the age-long endeavor of all philosophies in their aspiration for a city of man in which violence may progressively give way to wisdom.[15]

Here we have touched on the long-standing concern of philosophers and political leaders with debate as an instrument for dealing with society's problems. We can now understand why debate is pervasive. Individuals benefit from knowing the principles of argumentation and debate and from being able to apply these principles in making decisions and influencing the decisions of others. Society benefits if debate is encouraged, because free and open debate protects the rights of individuals and offers the larger society a way of reaching optimal decisions.

II. INDIVIDUAL DECISIONS

Whenever an individual controls the dimensions of a problem, he or she can solve the problem through a personal decision. For example, if the problem is whether to go to the basketball game tonight, if tickets are not too expensive and if transportation is available, the decision can be made individually. But if a friend's car is needed to get to the game, then that person's decision to furnish the transportation must be obtained.

Complex problems, too, are subject to individual decision making. American business offers many examples of small companies that grew into major corporations while still under the individual control of the founder. Some computer companies that began in the 1970s as one-person operations burgeoned into multimillion-dollar corporations with the original inventor still making all the major decisions. And some of the multibillion-dollar leveraged buyouts of the 1980s were put together by daring—some would say greedy—financiers who made the day-to-day and even hour-to-hour decisions individually.

---

14. Chaim Perelman and L. Olbrechts-Tyteca, *Traite de l'argumentation, La nouvelle rhetorique* (Paris: Presses Universitaires de France, 1958), sec. 7.
15. Chaim Perelman, *The Idea of Justice and the Problem of Argument,* trans. John Petrie (New York: Humanities Press, 1963), pp. 86–87.

When President George H. W. Bush launched Operation Desert Storm, when President Bill Clinton sent troops into Somalia and Haiti and authorized Operation Desert Fox, and when President George W. Bush authorized Operation Enduring Freedom in Afghanistan and Operation Iraqi Freedom in Iraq, they each used different methods of decision making, but in each case the ultimate decision was an individual one. In fact, many government decisions can be made only by the president. As Walter Lippmann pointed out, debate is the only satisfactory way the great issues can be decided:

> A president, whoever he is, has to find a way of understanding the novel and changing issues which he must, under the Constitution, decide. Broadly speaking ... the president has two ways of making up his mind. The one is to turn to his subordinates—to his chiefs of staff and his cabinet officers and undersecretaries and the like—and to direct them to argue out the issues and to bring him an agreed decision....
>
> The other way is to sit like a judge at a hearing where the issues to be decided are debated. After he has heard the debate, after he has examined the evidence, after he has heard the debaters cross-examine one another, after he has questioned them himself, he makes his decision....
>
> It is a much harder method in that it subjects the president to the stress of feeling the full impact of conflicting views, and then to the strain of making his decision, fully aware of how momentous it is. But there is no other satisfactory way by which momentous and complex issues can be decided.[16]

John F. Kennedy used Cabinet sessions and National Security Council meetings to provide debate to illuminate diverse points of view, expose errors, and challenge assumptions before he reached decisions.[17] As he gained experience in office, he placed greater emphasis on debate. One historian points out: "One reason for the difference between the Bay of Pigs and the missile crisis was that [the Bay of Pigs] fiasco instructed Kennedy in the importance of uninhibited debate in advance of major decision."[18] All presidents, to varying degrees, encourage debate among their advisors.

We may never be called on to render the final decision on great issues of national policy, but we are constantly concerned with decisions important to ourselves for which debate can be applied in similar ways. That is, this debate may take place in our minds as we weigh the pros and cons of the problem, or we may arrange for others to debate the problem for us. Because we all are increasingly involved in the decisions of the campus, community, and society in

---

16. Walter Lippmann, "How to Make Decisions," *New York Herald Tribune*, Mar. 3, 1960.
17. See Theodore C. Sorensen, *Decision-Making in the White House* (New York: Columbia University Press, 1963), p. 59.
18. Arthur M. Schlesinger, Jr., *Imperial Presidency* (Boston: Houghton Mifflin, 1973), p. 215.

Standard Agenda for Group Decision Making
■ Define and analyze the problem ■ Research the problem ■ Establish criteria ■ Generate solutions ■ Select best solution ■ Implement and monitor solution

general, it is in our intelligent self-interest to reach these decisions through reasoned debate.

When we make an individual decision, we can put it into effect if we control the necessary conditions. If we need the consent or cooperation of others to carry out our decision, we have to find a way of obtaining the appropriate response from them by debate—or by group discussion, persuasion, propaganda, coercion, or a combination of methods.

III. GROUP DISCUSSION

Decisions may be reached by group discussion when the members of the group (1) agree that a problem exists, (2) have compatible standards or values, (3) have compatible purposes, (4) are willing to accept the consensus of the group, and (5) are relatively few in number. When these conditions are met and when all relevant evidence and arguments are carefully weighed, group discussion is a reasoned means of decision making.

In February 1999, after the bitter and divisive House impeachment proceedings and subsequent Senate trial, President Bill Clinton was acquitted on two articles of impeachment. The vote on impeachment in the House occurred on straight party lines. Although there were some Republican defectors in the Senate vote, partisan tensions were heightened by the trial, as were tensions between the legislative and executive branches of the government. Despite the clash of personalities and the difficulties inherent in such partisan and interbranch differences, House and Senate leaders and President Clinton pledged to work together for the good of the country. Indeed a strength of American politics is that skilled leaders in both parties traditionally have been able to override political differences and enact at least some important legislation on which both parties could agree.

When a group has more than 15 or 20 members, productive discussion becomes difficult if not impossible. A group of senators can discuss a problem in committee, but not on the floor of the Senate. The Senate is too large for discussion; there debate must be used. Of course, informal debate may take place within the discussion process, and discussion may be a precursor of debate.[19] If the differences cannot be solved by discussion, debate is the logical alternative. Or if the group, such as a Senate subcommittee, reaches a decision by discussion, it may be necessary to debate it on the floor to carry the Senate as a whole.

Group decision making is best guided by a systematic procedure for problem solving. The first step requires that group members define and analyze the problem they are to address. They should determine the nature of the problem and its impacts, distinguishing causes from symptoms and measuring the relative importance of each. An important outcome of this step is an agreed upon statement of the problem. Second, they should research the problem, gathering and evaluating available information relevant to the problem as defined. The third step is perhaps the most important, and most often overlooked: establishing and prioritizing the criteria that will distinguish a successful solution. These criteria may be given numerical value. Fourth, the group members should generate a list of possible solutions through a process of brainstorming; and fifth, they should apply the criteria to the established list to select the best solution. Finally, the sixth step is to implement and monitor the solution, leading to reevaluation and in many situations, a return to step one.

Like an individual, a group may act on its decision only insofar as it has the power to do so. If it needs the consent or cooperation of others to carry out a particular plan, the group must use other means to secure their cooperation.

IV. PERSUASION

Purposeful **persuasion** is defined as *communication intended to influence the acts, beliefs, attitudes, and values of others.* Clearly, one method of persuasion is debate. Persuasion is not, however, limited to seeking carefully reasoned judgments, as is debate, nor does persuasion require logical arguments both for and against a given proposition. The "Marlboro Man" advertising campaign, for example, must have been judged as highly effective persuasion by the company that ran it for many years, but it did not seek the kind of carefully thought-out judgment that one associates with debate.

Frequently the persuader hopes to dominate the stage and avoid situations in which another side of the argument might be presented. Consider the cigarette companies, which accepted the ban on TV advertising without the prolonged court battle that many expected. The reason for this may have been that the TV stations were required to give equal time to public service announcements about the hazards of smoking. The tobacco companies apparently found it preferable to direct their advertising dollars to media that did not have an equal-time requirement. President Hugo Chavez of Venezuela recently made international headlines and prompted national protests when he failed to renew the license of

19. See James H. McBurney, James M. O'Neill, and Glen E. Mills, *Argumentation and Debate* (New York: Macmillan, 1951), p. 67.

Radio Caracas Television (RCTV), a popular television network, likely because it had been critical of him, thus effectively eliminating local opposition to his government.[20]

Persuaders select the type of persuasive appeals they believe to be best adapted to their audience. These may include such diverse communications as a picket line, a silent prayer vigil, a clever negative political commercial on TV, or the stately formality of a debate before the Supreme Court. (Audience analysis is considered in Chapter 15.)

Persuaders reach a decision on the problem before they begin the process of persuasion. They continue the process of persuasion until they solve the problem by persuading others to accept their decision or until they are convinced that further efforts are pointless. In trying to influence others, they may find it necessary or advantageous (1) to join with other persuaders and become propagandists or (2) to face the opposition and become debaters. Thus they must be familiar with the principles of argumentation and debate. This knowledge is also a defense against the persuasion of others. If we subject their appeals to critical analysis, we increase our likelihood of making reasoned decisions. And if persuaders advocate a decision we believe to be unsound, we may find it necessary to become debaters and advocate the conclusion we favor.

Unintended persuasion occurs when we receive a message not intended for us—for example, we overhear a private conversation in an elevator and are influenced by it—or when we unknowingly communicate to and influence others in an unintended way.

V. PROPAGANDA

Propaganda is the use of persuasion by a group (often a closely knit organization) in a sustained, organized campaign using multiple media for the purpose of influencing a mass audience. Historically propaganda has been associated with religious, social, or political movements. Today the term has been expanded to include commercial advertising campaigns. The term first came into common use in 1622 when Pope Gregory XV established the Sacred Congregation for Propagating the Faith. What, in the view of the faithful, could be more commendable than spreading the faith? In 1933, when Hitler appointed Dr. Joseph Goebbels as his minister of propaganda, the word took on a different connotation. From the standpoint of non-Nazis, what could be more evil than spreading Nazism? Even today *propaganda* often is perceived as a pejorative term. Imagine an official of a women's group saying:

> We've been conducting an extensive educational campaign to inform
> the public of the necessity of making abortion on demand available to

20. Christopher Toothaker, "Chavez Warns Foreign Critics," *The Miami Herald,* July 23, 2007, p. 8A.

women on welfare. It was going very well until the churches unleashed a bunch of propagandists to work against us.

Thus, in everyday language, *we* educate or give information, while *they* propagandize. Another example is President Chavez of Venezuela. He spoke to the United Nations in 2007, referring to President George Bush as "the devil." Later Chavez threatened to deport international visitors from Venezuela who were critical of him and his government.

Of course, the end does not justify the means. Propaganda, like persuasion, may be viewed as good or bad only to the degree that it is based on true evidence and valid reasoning. Examples of questionable methods may be found in the Allied propaganda in the United States prior to America's entry into World War I. At that time extensive use was made of distorted or false atrocity stories. Other examples may be found in communist propaganda from the former Soviet Union, which made extensive use of the technique of the "big lie." During Middle East crises both Israel and the Arab countries have conducted propaganda campaigns in the United States designed to sway public opinion in their favor. Each side obviously thinks of theirs as good and the other's as bad.

Examples of propaganda used for good purposes include the various campaigns designed to get the public to drive safely, to recognize the symptoms of cancer, and to practice safe sex; these examples are usually based on sound evidence and reasonable inference. Other examples include campaigns by churches to persuade people to act in accordance with the Ten Commandments and by charitable groups to raise funds for the homeless or for people with AIDS. Propagandists reach a decision on a problem before they begin the process of propaganda. They continue their campaign until they solve the problem by persuading others to accept their decision or are convinced that further efforts are pointless. In their efforts to influence others, propagandists may find it necessary or advantageous to confront their opponents and become debaters. In such cases they need knowledge of argumentation and debate. If their evidence is accurate, their reasoning valid, and their appeals chosen carefully, the campaign will have the greatest opportunity for success. If any of the conditions is lacking, however, the chances for success are diminished.

Similarly, knowledge of argumentation and debate is an important defense against the propaganda campaigns we constantly confront. Unless we subject propaganda to critical analysis, we will be unable to distinguish the good from the bad. We will lose our ability to make reasonable decisions and may fall prey to "hidden persuaders."

VI. COERCION

Coercion is defined as the threat or use of force. Parents employ coercion when they take a box of matches from a baby; society employs coercion when it confines criminals to prison; the nation employs coercion when it goes to war. A democratic society places many restrictions on the exercise of coercion. Parents

Methods of Decision Making

- Debate
- Individual Decision
- Group Decision
- Propaganda
- Coercion
- Combination of Methods

may not physically or mentally abuse their children; criminals may be sentenced to prison only after they have an opportunity to defend themselves in court; the United States may declare war only after the advocates of war win consent in Congress. President Bush found it prudent to obtain congressional approval for the use of force in Operation Enduring Freedom in Afghanistan and Operation Iraqi Freedom. In a democratic society coercion as a method of solving problems—by private individuals or the state—is generally prohibited except in special cases in which it has been found necessary after debate. A totalitarian society, by contrast, is characterized by sharply limited debate and by almost omnipresent coercion.[21]

Coercion may be employed to influence a decision. The coercive powers of the state represent a strong logical appeal against a decision to commit a crime, and for some individuals it may be the only effective appeal. In arguing in favor of policy propositions, affirmative debaters often provide for coercion in the plan of action they advocate. They may include an "enforcement plank" providing for fines, imprisonment, or some other penalty for those who do not obey or who try to circumvent the requirements of the plan. Alternatively they may advocate enforcement of the plan through existing legal structures.

A decision to employ coercion is likely to be socially acceptable and effective when that decision is made after full and fair debate. Baron Karl von Clausewitz's classic definition of war as the "continuation of diplomacy by other means" suggests that war—the ultimate form of coercion—is a method of problem solving to be selected after a careful debate on the possible risks and benefits.

VII. COMBINATION OF METHODS

It is often necessary to use a combination of methods in making a decision. The social context will determine the most suitable methods in a particular case.

The solution to a problem requiring the consent or cooperation of others may extend over a considerable period of time and may warrant use of all the

---

21. See Aleksandr I. Solzhenitsyn, *The Gulag Archipelago* (New York: Harper & Row, 1974).

methods of decision making. For example, through *individual decision* a person might determine that nonrefundable beverage containers cause unacceptable litter and should be prohibited.

Because that person is powerless to implement such a decision alone, he or she must use *persuasion* to influence friends to join in the effort. They may use the process of *group discussion* to decide how to proceed toward their objective. They might find it necessary to organize a group for raising funds and to work together for a period of months or years conducting a *propaganda* campaign directed toward the voters of the state. During this campaign many individuals might play a role in *persuading* or *debating*. Eventually a bill might be introduced into the state legislature.

After *discussion* in committee hearings and a number of *debates* on the floor of the legislature, a final *debate* determines the disposition of the bill. If the bill is enacted into law, *coercion* will be provided to ensure compliance. The validity of the law probably will be tested by *debates* in the courts to determine its constitutionality. When the law is violated, *coercion* can be applied only as the result of *debates* in the courts.

VIII. ETHICAL DECISION MAKING

In addition to making well-reasoned decisions, it is important to make decisions that are *ethical*. The consequences of a failure to consider ethical constructs when making decisions range from business failures (ENRON) to incarceration (Scooter Libbey), to the destruction of personal relationships. **Ethics** are a set of constructs that guide our decision making by providing standards of behavior telling us how we ought to act. While ethics may be based on or reflected in laws, they are not the same as laws. Similarly, we learn value systems and thus standards for ethical behavior from our communities and cultures, but that a behavior is a cultural standard or norm does not make it ethical.

According to Thomas White, there are two broad philosophical approaches to understanding ethical choices: **teleological** and **deontological**. The teleological approach is results oriented, and would focus on the good or bad consequences of an action or a decision. The deontological ethic is process or act oriented, and is based on the notion that actions have moral value.[22] Scholars at the Markkula Center for Applied Ethics at Santa Clara University have suggested that in making ethical decisions one ought to follow a framework through the following steps:

- Recognize an ethical issue
- Get the facts

---

22. Thomas White, "Philosophical Ethics," http://www.ethicsandbusiness.org/pdf/strategy.pdf. Adapted from Thomas White, "Ethics," in *Business Ethics: A Philosophical Reader* (New York: Macmillan, 1993).

- Evaluate alternative actions from various ethical perspectives
- Make a decision and test it
- Act, then reflect on the decision later[23]

Debate offers the ideal tool for examining the ethical implications of any decision, and critical thinking should also be ethical thinking.

How do we reach a decision on any matters of importance? We are under constant pressure to make unreasoned decisions, and we often make decisions carelessly. But which method is most likely to lead to wise decisions? To make wise judgments, we should rely on critical thinking. In many situations argumentation's emphasis on reasoned considerations and debate's confrontation of opposing sides give us our best, and perhaps only, opportunity to reach reasoned conclusions. In any case it is in the public interest to promote debate, and it is in our own intelligent self-interest to know the principles of argumentation and to be able to apply critical thinking in debate.

EXERCISES

1. *Individual decisions.* For one week, keep a journal of decisions you make. Separate them into trivial, somewhat important and very important decisions. How did you make your decisions? Upon what did you base your decisions? Can you identify a pattern based on level of importance?

2. *SPAR debates* (**SP**ontaneous **AR**gumentation). This is a classic introductory debate exercise.

   Format

Affirmative (Pro side) opening speech	90 seconds
Cross-Examination by Negative (Con side)	60 seconds
Negative opening speech	90 seconds
Cross-Examination by Affirmative	60 seconds
Affirmative closing speech	45 seconds
Negative closing speech	45 seconds

   Procedure
   Debaters step to the front of the room in pairs. One debater calls a coin flip. The winner may either choose the topic (from a list posted on the board) or the side they will defend. After two minutes of preparation time the debate begins. Each debater has a total one minute additional preparation time to be used during the debate. There should always be an on-deck pair of debaters preparing their arguments.

---

23. Manuel Velasquez, Dennis Moberg, Michael J. Meyer, Thomas Shanks, Margaret R. McLean, David DeCosse, Claire André, and Kirk O. Hanson, "A Framework for Thinking Ethically," Markkula Center for Applied Ethics, http://www.scu.edu/ethics/ practicing/decision/framework.html (downloaded July 20, 2007). This article appeared originally in *Issues in Ethics*, vol. 1, no. 2 (Winter 1988).

Possible topics
Honesty is always the best policy.
Slavery still exists today.
True love really does exist.
Violence is a necessary means to settle disputes.
Police are necessary for safety.
People should not eat meat.
The drinking age should be lowered to 18.
Smoking should be banned in all public places.
There is no such thing as Homeland Security.
Marijuana should be legalized.

3. *Group discussion.* Students should form groups of five to seven and using the standard agenda for group problem solving, complete the following exercise.

     As the most outstanding and well-respected students in your Ethics in Communication course, your professor has asked you to formulate a recommendation to her concerning a problem in the class.

     It has come to the attention of Professor Young that one of the students in the class plagiarized on an assigned paper. Sue M. Moral turned in a paper, more than half of which was actually written by her good friend Ben There. Ben had written the original paper for the same course two years ago, and suggested to Sue that she use his paper for her assignment. Since Professor Old had taught the course (since retired) when Ben took the course, Professor Young would be unlikely to recognize the work. Ben did not know that Professor Old had been so impressed with his paper that he had given it to Professor Young as a sample paper for her to keep on file. Professor Young also found out that Sue's roommate, Bye Stander, also a student in Ethics in Communication, knew about Sue's plagiarism, but did not inform Professor Young. In fact, Bye had agreed to photocopy Ben's paper for Sue, since she was making a trip to Kinko's for other reasons. The assignment counts 10 percent of the course grade. Sue has a "B" average on all other work in the class. Bye has an "A" average. Ben is still a major in the department. His "A" on the paper barely enabled him an "A" in Ethics in Communication. He hopes to graduate next semester with a "C" average.

     What, if any, action do you recommend Professor Young take?

4. *Persuasion.* Prepare a two-minute impromptu speech in support of your claim that "People should do _____" or "People should NOT do _____." Offer three reasons in support of your claim.

5. *Ethics.* Identify an ethical dilemma for decision making. Follow the framework suggested in the chapter to make a decision resolving the dilemma. Identify your ethical approach as teleological or deontological. An excellent source of hypothetical case studies is available at http://www.uvsc.edu/ethics/casestudies/

2

Applied and Academic Debate

On his first day of class in argumentation and debate, his professor asked Charles why he had chosen the course. Charles responded that "I always argue with my parents and friends. In fact, I often call my favorite radio sports-talk show to argue with the host. My mother is an attorney, and she sometimes practices her openings and summations for me. And I practically live online, defending myself on the Listserv I belong to and networking with my friends on the net. So I know all about argumentation and debate, and I'm good at it!" Charles correctly recognized that the principles of debate are important across many different fields of practical arguing. But he was not yet aware of the richness and diversity of debate practice.

Debate can be classified into two broad categories: applied and educational. **Applied debate** is conducted on propositions, questions, and topics in which the advocates have a special interest, and the debate is presented before a judge or an audience with the power to render a binding decision on the proposition or respond to the question or topic in a real way. **Academic debate** is conducted on propositions in which the advocates have an academic interest, and the debate typically is presented before a teacher, judge or audience without direct power to render a decision on the proposition. Of course the audience in an academic debate does form opinions about the subject matter of the debate, and that personal transformation may ultimately lead to meaningful action. However, the direct impact of the audience decision in an academic debate is personal, and the decision made by the judge is limited to identification of the winner of the debate. In fact, in academic debate the judge may be advised to disregard the merits of the proposition and to render her win/loss decision only on the merits of the support as presented in the debate itself. The most important identifying characteristic of an academic debate is that the purpose of the debate is to provide educational opportunities for the participants.

Miniglossary

Academic debate   Debate conducted under the direction of an educational institution for the purpose of providing educational opportunities for its students.

Applied debate   Debate presented before a judge or audience with the power to render a binding decision on the proposition.

CEDA   Cross Examination Debate Association.

Ethical   Being in accordance with the accepted principles of right and wrong that govern the conduct of a profession or community.

Forensics   An educational activity primarily concerned with using an argumentative perspective in examining problems and communicating with people.

Judicial debate   Debate conducted in the courts or before quasi-judicial bodies.

Mock trial debate   A form of academic debate that emulates trial court debating.

Moot court debate   An academic form of judicial debate used by law schools to prepare students for courtroom debate.

NDT   National Debate Tournament.

Nonformal debate   Debate that occurs in various contexts without formal or prearranged procedural rules.

Parliamentary debate   Debate conducted under the rules of parliamentary procedure (see Chapter 19). Also a form of competitive academic debate practiced under the auspices of organizations like the National Parliamentary Debate Association and the American Parliamentary Debate Association.

Special debate   Debate conducted under special rules drafted for a specific occasion—for example, presidential debates.

I. APPLIED DEBATE

Applied debate may be classified as special debate, judicial debate, parliamentary debate, or nonformal debate. After discussing each of these classifications of debate briefly, we will consider academic debate in more detail.

A. Special Debate

Special debate is conducted under special rules drafted for a specific occasion, such as political campaign debates. Examples include the Lincoln–Douglas debates of 1858, the Kennedy–Nixon debates of 1960, the Bush–Clinton–Perot debates of 1992, the Bush–Gore debates of 2000, Bush–Kerry in 2004, and the series of debates involving the candidates for the Democratic and Republican Partys' nominations during the 2007–2008 campaigns. These were formal debates, yet they were neither judicial nor parliamentary; they were conducted under special rules agreed on by the debaters. In an article published in the *Seattle Times*, Paul Farhi and Mike Allen described the process that led to the special rules for the Bush–Kerry debates in 2004:

> After weeks of private and reportedly heated negotiations, representatives of President Bush and Sen. John Kerry agreed earlier this week to three televised debates, with another for Vice President Cheney and Sen. John Edwards. The first presidential debate takes place Thursday at the University of Miami.
>
> And now, with the release of a 32-page 'memorandum of understanding,' we understand why it took so long. The document is crammed with sections and subsections spelling out almost every imaginable rule of engagement and detail about how the debates will look. Or will be prohibited from looking.
>
> In its precision and seeming fussiness, in its attempt at control, it often reads like an agreement between a concert promoter and a particularly demanding pop diva....

While the most important part of such agreements certainly has to do with the details governing the format and nature of questions or topics addressed, all details are considered. The authors continued,

> The agreement, for example, spells out the exact dimensions of the lectern to be used (50 inches high on the side facing the audience, 48 inches on the side facing the candidates) in the first and third debates, and how far apart those lecterns will be (10 feet, as measured from 'the left-right center' of one 'to the left-right center of the other'). It specifies the type of stools (identical, of equal height, with backs and footrests) that Bush and Kerry will sit on for the second, town-hall-style debate, as well as the arrangement (in a horseshoe) and nature of the audience. It specifies that it will consist of an equal number of 'likely voters who are "soft" Bush supporters or "soft" Kerry supporters,' soft being a polling term for people who might be willing to change their minds. There are details about the type of warning lights to be used if a candidate runs over his allotted time, about the moderators' conduct, about the coin flip that will be used to determine who goes first (the type of coin or number of flips isn't specified). There's even a codicil that might be called 'the perspiration clause,' since it alludes to every candidate's worst fear: an outbreak of Nixon-style flop sweat. The clause commits the nonpartisan producer, the Commission on Presidential Debates, to use its 'best efforts to maintain an appropriate temperature according to industry standards for the entire debate,'

although it's unclear what 'industry standard' temperature is, or even what industry the agreement is referring to.[1]

Debates between presidential candidates are now well established in the American political scene, and similar debates are often held between candidates in elections at all levels, from student government president to mayor to vice president. While the formats of these debates may leave much to be desired, they at least bring the candidates together and give voters a better opportunity to compare the candidates than they would otherwise have. Although this type of debate is most often associated with political figures and campaign issues, it may be used by anyone on any proposition or set of questions or topics. Opposing advocates merely have to agree to come together under the provisions of a special set of rules drafted for the occasion.

B. Judicial Debate

Judicial debate is conducted in the courts or before quasi-judicial bodies. Governed by the rules of a court of law, its purpose is the prosecution or defense of individuals charged with violation of the law or the determination of issues of law alleged to be applicable to specific cases before the court. Court TV and other television and even Internet access makes courtroom argument easily accessible to interested spectators.

Judicial debate may be observed in any court from the Supreme Court of the United States to a local court. In its academic form, judicial debate is known as **moot court debate** and is used by law schools to prepare students for courtroom debate. The impeachment trial of President Clinton during the winter of 1999 is a rare example of judicial debate held before the United States Congress under special rules establishing the Senate as a jury and presided over by the chief justice of the Supreme Court.

The principles of argumentation and debate apply to judicial debate. Because judicial debate is also concerned with sometimes highly technical rules of procedure—which may vary from federal to state courts, from one state to another, and from one type of court to another within a given state—the specific methods of judicial debate are not considered here. **Mock trial debate**, which emulates the form of trial court debating but without the emphasis on rules of procedure and admissibility, is considered in Chapter 18. Of course, moot court and mock trial debates are academic and not applied, as their judges do not render binding decisions on formal cases.

C. Parliamentary Debate

Parliamentary debate is conducted under the rules of parliamentary procedure. Its purpose is the passage, amendment, or defeat of motions and resolutions that

1. Paul Farhi and Mike Allen, "Rules of Engagement: Presidential Debate Details" *The Seattle Times,* Sept. 28, 2004; page updated 02:22 P.M., http://seattletimes.nwsource .com/html/politics/2002048299_webdebaterules28.html.

come before a parliamentary assembly. The practice of parliamentary debate may be observed in the Senate or House of Representatives, state legislatures, city councils, and town governing bodies, and at the business meetings of various organizations, such as the national convention of a major political party or a meeting of a local fraternity chapter. C-SPAN allows television viewers access to parliamentary debate in Congress, and local public television stations and radio stations may offer city or county government and school board meetings for public consumption.

In its educational or *academic* form parliamentary debate may be known as a model congress, a model state legislature, a model United Nations assembly, or a mock political convention. Intercollegiate debaters also compete in parliamentary debate tournaments, adapting the rules of procedure to the tournament context, with two-person teams competing. Of course, these simulations are not *applied debate*.

The principles of argumentation and debate apply to parliamentary debate. The special provisions of parliamentary procedure that also apply to this type of debate are discussed in Chapter 19.

D. Nonformal Debate

Nonformal debate is conducted without the formal rules found in special, judicial, parliamentary, and academic debate. This is the type of debate to which newspapers and television commentators typically are referring when they speak of the "abortion debate," the "immigration debate," and other controversies that arouse public interest. The term *nonformal* has no reference to the formality or informality of the occasion on which the debate takes place. A president's state-of-the-union address—a highly formal speech—may be a part of a nonformal debate. A rap session in a college dormitory—a very informal situation—may also be part of a nonformal debate.

Examples of nonformal debate can be found in national political campaigns, in community hearings or town hall meetings about water pollution or new school bond issues, in business meetings about corporate policy, in college conferences on matters of educational policy or the allocation of funds, and in election campaigns for student body officers. Nonformal debates occur in scientific and research realms, as in the debate over the ethics and implications of cloning. Talk radio and television provide forums for nonformal debate over issues ranging from lifestyle choice to sports, and many individuals participate in nonformal debate through Internet lists, networks, and chatrooms, including YouTube, Facebook, MySpace, and countless blogs and communities. For an example of a Listserv facilitating nonformal debate involving intercollegiate debaters and issues, visit http://www.ndtceda.com/. For nonformal debate about political campaign debates, visit http://www.debatescoop.org/.

At the family level nonformal debates may revolve around issues including the choice of a college or whether grown children should move back into the family home.

II. ACADEMIC DEBATE

As noted previously, academic debate is conducted under the direction of an educational institution to provide educational opportunities for students. Many schools and colleges conduct programs of academic debate. The issue here is not whether we will participate in debate—our participation is inevitable, because, sooner or later, most educated people will take part in some form of debate. The issue is whether our participation will be effective. Academic debate can teach us to become effective in this essential art.

A. The Background of Academic Debate

A history of academic debate would fill many volumes, but a few salient facts should be mentioned here. The origins of debate are lost in the remote reaches of history, but we know that people were debating at least 4,000 years ago. For example, Egyptian princes debated agricultural policy at the pharaoh's court (2080 B.C.). Chinese scholars conducted important philosophical debates during the Chou Dynasty (1122–255 B.C.). Homer's epic poems the *Iliad* and the *Odyssey* (900 B.C.) contain speeches—which the Roman rhetorician Quintilian cited as examples of the arts of legal pleading and deliberation—that may be regarded as embryonic debates. Aristotle's *Rhetoric* (384–322 B.C.) laid the foundation of argumentation and debate and is influential even today.

Although debate exists all over the world, it thrives in the context of democratic Western civilization. Former Secretary of State Henry Kissinger noted that American foreign policy that encourages the spread of democracy faces daunting problems in some cultures, such as Confucianism:

> Unlike democratic theory, which views truth as emerging from the clash of ideas, Confucianism maintains that truth is objective and can only be discerned by assiduous study and education of which only a rare few are thought to be capable. Its quest for truth does not treat conflicting ideas as having equal merit, the way democratic theory does. Since there is only one truth, that which is not true can have no standing or be enhanced through competition. Confucianism is essentially hierarchical and elitist, emphasizing loyalty to family, institutions, and authority. None of the societies it has influenced has yet produced a functioning pluralistic system (with Taiwan in the 1990s coming the closest).[2]

Of course, Confucianism is not the only culture to put stringent limits on debate. As we saw earlier, Muslim fundamentalists in Bangladesh favor executing anyone who debates the Koran.

Academic debate began at least 2,400 years ago when the scholar Protagoras of Abdera (481–411 B.C.), known as the father of debate, conducted debates

---

2. Henry Kissinger, *Diplomacy* (New York: Simon & Schuster, 1994), p. 638.

among his students in Athens. Corax and Tisias founded one of the earliest schools of rhetoric, specializing in teaching debate so that students could plead their own cases in the law courts of ancient Sicily.

Debate flourished in the academies of the ancient world and in the medieval universities, where rhetoric was installed as one of the seven liberal arts. What may have been the first intercollegiate debate in the English-speaking world took place in the early 1400s at Cambridge University between students from Oxford and Cambridge. The debating programs at British universities, which utilize a parliamentary format, have long been a training ground for future members of Parliament.

Debating has always been an important part of the American educational scene as well. Debating flourished in the colonial colleges; disputations were a required part of the curriculum, and debates were often a featured part of commencement ceremonies. Almost all the leaders of the American Revolution and the early national period were able debaters who had studied argumentation in the colonial colleges or in the community debating "societies," "lyceums," and "bees" that flourished throughout the country: "From the Spy Club at Harvard in 1722 to the Young Ladies Association, the first women's debating society, at Oberlin in 1835, the one common thread in literary societies was student interest in debating important issues."[3]

Intercollegiate debating began in the late 1800s, and interscholastic debating soon followed. In the early 1900s, however, intercollegiate debates were relatively rare. Normally a college would schedule only a few intercollegiate debates during an academic year, and large audiences would assemble to watch the few students who were privileged to participate in these unusual events.

Recognition of the value and importance of academic debate increased steadily during the twentieth century. Tournament debating was introduced in the 1920s, and by 1936 some educators were concerned about its increasing popularity.[4] But tournament debating did not become predominant until the late 1940s. From the 1920s to the 1940s, contract debating prevailed. A college debating team would send out contracts to other teams specifying details such as which team would argue which side of the proposition, how judges would be selected, and where the visiting team would be housed, and offering to reciprocate as host on some future occasion. When a sufficient number of signed contracts had been returned, teams would depart by car, bus, or train for a few days or a week or two of debating. Usually the schedule called for one debate a day, although in major cities like Boston, New York, Washington, and Chicago, two debates a day might be scheduled. On rare occasions teams traveled coast to coast in private railroad cars. A yearlong resolution was selected and announced to facilitate debaters' preparation, although individual tournaments might or might not adhere to the national resolution.

---

3. Charles DeLancey and Halford Ryan, "Intercollegiate Audience Debating: Quo Vadis," *Argumentation and Advocacy*, vol. 27 (1990), p. 49.
4. Alfred Westfall, "Can We Have Too Much of a Good Thing?" *The Forensic of Pi Kappa Delta*, Oct. 1936, p. 27.

In the post–World War II era, tournament debate became the predominant mode of debating. In 1947 the U.S. Military Academy began the National Debate Tournament (**NDT**) at West Point. Tournament debating proliferated, and teams soon could choose among many tournaments at nearby or distant colleges on almost any weekend between October and April. Swing tournaments evolved in which two colleges relatively close to each other would schedule back-to-back tournaments during the winter break so that, instead of one or two debates a day, teams could attend two tournaments in a week. A tournament would offer as many as twelve or more debate rounds in a single tournament. The NDT committee served to select and announce the yearlong topic in the summer.

In 1967 the American Forensic Association assumed responsibility for the NDT, which has been hosted by a different college each year since then. By 1967 the NDT had become the dominant force in intercollegiate debating, and virtually all teams geared their programs to winning a place in the NDT or emulated the practices of teams that were successful in the NDT. Debaters hoping to participate in the NDT debated a proposition announced in the summer before the academic debate season began. As in the NCAA basketball tournament, only a select number of teams are selected to participate in the National Debate Tournament.

In 1971 the Cross Examination Debate Association (**CEDA**) was established to provide an alternative to NDT debating—in part to meet a perceived need by placing greater emphasis on communication. (The use of cross-examination debating is no longer a distinguishing feature between the two approaches; since 1974–1975 the NDT has used the cross-examination format.) CEDA, which initially employed non-NDT policy propositions, started using value propositions in 1975. Two propositions per year—one for each academic semester—were debated. CEDA also established a sweepstakes system, which recognized the top debate programs in each region and in the nation. A point system was developed to reward successful debaters, both novice and experienced. (The NDT later adopted a similar point system with sweepstakes awards.) In 1986 CEDA established a national championship tournament open to any CEDA member. After a modest start as the Southwest Debate Association, CEDA emerged as the most widely used mode of intercollegiate debating.

In 1996 the fall CEDA topic was reselected as the spring CEDA topic, thereby creating a yearlong proposition, as was used by NDT. In addition, despite the nonpolicy or quasi-policy nature of the CEDA propositions from 1975 until 1996, by the mid-1990s most CEDA debates involved discussion of policies. These debates were very similar in content to those occurring among schools debating the NDT topic. Because CEDA debates had also adopted the stylistic characteristics common to NDT debates, the two debate groups differed little in debate practice. During their respective national tournaments in 1996, the NDT leadership communicated to CEDA that if CEDA adopted a yearlong policy proposition announced in the summer, NDT would adopt that proposition as well, creating a shared topic. CEDA did so, and thus the "merger" of CEDA and NDT occurred. CEDA and NDT maintain their separate ranking systems; however, teams now compete in tournaments previously closed to them by style, topic, and membership. Some teams and a majority of member schools in each organization compete in both the National Debate Tournament and the CEDA National Championship. Participation in the NDT is selective: Teams must qualify through a system of open bids and district competition. The CEDA tournament is open to any team representing a member school (remember that CEDA is an organization while NDT is a tournament).

Other debate organizations sponsoring team debates coexist with CEDA and NDT. The American Debate Association (ADA) was established in 1985 to foster the growth of "reasonable" rule-based policy debate.[5] ADA was concerned with keeping debate accessible to new debaters and new debate programs while maintaining academic integrity in its top-level debating. ADA has always debated within the NDT structure and utilized the NDT proposition. The National Educational Debate Association (NEDA) promotes debate with a focus on communication style and educational practice. NEDA selects its own propositions. The National Parliamentary Debate Association (NPDA) and the American Parliamentary Debate Association (APDA) sponsor competitive intercollegiate debate using a modified parliamentary format and featuring propositions chosen for individual debates or debate rounds. Lincoln–Douglas, or one-on-one, debate is organized through the National Forensic Association. The International Debate Education Association (IDEA) and the International Public Debate Association (IPDA) also work to promote academic debate. 1997 CEDA established an additional debate format called "public sphere debate," designed to provide competitive audience-style debate evaluated by nontraditional debate judges. The topic for public sphere debate was a narrowed or alternate version of the CEDA/NDT proposition. In 1999 CEDA eliminated the public sphere proposition and replaced it with a nonpolicy proposition (see Chapter 3). The nonpolicy proposition never gained much popularity and was abandoned in the 2002–2003 academic year.

In academic debate students must know and adapt to the preferences and expectations of the judges (see "Analysis of the Audience" in Chapter 15 and "Judging Philosophies" in Chapter 17). While CEDA and NDT have essentially merged as debate communities, new subcultures have developed based in part on styles of judging and debating. Constant change in argumentation styles and approaches create new challenges of adapting to unfamiliar audiences. Varying experience levels also affect the preferences and expectations of judges and coaches. Each of the various debate organizations and styles represents a set of unique approaches to the practice of debate.

B. The Organization of Academic Debate

Academic debate is by no means limited to the classroom and the argumentation course. As the previous discussion outlines, many colleges conduct programs of academic debate by organizing debating teams, which give students

---

5. For a more detailed consideration of NDT, CEDA, ADA, and other debate formats, see "Special Issue: A Variety of Formats for the Debate Experience," *Argumentation and Advocacy*, vol. 27, no. 2 (fall 1990).

opportunities beyond the traditional course offerings. Academic credit is often given for participation in the debate program—a program usually open to any qualified undergraduate. The director of forensics conducts the program to provide training opportunities for students new to debate and to maximize the challenge for more experienced students. CEDA, the American Forensics Association, the National Communication Association, IDEA, and other professional organizations, however, do promote scholarship and development of argumentation theory and teaching for all those interested in academic debate. They support research and learning to be applied in debate and argumentation classes, on-campus debating; and across the curriculum.

As the designation "director of forensics" suggests, many debating programs today have broadened their focus to include other forensic activities. "**Forensics** is defined as an educational activity primarily concerned with using an argumentative perspective in examining problems and communicating with people."[6] Recognizing that many forensics programs have been expanded to include a wide variety of public speaking and individual events in addition to debate, the 1984 definition continues:

> Forensics is viewed as a form of rhetorical scholarship which takes various forms, including debate, public address, and the interpretation of literature. Forensics serves as a curricular and co-curricular laboratory for improving students' abilities in research, analysis, and oral communication. Typically, forensic activities are conducted in a competitive environment so as to motivate students and accelerate the learning process. Forensics remains an ongoing, scholarly experience, uniting students and teachers, in its basic educational purpose.[7]

C. Values of Academic Debate

Because debating is an ancient discipline that is thriving in modern educational institutions, we should consider some of the values of academic debate. Although not all these values are unique to debate, a successful academic debate program is an important means of attaining them. Indeed, for many students it is the best, and sometimes the only, means of obtaining the benefits outlined here.

1. Debate Provides Preparation for Effective Participation in a Democratic Society. Debate is an inherent condition of a democratic society. Our Constitution provides for freedom of speech. Our legislatures, our courts, and most of our private organizations conduct their business through the medium of debate. Because debate is so widespread at decision-making levels, a citizen's ability to vote intelligently or to use his or her right of free speech effectively is

---

6. This definition, adopted at the Second National Developmental Conference on Forensics in Evanston, Illinois, in 1984, reaffirmed the definition adopted at the First National Developmental Conference on Forensics, held in Sedalia, Colorado, in 1974.
7. Second National Developmental Conference on Forensics.

limited without knowledge of debate. As we know from history, freedoms un-used or used ineffectively are soon lost. Citizens educated in debate can hope to be empowered to participate in the shaping of their world.

2. Debate Offers Preparation for Leadership.   The ultimate position of lead-ership is the presidency of the United States. Historian Arthur M. Schlesinger, Jr., cites two indispensable requirements that an effective president must meet. The first is "to point the republic in one or another direction. The second is to explain to the electorate why the direction the president proposes is right for the nation. Ronald Reagan understood, as Jimmy Carter never did, that politics is ultimately an educational process. Where Carter gave the impression of regarding presidential speeches as disagreeable duties, to be rushed through as perfunctorily as possible, Reagan knew that the speech is a vital tool of presidential leadership. His best speeches had a structure and an argument. They were well written and superbly delivered. They were potent vehicles for his charm, histrionic skills, and genius for simplification."[8]

It is interesting to note that Schlesinger's second requirement echoes the def-inition of argumentation given on page 5. Although few of you will become president, many will aspire to positions of leadership. And an indispensable re-quirement of leadership—not only in politics but in almost all areas of human endeavor—is that the leader explains why the direction proposed is right.

3. Debate Offers Training in Argumentation.   From classical times to the present, argumentation teachers have viewed debate as the best method of pro-viding training in this discipline. Debate offers an ideal opportunity for students to apply the theories of argumentation under conditions designed to increase their knowledge and understanding of these theories and their proficiency in their use. As an educational method debate provides excellent motivation for learning, because students have both the short-term goal of winning a decision or an award in a tournament and the long-term goal of increasing their knowl-edge and improving their ability. This combination of short-term and long-term motivations provides for an optimum learning situation. The constant monitor-ing of student achievement with immediate feedback and evaluations by debate judges gives frequent opportunities to encourage growth and progress and to de-tect and remedy misunderstandings.

4. Debate Provides for Investigation and Intensive Analysis of Significant Contemporary Problems.   Thoughtful educators have long been concerned that students and the general public often have only a superficial knowledge of significant contemporary problems. In addition to acquiring knowledge of the principles of argumentation, debaters also have a chance to investigate and ana-lyze the significant contemporary problems and relevant literature that form the basis of the propositions under debate. In the course of a debating career,

---

8. Arthur M. Schlesinger, Jr., *The Cycles of American History* (Boston: Houghton Mifflin, 1986), p. 293.

students will acquire a better-than-average knowledge of current problems, as well as skill in applying methods that will enable them to critically analyze the problems. As one authority points out, the true aim of rhetoric—the energizing of knowledge—is correlated with inquiry and with policy.[9] Through debate students learn how to acquire knowledge and how to energize that knowledge.

5. Debate Develops Proficiency in Critical Thinking.   Through study of argumentation and practice in debate, students participate in an educational process specifically designed to develop their proficiency in critical thinking. A number of studies have investigated whether college courses in argumentation and debate improve critical thinking. One researcher, Kent R. Colbert, found that, after a year's participation in either CEDA or NDT debate, the debaters significantly outscored the nondebaters on critical-thinking tests.[10] Debaters learn to apply the principles of critical thinking not only to problems that emerge in the relative comfort of research or a briefing session but also to problems that arise in the heat of debate.

6. Debate Is an Integrator of Knowledge.   Educators are constantly searching for methods of synthesizing knowledge. Debate is one way of achieving this goal:

> The exponents of a synthesis of knowledge and the broader view of a problem can [learn] from the practical experience and method of the arguer and discussant. Almost any problem at which the debater works cuts across these fields of knowledge.[11]

For example, in debating a proposition dealing with the issue of guaranteed annual wages, debaters must have at least a minimal familiarity with the principles of argumentation, economics, political science, sociology, psychology, finance, business management, labor relations, government, history, and philosophy. They will, of course, learn the principles and details of these disciplines through the appropriate departments of the college or through independent study; however, through debate they can integrate their knowledge of these various disciplines and bring them to bear on a significant contemporary problem. Debate offers a uniquely dynamic and energized environment within which students can learn. For many students debate is their first, and often their most intensive and valuable, experience in interdisciplinary studies.

7. Debate Develops Proficiency in Purposeful Inquiry.   Debate is preceded by inquiry. Debaters must be well informed about all the relevant aspects of the

---

9. See Charles Sears Baldwin, *Medieval Rhetoric and Poetic* (New York: Macmillan, 1928), p. 3.
10. Kent R. Colbert, "The Effects of CEDA and NDT Debate Training on Critical Thinking Ability," *Journal of the American Forensic Association,* vol. 21 (1987), pp. 194–201.
11. A. Craig Baird, "General Education and the Course in Argumentation," *The Gavel,* vol. 38, p. 59.

issue to be debated. The extent to which debate motivates students to undertake purposeful inquiry into significant contemporary problems, to apply the principles of critical thinking to those problems, and to integrate the knowledge acquired from various disciplines is suggested by a former college debater:

> In my four years of college debating, we worked on such vital real-world topics as aid for international development, the Constitutional right of privacy, trade policies on the Pacific Rim, and federal energy policies. Each of these big topics was subject to a range of interpretations and required in-depth research on subsidiary issues as well.
>
> Preparing to debate these subjects led me and many other debaters to do our first serious research. Debate introduced me to *Foreign Affairs*, the law reviews and indexes, *Business Periodicals Index*, the *Public Affairs Information Service*, *Dialog*, *Nexis*, *Datatimes*, *Dow Jones News/Retrieval*, and other databases.
>
> While numbers aren't everything, the fact is that the amount of research my partner and I did in just one year of debate exceeded the amount of research I did in preparing my master's thesis. Undoubtedly the research I had done for debate got me up to speed for the pressures of grad school and the competitive world of business.

Indeed, debaters frequently work on the cutting edge of contemporary problems, studying matters before they emerge as subjects of general public concern. As noted previously debaters seek out the scholarly journals in which significant problems are often first reported and discussed. The general public draws its information from television and the popular press, which may not report on these matters until months or years later. For example, many environmental concerns, such as the "greenhouse effect" and loss of rain forest were considered "exotic" topics by nondebaters who encountered them in the late 1970s. However, by the mid-1990s stories on these subjects were common in mass-circulation publications.

An examination of the lists of national intercollegiate debate propositions (see Appendices C and D) will reveal that debaters do in fact work on the cutting edge, considering major contemporary problems in advance of the general public. Perhaps the most striking example of foresight in discerning future public policy issues may be found in the then highly controversial 1954–1955 NDT proposition on the diplomatic recognition of communist China. It was not until President Nixon's historic visit to China 17 years later that the United States extended diplomatic recognition to China.

Learning how to conduct inquiry in sometimes unfamiliar fields and gaining practical experience in this kind of research will serve you well in many of your later pursuits.

8. Debate Emphasizes Quality Instruction.   Debate is based on a close tutorial relationship between faculty and students as well as experiential learning. Educators are worried about the negative effects of large classes and impersonal teaching, and debate classes offer an alternative by providing a tutorial relationship between faculty and students. Such classes usually are small and offer many opportunities for interaction between students and professor as they prepare for class debates or other class projects. This valuable process is enhanced by the feedback that usually follows such projects. Also, most of the educational activity of the debate program is carried out in a tutorial situation. The director of forensics or an assistant works with the two members of the debate team as they plan their research, develop their affirmative case, and plan their negative strategies. The coach may also work with groups of four students after a practice debate as they critique the debate in depth and plan for further improvement. Because this tutorial relationship is rarely limited to a quarter or a semester, but rather extends over four years, it provides a valuable opportunity for personalized education in the all-too-often impersonal world of higher education. Students benefit as well from interaction with their judges, who are talented educators from other colleges and universities. For example, community college student debaters may have hours of educational interaction with professors representing the nation's finest universities. Finally, in debate, the students are empowered with the direct responsibility for their own learning process. One cannot learn debate or acquire its skill sets without active, engaged participation.

9. Debate Encourages Student Scholarship.   Debate establishes standards of research and scholarly achievement that are rarely equaled in other undergraduate courses. Some students worry that the time they spend on debate may have a negative effect on their grades, but in fact the opposite is true. Intercollegiate debaters report that their work in debate is a significant factor in helping them do better on exams, write better term papers, and score higher on graduate school admissions tests. This, of course, is the predictable result of the benefits considered in this section. The scholarly skills that debaters develop in researching, organizing, presenting, and defending a debate case are directly transferable to many other academic pursuits.

Added to this is the challenge to do one's best that debate provides. In the classroom the professor typically makes "reasonable" assignments that the "average" student can fulfill. In intercollegiate debate, however, one's opponent is rarely "reasonable" or "average." As we noted in point 7, good debaters will do far more research than the average professor would ever expect for a term paper and will present it with far more skill and defend it far more effectively than would be required on a class assignment. Preparing for and participating in major tournaments can be a mind-expanding experience that encourages students to tap their full capabilities and enables them to realize their full potential.

Argumentation courses and intercollegiate debate are traditional training grounds for pre-law students. One study of 98 law school deans found that 69.9 percent would advise pre-law students to take a course in argumentation and 70.3 percent would recommend participation in intercollegiate debate. The deans also indicated that pre-law students "needed training in the skills of public speaking" (81.9 percent), "practical experience in the use of research techniques" (84.2 percent), "training in the application of the principles of logical reasoning" (89.6 percent), and "training in the techniques of refutation and rebuttal" (75.8

percent).[12] Not only are such training and experience valuable for pre-law students, they are important assets in many other areas of graduate study and in business and professional endeavors.

10. Debate Develops the Ability to Make Prompt, Analytical Responses.   In the 1988 presidential campaign Michael Dukakis—who had an 18-point lead in the early polls—let George Bush's attacks go unanswered. One of Bush's more effective salvos was to criticize Dukakis for vetoing a bill requiring teachers to lead the Pledge of Allegiance each day. "'Dukakis' strategy of shrugging off attacks suddenly stopped looking presidential and started looking weak,' said a top aide.... Months after Bush first raised the issue, Dukakis finally responded."[13] This failure to respond promptly and analytically to this and other attacks that Dukakis apparently judged to be frivolous was considered by many observers to be an important factor in Dukakis's defeat. In today's world of instant communication, candidates let attacks go unanswered at their peril (see Chapter 3). Politicians, business executives, and ordinary citizens may also find themselves in situations that require a prompt, analytical response. Students learn to do this in debate; cross-examination requires an instant response, and the response to an argument made in an opponent's speech must be prepared during the speech or in the brief time between speeches.

11. Debate Develops Critical Listening.   In their pioneer research on listening, Ralph G. Nichols and Leonard A. Stevens found that "on the average we listen at approximately a 25 percent level of efficiency."[14] If we allow our attention to wander while an opponent speaks, our reply will be ineffective and off the mark. And if we miss 75 percent of our opponents' arguments, we will surely lose the debate. Debaters quickly learn to listen to their opponents with sharply focused critical attention, recording their arguments precisely on a flow sheet (a specialized note-taking system used by debaters) so that their own responses are to the point—adapting the phrasing of their opponents and turning the subtleties and limitations heard to their own advantage. The ability to listen critically is widely recognized as an important attribute of the educated person. Nichols and Stevens found that a top executive of a large industrial plant reported "perhaps 80 percent of my work depends on my listening to someone, or upon someone else listening to me."[15] Debaters begin to develop this important skill of critical listening from their very first debate.

12. Debate Develops Proficiency in Reading and Writing.   Many debates are conducted in writing—for example, the daily "debates" on the editorial

---

12. From a paper by Don R. Swanson, "Debate as Preparation for Law: Law Deans' Reactions," presented at the Western Speech Communication Association convention (1970).

13. *Time,* Nov. 21, 1988, p. 47.

14. Ralph G. Nichols and Leonard A. Stevens, *Are You Listening?* (New York: McGraw-Hill, 1957), p. ix.

15. Nichols and Stevens, *Are You Listening?* p. 141.

page of *USA Today*. However, as a practical matter we most often think of debate as an oral argument. How then does debate develop proficiency in writing? Don't we merely "talk on our feet" when we debate? As we have seen, debate does indeed develop the ability to make prompt, analytical responses (see Point 10).

However, as we will discover, much of the debate is written prior to delivery. The first affirmative constructive speech is almost invariably a manuscript speech, which means that it is written and rewritten, revised and edited as the advocates try to develop the most effective statement of their position. In the same way many portions of other kinds of speeches and arguments are the products of careful writing and extensive rewriting, as well as skillful adaptation to previous speeches. Debaters must use clear, concise, powerful language to defend their positions. They build an extensive and precise vocabulary and develop a sense of clarity, which they bring to their writing.

The writing proficiency developed in debate pays dividends first by enabling debaters to present arguments more cogently and effectively. The skills learned in writing for debate carry over to many other fields. Students will find that they can apply the writing skills they learn from debate in writing term papers and in writing better answers to essay exams in their other classes. And after graduation students find that writing proficiency is highly valued in almost any business or profession.

Research conducted on Urban Debate League debaters has evidenced debate as an excellent tool to promote literacy training and development of reading skills. Reading aloud has the effect of building reading skills, even among those with very low reading capabilities. Participation in debate also builds vocabulary, as noted above, as students must learn to navigate complex academic, technical and challenging resource materials.[16]

13. Debate Encourages Mature Judgment.   Scholars tell us that many problems in human affairs result from a tendency to see complex issues in black-and-white terms. Educational debate gives students a chance to consider significant problems from many points of view. As debaters analyze the potential affirmative and negative cases, they begin to realize the complexity of most contemporary problems and to appreciate the worth of a multivalued orientation. As they debate both sides of a proposition, they learn not only that most contemporary problems have more than one side but also that even one side of a proposition embodies a considerable range of values. Sometimes at the start of an academic year, some debaters may, on the basis of a quickly formulated opinion, feel that only one side of a proposition is "right." After a few debates, however, they usually request an assignment on the other side of the proposition. By the end of the year (or semester), after they have debated on both sides of the proposition, they learn the value of suspending judgment until they have amassed and analyzed an adequate amount of evidence. The need to advocate one side of the proposition in a debate also teaches them that decisions cannot be postponed indefinitely. When they finally formulate

16. Linda Collier, "Argument for Success: A Study of Academic Debate in the Urban High Schools of Chicago, Kansas City, New York, St. Louis and Seattle," paper presented at the National Communication Association National Convention, 2004.

their personal position on the proposition, it may or may not be the same as at the beginning of the year. But now it will be a position they have reached after careful consideration, one they can defend logically.

14. Debate Develops Courage.   Debate helps students to develop courage by requiring them to formulate a case and defend it against strong opposition, under pressure. In debate students' cases will come under attack, and they might be tempted to push the panic button, beat a disorderly retreat, and avoid the confrontation. They cannot do this, however. The situation requires that they defend their position. They must have the courage of their convictions. They must discipline themselves, concentrate on the problem, organize their thoughts, and present a refutation. Well-prepared debaters find that they can defend their position, that their opponents are only human; as a result, they gain new confidence in themselves and in their ability to function in a competitive situation.

15. Debate Encourages Effective Speech Composition and Delivery.   Because composition and delivery of the debate speech are among the factors that determine the effectiveness of arguments, debaters need to select, arrange, and present their materials in keeping with the best principles of public speaking. Debating places a premium on extemporaneous delivery, requiring speakers to think on their feet. Typically debaters will speak before many different audiences: a single judge in the preliminary round of a tournament, a group of businesspeople at a service club, or a radio or TV audience. Each of these situations provides new challenges. Constant adaptation to the audience and to the speech situation helps debaters develop flexibility and facility in thinking and speaking.

Nervousness about public speaking is one of the most common fears for students and professionals. It can serve as a real and significant barrier to effective communication and ultimately to academic and professional success. Debate is an ideal arena for students to develop coping mechanisms allowing them to manage their speech anxiety. Because debate both requires and allows for substantial preparation, students develop confidence in their materials and passion for their advocacy. Debate provides a focus on the content over style, so the attention is on the arguments, not on the person. Student debaters may forget to be nervous as they have so much else to think about. And repetition of experience helps the students build confidence and learn to cope with their inevitable nervousness in such a way as to prevent it from impeding their objectives.

16. Debate Develops Social Maturity.   Intercollegiate debate provides an opportunity for students to travel to different campuses and meet students and faculty members from various parts of the country. It is not unusual for a team to participate in tournaments on the East or West Coast, in the Deep South, in the New England states, and in many points in between in the course of a year. Formerly there were eastern, midwestern, southern, and western styles of debating. But mass transportation has allowed debating to take place on a national scale, and so these regional differences have largely disappeared.

Exposure to both the businesslike atmosphere of the debate and the informal social situations that accompany most debates and tournaments helps students acquire social amenities, poise, and self-confidence. In the competition of a tournament or a classroom debate, they learn that they must accept victory or defeat gracefully and that they must respond courteously to the criticism of judge(s) regardless of their decisions. The educational benefits that come from meeting professors from a number of different colleges in informal settings can also be significant. In the college classroom, debaters will directly engage one another more than in most other courses. To debate is to express and to listen, to work together and to build community. One need not travel to encounter others with values and life experiences different from one's own, and the interaction afforded in the debate classroom and through the experience of sharing ideas through debate fosters this relationship building.

17. Debate Develops Multicultural Sensitivities.   As debaters learn to interact effectively with their colleagues, coaches, and judges in the debate environment, they will have the opportunity to engage individuals representing diverse cultural backgrounds. In the open debate context that celebrates free expression, students learn to communicate with sensitivity in a multicultural environment that may not be available on their home campus. Further, the nature of communication and argumentation demands that to be effective, debaters consider the implications of culture, values, and worldview on their cases and on their strategic approaches. To persuade a judge requires an understanding and sensitivity to their perceptual screen, and it is inescapable that argument premises are based upon foundations built at least in part by culture.

18. Debate Develops Computer Competencies.   The research conducted by debaters is frequently conducted online through various databases. Most debate teams travel with laptop computers and log on as soon as they check into their tournament accommodations. Debaters quickly become familiar with online data acquisition and use of computers to file and organize their data.

19. Debate Empowers Personal Expression.   In an academic environment, debate offers the participant a unique opportunity to express their ideas, experience, and voice. Rhetorical space—the opportunity to be respectfully heard—is guaranteed to the sincere participant. This opportunity to be heard is empowering and inspiring. Participants are able to learn from each other's experience and develop and grow as individuals and members of larger communities.

20. Debate Develops Problem-Solving Skills.   Policy debate demands that participants investigate and evaluate important social problems and creatively and critically apply solutions to those problems. Experience suggests that these abilities enable debaters to systematically evaluate situations and by utilizing reasoned measurement and ingenuity, discover appropriate solutions. Research also proves that debate training helps individuals find solutions to their own problems, and in particular, promotes nonviolent solutions to conflict. The

National Debate Project reports that debate reduces violence. Important new research is demonstrating that a significant correlation exists between the increased verbal skills associated with debate participation and decreased physical violence in both peer and domestic relations.[17]

21. Debate Develops Essential Proficiencies.   As we have seen, debate is an educational activity that provides students with the opportunity to develop proficiency in writing, thinking, reading, speaking, and listening. Educators and educational groups view these competencies as being vital to intellectual development. The consensus among major studies of education in the United States is that proficiency in oral communication is essential to academic competency. Consider the findings of the following studies:

1. The National Commission on Higher Education Issues identified the "fundamental competencies in reading, writing, speaking, mathematical techniques, and reasoning" as the requisite intellectual skills for the pursuit of higher education (*Summary Recommendations of the National Commission on Higher Education Issues*).

2. The National Commission on Excellence in Education echoed the same views and specified the same competencies, including both oral and written communication in its enumeration of necessary skills (*A Nation at Risk*, U.S. Department of Education, National Commission on Excellence in Education).

3. The Education Commission for the States' Task Force on Education for Economic Growth, whose members include governors, business leaders, and educators, assessed the critical needs of the education–commerce nexus and concluded that educational preparation for the "very competitive world of international commerce and trade" must include the essential language competencies of "reading," "writing," "speaking," and "listening" (*Action for Excellence*, Report of the Task Force on Education for Economic Growth, Education Commission for the States).

4. In its 1988 report the College Entrance Examination Board also listed "speaking and listening" among what it termed the "Basic Academic Competencies": "the broad intellectual skills essential to effective work in all fields of college study. They provide a link across disciplines of knowledge although they are not specific to any particular discipline. The Basic Academic Competencies are reading, writing, speaking and listening, mathematics, reasoning and studying" (*Academic Preparation for College*, The College Board).

5. In its proposal for strengthening public education, the Paideia Group specified the requisite intellectual skills for the educational process: "The skills to be acquired are the skills of reading, writing, speaking, listening, observing,

17. National Debate Project, http://communication.gsu.edu/ndp/benefits.htm, downloaded July 20, 2007.

measuring, estimating and calculating. They are linguistic, mathematical and scientific skills. They are the skills that everyone needs in order to learn anything, in school or elsewhere" (*Paideia Proposal,* the Paideia Group).

6. The American Association for the Advancement of Science, in a report prepared by the National Council on Science and Technology Education, stated that students should be able to "distinguish good arguments from bad ones" (*Project 2061 Phase 1 Reports,* the American Association for the Advancement of Science).

Debate is distinctive because of its unique dialectical form, providing the opportunity for intellectual clash in the testing of ideas. The creation of an argument is one of the most complex cognitive acts students can engage in. To create arguments, students must (1) research issues (which requires knowledge of how to use libraries and databases), (2) organize and analyze the data, (3) synthesize different kinds of data, and (4) evaluate information with respect to the quality of conclusions it may point to. To form the arguments after this process, students must (1) understand how to reason, (2) be able to recognize and critique different methods of reasoning, and (3) comprehend the logic of decision making. The successful communication of arguments to audiences reflects another cognitive skill: the ability to communicate complex ideas clearly with words. Finally, the argumentative interaction of students in a debate reflects an even more complex cognitive ability—the ability to process the arguments of others quickly and to reformulate or adapt or defend previous positions.[18]

III. ETHICAL STANDARDS FOR DEBATE

Because we use debate as a means of influencing human behavior, the mature, responsible advocate will be concerned with **ethical** standards for debate. To be conducted so that the benefits of debate are achieved, debate must be open, accessible, honest, and fair. Debate empowers its participants, but the power associated with debate participation carries with it personal responsibility. This responsibility includes honest and accurate representation of support materials and fair and open treatment of everyone involved. Debate in a free society demands civil behavior and fair treatment. To promote open participation, debaters should avoid language and behavior that would exclude or discourage the voices of any participants.

A. Ethical Practice

Ethical standards for debate practice occur on multiple levels. Some standards will vary by community and even by individual interpretations. For example, what is considered to be comprehensible or reasonable presentational style will

---

18. Adapted from "A Rationale for Forensics as Education," adopted at the Second National Developmental Conference on Forensics, Evanston, Illinois, 1984.

Ethical Guidelines for Students

The Second National Developmental Conference on Forensics

"Ethical Guidelines for Students"

Students participating in forensics are obligated to adhere to high ethical standards. Here we are concerned with the ethical choices students make for themselves, not with the standards to be applied by critics or judges. An ethical commitment by students is essential because the value of forensics is directly dependent on the integrity of those involved. For that reason, it is the duty of each student to participate honestly, fairly, and in such a way as to avoid communicational behaviors that are deceptive, misleading, or dishonest. Students should strive to place forensic competitions in a proper perspective as ethical decisions are pondered. The goal of winning must be evaluated within a framework that considers strategic choices in light of the educational value of such choices. Forensic contests are not ends in themselves but means to an end.

Furthermore, student participants must remember that forensics is an oral, interactive process. It is the student's duty to aspire to the objective of effective oral expression of ideas. When ideas are expressed in an unintelligible fashion, the forensic process is abused. The interactive dimension of forensics suggests that behaviors that belittle, degrade, demean, or otherwise dehumanize others are not in the best interests of forensics because they interfere with the goals of education and personal growth. The ethical forensic competitor recognizes the rights of others and communicates with respect for opponents, colleagues, and critics.

Student advocates should compete with respect for the principles and objectives of reasoned discourse. Students who invent definitions involving unwarranted shifts in the meanings of words fail to maintain a respect for the integrity of language. Students who deliberately employ specious reasoning as a stratagem fail to maintain a respect for the integrity of the forensic decision-making process....

Evidence plays an important role in forensic advocacy. Arguments can be no stronger than the evidence supporting them. If the evidence is misrepresented, distorted, or fabricated, the conclusions drawn are meaningless and ethically suspect. In order to understand these implications, the advocate should be familiar with the role of evidence in critical decision making, as well as with the methods of scholarship in discovering and recording evidence. The content of, and citations for, evidence used by advocates should be open to inspection by their opponents. Advocates should use only evidence that is in the public domain and, hence, open to critical evaluation by others.

Advocates should clearly identify, during their speeches, the source of all the evidence they use. Such identification should include available information relevant to the credibility of the author, the source of publication, and the date. Omitting the source of evidence denies the audience the opportunity to evaluate the quality of the information. Since the strength of evidence depends on the qualifications of the individual being quoted, this information is critical to any evaluator of the argument.

Advocates are responsible for the integrity of all the evidence they utilize, even when the evidence is not researched by the individual advocate. An advocate should not introduce evidence that is distorted or fabricated. In determining whether evidence has been distorted, the advocate should ask if the evidence deviates from the quality, quantity, probability, or degree of force of the author's position on the point in question. Any such deviation should be avoided, because such alteration can give undue rhetorical force to an advocate's argument....

Ethical Guidelines for Students (Continued)

Students competing in forensic contests share a unique opportunity to learn and to experience personal growth. This environment serves the goals of forensics best when student participants recognize their responsibility to preserve and promote opportunities for such a forensic education. Students should remember that forensic contests are often subject to public scrutiny and that reaction to forensic practices may aid or inhibit the future course taken by the forensic activity. Thus, students should carefully consider the values inherent in the claims they advance and in the behaviors they display. Communication that engenders ill will and disrespect for forensics ultimately reduces the utility of forensics for all who participate in it and should, therefore, be avoided.

As indicated at the outset, this document is intended to outline an ethic for the entire forensic community. Although it explicitly identifies certain direct participants in the activity, there are other, less centrally involved but nonetheless vitally important members of the community upon whom ethical responsibilities fall. Because forensics is an invaluable educational experience that can benefit all students, academic institutions may be ethically obligated to offer this experience and to commit the resources that will ensure its availability and quality. Similarly, alumni of forensic programs, having benefited themselves from this experience, may be ethically obligated to work for the continued availability of the experience for others. The future of forensics is in the hands of all members of the community.

Honest differences of opinion exist within the forensic community as to whether certain practices should be considered ethical or unethical. The surest guide to the debater and the director may be found in answering this question: "Am I more concerned with enduring ethical standards and educational objectives than with the short-term goal of winning a debate?" If the answer is an honest "yes," the decision about a particular practice will probably be an ethically sound one.

---

vary. Some standards, however, are agreed upon, and provide guidance for practice in all academic debate arenas.

First, the importance of competition must be kept in perspective. Many students enjoy debate largely due to its competitive nature. Because they are motivated to compete effectively, they work hard and immerse themselves in their debate preparation. This intensity of involvement results in great benefits to student debaters in achieving educational objectives and skill development. However, it should be remembered that competition is but a means to the more important educational ends.

Second, honesty and integrity should be maintained at the highest levels. The checks on honesty in the academic debate context are limited. In applied debate, opportunities to evaluate the accuracy of claims and support are available through methods including press coverage and legal checks on evidence history. Academic debate is time bound. For fair evaluation of evidence and reasoning it is vital that the highest standards of honesty be practiced.

Third, all participants should treat each other with respect. This may include appropriate language, nonverbal messages, and even choice of argumentation. The key is to honor each other's right to rhetorical space and to encourage open participation. To do so may require introspection, as disrespect may be communicated in subliminal and unintentional ways. Argumentation should be directed only at opponent's arguments and support, not at individuals or peoples.

Fourth, evidence standards require complete source citations and verbatim quotation. Fairness requires that evidence be gathered from published sources available to all participants. An advocate in debate is at a minimum ethically bound to provide reasons for their claims in the form of some type of proof.

B. Inclusion of All Participants

Debate provides a unique opportunity to learn from and about each other; across gender, culture, class, education, geography, and other differences. The opportunity to build bridges, however, can only be realized if participants become self-aware and work hard to create openness in their communicative behaviors. Socialization is a result of communicative behavior, and is insidious. However, the academic debate laboratory offers the opportunity to alter negative socializations and to substitute empowerment and respect. This positive change demands growth in awareness about those behaviors that devalue or discourage equality of participation. Growth of community requires respect and equality.

Research and personal narrative indicate that bias against woman and minorities exists in the community of intercollegiate debate. Any barriers to participation, whether intentional or not, are unethical and counterproductive. Barriers preclude the empowerment of many who would benefit from participation and denies those who do participate the richness of diversity. Discrimination and repression, of course, reflect practice in the academic world, business and industry, and in society at large. Fortunately, debate offers an ideal forum to discuss and change old and deep-seated bias. Tonia Green, a debater for the University of Louisville, presented a portion of her personal narrative as part of a debate at the District 6 National Debate Tournament Qualifier at Georgia State University in 2004.

> People continuously create false solutions for this flawed institution contributing to the pollution of the miseducation of life. I debate not just for competitive success but for a true purpose, by recognizing and not forgetting my social location as an African-American woman. My values as an African-American woman reflect my values as an African-American woman debater. "And that statement is more serious than the atom bomb and Saddam," as Lauryn Hill would say in her song, *Freedom Time.*

The Second National Developmental Conference on Forensics adopted "Ethical Guidelines for Students," which are recorded on pages 39–40 for your consideration. These guidelines provide a beginning outline for ethical practice.

EXERCISES

1. View a debate. Many are available online. What type of debate was it (applied or academic, etc.)? You may find debates at C-SPAN (http://www.c-span.org/), You Debate (http://youdebate.blogspot.com/), and countless other places.

2. *Listening.* Choose a story from the newspaper. Five student volunteers should leave the room, while one remains. Have one volunteer return, and have the in-the-room volunteer read the newspaper article aloud. No notes allowed, and after the first reading, the article will be discarded. Then call on the next person to return. The person who has just listened to the reading of the article should recount the story, including all details, to the new student. One at a time, have each student return and repeat the process. The rest of the class should observe. After all five have returned, have the class discuss what details were omitted, changed, or added.

3. Form teams of two to three people each. Each team should identify their candidate for President of the Argumentation and Debate class. Negotiate rules for a campaign debate. What should be the format, layout, etc.?

4. Working in teams, prepare a set of ethical standards to govern the debates in your class.

5. Form an online community consisting of your class. Your instructor may wish to do so through a course website, or you can create one. One easy way to facilitate this is to form a group at Yahoo! (http://groups.yahoo .com/). As a class, select a topic for debate and initiate an online debate.

3

Stating the Controversy

Debate is a means of settling differences, so there must be a difference of opinion or a conflict of interest before there can be a debate. If everyone is in agreement on a fact or value or policy, there is no need for debate; the matter can be settled by unanimous consent. Thus, for example, it would be pointless to attempt to debate "Resolved: That two plus two equals four," because there is simply no controversy about this statement. *Controversy is an essential prerequisite of debate.* Where there is no *clash* of ideas, proposals, interests, or expressed positions on issues, there is no debate. In addition, debate cannot produce effective decisions without clear identification of a question or questions to be answered. For example, general argument may occur about the broad topic of illegal immigration. How many illegal immigrants are in the United States? What is the impact of illegal immigration and immigrants on our economy? What is their impact on our communities? Do they commit crimes? Do they take jobs from American workers? Do they pay taxes? Do they require social services? Is it a problem that some do not speak English? Is it the responsibility of employers to discourage illegal immigration by not hiring undocumented workers? Should they have the opportunity to gain citizenship? Does illegal immigration pose a security threat to our country? Do illegal immigrants do work that American workers are unwilling to do? Are their rights as workers and as human beings at risk due to their status? Are they abused by employers, law enforcement, housing, and businesses? How are their families impacted by their status? What is the moral and philosophical obligation of a nation state to maintain its borders? Should we build a wall on the Mexican border, establish a national identification card, or enforce existing laws against employers? Should we invite immigrants to become U.S. citizens? Surely you can think of many more concerns to be addressed by a conversation about the topic area of illegal immigration. Participation in this "debate" is likely to be emotional and intense. However, it is not likely to be productive or useful without focus on a particular question and identification of a line demarcating sides in the controversy. To be discussed and resolved effectively, controversies must be stated clearly. Vague understanding results in unfocused deliberation and poor decisions, frustration, and emotional distress, as evidenced by the failure of the United States Congress to make progress on the immigration debate during the summer of 2007.

Miniglossary

A burden of proof   The obligation to prove what one asserts. Applies to both the affirmative and the negative, as any advocate forwarding a claim must provide support sufficient to overcome the natural presumption against that claim.

The burden of proof   The risk of the proposition; the obligation of the affirmative, in order to overcome the presumption against the proposition, to give good and sufficient reasons for accepting the proposition.

Burden of refutation   The obligation to refute, or respond to, opposing arguments. Applies to both the affirmative and the negative. Failure to fulfill the burden of refutation results in the acceptance of the unrefuted argument.

Presumption   A predisposition favoring a given side in a dispute. Describes a psychological state in which listeners and decision makers are predisposed to favor or oppose one side of a debate or an argumentative position.

Proposition   A statement of judgment that identifies the central issue in a controversy. May be a proposition of fact, value, nonpolicy, or policy.

Status quo   The existing state of things; the present system.

Someone disturbed by the problem of a growing underclass of poorly educated, socially disenfranchised youths might observe, "Public schools are doing a terrible job! They are overcrowded, and many teachers are poorly qualified in their subject areas. Even the best teachers can do little more than struggle to maintain order in their classrooms." That same concerned citizen, facing a complex range of issues, might arrive at an unhelpful decision, such as "We ought to do something about this" or, worse, "It's too complicated a problem to deal with." Groups of concerned citizens worried about the state of public education could join together to express their frustrations, anger, disillusionment, and emotions regarding the schools, but without a focus for their discussions, they could easily agree about the sorry state of education without finding points of clarity or potential solutions. A gripe session would follow. But if a precise question is posed—such as "*What* can be done to *improve* public education?"—then a more profitable area of discussion is opened up simply by placing a focus on the search for a concrete solution step. One or more judgments can be phrased in the form of debate propositions, motions for parliamentary debate, or bills for legislative assemblies. The statements "Resolved: That the federal government should implement a program of charter schools in at-risk communities" and "Resolved: That the state of Florida should adopt a school voucher program" more clearly identify specific ways of dealing with educational problems in a manageable form, suitable for debate. They provide specific policies to be investigated and aid discussants in identifying points of difference.

The Debate Proposition

- A proposition is a statement of judgment that identifies the central issue in controversy
- Those arguing in favor of the proposition present the *affirmative* side
- Those arguing against the proposition present the *negative* side

---

I. DEFINING THE CONTROVERSY

To have a productive debate, which facilitates effective decision making by directing and placing limits on the decision to be made, the basis for argument should be clearly defined. If we merely talk about "homelessness" or "abortion" or "crime" or "global warming" we are likely to have an interesting discussion but not to establish profitable basis for argument. For example, the statement "Resolved: That the pen is mightier than the sword" is debatable, yet fails to provide much basis for clear argumentation. If we take this statement to mean that the written word is more effective than physical force for some purposes, we can identify a problem area: the comparative effectiveness of writing or physical force for a specific purpose.

Although we now have a general subject, we have not yet stated a problem. It is still too broad, too loosely worded to promote well-organized argument. What sort of writing are we concerned with—poems, novels, government documents, website development, advertising, or what? What does "effectiveness" mean in this context? What kind of physical force is being compared—fists, dueling swords, bazookas, nuclear weapons, or what? A more specific question might be, "Would a mutual defense treaty or a visit by our fleet be more effective in assuring Laurania of our support in a certain crisis?" The basis for argument could be phrased in a debate proposition such as "Resolved: That the United States should enter into a mutual defense treaty with Laurania." Negative advocates might oppose this proposition by arguing that fleet maneuvers would be a better solution. This is not to say that debates should completely avoid creative interpretation of the controversy by advocates, or that good debates cannot occur over competing interpretations of the controversy; in fact, these sorts of debates may be very engaging. The point is that debate is best facilitated by the guidance provided by focus on a particular point of difference, which will be outlined in the following discussion.

II. PHRASING THE DEBATE PROPOSITION

In argumentation and debate a **proposition** is a statement of judgment that identifies the central issue in controversy. The advocate desires to have others accept or reject the proposition. Debate provides for organized argument for and against the proposition: Those arguing in favor of the proposition present the affirmative side; those arguing against it present the negative side. To promote intelligent and effective argumentation, a debate proposition must have certain characteristics.

A. Controversy

As stated at the beginning of this chapter, controversy is an essential prerequisite of debate. Thus the debate proposition must clearly state the controversy or reference the point of controversy.

B. One Central Idea

The most elegant proposition provides for the best debate and ultimately the most useful decision making. There should be a clear-cut yes/no answer to a single point of controversy to enable productive and sensible debate. Even though complexity is inevitable and many smaller questions will need to be answered to provide an answer to the broader propositional question, if a proposition has more than one central idea, it will lead to confusion. Consider the proposition "Resolved: That the Philosophy Club deplores abortions and lotteries as immoral." While some people certainly would agree with this proposition, there are really two subjects for argument here. Some might deplore abortions and approve of lotteries; others might take the opposite view. Two central ideas like these should be placed in separate propositions and debated separately. If this resolution were introduced into the Philosophy Club's parliamentary debate, any member of the club could move to amend the original motion into two separate motions. If the amendment were seconded and passed, then the two motions could be debated separately. The proposition addresses two controversies.

C. Unemotional Terms

The proposition should be stated in unemotional terms, without loaded language that might give a special advantage to the affirmative or the negative. Consider the proposition "Resolved: That cruel, sadistic experimenters should be forbidden to torture defenseless animals pointlessly." The heavily loaded, emotional language gives the affirmative an unreasonable advantage. "Resolved: That vivisection should be illegal" states the proposition in dispassionate terms. Although emotionally loaded terms have persuasive value, they have no place in a debate proposition.

Although probably no word is completely neutral to everyone, one can and must try to minimize the evaluative aspects of a proposition. The wording of the proposition must be such that reasonable participants on either side will accept it as accurately and dispassionately describing the controversy to be debated.

D. Statement of the Affirmative's Desired Decision

The proposition should represent a statement of the decision the affirmative desires. It should set forth the decision clearly and precisely so that, if adopted, the affirmative advocates will have achieved their purpose, yet maintain sufficient leeway for the affirmative to address a range of possible interpretations. The proposition "Resolved: That the power of the federal government should be increased" is vague and indefinite. If the affirmative should win a debate on such a proposition, what would have been accomplished? Nothing. After it was agreed that the powers of the federal government should be increased, another debate on the specific powers in question would be needed. For example, people who favored increasing the power of the federal government by allowing it to make military appropriations for three, rather than two, years might oppose an increase in the power of the federal government that would allow it to abolish the states. The phrasing of the proposition must be clear, specific, devoid of ambiguous terms, and precise in the statement of the desired decision. In particular, the direction of change should be identified, to draw a clear distinction for preparation and debating as to which side occupies which argumentative ground. For example, should there be more regulation or less?

Although the decision desired by the affirmative must be stated with precision, the proposition sometimes gives the affirmative considerable latitude in its analysis of the **status quo**—the existing state of things—and allows for the possibility of several plans in implementing that decision. For example, the proposition "Resolved: That the federal government should grant annually a specific percentage of its income tax revenue to state governments" indicates the general plan but allows the affirmative considerable latitude in analyzing the status quo and in developing the details of the plan. Thus some affirmatives might call for the plan to improve the financing of state and local services. Others might focus on specific problems, such as improved financing of the criminal justice or health care system. Still others might develop a quite different analysis and call for the adoption of the proposition as a means of checking the power of the military-industrial complex.

Such "open-ended" propositions realistically reflect the fact that different persons may support the same policy for a variety of reasons. As the saying goes, "Politics makes strange bedfellows," and in applied debate we often find unlikely combinations of legislators supporting a bill for widely different reasons.

The statement of the proposition should be affirmative in both form and intent. The proposition "Resolved: That the United States should not give direct economic aid to foreign countries" is in negative form. The use of negative phrasing is potentially confusing and needlessly complicates the advocates' task in presenting their case. By contrast, "Resolved: That the United States should offer foreign aid in the form of developmental assistance programs" allows affirmatives to clearly advocate particular aid programs.

The proposition "Resolved: That the jury system should be abolished" is negative not in its form but in its intent. The flaw here is that the proposition represents an interim goal and does not provide a clear, precise statement of the

---

Characteristics of an Effectively Worded Debate Proposition

- Controversy
- One central idea
- Unemotional terms
- Precise statement of the affirmative's desired decision

---

decision desired by the affirmative. If the jury system was abolished and nothing provided in its place, all accused criminals would go free, because there would be no means of trying them. But the proposition "Resolved: That juries should be replaced by a panel of three judges" represents a statement of a decision some affirmatives might advocate.

An important challenge for the framers of debate propositions is to find an appropriate balance between a very loosely worded proposition that fails to provide sufficient guidance for preparation and an overly restrictive or tightly worded proposition that overlimits the creativity of the advocates in interpreting the action required by the proposition. Considerations in selecting the appropriate degree of specificity may include the format, the context for debate, the nature and expertise of the participants, availability of support materials, the intended audience, and so on.

In addition to the criteria for a debate proposition, there are additional requirements for propositions in academic debate. (See the inset "Phrasing the Proposition for Academic Debate" on pages 49–50.) For CEDA and NDT debate, once several well-phrased propositions have been offered to the forensic community, a choice is made. (See the inset "Choosing the Proposition for Academic Debate" on page 51.) Individual tournament hosts design propositions to be debated in parliamentary debate rounds, and the National Forensic Association (NFA) and National Educational Debate Association (NEDA) choose their own propositions for Lincoln–Douglas and team debate, respectively.

III. PRESUMPTION AND BURDEN OF PROOF

A. The Status Quo

In debates about propositions of policy, affirmative advocates support change, usually favoring new governmental policy. Such supported change requires departure from the status quo, usually described in terms of currently existing structures or laws. The status quo is the current system or the way things are now. For example, at one time capital punishment was legal throughout the United States; it was the status quo. Then the Supreme Court ruled that existing capital punishment statutes were unconstitutional. The status quo then became one of no capital punishment. Subsequently some states enacted new capital punishment

Phrasing the Proposition for Academic Debate

The additional requirements for propositions used in academic debate involve significance, fairness, length, and ambiguity.

Significant Contemporary Problem

In choosing an issue for educational debate, directors of forensics not only look for a well-phrased proposition but also try to select one that will provide an opportunity for exploring a significant problem of current interest to students, judges, and audiences. Because the topic should be one on which information is readily available, national debate propositions deal with matters of current national or international concern. Some debate coaches favored the civil rights proposition selected by CEDA/NDT in 1998–1999 because they believed it helped to attract students, especially minority students, to debating. The 2003–2004 CEDA resolution, however, was criticized as too diffuse and obtuse to be interesting at first glance to new debaters.

Educators also seek an issue that will remain in the news and stay interesting during the academic year or semester so that debaters can continue to find new evidence and arguments. When the Supreme Court's right-to-privacy decisions were the subject of a national debate proposition, the educators who chose this issue did not expect that these decisions would be overruled during the year the proposition was being debated. But had this happened, the status quo on privacy might have changed so substantially as to render the proposition unsuitable for academic debate.

Sometimes the status quo may change dramatically and require substantial changes in affirmative cases without necessitating a change in the proposition. During the academic year in which the proposition concerning "federal control of the supply and utilization of energy" was debated, a number of such changes occurred. Early in the season some affirmative teams argued that "the Arab nations might embargo oil." Negative teams confidently denied this possibility, but the Arabs did in fact embargo oil early in the season. Some affirmative teams then argued for gas rationing as the only means of dealing with the oil embargo. As the academic year went on, however, it became apparent that, although some states had imposed limitations on gas sales, no real-world support existed for federal rationing. During that year many teams found it necessary to redraft their affirmative cases for almost every tournament, for the status quo changed repeatedly as new policies became operative or as new evidence became available. During the 2002–2003 academic debate season, a portion of the resolution became undebatable before the end of the debate year, as the SORT agreement, one of the policy actions called for in the proposition, was ratified by the U.S. Senate on March 6.

Equal Conflicting Evidence and Reasoning

In applied debates the evidence and reasoning may strongly favor one side. In the courts attorneys may defend clients when the evidence against them is almost overwhelming. In legislatures the minority leader may fight for an almost hopeless cause. In academic debate, however, the objective is not to secure or to prevent the adoption of a proposition. Rather, it is to use the proposition to provide opportunities to learn about argumentation and debate, as well as about the subject itself. For educational purposes preference is given to propositions that give both sides an approximately equal opportunity to build a strong case.

Single Declarative Sentence

In the interests of clarity, and because of the limited amount of time available, academic debate propositions should be limited to a single declarative sentence. In

Phrasing the Proposition for Academic Debate (Continued)

applied debates the proposition may be as long as necessary; for instance, a bill in Congress is a specialized form of debate proposition and may extend for many pages. Recent CEDA/NDT resolutions have violated this to some degree by offering lists of options to the affirmative. The trend has been for those options to be increasingly specific as to policies to be advocated, thus offering clarity for individual debates. Criticism has been directed at the failure of some resolutions (for example, the 2003–2004 CEDA/NDT Resolution) to offer a consistent theme and of some resolutions to be overly restrictive in dictating affirmative advocacy.

Avoidance of Ambiguity

Those wording a proposition for academic debate should seek to avoid excessive ambiguity while not unnecessarily limiting the debaters' opportunities to be creative in their interpretation of the terms of the proposition. The framers challenge, then, is achieve a balance between being too vague and too prescriptive. It is generally more effective to provide a clear direction of change in the wording of the proposition (for example, *increase* gun control, rather than *change* gun laws). The Second National Developmental Conference on Forensics made the following recommendations specifically for academic debate:

1. Take care when using any encompassing term such as *all, every,* or *any.*
2. Take care when using vague or compounding words or phrases such as *greater* or *any and all.*
3. Consult linguistics experts on the phrasing and interpretation of debate propositions.
4. Specify clearly the nature and direction of the change or decision.
5. Seek wording that will balance the need for maintaining interest over a period of time with the need to limit the topic in order to create a meaningful level of research and discussion.

laws that met the Supreme Court's criteria, and executions resumed in those states. Thus the status quo is that some states permit capital punishment under specific circumstances. But partisans on both sides are seeking to change this status quo: Some want to expand capital punishment to all states, whereas others want to abolish it.

B. Presumption

In debate **presumption** is a predisposition favoring a given side in a dispute. It describes the psychological predisposition of a listener or decision maker. Presumption may be viewed from two perspectives: the judicial perspective and the policy perspective. The judicial perspective offers a constant understanding of presumption: It always favors the status quo, or a presumed condition (for example, presumption of innocence). The judicial perspective may be used when the option exists of continuing the structure of the status quo. With this option there may, of course, be minor repairs and other modifications, but the essential features of the status quo will continue until good and sufficient reason is given to justify a change. This perspective is mandated in the courts, for example, where

---

Choosing the Proposition for Academic Debate

Each year, CEDA solicits topic papers from members of the debate community. Each topic paper provides an overview of a topic area, with discussion of the available literature, possible topic linkages and phrasings, and the relative merits of debating that topic area. In the spring the topic selection committee of CEDA, utilizing the topic papers to generate ideas, identifies at least three topic areas to be presented to the membership of CEDA. The membership votes for their preference among the problem areas, and the committee goes back to work to frame no fewer than three policy propositions within the chosen topic area, to be presented to the CEDA membership for final selection. The yearlong proposition, to be used by CEDA and the NDT, is announced in July. The ADA uses the CEDA/NDT proposition. NEDA and NFA Lincoln–Douglas select their own propositions. Parliamentary tournament debaters, as represented by APDA (American Parliamentary Debate Association) and NPDA (National Parliamentary Debate Association), use topics selected for each round of a given tournament as framed by the tournament hosts.

Research-based team debating in the tournament context makes use of national debate propositions indispensable. If students had to debate a different proposition for each tournament, or even if they attempted to debate a number of different propositions during the year, they would acquire considerable experience in research methods but might sacrifice the depth of research and experience in evidence-based debating. The first few academic debates on a new proposition are often tentative and experimental. After a number of debates on a proposition, the learning situation provides more depth.

Of course, alternative debate forums, including Parliamentary Debate (NPDA and APDA) offer different educational experiences and skill sets based on impromptu development of ideas and broad-based reading and research about a wide range of issues. Although such approaches may not offer the depth of research and argumentation, they are certainly valuable experiences in public advocacy and critical thinking.

Because much academic debating is on a national intercollegiate debate proposition, it is useful to know how such propositions are chosen. The care devoted to the selection of these propositions suggests something of the care that individual debaters should exercise in phrasing propositions for their own use. Similar standards should also be applied to resolutions for extemporaneous style debates such as those practiced in Parliamentary Debate Tournaments.

---

the accused must be presumed innocent (the status quo) until proved guilty. As a defendant is presumed innocent, the status quo is presumed acceptable until and unless a compelling case is offered to the contrary.

From the judicial perspective presumption favors the status quo. That is, the existing state of affairs will continue until good and sufficient reason is given for changing it. In debates using the judicial perspective, the presumption favors the status quo and the affirmative has **the burden of proof**—the risk of the proposition. Because change involves risk (and cost), the advocates of change must prove that it is worthwhile to take that risk. The advocates who affirm the proposition are required to prove their case. They must provide good and sufficient reason for adopting or accepting the proposition, and they must convince those who render the decision. If they do not fulfill the burden of proof, they will lose all that they hoped to gain from adoption of the proposition. These concepts are aptly summed up in the maxim "If it ain't broke, don't fix it."[1]

The policy perspective is used when change is inherent in the status quo. For example, in 2004 President Bush, the incumbent president, ran for reelection. That year the voters had the option of voting for Bush (the status quo) or for his opponent, John Kerry. Constitutional restrictions barred Bush from running for a third term in 2008; thus change was inevitable. Voters in the year 2000 did not have the option of supporting the status quo (voting for Clinton) but chose between two or more departures from the status quo, as in 2008. As is typical in such cases, one choice represented a greater change in the status quo than the other, as in 2000 the Republican candidate was perceived as more substantially different than the Democrat candidate.

From the policy perspective presumption favors the position that provides the greatest advantages while incurring the least disadvantages, or incurs the least risk due to the lesser degree of change. Put another way, presumption favors the position that is less risky or that incurs the least risk of harmful consequences. In debates on value propositions the presumption favors the position of the greater over the lesser value. For example, in debates on the "testing for controlled substances" proposition, the issue in many debates is whether "privacy" concerns outweigh "safety" concerns.

How does one determine the burden of proof in such cases? The classic rule of burden of proof applies: One who asserts must prove. Let us now look at a few examples to see how these concepts work. We will first consider some examples from the judicial perspective.

Do you favor a constitutional amendment defining marriage as the legal union of a man and a woman? A school prayer amendment to the Constitution? A right-to-life amendment to the Constitution? A balanced budget amendment? The status quo is the Constitution as it now exists. If you want to advocate a change to the Constitution, you have the burden of proof. In this case you must convince both branches of Congress to pass your amendment and then you must convince 38 states to ratify it. This is the burden of proof we place on those who want to change our Constitution.

The concept of presumption is a vital part of our legal system. Did Richard Roe rob the Cook County National Bank? Our laws explicitly require that a person be presumed innocent until proved guilty. The status quo is that Richard Roe is innocent, and the police department and the district attorney must convince a jury that he is guilty before he can be sentenced. (Unfortunately this principle of law is sometimes distorted. The accused in a well-publicized case may have a "trial by news media" and be "proved guilty" in the minds of the prospective jurors before the courtroom trial begins. British law is much stricter than American law in prohibiting pretrial publicity about the accused.)

---

1. A conservative English statesman, Viscount Falkland, expressed this famous dictum in 1641 in more stately prose: "When it is not necessary to change, it is necessary not to change."

The Richard Roes of this world move through the criminal justice system in relative anonymity; their cases rarely attract the attention of the media. The O. J. Simpson murder trial, however, drew unprecedented, worldwide attention. One TV reporter, commenting on the problem of choosing a jury for the trial, quipped; "Only someone who has been in a coma for the past few months hasn't heard about the O. J. case." The trials of Scott Peterson, Kobe Bryant, Martha Stewart, Phil Spector, Robert Blake, and Zacarias Moussaoui have drawn similar attention.

There are, however, some exceptions to this concept of presumption of innocence. For many years in contested tax cases, the taxpayer was in effect guilty until proved innocent—a clear violation of the presumption of innocence. This inversion of principle, however, had become the status quo and stood until, in a major ruling, the Fifth Circuit Court of Appeals put the burden of proof on the Internal Revenue Service (IRS).[2] The IRS Restructuring and Reform Act of 1998, also known as the "Taxpayer's Bill of Rights," legislatively shifted the burden of proof in certain legal proceedings from individual taxpayers to the IRS.

C. The Burden of Proof

In our law courts different standards prevail for the burden of proof in different circumstances. Before a grand jury only "probable cause" need be proved to secure an indictment; in a criminal trial the prosecutor must establish proof "beyond a reasonable doubt" to secure a guilty verdict; in a civil case the verdict commonly is based on a "preponderance of evidence." Outside the courtroom reasonable persons usually apply this standard and base their decisions in important matters on a "preponderance of evidence." The judge in legal proceedings will instruct the jury as to what constitutes "probable cause" or "reasonable doubt."

The concepts of burden of proof and presumption made the front page of the *New York Times* and other newspapers across the country when the Supreme Court ruled that in gender discrimination cases "an employer has the legal burden of proving that its refusal to hire or promote someone is based on legitimate and not discriminatory reasons." In the same decision the Court ruled that the employer has to show only by "a preponderance of evidence" that its reasons were legitimate, and not by the more rigorous standard of "clear and convincing proof" as required by a lower court.[3] Outside the courtroom we do not have predetermined definitions of what constitutes a "preponderance of evidence." Therefore a definition of that phrase may become a critical issue in the debate as the debaters try to convince the decision makers that theirs is a satisfactory definition within the context of the debate. (See Chapter 4.)

In certain situations in parliamentary debate, the affirmative must obtain a two-thirds or three-quarters majority to carry its burden of proof. In 1995 the proposal was advanced that Congress should require a three-fifths vote to enact

---

2. "Taxing News," *Newsweek,* July 8, 1991, p. 8.
3. *New York Times,* May 2, 1989, p. 1.

new taxes. By contrast, to convict Richard Roe of robbing the Cook County National Bank, the prosecutor must convince 100 percent of the jury. If one juror is not convinced of Roe's guilt, he cannot be convicted.

Sometimes the burden of proof may be greater than expected. In 1994 a majority of California voters thought they had won a victory when they approved Proposition 187, the anti–illegal immigration initiative. Their opponents, however, persuaded a federal court to delay enforcement of the initiative, arguing that federal, not state, laws governed the status of immigrants. A federal district court judge struck down the law as unconstitutional.

The burden of proof in enacting a new federal law is greater than that of obtaining a majority of one state's votes. To enact a new federal law, one must convince a majority of the House, a majority of the Senate, and the president. If the president vetoes the law, then the proponents must convince two-thirds of the House and two-thirds of the Senate. If the law is challenged in the courts, then its supporters may have to convince a majority of the Supreme Court. Let us now consider a few examples from the policy perspective.

In some cases, again, change may be inherent in the status quo. In such cases there is a presumption in favor of *a* change but not in favor of any *particular* change. A typical example may be found in the automobile industry, in which most companies make annual model changes. Even though new models come out every year, the designers advocating model X have the burden of proof to convince their company that model X is better than model Y or model Z or any other model under consideration. In some situations there is no status quo; for example, when it comes time to elect freshman class officers, there are no incumbents.

Thus, when the status quo provides for a change or when a change is inherent in the status quo, the advocates of a new policy or of possible change have the burden of proof. Similarly the advocates of a specific value (as in a debate on a proposition of value in which the affirmative advocates the specific value called for in the resolution) have the burden of proof. Again, the classic rule of burden of proof applies to all of these situations: One who asserts must prove.

The affirmative—the one advancing an assertion—has the burden of proof. The question then arises: What amounts to satisfactory proof? The answer depends on the rules governing the debate and the judgment of the person or group empowered to decide. At a minimum the affirmative must go more than halfway in convincing the decision makers. Thus, for example, if 49 percent of the members of your club vote for a motion and 51 percent vote against it, the motion fails. If 50 percent vote for the motion and 50 percent against it, the motion fails.

Note that there is a distinction between *the* burden of proof and *a* burden of proof, and that this distinction applies to both the judicial and the policy perspective. The burden of proof always rests on the affirmative, who must prove that the proposition should be adopted or accepted. However, **a burden of proof** may rest on either the affirmative or the negative. Whoever introduces an issue into the debate has a burden of proof. The advocate must support the argument he or she introduces. During a trial, for example, the prosecution may allege that Richard

Roe committed a robbery in Chicago. Richard Roe may claim that he was in New York at the time of the robbery. Richard Roe now has assumed a burden of proof; he must prove his alibi. In a debate on the "testing for controlled substances" proposition, if the negative introduces the argument that "privacy" concerns outweigh "safety" concerns, they have assumed a burden of proof.

D. The Burden of Refutation

Either side may also have a **burden of refutation**—the obligation to refute, or respond to, opposing arguments. This burden also referred to as the burden of "clash" rests on the advocate whose case is weakened by an argument advanced by an opponent. The advocate must refute that argument or suffer damage to the case. In Richard Roe's case, if Roe introduces evidence to establish that he was in New York at the time of the robbery, the prosecution has a burden of refutation. That is, the Chicago district attorney must refute that evidence or Roe will go free. In the "controlled substances" case the affirmative must refute the negative's "safety" argument or face a serious loss.

A tie is thus impossible in academic debate. The affirmative either carries its burden of proof or it does not. Even in a debate with one judge, a common situation in academic debate, a tie is impossible. If the judge discerns that both teams have done an equally good job, he or she must render a decision for the negative because the affirmative has failed to carry its burden of proof. Reasonable people follow this principle in making individual decisions. If the arguments pro and con are equal—if they simply cannot make up their minds—they decline to support the affirmative's proposal.

IV. TYPES OF DEBATE PROPOSITIONS

Debate propositions may deal with controversies of fact, value, or policy. We will first consider propositions of fact, then value, and finally policy.

A. Propositions of Fact

A proposition of fact is a type of descriptive claim. In a debate on a proposition of fact, the affirmative maintains that a certain thing is true, while the negative maintains that it is false. Our law courts are almost entirely concerned with propositions of fact. Examples of typical propositions of legal debates include "Resolved: That Richard Roe is guilty of robbery," "Resolved: That this is the last will and testament of John Doe," and "Resolved: That the plaintiff's constitutional rights were violated in this trial." Examples of typical debates on propositions of fact outside the courtroom include "Resolved: That the stock market will decline next year," "Resolved: That life begins at conception," "Resolved: That human activity causes greenhouse warming," and "Resolved: That others conspired with Lee Harvey Oswald to assassinate President Kennedy." This latter proposition of fact had been the subject of extensive public debate for years, and interest in it surged to new heights following the release of Oliver Stone's film *JFK*. Obviously a debate over a proposition of fact is not necessarily easy and may be a rich and important debate. In 2002 and 2003, the debate over the question of Saddam Hussein's ability to produce weapons of mass destruction was a debate of earth-shaking importance.

Propositions of fact also may be debated as precursors, or as a part of debates on propositions of value or propositions of policy, because it is frequently essential to establish relevant facts before reaching decisions about values or policies.

B. Propositions of Value

A proposition of value is a type of evaluative claim. Values are our beliefs about right and wrong, good and bad. So a proposition of value essentially makes a statement that something is good or bad. In a debate on a proposition of value, the affirmative maintains that a certain belief, value, or fact is justified, that it conforms to the definition or criteria appropriate to evaluate the issue. Examples of typical propositions of value include "Resolved: That abortion is immoral" and "Resolved: That television is a vast wasteland." One of the most prominent differences between a proposition of value and a proposition of policy is that the policy proposition requires the affirmative to propose a plan to implement the policy. The proposition of value does not provide for a plan. Rather, the affirmative seeks support for a claim that (1) endorses a value (for example, "Resolved: That compulsory national service for all qualified U.S. citizens is desirable") or (2) chooses one value over another (for example, "Resolved: That inflation is a greater threat to American society than is unemployment") or (3) rejects a value (for example, "Resolved: That the emphasis on competitive athletics is deleterious to American society").

Quasi-policy propositions are propositions that express a value judgment about a policy. Examples of typical quasi-policy propositions include the "compulsory national service" proposition just cited and many CEDA propositions prior to 1996, such as "Resolved: That a unilateral freeze by the United States on the production and development of nuclear weapons would be desirable." Although a plan is not explicit in quasi-policy propositions, it is implicit, and the debaters may need to debate the policy implications of the proposition. Between 1999 and 2002, CEDA selected both a policy and what they termed a "nonpolicy" resolution for each academic year. They defined a nonpolicy resolution as one "phrased so as to generally affirm the truth or value of an idea, condition, or action, but not to simply affirm the desirability or worth of future change."

A value may be a precursor of a policy. Once we have endorsed a value, the next logical step in most cases is to support policies consistent with that value. The intensity with which a value is endorsed or rejected will determine whether we adopt a *personal* policy or urge a *public* policy. A woman who favored the "abortion is immoral" proposition mentioned earlier might say, "Others may follow their own conscience; my values would never permit me to choose abortion." Intense partisans on both sides take a more activist stance and seek to have their values enacted into law. Of course, debaters might engage in a pleasant disputation on values that have no discernable policy implications—for example, "Resolved: That Washington was a greater president than Lincoln." A negative win on this debate implies no policy that we should tear down the Washington Monument or build Lincoln another memorial.

If we decide that "television is a wasteland," we might adopt a personal policy of watching much less television. If, however, we urge that the public support the value we have chosen, then a certain type of programming should, as a matter of policy, be eliminated from television and replaced with programming more beneficial to the public interest. The implications of such a policy are clearly a subject for examination by debaters and those who render the decision.

An example of fact and value judgments leading to policy considerations occurred in the first Bush–Dukakis presidential campaign debate in 1988. George H. W. Bush, who was known to favor the "sanctity of life" (a value proposition) and to regard abortions as "killings" (a fact position), was asked, "If abortions were to become illegal, do you think women who have them should go to jail?" (a policy position). Bush replied, "I haven't sorted out the penalties.... I'm for the sanctity of life, and once that illegality is established, then we can come to grips with the penalty side, and of course, there's got to be some penalties to enforce the law." This response was judged to be weak and ineffective by some observers. Michael Dukakis promptly focused on the policy implications of Bush's values: "Well, I think that the vice president is saying that he's prepared to brand a woman a criminal for making this decision."[4]

While we may sometimes debate facts, values, or policies by themselves, we will find that on many occasions it is necessary to consider all of them together.

C. Propositions of Policy

A policy proposition is a type of advocate claim. It calls for change. CEDA defines policy resolutions as those "phrased so as to affirm the value of future and specific governmental change, and suggesting a broad but predictable array of potential affirmative plans." In a debate on a proposition of policy, the affirmative maintains that a policy or course of action should be adopted. Most debates in legislative bodies are on propositions of policy. Examples of typical debates in Congress, state legislatures, and city councils include "Resolved: That the proposed tax bill should be enacted" and "Resolved: That the Senate should advise and consent to the nomination of Joseph Doakes as ambassador to France." In private organizations as well, most debates are on propositions of policy—for example, "Resolved: That the National Communication Association should hold its annual convention in Chicago" or "Resolved: That Compact Motors should pay a quarterly dividend of 50 cents per share of common stock" or "Resolved: That more dormitories should be established on this campus."

---

4. See the *New York Times*, Sept. 26, 1988, p. 11, for the full text of this exchange.

Recall that a plan to implement the policy is an essential part of the affirmative's case. In debates on policy propositions, propositions of value often arise as important issues. For example, in debates on the proposition of policy "Resolved: That the federal government should significantly strengthen the regulation of mass media communication in the United States," it was sometimes necessary to debate as essential issues "Resolved: That First Amendment rights are the most important of all our rights" and "Resolved: That pretrial publicity denies a fair trial to defendants in criminal trials" (both propositions of value).

The O. J. Simpson case raised many issues of fact, value, and policy. Was O. J. guilty of murder? This was a question of fact the trial intended to answer. During the pretrial hearings a friend of O. J.'s slain ex-wife wrote a book. Did this create prejudice against O. J.? While in jail awaiting trial, O. J. also wrote a book. Did this create prejudice in favor of O. J.? The media—from the tabloids to the mainstream press, from Court TV to the major networks—reported all of the events, gossip, rumors, and opinions surrounding the trial. Did the media's First Amendment right to report about the trial and events surrounding it outweigh O. J.'s right to a fair trial? Had O. J. been convicted, his lawyers might have sought to argue some of these questions of fact and value before the Supreme Court.

Had the prosecution sought the death penalty, the issue of whether to apply it would have become a question of policy to be debated by the jury in separate proceedings following a guilty verdict.

As another example, consider the Monica Lewinsky–Bill Clinton scandal. The House impeachment proceedings against President Clinton focused on propositions of fact. For its part the Senate considered the magnitude of the value implications and, finally, the appropriate policy action: Should President Clinton be removed from office? Just as questions of fact, value, and policy are interwoven in one of the twentieth century's most highly publicized murder trials and the historic proceedings against a president, they are also interwoven in the great debates on public policy and in the unpublicized debates that influence our everyday lives.

EXERCISES

1. Examine the following "propositions." Which are well phrased? Which violate the criteria of a well-phrased proposition? What criteria do they violate? Rephrase the incorrect propositions so they meet the requirements for academic debate.

   a. Inadequate parking facilities on campus
   b. The AIDS crisis
   c. Should our college abandon intercollegiate athletics?
   d. The present method of electing the president of the United States should be improved
   e. Affirmative action in college admissions

    f.   Gay/lesbian rights

    g.   Is politically correct speech a violation of free speech?

    h.   Our college should not adopt a multicultural curriculum

2.   Phrase one proposition of fact, one of value, and one of policy for each of the following areas:

    a.   Health Care

    b.   Education

    c.   Civility

    d.   The War on Terror

    e.   Tuition

3.   From the newspapers, newsmagazines, and radio and television broadcasts, and Internet discussions of the past week, identify what problems are currently being debated in Congress or in the nation. Phrase propositions of fact, value, and policy on five problems currently being debated nationally. Phrase these 15 propositions in a manner suitable for academic debate.

4.   From the newspapers, newsmagazines, radio and television broadcasts, and Internet discussions of the past week, find five examples of quasi-policy propositions currently being debated in Congress or in the nation.

5.   Prepare a five-minute speech for delivery in class in which you state a proposition of policy and demonstrate how it meets the criteria of a well-phrased proposition for academic debate.

6.   Consider the 2007–2008 NDT/CEDA debate proposition (see Appendix C). Reword it to better meet the criteria for an effective proposition.

4

Analyzing the Controversy

As we discussed in Chapter 3, effective debate begins with the identification of a controversy from which a proposition emerges or is framed. The proposition provides debaters a focus for preparation and argumentation, and allows the audience or judge a guideline for their decision. The proposition focuses the clash and ensures that arguments are pertinent to decision making. The proposition for debate may be formulated by one of the advocates in the debate, by agreement between the opposing advocates, or by someone other than the actual advocates. If a student at a business meeting of a college organization introduces the motion "Resolved: That the dues of this organization should be increased five dollars a semester," he or she is formulating a proposition for debate. Before Abraham Lincoln and Stephen Douglas held their famous debates, they agreed on the propositions they would use. The proposition may also be expressed in the form of a motion in parliamentary debate, and in our current political environment, candidates involved in campaign debates are presented propositions in the form of questions from moderators, audience members, or even YouTube contributors. Frequently an attorney first learns of the proposition to be debated in a court case when he or she is retained by a client in the form of formal legal charges or claims.

Regardless of how the proposition is chosen, our first task as advocates is to analyze the proposition and the area of controversy from which it is derived. When a chemist analyzes a compound, he or she breaks it down to its most basic elements to identify its makeup. Similarly, as debate advocates we must break the proposition down into its component parts, define the terms of the proposition, and then identify the issues involved. Words or terms in the proposition must be defined *within the context of the proposition.* For example, we cannot define, or even pronounce, the word *polish* until we know the context in which it is used. Analysis of the proposition's relationship to the problem area—the political, legal, social, or other relevant contexts from which it arises—may reveal other terms that require definition and new concepts that will aid in the development of issues.

Miniglossary

Definition of terms   The advocate's supported interpretation of the meaning of the words in the proposition.

Fiat   The convention in academic policy debate that, for the sake of argument, participants may assume implementation of a reasonable policy. This allows debaters to focus on the question of whether a policy *should* be adopted and to avoid as irrelevant arguments about whether the policy *would* be adopted.

Issues   Critical claims inherent in the proposition. Questions identifying points of controversy.

Stock issues   Those issues common to most debates on given types of propositions. In value debate they are definitive and designative; in policy debate they include harm, inherency, and solvency.

I. THE IMPORTANCE OF DEFINING TERMS

The **definition of terms**—the advocate's supported interpretation of the meaning of the words in a proposition—is an essential part of debate. In some instances the opposing advocates will agree right away on the definition of terms, and the debate will move on to other issues. In other cases the locus of the debate may be the definition of a key term or terms, and definitions become the "voting issue" that decides the debate. In all debates, however, a shared understanding of the interpretation of the proposition is necessary to guide argumentation and decision making.

Many intercollegiate debate propositions call for the "federal government" to adopt a certain policy. Often the term is self-evident in the context of the proposition, and no definition is necessary. In debates on the 2001–2002 CEDA proposition, "Resolved: That the United States Federal Government should substantially increase federal control throughout Indian Country in one or more of the following areas: child welfare, criminal justice, employment, environmental protection, gaming, resource management, taxation," the affirmative merely designated the appropriate federal agency (for example, The Bureau of Indian Affairs or the Environmental Protection Agency) to carry out its policy, and the debate moved on to other issues. However, sometimes other terms in the proposition (for instance, *Indian Country*) become critical issues of the debate. Not infrequently the negative will raise the issue of topicality and argue that the affirmative's plan is not the best definition, or interpretation, of the proposition. In debates on propositions of value, the clash over definitions or criteria may be crucial to the outcome.

In debates outside the educational setting, the same situation prevails. In some debates the definition of terms is easy and obvious—they need only be stated "for the record," and the debate proceeds to other issues. In other debates, however, the definition may be all-important. For instance physicians, clerics, and ethicists conduct long, hard-fought debates on the critical issue of when life begins: At conception? When the fetus becomes capable of surviving outside the womb? When the brain begins to function? Or at the moment of birth?

Exactly the opposite problem arose, and continues, in debates over the use of organ transplants. Does death occur when breathing stops? When the heart stops? Or when the brain ceases to function? Some states have debated this issue and adopted new definitions of death; in other states the debate continues. Similarly, environmentalists seeking protection from development for valued resources debate the definition of *wetlands* in public hearings; owners of sports franchises work to redefine players' salaries to fit within predetermined salary caps; and customers considering new product purchases study competing definitions of *value*. In February 2004, President Bush called upon the Congress to "promptly pass and send to the states for ratification, an amendment to our Constitution defining and protecting marriage as a union of a man and a woman as husband and wife." This advocacy by the president was an attempt to *define* "marriage" in such a way as to limit it to heterosexual couples. A public debate about the meaning of marriage, and its alternative, "civil union," ensued. Definitional debates have political, moral, and personal implications. What is poverty? Obesity? Adulthood? In 2007, the meaning of the term "surge" in reference to the United States military action in Iraq was hotly contested. Was this an expansion of the war or simply provision of necessary resources to achieve existing objectives? The 2007 immigration reform offered the opportunity for illegal immigrants working in this country to achieve citizenship through a cumbersome and expensive process. The reform legislation failed in part because it was termed "amnesty" by its opponents. Likewise, the definition of "terrorism" creates significant problems in our foreign policy.

Terms that do not actually occur in the proposition itself but that an advocate expects to use in the course of the debate may also require definition. For example, the words *cyclical, frictional,* and *hidden* did not appear in the proposition "Resolved: That the federal government should establish a national program of public work for the unemployed." Yet, because references to these types of unemployment likely recurred in debates on the proposition, the debaters needed to define them.

In debates on this same proposition, dictionary definitions of the individual words *public* and *work* would have done little to clarify the meaning of the proposition or to furnish a basis for argument. Advocates define the phrase *public work* rather than the individual words, and, by referring to the use of this phrase in legislation, they were able to provide a useful definition.

In analyzing the problem, advocates must carefully consider all possible definitions of all the terms. In presenting their cases, however, they will define only the terms that might be unfamiliar to their audience or about which they and their opponents might differ. In debating the proposition "Resolved: That Congress should be given the power to reverse decisions of the Supreme Court," it would probably be unnecessary to define *Congress* and *Supreme Court*. But it would be necessary to define *reverse* and *decisions,* because legal usage of these terms differs from popular usage, and opposing advocates sometimes interpret these words differently within the context of this proposition.

Consider the old brainteaser—when a tree falls in a forest but nobody hears it, does it make a sound? The answer, of course, is totally dependent on your definition of *sound*. If you define it as waves in the air, the answer is yes; if you define it as the subjective experience of hearing, the answer is no. The terms of a debate proposition may be defined in a variety of ways. To make the basis of the argument explicit, advocates should choose the method or combination of methods best suited to the requirements of the proposition and to the interests of the audience. It is important to define terms carefully to ensure a profitable debate.

II. METHODS OF DEFINING TERMS

A. Basic Methods

1. Example.   Giving an example is often an effective method of defining terms. In debates on the "national program of public work" proposition, affirmative teams sometimes defined their terms by saying, "By a national program of public work, we mean a program similar to the WPA of the 1930s." In this way they gave their audience a specific example of the type of program they proposed. Examples are generally discovered by debaters in the course of researching their issues and thus, they tend to appear in the literature related to the proposition or topic area.

2. Common Usage.   In the interest of accuracy and precision, debate propositions sometimes contain technical terms. Often these terms can be defined effectively by referring to common usage, or "common person" or "person on the street" definition. For example, in debates on the proposition "Resolved: That the requirement of membership in a labor organization as a condition of employment should be illegal," some affirmative teams defined an important term by saying, "By *labor organizations* we mean the type of organization popularly referred to as unions." This reference to common usage usually served to establish a definition acceptable to both teams and clear to the audience. Although the word *unions* would have served well as a definition, it would not have been an acceptable term for use in the proposition. Many important "unions" operate under the legal title of *brotherhoods, associations, federations,* or other names; and most important legislation regulating unions speaks of *labor organizations.* Had the word *unions* been used in the proposition, it might have led to some pointless quibbles as to whether such legislation would apply to organizations such as the railroad brotherhoods.

To qualify as common usage, a term must be commonly understood across lines of gender, age, and culture. The Senate confirmation hearings on Supreme Court Justice Clarence Thomas triggered an extensive public debate about "sexual harassment." Both men and women opposed it, but in many cases they had substantially different definitions of the term. The hearings, which dominated prime-time television and the front pages of newspapers, were generally ignored or given minimal coverage elsewhere in the world. This seems to indicate a cultural difference between the United States and many other countries in which sexual harassment is not a crime and the sexual behavior of politicians and other public figures is considered off limits to the media.

Similarly, when denying his involvement in a "sexual relationship" with White House intern Monica Lewinsky, President Clinton argued that, for him, oral sex did not constitute *sex* or a *sexual relationship.* He based his argument on the assumption that, for many (including himself), there is a clear distinction in common usage between the terms *oral sex* and *intercourse,* and that a definition of the terms *sex* and *sexual relationship* would refer only to the latter.

Of course, we do not require common global understanding for a term to be in popular usage in the United States. However, living in a multicultural society, we must be aware that cultural differences may influence how a term is perceived.

Sometimes terms in common usage are widely misunderstood. For instance, the *New York Times* called 12 A.M. and 12 P.M. "the trickiest times on the clock." Does 12 A.M. designate midday or midnight? Is 12 P.M. lunchtime or bedtime? Railroads avoid the problem by using schedule times such as 12:01 A.M. and 11:59 P.M. The military, too, avoids the problem by using 24-hour time; noon is 1200 and midnight is 2400. According to the nation's highest authority on time, the U.S. Naval Observatory, "there is no 12 A.M. or 12 P.M., only noon and midnight."[1] When time is critical, as it may be in contracts, on birth or death certificates, and in interpretations of other documents, it is advisable to use terms that are defined by a recognized authority.

Sources of common usage must be evaluated with care. One person's common usage may differ with another's for many reasons. An appeal to the judge or audience may fail if their sense of common interpretation differs from the debaters'. One source of common usage definitions is a general dictionary, including, for example, *Webster's, Oxford Collegiate,* and *American Heritage* dictionaries. Wikipedia or other "wiki" sources may provide useful references for common usage definitions, as they are generated and edited by a community of Internet users, not necessarily scholars or experts.

3. Authority. Some terms may be defined most effectively by referring to an authority qualified to state their meaning and usage. Dictionaries, encyclopedias, and books and articles by recognized scholars are often used as authority for a particular definition. In debates on whether "advertising degrades the quality of life in the United States," some debaters turned to the *American Heritage Dictionary* for their initial definitions of *degrades* and *quality of life.* Failure to consult the proper authority can lead to unexpected results. In one instance *Time* magazine chided the Nebraska legislature for failure to consult a recognized authority in drafting drug legislation, which resulted in a drug offender going free:

1. *New York Times,* Nov. 29, 1987, p. 19.

Burling was acquitted on largely lexicological grounds. The state legislature misspelled the drug's chemical name when it passed the bill that outlawed it in 1986. Thus Burling could not be convicted of possessing the substance specified by the lawmakers. The correct spelling is methylenedioxymethamphetamine, not methylenedioxyethamphetamine [note the omission of the letter *m*] as the law had it. Next time they ban a drug in Nebraska, they'd better consult a pharmacological dictionary.[2]

What is the definition of AIDS? The federal Centers for Disease Control (CDC) are the defining authority on matters of diseases. In 1993 the CDC adopted a broader definition of AIDS to include those infected with HIV who also had tuberculosis, pneumonia, or other illnesses. Under the new definition the number of AIDS cases increased overnight by 111 percent. The power to define a disease can create an epidemic or "eradicate" the disease.

We often hear that an appalling number of Americans are illiterate. What are the facts? Who can provide an accurate picture? The U.S. Census Bureau says that 95 percent of Americans are literate. (Of course, the Census Bureau can make mistakes, but no other source even remotely approaches the ability of the Census Bureau to gather population data.) Certainly this is primary evidence. But should we accept it as conclusive evidence? We could never question millions of individuals ourselves. But we might ask, how does the Census Bureau define *literacy?* The answer might surprise you: Anyone who said they attended school through the fifth grade was counted as literate![3] No effort was made to determine if these people could actually read or write. If we changed the definition to people who said they attended school through the third grade, the literacy rate would probably jump to 99 percent. If we required people to prove they could read and write at the fifth-grade level, who knows what the figure would be? The power to define literacy can change our nation's literacy rate to serve the interests of whoever defines the term.

Courts struggle every day to interpret the meaning of terms. Their precision in defining words important to enforcement of statutes can provide a powerful source of definition to the debater. In legal matters the only definition that counts is the one upheld by the Supreme Court. For example, what does *request* mean? Section 1915(d) of Title 28 of the United States Code states that federal district judges may "request" lawyers who practice before the federal courts to undertake uncompensated representation of the poor. Justice John Paul Stevens, in a dissenting opinion, held that *request* should be understood to mean "respectfully command." Justice William J. Brennan, Jr., held in the 5-to-4 majority opinion that "in everyday speech request means to ask, petition or entreat, not to require or command."[4]

---

2. *Time,* Dec. 12, 1988, p. 33.
3. John Silber, "Illiteracy and the Crisis of Our Society," *Bostonia* (spring 1994),
p. 48.
4. *New York Times,* May 2, 1989, p. 8.

Another problem of legal definition is exemplified by application of the term "obscenity" by courts in freedom of speech cases. To some extent, the term is defined by local standards, which are open to interpretation and application by the courts. Sources of definitions by authorities are wide and varied. Terms may be defined within the text of laws, court decisions, books, articles, websites, and other materials produced by experts and agencies. Field-specific dictionaries may often be helpful.

4. Operation.   Some terms are best defined if the advocate provides an operational definition and explains the function or special purpose represented by the terms in a specific context. Debates on the proposition "Resolved: That the nonagricultural industries should guarantee their employees an annual wage" required careful definition of the phrase *guarantee ... an annual wage*. Some affirmative advocates chose to provide an operational definition, defining these terms by presenting their plan. One debater said:

> We propose a plan whereby the employer places the sum of five cents per employee hour worked in a trust fund until that fund equals 50 percent of the average annual payroll of that company for the past five years. When an employee is laid off, he may then draw from his fund a sum equal to 75 percent of his average weekly pay for the previous year less such state unemployment compensation as he may receive for 52 weeks or until he is rehired.

> The use of operation as a method of definition is often linked with the presentation of a plan and is a helpful way of explaining a complex matter.

5. Negation.   Sometimes a term may be defined effectively by indicating what it does *not* mean. In debates on the nationalization of basic industries, some teams defined *basic industries* by combining negation with example. That is, they said, "We do not mean the corner drugstore, we do not mean retail businesses, we do not mean service businesses; we mean steel, autos, transportation, mining, oil, and gas."

6. Comparison and Contrast.   Some terms may be best understood if they are compared to something familiar to the audience or contrasted with something within the common experience of the audience. In debates on the "mass media" proposition, some negative teams offered a counterplan and proposed the creation of an agency "similar to the National Association of Broadcasters" to regulate newspapers. They then claimed an advantage from the fact that their plan called for voluntary regulation in contrast to the affirmative's proposal of federal regulation.

7. Derivation.   One of the standard methods of defining words is to trace their development from their original, or radical, elements. Thus, in a debate on fair

---

Methods of Defining Terms

- Example
- Common Usage
- Authority
- Operation
- Negation
- Comparison and Contrast
- Derivation
- Combination of Methods

---

employment practices, it would be possible to define the word *prejudice* by pointing out that the word derived from the Latin words *prae* and *judicium,* meaning "before judgment." Definition by derivation has limited use in argumentation and debate, because the advocate is usually concerned with the contemporary use of the word within a specific context.

8. Combination of Methods.   Because most propositions of debate contain several terms that must be defined, no single method is likely to be satisfactory for the definition of all of the terms. If any term is particularly difficult to define, or if it is of critical importance in the debate, the advocate may use more than one method of definition to make the meaning clear.

B. Providing a Satisfactory Definition

A satisfactory definition is one that meets the expectations of those who render the decision and provides reasonable guidance in interpreting the proposition.

In academic debate a judge may expect that a definition be *reasonable* or that it be the *best definition* in the debate. In applied debate the decision makers often have different expectations about decisions in different situations. As we saw in Chapter 3, the courts have different standards for defining the burden of proof in different situations. In our personal lives, too, we frequently apply differing standards. For example, our definition of "satisfactory medical care" would no doubt vary depending on whether we had a sprained ankle or a life-threatening illness.

In academic debate advocates sometimes offer unusual definitions—definitions that are not consistent with the expectations of the opposing advocates. The use of "trick" definitions to catch an opponent off guard or to gain some other advantage is specifically *not recommended*. A trick definition or the resultant case is one that the affirmative hopes in the first instance will find the negative unprepared and in the second instance will convince the judge to accept. One example of this occurred in debates on the proposition "Resolved: That greater controls should be imposed on the gathering and utilization of information about U.S. citizens by government agencies." Early in the season most negatives expected that the affirmative cases would deal with abuses of computerized credit information. But one trick case called for legislation to prohibit the gathering and utilization of information about citizens who used marijuana. (The affirmative argued that if the police and prosecutors were prohibited from gathering and utilizing such information, they would devote their time and energies to more important crimes.) Of course, once this case became well known, it lost an essential characteristic of the trick case—it no longer found negative teams unprepared. Advocates who depend on trick cases will find that usually they are quickly exposed and defeated by competent opposition. Not every unusual definition, however, should be regarded as a trick definition. The apparently unusual definition might take the opposing team by surprise only because they failed to thoroughly analyze the proposition.

Debaters are sometimes advised to look for the "original understanding" of the proposition. Such advice draws on important precedent: Attorneys arguing a case involving a constitutional issue before the Supreme Court may consult the debates that surrounded the adoption of the Constitution or the relevant amendment to discover the original understanding of the Founding Fathers. Most debate propositions, however, do not stem from constitutional issues, and there may be little or no record to provide evidence of the original understanding. Thus this well-intentioned advice is frequently of little value in academic debate.[5]

How, then, can one prove that a definition is satisfactory? The key is to give the decision makers good reasons to accept that definition.

What are some of the good reasons one might advance to prove that a specific definition is satisfactory? The reasons will differ with different propositions and different decision renderers, but some of the most frequently used criteria are listed in the inset on pages 70–71.

To prove that a definition is *reasonable,* one must establish that the definition meets the relevant criteria or standards. To prove that a definition is the *best in the debate* one must establish that the definition meets the relevant criteria in ways that are superior to opposing definitions.

C. The Meaning of Should and the Convention of Fiat

Most propositions on matters of policy contain the word *should (or ought)*—for example, "Resolved: That such-and-such should be done." In a debate on a policy proposition, **should** means that intelligent self-interest, social welfare, or the national interest prompts this action and that it is both desirable and workable. When the affirmative claims a policy "should" be adopted, it must show that the policy is practical—but it is under no obligation to show that it would be adopted. The affirmative must give enough detail to show that if implemented,

---

5. The extent to which "original understanding" should be used in legal debate is itself a subject of debate within the legal community. See Robert H. Bork, *The Tempting of America* (New York: Free Press, 1990). Throughout the book, Bork makes his argument for the use of "original understanding" and offers his critique of other methods.

it would work. It may be impossible, within the time limitations of the debate, for the affirmative to give all the details, but it must at least show the outline of its policy and indicate how the details could be worked out. For example, in a debate on federal funding for education, the affirmative could not reasonably be expected to indicate how much money each state would receive under its plan, but it would be obliged to indicate the method by which the amount of the grants would be determined. It would be pointless for the negative to seek to show that the affirmative's plan could not be adopted by demonstrating that public opinion is against it or that the supporters of the plan lack sufficient voting strength in Congress.

Consider that, at one time, public opinion and a majority of Congress were opposed to the income tax, yet when the advocates of the income tax demonstrated that it should be adopted, the Sixteenth Amendment was enacted. In the same way it could be demonstrated that, at a given time, the Eighteenth, Nineteenth, Twenty-first, and Twenty-sixth Amendments to the Constitution could not possibly have been passed. Too many people were opposed to prohibition, opposed to women's suffrage, opposed to the repeal of the Eighteenth Amendment, or opposed to lowering the voting age to 18. Yet all these amendments were passed after the advocates of these measures won debates showing they *should* be adopted. Thus in an academic debate on a policy proposition, *constitutionality is never an issue*. If the affirmative proves that a certain policy should be adopted, it has also proved that, if necessary, the Constitution should be amended. In the same way, if the affirmative's proposal is currently illegal or outside the scope of existing law, it has, by showing that its proposal should be adopted, demonstrated that the necessary enabling legislation should be enacted.

Thus in academic debate the negative cannot argue that "Congress will never pass the affirmative's plan" and proceed to prove that, because of attitudinal barriers, political interest, or some other reason, the affirmative can never get enough votes to enact its proposal. The affirmative may simply call upon "fiat," where for the sake of the argument they will assume the hypothetical enactment of the proposal and focus on their advocacy that Congress *should* enact the plan. The affirmative need only demonstrate that its proposal ought to be adopted; it need not consider the political or attitudinal barriers that so far have prevented its enactment, although it may have the obligation of defending the merits of its proposal against the potential political and/or attitudinal consequences of enactment.

The negative must avoid the "should-would" argument, which is pointless in academic debate.[6] The point is not **would**—but *should*—the affirmative's proposal be adopted. The negative may, of course, focus on the workability of the

---

6. "Should-would" arguments may be of considerable importance in applied debate. A political leader might feel that a certain policy should be adopted but, recognizing that it would be impossible to marshal sufficient support, decide not to fight for it, preferring to conserve energy and credibility for more viable policies. For example, some of President Reagan's advisors urged that the Constitution should be amended to ban abortions and to permit school prayer. Reagan sympathized with their proposals but declined to lead an all-out legislative battle for them, apparently feeling Congress would never enact them.

Criteria to Prove a Satisfactory Definition

Debate often focuses on the relative merits of competing definitions. Standards that support the definitions offered as satisfactory provide valuable measures for comparison of differing interpretations. The debater is well advised to choose definitions that meet valid criteria.

1. *Prove that your definition is officially stipulated as the correct one for this resolution.* This criterion is of great value in the law courts, where many definitions are stipulated by statute and have been upheld by the highest courts so often that appeal is pointless. Elsewhere a *kilogram* is defined by an international agreement; a *watt* is a standard unit of measure in the United States; *drugs* are defined by official pharmacopoeias. Less common terms like *black hole, gigaflop, pulsar,* and *quasar,* although not officially defined, have universally accepted definitions in the scientific community. Of course, any definition could be changed, but changes in official or universally accepted definitions come only after exhaustive debate.

2. *Prove that your definition is grammatically correct.* Presumably the framers of the proposition are knowledgeable in the conventions of English grammar and syntax, each word in the proposition is there for a good reason, and each word further refines the meaning of the sentence. Thus you must prove that your definition considers all the terms of the proposition and that none of the terms is redundant or contradictory.

3. *Prove that your definition is derived from the appropriate field.* Many propositions contain specialized terms. If the subject is nuclear weapons, you must prove that your definition is the one used by nuclear physicists. If the subject is economics, you must prove that your definition is the one used by economists.

4. *Prove that your definition is based on common usage.* Many of the terms in debate propositions are words in common usage. Because debate is a public activity, you must be able to prove that your definition is consistent with the common usage of the general public.

5. *Prove that your definition is consistent with policy makers' or value makers' usage.* Debaters are arguing that we, the public, should adopt or reject a certain policy or value. You must prove that your definition is consistent with the usage of the makers of policy and value in the public forums; for example, you would need to prove that your definition is consistent with the definition used in congressional debates on the subject.

6. *Prove that your definition meets the original understanding of the proposition's framers.* (Cautions against this method are given in the section "Providing a Satisfactory Definition.") This criterion may be compelling to some judges and to some legal scholars in applied debate in the courtroom. But the original understanding of the people who framed a proposition for academic debate or for applied debate outside the courtroom is often elusive, and it may even be impossible to discover.

7. *Prove that your definition provides a clear distinction between what legitimately fits within the definition and what is excluded by the definition.* It is important that definitions clearly distinguish between affirmative ground and negative ground.

8. *Prove that your definition would provide a fair division of ground.* That is, prove that, if interpreted as you suggest, there would be fairly equal ground for both affirmatives and negatives to use for development of their plans, counterplans, and argumentative positions. Included here might be justification for your definition based on the educational merits of such a definition: Is it better to provide a narrow

Criteria to Prove a Satisfactory Definition (Continued)

but deep interpretation of propositional terms or a broad but shallow interpretation? In addition, you may want to suggest that, in the interest of fairness and prior notice, a definition should provide clear and predictable limits within which advocates may analyze and interpret the resolution.

Note that the debater will rarely use all these criteria to prove that the definition used is satisfactory. In fact, some of the criteria will contradict others. Initially the definition is stated succinctly with only the minimum evidence essential to establish the claim. Only if the definition comes under attack does the debater move to a full-scale justification of the definition. The most important function of these criteria is to provide a way for judges to weigh competing definitions and decide which is most satisfactory for a given debate.

To successfully attack an opponent's definition, one must prove that the definition does not meet one or more of the criteria just discussed. Note, too, that the criteria listed here, although widely used, are not all-inclusive. Depending on the nature of the proposition, other criteria may be discovered and applied to prove or disprove the claim that the definition is satisfactory.

policy and try to demonstrate that a given policy, if adopted, would not work or would produce significant disadvantages.

For example, in debating the "government control of the supply and utilization of energy" proposition, the negative could not argue that Congress would not pass gasoline rationing because it is so unpopular with members of Congress and their constituents. The affirmative could simply fiat rationing—that is, argue that it *should* be passed and assume, for the sake of argument, that it has been implemented. However, the negative could argue that, because rationing is so unpopular, it would not work; that there would be widespread violations and black markets; that the system would break down; and thus that the affirmative could not achieve any advantage.

Fiat is the convention in an academic policy debate that, for the sake of argument, participants may assume implementation of a reasonable policy. This allows debaters to focus on the question of whether a policy *should* be adopted and to avoid as irrelevant arguments about whether the policy *would* (or *will*) be adopted. The purpose of fiat is to require the debaters to debate the merits of the proposition, and not the political machinations of how one might garner the votes necessary for enactment. However, the political fallout of plan adoption may be subject to debate. Fiat is generally thought to assume that the plan has been implemented through "normal means." Normal means in our governmental system includes deal making and compromise. Implementation of an affirmative proposal might be argued to require use of political capital, which would then be lost at the cost of the potential implementation of other policies or actions.

Note, too, the limitations of fiat: Fiat is not a real power. The affirmative may use fiat to focus on *should,* but fiat goes no further. The affirmative may not "fiat" that advantages will flow from its plan; the advantages must be proved. The affirmative may not "fiat" attitudes; for example, the affirmative may not "fiat" that all citizens will love gas rationing and will eagerly comply with the plan. Fiat is not a magic wand; it may not be used to make a plan work. (Some additional uses and limitations of fiat power will be considered in Chapter 12.)

Another way to approach fiat is to consider it as it relates to the "agency" or ability to invoke change held by the debaters as activists and advocates. Such an approach recognizes that the traditional use of fiat is hypothetical; at the end of a debate when a judge votes for the affirmative, of course, the plan does not in reality become law. The true agency or power of the debaters as advocates is to influence the participants in the immediate debate itself. Therefore, the debate as an act of advocacy should be the focus of the participants, and the decision rendered by the judge is about the debaters rather than the hypothetical plan they are debating. Based on such an approach, critical and philosophical implications of the rules and contexts of the debate itself, the performances of the debaters (including their advocacy and language use), and the underpinnings of the structural framework of policy advocacy and debate practice are all subject to debate. Critical and performance-based approaches built on the idea that "fiat is illusionary" have grown in popularity in tournament practice. Proponents point to debates that are more relevant to the lives of participants (judges and debaters) and to a greater sense of involvement and activism by debaters. Opponents note that debates may lack clear points of clash or concrete comparison (as is provided by the policy comparison facilitated by traditional fiat).

III. ISSUES

Issues are those critical claims *inherent* in the proposition that the affirmative must establish. They may also be thought of as places where groups of arguments converge or points of clash subordinate to the proposition. Issues also suggest checklists or categories of arguments to be addressed by the participants in a debate or argumentative situation.

In a traditional policy debate, the negative must defeat at least one "stock" issue to win (although, the stock issues will be measured in relation to one another). **Stock issues** are those issues common to all debates on similar types of propositions, or standard claims that are applicable to many propositions. Issues may be readily recognized, because they are questions with answers that directly prove or disprove the proposition. If the issues are established, then the proposition must prevail. As debaters begin analysis of the proposition, they phrase the issues as questions—for example, "Did John Doe kill Richard Roe with malice?" Issues in the analysis stage are phrased in the form of questions to which the affirmative must answer yes. Of course, the negative must answer no to at least one issue or there is no debate. When the issues are presented in a debate, the advocate phrases them as declarative sentences—for example, "John Doe killed Richard Roe with malice." Stock issues will be considered in detail in the following sections.

Potential issues are all of the possible answers to the stock issue questions. In any given debate, however, it is unlikely that all of the potential issues will be used. (See the section "Discovering the Number of Issues" later in the chapter.)

Admitted issues are issues that one side concedes, or chooses not to challenge. For example, in debates on the proposition "Resolved: That the federal government should implement a program that guarantees employment opportunities for all U.S. citizens in the labor force," some affirmatives introduced the issue "millions of U.S. citizens are unemployed." In view of the evidence the affirmative could have produced to support this issue, many negative advocates readily admitted this issue. Some negatives introduced the issue "millions of unemployed do not suffer economic hardship." In view of the evidence the negative could have produced to support this issue, many affirmatives quickly concede this issue. It is usually a wise policy for debaters to concede those issues they cannot win and concentrate on those issues they have a chance of winning.

The *issues of the debate* are the issues that actually are introduced into the debate and on which the opposing advocates clash. For example, the potential issues on a certain proposition might be: A, B, C, D, E, F, G, H, I, and J. The affirmative might introduce issues A–F. The negative might admit issues B and C, introduce issue G, and seek to refute issues A, D, E, and F. The potential issues H, I, and J were not introduced by either side and thus did not enter into this debate. The issues of this debate were A, D, E, F, and G.

The *ultimate issue* or *voting issue* arises when there is only one issue remaining in dispute, or when all remaining issues rest upon that single voting issue. In some debates the clash may narrow down to one contended issue, which becomes the ultimate issue. In the preceding example the affirmative might have won issues A, D, E, and F early in the debate, leaving only issue G in dispute. Issue G thus would become the ultimate issue of this debate.

Contentions are statements offered in support of an issue. (Contentions may also be referred to as observations or even "main points.") Pertinent evidence is organized into cogent arguments to support each issue. Usually several contentions are offered in support of an issue. The affirmative may fail to establish some of the contentions and still win its case, provided that the remaining contentions have enough substantiating force to establish the issue.

A. Discovering the Issues

One of the first problems confronting the advocate in preparing to debate a proposition is discovering the issues. In a courtroom debate the issues are often stated explicitly in the law applicable to the case before the court. For example, if the proposition before the court was, in effect, "Resolved: That John Doe murdered Richard Roe," in most jurisdictions the issues would be:

1. Richard Roe is dead.
2. John Doe killed Richard Roe.
3. John Doe killed Richard Roe unlawfully.

4.   John Doe killed Richard Roe following premeditation.

5.   John Doe killed Richard Roe with malice.

If the prosecution failed to prove any one of these issues, John Doe could not be convicted of murder. However, he might be convicted of manslaughter or some other lesser charge if some of the issues were proved.

In debates outside the courtroom, the issues are seldom so explicitly stated. It is up to the advocates to discover them using one of several methods. First, a careful definition of the terms of the proposition will aid the advocate in discovering some of the issues of the debate. As the terms are defined, important aspects of the proposition will become apparent and reveal at least some of the issues. For example, in debates on "a national program of public work for the unemployed," the definition of the word *unemployed* was important. If unemployed was defined as including homemakers who were seeking part-time work, this definition suggested the issue question "Do the unemployed have the skills necessary for a public work program?"

Second, stock issues—the standard questions applicable to many propositions—may be used profitably in the early analysis of the problem. As standard questions they are not sufficiently specific to the issues of a particular proposition, but they often aid the advocate in the formulation of the actual issues.

1. Stock Issues on Propositions of Value.   The stock issues in a debate on a proposition of fact or value are drawn from the two basic elements of the affirmative case: definition and designation. Because academic debate is more often concerned with propositions of value than with propositions of fact, we will refer to propositions of fact only briefly and consider propositions of value in much more detail.

In their briefest form the stock issues may be phrased as follows:

1.   Definitive issues

   a.   What are the *definitions* of the key terms? As discussed above, the terms in the proposition must be defined in order to establish an interpretation of the proposition itself. This will necessarily include definition of the value(s) explicitly or implicitly identified as points of controversy.

   b.   What are the *criteria* for the values (or for interpretation of definitions)? The values provide the points of clash for the debate, but in order to consider competing values, criteria or devices for measurement of the values must be provided. In the case of fact-based or descriptive definitions, some method for testing the definitions may be called for.

2.   Designative issues

   a.   Do the facts *correspond* to the definitions? Examples provided in support of or in opposition to the proposition are relevant only inasmuch as they are relevant to the terms as defined in 1a; advocates must present proof that their examples are indeed consistent with the definitions and interpretations they have provided.

Stock Issues on Propositions of Value

1. Definitive Issues
   a. Definitions
   b. Criteria
2. Designative Issues
   a. Correspondence
   b. Application

---

   b.   What are the *applications* of the values? At this point, debaters must apply the criteria established in 1b to the facts presented in 2a.

With this brief outline in mind, we can proceed to a more detailed consideration of the stock issues.

Let us turn first to the murder trial of John Doe that we just considered. This trial, of course, is a debate on a proposition of *fact*. The definitive issue in this trial is the legal definition of murder. The designative issues in this trial are the five issues—Richard Roe is dead, John Doe killed Richard Roe, and so on—that the prosecuting attorney must prove in order to establish that the facts correspond to the definition of murder, thus proving that Joe Doe is guilty of murdering Richard Roe.

In a trial court debate on a proposition of fact, the issues are often neatly spelled out in the applicable law. In most debates outside the courtroom, however, the issues must be discovered by a careful analysis of the proposition. Consider the value proposition "Resolved: That commercial television is more detrimental than beneficial to American society." What are the definitions of the key terms? We will certainly have to define *commercial television* and *American society*. What are the criteria by which to define the value terms *detrimental* and *beneficial?* (You may want to refer to the discussion on how to provide a satisfactory definition.)

As we consider the application of the values, we may discover additional issues. The affirmative might argue that "detrimental" applies to programming that emphasizes sports, soap operas, and escapist entertainment, whereas "beneficial" applies to programming that emphasizes classical drama, classical music, and scholarly lectures. The negative might reply that the application of such values would drive viewers away, which in turn would drive sponsors away. With little or no advertising revenue, the television stations would have to turn to the government for revenue; thus the government should become the arbiter of television programming. Such government control, the negative might argue, would be far more detrimental than the programming the affirmative indicted. The affirmative might respond by arguing that the application of its values would raise the intellectual level of American society, that in time the public would come to appreciate its "beneficial" programming, and that the quality of American society would be improved.

Note that as the debaters began to consider the policy applications of the values, they moved into a quasi-policy debate. In such debates the negative may well offer "value objections" that are very similar to the policy issue of "disadvantages." Additional issues long associated with policy debate become essential in quasi-policy debate. Because quasi-policy debate involves policy issues, we will consider them next.

2. Stock Issues for Propositions of Policy. The stock issues for the proposition of policy are drawn from the three basic elements of the affirmative case: harm, inherency, and solvency. In their briefest form, the stock issues may be phrased as follows:

1. Harm
   a. Does a compelling problem exist in the status quo?
   b. Is the problem quantitatively important?
   c. Is the problem qualitatively important?

2. Inherency
   a. Are the causes of the problem built into the laws, attitudes, and/or structures of the status quo?
   b. Absent a significant change in policy action, is the problem likely to continue?

3. Solvency
   a. Is there a workable plan of action?
   b. Does the plan solve the problem?
   c. Does the plan produce advantages?
   d. Do the advantages outweigh the disadvantages?

With this brief outline in mind, we can proceed to a more detailed consideration of the stock issues.

Is there a justification for a change in the status quo? That is, are there specific needs, problems, undesirable factors, shortcomings, unmet goals or criteria, unattained advantages, or alternative justifications that constitute good reasons for changing the status quo? Are these conditions significant enough to warrant a change in the status quo? (Significance may be demonstrated either quantitatively or qualitatively, or, best of all, in both ways.) The HARM issue addresses existing evil in our world. We would not act to implement change unless we are convinced that there is a cost to not acting. Harm requires advocates to address the importance and compelling nature of existing problems.

The INHERENCY issue considers the likelihood that absent our positive action, the HARM will continue. Advocates may need to address questions in-

---

Stock Issues for Propositions of Policy

---

1. Harm
2. Inherency
3. Solvency

---

cluding: Are these conditions inherent in the status quo? Are they caused by the status quo? (Inherency may be demonstrated as being structural, attitudinal, or, again best of all, in both ways.) Is it impossible to eliminate these conditions by repairs, adjustments, or improvements within the framework of the status quo? Is any negative proposal to repair or adjust the problems of the status quo unsatisfactory? And most importantly, if we do not act, will the harms continue into the future?

The issue of SOLVENCY considers the proposed solution and focuses on policy comparison. Is there a plan to solve the problems cited as justification for adopting the proposition? Is the plan topical—that is, is it directly related to the proposition? Is the plan workable? Does the plan have solvency—that is, will it solve the problems? Is any possible negative counterplan topical and thus capable of being absorbed into the affirmative's plan? Is any counterplan unworkable or lacking in solvency?

Will the plan achieve the claimed advantages? That is, will it satisfy the justification offered by the affirmative, meet the needs cited by the affirmative, and attain the goals or criteria cited by the affirmative? Will the plan produce no disadvantages as great as or greater than those existing in the status quo? Will any possible negative counterplan produce greater disadvantages than the status quo or the plan? Are the advantages inherent in the plan—that is, will they necessarily flow from the adoption of the plan? Are the advantages unique to the plan—that is, can they be obtained without adopting the plan? Are the advantages significant? Do they outweigh the disadvantages?

3. Using Stock Issues.　After carefully defining the terms of the proposition and the related terms from the area of controversy, and applying the appropriate stock issues, the advocate will formulate a preliminary statement of the potential issues of the debate.

Both the affirmative and the negative use stock issues in their analysis. Affirmatives use stock issues as they seek to discover the issues they will advance. Negatives use stock issues as they seek to anticipate the issues they must refute and the issues they will advance, such as disadvantages.

A practical method for the advocate to follow in beginning analysis involves two basic steps. Note that this is a checklist for the process of preparation, not for actually debating the issues.

1. Phrase the stock issue as a question: Is there a justification for a change in the status quo of the type called for in the resolution? Is the problem inherent in the status quo? and so on.

2. Answer each of these questions with the statement of a potential issue of the debate.

The following example shows how the stock issues may be used.

Some debaters started their analysis of the proposition "Resolved: the United States Federal Government should establish an energy policy requiring a substantial reduction in the total nongovernmental consumption of fossil fuels in the United States." Their preliminary research helped them quickly identify many problems related to energy use. These problems included the risks inherent in nuclear power generation, the dangers of reliance on foreign oil and the harms to the environment caused by the burning of fossil fuels, including air pollution and contributions to global warming. In addition, they found many advocates for various solutions to these problems. As they defined the terms in the proposition, they recognized that they would have to select an agent of implementation from within the United States Federal Government, and that they would need to advocate a set of actions built specifically around energy policy. For example, new tax credits to encourage use of alternative energy sources might not be considered "ENERGY" policy. And, their policy must reduce the CONSUMPTION of a particular type of resources: FOSSIL FUELS.

As these debaters continued their preliminary research, they decided that a major evil in the status quo was that through their unnecessarily high consumption of gas, private automobiles needlessly generated excessive emissions of greenhouse gases and created a dangerous reliance on imported oil. They also found that even though a federal government policy existed to decrease consumption of fossil fuels by placing CAFE (Corporate Average Fuel Economy) limits on the fleets of automobile manufacturers, those standards were too low and there was an important loophole: Light trucks that exceed 8,500 lbs gross vehicle weight rating (GVWR) did not have to comply with CAFE standards. These vehicles included very popular pickup trucks, sport utility vehicles, and large vans, thus undermining the existing energy policy. Establishment of a new policy in the form of stricter CAFE standards was warranted. This research led them to formulate the following potential harm issue:

Excessive consumption of fossil fuels is a major problem. In analyzing the harm, they recognized that although it was still debatable, in general, it was the conclusion of a consensus of scientists that by creating auto emissions, humans contributed to global warming, and that the consequences of that would be catastrophic. In addition, human health was negatively impacted by the air pollution created by auto emissions, and independently, relying on a largely foreign supply of oil put the United States at greater risk of economic disruption and foreign policy danger, including wars.

They found these problems to be inherent, since the American economy was dependent on the use of personal automobiles for transportation, and because the attitudes of consumers tended to favor less efficient cars. Therefore, some regulation was called for, but existing restrictions had proved insufficient, and were circumvented by the loophole on light trucks. More research indicated that auto manufacturers could comply with a higher standard, including the closing of the light truck loophole. The plan would work, and it would reduce consumption of fossil fuels in the form of gas, thus reducing incrementally the reliance on foreign oil and contributions to greenhouse warming.

These potential issues represented the debaters' preliminary analysis of the problem. At this point they had moved from general stock questions to potential issues specifically adapted to the proposition. Their next task was to test these potential issues by further research to determine whether the evidence would in fact support the claimed issues. The debaters had to discover whether there were effective objections to their plan—whether their plan would produce disadvantages greater than the claimed advantages. There would certainly be disadvantages to increasing CAFE standards. American automakers were behind their foreign competitors in the production of high mileage cars. And, some safety and convenience might be sacrificed in order to reduce emissions. On the basis of further study, the debaters no doubt modified their potential issues and tried them out in a few practice debates. Experience led them to rethink some or all of the potential issues. They had, however, taken the essential first step: They had moved from the general to the specific and had begun a meaningful analysis of the proposition.

In similar fashion the advocate who is debating propositions of value must analyze the subject area and move from the general stock issues to the specific issues inherent in the proposition. Using the "commercial television" proposition, consider a real-world example of value (and later policy) debate that took place a few years ago and continues to the present, although in a somewhat different form. Opponents of cigarette commercials on television argued that such commercials were "detrimental," and they established the criterion that "encouraging sales of products that caused illness and death was detrimental." Turning to the next issue, the affirmative sought to demonstrate that the subject met the criterion by drawing on the Surgeon General's Report, which claimed a link between cigarette smoking and illness and death. Significance was established by the same report, which claimed a link between cigarette smoking and many thousands of deaths. The inherency issue gave the affirmative the most difficulty. People had been smoking cigarettes for years before commercial television came into existence, and cigarette manufacturers were also advertising lavishly in other media. The debate came to an inconclusive end when the negative withdrew from the field. The law required that equal time be given to antismoking commercials, and the cigarette companies decided to direct their advertising to media that did not have the equal-time requirement.

B. Introducing the Issues

1. Introduction by Either Side.   In both value and policy debate the affirmative must introduce the issues necessary to establish a prima facie case—one that

---

Issues (Critical Claims Inherent in the Proposition)

- *Stock Issues* are those issues common to all debates on similar types of propositions or standard claims that are applicable to many propositions.
- In a traditional policy debate, the negative must defeat at least one stock issue to win.
- *Potential issues* are all of the possible answers to the stock issue questions.
- *Admitted issues* are issues that one side concedes or chooses not to challenge.
- The *issues of the debate* are the issues that actually are introduced in the debate and on which the opposing advocates clash.
- The *ultimate issue* or *voting issue* arises when there is only one issue remaining in dispute or when all remaining issues rest upon that single voting issue.
- *Contentions* are statements offered in support of an issue.

---

provides good and sufficient reason for adopting the proposition. As a starting point a prima facie case must provide effective issue statements to answer each of the stock issue questions. (See the first section in Chapter 11.) If the negative detects flaws in the affirmative case, it has the responsibility of introducing the appropriate issues to refute the affirmative. For example, the affirmative case should be so clearly topical that it is unnecessary for the affirmative to prove that it is. In such a case it is clearly pointless for the negative to attack it, and this issue will not be argued. If the affirmative case is not topical, however, the negative may "attack topicality." (See Chapter 13 for a consideration of the issues the negative may introduce.) If the affirmative is using a "needs analysis" case, it will certainly introduce one or more "need" issues. In proving these issues, the affirmative might argue that the status quo cannot be repaired, or it might wait to see if the negative provides repairs and then argue the specific negative repairs. Workability, for example, might become a critical issue, and it might be introduced by either side. In debates on the Twenty-sixth Amendment, workability was never argued (because it was self-evident that the voting age could be lowered to 18), the affirmative did not have to prove it, and it would have been pointless for the negative to attempt to disprove it. In debates on the "further development of nuclear weapons" proposition, workability invariably was a critical issue. The negative was almost certain to introduce the issue. Recognizing this possibility, some affirmatives sought to preempt the argument by introducing the issue first. The affirmative would claim "advantages" for their plan and be prepared for a negative attack on this issue. The issue of "disadvantages," however, was argued only if the negative introduced it.

Clearly advocates must discover and prepare to deal with *all* potential issues of the proposition—not merely those they find it most convenient to deal with. Any potential issue may become an issue of the debate.

Note that, although the affirmative must carry all of the stock issues, it is not necessarily required to carry all of the contentions. In the example about wiretaps and organized crime, the affirmative had to carry the stock issue of advantage. Simply carrying the first advantage contention (the plan would provide an effective weapon against organized crime) might be sufficient to do so, even if the affirmative lost the second and third advantage contentions.

2. The Counterplan.   One of the potential issues of any policy debate is whether the plan proposed by the affirmative is the best possible way to solve the problems of the status quo. The negative, however, may find it desirable to admit that certain problems exist in the status quo and may introduce a counterplan to meet these problems, as is shown in Chapter 13. A counterplan is an alternative policy action, different from the plan, which if accepted would be a reason to reject the affirmative plan. In such a case the negative introduces this issue, and the affirmative may then argue that the counterplan (1) is topical and thus provides support for the affirmative resolution, (2) is not competitive with the affirmative plan and thus is not a reason to reject the plan, (3) is not workable, (4) lacks solvency, or (5) produces disadvantages greater than the status quo or the affirmative's plan.

C. Discovering the Number of Issues

The number of issues varies from one proposition to another and can be discovered only by careful analysis of the problem. In general, although there will be many arguments in a debate, the number of issues is rather small. There are usually four to six issues in dispute in the typical intercollegiate debate. If advocates claim a large number of "issues," they may be confusing supporting contentions with issues. It is usually to the advantage of the affirmative to try to narrow the number of issues of the debate. If, for example, the affirmative can secure the admission of the negative or can quickly establish three out of four issues, then it can concentrate on proving the remaining issue. It is usually to the advantage of the negative to seek to establish as many issues of debate as possible. By keeping the maximum possible number of issues in dispute, the negative hopes to force the affirmative to prove every issue and to deny the affirmative the opportunity of concentrating on a few issues of its own choosing. Either team, however, may find it advisable to drop a nonessential issue it is losing and concentrate on the critical issues it feels it can and must win.

In debates on the "guaranteed employment opportunities" proposition, as mentioned previously, the affirmative had excellent evidence to establish the issue "millions are unemployed." Many negatives chose to admit the issue and concentrated on other issues. Some, however, adopted the strategy of clashing with this issue: They argued that the figures were flawed, in that they included millions of short-term unemployed who sustained no real harm from brief unemployment. This contention, of course, forced the affirmative to spend time reestablishing the issue at the cost of devoting less time to extending or defending other issues.

Neither side can manufacture issues simply to waste its opponent's time—capable advocates would quickly expose such a trick. Both teams have an obligation to develop the issues essential to their position. It is wise strategy, however, to drop a noncritical, lost issue and concentrate on the issues that can be won. If an affirmative effectively answered the negative's topicality attack or a disadvantage argument, the negative might choose to drop those issues, concentrate on a disadvantage that it felt it was winning, and argue that this disadvantage alone outweighed all of the affirmative's advantages. Thus it is typical to find fewer issues in contention at the close of the debate than there were at the beginning.

D. Phrasing the Issues

The issues must be so phrased as to provide maximum logical and persuasive impact on those who render the decision. First, each issue must be phrased to preview and then bring into focus the line of argument to be developed. Second, each issue must be phrased persuasively. Third, each issue must be phrased concisely. Fourth, taken as a whole, the issues must be phrased to provide a coherent organization for the case and allow a smooth transition from one issue to another. (Students will find it worthwhile to review Chapters 15 and 16 as they begin to put their phrasing of the issues into final form.)

Some students debating "Resolved: That executive control of U.S. foreign policy should be significantly curtailed" wanted to limit executive control by prohibiting the executive from carrying out covert operations in foreign countries. They *might* have phrased the first need issue as "American foreign policy objectives of combating terrorism, totalitarianism, protecting the innocent, and preserving peace are seriously impeded when it becomes a matter of public knowledge that the United States has in fact engaged in covert operations to overthrow hostile regimes." They *might* have phrased the second issue as "Neither reducing the number of covert operations nor limiting covert operations to those most likely to succeed will effectively avoid the adverse publicity that will follow when the operations become public knowledge." Instead, they wisely phrased the issues as "Discovery of covert operations undermines American objectives" and "The only way to prevent discovery is to end all operations."

The phrasing actually used is clearly superior and meets the criteria considered earlier in this section. Most often, however, the issue will first occur to an advocate in a rambling, disjointed form. The experienced advocate knows that well-phrased issues are the result of careful rewriting and skillful editing.

Well-phrased issues give advocates in academic debate one of the best opportunities to "take control of the flow sheet" and lodge their arguments, *exactly as they want them stated,* in the mind of the judge and on his or her flow sheet. The flow sheet is the detailed set of notes taken by the judge as a record of the debate.

The importance of phrasing issues with precision is by no means limited to students in academic debate. In almost any circumstances advocates are more likely to achieve their objectives if they state the issues crisply and coherently. The importance of well-phrased issues becomes even more critical if advocates attain enough prominence to be quoted on a radio or television news program.

These advocates soon recognize that their entire speech is almost never presented; rather, they are lucky if as much as a 20-second "clip" or "sound bite" is used. In such circumstances wise speakers quickly learn to phrase their issues effectively. The same considerations apply to newspapers, which often quote portions of a speech but only infrequently publish full texts.

E. Phrasing the Substructure of the Issues

The same considerations that apply to the phrasing of the issues also apply to the substructure of the issues. The contentions—that is, the supporting arguments used to establish an issue—must be phrased with care so that they, too, have the maximum logical and persuasive impact.

Consider the substructure of the issues cited in the previous section:

I.   Discovery of covert operations undermines American objectives.
   A.   Discovery strengthens totalitarianism.
   B.   Discovery strengthens terrorism.
   C.   Discovery injures the innocent.
   D.   Discovery threatens peace.
   E.   Discovery encourages terrorists.

II. The only way to prevent discovery is to end all operations.

   A.   Discovery of some operations is inevitable.
   B.   Discovery is unpredictable.

The reiteration of the concept of "discovery" on which this advocate wished to focus and the concise phrasing of the contentions helped the advocate to establish the case more effectively.

F. Considering the Decision Makers

Advocates must consider the attitudes and values of those who render the decision as they decide what issues they will introduce and how they will handle them. In debating the "Comprehensive medical care for all citizens" proposition, some debaters quickly discovered the issue "Comprehensive medical care for all citizens will inflate taxes by prolonging lives." The argument was irrefutable. If the plan worked as well as the affirmative claimed it would, the negative could prove that vast numbers of elderly indigents would linger on for years in an unproductive state consuming more and more tax dollars in medical and welfare costs. Despite the overwhelming logical force of the argument, the debaters decided against introducing the issue. They felt the values of most American audiences are such that they would reject the idea of denying poor people medical care so that they might die earlier and thus save on taxes.

Before a group of business managers, the "cost issue" is one that the negative will almost certainly argue if the plan requires the expenditure of tax monies. The negative will maximize the tax burden, while the affirmative will seek to minimize it. Businesspeople are well aware of their existing tax burden and are predisposed to resist any new or additional taxes. Cost may well become the critical issue of the debate and provide the negative with its best opportunity of winning. Before student groups, by contrast, negatives often find that the cost issue is less critical. Many students are beneficiaries of tax-spending programs and have not yet felt the personal burden of paying heavy taxes. Before such audiences the negative may decide to drop the cost issue or argue that the affirmative plan will "distort social priorities" because its cost is so great that it precludes or reduces other, more desirable programs. Thus, in arguing the "medical care" proposition, some negatives maintained that more lives would be saved and the quality of life improved if the money were spent to provide better food and housing for the poor, rather than on medical care.

Even the highly qualified professional judges ideally found in academic debate cannot totally divorce themselves from their value systems. Thus, if in a debate on the "medical care" proposition, a negative introduced as a counterplan the issue "euthanasia for anyone hospitalized more than once a year," it must expect that the judge will evaluate almost any affirmative objection as sufficient to defeat the counterplan.

As students begin to make final selection of issues and to plan their handling of those issues, they may find it helpful to study Chapter 15, especially the section "Analysis of the Audience."

EXERCISES

1. Working in pairs, find competing definitions for each of the terms listed below. Have a debate in which you each defend one of the definitions as superior to your opponent's. Alternate with four speeches, none to exceed one minute.

   Terrorism
   Poverty
   Sufficient Health Care
   Family Values
   Middle Class
   Responsibility
   Respect
   Adult
   Freedom
   Privacy
   Obesity
   Beauty
   Leadership
   Quality of Life

2. Working in teams, select a policy proposition (this could be one you for-
    mulated in Exercise 2 from Chapter 3). Define key terms and prepare an
    interpretation of the proposition. Then outline a case addressing potential
    Harms, Inherency, and Solvency.

3. From recent newspapers, newsmagazines, or news websites, find an example
    of an argumentative speech on a proposition of policy by a public speaker. A
    candidate's answer to a moderator's question in a political campaign debate
    would be an excellent choice. Identify the "proposition" or central argu-
    ment made by the speaker and state the issues set forth. If necessary, rephrase
    the speaker's words to form a clear and correct statement of the proposition
    and issues; be careful, however, to preserve the speaker's ideas. Do you agree
    with the speaker's choice of issues?

4. Prepare a three-minute speech for delivery in class in which you (a) state a
    proposition of policy or value as determined by your instructor, (b) define
    the terms, and (c) state the issues. The class will be asked to evaluate the
    three parts of your presentation. Prepare an outline of this speech to give to
    your instructor.

5

Exploring the Controversy

Once the controversy has been analyzed and the statement of the potential issues has been formulated, the next step is to explore the controversy. Advocates who want to present their position intelligently and to convince others to concur with them must be thoroughly familiar with the controversy. They must undertake an organized program of research so that they can explore fully all relevant aspects of the issues. Careful research will provide a firm foundation for the case they will build. And the potential issues formulated in the analysis of the controversy will help to give direction to their exploration of it. The processes of analyzing and exploring the controversy are interwoven, and advocates will move from one to the other as long as they are concerned with the proposition. They must be innovative and creative in their search for evidence and issues, and they must be coolly and dispassionately analytical in evaluating findings and planning further research. On the basis of their exploration, they may find it necessary to rephrase the issues they originally developed or to develop new issues, or even to revise the proposition.

In formal debate, a restatement of the proposition cannot be done unilaterally; it requires the consent of all parties concerned. The intercollegiate debater, the trial attorney, and other advocates often must debate a proposition not subject to revision. In informal debate in government and business, advocates—for persuasive purposes—often attempt to change the wording and meaning of the proposition unilaterally. For example, opponents of abortion prefer to speak of the "right to life," and supporters of euthanasia prefer to state their proposal as "death with dignity" rather than as "mercy killing." In parliamentary debate the proposition may be amended by a simple majority vote; in many conference and discussion situations, the problem may be revised by informal action. In any event advocates continually explore the issues and revise the case on the basis of new information.

Miniglossary

Brainstorming   A method of shared problem solving in which all members of a group spontaneously contribute ideas. Individuals may use brainstorming by rapidly generating a variety of possible solutions.

Brief   An organized set of prepared arguments with supporting evidence.

Card   Debate jargon for a single item of quoted material used in support of an argumentative claim.

Search engine   A computer program that works to retrieve and prioritize information within a computer system.

Think tanks   Groups of experts who conduct research and prepare reports in support of their inquiry and advocacy concerning issues of various concerns including public and governmental policy, business, science, and education.

Wikis   The term "wiki" is Hawaiian for *quick*. Wikipedia is the most famous. Groups of readers contribute to the development of materials, including contribution of content as well as editing.

I. BRAINSTORMING FOR IDEAS

Traditionally advocates try to develop cases by a careful, orderly, deliberate, logical process. Although the case they ultimately present must be logically sound, advocates sometimes find it advantageous to shorten the logical processes while gathering ideas for their case. Sometimes the solution to a problem is found by means of an "intuitive leap," a "hunch," a "lucky break," an "inspiration," or "serendipity." The advocate might simply happen to look into an obscure reference and make a critical inference or find exactly the piece of evidence needed to complete a chain of reasoning. The advocate might consider a seemingly improbable plan "just for the fun of it" and find that it meets his or her needs perfectly. Or the advocate might follow up an apparently irrelevant lead and uncover an important precedent, or consider an impractical proposal that will lead to a highly practical solution.

A dramatic example of how one may use inferences to make a creative leap from sketchy data occurred when an inference reader in the CIA was assigned to read native-language newspapers of a hostile regime. The reader noted that a small town's soccer team, perennial losers, suddenly began winning games and catapulted to the top of their league. At the inference reader's urging, an overflight was made of the town, revealing a nuclear installation. The regime had carefully camouflaged the installation but had forgotten that its technicians would notably improve the town's soccer team. Thus skilled inference reading revealed an important secret.

It is for the express purpose of uncovering ideas that might otherwise be ignored or delayed that the advocate uses **brainstorming**: a method of shared problem solving in which all members of a group spontaneously contribute ideas. Individuals also may use brainstorming by rapidly generating a variety of possible solutions. Many situations arise in which it may be profitable to use brainstorming: in defining terms or discovering issues, in finding materials for an argument, in connection with the problems of evidence or reasoning, and in building the case. Although brainstorming is not a substitute for the ways of dealing with problems considered in other chapters, it is a supplement that can help in many situations.

In a typical brainstorming session the participants make a deliberate effort to create an informal atmosphere in which everyone is encouraged to contribute and no one is permitted to criticize. They are usually most successful when following certain guidelines; the inset on page 89 summarizes the process.

Brainstorming is often deceptively simple—the ideas generated may evoke the comment that "anyone could have thought of that." This is often true. The point is that, in many cases, no one had thought of the idea earlier, and perhaps no one would have thought of that particular idea had it not been for the brainstorming session. Many of the ideas that emerge in brainstorming sessions are pure "fluff." However, if only one important idea evolves that otherwise might never have been considered, the time has been well spent.

One group of college students debating a "national program of public work for the unemployed" found early in the season that their affirmative teams were having difficulty with their plan, which called for a massive program of urban renewal to provide jobs. Their negative opponents were defeating the plan by pointing out that few of the unemployed had the skills necessary for construction work. The debaters held a brainstorming session from which evolved the idea that the affirmative plan did not have to call for construction work. Then they proceeded to develop a new plan that called for conservation, service, and maintenance work that unskilled persons could easily perform. This plan might have evolved by some other means, of course, but this particular group of advocates was unable to develop an effective plan until they brainstormed the problem.

An excellent place to start when brainstorming and beginning research on a CEDA/NDT resolution is the topic paper produced during the topic selection process. These papers are readily accessible through the Cross Examination Debate Association (http://cedadebate.org/), and specifically at the CEDA Topic home page (http://www.cedatopic.com/). The topic paper reflects the brainstorming and research already done by others and provides a bibliography of primary sources relevant to the proposition. The topic blog also records the community brainstorming and discussions guiding topic selection and wording.

II. LOCATING MATERIALS

Whether in the library or elsewhere, research today generally begins on a computer. Online research through Internet sources and databases can be productive,

Guidelines for Brainstorming

1. *Limit the size of the group.* Brainstorming has been found to work better in small groups. Fifteen is usually considered to be the maximum workable size, and groups with as few as two or three members have been effective. It is even possible for an individual to brainstorm alone.

2. *Limit the time devoted to a brainstorming session.* Because the objective of brainstorming is to produce a large number of ideas and to avoid any critical evaluation during the session, it is usually desirable to limit a session to one hour or less. Many profitable sessions have been limited to between 20 and 40 minutes.

3. *Announce the problem in advance.* The person calling the brainstorming session should state the problem he or she wants the group to consider, either at the start of the session or a day or two in advance.

4. *Encourage all participants to contribute.* Because the objective is to secure the maximum possible number of ideas, everyone should participate. The leader can encourage contributions by creating a friendly, informal atmosphere. Participants should not only originate ideas but also modify and extend ideas presented by others.

5. *Don't follow any organized pattern.* Whereas traditional discussion follows a careful pattern of reflective thinking, brainstorming deliberately follows no pattern. The objective is to provide an atmosphere for the trigger effect, in which an idea, even a bad or irrelevant one, once expressed, may trigger a good idea.

6. *Don't permit any criticism or evaluation of ideas.* Because criticism at this stage tends to discourage contributions and decreases the possibility of the trigger effect, the leader must suppress criticism and strive to maintain an atmosphere in which everyone feels free to contribute.

7. *Record all ideas.* In the most widely used method two or three members of the group write ideas on a blackboard as rapidly as they are expressed. Other methods include the "idea tree"—whereby a short pole is set in the center of the table and participants write out their ideas and attach them to the "tree" with adhesive tape—and the "cracker barrel"—whereby a basket is placed on the table and participants write their ideas on pieces of paper and toss them into the "barrel." Whichever method is used, all ideas should be recorded and forwarded to the person or group responsible for evaluation.

8. *Subject all ideas to rigorous evaluation.* Only when the brainstorming session is over and the ideas have been recorded in some usable form should they be subjected to thorough evaluation. Sometimes the ideas are duplicated and sent to the participating individuals for their evaluation. In many cases they are forwarded to a policymaking group or to the individual responsible for making decisions for screening and testing. The ideas gathered during brainstorming may serve as springboards for concepts that will be developed more fully during evaluation.

and libraries generally have online research capabilities, which often can be accessed from remote sites. But one way or another, advocates are well advised to turn to the library for their first sources of material. Because library computer facilities, resources, physical arrangements, and loan policies vary enormously,

---

Questions to Ask in Locating References

---

1. *Who is concerned with the proposition?* Persons and organizations concerned with a problem might include those with an academic interest in it, those interested in the potential influence of the proposition, and even those currently unwilling to take a public stand on the problem. For example, in seeking information on the "higher education" proposition, the answer to the question "Who is concerned with the proposition?" would include the various associations of educators, economists, political scientists, businesspeople, labor organizations, and organizations in other related fields. The scholarly associations and their journals seldom take an official position for or against legislation, but their journals contain important articles about contemporary problems in the area of their special interest. The education journals, in particular, yielded a number of significant articles on this proposition.

2. *Who is interested in securing the adoption of the proposition?* The answer to this question will often lead to one of the most prolific sources of information. A search for information on "higher education" would lead an advocate to the Department of Education, for example, which took the lead in presenting the administration's arguments in favor of the proposition.

3. *Who is interested in preventing the adoption of the proposition?* The answer will often lead to another prolific source of information. The advocate interested in "higher education" found, for example, that the National Association of Manufacturers published a good deal of material opposed to the proposition.

---

advocates are well advised to familiarize themselves with their library's collections and organization so that subsequent searches for information will be purposeful and effective. Librarians are usually eager to assist individuals doing serious research and can provide valuable aid.

A. Background Material

Gather background material to give you direction and help you learn about your topic. Encyclopedias and dictionaries, including Wikipedia, can provide a good start. The free online English dictionary, http://www.yourdictionary.com, provides excellent resources and services including definitions, thesaurus entries, spelling, pronunciation, and etymologies. The *Oxford English Dictionary* and *Oxford Reference* are also available online, as is *Merriam-Webster's Collegiate Dictionary*. The objective of the researchers in this stage is not to gather proof for argumentation, but to learn about the terms and issues relevant to the proposition and develop ideas about their future research. Find relevant resource materials in the reference section of your library, and test out various combinations of keywords across different search platforms. Exploration usually begins with the acquisition of general information on the problem. As the advocate acquires some general knowledge of the problem, he or she is in a position to develop more specific lines of inquiry and to seek more specialized information.

B. Books

Use catalogs to find books. Obviously different sorts of publications provide different sorts of content. In general, books may offer the advantages of both depth and breadth of information. Of course they may not be as current as newspapers or magazines, or even scholarly journals. However, especially in the early stages of researching a topic, books can provide important background. Every library will have its own catalog, and you may wish to access the Library of Congress catalog to help you discover relevant books. An excellent resource is WorldCat (http://www.worldcat.org/), self-described as the world's largest network of library resources. In addition, you may visit commercial online bookstores (Amazon and Barnes & Noble are two such vendors) to identify books and even read reviews then find links to other related books. Once you have secured some relevant books, they can lead you to more. Follow the footnotes and seek out the materials listed in the bibliographies of relevant books.

C. Periodicals

Use indexes to seek out periodicals. Because advocates are most often concerned with a proposition of current interest, they may expect that information relating to the proposition will appear from time to time in the daily newspapers, weekly newsmagazines, and monthly magazines. Online availability makes information dissemination possible immediately. In fact, in some cases debaters may wish to subscribe to daily e-mail delivery of newspapers or relevant bulletins. Resourceful advocates constantly scan current publications for articles related to their problem. Their daily reading should include the *New York Times* and at least one other metropolitan daily. The Sunday *New York Times'* "Week in Review" section is a helpful summary of current events. Weekly reading should include newsmagazines like *Time, Newsweek,* and *U.S. News & World Report*. If the proposition is related to a particular field, advocates should add the special publications of that area to their research list. For example, if they are concerned with a business problem, they should read the *Wall Street Journal,Business Week, Fortune,* the *AFL-CIO News,* and the *Monthly Labor Review,* together with some of the trade papers and newsletters of the specific area under consideration.

Advocates should make a special point of reading publications with different editorial policies. Much of their opponents' evidence and argument may come from publications with which they disagree. If they study this information in its original source, they will be in a better position to deal with it in the debate.

Most major journals and periodicals are available (at least in part) on the Internet. In addition, a number of quality journals are only available online. The list of available sources is practically endless. For example:

Newsweek	http://www.msnbc.msn.com/site/ newsweek/
CNN	http://www.cnn.com/
New York Times	http://www.nytimes.com/
Salon	http://www.salon.com/
Slate	http://slate.msn.com/
The Economist	http://www.economist.com/
The New Republic	http://www.tnr.com/
Time Magazine	http://www.time.com/time/
Truthout	http://www.truthout.org/
U.S. News & World Report	http://www.usnews.com/
Wall Street Journal	http://www.wsj.com/
Washington Post	http://www.washingtonpost.com/

A more productive way to locate periodical information is through a subject or keyword search through one or more of your library's general indexes. These indexes will guide you to a wide range of newspapers, magazines, journals, e-journals, and other sources. There are quite a few available services, but they generally require membership for access, so you will have to investigate your own access. Even when index services overlap, they each have their own unique collections and idiosyncrasies. It is wise to conduct a variety of searches in different locations. Some of the best available indexes include InfoTrac, LexisNexis, NewsBank, Alternative Press Index, World News Connection, Wilson Web (various collections, including Readers' Guide Full Text and Readers' Guide Retrospective), ProQuest Research Library, Public Affairs Information Service (PAIS) International, LegalTrac, OCLC FirstSearch, EBSCOhost, and Expanded Academic ASAP.

More-specific indexes are available to guide you to more-focused discipline specific materials and scholarly journals. Scholarly publications are distinct from publications offering substantive or general interest news and are more credible and usually more specific. One can often recognize a scholarly journal in a number of ways. Often its title includes the name of a specific professional organization (*Journal of the American Medical Association*) and may even include the word "journal." Articles are likely to include an abstract, which is a descriptive summary of the article contents at the beginning of the article, and they will have an academic appearance without exciting photographs or color graphics. They will always cite their references in the form of footnotes and endnotes, and will list a number of editors and reviewers. Articles in scholarly journals are "peer reviewed" and competitively selected for publication. They therefore represent extensive and high quality research and careful evaluation. This helps to ensure a higher level of credibility and believability than other periodicals. Numerous field-specific indexes, like Communications & Mass Media Complete and Family & Society Studies Worldwide may guide researchers to scholarly journals in their areas of interest. Be sure to check your library for available indexes in the disciplines appropriate to your topic. General indexes for scholarly publications include JSTOR: The Scholarly Journal Archive, Google Scholar, and ERIC (Educational Resources Information Center).

D. Government Sources

Access Government Documents. Much useful research, information gathering, policy analysis, and debate sponsored by and conducted by the United States federal government are easily available and extremely useful to the academic debater. During Bill Clinton's presidency, White House documents became available online (http://www.whitehouse.gov/) and when Newt Gingrich became Speaker of the House, congressional documents also became available online (http://www.access.gpo.gov/congress/). Indeed, increasingly, all sorts of government documents are becoming available online at little or no cost (http://www .gpoaccess.gov/index.html). These documents have long been available in hard copy in government library depositories; check with your library for availability and best means of access.

E. Databases

Seek out databases. Databases collect information from various locations and organize them for access and use. The debater is most interested in those databases, accessible through libraries, in which publications and sources of information are organized for easy access. A particularly helpful database for academic debaters is CQ Researcher (and CQ Weekly). CQ stands for *Congressional Quarterly*. This source provides excellent information by collecting reports about issues of public policy and presenting them in a useful and readable format.

F. Think Tanks

Access **think tanks**. These are groups of experts who conduct research and prepare reports in support of their inquiry and advocacy concerning issues of various concerns including public and governmental policy, business, science, and education. For some think tanks, their mission is primarily research; others are unabashed promoters and lobbyists. They may be funded as nonprofit organizations, in which case they avoid political affiliation, or privately. Some well-known think tanks (certainly not an exhaustive list), categorized by their political inclinations are:

Conservative

- American Enterprise Institute
- Claremont Institute
- Competitive Enterprise Institute
- Project for the New American Century
- Heritage Foundation

Liberal

- Brookings Institution
- Center on Budget and Policy Priorities
- Center for American Progress
- Center for Economic and Policy Research
- Center for Progressive Reform

Libertarian

- Cato Institute
- Ayn Rand Institute

Nonpartisan

- Aspen Institute
- Atlantic Council of the United States
- Center for Strategic and International Studies
- Council on Foreign Relations
- Woodrow Wilson International Center for Scholars

G. The World Wide Web

Search the web. Many students are tempted to begin their research with an Internet search. This is ill advised. The World Wide Web, or the Internet, is the cumulative collection of images, text, video, and other materials that have been organized and stored on computers called web servers by a wide range of individuals, businesses, and organizations. The output of any keyword search is likely to be huge. Web pages or websites range from collections of high-quality research materials posted by nonprofit think tanks and academic associations to social networking sites, personal diaries, and commercial materials. Much useful information is available to the web searcher, but the challenge (and it is a huge challenge) is to efficiently locate and identify material of worth and to critically evaluate its quality. A debater accessing an article in a scholarly journal knows the article has been carefully reviewed and edited and represents some level of reliability and credibility. This is not so for a website. In this section, we will consider how to search the web, how to assess the credibility of a website, and some dangers to avoid.

Searching the web begins with a **search engine**. This is a computer program that works to retrieve and prioritize information within a computer system, in this case, the Internet. There are literally hundreds of available search engines; as of 2007, 80 percent of users turned to the two most popular: Google and Yahoo!. To use a search engine, begin with a keyword search. Enter relevant terms into the search space. Use the "Boolean search operators" AND and OR to limit your search in different ways. For example, George W. Bush AND "gay marriage" will find material that contains references to both President Bush and to gay marriage; using OR will find materials with references either to the president or to gay marriage, or to both the president and gay marriage. Please note that without the quotation marks, the above search will also turn up references to Bush and gay, and to Bush and marriage. Many engines will also allow use of NOT as an operator. This typically is offered as BUT NOT or AND NOT. For example, George W. Bush BUT NOT gay marriage will turn up materials including references to President Bush, but excluding any materials that also reference gay marriage. Another Boolean operator is the word NEAR. Bush NEAR Iraq should turn up materials in which Bush appears within 10 or 25 (depending on the search engine) words of Iraq in the text of the article. Even more useful are the characters + (for the word AND), - (for the word NOT), and "" (to enclose a phrase).

Websites are not equal in their credibility. Here are some types of websites:

- Personal home pages. These are developed and posted by individuals. They may include family pictures and hobbies, but they may also offer opinions and even academic or research papers, resumes, and other informative materials. Personal home pages may include blogs (weblogs, or journals) or social networking sites.

- Special interest sites. These may be posted by clubs, community organizations, or special interest groups. They are inherently biased, as they are created to promote or facilitate their interest. For example, they may promote a political issue (gun control), and community initiative (a proposed dog park), or a hobby (paintballing).

- Professional sites. Such websites are official functions of professional organizations, institutions, or individuals. They may provide useful information about the work of the web poster, and may offer quality research, advice, information, and opinion. While they may exist to promote a for-profit business, the information at the site is free and offered as a service.

- Commercial sites. A large number of websites are advertisements, portals for online sales, or catalogs. These include giant online businesses (Amazon.com), brick and mortar businesses with web presence (Barnes & Noble), and at-home entrepreneurship.

- Publications. Newspapers, journals, and magazines generally publish online in addition to their hard copy publication, and some journalistic publications are strictly online (e-zines). For many, the web is simply another medium for their credible journalism. However, anyone can publish his or her own material to the web. The line between a personal home page and a respected blog is a fine one.

- Wikis. The term "wiki" is Hawaiian for *quick*. Wikipedia is the most famous. Groups of readers contribute to the development of materials, including contributions of content as well as editing. They can be extremely helpful in understanding a concept, but are not necessarily credible as sources of qualified information, research, or opinion.

How does one navigate this wide range of varied information? Some standards for all evidence will be explored in the next chapter. Some things to look for include: Is the author of the information clearly identified? What can you learn about her/him? Are the author's credentials sufficient to lend credibility to the subject? Is the corporate author or sponsoring organization clearly identified? What is their likely bias or reputation regarding the topic? Are the date of publication and the date of the information available? Is it current? Is there a list of works cited? What type of website is it? Are they selling a product or service? Can you learn anything relevant about the site from its web address? For example, the last three letters will indicate the following: .edu (education sites), .gov (government sites), .org (organization sites), .com (commercial sites), and .net (network infrastructures).

Finally, do not assume that because a website looks professional that it is credible. Graphics are easy to navigate, and the Internet is accessible to everyone, regardless of integrity. For example, if you click on http://www.wto.org/, you will visit the legitimate website of the World Trade Organization (WTO). If you visit http://www.gatt.org/, you will visit a sham website that has been made to look like the WTO site, but offers subtle (and not so subtle) false stories in an attempt to ironically criticize the WTO. If you happened onto the sham site without any other knowledge about the World Trade Organization, you would read stories that, among other things, promote formalized slavery. While the fake site is a clever criticism of the WTO, it is not factually representative.

H. Direct Communication

Information may also be obtained through interviews and correspondence. The answers to the three questions in the inset on page 90 will suggest people the advocate should try to interview or correspond with.

Caution: Interviews and correspondence will provide both leads to evidence and evidence that is admissible in the debate. It is important to know the difference between the two types.

1. Interviews.   Interviews with subject-matter experts can be valuable sources of information. The value of any interview depends to a considerable extent on our advance preparation; carefully planned preliminary research will enable us to ask meaningful questions. The student debater is in an excellent position to secure interviews with faculty members. Furthermore, interviews often can be arranged with members of Congress, business executives, labor leaders, and others who have special knowledge of the subject of the debate proposition.

Consider a hypothetical case: In the course of an interview with Dr. Hamilton, an economics professor on your campus, you might ask about a study that your opponents cited and that you found particularly difficult to refute. If Dr. Hamilton replies, "The Back Bay Study is seriously flawed because it failed to consider …," you have a *lead*. You can't quote Dr. Hamilton's statement in a debate because, within the limitations of academic debate, you cannot prove you are quoting this professor accurately. At the first opportune moment, ask Dr. Hamilton, "How can we document the flaws in this study?" If Dr. Hamilton replies by citing a scholarly article in an economics journal, and if your examination of the article provides a detailed statement of the flaws in the Back Bay Study, you are covered. By citing the article to which the economics professor gave you a lead, you now have evidence that is admissible in the debate.

There are many other important interviews the advocate can study. Radio and television stations often present interviews with national or world figures on problems of contemporary importance. (*Meet the Press, Hardball, Face the Nation,* and *Frontline* are examples.) Magazines also often publish interviews in which prominent persons are quizzed about important problems; these can serve as important sources of information. Websites and blogs offer interviews as well as personal statements by noted experts. Note that the same distinction between leads and admissible evidence applies here. An interview in a magazine clearly is admissible evidence; it is available in the public record and may be used without any question on that score. However, your recollection of what the secretary of the treasury said on *Meet the Press* last Sunday is just that—your recollection. As such it constitutes a lead and nothing more. Of course, if the Monday newspapers quote the secretary's statement, you have admissible evidence. Otherwise you must request a transcript of the program, and you cannot use the evidence until the transcript arrives.

In academic debate, convention wisely requires that the advocate document evidence from sources available in the public domain.

2. Correspondence.   Correspondence is often a fruitful source of information. A helpful starting point in the search for information is the list of associations and societies in the United States published in Associations Unlimited. Hundreds of organizations are listed, ranging from "Abolish Capital Punishment, American League to" through "Zoologists, American Society of." Most of these organizations, as well as many other special interest groups, will respond to thoughtful letters or e-mail correspondence asking intelligent questions in the area of their concern.

Often advocates will discover organizations that strongly support or oppose the proposition under consideration. Some of these groups maintain elaborate propaganda agencies. Through correspondence advocates may obtain press releases, special papers, data sheets, pamphlets, booklets, and other materials not ordinarily available through libraries. Here, too, it is important to note the distinction between a lead and admissible evidence. For example, suppose that, in response to your request for a transcript of the House Hearings on Unemployment, your representative not only sends you a copy but adds a personal note stating, "I feel these hearings are unnecessarily gloomy. My view is that we will see a substantial drop in unemployment beginning in the next quarter." The hearings, of course, are admissible evidence. But the letter is not because, within the limitations of academic debate, it is impossible to authenticate the letter. It is, however, a valuable lead. Phone your representative immediately and ask whether the prediction can be documented. If your representative refers you to a recent think-tank study that has gone unnoticed in the press, you may—when you get a copy of the study—have valuable admissible evidence.

Sources of Debate Materials

- Reference Materials
- Books
- Periodicals
- Government Documents
- Databases
- Think Tanks
- Websites
- Direct Communication

III. READING WITH A PURPOSE

Advocates can make brainstorming work by preparing a carefully drafted outline of the ideas and sources suggested in brainstorming. From this list they should develop a bibliography to use in research and a list of publications to monitor. While doing research and monitoring, they can revise and refine the bibliography and list of monitored publications. This process of brainstorming, research, and revising will continue until the first debate, which will often trigger further brainstorming and research that will continue as long as the proposition is debated.

When students are asked to monitor the daily press or weekly newsmagazines, they sometimes protest, "But I don't have time to read all those newspapers and magazines." Perhaps they do not have time to read an entire newspaper every day, but when they read for the purpose of finding information on a specific problem, they do not need to read the entire paper. It takes only a few minutes to scan the bulky *New York Times* to determine whether it contains an article on, say, inflation, unemployment, population stabilization, or an international conflict.

Whether research is conducted in through an online index, database, or search engine, effective use of *keywords* is critical to productive gathering of information. The advocate must be familiar with the jargon of the relevant field and the workings of the index or search aid to know what keywords to look for, how to combine them, and how to broaden or narrow a search. The researcher also must become familiar with the language used by those writing about the controversy. As the researcher becomes more familiar with the relevant literature, he or she will know better how to limit searches by dates and types of materials and thus how to more efficiently zero in on relevant data.

Try to map out the argument as best you can before you start researching. Keep a physical map of it (either on the computer or written down), and add to it as your research progresses. The point is to be aware of all the different components of the argument, so you recognize a card when you see it. Develop a list of keywords or phrases that go along with your argument. Try to determine if the literature uses any other words or phrases interchangeably. This will give you different options when you are looking for articles. Copy and investigate the footnotes. Sometimes you might randomly find a title that looks interesting. Or, if you find some helpful information, and there is a footnote for it, look it up as it will probably help you. Search for similar articles by the same author. Find their website, or the website of the publication they write for or organization they represent. Or, just Google their name and explore. But if an author writes about an issue, odds are there is more of their work somewhere.

IV. READING CRITICALLY

More literature is available on any contemporary, controversial problem than advocates could possibly read in the time available. Research, then, must be planned for both breadth and discrimination, so that time is used efficiently. Advocates must seek out sources representative of the various points of view related to the problem in order to understand possible lines of argument. Because much writing on any contemporary problem is likely to be a restatement of other writings, or a superficial treatment, discriminating advocates will seek out original sources, articles in scholarly or professional journals, writings by qualified authorities, and reports by competent and objective persons, giving preference to sources with established reputations for accuracy.

An article on nuclear weapons appearing in the *Bulletin of Atomic Scientists,* for example, is more likely to contain accurate and significant information than is an article on the same subject in the Sunday supplement of a local newspaper. The full text of the secretary of state's speech on a foreign policy problem may contain some carefully phrased qualifications that are omitted in the brief summary appearing in a newsmagazine.

Advocates cannot read everything written about the problem. So they must be critical in their reading to select representative, authoritative, accurate, and significant material for careful, detailed study.

V. RECORDING MATERIALS

In the early exploration of a problem, advocates should adopt a systematic method of recording materials so they may readily use the information assembled from many different sources. Advocates may use any method—index cards, legal pads, filing cabinets, computer data files—that their needs dictate and their resources permit. Many advocates develop a portable library that they can take with them on the campaign plane or into the boardroom, the courtroom, or the classroom. Intercollegiate debaters have developed a successful method of recording materials by using thousands of file folders (or dozens of accordion-style expandable files) stuffed with letter-sized briefs, assembled in boxes or tubs carried with the aid of hand trucks or carts. Although the advocate may use only a relatively few briefs in any one debate, experienced CEDA/NDT debaters find it desirable to have thousands of pieces of information immediately available to meet the many possible arguments presented by their opponents. A few industrious debaters have successfully created electronic filing systems that they can access quickly and easily for reference during the course of a debate. This is certainly the future!

At one time intercollegiate debaters stored their material on index cards, filed in recipe boxes or long file drawers. Today debaters find it more efficient to organize page-sized **briefs** into file folders and expandable files. However, they often still refer to one item of information as a **card** even though it is generally a quotation or statistic read from a full-sized sheet of paper. As you conduct your research, your goal is to accumulate *cards*, and to organize cards so as to construct argument briefs.

How much evidence does one need in applied debating? The short answer is: whatever it takes to win the argument. In a class debate a few dozen well-chosen evidence cards may be sufficient. By contrast, some lawsuits have required literally truckloads of evidence. Most advocates prefer to have too much rather than too little evidence available to them. In academic debate, if some seldom-used evidence becomes critical, you must either have it with you or lose whatever issue the evidence might win for you if it were available.

While researching and reading source material, advocates should have a system on which to record (1) all information that may help in supporting their stand on the proposition and (2) all information that may be of help to opponents. Begin by organizing cards.

There are three parts to a card. The tag (a one sentence explanation of the card), the citation or cite (the source of where the card comes from, including author and publication), and the card itself. Make sure to get the full or complete citation. This includes the author, where it was published, the date of publication, the volume or issue number, and the website if it is online. If you are referencing a book, include the editor (if there is one). If it is one chapter of a book, include the chapter name as well as the book name.

Make sure to get the person's qualifications. Newspapers will often just have a staff writer, which is their qualification. But in books or journals, those people usually have credentials. Even if the credentials are not listed, search for them online. Do a Google search for the name, or look in *Who's Who*. If five minutes of looking saves you a debate because your key evidence comes from a Ph.D. professor of physics at Cornell University instead of some dude from the *Pittsburgh Post Gazette,* it is well worth it.

If you are on an Internet source with no apparent date, look closely on the website. Often there is a copyright symbol at the bottom and a year, indicating when the material was last updated or "published." If nothing is available after rigorous searching, use the Date of Access (DOA). Make it clear in the citation that the date referenced is the date that the material was accessed, and not necessarily when it was published.

Put brackets around the beginning and end of the material to be quoted in the card. This will help you process it later. If you are "cutting" cards on

Cutting Cards on the Computer

A. Creating and Using a Document Template

1. Open a blank Word document. Save the file as a template by clicking "File ... Save As." Change the file name to "debate template" and where it says "Save as type" choose "Document Template."

2. Adjust the page margins. Go to "File ... Page Setup ... Margins." For Mac, go to "Format ... Document." Change the top and bottom margins to 0.5", and both side margins to 0.8".

3. Open the Styles palette. On Windows, click "Format ... Styles and Formatting." On Mac, click "Format ... Style." Either a new sidebar will appear on the right (Windows) or another menu will pop up (Mac).

4. First, create the style that will normally appear whenever you put something into Word. This is the Normal style. Find "Normal" on the menu and click "Modify." Under "Formatting" change to Arial, 11 pt. font. Make sure to click "Add to template" or "Save to template" before clicking OK.

5. Next, create the style for block headings; this will be Heading 1. Scroll down the menu to the "Heading 1" style. Click "Modify." Under "Formatting" change to Arial, 18 pt. font, Bold, single underline, and center aligned. Then give it a shortcut key. Click on "Format ... Shortcut key" and assign one. With Windows, choose F2. With Mac, the function keys are already taken, so choose Control + 1. Make sure to click "Add to template" or "Save to template" before clicking OK. ONLY use Heading 1 for block titles. Right after you type a title and hit Enter, make sure to switch out of Heading 1. This is very important for indexing.

6. Now, choose a style for citation headings. Under the Styles menu, choose "Heading 2." Click "Modify." Under "Formatting" change to Arial, 12 pt. font, Bold, and single underline. Then give it a shortcut key. Click on "Format ... Shortcut key" and assign one. With Windows, choose F3. With Mac, the function keys are already taken, so choose Control + 2. Make sure to click "Add to template" or "Save to template" before clicking OK.

7. Now, create a style for tags. Under the Styles menu, choose "Heading 3." Click "Modify." Under "Formatting" change to Arial, 12 pt. font, Bold, no underline. Then give it a shortcut key. Click on "Format ... Shortcut key" and assign one. With Windows, choose F4. With Mac, choose Control + 3. Make sure to click "Add to template" or "Save to template" before clicking OK.

8. "Paste Special" is a function that allows you to copy large amounts of text (retrieved from a website, for instance) and paste it into the Word document WITHOUT any of the graphics or other inserts from the web page. "Paste Special" allows you to paste JUST the text, which is what debaters want. Once you have something copied from another source (for example, a web page or PDF file), click on "Edit" and then "Paste Special." Then choose "Unformatted Text" to paste it as text only.

9. That was a long process. For convenience sake, add "Paste Special" to your customized toolbar. Under the "Tools" option, click on "Customize ... Toolbars." For Windows, you can also just right click the toolbar and click either "Add icons" or "Customize." A new menu will pop up—click on the "Commands" section. On the available menu, click on "Edit" and then find "Paste Special." Drag "Paste Special" to your toolbar at the top of the document. This should add that button to your toolbar. Now, you can just click on that button directly to paste.

Cutting Cards on the Computer (Continued)

10. Result: If you have done all of this correctly, your document should be nicely formatted. When the Normal font is selected, and you Paste (Special) something into it, the text will appear exactly as you designated. When you press F2 (or Ctrl + 1 for Mac), it should automatically center and allow you to create a block heading. Continue using the commands to enter in tags, cites, and the "normal" text for cards, and you will have a perfectly formatted file.

B. Indexing Files on the Computer

1. You should have used Heading 1 for each of your block titles. These will form the index. Go to "Insert … Reference … Index and Tables … Table of Contents." Where it says "Show levels" scroll down to 1. Once you click OK, it will paste an Index wherever the cursor was.

2. If there are all sorts of other things (not just brief titles) that come up on the index, that means that you didn't change out of Heading 1 before you moved on from that block title. Simply find the page where the error was made, select the text that is appearing as Heading 1, and change it to Normal. You may have to re-underline it. But, the point is, make sure ONLY the file titles are in Heading 1 format.

the computer, when you are finished cutting the card, paste the citation above it immediately. Do not put a tag that the card does not support. It is better to acknowledge the card for what it is, and connect it with other cards that together tell a story. That is much better than trying to claim that one card says the whole thing, and then you look like a fool in a debate. If you are cutting cards from a hard copy source (not on computer), you have to process them, which involves printing up a list of citations, cutting out the cards, and pasting or taping them to the appropriate cites. This is called *processing*. Make sure to process your evidence shortly after you cut it.

You should tag your evidence as soon as you cut it. Don't just leave it with brackets on the side. If you are on the computer, you can type a tag right after you cut the card. If you are reading a printed source, write the tag to the side. You still have the option to change the tag before you print or block the card (adding it to a brief), but having some sort of tag there is necessary to categorize and sort.

VI. ORGANIZING MATERIALS

Not only must advocates have a wealth of information, but that information must be instantly available to them. The method considered here is used by intercollegiate debaters, but it may be adapted to any type of advocacy.

First, the advocate should classify information as *affirmative* or *negative,* and classify the type of argument (disadvantage, case/solvency, counterplan, etc.), perhaps indicating these classifications by an abbreviation placed on each card or by different colors of cards. Next, the advocate should classify the cards according to the issues developed. The affirmative file will consist of the issues necessary to develop the affirmative case together with the evidence necessary to establish the case in the first affirmative speech and to defend and extend the case in the second affirmative speech and rebuttals.

A system of indexing the files should be developed to enable the advocate to locate any brief quickly. After evidence has been "cut" (tagged and marked) and "processed" (attached to its relevant citation), it is ready to be "sorted." Here, you go back to your map of the argument or file. Make sure you have categories for as much of the argument as possible. Make separate piles for every category (even for different subcategories), and organize your big stack of cards into each pile. Sometimes a card will not fit under any category, and you have to create a new one. It is important to physically see the file laid out so you can tell if there are any holes to fill. Once the file is sorted, you are ready to block.

Blocking is the creation of argument briefs, prepared and evidenced arguments ready to be presented in a debate. You may wish to begin by putting your name in the top left corner. Put the title of the block in the top center of the page. Put the name of the file on the top right of the brief. Put your tag, cite, and card down on the page.

Make an index for the file on the top right, place the number for that page in the block. For instance, if it is the first piece of paper under a four-page impact extension block, put 1 / 4. If it is the second page in a six-page answers to block, put 2 / 6. Place the page number on the bottom right of the file. Do not number until you are certain the file is finished, or until you have produced an index.

The objective is to provide as many subheadings as necessary (separate files) while keeping related information together (within files and among groups of related files) to make essential information instantly available. Color coding may be used to indicate subdivisions, and highlighting and underlining will indicate "cards" (selected quoted material) and portions of cards with particularly important information. The examples shown here are drawn from the files of student debaters, but any advocate who must organize a large mass of data must develop some comparable system.

In some cases advocates will find that a given piece of information might appropriately be placed under more than one classification. Multiple cards recording the same information should be prepared and inserted in the proper places, with cross-references to other locations to avoid repetition.

Careful exploration of the problem is essential to intelligent advocacy. Reasonable and prudent people will give little time and less credence to advocates who don't seem to know what they're talking about. Debaters who thoroughly study the appropriate sources of information, carefully conduct their research, read purposefully and critically, record materials accurately, and organize effectively are taking an important step toward responsible and effective advocacy. Only well-prepared advocates can hope to gain and hold the attention of a critical audience, perform well against well-informed opponents, and secure a decision from reasonable judges.

EXERCISES

1. *Brainstorming.* Working in groups of five, brainstorm a list of causes and possible solutions to the problem of childhood obesity (or substitute any significant social issue; you may wish to brainstorm an issue for classroom debate). This should culminate in a "map" for your research.

2. Find one card from each of the seven sources of debate materials (excluding direct communication) relevant to issues identified in Exercise 1 (or identify a social issue and collect one relevant card from each type of source).

3. *Treasure hunt.* Find a recent book or scholarly article about the topic identified in Exercise 1 (or choose a topic of social importance). Use the bibliography to identify another source, go to that source, and find another relevant source in its bibliography. Continue until you have visited five sources.

4. Begin with a topic of social importance. Identify as many keywords and combinations of keywords as you can to guide your online research of the topic.

5. Begin with a topic of social importance. Locate one of the six types of websites relevant to the topic. Evaluate the quality of each as a source of debate information.

6

Evidence

In order to justify the invasion of Iraq rather than to continue a U.N.-sponsored inspection regime in Iraq, President Bush in 2002 and 2003 offered "evidence" of Iraqi-sponsored programs to develop and stockpile weapons of mass destruction (WMDs), in violation of U.N. resolutions. This evidence included claims of intelligence information that could not be detailed. Was the evidence offered by the Bush administration sufficient? The war ensued with the support of the majority of the American people, even in the face of opposition by many of our allies including France and Germany. After the end of major combat was declared, when weapons of mass destruction had not been discovered, contenders for the Democratic nomination to the presidency and other opponents of the war offered that failure to find WMDs was evidence that the war was unwarranted. Was their argumentation well founded?

Evidence is the raw material of argumentation. It consists of facts, opinions, and objects that are used to generate proof. The advocate brings together the raw materials and, by the process of reasoning, produces new conclusions. We cannot undertake critical thinking without a sound basis of evidence. The use of evidence is not limited to debates—although debates give us an excellent means of learning about evidence. Even in unstructured disputes in informal settings, we must necessarily seek out evidence. Who won the first Heisman trophy? Just what does your warranty cover? Did the campus paper really say that? Those and countless other matters are best settled by referring to the appropriate evidence.

The impact that the evidence will have on the decision renderers will depend on their perceptions and values. In intercollegiate debate judges are expected to evaluate evidence coolly and dispassionately, setting aside any preconceived notions and weighing the data critically. This is a good model for us to follow when we are called on to make important decisions. Yet we must recognize that, in almost any situation, the judge or the audience will be influenced by the *source* of the message (that is, the advocate or the publication the advocate quotes), the *message* itself, and the *channel* (for example, face-to-face communication, radio, or television). The judge will be affected by all these factors as a *receiver* (that is, the receiver's values and perceptions affect his or her evaluation of evidence). This is no less true in the

---

Miniglossary

Casual evidence   That which is created without an effort being made to create it and is not designed for possible future reference.

Conclusive proof   Evidence that is incontrovertible, either because the law will not permit it to be contradicted or because it is strong and convincing enough to override all evidence to the contrary and to establish the proposition beyond reasonable doubt.

Corroborative proof   Strengthening or confirming evidence of a different character in support of the same fact or proposition.

Direct evidence   That which tends to show the existence of a fact in question without the intervention of the proof of any other fact.

Evidence   Consists of facts, opinions, and objects used to generate proof.

Evidence aliunde   Evidence that explains or clarifies other evidence.

Extrajudicial evidence   Evidence that is not admissible in court; such evidence may be used outside the court.

Indispensable proof   Evidence without which a particular issue cannot be proved.

Judicial evidence   Evidence that is admissible in court.

Judicial notice   Evidence introduced into argument without the necessity of substantiation; it is assumed to be so well known that it does not require substantiation.

Negative evidence   The absence of evidence that might reasonably be expected to be found was the issue in question true.

Partial proof   Used to establish a detached fact in a series of facts tending to support the issue in dispute.

Prearranged evidence   That which is created for the specific purpose of recording certain information for possible future reference.

Presumptive evidence   Evidence that tends to show the existence of a fact by proving other, related facts.

Primary evidence   The best evidence that the circumstances admit; original or firsthand evidence that affords the greatest certainty of the matter in question.

Public records   All documents compiled or issued by or with the approval of any governmental agency.

Public writings   A frequently used source of evidence that includes all written material, other than public records, made available to the general public.

Secondary evidence   Evidence that by its nature suggests the availability of better evidence in the matter in question.

academic debate than in other argumentative contexts, despite judges' best efforts to divorce themselves from their own personal judgments.

We probably could establish, after some debate that the unemployment rate in the United States is 4.5 percent. Once that fact was established, we would proceed to the more difficult matter of establishing that 4.5 percent was an acceptable or unacceptable rate of unemployment. The college professor serving as debate judge would probably feel empathy for the scholarly opinion of a professor of economics. An unemployed audience member might attach the most weight to a labor leader's view. A banker in the audience might be most impressed by a statement from the chair of the Federal Reserve Board. A student in the audience might evaluate the evidence on the basis of personal experience: Is unemployment a remote concept considered only in economics classes, or was one of the student's parents just laid off at the auto plant?

In previous chapters we considered how advocates assemble and organize information as they analyze and explore the problem. In this chapter we will consider the evidence itself, and in the next chapter we will consider tests to be applied to evidence. Subsequent chapters will consider the composition of the case (Chapter 15) and the delivery of the case (Chapter 16), thereby highlighting the interrelationship of evidence with source, message, channel, and receiver. By understanding evidence and its interrelation with communication, we will be in a better position (1) to evaluate arguments presented for our decision and (2) to construct good reasons to serve as justification for the decisions we desire to secure from others.

Evidence may be classified as direct or presumptive. **Direct evidence** is evidence that tends to show the existence of a fact in question without the intervention of the proof of any other fact. For example, in a debate on "tax sharing," the claim that "43 states now have state income taxes" could be established or refuted by reference to the Internal Revenue Service, or some other reliable source. In argument direct evidence is most frequently used to establish supporting contentions rather than to prove the proposition itself. If irrefutable evidence existed in proof of the proposition, there would be no point in debating it. At one time, for example, the proposition "Resolved: That the United States can land men on the moon" was debatable. Today there is simply no point in debating the proposition (although a Fox TV program and a number of websites have emerged that contend that the moon landing was a hoax; see http://www.apollo-hoax.me.uk/index.html.

Presumptive evidence, or indirect or circumstantial evidence, is evidence that tends to show the existence of a fact in question by proving other, related facts—facts from which the fact in question may be inferred. In debates on the "hazardous waste" proposition, for example, students had many occasions to argue presumptive evidence. When someone lived (usually unknowingly at the time) near a site where hazardous waste had been buried and contracted cancer years later, could it be presumed that the hazardous waste was the cause of the cancer? Many civil suits turned on this issue, and many state legislatures enacted laws addressing this question. In many cases the courts ruled that the presumption was strong enough to justify a verdict for the plaintiff.

As a practical matter much time and effort is spent on presumptive evidence. "But you can't convict a person on circumstantial evidence!" students sometimes

Evidence
■ *Evidence* is the raw material of argumentation
■ *Direct evidence* tends to show the existence of a fact in question without the intervention of the proof of any other fact
■ *Presumptive evidence,* or indirect or circumstantial evidence, is evidence that tends to show the existence of a fact in question by proving other, related facts, from which the fact in question may be inferred

protest. On the contrary, many people *are* convicted on the basis of circumstantial evidence. If there is strong direct evidence of the guilt of the accused, the case seldom comes to trial; under such circumstances the accused usually finds it advisable to "plea bargain" (plead guilty to a lesser charge in exchange for a lighter sentence).

I. SOURCES OF EVIDENCE

Evidence is introduced into an argument from various sources. By understanding the uses and limitations of the sources of evidence, we will be more discerning in reaching our own decisions and in developing arguments for the decisions of others.

A. Judicial Notice

Judicial notice is the quickest, simplest, and easiest way of introducing evidence into an argument. **Judicial notice** (the term is borrowed from the courts) is the process whereby certain evidence may be introduced into an argument without the necessity of substantiation; it is assumed to be so well known that it does not require substantiation. In almost any argument it is necessary to refer to various matters of common knowledge in order to lay the foundation for other evidence to be introduced later and to set the argument in its proper context. Certain matters, which we might reasonably expect any well-informed person to know, may be presented as evidence simply by referring to them. Certain cautions, however, must be observed in the use of judicial notice.

1. The Evidence Must Be Introduced. Advocates cannot expect those who render the decision to build a case for them; they cannot plead, "But I thought everybody knew that." If certain evidence is important to an understanding of the case, then the advocate must introduce that evidence. The Supreme Court summed up this principle, which applies to legal pleadings and to other types of argumentation, when it ruled, "A judge sees only with judicial eyes and knows nothing respecting any particular case of which he is not informed judicially."

2. The Evidence Must Be Well Known. The instrument of judicial notice may be used only for those matters that are truly common knowledge. For example, when the "energy" proposition was debated, the existence of an oil shortage could be established by judicial notice; the extent of the shortage was another matter, however. To establish this, the debater had to produce evidence that would likely be attacked with conflicting evidence. If advocates introduce little-known evidence merely by judicial notice, they may anticipate some doubt in the minds of those who render the decision. The Supreme Court made this sound principle of argumentation a part of our legal structure when it ruled, "Courts should take care that requisite notoriety exists concerning the matters on which they take judicial notice, and every reasonable doubt upon the subject should be resolved in the negative." (A "perfect example" of judicial notice is considered in the Chapter 8 section "Modal Qualifications.") Note that well-known evidence is often perishable. For example, the bombing of Pearl Harbor is burned indelibly in the minds of one generation of Americans; the assassination of President Kennedy is firmly implanted in the minds of another generation of Americans. They can tell you where they were, who they were with, and what they were doing at the time they learned of these events. But you may or may not remember the dates or any details of these events from reading about them in school years after they occurred. You probably do, however, recall the date of the terrorist attacks on the World Trade Center in New York City and the Pentagon. Those events are well known to you.

3. The Evidence May Be Refuted.   Evidence offered by judicial notice is usually presented in the expectation that it will be accepted without question by the opposition. But such evidence, like all evidence, is subject to possible refutation. In debates on "right-to-work" laws, for instance, some affirmative debaters sought to establish by judicial notice that "there is widespread corruption in labor unions." Negative debaters, however, usually refused to allow this claim and introduced evidence designed to refute it.

In presenting evidence through judicial notice, the advocates ask, in effect, that their opponents and those rendering the decision suspend the tests of evidence and accept their assertion as an established fact not requiring proof. Opposing advocates allow such evidence to go unchallenged at their peril. If the evidence actually is irrefutable, there is no point in raising an objection. But if the evidence is refutable and the opposing advocates fail to raise an objection, then they have only themselves to blame if those who render the decision accept the evidence as an established fact.

The use of judicial notice is not uncommon in academic debate. It is most likely to be found toward the end of the academic year, when a certain body of evidence and argument related to the current national debate proposition has become common knowledge in the forensic community. In these circumstances judicial notice will be effective if (1) the evidence is so well known to the opposing team that it will concede the point by not attempting to refute it, and (2) the evidence is so well known to the judge(s) that it will weigh in the decision as if it were fully developed rather than merely asserted.

Judicial notice is not limited to the courtroom or academic debate, however. It may be used in any circumstances in which the evidence is, in fact, well known to those who render the decision. Thus an executive at a board meeting might argue, "We can't use this incentive plan—remember Ernst & Whinney's report on how it would affect our tax situation?" If the report is well known to the board, and if all members accept its conclusion that the incentive plan would hurt the company's tax position, the proposal may well be defeated by this brief use of judicial notice. The advocate must remember that what is well known to the "in-group" may be unfamiliar to others. Thus the use of a critical piece of evidence by judicial notice might be devastating in the final round of a major tournament but ineffective in an exhibition debate before a Kiwanis club. Similarly, the brief reminder that might clinch an argument before knowledge-able board members might be meaningless at a stockholders' meeting; the stock-holders of a large corporation could not be expected to be familiar with the details of every report submitted to the board of directors.

B. Public Records

Public records are often used as a source of evidence. On many matters they are the most important evidence, because private individuals or organizations lack the authority or resources to assemble much of the evidence that can be found only in public records.

Public records include all documents compiled or issued by or with the approval of any governmental agency. In this category are such diverse materials as the *Congressional Record,* federal and state statute books, birth certificates, deeds, reports of congressional hearings, and the minutes of a town meeting. Official records are usually highly regarded. The fact that they are public records, how-ever, does not mean that they should be accepted uncritically. A public record containing the report of a congressional committee might be the best possible source of information on the amount of money the United States spent on direct economic aid to foreign countries in a certain year, because the committee has the power to compel officials to produce their records and testify under oath. The same report might contain the testimony of witnesses on the value of this economic aid. Their testimony would not necessarily be the best possible expert opinion on that subject, however: They might be impartial authorities, or they might be highly prejudiced lobbyists.

C. Public Writings

Public writings, another frequently used source of evidence, include all written material, other than public records, made available to the general public. In this category are such diverse materials as the *Encyclopedia Britannica* and the *Weekly World News,* a college textbook and the campus humor magazine, the *World Almanac* and *The Great Gatsby,* and a Brookings Institution report and an astrol-oger's chart. Some public writings command high prestige and are likely to be accepted readily; others are more likely to be disbelieved than believed. Obviously the value of public writings varies tremendously.

D. Private Writings

Caution: Private writings and testimony of witnesses, like the interviews and correspondence considered in Chapter 5, will provide both *leads* to evidence and evidence that is *admissible* in the debate. As noted previously, the advocate needs to know the distinction.

Private writings include all written material prepared for private rather than public use. Some private writings are designed to become public records at a later date. Wills, for example, become public records when they are probated; contracts become public records if they are brought into court for adjudication. Any private writing may become a public record if it is included in the records of a court or a governmental agency, or it may become a public writing if it is made available to the general public. Most private writings, however, are prepared for a limited circulation among selected individuals. In this category are such diverse materials as a privately owned company's financial statement prepared by a certified public accountant, a student's class notes, a diary, and a personal letter.

Private writings may be carefully prepared documents designed to report events with great precision and to reflect considered judgments, or they may be incomplete and studded with offhand comments or facetious remarks. Because private writings constitute an important source of evidence, care should be taken to determine who prepared the document and under what circumstances. Note that personal letters are not customarily introduced as evidence in academic debate. The reason may be that it is usually impossible to authenticate a personal letter within the limitations of an academic debate. Thus, if private writings become public writings, they are clearly admissible in the form of public writings. If they remain private writings, they are leads that may guide one to admissible evidence.

Computers have created a gray area of public/private writing. E-mail or comments on an electronic bulletin board are similar to postcards. That is, they're public in the sense that many people have easy access to them, but they're private in the sense that they are often intended for one person or a small group of people. The test here is the context in which the evidence is found. If it is stored in a database available to the general public, it is clearly a public writing and admissible as evidence. If the evidence is only fleetingly available, it must be treated as a lead. Note, too, that there is the problem of verifying such evidence. (The Chapter 7 section "Verifiable Evidence" discusses this issue in more detail.)

E. Testimony of Witnesses

The testimony of witnesses is one of the most common sources of evidence. Testimony in court or before a governmental body is usually given under oath and is subject to penalties for perjury or contempt. Testimony outside the courtroom or hearing room is not subject to the same legal restrictions and is usually more informal. For example, management officials usually give testimony on the operation of their company at a stockholders' meeting; the president of a company may ask the plant superintendent for an oral report on the utility of a new machine; the college freshman may ask a sophomore for advice on what courses to take. In fact, much of our day-to-day business and social activity is based on the testimony of witnesses.

The value of such testimony may vary considerably. Clearly the testimony of a witness at a congressional hearing is readily admissible by citing the hearings. The "testimony" of your political science professor in a classroom lecture is *not* admissible in academic debate, but it may constitute a valuable lead that will enable you to find admissible evidence.

F. Personal Inspection

When personal inspection is used as a source of evidence, something is presented for examination to the persons rendering the decision. For instance, the automobile sales person may invite customers to lift the hood and inspect the motor; a stockbroker may show the financial statement of a company to a client; or a senator may bring a bag of groceries into the Senate chamber for use during a speech on nutrition. College students frequently are asked to perform personal inspections. For example, the geology professor may offer a sample of rock for the class to examine; the economics professor may sketch a supply-and-demand curve on the board; or the music professor may play a portion of a recording for a music appreciation class.

Personal inspection is frequently used in courtroom debates: Attorneys show juries and judges the murder weapon, arrange for them to visit the scene of the crime, or show them the plaintiff's injuries. Evidence presented through personal inspection has been carefully selected and arranged by someone to support a particular argument; it must therefore be examined with care.

Sources of Evidence

- Judicial Notice
- Public Records
- Public Writings
- Private Writings
- Testimony of Witnesses
- Personal Inspection

II. TYPES OF EVIDENCE

A. Judicial or Extrajudicial Evidence

Evidence is usually classified as judicial or extrajudicial. **Extrajudicial evidence** is also known as "extralegal" or "incompetent" evidence. The word *incompetent* has no negative connotation when used in this sense, but merely means "not admissible in court"; such evidence may be used outside the court. Thus extra-judicial evidence is used to satisfy persons about the facts requiring proof in any situation other than a legal proceeding and is subject only to the usual tests of evidence. **Judicial evidence**, also known as "legal" or "competent" evidence, is evidence that is admissible in court. Such evidence must satisfy not only the usual tests of evidence but also the various technical rules of legal evidence.

In legal proceedings certain otherwise perfectly good evidence is excluded. For example, if we are trying to decide whether a certain man's testimony is trustworthy, we are interested in knowing whether he has a criminal record. Such evidence, however, is often excluded from courtroom debates. Thus, if someone says, "That evidence couldn't be admitted in court," the objection is irrelevant unless the debate actually is taking place in court.

The famous O. J. Simpson murder case educated the public on these terms. For weeks there was intensive media coverage of the pretrial hearings. During these hearings the defense and prosecuting attorneys debated whether the results of DNA testing, O. J.'s history of spousal abuse, and other matters were judicial evidence. If judicial, such evidence would be admissible to the trial. Similarly, the admissibility of the prior sexual history of the alleged victim in the Kobe Bryant rape trial was an issue for the court to consider and drew public attention.

B. Primary or Secondary Evidence

Evidence is often classified as primary or secondary. **Primary evidence** is the best evidence that the circumstances admit. It affords the greatest certainty of the matter in question, and it is original or firsthand evidence. **Secondary evidence** is evidence that falls short of this standard, because by its nature it suggests there is better evidence of the matter in question. Thus an examination of this chapter and Chapter 7 of this book is primary evidence that the book contains two chapters on evidence; someone's statement that this book contains two chapters on evidence is secondary evidence.

In debates on a law enforcement proposition, for example, students came across many newspaper and magazine stories quoting the FBI as reporting that the crime rate had gone up 16 percent that year. These stories, of course, were secondary evidence of the FBI's report. Thoughtful debaters checked the primary evidence: the FBI's report itself. There they found the caution that the statistics should not be used for year-to-year comparisons. One reason for this caution was that, in 1995, many police departments across the country switched from the Uniform Crime Report (UCR) system of reporting crimes to the national incident-based system. The incident-based system required the police to report each crime that occurs during an incident. Under the UCR system police reported only one crime per incident—the most serious crime. Thus, if someone broke into a home and robbed and raped a woman the UCR would report that event as a rape. In the incident-based system it is reported as three separate incidents: as breaking and entering, as grand theft, and as a rape—and possibly other crimes as well. Indeed, up to 10 separate crimes could be reported for a single occurrence in the incident-based system. The fact that the incident-based system reported and counted many more crimes was not statistically valid evidence of any change in the number of crimes actually committed. Many secondary sources omitted this caution, and debaters who depended on this secondary evidence sustained embarrassing defeats at the hands of debaters who had sought out the primary evidence.

Primary evidence is stronger than secondary evidence because there is less possibility of error. Secondary evidence is weaker than primary evidence because it does not derive its value solely from the credibility of the witness, but rests largely on the veracity and competence of others. In any argument the prudent advocate seeks to use primary evidence whenever possible.

C. Written or Unwritten Evidence

Written evidence is evidence supplied by writings of all kinds: books, newspapers, and magazines, as well as less frequently used types of writing, such as Roman numerals carved on the cornerstone of a building. *Unwritten evidence* includes both oral testimony and objects offered for personal inspection.

In arguments outside the courtroom, written evidence generally is given greater weight than oral evidence, because it is easier to substantiate. In a recent intercollegiate debate a negative speaker introduced unwritten, secondary evidence by saying:

> Last week I had the opportunity to talk with the senator when he visited in my hometown, and he told me that ...

Then the negative debater quoted a statement strongly critical of the affirmative's position. An affirmative speaker replied to this by using written evidence:

> We have no way of knowing how accurately the negative quoted the senator or of knowing what the senator said in a private interview. However, we do have a record of the considered opinion of the senator on this subject as he expressed it in an article in the *New York Times Magazine* of last week when he stated ...

The affirmative debater then quoted a carefully qualified statement that indicated only minor reservations about the affirmative's position. Which of the speakers quoted the senator correctly? Perhaps both. The senator may have changed his mind; or, more likely, the two statements represented the difference between an offhand comment and a considered opinion. In any event the judge accepted the statement of the affirmative speaker, because he could better substantiate his evidence.

On the other hand, we often accept and act on oral evidence even when it is hearsay. If a professor says to some students, "Last night the dean told me that the president told him that the trustees have decided to raise the tuition next year," the students might well decide immediately that they will have to raise more money for next fall's tuition. As noted in Chapter 5, although unwritten evidence is not used in academic debate, it may provide valuable leads to written evidence, which can be used in academic debate.

D. Real or Personal Evidence

Real evidence is furnished by objects placed on view or under inspection. In the courtroom real evidence may consist of fingerprints, scars, or weapons. Outside the courtroom a farmer may be asked to inspect test plots in which different types of seed are used; a customer might be invited to taste a new food product; a student might be invited to examine a famous painting in a museum; or a customer might be asked to test drive a new car.

We are constantly offered pseudo- or real evidence in the form of print advertisements and TV and radio commercials. Vast sums of money are lavished on producing evidence designed to convince us to buy a product or vote for or against a candidate. Pictures of a car effortlessly speeding along a mountain road or of an opposition candidate caught at a particularly inept moment are offered as "real" evidence of the performance of the car or of the candidate's qualifications. It is important to realize that such "real" evidence is selected and prepared by someone. Consequently, if we hope to make a critical judgment about this evidence, we must apply the appropriate tests of evidence both to the evidence itself and to the persons who prepared it.

Personal evidence is evidence furnished by persons, and it may be in the form of oral or written testimony. The credibility we attach to personal evidence depends in large part on the competence and honesty we attribute to the person providing the testimony.

E. Lay or Expert Evidence

Evidence is usually classified as either lay or expert. As a practical matter, however, it is often difficult to distinguish between the well-informed layperson and the expert. Representatives and senators, for example, may or may not be experts on the subjects they speak about. However, because their official position gives them unusual opportunities to acquire special knowledge on many subjects, audiences often regard them as experts. The able intercollegiate policy debater who has spent an academic year in a superior forensic program studying a national debate proposition might be qualified as a minor expert on that proposition.

Lay evidence is provided by persons without any special training, knowledge, or experience in the matter under consideration. Such evidence is useful in areas that do not require special qualifications. For example, in debates on "right-to-work" laws, the testimony of "rank-and-file" union members or managers of small businesses was frequently important. These people often had no special knowledge of law, economics, sociology, or even unions. But they were able to give important evidence as to how certain union practices had affected them.

In general the courts will allow laypersons to testify on matters of fact but will not allow them to testify as to their opinions. This limitation may apply in argumentation outside the courtroom as well. Laypersons, assuming they meet the qualifications of a good witness, are usually competent to testify on a matter of fact they have observed; however, their opinion of the significance of the fact is another matter. Thus the testimony of a rank-and-file steelworker as to how many members of his or her local attended the meeting at which a strike vote was taken would be good evidence, assuming that the steelworker was an honest and competent person. However, his or her opinion about the effect of a steel strike on the national economy could not be considered as more valuable than that of any other layperson of comparable education and intelligence. Only an expert, in this case probably an economist, could give a meaningful opinion.

Expert evidence is evidence provided by persons with special training, knowledge, or experience in the matter under consideration. In the courtroom expert testimony is permitted only when the inference to be drawn requires something more than mere everyday experience. For example, an expert would be required to infer the mental state of an accused person based on the accused's behavioral characteristics. Similarly, in argumentation outside the courtroom, expert testimony should not be used unnecessarily.

The courts further require that the special competence of experts be established before they are allowed to offer opinion evidence. It is advisable to follow this practice in all argumentation. Remember that an expert is a maven in certain areas only and is a layperson in all other areas.

The qualifications of a witness should be studied carefully before that individual is accepted as an expert. That persons are well known or that their views appear in print does not establish them as experts. Intercollegiate debaters are constantly required to distinguish between the expert and the pseudoexpert. Each year the national debate proposition deals with some subject of contemporary significance, about which a number of articles appear in the press. Some are thoughtful analyses written by experts; others are superficial treatments turned out under the pressure of a deadline by writers who may know less about the subject than the typical college debater.

"Argument from authority" is a phrase sometimes used to indicate that expert opinion is presented to establish a contention in an argument. Expert opinion should be used only when some issue cannot be established readily by other evidence. Intercollegiate debaters and others who cannot establish themselves as experts often find it advantageous to introduce the opinions of experts to sustain certain contentions. Thus in debates on the "compulsory wage and price controls" proposition, some negative speakers contended that controls merely intensified inflationary pressures, whereas affirmative speakers maintained that they were the solution to inflation. The judges in these debates had little basis for accepting the opinion of one college student over that of another. Consequently the debaters found it necessary to introduce as evidence the opinion of experts who commanded the respect of the judges.

In any matter likely to be the subject of a debate, there will probably be expert opinion on both sides. Economists will differ on the merits of a certain tax policy; physicians will differ on the merits of a certain drug; lawyers will differ in their opinion about whether a certain merger violates the antitrust laws; advertising people will differ on the merits of a certain advertising campaign. An important task in both applied and academic debates is establishing a preponderance of expert opinion—not by simply marshaling *more* experts than the opposition but by using testimony from *better qualified* experts whose opinions may be related directly to the matter at hand.

The scientific study is a form of expert evidence that advocates eagerly seek out in an effort to establish greater credibility for their claims. Arguments about the credibility of studies are often crucial to the outcome of a debate. Debate educator Sara Newell maintains that a study is *unique* in that we are provided not only with opinions (the conclusions of the study) but also the facts (observations/data) on which those opinions are based; we are provided not only facts but also with an explanation of how the observations were made; and we are provided not only statistics but also with an expert interpretation of the statistics. A study then is evidence which includes an argument for its own credibility. This unique combination gives a study the potential to "carry more weight," to be more conclusive and more credible than other types of evidence.[1]

Advocates who introduce studies into a debate must be prepared to give good reasons that the studies should be accepted; those whose case is harmed by the studies must be prepared to give good reasons that the studies should be rejected. Newell offers these recommendations:

> Reasonably, the person who introduces the study into the round needs to give some standard or warrant for the credibility of the study. Three major factors determine the extent of proof necessary: (1) the controversial nature of the study's conclusion, (2) the existence of counterstudies, and (3) the importance or controversy of the policy claim. The warrant may range anywhere from general qualification of the expertise of the researcher, to evidence from other sources proclaiming the study to be good or acceptable, to specific explanation and support for the external and internal validity.... The arguments indicating a study are generally of five types. In hierarchical order, according to persuasive power, they are (1) counterstudies disprove, (2) the study is flawed—specific indictments by experts, (3) the study is flawed—general indictments by experts, (4) the study is flawed—specific indictments by the debater, and (5) general indictments by the debater. "The study is flawed" just means that something is wrong with either the internal or external validity.[2]

---

1. Sara E. Newell, "The 'Study' as Evidence and Argument in Academic, Policy Debate," in *Proceedings of the Summer Conference on Argumentation,* ed. Jack Rhodes and Sara Newell (sponsored by the Speech Communication Association and the American Forensic Association) (privately published, 1980), p. 296.
2. Newell, "The 'Study' as Evidence and Argument in Academic, Policy Debate," p. 302.

F. Prearranged or Casual Evidence

Prearranged evidence is created for the specific purpose of recording certain information for possible future reference. Many public records and public writings are of this type. Political leaders often try to get their views "on the record," so that at election time they will have evidence that they supported measures of interest to their constituents. The average person has a considerable amount of prearranged evidence: birth certificates, driver's licenses, marriage certificates, deeds to property, social security cards, insurance policies, receipts, canceled checks, contracts, military discharge papers, transcripts of college records, and so on. Prearranged evidence is valuable because it is usually created near the time that the event in question took place; also, because it is intended for future reference, it is usually prepared with care. At the same time, because this kind of evidence is *arranged,* it may be subject to the influence of those arranging it.

Casual evidence is created without any effort being made to create it and is not designed for possible future reference. For example, when a newspaper photographer snapped a human-interest picture of a "Good Samaritan" helping a motorist whose car had broken down and was blocking rush-hour traffic, he had no intention of creating evidence. It simply happened to be a light news day, and the editor decided to run the picture with the names of the motorist and the Good Samaritan together with a brief story about the traffic tie-up. Some months later that casual evidence became important evidence in a criminal trial in which the Good Samaritan was accused of bank robbery. The circumstantial evidence against the Good Samaritan was strong: His car matched the description of the robber's car, even to a similar dent on the left rear fender; his physical description matched that of the robber; he had no alibi; and he could not remember where he had been at the time of the robbery four months earlier. His future looked bleak until his attorney, doing research on an unrelated case, happened to come across the newspaper story, which established that, at the time of the robbery, his client had been in a city 100 miles away. This casual evidence led to a prompt acquittal.

Casual evidence is valuable because the party concerned did nothing to create the evidence. In the robbery trial example the accused did not know a photographer was coming to the scene of the traffic jam, and he did not ask to have his picture taken or published. As the accused did nothing to create the evidence, the jury was all the more ready to believe it was genuine and not a prepared alibi. The weakness of casual evidence is that its value is usually not known at the time it is created, often no effort is made to preserve it, and later efforts to recall events may be subject to uncertainty. In this case it was sheer luck that the picture appeared in the paper together with the accused's name and the fact that it was taken at the height of the morning rush hour on a particular day.

Caution: Databases contain both prearranged and casual evidence. LexisNexis, for example, may carry the text of a Supreme Court decision. This decision was prepared with care by the justices and transcribed with care by a staff familiar with legal usage and terminology. This is prearranged evidence prepared with every expectation that it will be quoted in serious debate.

By contrast, a comment on that decision found on an electronic bulletin board might be very casual evidence—a flamingly indignant, off-the-cuff, impassioned outburst. The author, if one could be found, might well disavow it as a momentary outburst not intended as a serious, scholarly, for-the-record critique of the decision.

G. Negative Evidence

Negative evidence is the absence of evidence that might reasonably be expected to be found were the issue in question true. For example, if the name of a person cannot be found in an official list of graduates of your college, this is negative evidence that he or she did not graduate from the school. Negative evidence played an important part in at least one presidential election. In 1884 a New York clergyman called the Democrats the party of "rum, Romanism, and rebellion" in a speech at a reception attended by James Blaine, the Republican candidate. Blaine's failure to repudiate this statement was taken by many voters as negative evidence that he agreed with it. Some historians regard this as the critical turning point in the election in which Blaine was defeated and Grover Cleveland elected.

Negative evidence was highly important in the investigations of the assassination of President Kennedy. Official investigations established that *no evidence* of a conspiracy existed. Yet rumors of conspiracies persist and have spawned many books, articles, and television programs, as well as the controversial Oliver Stone film *JFK*. Is the absence of any evidence of a conspiracy proof that there was no conspiracy? Or is it proof that the investigators were not thorough enough?

Negative evidence must be introduced into the argument with care. Advocates should claim negative evidence only when they are certain there is an absence of the evidence in question.

Even if careful investigation establishes that the evidence is indeed missing, is it missing for the reason claimed? This difficulty of negative evidence can be illustrated by a case from World War II. Germany developed and stockpiled huge amounts of the deadly nerve gases Tabun, Sarin, and Soman.[3] German scientists who studied Allied scientific journals found no reference to these chemicals. Because this absence of any reference to these chemicals was exactly what one would expect to find as the result of efficient censorship, the Germans concluded that the Allies also had developed the gases and probably had large supplies on hand. The fear of retaliation apparently led the Germans to decide not to use their gases during the war. Actually the chemicals were not mentioned in the Allied journals simply because no Allied scientist had discovered them. Their existence was unknown until Allied troops stumbled on the German supplies after V-E Day.

---

3. These compounds are designated GA, GB, and GD in the United States; their less volatile liquid counterparts are known as V-agents.

Richard Bernstein's commentary on historian David Irving's *Hitler's War* considers a perplexing problem of negative evidence.[4] In his book Irving made the extraordinary assertion that the Nazi's extermination of the Jews was carried out without the Führer's knowledge. Irving argued that Hitler never committed to writing any order implementing the "Final Solution." In the absence of evidence that Hitler did know, Irving concluded that he did not—a classic case of negative evidence. Other historians have argued that this is a biased view because Hitler used code words to make his wishes known to his followers.

A more recent problem of negative evidence arose when many veterans of the Gulf War complained of a mysterious malady, the Persian Gulf syndrome, which they attributed to Iraq's use of chemical or biological weapons. When questioned by a congressional committee, representatives of the Department of Defense and the CIA testified that they had no convincing evidence that such weapons had been used, but they were not willing to guarantee that exposure had not occurred.

> The intelligence community has an expression, "Absence of evidence is not evidence of absence," said John T. Kriese, chief officer for ground forces at the Defense Intelligence Agency. I cannot say there was no CW [chemical warfare] use or BW [biological warfare] contamination. From everything I know my judgment is that it was not used. [But] I think it's impossible to prove a negative.[5]

Failure to discover evidence of Saddam Hussein's development and stockpiling of weapons of mass destruction in Iraq after Operation Iraqi Freedom was used to argue that American intervention had not been justified.

Fortunately we are rarely faced with such complex tasks as confront intelligence agencies seeking to discover an enemy's capabilities. Consider this typical use of negative evidence in everyday affairs: An executive receives a tempting offer to purchase some merchandise from an out-of-town firm. The price is favorable, but she does not know whether the firm will really deliver merchandise of the quality claimed. The executive directs an assistant to look into the matter. The assistant calls the Better Business Bureau in the firm's city and inquires. The reply indicates that the firm has been doing business in that city for 25 years and that only six complaints have been received about the firm in the past year, with all adjusted to the satisfaction of the customers. The executive would probably take this lack of unsettled complaints as satisfactory negative evidence that the firm is reputable.

H. Evidence Aliunde

Evidence aliunde, also known as "extraneous" or "adminicular" evidence, explains or clarifies other evidence. Often the meaning or significance of evidence

---

4. Richard Bernstein, "Culling History from Propaganda," *New York Times,* Apr. 24, 1994, sec. 4, p. 4.
5. *New York Times,* May 26, 1994, p. A12.

is not apparent on the presentation of the evidence per se; therefore, that evidence must be explained by the presentation of other evidence. In debates on free trade, for example, some debaters introduced as expert evidence the opinion of certain economists that free trade would be beneficial because it would permit the operation of the principle of comparative advantage. Unless those who rendered the decision understood the principle of comparative advantage, this evidence would be of little value until the debaters introduced additional evidence to explain the concept.

Evidence is used in extraordinarily complex combinations in argumentation. One piece of evidence may often be classified under several types. For example, in a debate on the "increase exploration and/or development of space" proposition, one affirmative speaker offered the following evidence from *Time* magazine to establish an advantage:

> One of the six crewmembers [of the aborted *Discovery* mission] is Charles Walker, 35, an engineer with McDonnell Douglas and the shuttle's first ambassador for private enterprise. Walker's in-flight task is to concoct a mystery drug for Johnson & Johnson, using a technique called electrophoresis, which in the zero gravity of space can separate biological compounds 700 times as efficiently as on earth. Judging by the many clues the principals have dropped, the substance *could be a one-shot cure for diabetes.*

The identification of the types of evidence represented by this statement will help us to analyze it. Obviously it is written evidence from a public record—that is, *Time.* Clearly it is secondary evidence, because *Time* isn't telling who the "principals" are. It *may* be expert evidence, as suggested by the use of the word *principals,* but we don't know who made the statement or what the credentials of the principals are. It is probably unwritten evidence; "clues" tend to be "dropped" in off-the-record comments. Certainly, had the clues appeared in, say, the *New England Journal of Medicine, Time* would have cited such a prestigious source. This evidence in its current form is useless, as the affirmative debater who used it—just once—quickly found out. Clearly evidence aliunde is needed to clarify this evidence before it will have real impact in establishing the value of preparing biological compounds in space.

I. Alternative Forms of Evidence

If the development of argumentation is considered outside the traditional logical construct, importance of emotional content and alternative viewpoints may become relevant. Classroom and tournament debaters derive most of their evidence from published sources. These sources represent well-educated experts from academe, particular content fields, government, and other privileged positions. In other words, the sources of most quoted evidence are economic and social elites within their respective societies. Thus, they have access to traditional publication in academic journals, periodicals, and other materials. They may be perfectly

---

Types of Evidence

- Judicial or Extrajudicial Evidence
- Primary or Secondary Evidence
- Written or Unwritten Evidence
- Real or Personal Evidence
- Lay or Expert Evidence
- Prearranged or Casual Evidence
- Negative Evidence
- Evidence Aliunde
- Alternative Forms of Evidence

---

qualified to offer opinions and conclusions about problems of general concern, but their viewpoints may be limited by standpoint. Therefore, it is beneficial at times for debaters to offer their own nontraditional forms of proof, and those of marginalized or disenfranchised persons. The form of such evidence may be in narrative, poetry, prose, art, music, or hip-hop. The content, although challenging to measure, can be powerful and emotional, and can offer viewpoints excluded by traditional standards.

III. THE PROBATIVE FORCE OF EVIDENCE

We are concerned not only with the sources and types of evidence but also with its *probative force*. Evidence may only partially substantiate an issue, or it may be strong enough to justify the claim conclusively in the minds of those who render the decision. Baseball fans engaged in a pleasant disputation on the question "Who won the Most Valuable Player award last year?" will probably settle the matter conclusively by reference to a standard almanac. But if the question is, "Who was the greatest baseball player of all time?" a conclusive answer is probably impossible; the game has changed too much over the years. Ty Cobb and Babe Ruth unquestionably are greats of yesteryear, but there is no practical way of comparing them with today's greats. Thus the standards necessary to establish a conclusive answer probably could not be agreed on. The debate over the 2003–2004 NCAA Division I-A national football championship would be no less challenging. Both Louisiana State and Southern California made claims to the championship, and the standards of the NCAA and its Bowl Championship Series did not resolve the issue. If all involved could agree on the standards, there would have been only one champion.

The often-heard question "If we can put a person on the moon, why can't we solve the problem of homelessness or clean up the inner cities?" provides an excellent example of the probative force of evidence. Once the political decision was made to spend the money to put a person on the moon, the problem was limited to its scientific and engineering aspects. The scientific and engineering communities had developed agreed-on standards that allowed them to establish conclusive proof that a moon landing could be made, and the mission was accomplished. Solving homelessness or cleaning up the inner cities, however, depends not only on accepted scientific and engineering facts but also on complex political and social problems involving conflicting values and perceptions. Thus the decision renderers will determine the probative force of evidence, and the task of the advocates remains that of discovering evidence that will have the desired impact in justifying their claim.

A. Partial Proof

Partial proof is used to establish a detached fact in a series of facts tending to support the issue in dispute. In debating the proposition of "guaranteed annual wages," affirmative debaters sometimes sought to introduce evidence of seasonal fluctuations in employment as partial evidence in support of their need issue. In a murder trial the prosecution usually has to introduce evidence to prove malice on the part of the accused toward the murdered person—partial evidence in the series of facts the prosecution will seek to establish in order to prove the charge of murder. Evidence that only partially substantiates the advocate's contention is of little value in itself. However, when several pieces of partial evidence are combined, their effect may be powerful. Indeed, taken together they might become conclusive.

B. Corroborative Proof

Corroborative proof, also known as "cumulative" or "additional" proof, is strengthening or confirming evidence of a different character in support of the same fact or proposition. For example, in debates on "free trade," some advocates sought to show that free trade would harm domestic industry. Evidence showing a specific industry that would be harmed was of some value in establishing this contention. Evidence that a number of industries would be harmed made the contention stronger. Similarly, a defendant in a trial might claim that he was out of town on the day the crime took place. One witness who saw him in another city on the day in question could furnish evidence of his alibi, but his alibi would be stronger if he could produce several witnesses to corroborate his story.

C. Indispensable Proof

Indispensable proof is evidence without which a particular issue cannot be proved. In courtroom debates it is relatively easy to identify indispensable evidence. In a murder trial, for example, the prosecution must introduce evidence to establish the actual death of the person alleged to have been murdered.

The Probative Force of Evidence

- Partial Proof
- Corroborative Proof
- Indispensable Proof
- Conclusive Proof

In argumentation outside the courtroom, the indispensable evidence necessary to establish the proposition is usually less well defined than in legal proceedings, but careful examination of the proposition will indicate certain matters that must be proved. For instance, in a debate on "wage and price controls," the affirmative must introduce evidence showing that such controls will work to control inflation.

D. Conclusive Proof

Conclusive proof is evidence that is incontrovertible, either because the law will not permit it to be contradicted or because it is strong and convincing enough to override all evidence to the contrary and to establish the proposition beyond reasonable doubt. Evidence that may not be contradicted in legal proceedings varies from one jurisdiction to another. Outside the courtroom no evidence is safe from refutation, and no evidence is conclusive or acceptable on its merits alone. The advocate always seeks to find such evidence, but on matters likely to be the subject of debate, conclusive evidence that applies directly to the proposition is seldom available. Obviously, once conclusive evidence is presented on a proposition, that proposition is no longer debatable. More often such evidence is found to support subsidiary matters related to the proposition. In debates on "right-to-work" laws, for example, some advocates were able to introduce conclusive evidence of corruption in labor–management relations; they were not able, however, to introduce conclusive evidence that "right-to-work" laws would eliminate such corrupt practices.

Evidence is an essential ingredient in all argumentation. We cannot make intelligent decisions without evidence. The value of one piece of evidence, however, may differ considerably from that of another. Therefore, when we evaluate evidence presented to us for our decision, we must accept the good and reject the defective. Likewise, when we seek the decision of others, we must evaluate evidence carefully so that we use sound evidence in our case. We must also be able to evaluate the evidence of our opponents so that we can expose their defective evidence. Those seeking to reach a reasoned decision on evidence will find it desirable to apply the tests of evidence considered in the next chapter.

EXERCISES

1. Select one contention related to the current CEDA/NDT national inter-
    collegiate debate proposition, as your instructor specifies. Bring to class two
    examples of each of the following classifications of evidence:

    a. Direct evidence to prove this contention
    b. Presumptive evidence in support of this contention

2. From newspapers or newsmagazines published within the past week, find
    examples of the use of the following sources of evidence to support a
    contention:

    a. Judicial notice
    b. Public records
    c. Public writings
    d. A source that was originally a private writing
    e. Testimony of a witness. Write a brief paper in which you classify the
        evidence, identify the contention advanced by the writer, and attach a
        clipping of the supporting evidence.

3. Obtain the text of a recent public speech by a well-known national figure or
    an editorial in a newspaper or newsmagazine on a matter of current impor-
    tance. Classify the evidence:

    a. By type
    b. By the probable probative force the evidence had on the audience ad-
        dressed by the speaker

4. Attend an intercollegiate debate and take careful note of the evidence pre-
    sented in the debate. Prepare a brief paper in which you classify evidence:

    a. By type
    b. By the probable probative force it had on the judge

    Compare this with the paper you prepared for Exercise 3. Who used
    more evidence, the public figure or the debaters? Why? Who did the better
    job of giving the audience good reason for accepting the evidence?

7

Tests of Evidence

Evidence is the raw material of argumentation. It provides the building blocks with which the advocate constructs the case. If the evidence is accurate, the advocate can construct a strong case; if the evidence is weak or flawed, the case can never be sound. Furthermore the advocate is often confronted with conflicting evidence. For instance, as the "University of California–Berkeley Wellness Letter" once observed, studies have shown that caffeine raises, lowers or does not alter blood pressure; increases, decreases or does not alter heart rate; stimulates respiration or does not affect it; raises or does not raise metabolic rate; raises or does not raise glucose concentration; raises or does not raise cholesterol levels.[1]

A Harvard University researcher found no evidence that normal caffeine consumption poses any sort of health hazard. A Stanford University study found that decaffeinated coffee caused a 7 percent increase in cholesterol. And a Boston University study suggested that five or more cups of coffee a day—regular or decaf—can cut the risk of developing colon cancer by 40 percent. Conflicting evidence is not limited to medicine but can be found in every field of human affairs. Thus we must consider the tests of evidence.

I. USES OF TESTS OF EVIDENCE

The previous chapter considered the sources and the types of evidence; this chapter considers tests that may be applied to evidence. These tests have three important uses.

A. Testing the Credibility of One's Own Evidence

In constructing their cases advocates will discover a great deal of evidence. Before they use any of it, they should apply the tests of evidence, rejecting

---

1. *AARP Bulletin*, vol. 31, no. 1 (Jan. 1990), p. 6.

Miniglossary

Clear evidence   Proof that supports exactly what it is intended to support with precision and definitional clarity.

Counterintuitive rejection of evidence   Evidence the audience rejects in the first instance because they "know" it is wrong—for example, that employment causes harms.

Intuitive acceptance of evidence   Evidence the audience accepts in the first instance because they "know" it is right—for example, that unemployment causes harms.

Psycho-facts   Beliefs that, though not supported by hard evidence, are taken as real because their constant repetition changes the way we experience life.

Reliable evidence   Evidence from a trustworthy source, with a reputation for honesty and accuracy in similar matters and consistency in commenting on the matter.

Sufficient evidence   A fair preponderance of evidence.

Verifiable evidence   Evidence which may be authenticated, confirms, and/or substantiated.

---

weak and inconclusive evidence and retaining only what stands up under examination. By applying the tests of evidence, they may also anticipate the probable refutations of their opponents and prepare to meet them.

The tests of evidence should also be applied to problems outside the debate situation. For instance, the political leader must weigh intelligence reports; the executive must evaluate reports of market trends; and the college student must appraise studies of employment opportunities in various fields. Throughout life we all have to formulate propositions, gather evidence related to those propositions, and evaluate that evidence as a part of the process of making decisions. Intelligent self-interest and our sense of responsibility to those affected by our decisions require that we apply the tests of evidence with care.

B. Testing the Credibility of Evidence Advanced by an Opponent

While preparing their own cases, advocates must also look for evidence that opponents will find useful, apply the appropriate tests to it, and plan a refutation. As a debate develops, advocates will discover the actual evidence used by opponents and be prepared to test and refute it during the debate.

Questions for Testing Evidence Credibility

In general, affirmative answers to these questions imply that the evidence is credible; negative answers imply a weakness in the evidence.

Is there enough evidence?

Is the evidence clear?

Is the evidence consistent with other known evidence?

Is the evidence consistent within itself?

Is the evidence verifiable?

Is the source of the evidence competent?

Is the source of the evidence unprejudiced?

Is the source of the evidence reliable?

Is the evidence relevant?

Is the evidence statistically sound?

Is the evidence the most recent available?

Is the evidence cumulative?

Is the evidence critical?

Note that the responsibility for applying the tests of evidence and for refuting evidence rests on the party whose case is damaged by the evidence. If certain evidence used by our opponents adversely affects our case but we do not refute it, the decision renderers may accept even weak evidence at face value. The absence of refutation may actually enhance the value of the adverse evidence.

C. Testing the Credibility of Evidence Advanced for a Decision

Although we may participate in only a few debates over a lifetime, we constantly have to make decisions. As citizens, as consumers, and simply as social beings, we are confronted with evidence that we must evaluate almost daily. Thus, if we do not properly evaluate the evidence of a political candidate's qualifications, we may share the responsibility for a poor government; if we do not evaluate the evidence of the merits of a product, we may be inconvenienced or may lose money. In fact, whenever we fail to apply the tests of evidence, we run the risks inherent in an unwise decision. The rewards of applying these tests are correspondingly great. As we apply them, we increase our opportunities for making sound decisions and gaining all the benefits that come with wise decisions.

II. TESTS OF CREDIBLE EVIDENCE

The tests of credible evidence considered have their roots in the long history of argumentation and should give advocates a reliable system for evaluating evidence. The tests of evidence can be stated in the form of questions; the inset on page 128 lists these questions. As indicated in the previous chapter, all evidence obviously does not have the same degree of cogency, and thoughtful persons test the degree of cogency that decision renderers are likely to assign to the evidence. Let's now discuss the tests in detail.

A. Sufficient Evidence

The advocate must provide enough evidence to support the issue being disputed. How much is enough? When we begin our research, we may find some credible evidence in support of our position. But in debatable matters there will be credible evidence on the other side as well. Advocates therefore must provide evidence that is more convincing than the opposing evidence. Naturally they seek conclusive evidence, but because this is often unavailable, they have to settle for **sufficient evidence**—that is, for a fair preponderance of evidence. In the civil courts the verdict is based on a "preponderance of evidence." In important matters outside the civil courtroom, reasonable people also usually apply this standard in making decisions. The national intercollegiate debate propositions, for example, always have some evidence—but less than conclusive evidence— available for each side. Usually the ability of the advocates determines which side will establish a fair preponderance of evidence. Remember that in an argumentative situation the advocates try to convince those who render the decision rather than to convince their opponents.[2] They need to persuade only those who judge the debate that they have a fair preponderance of evidence.

B. Clear Evidence

The advocate must provide evidence that is clear or that, by means of evidence aliunde, can be made clear. For instance, in a classroom debate on the "mass media" proposition ("Resolved: That the federal government should significantly strengthen the regulation of mass media communication in the United States"), an affirmative team built a case to ban violence on television. The debaters were delighted to discover a newspaper article by a psychiatrist and research director of the National Coalition on Television Violence in which he said: "The surgeon general's expert panel concluded the evidence is overwhelming. Violent

---

2. In some argumentative situations the opponent may render the decision by conceding. For example, in a civil suit for personal injury damages, the defense attorney may try to convince the plaintiff's attorney that his or her case is so weak that it would be better to accept a modest out-of-court settlement than to run the risk of the jury's awarding no damages—or, of course, vice versa.

entertainment has a harmful effect on viewers."[3] At first the debaters thought they had found an excellent source that seemed to be saying exactly what they wanted. But was the evidence clear? Without evidence aliunde it is not clear. (See the Chapter 6 section "Evidence Aliunde.") What is meant by violence? Professional football or professional hockey? Saturday morning cartoons? A drama featuring a few murders? Nor is it clear what "harmful" meant—something trivial or something catastrophic? The negative would have quickly pointed out the lack of clarity in this particular piece of evidence. The affirmative debaters wisely decided to seek additional evidence to clarify this evidence in the mind of the judge. Their further research turned up evidence that the surgeon general's report was 16 years old. They decided that if Congress had not acted on the report in 16 years, they must have found the evidence unconvincing. The affirmative decided they would seek evidence that was clear, primary (see Chapter 6), and recent (see the section "The Most Recent Evidence" later in this chapter).

C. Evidence Consistent with Other Known Evidence

Advocates must determine whether their evidence is consistent with other known evidence. If it is, they may be able to strengthen their evidence by corroborative evidence. If it is not, they have to be prepared to show that their evidence is more credible than other known evidence or that other known evidence is not applicable in this particular case. For instance, if business executives offer evidence that the unit cost of a certain product will decrease as production increases; their evidence is consistent with the experience of many manufacturing firms. Thus this evidence will be consistent with other known evidence.

This test, however, clearly does not prohibit the advocates from using or considering evidence inconsistent with other known evidence. For example, in debating the "guaranteed employment opportunities" proposition, some students found evidence indicating, as we would expect, that unemployment was correlated with ill health, divorce, child abuse, crime, and suicide. This finding was consistent with other known evidence and provided the students with recent studies on the very point they wanted to make. Other students, researching the same proposition, came across other studies indicating that the stress associated with employment and the hazards of on-the-job accidents were also correlated with ill health, divorce, child abuse, crime, and suicide. Given the widespread acceptance of the work ethic in American society, based on **intuitive acceptance of evidence**, most audiences would probably accept the evidence because they "know" that employment is good and unemployment is bad. When offered such evidence, we tend to nod in agreement and think, "Sure, that's obvious." Those debaters who used the second piece of evidence likely encountered **counterintuitive rejection of evidence**, whereby audiences reject the evidence because they "know" it is wrong. When debaters find it necessary to use counterintuitive evidence, they must demonstrate to the decision renderers

---

3. Thomas E. Radecki, "We Must Curb TV Violence," *USA Today*, Oct. 24, 1988, p. A10.

that their experts' credentials are superior and that their experts' evidence is more recent. They also have to supply other good reasons why the counterintuitive evidence—evidence inconsistent with other known evidence—should be accepted in the particular case.

Psycho-facts are related to intuitive and counterintuitive evidence. Economist Robert Samuelson defines **psycho-facts** as "beliefs that, though not supported by hard evidence, are taken as real because their constant repetition changes the way we experience life."[4] For example, many people believe that asbestos in schools poses a health hazard to schoolchildren. But as Supreme Court Justice Stephen Breyer showed, the asbestos panic was a costly mistake.[5] Samuelson noted that the risk of police dying on the job is 1 in 4,500, the risk of dying from an airplane crash is 1 in 167,000, and the risk of dying from lightning is 1 in 2 million—while the risk of dying from asbestos in schools is 1 in 11 million. (All data are annual.)

Advocates should not disregard evidence simply because it is inconsistent with other known evidence or considered counterintuitive. Many beliefs now widely held were once considered counterintuitive. However, the advocate should recognize that this evidence has to be considered especially carefully. The advocate must be prepared to have the evidence attacked by opponents and must anticipate possible audience resistance. In most fields, of course, some known evidence is available on either side of a proposition. For example, with regard to trends in the stock market, there is probably some evidence indicating a rise and some indicating a decline.

D. Evidence Consistent Within Itself

Advocates should study the evidence carefully and determine whether it is consistent within itself. For example, in debating the proposition "Resolved: That United States law enforcement agencies should be given significantly greater freedom in the investigation and/or prosecution of felony crime," some affirmative debaters cited evidence of an alarming increase in the number of rapes (going on to argue that the affirmative's plan for a change in the way rape trials were conducted was necessary). Well-prepared negative debaters turned to the same source and quoted the following:

> The rates are for reported crimes only. In many cases society's attitude about a crime is a significant factor in whether or not it will be reported. Rape is a classic example; only a few years ago the woman was assumed "to have asked for it" and vast numbers of women were too ashamed to report the crime. Today Rape Crisis Centers are widely available to help and counsel the victim; "date rape," a term unheard of until recently, is now a recognized phenomenon.

---

4. Robert J. Samuelson, "The Triumph of the Psycho-Fact," *Newsweek,* May 9, 1994, p. 73.
5. Stephen Breyer, *Breaking the Vicious Circle Toward Effective Risk Regulation* (Cambridge, Mass.: Harvard University Press, 1994), p. 26.

Thus, while the statistical tables did show an increase in the crime of rape, the text of the document itself contained a serious disclaimer about the accuracy of the statistics. The evidence was not consistent within itself. The negative argued that the increased reporting proved that women were now willing to go to trial and that the affirmative's plan to change the way rape trials were conducted was unnecessary.

Here's another example: A group campaigning for a higher tax rate for a local school district issued a pamphlet in which they maintained that the additional revenue would go for increased teachers' salaries—an increase they argued was necessary to maintain quality education in the school district (quality education was a popular issue in this school district). Examination of the proposed budget printed in the pamphlet, however, showed that most of the additional tax revenue would go for the purchase of additional school buses and to pay bus drivers and bus maintenance workers (busing was an unpopular issue in this school district).

A newspaper editor's nightmare may be found in the following example, which appeared in a major metropolitan newspaper:

U.S. Report Riles Currency Market

Yen Falls to Post-War Low on News from Treasury

WASHINGTON—The dollar fell to a post–World War II low against the yen yesterday after the U.S. Treasury issued a report saying a strong yen would help reduce the swelling U.S. trade deficit with Japan.

Clearly the headlines and the text of the story are inconsistent with one another.

E. Verifiable Evidence

Advocates must always be able to verify their evidence—that is, authenticate, confirm, and substantiate it. In gathering evidence advocates should carefully check evidence against other sources to satisfy themselves about its validity before presenting it, and they should present whatever supporting evidence may be necessary to their audience. They should also carefully identify the source of their evidence so that those who render the decision can verify it themselves if they wish. For example, in a debate on economic policy, a speaker might say, "According to *Newsweek,* December 26, inflation fell from 13 percent to 4 percent during the last eight years." The audience could then consult *Newsweek* and verify that the magazine did make that statement. In most debates this would probably be enough to establish the claim about the budget. If the audience were skeptical or doubted the magazine's accuracy, the speaker might want to offer a further opportunity for verification by citing the appropriate fiscal-year reports of the Treasury Department's Office of Management and Budget or the appropriate *Economic Reports of the President.* Verification of a claim, of course, is more impressive if one can demonstrate that various independent sources verify the claim. (We discuss cumulative evidence in a later section.)

Caution: Some evidence from databases is easily verifiable; other such evidence is highly perishable and may be impossible to verify. Suppose, for example, that the critical piece of evidence in a debate is a quotation from last week's *Wall Street Journal.* The affirmative has a printout of the quote; the negative challenges the accuracy of the printout. If the matter is really crucial, the judge can call up the quotation on a computer and determine the accuracy of the affirmative's printout. If, however, the quotation in question is from a week-old comment on a computer bulletin board, it will probably be impossible to verify. Such comments are routinely deleted after 48 hours. Thus we offer this admonition: *Never use evidence that cannot be verified.*

F. Competent Source of Evidence

Advocates must determine whether the source of the evidence is actually qualified to testify on the matter at issue. When the source of evidence is a *layperson,* the following tests should be applied.

1. *Did the witness have an opportunity to observe the matter in question?* A popular journalist once spent a week in Cuba and on his return wrote an article entitled "Castro's Secret Plans for Central America." One might reasonably ask if the writer, who was an experienced journalist but a layperson on matters of foreign policy and espionage, actually had an opportunity to learn about secret decisions made by a tightly controlled totalitarian regime.

2. *Was the witness physically capable of observing the matter in question?* A trial witness once claimed that he would be able to identify a robber he had seen at a distance of approximately 100 yards, yet he was unable to read a clock in the courtroom 30 yards from the witness stand. One might reasonably ask if the witness was physically capable of seeing the person he claimed he saw.

3. *Was the witness mentally capable of reporting his or her observations?* A defendant at a certain trial testified in great detail about the routine events of a business day five years earlier, but he was unable to recall any details of other business days at approximately the same time. One might reasonably ask if the witness was mentally capable of recalling all of the details he claimed he remembered.

A person's power of observation may be influenced by circumstances surrounding the event. A standard psychology class experiment involves two individuals who rush into the classroom, fight, and then rush out. When asked to describe the incident, students often give widely differing reports. We must know, too, whether the witness had any interest in making a mental effort to observe and remember the event. How many people attended last year's commencement ceremonies at your college? Ask a few people who were present. Probably very few made any effort to count the audience.

When the source of evidence is an *expert,* the following tests would be applied in addition to the tests applicable to a lay witness.

4. *Does the witness have official signs of respectability?* If claiming to be a physician, does the witness have a medical degree? If claiming to be an economist does the person have a doctorate in that field? In other words, does the witness have expert credentials? The fact that a physician has all the proper credentials of a surgeon does not, of course, guarantee that the operation will be a success. However, even though some persons without proper credentials have performed successful surgery, few of us would care to entrust our lives to an amateur brain surgeon.

5. *Is the witness well regarded by other authorities?* If an expert witness is highly regarded by others in the field in which he or she claims special competence, then the opinions have added weight. If a physician is an officer of the appropriate medical associations, is accredited in a specialty, has presented papers at medical conventions, and is a professor of medicine at an accredited medical school, then it is reasonable to conclude that this person is well regarded by other authorities in medicine. Advocates should look for similar signs of professional regard for other types of experts.

G. Unprejudiced Source of Evidence

Advocates must determine whether the source of evidence is prejudiced. In many cases people testify about matters in which they have an interest, and in some cases those who have a personal stake in the matter are the only witnesses available. Are these individuals free from prejudice? Do they report matters objectively, or do they slant them in a manner favorable to their own interests? The advocate must determine whether the witness has an interest in the matter at issue and whether this interest is likely to influence his or her testimony.

Traditionally presidents are evaluated after their first 100 days in office. When President Clinton reached that landmark, one major city newspaper ran the front-page headline "Clinton Has Good Marks for His First 100 Days." Sounds impressive, doesn't it? The critical question, of course, is who gave Clinton the good marks? The first paragraph of the story gave the answer: "President Clinton acknowledged yesterday that he had underestimated the power of the Republicans who killed his jobs bill but gave himself good marks overall for his first 100 days in office." Obviously Clinton is not an unprejudiced source of evidence on the question of how he did in his first 100 days in office. If students were permitted to assign their own grades, membership in Phi Beta Kappa would grow by several thousand percent.

In the famous Rodney King case in Los Angeles, King was arrested for speeding and resisting arrest and was taken to a hospital after being beaten by the police. King charged police brutality. The police responded that he was resisting arrest and that they had to use reasonable force to restrain him. Another man, who had no connection with King or the police and who just happened to witness the arrest, videotaped the event. The tape was the *crucial* piece of evidence in this case. In the lengthy legal proceedings that followed this incident, two different juries interpreted the incident differently. No one, however, challenged the fact that the man who videotaped the event was unprejudiced. Note also that this is an example of casual evidence (see Chapter 6). The man with the camcorder did not set out to collect crucial evidence; he was merely trying out a newly acquired gadget.

Whenever possible, it is best to seek out evidence from an unprejudiced source. The *reluctant witness* is the witness who furnishes evidence against his or her own interests or prejudices. This evidence, of course, is even stronger than that from a disinterested source. For example, throughout his long fight against impeachment, President Nixon had counted on Republican loyalists who had ably defended him in the House Judiciary Committee proceedings. When new evidence was released after the committee hearings concluded, Nixon at first glossed over its importance. But within hours of the release of the transcripts, all Republican members of the committee indicated that the new facts "were legally sufficient to sustain at least one count against the president" and that they would vote for impeachment. Apparently this reluctant reversal of their previous position was a major factor in convincing Nixon his case was hopeless. Three days later he resigned.

H. Reliable Evidence

Advocates must determine whether the source of evidence is trustworthy. Does the source have a reputation for honesty and accuracy in similar matters? Presidential elections afford interesting examples of the reliability of sources of evidence. Official results of presidential elections are not known until several days after the election. But the national news services have established such a reputation for reliability in reporting results that we invariably accept and act on their unofficial returns, which are announced the night of or the day following the election. While the final result of the 2000 election was long delayed, the media coverage of the historic court battles was generally considered to be reliable. Similarly the polls predicting the results of presidential elections have earned a reputation for accuracy and are generally considered to be **reliable evidence**. By contrast, evidence offered by the candidates themselves predicting the outcome of elections is notoriously unreliable. Typically front-runners in the polls will downplay the importance of the polls for fear their supporters will become overconfident and fail to turn out the vote, which could lead to a defeat. Candidates who are trailing in the polls also minimize the importance of the predictions for fear their supporters will become discouraged and fail to turn out to vote, leading to a crushing defeat.

If advocates can demonstrate that the source of their evidence is reliable, they increase the credibility of that evidence. If they can demonstrate that the source of their opponent's evidence is not reliable, they have cast doubt on that evidence.

I. Relevant Evidence

Advocates must determine whether the evidence is actually related to the matter at issue. Sometimes evidence is offered that is not relevant to the issue or that only seems to be relevant. For instance, the popular phone-in polls using the 900 area code generate dubious evidence. The public is asked to call different numbers to register yes or no votes, or to express preferences for different candidates. The deficiency is that only those who feel strongly enough to pay for this toll call are likely to phone in, and, of course, those who feel *very* strongly can make multiple calls— not exactly relevant evidence of how the general public would vote.

J. Statistically Sound Evidence

Occasionally advocates may find it necessary to use evidence in the form of statistics; however, such evidence should be introduced into a speech only when absolutely necessary. President Reagan, for example—who could draw on all the resources of the federal government for statistical evidence—would use statistics in a speech only if he could not make his point without them. When he did use statistics, he would "round off" and simplify the figures and dramatize them as much as possible. This is a sound practice for all speakers to follow, because most audiences find statistics uninteresting, difficult to follow, and easy to forget. Statistical evidence is always prepared by someone, is almost always written evidence, and is usually expert or allegedly expert; it is therefore subject to the usual tests of evidence. Strictly speaking, there are no special tests for statistics that are not implied in the other tests of evidence. However, because the form of statistical evidence is specialized, certain tests will help advocates evaluate this evidence.

1. Have Accurate Statistics Been Collected?   Many people are reluctant to appear socially unacceptable or uninformed. When a pollster calls, they tend to give what they think is a socially acceptable response—they say they intend to vote when they don't, offer what they believe to be less controversial opinions, or express some arbitrary view to cover up their ignorance of an issue. In one study almost a third of the respondents offered an opinion when asked about the nonexistent "Public Affairs Act." With regard to phone surveys, it should be noted that women answer the phone 70 percent of the time. A poll that doesn't take this into account by making extra calls to get enough men is likely to be skewed. Advocates have to search for evidence that will establish the accuracy of the statistics collected.

2. Have the Statistics Been Classified Accurately?   If you want the best place to go skiing, what do you look for? The folks at Rand McNally ignored Colorado's world-class resort areas in their list of the 10 best cities for skiing, ranking Detroit first, Los Angeles second, and Akron-Canton, Ohio, third. "This is insane!" protested Colorado ski resort owners. Six of their state's ski resorts are among the nation's 10 busiest, with Vail the top pick of skiers. But the author of *Sports Places Rated: Ranking America's Best Places to Enjoy Sports* said the rankings made "perfect sense." They were based on federally defined metropolitan statistical areas, and all of Colorado's world-class ski resorts are just outside such areas. The scoring was based on the total ski lift capacity within the metropolitan area where the city was located. Detroit has five ski areas in its three-county metropolitan area, but none of them are on mountains. Should we classify the best places for skiing by chairlift capacity in metropolitan statistical areas or by the size of the slopes?

Students debating a proposition on direct foreign economic aid learned the importance of accurate classification of statistics. Some sources listed foreign aid expenditures as amounting to billions of dollars; others listed these expenditures as $700 million, $500 million, or other amounts. The difference depended on how the person preparing the statistics classified military aid, defense support, technical assistance, and other types of aid.

3. Has the Sampling Been Accurate?   The ratings of television programs are based on such tiny samples that some congressional observers wonder if they are not meaningless. Some statisticians claim they can predict a presidential election with only a few thousand respondents—if they have just the right proportion of urban residents, farmers, northerners, women, African Americans, college graduates, manual laborers, naturalized citizens, and so on.

Getting such a representative sample, however, is difficult. Many pollsters would rather interview prosperous-looking people who live in good residential areas than go into the slums to find the requisite number of unskilled laborers. Some ghetto dwellers view pollsters as representatives of "the Establishment" and refuse to reply to questions or give misleading answers. A number of psychological studies are based on responses given by college sophomores—mainly because many sophomores are enrolled in psychology classes, and it is convenient to test them. But are college sophomores representative of the general public?

4. Have the Units Been Accurately Defined?   A kilowatt-hour is a reasonably well-defined unit, but what is a "workweek"? Students debating a proposition on guaranteed annual wages discovered that there are many different definitions for this term. When Russia ordered an army division into Chechnya, some observers, thinking of the awesome Red Army divisions of the Cold War era, expected that the rebellion would be crushed in a few days. The Russian army divisions, however, were not the same units as their predecessors, and the military campaign was a fiasco. Even such seemingly familiar and easily understandable units as "the family" require accurate definition: That unit is defined one way for tax purposes, another way in housing statistics, and in still other ways in other statistics.

5. Are the Data Statistically Significant?   Almost any set of statistics will show certain variations. Are the variations significant? Statistical differences are considered significant only if the sample is sufficiently large and representative, and if allowance has been made for the necessary margin of error, seasonal fluctuations, and other factors. If one student scores 120 on an IQ test and another student scores 121, the difference is not statistically significant. If you toss a coin 10 times and it comes up heads 8 times, the result is not statistically significant. Figures showing the extent of unemployment in December and June are not significant unless seasonal differences have been taken into account.

6. Is the Base of the Percentage Reasonable?   Whenever statistical evidence is reported in percentages, the advocate must discover the base from which the percentage was determined. Has the value of the American dollar gone up or down? It all depends on the date used as the base. During the Summer Olympics in Los Angeles in 1984, things were so peaceful that the police insisted that crime in certain sections had somehow dropped 250 percent. *Newsweek* noted wryly, "Anything over 100 percent seems to imply that some lawbreakers had switched to performing good deeds."

7. Do the Visual Materials Report the Data Fairly?   Statistical evidence is often reported in visual form. Visual materials are helpful in overcoming audience apathy toward statistics and, when prepared correctly, in clarifying complex data. However, visual materials can distort statistical evidence. Therefore the advocate must determine whether the various charts, diagrams, and other visual materials really interpret the data fairly. For example, assume that the following figures for the production of widgets are absolutely accurate:

	United States	Japan
Last year	1,000,000	5,000
This year	1,010,000	10,000

Now consider the graphs in the box on page 139 and the way they slant these figures. In the first two the choice of units for the vertical axis of the graph produces two quite different pictures; in the third one the height of each bar is reasonably accurate, but a distorted picture is created by using a much wider bar for Japan. The caption above each graph adds to the distortion.

These few simple examples only begin to suggest the possibility of distortion in visual materials. Advocates should carefully examine each visual aid presented in the argument to determine whether it accurately represents the data.

8. Is Only Reasonable Precision Claimed for the Statistics?   If greater precision is attributed to the statistics than they deserve, it may lead to unwarranted conclusions. How many battered women are there in the United States? *Time* reported that 4 million American women are assaulted by a "domestic partner" each year. *Newsweek* reported that the number of women beaten by "husbands, ex-husbands and boyfriends" was 2 million a year. As *Newsweek* noted, this is terrible. Not only because of the implication that either *Time* or *Newsweek* is wrong by a factor of 2, but because the divergence reflects society's actual state of ignorance on such an important and theoretically verifiable statistic. Nor is this a problem unique to the question of how many men beat their wives. Great issues of public policy are being debated by people who have no idea what they're talking about.[6] Both *Time* and *Newsweek* acted in good faith and used

---

6. "The Numbers Game," *Newsweek*, July 25, 1994, p. 56.

Visual Materials: Examples

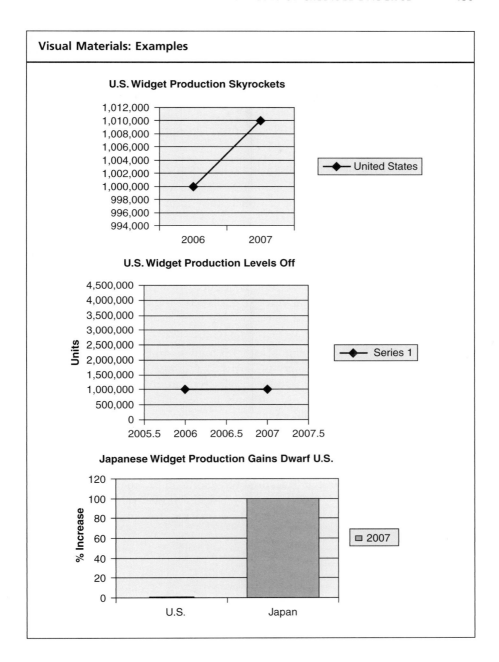

credible sources. The problem was that even apparently credible sources can arrive at widely different statistical conclusions.

In their desire to satisfy the demand for quantification, journalists, legislative reference clerks, supposedly serious scholars, special interest groups, and others often provide us with "imaginary numbers."[7] Thus we should view with a healthy suspicion statistics that come from sources less interested in precisely measuring a given problem than in showing that it's even worse than anyone thought. "People who want to influence public policy have a real strong feeling that the end justifies the means," says Cynthia Crossen, a *Wall Street Journal* reporter and author.[8]

Consider the following examples of imaginary numbers that have appeared in the media:

Estimates of the number of homeless range from 223,000 to 7 million.

A U.S. senator announced that 50,000 children are abducted by strangers each year. A Department of Justice study found fewer than 5,000 stranger abductions a year.

One source claimed that 150,000 women die annually of anorexia. Another source reported there are 150,000 cases of anorexia a year, almost none of them fatal.

The American Medical Association announced that family violence kills nearly 10,000 women a year. An FBI report found that a total of 4,000 women were murdered a year.

Crossen noted that the "Survey of Childhood Hunger in the United States" offered as its "key finding" that 11.5 million American children under age 12 were either hungry or "at risk" of hunger. The "at-risk" category is often a fruitful one for social action groups seeking to magnify a problem. The term *at risk* can easily be defined to raise or lower the number by several million.

When you read about such wide discrepancies in the statistics on such important matters as these, do you wish you could find the truth of the matter?

9. Are the Data Interpreted Reasonably?   Sometimes "the thing speaks for itself" and no interpretation is necessary.[9] Usually, however, someone reports the data and draws conclusions from them—and that someone may support a

---

7. This term is used here to indicate numbers that come from the writer's imagination, with little or no warrant from the real world. In higher mathematics an imaginary number is a multiple of the square root of -1.

8. "The Numbers Game," p. 57.

9. The legal maxim is *res ipsa loquitur.* A classic example would be a surgical operation, after which a sponge is found in the patient's abdomen. The patient, who was under anesthesia at the time, cannot testify that the surgeon did anything wrong. Usually there are no witnesses to the wrongdoing; if any of the other physicians or nurses present at the operation had noticed the error, they would have told the surgeon, who would have corrected the situation before the incision was closed. The plaintiff's lawyer would argue *res ipsa loquitur:* Sponges simply are not supposed to be left in a patient's abdomen; therefore the surgeon must have done wrong. The *res ipsa loquitur* argument, although powerful in this case, is not necessarily conclusive. Now, however, the surgeon's lawyer would have the burden of proving that the sponge had somehow been introduced into the patient's abdomen by some other surgeon at some other time.

particular point of view. For example, assume that the following figures on the cost of widgets are absolutely accurate:

Month	Cost of Widgets	Increase (%) from January	Increase (%) from Previous Month
January	$1.00	—	—
February	$1.10	10	10.0
March	$1.20	20	9.6
April	$1.30	30	9.1
May	$1.40	40	7.8
June	$1.50	50	7.1
July	$1.60	60	6.7
August	$1.70	70	6.2

With these data before them, the advocates may make a number of accurate but different statements. On the one hand they might say, "The price of widgets has increased by 70 cents in eight months." Or they might say, "The price of widgets soared a staggering 70 percent in runaway inflation in just eight months." On the other hand, the advocates might take a more sanguine view and say, "Last month the price of widgets rose only 6.2 percent." Or they might report, "Inflation is ending; for the sixth consecutive month there has been a decreasing rate of increase in the cost of widgets."

As another example, consider which is safer, travel by air or travel by car? The statistical method favored by the airlines examines passenger-miles traveled. To reach this figure, multiply the number of passengers in a plane or car by the number of miles flown or driven by each vehicle. Viewed this way, scheduled commercial airline travel had 0.06 deaths for each 100 million passenger-miles flown in the most recent 10-year period; cars had 2 fatalities for each 100 million passenger-miles driven in the same period. This suggests that commercial airplanes are 33 times safer than cars.

However, if you prefer driving to flying, you might prefer the vehicle-miles method, which completely ignores how many people are in the vehicle. Viewed this way, commercial airplanes had 6.6 fatalities per 100 million vehicle-miles, while cars had only 3 fatalities for each 100 million vehicle-miles. This method suggests that cars are more than twice as safe as commercial airplanes.

Clearly the advocate should review statistical data in as much detail as possible and determine if the interpretation is reasonable or if other equally reasonable interpretations are possible.

10. Are the Questions Unbiased?   Even polls taken by highly regarded professional pollsters at almost the same time can produce dramatically different results depending on how the question is phrased. *USA Today* provided a striking example of this. In a poll taken by Lou Harris Associates, commissioned by Planned Parenthood, the question was:

> Do you favor or oppose that Supreme Court decision preventing clinic doctors and medical personnel from discussing abortion in family planning clinics that receive federal funds?

Oppose	65%
Favor	33%
Not sure	2%

In a poll taken by the Wirthin Group, partly paid for by the National Right to Life Committee, the question was:

> The U.S. Supreme Court recently ruled the federal government is not required to use taxpayer funds for family planning programs to perform, counsel, or refer for abortion as a method of family planning. Do you favor or oppose this ruling?

Favor	48%
Oppose	48%
Don't know/refuse	4%

Even so seemingly a minor change as using or not using a married woman's maiden name may produce a significant change in the public's perception of her. GOP pollster Fabrizio McLaughlin found that Americans gave "Hillary Clinton" a favorable/unfavorable rating of 56.8 percent to 25.6 percent, while "Hillary Rodham Clinton" got 49.4 percent to 30.6 percent—almost a 13 percent difference.[10] Guess how GOP politicians referred to former President Clinton's wife thereafter.

The perspective, or spin, given to a question may have a profound effect on the response elicited (see the Chapter 15 section "Emphasis"). We might be surprised and worried if the same person expressed radically different judgments depending on how the question was put to him or her. Yet that happens frequently. For example, a group of doctors was asked:

> Imagine that the United States is preparing for the outbreak of an unusual disease, which is expected to kill 600 people. Two alternative programs to combat the disease have been proposed. Assume that the exact scientific estimate of the consequences of the program is as follows: If program A is adopted, 200 lives will be saved. If program B is adopted, there is a ⅓ probability that 600 people will be saved and a ⅓ probability that no people will be saved. Which of the two programs do you favor?

The vast majority of doctors (72 percent) opted for program A. Another group of doctors was given the same "cover story" as the first, but they were asked to choose among the following alternatives:

---

10. *Time,* Apr. 5, 1993, p. 15.

If program C is adopted, 400 people will die. If program D is adopted, there is a ⅓ probability that nobody will die, and a ⅔ probability that 600 people will die. Which of the two programs do you favor?

Only 22 percent of the doctors opted for program C. The odd thing is that C is merely a different way of phrasing A.[11] And D, of course, is only a different way of phrasing B. So the spin can really make a difference. Advocates should be aware of spin control and give careful consideration to how the question is phrased.

11. Are the Statistics Meaningful to the Audience?   Tournament debaters speak of millions, billions, and trillions as casually as if they were members of the House Appropriations Committee. This is accepted in tournament debates, because the evidence is usually familiar to all. Before a general public audience, however, an effort must be made to make these numbers meaningful to the lay-person. Consider this example:

> It takes only about 11½ days for a million seconds to tick away, whereas almost 32 years are required for a billion seconds to pass. And a trillion? The Neanderthal man finally disappeared about a trillion seconds ago. Thus when we speak of $2 trillion, we're talking the dollar equivalent of twice the length of the existence of human-kind, compared with the 11½ days worth of dollars most of us aspire to win in the lottery.[12]

As we saw earlier, statistics may be interpreted in a number of ways. Naturally the advocate will want to put a favorable spin on the statistics (again, see the Chapter 15 section "Emphasis"). When columnist George Will opposed legislation that would have put a limit on the amount of money that could be spent on political campaigns, he deprecated the proposal by saying that "in 1992 congressional races involved a sum equal to 40 percent of what Americans spent on yogurt."[13] Most Americans spend only a trivial sum for yogurt—and 40 per-cent of trivial really is inconsequential. Thus Will's spin suggested that there was hardly any need for the legislation he opposed.

K. The Most Recent Evidence

Old evidence may sometimes be more valuable than recent evidence. If we want to know certain facts about the voyage of the *Mayflower,* a document dating from 1620 may be more valuable than one dating from 1920. A map made in A.D. 1000 was important evidence supporting the claim of many scholars that Leif

11. Leo Katz, *Bad Acts and Guilty Minds: Conundrums of the Criminal Law* (Chicago: University of Chicago Press, 1987), pp. 4–5.
12. Molly Ivins, "Getting It Sort of Right—By the Numbers," *Cleveland Plain Dealer,* Apr. 30, 1993, p. C6.
13. George Will, "So, We Talk Too Much?" *Newsweek,* June 28, 1993, p. 68.

Erikson's Norsemen reached Labrador, the New England coast, and Martha's Vineyard long before Columbus "discovered" the New World.

Often, however, the most recent evidence is the best evidence. If the facts of a situation can change, or if opinions about a certain matter tend to be revised, we want the most recent information available. For instance, this month's Bureau of the Census estimate of the population of the United States is more valuable evidence of the size of the population than a report issued by the same bureau a year ago.

In many cases more recent evidence, simply because it is more recent, is enough to refute older evidence. In debates on the "mass media" proposition, some affirmative teams called for a ban on the advertising of diet drinks containing saccharin. Their justification was that a several-year-old Canadian study indicated a 60 percent greater risk of bladder cancer among saccharin users. The value of this evidence sharply depreciated when, three-quarters of the way through the debate session, a series of new studies appeared that reported "there is no saccharin-induced epidemic of bladder cancer in this country" and that people who use moderate amounts of saccharin "can be assured that their excess risk of cancer, if present at all, is quite small and little cause for concern." Because new evidence is constantly appearing on matters that are likely to be subjects of debate, advocates should make a special point of gathering the most recent evidence and allowing for it in their case.

L. Cumulative Evidence

Although one piece of evidence is sometimes enough to support a point, advocates are usually in a stronger position if they can offer several pieces of evidence from different sources or of different types to substantiate their contentions. In debates on the issue of nuclear power plant safety, for example, the opinion of one eminent scientist might be offered to establish a certain contention. This contention would be more firmly established, however, if the advocate could show that the same conclusion was shared by, say, the Nuclear Regulatory Commission, the Union of Concerned Scientists, the Institute of Nuclear Power Operations, and the National Academy of Sciences.

M. Critical Evidence

We may have much evidence, but do we have the critical evidence—the evidence we really need in a particular situation? In many cases evidence made available to us is distorted. That's the reason the Food and Drug Administration has phased in new regulations governing food labeling and advertising. *Time* magazine reported the following:

> Budget Gourmet Light and Healthy Salisbury Steak, which are labeled "low fat," derive 45% of its total calories from fat.
>
> Diet Coke contains more than one heavily advertised calorie per can (so does Diet Pepsi).

There is no real fruit—just fruit flavors—in Post Fruity Pebbles.

Honey Nut Cheerios provide less honey than sugar and more salt than nuts.

Mrs. Smith's Natural Juice Apple Pie contains artificial preservatives. The word *natural* refers to the fruit juice used to make the pie.

If you can't trust Mrs. Smith, whom can you trust?[14]

In the Persian Gulf War *the* critical question for Iraq was where the coalition would attack. General Norman Schwarzkopf provided ample evidence, in the form of air and naval bombardment, that the attacks would come from the south and the east. Saddam Hussein thus concentrated his forces to meet attacks from these directions. While escalating the bombardment in the south and the east, Schwarzkopf, in what he later called his "Hail Mary play," moved more than 200,000 troops across as much as 300 miles of desert in 10 days without Saddam Hussein's knowledge and attacked on Iraq's weak western flank.

III. TESTS OF AUDIENCE ACCEPTABILITY

In addition to tests of evidence credibility, the advocate must also apply tests of audience acceptability. Some evidence that might appear credible may not be acceptable to the audience; therefore the advocate must consider not only how the audience views the credibility of the evidence but also the acceptability of the evidence to the audience. The audience, of course, may be a single judge in an academic debate, the whole voting population of the United States in a presidential election, or any group of decision renderers. One method of audience analysis is considered in Chapter 15; only certain tests of audience acceptability are considered here. These tests can be stated in the form of questions (see the accompanying inset on page 146). Let us now discuss these tests in detail.

A. Evidence Consistent with Audience Beliefs

A negative answer to the tests of evidence previously considered implies some weakness in the evidence. A negative answer to the question of consistency with audience beliefs, however, does not carry such an implication; obviously advocates occasionally have to use evidence inconsistent with audience beliefs. But when they use such evidence, advocates should anticipate audience resistance to it and take steps to overcome this resistance. This means that they must analyze their audiences and determine their beliefs on the various pieces of evidence they plan to use. (Recall the discussion of intuitive and counterintuitive evidence.)

An excellent example of how the audience's beliefs condition their response to political candidates occurred in the 1988 presidential election. In the Democratic primaries Michael Dukakis proudly *boasted* that he was "a card-carrying

14. *Time,* July 15, 1991, pp. 52–53.

Questions for Testing Audience Acceptability

In general, affirmative answers to these questions indicate that the evidence will probably be acceptable to audiences; negative answers indicate that it probably will not be acceptable.

Is the evidence consistent with the beliefs of the audience?

Is the source of the evidence acceptable to the audience?

Is the evidence suited to the level of the audience?

Is the evidence consistent with the motives of the audience?

Is the evidence consistent with the norms of the audience?

Is the evidence documented for the audience?

---

member of the American Civil Liberties Union." The liberal Democrats who voted in the primaries saw this as evidence that Dukakis's views were consistent with theirs. This evidence was credited with contributing to his winning the nomination. But in the general election George Bush *accused* Dukakis of being "a card-carrying member of the ACLU." In the general election many more conservative voters saw this as evidence that Dukakis's views were inconsistent with theirs. This evidence was credited with contributing to Bush's victory.

The importance of audience beliefs is not limited to political campaigns; there are ardent partisans for nonpolitical issues as well. Experienced advocates recognize that many audiences will contain partisans who will interpret evidence from the point of view of their own beliefs. Advocates need to find evidence that will be acceptable to as many members of the audience as possible.

B. Source Acceptable to the Audience

The level of source acceptability does not imply any weakness in the evidence itself; rather, it indicates a problem advocates have to overcome. We know that audiences tend to believe some sources more than others. If evidence comes from a source that has high prestige in the minds of audience members, they are likely to accept it automatically; if it comes from a source without special prestige for the audience, it has to stand on its own merits; if it comes from a source the audience has little or no respect for, it may be discredited regardless of its intrinsic merits. Advocates, then, should try to use sources of evidence that are acceptable to the audience. If they find it necessary to use sources with low prestige, they must establish the credibility of the sources, at least in this special case. When they find it absolutely essential to use sources the audience is hostile to, they have to overcome this hostility.

An excellent example of this problem occurred when the proposition "the federal government should control the supply and utilization of energy" was debated. When the Arabs embargoed oil and raised prices in the 1970s, many parts of the country experienced serious shortages, and prices rose sharply. How much of the shortage was due to the embargo? How much of the price increase was caused by the increase in the price of imported oil? The oil companies had one answer; governmental agencies had another; consumer advocates had a third answer. Which source would the audience believe? It depended almost entirely on the audience's attitude toward the various sources. One debater solved the problem by citing figures from consumer advocate Ralph Nader and argued that, because even Nader admitted that imports were down X percent, the audience should accept that figure as accurate. The proconsumer members of the audience felt they had to agree with their hero; and the probusiness members of the audience, while believing the actual figure to be much higher, were pleased to see an old rival admit there was some truth on their side. As Carl Hovland and his colleagues pointed out:

> The debater, the author of scientific articles, and the news columnist all bolster their contentions with quotations from figures of prestige.... When acceptance is sought by using arguments in support of the advocated view, the perceived expertness and trustworthiness of the communicator may determine the credence given them.... Sometimes a communication presents only a conclusion, without supporting argumentation, and its acceptance appears to be increased merely by attributing it to a prestigious or respected source.[15]

If, for example, advocates wished to cite certain evidence that had appeared in the *New York Times, National Geographic, Ladies Home Journal,* and *Field and Stream,* they would be well advised to cite the source with the highest prestige for their audience. Hovland and colleagues found that the credibility of a message seems related to the particular magazine in which it appears.[16] Students debating the "law enforcement" proposition found confirmation of this fact. Some excellent articles relating to the proposition, written by highly regarded, well-qualified sources, appeared in *Playboy* magazine. When the debater said, "As Superintendent Parker said in last month's *Playboy* ...," audiences usually interrupted the quotation with chuckles. Apparently the audiences associated the magazine more readily with the pictures of naked women for which it is famous than with the quality articles it sometimes publishes. President Carter learned that lesson when an interview he had granted appeared in *Playboy* shortly before the presidential elections. The interview generated more negative publicity for Carter than almost any other single incident in the campaign and led him ruefully to admit during the third television debate of the campaign, "If I should

15. Carl L. Hovland, Irving L. Janis, and Harold H. Kelley, "Credibility of the Communicator," in *Dimensions in Communication,* 2nd ed., ed. James H. Campbell and Hal W. Hepler (Belmont, Calif: Wadsworth., 1970), p. 146.
16. Hovland, Janis, and Kelley, "Credibility of the Communicator," p. 147.

ever decide in the future to discuss my deep Christian beliefs ... I'll use another forum besides *Playboy*."[17]

C. Evidence Suited to Audience Level

It's important that the evidence not be too technical or too sophisticated for the audience to understand. In debates on the issue of nuclear power plant safety, some of the primary evidence was so technical that it could be understood only by a physics maven. When debating before lay audiences, the advocates were forced to discard the primary evidence and turn to secondary evidence that made approximately the same point in simpler terms. One debater summed up such evidence by saying, "You don't have to be a rocket scientist to understand that if a nuclear plant blows up, there goes the neighborhood—Maine, Vermont, New Hampshire."

D. Evidence Consistent with Audience Motives

Advocates occasionally have to use evidence not in keeping with the values and attitudes of the audience. In these cases they should expect audience resistance. Some advocates debating the "mass media" proposition used cases calling for restraints on publication of information about the identity of CIA agents (giving as their justification that events in Iran and Afghanistan necessitated increased U.S. intelligence-gathering capabilities). Some judges, thinking of earlier CIA abuses, ignored the affirmative's carefully qualified plan and said, "I simply cannot vote to give the CIA unchecked powers."

E. Evidence Consistent with Audience Norms

Certain audiences have well-defined norms for evaluating evidence, and the advocate must be aware of and adapt to these norms. Someone arguing a point of law before a group of lawyers will find that they have definite ideas about how legal arguments should be made. In the same way scientists, physicians, accountants, policymakers, philosophers, and others usually impose specific standards for evaluating evidence. For example, the norms that a group of scientists imposes on evidence used to establish a scientific hypothesis will be much more rigorous than the data needed to establish a proposition before a lay audience.

F. Evidence Documented for the Audience

We saw earlier that evidence must be verifiable. To give the audience the opportunity to verify evidence, a speaker has to provide documentation within his or her speech at the time of evidence presentation. In an academic debate the judge expects this documentation, and a good debater will fulfill the judge's ex-

---

17. See Paul F. Boller, Jr., *Presidential Campaigns* (New York: Oxford University Press, 1984), p. 352.

pectations. In fact, the National Debate Tournament, the American Debate Association, the American Forensic Association, and the Cross Examination Debate Association provide guidelines for ethical and fair use of debate evidence. CEDA's constitutional bylaw (bylaw XV, Section I-C of the CEDA Constitution, revised March 7, 2007) is particularly clear:

> C. Use of Debate Materials. The primary creation of argument and the primary research effort in CEDA debate must be the student's. Students who rely on briefs written or evidence researched by faculty or graduate assistants, on handbook evidence rather than library research, or materials and evidence traded among programs fall short of the goal of maximizing their development as competent arguers and users of evidence. Evidence plays a key role in debate. It is important, therefore, that debaters use evidence responsibly. Responsible use of evidence includes accurate recording and documenting of material, as well as avoidance of plagiarism, misrepresentation, distortion, or fabrication. Debaters are responsible for the integrity of all the evidence they use. Debaters should clearly identify and qualify, during their speeches, the source of all the evidence they use. Omitting the source of evidence denies opponents, judges and the audience the opportunity to evaluate the quality of the information. Claiming another's written or spoken words as one's own is plagiarism, a very serious offense against responsible scholarship. Debaters should use only evidence which is in the public domain and, hence, open to critical evaluation by others. Debaters should not fabricate, distort, or misrepresent evidence. If evidence is misrepresented, distorted, or fabricated, the conclusions drawn from it are meaningless and ethically suspect. Fabrication of evidence refers to falsely representing a cited fact or statement of opinion as evidence when the material in question is not authentic. Distorted evidence refers to misrepresenting the actual or implied content of the factual or opinion evidence. In determining whether evidence has been distorted, debaters should ask if the evidence deviates on the particular point in question. Any such deviation should be avoided because such alteration can give undue rhetorical force to an advocate's argument. Distortions include, but are not limited to:
>
> 1. quoting out of context;
> 2. misinterpreting the evidence so as to alter its meaning;
> 3. omitting salient information from quotations or paraphrases;
> 4. adding words to a quotation which were not present in the original source of the evidence without identifying such as addition;
> 5. failure to provide within a reasonable time complete documentation of the evidence [name of author(s), source of publication, full date, page numbers, and author(s) credentials when available in original] when challenged.

To avoid any misunderstanding, the full source information should be presented *in the speech*. As any student of communication theory knows, not only the debate judge but the general public as well reacts to documentation. As Paul Rosenthal points out:

> Verifiability is the primary linguistic factor in enforcing a statement's credibility, not because the listener *will* verify the statement but because he or anyone else *can* verify it.... This opens up the possibility that measurement of the degree of verifiable content in a message may provide an index of its credibility to the receiver.[18]

An experimental study by Helen Fleshler and her colleagues led them to conclude:

> It is evident that message documentation was the primary variable that determined evaluations of message and speaker. Concrete message documentation resulted in significantly more positive evaluations of the message and the speaker.[19]

Here's an example of how people respond to documentation: Peggy Noonan, a speechwriter for Presidents Reagan and George H. W. Bush, used the image of "a thousand points of light" in the elder Bush's acceptance speech. The phrase captured the public's imagination, and for months the media speculated about its origin. Noonan described her reaction to a newspaper story about the phrase:

> C. S. Lewis had used the phrase "a thousand points of light" in one of his science-fiction books, which did surprise me. I hadn't read it, but *I assume the* Times *was right because it cited the page number of a specific edition, a show of confidence that suggests the writer had the book in his hands as he wrote.* People ask me now if that's where it came from. I say no.[20]

EXERCISES

1. Find three advertisements in newspapers published during the past week in which advertisers use evidence to support their arguments. Apply the appropriate tests of evidence to the advertisements. Attach copies of the ads to your paper.

---

18. Paul I. Rosenthal, "Specificity, Verifiability, and Message Credibility," *Quarterly Journal of Speech,* vol. 57 (Dec. 1971), p. 400. Italics in original.
19. Helen Fleshler, Joseph Ilardo, and Joan Demoretcky, "The Influence of Field Dependence, Speaker Credibility Set, and Message Documentation on Evaluations of Speaker and Message Credibility," *Southern Speech Communication Journal,* vol. 39 (summer 1974), p. 400.
20. Peggy Noonan, *What I Saw at the Revolution* (New York: Random House, 1990), p. 313. Emphasis added.

2. Find three editorials in newspapers published within the past week in which the writer uses evidence to support his or her argument. Apply the appropriate tests of evidence to the editorials.

3. Find three examples of the use of statistical evidence in newspapers or newsmagazines published during the past week. Apply the appropriate tests of evidence to the statistics.

4. Find three examples of the use of graphic aids to present statistical evidence in newspapers or newsmagazines published in the past week. Apply the appropriate tests of evidence to the visual aids.

5. Prepare a three-minute speech for presentation in class in which you develop an argument supported by carefully chosen evidence. Other class members will be invited to apply the tests of evidence to see if your evidence is sound. Prepare an outline of your speech in which you indicate the types of evidence used, and give this outline to your instructor.

6. One point debates. Divide into teams of two. The first debater will make a claim supported by evidence (select one of your cards blocked in the previous chapter). The second speaker (the opposing team) will challenge your evidence applying the appropriate tests of evidence to discredit it. The third speaker will defend the initial card against the challenges made, supporting the original point, and the fourth debater will answer the arguments made by the third debater.

8

The Structure of Reasoning

For centuries philosophers, rhetoricians, debaters, and others have been concerned with the structure of reasoning. In this chapter we consider what are now the two most common structures. We turn first to the structures of Aristotle, whose syllogism and enthymeme have been standard tools of reasoning for centuries and are still the basis of much reasoning. Next we turn to a contemporary logician, Stephen Toulmin, whose concept of the elements of any argument—claims, grounds, warrants, backing, modal qualifications, and possible rebuttals—has come into common use.

The formal structure of these methods of reasoning gives us special opportunities to make astute analyses of lines of reasoning and to test their validity. The methods and terminologies of both the classical and the contemporary structures are now widely used in argumentation, and students should have a working knowledge of both.

I. THE CLASSICAL STRUCTURES

Two special forms of deductive reasoning are the syllogism and the enthymeme. Plato was the student of Socrates and the teacher of Aristotle. Plato was also a critic of rhetoric. He was suspicious of the power and influence of rhetoric over unsophisticated people. He preferred the philosophical method of formal inquiry known as "dialectic." Dialectic, in which a question-response process is followed, is guided by rules of formal logic in which interlocutors begin with a set of questions in their search for answers and ultimately, truth. Rhetoric, which involves uninterrupted argumentation or speech, begins with an answer and then provides proof to persuade an audience of the probable truth of that answer. Aristotle recognized the importance and value of both dialectic and rhetoric in a democratic society, and argued that for the dialectical syllogism, there was the counterpart of the rhetorical enthymeme. Both are useful to the debater in different ways.

Miniglossary

Backing   Additional evidence and reasoning advanced to support a warrant.

Categorical syllogism   A syllogism in which the major premise is an unqualified proposition. Such propositions are characterized by words like *all, every, each,* and *any,* either directly expressed or clearly implied.

Claim   The conclusion we seek to establish by our arguments.

Conditional syllogism   A syllogism in which the major premise deals with uncertain or hypothetical events. Usually identified by *if, assuming, supposing,* or similar terms, either expressly stated or clearly implied. Also known as a *hypothetical syllogism.*

Disjunctive syllogism   A syllogism in which the major premise contains mutually exclusive alternatives. Usually indicated by such words as *either, or, neither, nor, but,* and *although,* either expressly stated or clearly implied.

Enthymeme   (1) A *truncated* syllogism, in which one of the premises or the conclusion is not stated. (2) A syllogism based on probability, signs, and examples, whose function is rhetorical persuasion. Its successful construction is accomplished through the joint efforts of speaker and audience.

Grounds   Evidence and reasoning advanced to establish the foundation of a claim.

Modal qualification   The degree of cogency we attach to our claim.

Rebuttal   Evidence and reasoning introduced to weaken or destroy another's claim.

Syllogism   A systematic arrangement of arguments consisting of a major premise, a minor premise, and a conclusion.

Warrant   Evidence and reasoning advanced to justify the move from grounds to claim.

By understanding the structures of syllogism and enthymeme for the purpose of analysis, we can apply the appropriate tests of formal validity and of rhetoric to the reasoning we encounter as we explore a problem, to the reasoning we develop for our own case, and to the reasoning we meet in our opponent's case.

A. Syllogisms

Syllogisms are deductive forms of argument, proceeding from generalization to specific application. We will discuss three types of syllogisms: (1) categorical, (2) disjunctive, and (3) conditional. First, however, we should consider the structure of all types of syllogisms. The **syllogism** is a systematic arrangement of arguments:

1. A *major premise,* which is a proposition stating a generalization ("All A's are B's")
2. A *minor premise,* which is a proposition stating a specific instance related to the generalization ("C is an A")
3. A *conclusion,* which necessarily must follow from these premises ("Therefore, C is a B")

The following is an example of syllogistic reasoning:

All legally insane persons are incompetent to make binding agreements.
(*major premise*)

John Doe is legally insane. (*minor premise*)

Therefore, John Doe is incompetent to make a binding agreement.
(*conclusion*)

Note that the argument begins with a sweeping generalization and ends with a specific claim about Doe. In the dialectic method, interlocutors would challenge each premise vigorously in order to ascertain its truth.

In the various examples of syllogisms that follow, assume for now that each premise is absolutely true. We will focus first only on the structure of the argument; later we will consider the truth of the premises (in the section "Formal Validity and Material Truth").

1. The Categorical Syllogism.   In the **categorical syllogism**, the major premise is an unqualified proposition. These propositions are characterized by words like *all, every, each,* and *any,* either directly expressed or clearly implied. The example above represents the categorical syllogism.

Some scholars object to this aspect of the categorical syllogism, pointing out that it is difficult to make unqualified generalizations. After all, for example, all legally insane persons are not the same; the nature and degree of their illnesses, the types of treatment they require, and their chances of recovery differ widely. They are identical, however, in that they are all incompetent to make legally binding agreements as long as they are legally insane. For practical reasons we treat many matters as identical and make unqualified generalizations about them. Advocates have to try to determine when it is practical or necessary to make unqualified generalizations, within a specific context, and when it is prudent or necessary to recognize the differences in apparently identical matters.

Certain tests may be applied to validate or dismiss the integrity of the categorical syllogism.

2. The Disjunctive Syllogism.   The **disjunctive syllogism** is a syllogism in which the major premise contains mutually exclusive alternatives. The separation of alternatives is usually indicated by such words as *either, or, neither, nor, but,* and *although,* either expressly stated or clearly implied.

Tests: Categorical Syllogism

---

1. *The categorical syllogism must have three terms—no more and no less.* These terms may be represented by the letters A (middle term), B (major term), and C (minor term). Here's an example:

   MAJOR PREMISE: All A's are B's.

   MINOR PREMISE: C is an A.

   CONCLUSION: Therefore, C is a B.

2. *Every term must be used twice in the categorical syllogism—no more and no less.*

3. *A term must be used only once in any premise.*

4. *The middle term must be used in at least one premise in an unqualified or universal sense.* In the syllogism on legal insanity (see page 154), the middle term was correctly distributed, referring to *all* legally insane persons. The middle term is incorrectly distributed in the following example, because (A) is qualified by the word "some."
   (some). Consequently, the conclusion of this syllogism is invalid.

   MAJOR PREMISE: Some politicians (A) are corrupt (B).

   MINOR PREMISE: Calvin Hobbes (C) is a politician (A).

   CONCLUSION: Therefore, Calvin Hobbes (C) is corrupt (B).

5. *A term may be distributed in the conclusion only if it has been distributed in the major or minor premise.* The following is an example of an *illicit major*—a major term that is distributed in the conclusion but not in the major premise.

   MAJOR PREMISE: All leftists (A) want the United States to cut defense spending (B).

   MINOR PREMISE: Congressman Zilch (C) is not a leftist (A).

   CONCLUSION: Therefore, Congressman Zilch (C) does not want the United States to cut defense spending (B).

When the major premise is fully stated—"All leftists are *among those* who want the United States to cut defense spending"—it becomes apparent that the major term (B) is not used in a universal sense in the major premise and thus may not be distributed in the conclusion. Congressman Zilch might be a pacifist.

The following is an example of an *illicit minor*—distributed in the conclusion but not in the minor premise.

   MAJOR PREMISE: All union presidents (A) favor the union shop (B).

   MINOR PREMISE: All union presidents (A) are members of unions (C).

   CONCLUSION: Therefore, all members of unions (C) favor the union shop (B).

Tests: Categorical Syllogism (Continued)

In this example the minor term (C) is distributed not in the minor premise but in the conclusion. When the minor premise is fully stated—"All union presidents are *some* members of unions," it becomes apparent that the minor term (C) has not been distributed and that consequently the conclusion is invalid. The only conclusion that could be drawn from these premises is that *some* union members favor the union shop.

6. *At least one of the premises must be affirmative.* Obviously no valid conclusion can be drawn from two negative premises. Here is an example:

MAJOR PREMISE: No Democratic senators (A) will vote for this bill (B).

MINOR PREMISE: Senator Eliot (C) is not a Democratic senator (A).

CONCLUSION: Therefore, Senator Eliot (C) will _____?

7. *If one premise is negative, the conclusion must be negative.* Here's an example:

MAJOR PREMISE: No Republican senators (A) voted for this bill (B).

MINOR PREMISE: Senator Eliot (C) is a Republican senator (A).

CONCLUSION: Therefore, Senator Eliot (C) did not vote for this bill (B).

MAJOR PREMISE: Either Congress will amend this bill or the president will veto it.

MINOR PREMISE: Congress will not amend this bill.

CONCLUSION: Therefore, the president will veto it.

The validity and soundness of the disjunctive syllogism may also be tested.

3. The Conditional Syllogism. The **conditional syllogism**, also known as the *hypothetical syllogism,* is a syllogism in which the major premise deals with uncertain or hypothetical events that may or may not exist or happen. The conditional event is usually indicated by *if, assuming, supposing,* or similar terms, either expressly stated or clearly implied. For example, the following conditional syllogism was used in debates on the proposition "Resolved: That the federal government should adopt a program of compulsory wage and price controls":

MAJOR PREMISE: If the present measures have reduced greenhouse emissions, then we will not need to implement a carbon tax.

MINOR PREMISE: Present measures have not reduced greenhouse emissions.

CONCLUSION: Therefore, we will need to implement a carbon tax.

The major premise of the conditional syllogism contains an *antecedent* statement, which expresses the conditional or hypothetical event under consideration, and a *consequent* statement, which expresses the event that is maintained as necessarily following the antecedent. In the example just given, the antecedent statement begins with the word *if* and the consequent statement begins with the

---

Tests: Disjunctive Syllogism

1. *The major premise of the disjunctive syllogism must include all of the possible alternatives.* For example, after tribal wars broke out in Africa, some thought severe food shortages might occur and called for the United States to send massive food shipments to Africa. The argument went like this:

    MAJOR PREMISE: We must send food to Africa or millions will die.

    MINOR PREMISE: We don't want millions to die.

    CONCLUSION: Therefore, we must send food to Africa.

    Negative advocates who encountered this syllogism recognized that the major premise did not include all possible alternatives. They pointed out that the African country under consideration not only produced enough food to feed itself but normally had ample food for export. The problem was not a food shortage but a genocidal tribal war. Food was rotting in the fields while rival tribes battled, destroying the transportation system. Thus unloading food on docks at the country's ports—even if that could have been done—would have been useless, because the ports were under siege and the roads were impassable.

2. *The alternatives presented in the disjunctive syllogism must be mutually exclusive.* Those who opposed sending food to the African country argued that the war and not a food shortage was the major cause of deaths. They argued that only a major effort by the United Nations could end the war. They maintained that sending food without ending the war would merely increase deaths, because the rival tribes would intensify the war to gain control of the food supplies.

3. *The minor premise must affirm or contradict one of the alternatives given in the major premise.* If the minor premise neither affirms nor contradicts one of the alternatives in the major premise, no valid conclusion is possible. Here is an example:

    MAJOR PREMISE: Congress must either raise taxes or reduce federal expenditures.

    MINOR PREMISE: Members of Congress will not cut their own salaries.

    CONCLUSION: Therefore, Congress must _____?

    Because congressional salaries are only a minor part of all federal expenditures, the premise that members of Congress will not cut their own salaries might more accurately be phrased as "Members of Congress will not reduce *some* federal expenditures." Even though congresspersons will not cut their own salaries, it is possible for them to reduce *other* federal expenditures; therefore this premise neither affirms nor contradicts one of the alternatives in the major premise.

---

word *then*. The *if-then* relationship is a convenient way of expressing the major premise in a conditional syllogism.

Certain tests may be applied to the conditional syllogism.

Tests: Conditional Syllogism

1. *The minor premise must affirm the antecedent or deny the consequent.* If the minor premise affirms the antecedent, the conclusion must affirm the consequent; if the minor premise denies the consequent, the conclusion must deny the antecedent. Consider this example:

MAJOR PREMISE: If the interest rate on treasury notes increases, then more of these notes will be purchased.

MINOR PREMISE: The interest rate on treasury notes will increase.

CONCLUSION: Therefore, more of these notes will be purchased.

Note that in this case the minor premise affirms the antecedent and the conclusion affirms the consequent. The following example does just the opposite:

MAJOR PREMISE: Either the Extended Medical Care Act will provide for rationing or it will not pass.

MINOR PREMISE: Rationing will not be provided for in the Extended Medical Care Act.

CONCLUSION: Therefore, the Extended Medical Care Act will not pass.

2. *If the minor premise denies the antecedent or affirms the consequent, no valid conclusion can be drawn.* Here's an example:

MAJOR PREMISE: If the interest rate on treasury notes increases, then more of these notes will be purchased.

MINOR PREMISE: The interest rate on treasury notes will not increase.

CONCLUSION: Therefore, _____?

In this example the absence of an increase in interest rates will not lead to more of these notes being purchased. However, (because a change in any of a number of fiscal or monetary policies might lead to more of these notes being purchased), one cannot conclude that more notes will *not* be purchased. Thus, when the minor premise denies the antecedent, no valid conclusion can be drawn. Now consider this example:

MAJOR PREMISE: Either the Extended Medical Care Act will provide for rationing or it will not pass.

MINOR PREMISE: Rationing will be provided for in the Extended Medical Care Act.

CONCLUSION: _____?

Even if rationing is provided for, numerous other factors might prevent passage of the Extended Medical Care Act. Thus, when the antecedent statement affirms the consequent, no valid conclusion can be drawn.

B. The Enthymeme

1. Definitions of the Enthymeme.   The rigorous rules of the syllogism make it a valuable instrument for testing arguments. But these rules also limit the situations in which it can be used. We rarely talk in syllogisms; we are more likely to express our arguments in less-than-complete syllogisms. Also there are many situations in which we must deal with probabilities rather than certainties. In these circumstances we make use of the enthymeme. Because there are two discrete concepts involved, there are two definitions of the **enthymeme**.

The first definition of the enthymeme—as a *truncated (shortened) syllogism*—is extremely important to the advocate. As noted, people usually do not talk in syllogisms.

Many arguments are expressed in the form of enthymemes. In a debate on federal aid for higher education, we might hear this argument: "This plan would lead to federal control and is undesirable." Expressed in the form of an enthymeme, this argument would look like this:

MAJOR PREMISE: This plan leads to federal control.

CONCLUSION: Therefore, this plan is undesirable.

As advocates encountering this enthymeme, we would immediately look for the unstated major premise. If the unstated major premise were "*Some* forms of federal control are undesirable," we would recognize that the middle term is not distributed and that therefore the conclusion is formally invalid. If the unstated major premise were "*All* forms of federal control are undesirable," the conclusion would be formally valid, but we might want to question the material truth of the major premise.

Thus, when we encounter enthymemes in an argument—and we will often encounter them—we should look for the unstated premise and determine whether the conclusion logically follows that premise or whether the unstated premise is materially true. In discovering the unstated premise, we may open up important avenues of analysis.

Two Definitions of the Enthymeme

1. The enthymeme is a *truncated* syllogism in which one of the premises or the conclusion is not stated.
2. The enthymeme is a syllogism based on probabilities, signs, and examples, whose function is rhetorical persuasion. Its successful construction is accomplished through the joint efforts of speaker and audience, and this is its essential character.[*]

[*] Lloyd F. Bitzer, "Aristotle's Enthymeme Revisited," *Quarterly Journal of Speech*, vol. 45, no. 4 (1959), p. 408.

Sometimes advocates may find it psychologically advantageous to omit the conclusion. If the major and minor premises are clearly stated, the audience or judges will draw the conclusion and may hold it more firmly because they reached it "on their own." Or advocates may be able to make an unpleasant point without actually stating it. Thus a professor might say to a student, "Anyone who failed the midterm exam must get a B or better on the final to pass the course. You failed the midterm." The professor would no doubt get the message across without verbalizing it; and the student, drawing the inevitable conclusion, might be motivated to put extra effort into preparing for the final.

The enthymeme—as the term is used in the second definition (with the focus on probabilities, signs, and examples and on construction through the joint efforts of speaker and audience)—may or may not omit one of the premises or the conclusion. This definition of the enthymeme is also important to the advocate, who is often concerned with probability rather than certainty and who often wishes to build on premises already established in the mind of the audience.

Affirmative advocates of a policy proposition argue for implementation of some *plan of action,* which they claim will have substantial benefits. Negative debaters may argue that the affirmative's plan should be rejected on the basis of its costs (see Chapters 12 and 13). For example, many negative debaters use this objection to the cost of an affirmative plan:

MAJOR PREMISE: All plans that cause inflation should be rejected.

MINOR PREMISE: This plan *may* cause inflation.

CONCLUSION: Therefore, this plan should be rejected.

In this case the debater hoped the audience was predisposed to oppose inflation and would thus join with the debater in building the enthymeme by accepting the major premise. Syllogistically this argument proves absolutely nothing. It has a formal validity of zero. The syllogism is a logical instrument for dealing with certainty; it is concerned with all of the factors in a certain classification and with matters that necessarily and inevitably follow from certain premises. However, many problems the advocate must consider are not subject to certainty or to absolute proof. If the negative can establish a reasonable degree of cogency for its argument—if it can establish a reasonable probability that the plan will cause inflation—it might well win the decision.

Another enthymeme was used in some debates on the tax-sharing proposition:

MAJOR PREMISE: All tax programs that encourage urban sprawl are undesirable.

MINOR PREMISE: The affirmative's plan of tax sharing may encourage urban sprawl.

CONCLUSION: Therefore, the affirmative's plan of tax sharing is undesirable.

In this case the debater hoped the audience was predisposed to oppose urban sprawl and so would join with the debater in building the enthymeme by accepting the minor premise. At the time of these debates, the negative could cite some evidence to support the minor premise, and the affirmative could cite some evidence to refute it. Assuming neither side could establish certainty, the decision on this clash would go to the side establishing a fair preponderance of evidence.

Enthymemes, like syllogisms, may be classified as categorical, disjunctive, and conditional. The same tests used to determine the formal validity of a syllogism may be used to determine the formal validity of an enthymeme. Although the enthymemes just cited are invalid as syllogisms, they are formally valid as enthymemes. Thus, if advocates can establish a preponderance of probability to support their arguments and can get the audience to join with them in the construction of the enthymeme, they may persuade reasonable people to accept their conclusions.

The following enthymeme, however, is formally invalid; thus, regardless of the degree of probability attached to the premise, the conclusion is worthless:

MAJOR PREMISE: Some domestic industries are not harmed by Chinese imports.

MINOR PREMISE: Textiles are a domestic industry.

CONCLUSION: Therefore, textiles are probably not harmed by Chinese imports.

The fallacy of an undistributed middle term—"*some* domestic industries"—renders the conclusion of this enthymeme formally invalid.

2. Chain of Enthymemes.   Arguments are often stated in the form of a chain of enthymemes. A speaker may state only the conclusion of an enthymeme, use that as one premise of a second enthymeme, state the conclusion to the second enthymeme without indicating the other premise, and continue in this way to build a chain of enthymemes. The omitted portion of the enthymeme sometimes will be evident and uncontestable; other times, however, it may not be apparent or may be subject to refutation. Consequently advocates should recognize and analyze a chain of enthymemes, seek out the omitted portions of the argument, restructure the argument in syllogistic form, and apply the appropriate tests.

Advocates will often find it advantageous to begin to build a chain of enthymemes in the minds of the listeners. As Aristotle advised: "Our speaker, accordingly, must start out from ... the [actual] opinions of the judges [audience], or else the opinions of persons whose authority they accept. And the speaker must make sure that his premises do appear in this light to most, if not all, of his audience. And he must argue not only from necessary truths, but from probable truths as well."[1]

Thus, if the advocate were speaking before a civil liberties group, analysis of the audience might lead him or her to conclude that the group would support the major premise, "Privacy is an important value guaranteed by the U.S. Constitution." Building on this premise in the minds of the audience, the advocate might begin the argument by stating, in effect:

---

1. Aristotle, *Rhetoric*, II, 22.

MINOR PREMISE: The USA Patriot Act violates our right of privacy.

CONCLUSION: Therefore, the USA Patriot Act must be repealed.

Or, if the speaker were addressing a gun club, analysis of the audience might lead him or her to conclude that the group would support the major premise, "The right of the people to keep and bear arms shall not be infringed." Building on this premise in the minds of the audience, the speaker might begin the argument by stating, in effect:

MINOR PREMISE: The Gun Registration Act infringes on our right to keep guns.

CONCLUSION: The Gun Registration Act is unconstitutional.

Advocates should analyze their decision renderers carefully and seek out opportunities to build a chain of enthymemes on the premises already established in the minds of the audience or judge (see the Chapter 15 section "Analysis of the Audience").

C. Formal Validity and Material Truth

In the syllogisms and enthymemes considered thus far, we have assumed that each premise of each syllogism is *absolutely* true and that each premise of each enthymeme is *probably* true. If they are true, the conclusions drawn from the formally valid syllogisms are matters of absolute certainty, and the conclusions drawn from the formally valid enthymemes must be accorded the degree of cogency appropriate to the probability found in the premises. If, however, any of these premises is false, then its conclusion is worthless regardless of the formal validity of the construction:

MAJOR PREMISE: Any child can make a spaceship.

MINOR PREMISE: John is a child.

CONCLUSION: Therefore, John can make a spaceship.

This syllogism unquestionably is formally valid. Assume that John really is a child; the minor premise is then materially true. The major premise, however, has no foundation in fact. Obviously the conclusion is worthless.

Note that a materially true conclusion is not proof that the premises are materially true or that the syllogism is formally valid. Consider the following syllogism:

MAJOR PREMISE: All nations that have received direct economic aid from the United States are now military allies of the United States.

MINOR PREMISE: Canada has not received direct economic aid from the United States.

CONCLUSION: Therefore, Canada is a military ally of the United States.

The proof of this conclusion must come from a source other than this syllogism.

To establish the material truth of a premise, the advocate must apply the tests of reasoning and the tests of evidence considered earlier. Because many premises are, in fact, conclusions from other syllogisms or enthymemes that may or may not have been stated in the argument, the appropriate tests of formal validity should be applied to them.

II. THE ELEMENTS OF ANY ARGUMENT

Whereas formal logic provides for rigorous testing of arguments based on almost mathematical rules, most human decisions, even by critical audiences, are made on a basis of more practical reasoning. Therefore in debate, more often than not, the test of an argument is not whether it is true or false, but rather, is it strong or weak.

Philosopher Stephen Toulmin offers a model for better understanding the structure of practical reasoning that occurs in any argument. He maintains that six elements can be found in any wholly explicit argument: (1) claims, (2) grounds, (3) warrants, (4) backing, (5) modal qualifications, and (6) possible rebuttals.[2] We consider each in turn.

A. Claims

The **claim(s)** element of the argument is the conclusion we are trying to establish by our argument. Our claim might be the proposition itself—for example, "Resolved: That the federal government should significantly strengthen the regulation of mass media communication in the United States" or "Resolved: That the federal government should significantly curtail the powers of labor unions in the United States." In practice, to establish those claims, we would first have to establish a series of other claims—for instance, "Banning publicity will reduce terrorism" or "Work sharing will reduce unemployment in the United States."

B. Grounds

Once we have made a claim, we must advance **grounds**—evidence and reasoning to establish the foundation of our claim. We have to provide good reasons to establish that our claim is solid and reliable. The grounds represent what we have to go on.

C. Warrants

Once we have made a claim and indicated the grounds for that claim, we must provide a **warrant**—evidence and reasoning advanced to justify the move from the grounds to the claim. We need to establish that the evidence and reasoning we have offered as grounds apply in this particular instance.

---

2. Stephen Toulmin, Richard Rieke, and Allan Janik, *An Introduction to Reasoning* (New York: Macmillan, 1979), p. 25.

Let's consider how affirmative advocates on the proposition "Resolved: That the federal government should significantly strengthen the regulation of mass media communication in the United States" used these three elements of argument: If the advocates have provided good evidence and reasoning to establish their grounds and to support their claim, they will have taken important steps toward establishing their claim.

Let's continue now with a consideration of the other elements of argument.

D. Backing

Our warrant will not be accepted merely on our say-so; we have to provide **backing**—additional evidence and reasoning to support our warrant. Applying this element to our mass media example, we expand our diagram:

We see that the warrants are not self-validating.[3] Therefore, we need to provide additional evidence and reasoning to sustain our warrant in the form of backing.

E. Modal Qualifications

When we have considered the grounds, warrant, and backing offered in support of our claim, we are in a position to qualify that claim—that is, to express the

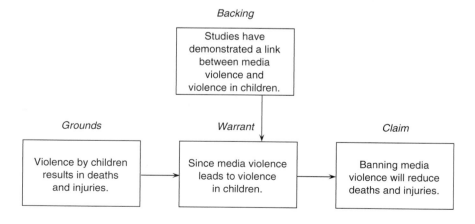

---

3. Toulmin, Rieke, and Janik, *An Introduction to Reasoning*, p. 58.

degree of cogency (considered in detail in Chapter 9) that we can attach to our claim. The degree of cogency, or **modal qualification**, we can attach to our claim may vary from certainty to possibility.

Let's consider an example in which the modality can be precisely verified:

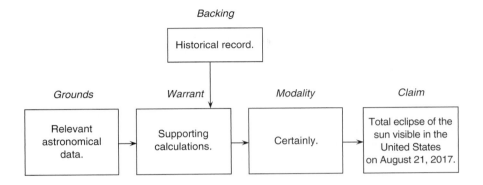

Students are invited to check with the astronomy department of their university: Do the professors there agree with the modality or degree of cogency assigned to this claim? Note that after August 21, 2017, this claim will become a perfect example of judicial notice (see Chapter 6). If "everyone" knows that there was a total eclipse of the sun on that date, we only have to mention the fact to establish the claim. Because the eclipse of 2017 will be the first eclipse of the sun visible in the United States since July 11, 1991, it will undoubtedly be a well-publicized event. Only after a lapse of some time after the event will it be necessary to introduce evidence to support the claim.

Consider another example: Will the United States send a manned space expedition to Mars in 2013? Will the United States and another country send a joint manned space expedition to Mars 2013? In that year Mars will come relatively close to Earth. Scientists have made such proposals. However, an affirmative answer to these questions *cannot* be given with *certainty* until we are much closer to that date. Although eclipses and the orbits of planets can be predicted with certainty far in advance, the decisions of nations—and their ability to carry out these decisions—cannot be predicted with anything approaching the same precision.

Advocates rarely deal with certainty; usually they are concerned with establishing a lesser degree of cogency. As an example, let's consider an argument that was made in the final round of an NDT tournament:

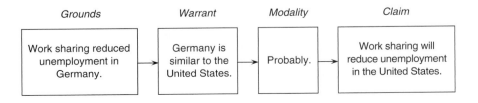

Did the advocates assign a reasonable degree of cogency (modal qualification) to their claim? Not surprisingly the negative did not let this claim go unchallenged. In fact the negative debaters did exactly what we would expect them to do—introduce rebuttal—which brings us to the last of Toulmin's elements of argument.

F. Rebuttals

As is discussed in detail in Chapter 14, **rebuttal** involves introducing evidence and reasoning to weaken or destroy another's claim. In the debate on work sharing, the negative introduced rebuttal designed to destroy the degree of cogency that the affirmative assigned to its claim.

With the rebuttal and its backing now before us, we will either have to drop the claim or assign to it a much lower degree of cogency (modality). Depending on the evidence and reasoning the negative has used in its rebuttal, the chance that work sharing will reduce unemployment in the United States has now been lowered from a probability to at best a possibility.

Rebuttal, then, may be seen as an element of argument that may block or impede the movement of argument from grounds to claim and force us to reconsider and to define more precisely the degree of cogency we assign to our claim.

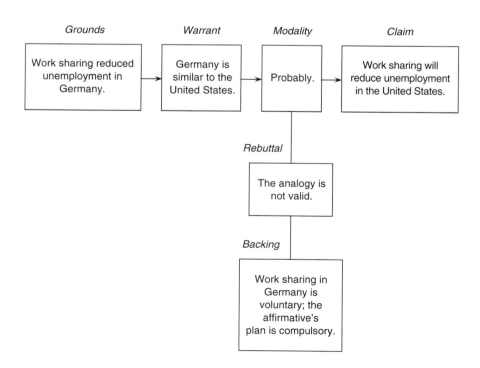

III. EXTENDING THE ELEMENTS OF AN ARGUMENT

The samples we have considered are brief. In an actual argument or debate, the elements of argument are often extended and complex. In the example just discussed, the negative built on their backing, "Work sharing in Germany is voluntary; the affirmative's plan is compulsory," to establish a disadvantage and advanced a revised version of that backing as grounds, "Unions despise compulsory work sharing," for their claim that "Unions will strike":

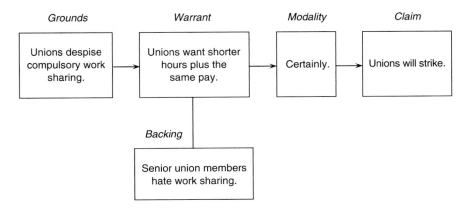

Naturally the affirmative responded with a rebuttal of its own, challenging the claim that the unions would certainly strike. Still more arguments were built on the strike argument as the opposing teams introduced evidence and reasoning to establish that the strikes would have a devastating impact on the economy or that the strikes wouldn't happen at all or that they would have only minimal impact on the economy.

Another example, with more obvious flaws, may help to clarify:

Grounds

Barack Obama is a tall man.

Warrant

Because tall men make great presidents,

Claim

Barack Obama would be a great president.

Backing

Research suggests a strong correlation between highly rated presidents and height.

This argument seems outrageous, yet presidential candidates are careful to emphasize their height during campaigns. A major point of conflict occurred during negotiations to arrange the stage for the Dukakis versus Bush debates of 1988. Bush was significantly taller than Dukakis, and his campaign team did not want to allow Dukakis to stand on a riser to equalize height during the debate. So there seems to be at least some validity to the above argument. Is it a strong argument? Kerry's height can be measured. Analysis would isolate the key to this argument as the warrant, and how well it would be received by the intended audience.

Careful evaluation of the elements of argument will allow the advocate to detect flaws in an argument and thus to launch an attack on an opponent's argument or to replace or repair a flawed argument intended to support the advocate's own position.

EXERCISES

1. Find an argumentative editorial published in a daily newspaper within the past month. Restate the arguments in the form of syllogisms or enthymemes. Analyze these arguments. Show why they are or are not formally valid.

2. Find an argumentative editorial as in Exercise 1. Lay out the major arguments in the form considered in Sections II and III of this chapter. Does the warrant justify the movement from grounds to claim? Has the writer established the modality of the claim accurately? Has sufficient backing been provided when needed? Have possible rebuttals been considered?

3. Select a major argument from the debate in Appendix B. Lay out the argument in the form considered in Sections II and III of this chapter. Apply the questions listed in Exercise 2.

4. Select a major argument from the debate in Appendix B. State the argument as a syllogism. Does it meet the appropriate tests of a syllogism?

5. Select a major argument from the debate in Appendix B. State the argument as an enthymeme. Show why the enthymeme is or is not formally valid. If a premise is omitted, supply the omitted premise. Does the enthymeme establish a reasonable degree of probability?

9

Types of Reasoning

Reasoning is the process of inferring conclusions from premises. The premises may be in the form of any of the various types of evidence; they may be stated as propositions; or they may be statements of conclusions reached through prior reasoning. Thus advocates use the premises they have previously established or asserted, and by a process of reasoning, they try to establish something new—a conclusion they want their audience to accept. If the audience perceives the premises as well grounded and the reasoning as rhetorically sound, it will be likely to accept the conclusion.

I. THE DEGREE OF COGENCY

The **degree of cogency** is the extent to which an argument is both sound and intellectually compelling because it is well founded in fact, logic, or rationality. (As we saw in Chapter 8, Toulmin used the term *modal qualification* to express this concept.) The degrees of cogency are certainty, probability, plausibility, or possibility. These may be thought of as existing on a continuum, represented by the following diagram.

These degrees of cogency are not discrete compartments; rather, they are terms used to suggest the relative compelling force of various logical proofs.

Cogency Continuum

Absolute   A scintilla
truth   of truth

Certainty
....................Probability
....................Plausibility
....................Possibility......................

Miniglossary

Analogy, reasoning by   The process of making a comparison between two similar cases and inferring that what is true in one case is true in the other.

Causal reasoning   The process whereby one infers that a certain factor (a cause) is a force that produces something else (an effect).

Deduction   Argument that begins with a broad generalization and moves to a more specific application or conclusion.

Degree of cogency   The extent to which an argument is both sound and intellectually compelling because it is well founded in fact, logic, or rationality.

Example, reasoning by   The process of inferring conclusions from specific cases.

Induction   Argument that begins with a specific case and moves to a broader generalization.

Sign, reasoning by   The process of inferring relationships or correlations between two variables.

A. Certainty

Certainty is associated with absolute truth. If a conclusion is a certainty, all competent observers are in agreement. Relatively little of the advocates' time is concerned with this degree of proof. But few matters of human affairs actually are subject to proof as certainty. Advocates' efforts usually are in the realm of probability; they have to try to demonstrate that their conclusions have a degree of credibility warranting acceptance. In criminal courts, which demand the highest standard of proof, all elements of the case must be proven "beyond a reasonable doubt," or what has been estimated to be over 90 percent certainty. Outside the criminal courts we are often required to make decisions based on a lesser degree of certainty. For example, the secretary of the treasury, even with all of the resources of the federal government at his or her disposal, cannot establish as a certainty the proposition that a given tax bill will raise X dollars in revenue. Students who debated tax sharing and higher education found that estimates of state sales tax revenues and the yield from school tax levies were often inaccurate. Furthermore, matters that are a certainty are, by definition, not appropriate subjects for debate. Matters that are a certainty, however, are often used as part of the evidence and with reasoning are used to establish new conclusions.

We should note that it is not only the evidence itself but the way it is perceived that will determine certainty and the other degrees of cogency. If our ego, politics, finances, or other interests are involved in the matter, our evaluation of the evidence will vary. While the judge or audience can consider some matters dispassionately and objectively (fortunately, this is usually the case with judges in academic debate), at other times advocates have to be aware of audience attitudes and adapt their cases, reasoning, and evidence to their listeners' interests (see Chapter 15).

B. Probability

Probability is associated with a high degree of likelihood (but *not* certainty) that a conclusion is true. As advocates we will spend much of our time trying to prove that our propositions have a high degree of probability and are more probably true than those of our opponents. For example, no method of contraception is 100 percent effective; even sterilization fails at times, and other methods range from 76 percent to 97.6 percent in their effectiveness. Thus, in choosing contraceptives, people are basing their decisions on probabilities. In the physical sciences the degree of probability of a proposition being true can be established with great precision; often thousands of cases can be examined under carefully controlled conditions. In other areas, however, it is not always possible to measure as accurately and to control as precisely the variables affecting the proposition. In civil courts the standard of proof is the preponderance of evidence; this means a 51 percent chance of being true. Outside the civil courts the necessary degree of cogency depends on the situation. For example, the secretary of the treasury, in seeking to establish the proposition that a given tax bill will raise X dollars in revenue, will have to qualify his or her statement. That is, he or she will have to say that *if* the present level of employment is maintained, *if* spending is continued at the present level, *if* there isn't an international crisis, and *if* various other relevant factors don't change, then it is reasonable to assume that the tax bill will raise X dollars.

C. Plausibility

Plausibility is associated with a lesser degree of likelihood that a proposition is true. Advocates will use arguments having this degree of proof only when no better arguments are available. The ancient Sophists often used this type of proof; modern propagandists do so as well. Arguments of this type are sometimes superficial or specious and have limited probative force for the thoughtful listener or reader. Sometimes, of course, we are forced to make decisions simply on the basis of plausibility, if this relatively low degree of cogency is the best available. Many life-or-death surgical decisions are made on this basis. When a new surgical procedure is first developed (heart transplant, for example), the surgeon tells the patient, in effect, "If you go on as you are, all our experience indicates that your condition will continue to deteriorate and you will die within a few months. We've developed a new surgical procedure that *could* help you. We've had some successes with this new procedure, but frankly it's still experimental and we don't have enough data to make firm estimates." Given this set of circumstances, would you take the gamble?

D. Possibility

Possibility is associated with a low degree of likelihood that a proposition is true. The advocate has only limited use for proofs with this degree of cogency and will always seek proofs having greater logical force. Until the closing weeks of the baseball season, for example, a mathematical possibility usually exists that the last-place team could win the division pennant. If such a possibility requires, however, that the last-place team win all its remaining games and that the top three teams lose all their remaining games, this possibility would not warrant serious consideration. Sometimes, of course, we are forced to make decisions when proofs with this low degree of likelihood are the best available. When debating the proposition "Resolved: That the federal government should establish a national program of public work for the unemployed," some affirmative teams argued that the proposition should be adopted because a major recession might occur in the future and that such a program should be established in case it needed to be put into effect at the onset of the recession. At the time the proposition was debated, the country was enjoying a period of prosperity and there was no evidence of a recession in the foreseeable future. But some affirmative teams argued successfully that on the basis of all our previous experience a recession was a possibility for which we should be prepared.

Recall the evidence considered in the Chapter 6 section "Evidence Aliunde" regarding the debate on the proposition to increase space exploration: "the substance *could* be a one-shot cure for diabetes." As we saw, this evidence as presented is useless. But let's assume for a moment that the pharmaceutical company hoped to develop such a substance; after all, that's entirely *plausible*, indeed *probable*. Let's assume further that the company had conducted exhaustive studies indicating that, by using certain techniques in the zero gravity of space, such a substance *could* be produced. Yet, prior to actual testing in space, one can only say "could." Until the experiment was actually performed in zero gravity and the results carefully evaluated, no one could say positively that the substance would in fact be a one-shot cure for diabetes. Yet, given the rewards that would come from such a discovery, it's entirely reasonable to believe that investors would risk large sums of money on the long odds.

The effort to develop the next generation of computer chips provides another example. Although it is generally agreed that such a computer chip will come about, highly competent engineers have different ideas about how it should be designed. At this time no one actually knows how or when it will be developed, but the cost-benefit ratio of being the first to develop a new-generation computer chip is so great that billions of dollars are being poured into research on this project.

The balance of this chapter will consider the types and uses of the tests of reasoning. We first discuss general tests applicable to all types of reasoning. Then we cover specific tests for (1) reasoning by example, (2) reasoning by analogy, (3) causal reasoning, and (4) sign reasoning.

II. TESTS OF REASONING AND THEIR USES

Obviously all reasoning does not have the same degree of cogency. Therefore, it's important to test reasoning to determine the degree of probability of the conclusions. Often more than one type of reasoning is involved in a given line of argument, making it necessary to apply all the appropriate tests to each piece of reasoning. There are three uses for the tests of reasoning.

A. To Test the Validity of One's Own Reasoning

In the construction of a case, advocates will discover much reasoning advanced by others and will develop tentative lines of reasoning of their own. Before incorporating any of this reasoning into their cases, they must apply the tests of reasoning so that they may reject invalid reasoning and include only what will stand up under scrutiny. By applying the tests of reasoning, they can anticipate the probable lines of refutation by their opponents and prepare their counterrefutation. These tests of reasoning should also be applied outside the debate situation. For example, as college students weigh the propositions that they should enter law school, or medical school, or a certain field, their future happiness and success require that they carefully apply the tests of reasoning to the arguments supporting these propositions.

B. To Test the Validity of the Reasoning Advanced
by the Opposition

In preparing cases advocates have to try to discover the probable lines of reasoning their opponents will use, apply the appropriate tests to this reasoning, and plan refutation of it. In the course of the debate, they should be prepared to apply the appropriate tests as their opponent's actual lines of reasoning are presented and to develop their refutations accordingly.

C. To Test the Validity of Reasoning Advanced for a Decision

Often we may seek neither to advance our own arguments nor to refute arguments of others; rather, we function as decision renderers to whom various lines of reasoning are directed. As citizens, we are the target of arguments advanced by political parties. To function as responsible citizens, we have to apply the tests of reasoning to these arguments. If we plan to buy a car, or stock, or a house, or make any other significant purchase, our own self-interest compels us to apply the tests of reasoning to the arguments advanced by the salesperson. In fact any time we have to make a decision of any significance, common sense dictates that we apply the tests of reasoning to the factors relating to that decision with a degree of rigor directly related to the importance of the decision.

In the course of the debate, we and our opponents are presenting reasoning to the audience or judges for their decision. The audience or judges will make a judgment as to what degree of cogency they assign to the conflicting arguments. We must be in a position to advance good reasons that they should accept our arguments and reject the reasoning of our opponents.

III. GENERAL TESTS OF REASONING

The general tests that should be applied to all types of reasoning are drawn from the section "The Elements of Any Argument" in Chapter 8. Once a claim is advanced, we have to apply these general tests to the supporting elements of the argument. The tests, of course, must be specific to the particular argument being considered. An affirmative answer to the following test questions implies that the reasoning is sound; a negative answer may imply the presence of a fallacy.

1. *Are the grounds solid?* Have good reasons been given to establish the foundation of this claim? Have reliable evidence and reasoning been provided to establish grounds for the claim?

2. *Does the warrant justify the claim?* Have sufficient evidence and reasoning been given to provide good reasons justifying the movement from grounds to claim in this specific instance?

3. *Is the backing adequate?* In many cases the warrant or rebuttal is not sufficient to stand alone. Have additional evidence and reasoning been provided to establish adequate backing?

4. *Has the rebuttal been properly evaluated?* Almost any argument is subject to rebuttal. Have sufficient evidence and reasoning been provided to offset or minimize the rebuttal? Has the rebuttal been properly evaluated?

5. *Has the degree of cogency (modal qualification) been properly determined?* As we have seen, the degree of cogency or modal qualification that may be attached to a claim may vary from certainty to possibility. Has the degree of cogency assigned to this particular claim been established accurately and precisely?

IV. TYPES OF REASONING AND TESTS
FOR EACH TYPE

Reasoning is often classified as deductive or inductive. *Deductive* reasoning moves from general to specific. Syllogisms are deductive forms of argument. For example, all men are mortal (broad generalization or premise), Socrates is a man (more specific); Socrates is mortal (most specific). Deductive reasoning claims to establish the certainty of a conclusion. *Inductive* reasoning moves from specific cases to generalizations. For example, "I had Pad Thai at the new Thai Restaurant last night and it was very good" (one specific case of my meal at the new restaurant); "I can therefore safely conclude that this is an excellent restaurant" (refers to a broader number of cases), and in fact, "I would have to say that Thai food is excellent!" (even broader). Inductive reasoning claims to establish a lesser degree of cogency for its conclusion. Irving Copi points out:

> Although every argument involves the claim that its premises provide evidence for the truth of its conclusion, only *deductive* argument involves the claim that its premises provide *conclusive* evidence.... An inductive argument, on the other hand, involves the claim not that its premises give conclusive evidence for the truth of its conclusion, but only that they provide *some* evidence for it.... Inductive arguments may, of course, be evaluated as better or worse, according to the degree of likelihood or probability which their premises confer upon their conclusions.[1]

As a practical matter, advocates use both **deduction** and **induction**, moving back and forth from one to the other many times while developing or analyzing an argument. The intermingling of deduction and induction will become apparent as we consider the principal types of reasoning and their related tests.

A. Reasoning by Example

The process of **reasoning by example** consists of inferring conclusions from specific cases. This process may be represented as follows:

Sometimes a single case may be used to establish the conclusion or generalization. More often a number of cases will be offered as the basis for the conclusion. Reasoning by example is a form of inductive reasoning and involves either cause or sign reasoning, because the advocate is trying to show that the examples or cases are a cause or a sign of the conclusion presented.

Advocates make frequent use of reasoning by example. In debating the proposition "Resolved: That the United States should discontinue direct economic aid to foreign countries," some affirmative teams tried to establish the argument that recipient nations resented direct economic aid. They offered as examples a series of statements by various foreign leaders, maintained that these statements expressed resentment toward direct economic aid, and from these cases drew the conclusion that resentment against such aid was widespread. Other affirmative teams debating this proposition maintained that direct economic aid was wasteful. They offered examples of expenditures of direct economic aid monies,

---

1. Irving M. Copi, *Introduction to Logic,* 3rd ed. (London: Macmillan, 1968), pp. 20–21.

maintained that these expenditures were unwise, and from these cases drew the conclusion that direct economic aid was wasteful.

The following questions serve as tests for reasoning by example:

1. *Is the example relevant?* Advocates should determine whether the cases offered are relevant to the matter under consideration. Some negative teams, refuting the argument that recipient nations resented direct economic aid, were quick to point out that some of the statements quoted by the affirmative were criticisms of U.S. foreign policy generally, not of direct economic aid specifically. They also noted that the statements quoted by the affirmative were criticisms of U.S. military aid, not of direct economic aid. These negative teams demonstrated that the examples offered by the affirmative were not relevant examples of criticism of direct economic aid, however accurate they might be as examples of criticism of other aspects of U.S. foreign policy. In this way they refuted the conclusion drawn from the examples.

2. *Is there a reasonable number of examples?* Although a single example may be used to establish a generalization or conclusion, the advocate's position is usually stronger with supporting examples. Even a carefully controlled laboratory experiment is usually not accepted as establishing a conclusion until it has been repeated with the same results by other competent scientists—and, in medicine, not until thousands of cases have been studied.

   How many cases are enough? One method of obtaining enough cases is to make a complete enumeration. For example, you could ask all the students in your argumentation class whether they own computers and then draw the conclusion that X percent of the students own computers. Complete enumeration, however, has obvious limitations, because it is often difficult or impossible to consider every case. Therefore, advocates have to present enough cases to convince a reasonable person that there is a high degree of probability that a conclusion is correct.

   Some negative teams, answering the argument that direct economic aid was wasteful, did not attempt to refute the examples. Rather, they maintained that three or four examples of waste among thousands of projects were not sufficient to justify the conclusion that such aid, as a whole, was wasteful. Some negative teams carried this refutation a step further; they introduced reports of congressional committees that had studied large numbers of projects and had found that such projects were, on balance, useful. Thus, although time limitations will often prevent our citing a large number of examples directly, we may give a few examples to illustrate our point and then, to substantiate our conclusion further, offer the testimony of persons who have studied large numbers of cases.

3. *Do the examples cover a critical period of time?* In many cases the time at which the examples were studied or the time period covered by the examples may be critical. The advocate should try to find examples representative of the period of time critical to the argument. Suppose, in debating direct economic aid, the affirmative had chosen all of its examples of waste from the first year or two of the operation of the aid program. The negative might have maintained that

some errors in administration could be expected at the start of a new program and that the affirmative had offered no examples of waste in the recent or current operation of the program. Public opinion polls taken during election years often provide dramatic evidence of the importance of obtaining examples from the critical period of time. After the Persian Gulf War, President Bush's popularity in the polls soared to near unprecedented highs. Many of the front-runners for the Democratic nomination dropped out of the race, apparently believing Bush was unbeatable. The critical period of time, however, was November 1992. By then, Bush had dropped to second place in a three-way race, and Clinton won by a plurality.

4. *Are the examples typical?* The advocate must determine whether the cases offered are really representative. In Senate debates on labor legislation, some senators have cited examples of corrupt labor practices and called for legislation to regulate labor unions. Other senators have opposed this legislation, maintaining that the few examples of corruption were not typical of labor unions generally.

5. *Are negative examples noncritical?* Advocates must discern whether the negative examples they discover are critical or noncritical. In matters of policy, it is unlikely that all of the examples will support one conclusion. Some examples may well be negative or contrary to the conclusion. In considering direct economic aid, advocates will find examples of waste and examples of excellent management; in considering employment practices, advocates will find examples of firms that practice discrimination and examples of firms that do not. They should remember that they are concerned more often with probability than certainty. They should not attempt to show that *all* direct economic aid projects are wasteful; rather, they should try to show that the examples of wastefulness warrant the conclusion that waste is inherent in the program and that direct economic aid should be discontinued. On almost any proposition the opponents are likely to have negative examples; advocates must anticipate these examples and be prepared to offer adequate evidence that the examples are noncritical and do not invalidate their conclusion.

Reasoning by example may also be analyzed by laying out the argument as outlined in the section "The Elements of Any Argument" in Chapter 8. For example, assume the advocate claims there are practical alternatives to nuclear power, as the following diagram shows.

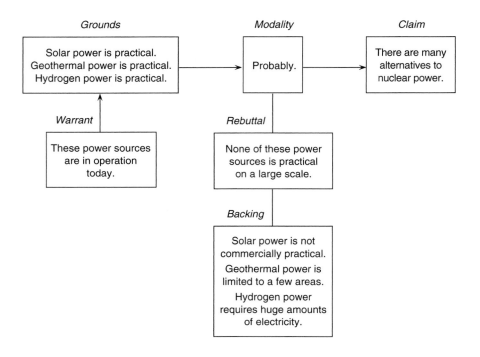

B. Reasoning by Analogy

The process of **reasoning by analogy** consists of making a comparison between two similar cases and inferring that what is true in one case is true in the other. Reasoning by analogy is a form of inductive reasoning, in which the advocate seeks to show that the factors in his or her analogy are either a cause or a sign of the conclusion presented. This process may be represented as follows:

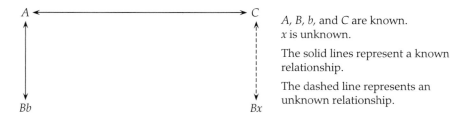

In this diagram *A* might represent Megalopolis, *Bb* might represent the type of city income tax in effect in Megalopolis, *C* might represent Gotham, and *Bx* might represent the type of city income tax proposed for Gotham. An advocate using reasoning by analogy might argue that, because a certain type of city income tax was desirable in Megalopolis, a similar city income tax would be desirable in Gotham. Similarly, in debating the proposition "Resolved: That the federal government should grant annually a specific percentage of its income tax revenue to the state governments," some negative teams tried to show that, because state income taxes were effective revenue producers for some states, other states could also use these taxes effectively.

Analogies may be literal or figurative. The analogy is *literal* when the cases compared are in the same classification, as are Megalopolis and Gotham (if we accept these as metropolitan cities for the purposes of our illustration) or the various state governments. The analogy is *figurative* when the cases compared are in different classifications—as in the statement "This car is a lemon!" A book reviewer made clever use of a figurative analogy when he noted, "Writing about the business of baseball is like writing about the music in topless bars." However fascinating the thrust and parry of management and labor, however clever the stratagems and costly the miscalculations of the opposing sides, they are not why people go to baseball games.[2]

These analogies have zero value as logical proof. They do, however, make their points effectively by utilizing *imagery* (a factor of style considered in detail in Chapter 15).

Carefully developed literal analogies may be used to establish a high degree of probability. Figurative analogies, on the other hand, have no value in establishing *logical* proof. If well chosen, however, they may have considerable value in establishing *ethical* or *emotional* proof, in illustrating a point, and in making a vivid impression on the audience.

The following questions provide tests for reasoning by analogy:

1. *Are there significant points of similarity?* Advocates should determine whether significant points of similarity exist between the cases compared. In making an analogy between Megalopolis and Gotham, the advocate might be able to discover a number of significant points of similarity. For instance, both might have approximately the same population; both might have comparable inner-city problems; both might have suburbs of about the same size and affluence; and both might have about the same ratio of heavy industry to service businesses. Unless the advocate can demonstrate some significant points of similarity between the cases, no analogy can be made.

2. *Are the points of similarity critical to the comparison?* It is not enough for the cases to have some significant similarities. The existence of significant points of similarity makes an analogy possible, but the analogy cannot have a reasonable degree of cogency unless it can be demonstrated that the cases are similar in critical points. We could easily demonstrate, for example, some points of similarity between a water pump and the human heart. We would not conclude, however, that a mechanic is qualified to repair both. Similarly, as indicated, we could find many significant similarities between Megalopolis and Gotham; however, in arguing that a certain type of city income tax is equally desirable in both cities, we would find these similarities noncritical. To support an analogy involving a city income tax, we would have to

---

2. Alan Abelson, "Barbarians at the Ball Park," *New York Times Book Review,* Apr. 10, 1994, p. 3.

determine, for example, whether similar state income tax laws applied in both cities or whether there were similar state and city sales taxes in effect in both cities, similar reciprocity provisions for suburban city income taxes, similar taxes of other types, or similar financial policies. In other words we would have to demonstrate that the two cities were similar in critical points.

3. *Are the points of difference noncritical?* Advocates will discover that no two cases are identical in every respect. Even when two cases are similar in critical points, there will still be certain points of difference. Advocates need to determine whether the points of difference are critical or noncritical. This often depends on the context in which the comparison is made. For example, "identical" twins are usually similar in many respects, yet they have different fingerprints. This apparently minor difference might become critical and outweigh all similarities in a case in which the identity of one of the twins was the issue and fingerprint evidence was available. As another example one might point to a low level of malpractice suits against British physicians and the soaring rate of malpractice suits against American physicians and argue that British physicians must be providing much better medical care. In support of this one could argue that an injured British patient would be just as willing to sue as an injured American patient, so the only possible reason for the difference in the ratio of malpractice suits must be the quality of medical care. But there are critical differences in British and American law. In Britain the contingency fee is prohibited; in America it is almost the sole means of financing malpractice suits. Another critical difference is that in Britain all malpractice suits are held before a judge; in America almost all such suits are heard by juries. To defend an analogy, the advocate must be prepared to demonstrate that the similarities outweigh the differences in the cases compared and that the differences are not critical to the matter at issue.

4. *Is the reasoning cumulative?* An analogy is strengthened if it can be demonstrated that more than one comparison can be made in support of the conclusion. For instance, in defending the proposition that a city income tax would be advantageous in Gotham, the advocate would strengthen his or her case by making analogies not only between Gotham and Megalopolis, as mentioned, but also between Gotham and other comparable cities having city income taxes. If we were able to demonstrate that the similarities between the cities compared were critical and that the differences were noncritical, we would strengthen our case by using cumulative analogies.

5. *Are only literal analogies used as logical proof?* Advocates should remember that only literal analogies may be used to establish logical proof.

Figurative analogies are useful as illustrations, but they have no probative force. When confronted with a figurative analogy, advocates should be prepared to demonstrate its shortcomings as logical proof.

Reasoning by analogy may also be analyzed by using the elements of any argument. For example, assume the advocate claims that British medical care is better than American medical care, as the following diagram shows.

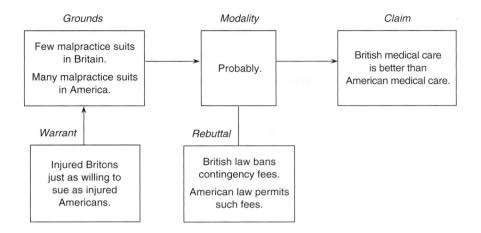

C. Causal Reasoning

In the process of **causal reasoning**, one infers that a certain factor (a cause) is a force that produces something else (an effect). This process can be represented as follows:

$$C \qquad\qquad\qquad E$$
$$\text{(inferred)} \longrightarrow \text{(known)}$$

The same process can be used in reverse. That is, if an effect is known to exist, it may be reasoned that it was produced by a cause. This process may be represented as follows:

$$C \qquad\qquad\qquad E$$
$$\text{(inferred)} \longleftarrow \text{(known)}$$

Causal reasoning, whether cause-to-effect or effect-to-cause, usually involves generalization. In using causal reasoning the advocate tries to show *why* the proposition is valid. The National Weather Service, for example, regularly reports the existence of low-pressure areas and other phenomena (causes) and predicts that we will have rain (an effect) tomorrow. The fact that the weather service is not always right emphasizes the point considered earlier: We often deal with matters in the realm of probability because we cannot establish certainty. Recall that in debates on the discontinuance of direct economic aid, some affirmative teams tried to show that this aid caused resentment among recipient countries. Continuing this argument, those advocates reasoned that if direct economic aid (the cause) were discontinued, then criticism (the effect) would also be eliminated. Conversely the proponents of such aid argued that it was producing desirable effects.

Advocates must, of course, recognize that many causes are at work in any problem under consideration; at the same time they should try to discern the practical, effective cause or causes in the matter at issue. Many debates on human affairs revolve around causal matters. The supporters of a national program of public work for the unemployed, for example, saw such a program as a cause that would produce many desirable effects, whereas opponents saw it as a cause that would produce many undesirable effects. Causal reasoning influences our thinking on personal matters as well. Students may go to college because they see a college education as a cause that they hope will produce desirable effects in later life.

The problem, as we apply the tests of causal reasoning, is to discern the significant, practical, and effective causes in the matter at issue. The following tests of reasoning may be applied either to cause-to-effect or to effect-to-cause reasoning:

1. *Is the alleged cause relevant to the effect described?* Some observers have claimed that an increase in sunspot activity causes a rise in the stock market. Is there a relevant cause-and-effect relationship between these two phenomena? Most competent authorities have not been able to discern it. One college debater recently informed her professor that she expected to win because it was snowing the day the tournament began and she had previously won a tournament when snow had fallen at the start of the event. Her remark was facetious, of course, because she recognized that there was no causal relationship between snowfall and winning a tournament. Yet this kind of reasoning has formed the basis of many superstitions. The superstition that breaking a mirror will cause seven years of bad luck, for example, is based on the assumption that a cause-to-effect relationship exists when in fact there is no such relationship. Unless and until a causal link can be established between an alleged cause and an alleged effect, one cannot hope to develop causal reasoning.

2. *Is this the sole or distinguishing causal factor?* Advocates should determine whether the alleged cause is the only causal factor in producing the effect under consideration or, if not, whether it is the distinguishing causal factor. In debates on the proposition "Resolved: That the federal government should significantly strengthen the regulation of mass media communication in the United States," some affirmative advocates used cause-to-effect reasoning to argue that television commercials for sugar-laden cereals caused children to eat these products, which in turn had deleterious effects on their health. In countering this line of reasoning, some negatives argued that children naturally liked sweet foods and would eat sugar-laden cereals even if commercials for these products were banned from television.

Some negative advocates extended their argument by claiming that, if television commercials for these products were banned, the manufacturers would simply shift their advertising to newspapers, magazines, and billboards (that is, media not affected by the affirmative's plan) and that these media would produce the same effect as the television commercials had. Thus the negative advocates claimed that television commercials were neither the sole nor the distinguishing causal factor in children's consumption of sugar-laden foods. The advocate should therefore be prepared to demonstrate that the alleged cause is the sole or distinguishing causal factor.

3. *Is there reasonable probability that no undesirable effect will result from this particular cause?* Usually a given cause will produce various effects in addition to the effect under consideration. Will these other effects be desirable, unimportant, or undesirable? If desirable, they will aid those advocating this particular cause; if unimportant, they will have no adverse impact; if undesirable, they may provide good reason for rejecting the arguments in support of this cause. In debates on the mass media proposition some negative teams developed a disadvantage argument by maintaining that, if the affirmative's plan of banning television commercials for sugar-laden cereals were put into effect, it would drastically reduce the demand for sugar and would cause widespread unemployment among sugar producers; the harms resulting from this unemployment would far outweigh any minor harms related to sugar consumption.

   Some readers of this book can verify the following example from their own experience: Penicillin is a very effective cause for producing certain very desirable effects in some types of illness. Yet in some persons penicillin causes effects that are so undesirable that its use is contraindicated. The possible good effects are outweighed by the undesirable effects. Thus advocates have to determine what other effects will be produced by the cause they speak for and be prepared to demonstrate, at the least, that these other effects are not undesirable.

4. *Is there a counteracting cause?* When an effect that will take place in the future is the factor under consideration, it is necessary to determine that no counteracting cause, or causes, will offset the alleged effect. In debating the mass media proposition, some affirmative teams argued for a ban on the sale of pornographic material. Some negative teams developed a series of plan-will-not-achieve-claimed-advantage arguments by claiming that the sale of pornographic materials would continue virtually undiminished under the affirmative's plan because of certain counteracting causes. Specifically they argued that (1) the courts would find it difficult or impossible to define pornography; (2) the affirmative's figures on the sales of pornographic material proved that a vast market exists for such materials, which meant that the criminal elements that produced it would have a strong incentive to circumvent the law; and (3) prosecutors would be reluctant to prosecute pornography cases, because prosecuting cases with little hope of obtaining convictions would be a waste of tax dollars. Thus advocates must be prepared to demonstrate that other causes at work in the situation will not counter the effect they claim a certain cause will produce.

5. *Is the cause capable of producing the effect?* Often various factors occur prior to a given event, yet these factors cannot be considered as causing the effect until it can be established that they are capable of producing it. For example, did the assassination of Archduke Ferdinand at Sarajevo cause World War I? Although this incident did immediately precede the outbreak of that war, assassination of members of European royalty was not an unusual occurrence, and such occurrences typically did not cause wars. Most thoughtful

historians do not regard this assassination as a cause capable of producing World War I, and so they assign other causes to that war.

In debating the "guaranteed employment opportunities" proposition, many affirmative teams argued that their plan would create jobs, thus guaranteeing the employment opportunities called for in the resolution. Of course, they had to prove that their plan was capable of generating several million new jobs.

When Geraldine Ferraro became the Democratic vice presidential nominee in 1984, many supporters believed that her presence on the ticket would cause large numbers of women to vote Democratic. This causal reasoning turned out to be faulty; President Reagan won a majority of the women's votes.

In debating, as in politics and many other contexts, a plan is often proposed as a cause that will produce a particular desired effect.

6. *Is the cause necessary and sufficient?* A *necessary* cause is a condition that is essential to producing the effect. Oxygen, for instance, is a necessary condition for fire. Oxygen alone will not cause fire, but we cannot have fire without it. Once we have identified the necessary condition for an event, we can *prevent* that event from occurring by removing one of the necessary conditions. In debating the "curtail executive control of foreign policy" proposition, some affirmatives argued that, when exposed *necessarily,* covert operations caused harm to U.S. foreign policy, and so they advocated prohibiting the executive from carrying out covert operations.

    A *sufficient* cause is a condition that automatically produces the effect. As the inventor of the guillotine well knew, decapitation is sufficient cause for death. The difference between a necessary and a sufficient cause is that, although a necessary condition must be present, it will not by itself produce the effect. The sufficient cause is by itself enough to produce the effect. Most often a sufficient cause is a collection of necessary causes all present at one time and place. For instance, oxygen, a combustible material, and the combustion point are all necessary conditions to fire. Together, all three constitute the sufficient cause for a fire. Once we have identified the sufficient conditions for an event, we can *produce* the event by bringing the sufficient conditions together. In debating the comprehensive health care proposition, some affirmatives argued that, if the government provided free medical care, trained more physicians and other medical personnel, and built more medical facilities, the *necessary* result would be better health for all citizens.

7. *How does a new cause affect the system?* In debates on the comprehensive health care proposition, some affirmatives claimed as a need better medical care for slum residents and cited tragic cases of children bitten by rats as a need for providing medical care in slums. Some negatives countered by arguing that there would be little point in treating the rat bite and then sending the child back to the slum home to be bitten again by another rat. Instead of spending the money on medical care, they argued, it would be better spent on pro-

viding better housing, better food, and other improved conditions for slum dwellers.

Causal reasoning may also be analyzed by using the elements of an argument. For instance, assume the advocate claims that the cost-of-living index will go up because of a recent increase in the cost of meat, as the diagram indicates.

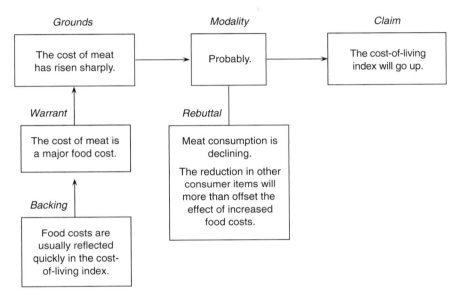

D. Reasoning by Sign

The process of **reasoning by sign** consists of inferring relationships or correlations between two variables. Here one argues that two variables are so closely related that the presence or absence of one may be taken as an indication of the presence or absence of the other.

Reasoning by sign involves reasoning by analogy, by example, or from effect to effect as the advocate seeks to show that a proposition is valid. (In causal reasoning, you will remember, the advocate seeks to show *why* a proposition is valid.) We use reasoning by sign when we note that the leaves are falling from the trees and take this as a sign that winter is coming. The attribute is a part or a characteristic of the substance or totality with which we are concerned. In reasoning by sign the advocate may reason either from the attribute to the substance or from the substance to the attribute.

If one variable may be taken as a sign of another, the relationship between the variables is *reciprocal*. The relationship between the variables is *nonreciprocal* when one variable may be taken as a sign of the other but the second variable is not a reliable sign of the first. For instance, if a person is president of the United States, we may take this as a sign that he or she is at least 35 years old.

Obviously, we cannot take the fact that a person is 35 years old as a sign that he or she is president of the United States.

In debating the proposition "Resolved: That the United States should extend diplomatic recognition to Cuba," some negative advocates argued that we should not adopt the proposition because diplomatic recognition was a sign of approval of the government in question.

The following questions serve as tests of reasoning by sign:

1. *Is the alleged substance relevant to the attribute described?* It is necessary to determine whether there really is a sign relationship between the substance and the attribute under consideration. Some affirmative advocates, in meeting the argument that diplomatic recognition would be a sign of approval, maintained that diplomatic recognition is not a sign of approval. In support of this, they pointed out that the United States extended diplomatic recognition to many regimes that followed policies we did not approve of; they maintained that no sign relationship exists between approval of a government and diplomatic recognition of that government. Unless and until advocates can demonstrate that a sign relationship exists between the substance and the attribute under consideration, they cannot develop sign reasoning.

2. *Is the relationship between substance and attribute inherent?* Advocates have to determine whether the relationship between substance and attribute is inherent or merely incidental. A political commentator once noted that the Cubans greatly increased the number of attachés at their embassy in a certain Central American country. He took this action as a sign that the Cubans were planning to increase their aid to forces seeking to overthrow that country's government. But was the relationship inherent? On some occasions this type of action has been a sign of an attempt to overthrow a government. More often, however, it has merely meant an increased propaganda or trade campaign.

3. *Is there a counterfactor that disrupts the relationship between substance and attribute?* It is necessary to determine that no counterfactor or factors disrupt the relationship. An increase in the number of attachés that one country assigns to another may under some conditions be a sign that the country increasing its embassy personnel plans to invade. For example, when the United States expanded its embassy in the People's Republic of China, no one took this as a sign that the United States planned to overthrow the People's Republic; too many counterfactors disrupted that sign relationship.

4. *Is the sign reasoning cumulative?* Reasoning by sign is strengthened by a demonstration that more than one sign relationship can be presented in support of the conclusion. An upturn in durable-goods orders might be a sign that an economic slump is ending. But this sign by itself is a relatively weak indicator. If other signs can be found—such as increases in a number of indicators (productivity rate, orders for plants and equipment, orders for consumer goods, and new residential building permits)—the accumulation of a series of signs may add up to a conclusion with a high degree of cogency.

Sign reasoning can also be analyzed by using the elements of any argument. For instance, assume the advocate claims that the economy will improve in the next few months, as in the accompanying diagram.

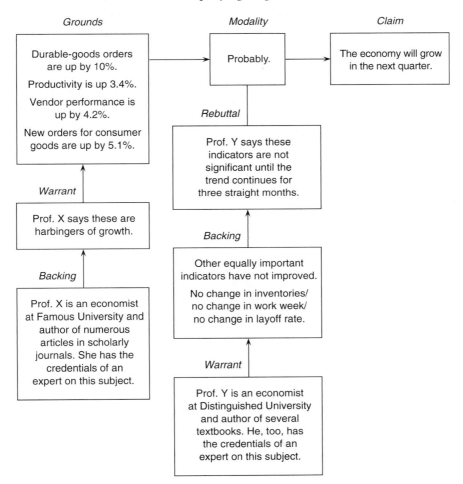

EXERCISES

1. Prepare an argument for presentation in class in which you develop one closely reasoned argument. You may wish to present one of the evidenced arguments developed in Chapter 5. Other members of the class will be asked to apply the tests of reasoning to your argument to see whether it is valid.

2. Bring to class examples of each of the four types of reasoning considered in this chapter. Draw your examples from newspapers or newsmagazines published within the past week. Apply the appropriate tests of reasoning to each example.

10

Obstacles to Clear Thinking

Clear thinking is essential to all intelligent decision making. From the moment we begin to explore a problem until the end of the final debate on that problem, we have to constantly be on guard against obstacles to clear thinking. The obvious obstacles are readily detected. One type of obstacle, however, that is more subtle, and hence more deceptive, is called a fallacy. At first glance the error, unreasonableness, or falseness of the fallacy is not apparent, for the statement has the appearance of truth or reasonableness. Richard Whately defined a **fallacy** as "any unsound mode of arguing, which appears to demand our conviction, and to be decisive of the question in hand, when in fairness it is not."[1]

Fallacies are usually easy to detect in isolation, but woven into the context of an argument, they may go unnoticed unless we are on guard. Debate gives those who render decisions one of the strongest protections against fallacies. Not only do they have the opportunity to detect fallacies themselves, but there is the added safeguard that the opposing advocates are motivated to point out fallacies in one another's cases.

Fallacies may be used accidentally or deliberately. Some advocates intentionally introduce fallacies into their arguments to exploit their listeners or readers and secure an unfair decision. Contemporary examples of apparently deliberate use of fallacies can be found in any international crisis as the hostile parties create propaganda to sway world opinion. Much of this propaganda is prepared by persons intelligent enough to recognize the fallacies they are using. But some fallacies may be introduced into arguments unintentionally by well-meaning people. Advocates must be alert for obstacles to clear thinking at all times and from all sources.

For convenience fallacies are classified here under various groupings and subgroupings. In actual argument fallacies often are interwoven, and a fallacious argument may be a complex of several fallacies. In exposing fallacies in our opponent's case, we will do little good by exclaiming, "Aha! In his last statement my opponent committed the fallacies of circulus in probando and per negationem consequentiae!" Although we may wish to identify and classify a fallacy for our own convenience, our task in the debate is not to name the fallacy but to show those who render the decision how or why the

---

1. Richard Whately, *Elements of Logic* (Boston: James Munroe, 1848), p. 143.

Miniglossary

Ambiguity   Arises when the meaning of a word, phrase, or passage may reasonably be interpreted in two or more ways.

Appeal to ignorance   Advocates maintain that something cannot be so because they, or the audience, have never heard of it.

Appeal to tradition   Support for an argument is based on customary and historical support for the argument.

Arguing in a circle   Occurs when one assumes as a premise for the argument the very conclusion one intends to prove.

Bandwagon   Support for an argument based on its popular support by a large number of people.

Fallacy   Any unsound mode of arguing, which appears to demand our conviction, and to be decisive of the question at hand, when in fairness it is not.

Denying a valid conclusion   Advocate admits or cannot refute the premises of an opponent, yet denies the conclusion that logically follows from these premises.

Grammatical structure   Reasoning based on meaning distorted by incorrect or imprecise grammar.

Hasty generalization   Argument from example in which the inference, or movement from specific example to generalization, is made on the basis of insufficient evidence, either nonrepresentative example(s) or an insufficient number of examples.

Incomplete comparison   A type of grammatical fallacy in which the point of comparison is missing or not clearly identified.

Irrelevancy   An argument in which proof is carried beyond its reasonable limits, and therefore does not pertain to the claim.

Loaded language   Use of emotionally charged words in an effort to establish a conclusion without proof.

Non sequitur   A conclusion that does not follow from the premises or evidence on which it is based.

Popular appeal   An advocate tries to win support for a position by maintaining that he or she is merely an "ordinary person" like everyone else.

Post hoc   Assuming a causal relationship where none has been proved.

Pseudoargument   Fallacy created (by accident or design) by distortion, confusion, manipulation, or avoidance of the matters at issue or by substitution of matters not germane to the issue.

Pseudoquestion   An advocate asks an unanswerable, "loaded," or ambiguous question or series of questions, or asks a question based on a false assumption.

> Miniglossary (Continued)
>
> **Repeated assertion** An argument is presented as proof for itself.
>
> **Special pleading** Urging that an exception be made to an accepted line of reasoning.
>
> **Straw argument** Setting up an issue merely so it can be knocked down.
>
> **Structured response** A pattern is established leading to an improper or unsupported conclusion.
>
> **Verbalism** The abundant use of words without conveying much meaning.

matter in question is fallacious. This task is complicated by the fact that fallacies are often field dependent—that is, they must be considered in context. As Stephen Toulmin points out, "Most disturbingly to some people, arguments that are fallacious in one context may prove to be quite solid in another context. So we shall not be able to identify any intrinsically fallacious forms of argument; instead we shall try to indicate why certain kinds of argument are, in practice, fallacious in this or that kind of context."[2]

One helpful way of exposing fallacies is to focus attention on the warrants (considered in Chapter 8) and see whether the expressed or implied warrant justifies the claim made.

Some hold that there is no such thing as a fallacy; rather there is a failure to apply the appropriate tests of evidence or reasoning or language. In this chapter the conventional fallacies are discussed and the appropriate tests recommended. The use of the concept of fallacies provides us with a means of double-checking our arguments and those of our opponents.

I. FALLACIES OF EVIDENCE

Theater or film advertisements sometimes provide examples of fallacious use of evidence. One critic wrote of a Broadway musical:

> *Interlude* represented an inept effort to make a dull story palatable by adding music. Unfortunately one brilliantly executed dance number in the first act was not enough to keep the show moving. Lavish costuming could not overcome the basic fact that the female lead simply does not have an adequate voice for the theater. The comedy routines showed brief flashes of inspiration, but they could not relieve the overall pedestrian pace of *Interlude*.

The newspaper advertisements quoted the reviewer as saying, "*Interlude* ... brilliantly executed ... lavish costuming ... flashes of inspiration." We can guard against this kind of fallacious use of evidence by asking, "Is any evidence omitted?"

2. Stephen Toulmin, Richard Rieke, and Allan Janik, *An Introduction to Reasoning* (New York: Macmillan, 1979), p. 157.

Fallacies of Evidence

- An unsupported assertion is often presented as if it were a complete argument
- Violation of the tests of evidence discussed in Chapter 7 reveal fallacies of evidence

---

One of the most common fallacies of evidence is the use of the unsupported assertion. Here the speaker offers no evidence to support a statement; he or she asks us to assume that something is so merely because he or she says it is so. The high-pressure used car salesperson may tell a customer, "This car is in perfect condition. You'd better buy it now before someone else gets it." The prudent buyer would not accept this unsupported assertion but would look for evidence of the condition of the car. We can guard against this fallacy by asking, "Is the contention an unsupported assertion?"

The tests of evidence discussed in Chapter 7 can help us identify other fallacies of evidence.

II. FALLACIES OF REASONING

Not only must we guard against fallacies of evidence, but we must also be alert to possible fallacies in each of the types of reasoning we considered earlier.

A. Example

A speaker who maintained that the public schools are failing to educate our children offered as proof the following examples of their "failure":

> Last year 23 percent of the graduates of North High School who went to Omega State University were required to take remedial English; 37 percent of the North High graduates at Omega were required to take remedial math. I could cite dozens more examples of the failure of our schools, but this is enough to prove that we need a statewide system of competency testing before we grant high school diplomas.

Are you willing to accept this as an accurate picture of conditions statewide? Are the North High students typical of all students in the state? Are the North High students who go to Omega State typical of North High students in general? We can quickly expose this fallacy by asking, "Are the examples given typical of the whole?"

Another common fallacy of reasoning by example is committed by the person who knows two or three motorcyclists who have criminal records and concludes, "They're all drug dealers." Here one should ask, "Have sufficient examples been given?" A **hasty generalization** based on insufficient evidence often leads to unsound conclusions that will not be accepted by those who render the decision.

Additional questions that can help us guard against other fallacies of reasoning by example can be found in the Chapter 9 section "Reasoning by Example."

B. Analogy

A Russian leader once told an American visitor: "With the death of communism, Russia is now completely democratic. We even have competing candidates running for some offices." The American exposed the fallacy in this analogy by replying, "You have started toward democracy, but you still have a way to go. In America we have at least two well-established political parties and we are ruled by laws, not by decrees." In this case the American applied the question, "Are there critical differences in the factors compared?" Her answer pointed out two essential differences between American and Russian governments.

Additional questions that will help us detect fallacies in reasoning by analogy can be found in the Chapter 9 section "Reasoning by Analogy."

C. Cause

Many causal factors are at work in most situations. For example, following the disastrous 1989 oil spill in Prince William Sound, Alaska, oil prices rose dramatically nationwide. Some consumer advocates were quick to charge that the price increase was excessive. Industry experts, however, pointed out that the price increase was only partially related to the costs of cleaning up the spill; OPEC had earlier decided to decrease oil production, and new EPA regulations had just come into effect tightening fuel-grade requirements. Was the price increase due solely to the costs of cleaning up the oil spill, or was it caused by a combination of factors? Fallacies of this type may be detected by asking, "Is a partial causal relationship treated as the sole or distinguishing causal factor?"

Additional questions we may ask to expose fallacies of causal reasoning are found in the Chapter 9 section "Causal Reasoning."

D. Sign

The ability to use reasoning by sign effectively is an essential part of the work of all who seek rational decisions. The physician, for example, must constantly be on guard against fallacies in interpreting signs. In diagnosing a case, the neurologist may look for the Babinski sign, a certain type of movement of the toes after stimulus. This sign is apparently inherent in certain types of illness and, when found in adults, is taken as an indication of the presence of disease of the corticospinal pathway. The Rossolimo sign, a certain type of flexing of the toes after stimulus, indicates disease of the pyramidal tract. It is a much less reliable sign, however, because it is sometimes absent when the disease is present and it

---

Fallacies of Reasoning

For each, the fallacy represents a violation of the tests identified for each category in Chapter 9.

- Example
- Analogy
- Cause
- Sign

---

is sometimes found in healthy individuals. All who use reasoning by sign should be on guard against fallacies that might lead to false conclusions.

Questions that can help us detect fallacies in reasoning by sign in argumentative situations are considered in the Chapter 9 section "Reasoning by Sign."

III. FALLACIES OF LANGUAGE

The fallacies of language are often interwoven with other fallacies. Some of the more common fallacies of language that advocates should guard against are discussed here.

A. Ambiguity

Ambiguity arises when the meaning of a word, phrase, or passage may reasonably be interpreted in two or more ways. For example, what does a speaker mean when saying, "I favor the American way of doing things"? A candidate for public office once campaigned on the slogan of "more teamwork in government." "Teamwork" may sound good, but what does it mean? A government official recently testified that he had not received any "improper" gifts from a constituent and that he had not made any "unreasonable" requests of governmental agencies on behalf of this constituent. His opponents viewed these same activities as "corruption" and "influence." Such terms as *feminist, family values, egalitarian, multicultural, liberal, conservative,* and *middle of the road* have so many different meanings to so many different people that they are often ambiguous.

B. Verbalism

Verbalism refers to the abundant use of words without conveying much meaning. There is a story of a politician who, seeking to avoid taking a position on gun control legislation, said, "The question is not a simple one. Indeed anyone could say—and they would be more or less right—that it is complex. In the second instance there is the First Amendment to the Constitution. I mean in the first place there is the Second Amendment—or whatever. This is perfectly clear until you get to the part that isn't. About the militia that is. And I wonder what the Founding Fathers would say about that? And why it isn't. When I was a boy my father took me hunting and fishing. And I was duck hunting only last month. I think fathers should take their sons hunting unless they have daughters. And more recently the Tenth Amendment business. And, of course, daughters should go hunting too. And we need to look at this thing from the law and order point of view as well also."

C. Loaded Language

Loaded language provides many possibilities for obstacles to clear thinking. **Loaded language** involves the use of emotionally charged words in an effort to establish a conclusion without proof. In a recent political campaign one candidate declared, "The time has come to throw this do-nothing, corruption-riddled administration out of office." Obviously such an administration should be thrown out of office, but the mere use of these labels did nothing to prove that the administration was guilty of either of the charges.

Loaded language, or name-calling, is too often used in political campaigns. The *New York Times* reported this example:

> What's in a name? When it comes to winning elections, it could be everything. In fact, here is some choice advice for candidates about names to call your campaign opponents and yourselves.
>
> Call your opponent a "sick, pathetic, liberal, incompetent, tax-spending traitor." Reserve for yourself the label "humane, visionary, confident, candid, hard-working reformer."
>
> Saying good things about yourself and bad things about your opponent may seem basic, in life as much as in politics. But now, this specific advice on which names to use has been drawn up and a list is being distributed to Republican state legislative candidates across the country.[3]

A more creative example of loaded language was reported from a Florida senatorial campaign by *Time* magazine:

> [George] Smathers used fancy language to convey sinister meanings to benighted rural listeners. "Are you aware that Claude Pepper is known all over Washington as a shameless extrovert? Not only that, but this man is reliably reported to practice nepotism with his sister-in-law, and he has a sister who was once a thespian in wicked New York. Worst of all, it is an established fact that Mr. Pepper before his marriage habitually practiced celibacy."

Pepper was defeated by 67,000 votes. "On election night people came up to our house in cars, shouting obscenities, cheering the fact that I had been defeated," Pepper recalls. "They wanted to destroy me and just about did."[4]

---

3. *New York Times,* national edition, Sept. 9, 1990, p. 18.
4. *Time,* Apr. 25, 1983, p. 29.

Fallacies of Language

- Ambiguity
- Verbalism
- Loaded Language
- Grammatical Structure

D. Grammatical Structure

Grammatical structure can, and often does, alter the meaning of a sentence. At a recent Republican convention the first draft of the party platform contained the sentence "[Republicans] oppose any attempts to increase taxes which would harm the recovery and reverse the trend to restoring control of the economy to individual Americans." A harmless bit of political rhetoric; of course everyone would oppose *harmful* tax increases, yet the door was left open to *unharmful* tax increases. The party's conservatives fought "The Battle of the Comma" and changed the sentence to read, "oppose any attempts to increase taxes, which would harm the recovery and reverse the trend to restoring control of the economy to individual Americans." The sentence, as punctuated with the comma, held *all* tax increases to be harmful. When the sentence was read aloud, the presence or absence of a pause would indicate the presence or absence of a comma.

    Incomplete comparison is another grammatical fallacy—for example, "The present foreign aid program is unquestionably more effective." More effective than what? The advocate must guard against these hazards of grammatical usage.

IV. FALLACIES OF PSEUDOARGUMENTS

Pseudoarguments are fallacies created (by accident or design) by distortion, confusion, manipulation, or avoidance of the matters at issue or by substitution of matters not germane to the issue. Some common fallacies are considered here.

A. Offering Irrelevancy

The fallacy of **irrelevancy** carries an argument beyond its reasonable limits. For example, some opponents of "right-to-work" laws argued that these laws did not provide jobs for the unemployed. These laws were intended not to provide jobs but merely to eliminate the requirement of union membership as a condition of employment. It would be just as reasonable to criticize the polio vaccine because it does not prevent pneumonia.

B. Arguing in a Circle

The fallacy of **arguing in a circle** occurs when one assumes as a premise for the argument the very conclusion one intends to prove. For example, consider this exchange: "William Shakespeare is a greater writer than Danielle Steel because people with good taste in literature prefer Shakespeare." "How do you know who has good taste in literature?" "Why, that's simple; people with good taste in literature prefer Shakespeare to Danielle Steel." Even though Shakespeare is undoubtedly a greater writer than Steel, this circular argument does not prove the claim.

C. Ignoring the Issue

In a debate on the proposition "Resolved: That the United States federal government should significantly increase exploration and/or development of space beyond the Earth's mesosphere," an affirmative team proposed a particularly weak and ineffective plan. In a thoughtful, closely reasoned refutation, the negative demonstrated that the affirmative's plan was completely unworkable. In their remaining speeches the affirmative speakers completely ignored the issue of the workability of their plan; instead they spent their time claiming the great advantages that would come from their plan. By ignoring the issue, the affirmative lost this debate.

D. Baiting an Opponent

Sometimes advocates will bait their opponents by insulting them, attacking them personally, criticizing their friends, or doing anything that will cause them to lose their tempers. Once advocates lose their cool, they are likely to lose control of the argument and make reckless statements that will undermine their case. Advocates can defend themselves against this kind of baiting only by holding their tempers during the argument.

E. Repeating an Assertion

The fallacy of **repeated assertion** occurs when an argument is repeated, with the repetition treated as proof. In a debate on guaranteed annual wages, members of the affirmative team stated repeatedly, without offering any proof, that American working persons need a guaranteed annual wage. A negative speaker, exposing this fallacy, pointed out that saying something three times did not make it true. This fallacy is not always so easily brushed off, however. Adolf Hitler developed to a fine art the technique of repeating a "big lie" so often that many came to believe it.

F. Structuring a Response

The fallacy of **structured response** is often found in cross-examinations or any other situation in which the advocate has an opportunity to ask a series of questions. The advocate first asks a series of unimportant questions, which the respondent must answer in a predetermined way, until the pattern of a response has been established. Then the critical question is asked. An old routine of insurance salespersons, for example, goes something like this: "You love your spouse, don't you?" "You love your children, don't you?" "You want your children to go to college, don't you?" "You want your family to continue to live in this lovely house, don't you?" "If something should happen to you, you want your family to be provided for, don't you?" "You would still want your children to go to college, wouldn't you?" "You want to provide protection for them, don't you?" "To be safe, don't you feel you should sign your name on this routine form today?" Any prospects who have been lulled into a series of "yes" responses may find that they have signed an application for insurance without fully realizing the commitment they have undertaken.

The structured response was used effectively by Senator Edward Kennedy at the 1988 Democratic Convention, when after each recitation of supposed Republican shortcomings he asked, "Where was George?" (The Republican candidate, Vice President George Bush, had stated that he was not present when certain controversial decisions were made.) The partisan audience quickly picked up the theme and chanted "Where was George?" along with Kennedy as he continued the list.

G. Special Pleading

The fallacy of **special pleading** occurs when advocates accept a line of reasoning and its conclusions but urge a special exception for their case. Examples of special pleading are sometimes found in Congress. In the early 1990s, for instance, there was tremendous pressure on Congress to produce a balanced budget. Virtually all members of Congress favored a balanced budget—but not, of course, at the expense of cutting from the budget any items of interest to their constituents.

H. Substituting the Person for the Argument

This fallacy involves attempting to have an argument accepted or rejected not because of any merit or defect intrinsic to the argument but because of the character of the person advancing the argument. For example, some people said that compulsory wage and price controls should be rejected because Socialists favored them. Conversely it may be argued that because someone is good in some respect, his or her arguments on some other matter must also be good. To counter the prosecution's claim that his or her client shot a business rival, the defense attorney in a murder trial might try to present the client as, for example, a kindly man who helps old ladies across busy streets, who is good to his wife and his children, who gives generously to charities, and who sings in the church choir. Traditionally the country rallies behind the president at the time of an international crisis, the theme being, "We must support the president during this crisis." Thus Roosevelt during World War II, Kennedy at the time of the Cuban missile crisis, and Bush during Operation Desert Storm enjoyed great initial support for policies that later came under criticism. President George W. Bush relied on such support when he began his presidential reelection campaign in 2004 with spot advertisements reminding voters of the ongoing war on terrorism by presenting images of the twin towers of the World Trade Center.

Note that an argument about a person is legitimate when the character of the person is intrinsic to the matter at issue. Evidence that John Doe was a child molester would be legitimate if the issue were his employment as a teacher. Evidence that Jane Roe was a convicted embezzler would be germane if the issue were her employment as an accountant. These examples emphasize the point made at the beginning of this chapter that fallacies are often field dependent. Doe's sexual activities or Roe's criminal record are critical, legitimate evidence in the context considered here; they would be irrelevant and thus fallacious in many other contexts.

I. Substituting Bombast for Argument

When no evidence or reasoning is available, advocates may sometimes attempt to support their argument by sheer noise and histrionics. In a debate on the mass media proposition, for example, a novice debater inserted in her affirmative case the impromptu claim that the federal government had a moral obligation to mandate a massive increase in the number of hours of closed-captioned programs that television stations provided for the hearing-impaired. The next negative speaker, in cross-examination, asked her to define moral obligation. Caught in her error, she replied with more hope than confidence, "My partner will define the term in the second affirmative." The second affirmative speaker, now on the spot, frantically searched his evidence files but was unable to find a single scrap of evidence defining moral obligation or any notion of lines of argument that he could use to support his colleague's claim. There may have been some arguments to support this assertion, but they were not available at that moment. In desperation he decided to bluff his way by *bombast*. In a voice seemingly choked with emotion, he said, "The negative has asked us to define 'moral obligation.'" Eyes flashing with apparent righteous indignation, he glared at his opponents: "We all know what 'moral obligation' is!" Pounding the lectern with his fist, he cried, "A 'moral obligation' is a 'moral obligation'!" The negative, cowed by these histrionics, never dared mention the subject again. Had the next negative speaker, in sharp contrast to the bombast of the affirmative, calmly and thoughtfully pointed out the absurdity of the affirmative's definition, he might well have punctured the balloon the affirmative speaker had used so effectively to conceal his lack of an adequate answer to a reasonable question.

J. Denying a Valid Conclusion

The fallacy of **denying a valid conclusion** occurs when an advocate admits or cannot refute the premises of an opponent yet denies the conclusion that logically follows from these premises. For example, in a debate on federal aid for higher education, one negative team admitted that more money was needed for education and that the money must come from either the federal government or state and local governments. Furthermore the negative was unable to refute the affirmative's argument that many state and local governments could not increase their aid to education. The logical conclusion from the admitted and unrefuted premises was that the federal government was the only source of the needed money, but the negative attempted to deny this valid conclusion. The negative team's error was twofold. They admitted too much and failed to advance arguments they could have used. Other negative teams successfully argued that state and local governments could increase their aid to education and that the dangers of federal control outweighed the benefits of federal funds.

K. Using Popular Appeal

The fallacy of **popular appeal** occurs when an advocate tries to win support for a position by maintaining that he or she is merely an "ordinary person" like everyone else. This approach was popular with rural politicians at the turn of the nineteenth century and is still common today. During the 1988 presidential campaign Michael Dukakis liked to contrast his "son of immigrants" background with the "preppy" image of Vice President George Bush by proclaiming, "My friends, there is only one country on the face of the earth where this son of immigrants could aspire to be the president of the United States, and that's the United States." As the governor of Massachusetts, the son of a millionaire physician, and a Harvard Law School graduate himself, Dukakis was, of course, not exactly a typical son of immigrants. And one might be forgiven for asking where else but the United States could one reasonably aspire to be president of the United States?

Another aspect of the same fallacy is the **bandwagon** technique—arguing that something should be done because "everybody" is doing it. In many political campaigns both candidates will proclaim their confidence that they will win by an overwhelming majority. They hope by this method to induce many undecided voters to vote for them simply because they are going to win anyway. Only one brand of cigarettes or soap or any other type of product can be the most popular, yet note the number of companies that claim their product is the most popular. They hope their product will be bought because "everyone" is buying it.

L. Offering a "Straw Argument"

The fallacy of the **straw argument** occurs when advocates set up an issue merely so they can knock it down. Sometimes they attack a minor argument of their opponents and claim that they have refuted the whole case. Or they might refute an argument their opponents did not advance and claim that they have thus refuted their opponents' position.

An example of this fallacy occurred in a debate on the proposition "Resolved: That the federal government should implement a program which guarantees employment opportunities for all United States citizens in the labor force."

Many affirmative plans were vulnerable to attack on the grounds that the plan to regulate businesses would be burdensome and would negatively affect those businesses. One affirmative team prepared for such an argument by carefully designing its plan to include tax credits to decrease the burden on businesses. A negative team, meeting this affirmative, failed to note the tax credits in the affirmative plan and ran its own prepared argument briefs attacking the plan on the basis of the increased cost of regulations. This was an attack on a "straw argument," which the affirmative quickly pointed out and the judge duly noted.

M. Appealing to Ignorance

The fallacy of the **appeal to ignorance** occurs when advocates maintain that something cannot be so because they, or the audience, have never heard of it. Uninformed persons, for example, at one time declared the telephone to be an impractical gadget because "Everyone knows you can't talk over wires." Another example of the appeal to ignorance occurred in a debate on guaranteed employment opportunities. The concept of "cyclical fluctuations" was important in many of these debates. One freshman debater, who had not yet taken his first economics course, had never heard of the term when he met it in an early-season debate. Faced with an unknown concept, he stoutly maintained, "Well I never heard of, ah, uh, those, err, fluctuations, and I certainly don't think they influence our economy." The appeal to ignorance did not work in this instance—the judge had heard of cyclical fluctuations.

Unfortunately the appeal to ignorance is sometimes successful with an uninformed audience. The defense against this fallacy is to provide the audience with the knowledge necessary to understand the argument. But this is not always easy. Before the moon landings, it would have been almost impossible to refute the argument "Of course, you can't get to the moon, that's science fiction" before a popular audience without giving a lengthy technical explanation. In fact the explanation would have probably had to be so lengthy and technical that it could not be presented within the available time.

N. Asking Pseudoquestions

The fallacy of the **pseudoquestion** occurs when an advocate asks an unanswerable, "loaded," or ambiguous question; or a question based on a false assumption; or so many questions that an opponent cannot possibly answer them adequately within the available time. An example of this type of question is, "Have you stopped cheating on examinations?"

Another example of this type of fallacy occurred when a second negative speaker posed a series of 11 pseudoquestions about the plan. If the first affirmative rebuttalist had attempted to answer them, she would never have had the time to get to the "case-side" arguments and probably would have lost the debate. Rather than trying to answer the questions individually, she grouped them: "The first seven questions have to do with funding; please group them and note that our funding plank clearly provides.... The next four questions have to do with enforcement; please consider these together and note that our enforcement plank provides for...." In this way she was able to dispose of the 11 questions quickly and effectively and thus meet her responsibilities for defending the plan and the case.

O. Appealing to Tradition

The fallacy of the **appeal to tradition** occurs when the advocate maintains that we should follow a certain policy because we have "always" done things that way. Thus a negative speaker, in a debate on a proposition on comprehensive medical care for all citizens argued against the affirmative's plan by saying it was unnecessary because physicians and hospitals had always provided free medical care for the indigent. The fact that something has been a long-standing tradition does not prove its merit. As a famous senator once pointed out, murder and larceny have been practiced in all nations in all ages, but this does not make either murder or larceny meritorious.

P. Posing a Non Sequitur

Thus far we have avoided the Latin names of fallacies, but the **non sequitur**— which is simply a conclusion that does not follow from the premises or evidence on which it is based—is best known by its Latin designation. In the medical care debates, some affirmatives cited evidence showing that many people could not afford medical care and then argued that the government should provide free medical care for all citizens. In other debates some negatives argued that the affirmative plan would be administered by a government agency and so would be inefficient. Bureaucracy does have a bad reputation—but it does not follow that all government agencies are inefficient.

Q. Arguing Post Hoc

This title is shorthand for the longer Latin phrase *post hoc ergo propter hoc,* meaning "after the fact, therefore because of the fact." The fallacy of **post hoc** lies in assuming a causal relationship where none has been proved. American history provides one of the best known illustrations of this fallacy. Every American president elected at a 20-year interval since 1840 died in office (Harrison, Lincoln, Garfield, McKinley, Harding, Roosevelt, and Kennedy) until Ronald Reagan broke the morbid chain of coincidence. A remarkable coincidence, surely, but their election in a particular year was hardly the cause of their death.

Obviously there are many fallacies, and the possibility of their being introduced into arguments is almost unlimited. As advocates, we must constantly be on guard against these obstacles to clear thinking, not only in statements of others but in our own statements as well.

Fallacies of Pseudoarguments

- Offering irrelevancy
- Arguing in a circle
- Ignoring the issue
- Baiting an opponent
- Repeating an assertion
- Structuring a response
- Special pleading
- Substituting the person for the argument
- Substituting bombast for argument
- Denying a valid conclusion
- Using popular appeal
- Offering a "straw argument"
- Appealing to ignorance
- Asking pseudoquestions
- Appealing to tradition
- Posing a non sequitur
- Arguing post hoc

EXERCISES

1. Find the full text of a recent speech by a public figure. Find the speech on-line and listen to it as you follow along with the text. You may also wish to compare this with excerpts of the speech printed in the newspapers or newsmagazines. Do you find a fallacy of omitted evidence? Remember, there is a big difference between an accurate condensation and the fallacy of omitted evidence.

2. Analyze some newspapers and newsmagazines published within the last month. Locate five fallacies in the editorial or news sections of these publications, and locate five fallacies in the advertisements.

3. Some of the following statements contain one or more fallacies. List the fallacies you discover in these statements.

   a. The Championship Tally and Sharmin Kennels use Wags Dog Food exclusively. Get Wags Dog Food for your dog today!

   b. Canada has nationalized its health care. The same system would work well in the United States.

   c. Gun control laws are bad; that's how Hitler came into power in Germany.

   d. *Q:* What will be the cost of this plan during its first five years of operation? *A:* Our country owes a debt of gratitude to the farmer. The farmer represents the American way of life. Farmers are good people. They live close to the soil. They have not come under the influence of Socialist union bosses or Eastern intellectuals.

    e.   Why is it that the Democratic party always leads this country into war and the Republican party always leads us into depression?

4.   Create or find an example of each type of fallacy identified in the chapter.

11

Requirements of the Case

When Zenia and Alex began to prepare for the upcoming debate season, one of their primary jobs was to develop their **case**, defined as the operational strategy drafted by the advocates on one side of the proposition for the purpose of coordinating their reasoning and evidence and presenting their position with maximum effectiveness. Their first task is to develop their affirmative case area, providing positive support for the proposition. The proposition not only provided the parameters within which they could select and develop a case but also offered many case opportunities. After analyzing and exploring the controversy offered by the proposition, they narrowed their focus to an affirmative case area. From the available options the affirmative has to select the one most likely to overcome the negative's opposition and to win favor with those who render the decision. They knew they would debate both sides of the proposition, because when they debated on the negative side of the proposition, they might debate any number of possible affirmative cases. Thus they also had to develop negative strategies.

When several advocates on one side of a proposition seek to coordinate their efforts in securing a decision, the drafting of a case becomes a team or group function. Most debates conducted in nonacademic parliamentary debate situations, most major courtroom debates, and most academic debates are team functions. If the advocates on a given side of a proposition fail to coordinate their efforts and to agree on a case, they reduce their effectiveness and leave themselves open to attack by their opposition, who will be quick to point out inconsistencies in their position. Even in a huge undertaking like a national political campaign, which involves literally thousands of advocates on each side, an effort is made to provide a highly specialized form of case in the statement of the party platform. The party leaders hope that members of their party will subscribe to this platform, or case, and use it as the basis for their campaign speeches. In practice, of course, there are numerous deviations by campaign speakers, and, if these deviations are serious enough, they may affect the final outcome of the campaign.

The two debaters in an intercollegiate tem debate—like a block of senators in Congress or a battery of lawyers before the Supreme Court or the party spokespersons in a presidential campaign—will draft their case by carefully considering the

---

Miniglossary

Brief   A set of preprepared answers to anticipated arguments of the opposition.

Case   The operational strategy drafted by the advocates on one side of the proposition for the purpose of coordinating their reasoning and evidence and presenting their position with maximum effectiveness.

Presumption   The psychological predisposition of the judge or a predisposition favoring a given side to a dispute.

Prima facie case   A case that in and of itself provides good and sufficient reason for adopting the proposition. It must provide effective issue statements to answer each of the stock issue questions.

---

various requirements of the case. Even the single Lincoln–Douglas debater will carefully consider the demands of preparing the case.

I. REQUIREMENT TO PRESENT
A PRIMA FACIE CASE

The first requirement of any affirmative, whether debating a value or policy proposition, is that it must present a **prima facie case**—one that in and of itself provides good and sufficient reason for adopting the proposition. In order to overcome the *presumption* opposing the proposition, the affirmative must fulfill their *burden of proof* by presenting such a case. As a starting point a prima facie case must provide effective issue statements to answer each of the stock issue questions. (See the section "Discovering the Issues" in Chapter 4.) The affirmative's case on a value proposition must address definitive issues and designative issues. On a policy proposition the affirmative case includes harm, inherency, and solvency issues. Moreover the case must be both structurally and qualitatively strong enough to be logically self-sufficient. It must convince a reasonable and prudent person, and it must stand on its own merits until or unless it is refuted.

A. Presumption

Before a debate ever starts, the judge (as a thinking person) assumes some things. Presumption describes these assumptions. **Presumption** is therefore the psychological predisposition of the judge or audience. Generally, judges of policy debate begin with the assumption that things are ok and should not be changed unless some advocate can convince them otherwise. Remember that a policy resolution calls for a change. Presumption for keeping things the way they are ("the way things are" is also referred to as the *status quo*) exists because we tend to believe in the adage, "If it ain't broke, don't fix it!" Further, change can be costly and risky. You don't make a major change in your life if you do not recognize the need for that change, in part because it involves a risk of the unknown to make that change.

Another way to think of presumption in a debate is to recognize the natural skepticism of the debate judge as a thinking person. Because we are skeptical, if a person makes an assertion (for example, the statement advocating change that is the resolution), we question that assertion and accept it as valid only when it has been proven. This describes the assumption of the debate judge that "he or she who asserts must prove," or as someone from Missouri would say, "Show me!"

Finally, presumption may be thought of as "a predisposition favoring a given side to a dispute." Thus, in a typical, traditional debate about a policy resolution, there is a predisposition favoring the negative (opposing the affirmative). Because the affirmative must advocate a major policy change, the negative is ahead before the debate ever starts.

Because presumption favors one side or the other (usually the negative), a debate cannot end in a tie: Presumption will tilt the balance in favor of one of the sides in the debate.

B. Burden of Proof

Affirmatives, then, not only have to defeat the negative team; they first have to overcome presumption. Just as the prosecution in a criminal trial must prove the defendant "guilty beyond a reasonable doubt," the affirmative must prove it is a good idea to change the status quo (the ways things are) and adopt a radical change. In order to overcome presumption, they must meet their *burden of proof*. The burden of proof requires the affirmative to prove convincingly with evidence, analysis, and reasoning that there is sufficient justification to alter the status quo and adopt the policy change advocated by the resolution. (Recall that there is *a* burden of proof for any argument forwarded within the debate.) The affirmative meets their burden of proof by establishing a prima facie case for the resolution. Prima facie means "at first look," thus a prima facie case is one that is convincing when the judge first sees it, even before the negative team argues against it. It is logically whole, and leaves all obvious questions answered. If the affirmative fails to present a prima facie case, they do not meet their burden of proof or overcome the substantial presumption against the resolution.

C. Prima Facie Case

A prima facie case is one that is persuasive, on its face, to a reasonable judge. In order to be persuasive, this prime facie case should present *arguments* consisting of evidence and reasoning in support of the proposition. In any debate, lots of arguments will be presented. These arguments, to be persuasive, must be offered in support of the *stock issues*. Issues are places where arguments converge.

This requirement is unique to the affirmative. Although Lincoln–Douglas debaters often refer to the "negative case," in team policy debate, the term *case* is the vernacular for the affirmative's prima facie case. We will consider additional requirements of the case: (1) those that apply to value propositions, (2) those that apply to policy propositions, and (3) those common to both value and policy propositions.

Remember that some value propositions are quasi-policy propositions and that, although we may sometimes debate facts, values, or policies by themselves, we will often find it necessary to consider all of them together. (See the Chapter 3 section "Propositions of Value.") Thus it is important to know the requirements that apply to both value and policy propositions.

II. GENERAL CASE REQUIREMENTS

A. Requirements Imposed by the Characteristics of Decision Renderers

Because advocates naturally want to win the decision, they must carefully consider the person or persons who will render the decision and adapt their case accordingly. The objective is not only to develop a case that is intellectually satisfying; it is to develop a case convincing enough to those who render the decision that they will vote for it. For instance, in debating the mass media proposition, the affirmative would do well to develop different cases for use before audiences consisting of PTA members, television station managers, and supermarket executives. If the decision is to be rendered by a critic judge or panel of judges, the debaters should adapt their case to these key individuals. In most intercollegiate debates a single judge scrupulously seeks to render the decision solely on the basis of which team did the better debating. However, as we will see in Chapter 17, judges often do have a specific judging philosophy or preferred decision-making paradigm; experienced debaters find out about these preferences and adapt to them. For example, Judge A might be an issues judge, Judge B might prefer the policymaker paradigm, Judge C might be an evaluator of argument, while Judge D might like counterplans.

The debater should be aware that in applied debates the judge or judges are often influenced by the reactions of the nonvoting audience. In messages to Congress, for example, the president may deliberately use the audience to influence those who render the decision. Supposedly these messages are addressed to the Congress, which will render a decision on the message by voting for or against the legislation the president proposes. In fact, however, the president frequently tries to go over the heads of Congress and to present a case to the people in the hope that they will pressure Congress to vote as the president wishes. Presidents Franklin D. Roosevelt and Ronald Reagan in particular raised the technique of going over the heads of the audience to an art form and skillfully applied great pressure on Congress. We know that legislators frequently are influenced by letters, phone calls, and e-mail from home and that juries are not impervious to the reactions of spectators in the courtroom. Sometimes a speaker will have the even more complex task of simultaneously addressing two quite different audiences. For example, in the 1980 Mariel boat lift Fidel Castro allowed 125,000 Cubans, many of them criminals, to flee to the United States. In response, Attorney General Janet Reno sought to send strong messages to two distinct audiences. On the domestic front, her announcement of a partial block-ade sought to demonstrate to Florida that the administration was on top of a potentially explosive situation. On the diplomatic front, her announcement aimed to warn Castro not even to try to engineer a Mariel II.[1]

Most frequently, as students or citizens, we will try to influence a single in-dividual or a small group of individuals. In these cases we should try to learn as much as possible about the key individual/group and adapt our case accordingly. Although the key individual/group will be the focal point of our presentation, the desirability of securing a favorable response from the nonvoting audience should not be overlooked, because this response may influence the person who renders the decision. In a certain large corporation, for example, the purchasing manager had the sole authority to determine the make of automobile that would be purchased for the salespeople. After ordering a fleet of B cars, he confided to a friend, "A cars are really better, but the salespeople wanted B. There wasn't a great deal of difference between the two, so I let the salespeople have the one they wanted." Apparently the advocates for B cars did the better job of influenc-ing the nonvoting audience.

B. Requirements Imposed by the Occasion

Argument takes place not in a vacuum but in a specific context of time and place and with a certain relationship to events that precede and follow the argumenta-tive speech or writing.

In intercollegiate debate, tournament situations call for certain social ameni-ties, gracious references to the opposing team, a courteous exchange with the judge, and a certain air of poised informality. The final round of a national tour-nament requires a gracious reference to the host college and the opposing team and a judicious mixture of formality and wit. An international debate requires well-chosen references to international relationships and to the visitors' nation and customs.

The necessity of adapting to the occasion applies to all advocates. Speakers on the highest governmental level face this same requirement. A dramatic exam-ple of the occasion's influencing the debate may be seen in America's entry into World War II and in the beginning of Operation Desert Storm. In 1941, when President Roosevelt asked Congress for a declaration of war, he gave a brief speech dealing only with the events of the previous day. His proposal became law within an hour after he finished speaking, and there was only one dissenting vote. In 1991, when President Bush sought congressional approval for the use of military force against Iraq, Congress debated for three days, during which time

---

1. *New York Times*, Aug. 13, 1994, p. 6.

Bush vigorously lobbied for his proposal. When Congress finally gave its approval, there were a number of dissenting votes. The difference in the approaches used by the two presidents showed an awareness of the different situations involved—a sneak attack at Pearl Harbor in 1941 versus allowance for more time for the United Nations embargo to take effect in 1991. The advocate, whether a college student or a president, should be aware of the occasion and adjust to it.

C. Requirements of Clarity and Relevancy

A debate case obviously has to be clear, interesting, relevant, and succinct, because time is always limited in a debate. In intercollegiate debates strict time limitations are imposed. In other debates factors such as limitations of radio or television time, a preestablished time of adjournment, and practical considerations like audience attention span and interest level limit the time available to the advocates. Well-prepared affirmatives, therefore, always have at their disposal more material than they can possibly use in the time available. From the materials available to them, the advocates utilize the items that are clearest, most interesting, and most relevant to their purpose. Debaters speaking on the proposition "Resolved: That law enforcement agencies in the United States should be given greater freedom in the investigation and prosecution of crime" before a Massachusetts audience would certainly have wanted to include references to the widespread criminal activity exposed by a Massachusetts crime commission at the very time this proposition was debated.

Well-prepared debaters will have several items of evidence available to support each issue of their case. Many of these items may have approximately equal value in fulfilling the logical requirements of the position. Debaters should select those that will make their presentation most clear and interesting to the specific audience and most relevant to their overall purpose. A good rule for advocates is to be sure that everything included in their case is specifically relevant to their purpose and to exclude ruthlessly anything else. We should note that the social amenities of the debate and certain other factors of persuasion may not be relevant to the logical proof of the case. But they are relevant to the debater's purpose, which is to secure a favorable decision.

The sequence in which the issues and materials of the case are presented is extremely important. Occasionally debaters may want to arrange materials so as to achieve maximum effect, even if this means a violation of logical organization.

D. Requirements Imposed by the Probable Case of the Opposition

The advocates' task is not to overcome all possible opposition to their case; it is to overcome the specific case presented by their opponents within the context of a given debate. To do this, debaters must try to anticipate the position their opponents will take. The advocates can gain a real understanding of the problem only when they have thoroughly analyzed both sides of the proposition.

Effective advocates must consider the most likely arguments against their positions and map out strategic approaches to avoid those arguments, preempt them, or establish positions from which they can later generate answers to their opponents' arguments.

Salespersons, lawyers, generals, diplomats, and others devote a considerable portion of their time to estimating the probable moves of their opponents and to planning their own actions so as to anticipate and defeat the opposition. Advocates should carefully think through the probable moves of their opponents and be prepared to meet them. Many teachers of argumentation, from classical times to the present, have encouraged students to debate on both sides of the proposition selected for academic debate. Most contemporary intercollegiate debate tournaments are structured to provide students with just such an opportunity. This procedure gives participants a chance to acquire knowledge of both sides of the proposition and of the requirements of both affirmative and negative cases. Few teachers of argumentation are interested in training propagandists for or against a given proposition. Rather, they are interested in using the proposition as an educational tool by which they can teach the theory and practice of argumentation. A student would not, of course, be asked to publicly advocate a position contrary to his or her convictions, and such a problem rarely arises in academic debating. National academic debate propositions usually deal with matters on which the average student has an open mind. After a number of debates on both sides of the proposition, the student is better able to formulate a judgment based on an intelligent analysis of the problem.

E. Requirements of Consistency

If the two advocates in an academic debate allow themselves to present contradictory or inconsistent arguments, the result is almost certain to be defeated. The same consideration applies outside academic debate. During the energy crisis, when gasoline prices were soaring, oil company executives had to coordinate their position carefully when speaking in public. Before their stockholders there was a temptation to point with pride to the profits they had made. That is, after all, what corporate executives are supposed to do—and increased profits are an excellent justification for increased executive salaries and bonuses. At the same time other executives were testifying before congressional committees and various regulatory commissions. Here there was a temptation to minimize their profits and to emphasize how poorly the oil companies had done in comparison to other industries. If their statements revealed inconsistencies, they could expect unfavorable action from at least one audience.

F. Requirements of Flexibility During the Debate

As advocates, although we make the best possible estimate of the opposition case, we should remember that we can only estimate the position our opponent might take; we can never be sure. If we set up our case too rigidly, we may find ourselves unable to adapt to the case actually presented by our opponent, and we may be seriously handicapped by the inflexibility of our own position. We would do well to follow the example of Winston Churchill, one of the most skilled parliamentarians of the twentieth century. Churchill carefully estimated the probable course of debate in Parliament and often appeared with seven or eight different, carefully prepared speeches. Once he learned the precise position his opponents had taken, he would select the most appropriate speech. Of course this is exactly what today's skilled debaters do.

Negative advocates, for example, develop a variety of **briefs** against possible affirmative positions. Once the affirmative has committed itself to a specific position, the negative then selects the appropriate preplanned briefs, adapts them to the affirmative arguments, and launches the attack. Their file may be titled "answers/to" the various possible arguments of the opposition.

The advocate's case should be sufficiently flexible to allow for adaptation during the debate itself. If several advocates join together to build a case, they should decide in advance what position they will take if the opposition presents a given course of argument, and they should be able to make a smooth transition to a different and previously prepared position. In academic debate such adaptation typically occurs in the affirmative case at the start of the second affirmative speech. At this point, as at many others during the debate, there is a high premium on flexibility. Although the attacks may be anticipated, their exact form cannot be known until the first negative presents them. Then the second affirmative needs to move swiftly, smoothly, and consistently to refute the attacks made by the negative and must extend the issues introduced by his or her colleague. Effective advocates carefully estimate the probable case of their opponents and prepare to meet that case. They also consider carefully every possible position their opponents may take and thoroughly prepare both their defense and their attack for each of these positions. There is an answer for almost every argument that can be introduced into the typical debate dealing with probabilities.

In a debate the clash usually does not end with our advancing a line of argument and our opponent's meeting that argument with an answer. We should assume that our opponent is well prepared and has counterargument ready for each of the major contentions of the debate. Therefore, we must prepare an answer not only for each of the probable arguments of our opponent but also for each counterargument that this opponent is likely to advance in support of his or her original contentions. In this way we can prepare our arguments in depth. Not only will we be ready to meet our opponent on the first level of argument—the initial clash of argument and counterargument—we will also have additional evidence and arguments at our disposal that we can use to reinforce our initial position through however many exchanges are necessary to sustain our position. This preparation is reflected in the debate card file, which should contain the evidence and argument we plan to use initially, as well as supplementary materials we hold in reserve in case we need to draw on them.

EXERCISES

1. Consider the value proposition "Resolved: That violence is a justified response to political oppression."

   a. What are the likely definitive issues?
   b. What are the likely criteria for the values?
   c. Do the facts correspond to the definition?
   d. What is the application of the values?

2. Consider the value applications of the proposition in Exercise 1.

   a. What value applications is the affirmative most likely to claim? Are they significant quantitatively? Qualitatively?
   b. What value objections is the negative most likely to advance? Are they significant quantitatively? Qualitatively?
   c. Are the value objections significant on balance when contrasted with the value applications?

3. In the quasi-policy proposition "Resolved: That throughout the United States more severe punishment for individuals convicted of violent crime would be desirable," what additional issues must be considered?

4. Consider the requirement to prove inherency in a debate on the current CEDA/NDT intercollegiate proposition.

   a. Are there inherent needs in the status quo for adopting the proposition?
   b. Are there structural barriers that prevent the status quo from solving the problem?
   c. Are there structural gaps that prevent the status quo from solving the problem?
   d. Are there attitudes that prevent the status quo from solving the problem?
   e. Can the affirmative successfully argue existential inherency?

5. Consider the requirement for proving significance in a debate on the current CEDA/NDT intercollegiate proposition.

   a. If the affirmative claims there is a need to change the status quo, is this need significant quantitatively? Qualitatively?
   b. Is the plan a significant change quantitatively in the status quo? Qualitatively?
   c. Are the advantages significant quantitatively? Qualitatively?
   d. Are the advantages on balance significant when contrasted with the likely disadvantages that a negative will claim?
   e. Are the disadvantages significant quantitatively? Qualitatively?
   f. Are the disadvantages significant on balance when contrasted with the likely advantages that an affirmative will claim?

6. Consider a plan currently being debated in Congress, in your state legislature, or by the governing body of your college. Apply the questions on in-

herency listed in Exercise 4. Apply the questions on significance listed in Exercise 5.

7. What are the requirements that might be inherent in the attitudes, interests, and intellectual capabilities of each of the following if they were asked to judge a debate on the value proposition identified in Exercise 1? On the current CEDA/NDT proposition?

    a. A labor union official
    b. The president of a local chamber of commerce
    c. The president of a local chapter of the National Organization for Women
    d. A fundamentalist preacher
    e. An imam
    f. A rabbi
    g. A lawyer for the American Civil Liberties Union
    h. The members of a local parent–teacher association
    i. The members of a local Rotary Club
    j. The students at a high school assembly program
    k. A professor of argumentation
    l. A member of Congress

12

Building the Affirmative Case

In this chapter on the affirmative case and in the following chapter on the negative case, we will begin with value propositions and conclude by considering policy propositions. You will notice that, in this chapter and the next, more space is devoted to policy debate than to value debate. The reason is simple: Most team topic debaters participate in policy debate. Also debating policies requires advocates to address issues of fact and value in addition to fundamental policy questions.

Team topic policy debate as now exemplified by debate at the National Debate Tournament, has been around since 1920 (the first National Debate Tournament was in 1947.) CEDA did not begin using value propositions until 1975 and adopted only policy topics beginning in spring 1995. Since the 1996-1997 academic year CEDA and NDT have shared the same yearlong policy topic. Not surprisingly, given policy debate's 55-year lead, more research and writing have been done in the policy area. Lincoln–Douglas debaters sometimes use policy or quasi-policy topics, and parliamentary debaters also use a variety of types of topics, including policy ones.

The CEDA national proposition "Resolved: That United States military intervention to foster democratic government is appropriate in a post cold war world" is an excellent example of the blurring of the value-policy distinction. This *quasi-policy* proposition prompted most affirmative teams to use policy paradigms and in many cases to offer plans. Plans, as we will see, are a hallmark of policy debate. This is a clear example of debaters broadening their horizons and reaching out to previously untapped sources of argumentation theory.

Knowledgeable negative teams meeting such cases wisely responded by also turning to policy debate theory and offered disadvantages—which, as we will learn, are another hallmark of policy debate—as well as counterplans to the affirmative's case. One observer of CEDA debate in the early 1990s notes: "At those tournaments meeting the characterization of the national circuit virtually every round will feature an affirmative defending more or less specific policies … while the negative articu-

---

Miniglossary

Advantages The benefits or gains that the affirmative claims will result from adopting its plan, which must be shown to outweigh the disadvantages.

Application In debating a proposition of value case; the measure of effect in accepting the value, or concrete implication of the value.

Attitudinal inherency Suggests that attitudes prevent solution of the identified problem within the status quo.

Comparative advantage case Situation in which the affirmative accepts the goals of the status quo and argues that its plan is a better way of attaining these goals and that its plan will produce greater advantages than the status quo.

Criteria The standard on the basis of which a decision is to be made. A major issue in value debate; sometimes used in policy debate.

Harm Refers to the evils or important problems existing in the status quo and requiring remedy.

Intrinsic A factor is intrinsic if it is embedded within the essential nature of a thing or is an inherent characteristic or consequence of the thing.

Impact A substantial measure of importance.

Plan The affirmative's method of solving the problems claimed in the justification as needs or harms. It must produce the advantages claimed by the affirmative.

Qualitative significance The compelling nature of a harm as diminished quality of life or denial of some important value.

Quantitative significance Numerical, observable, and concrete measure of the harm

Solvency The ability of a plan to work and to reduce the harm identified by the affirmative.

Structural inherency Demonstrates that the harm is permanently built into the status quo; consists of law, court decisions that have the force of law, and societal structures.

Turnaround argument Converting a negative's disadvantage into an affirmative advantage. In common usage any statement that one turns against the originator.

---

lates equally specific [disadvantages]."[1] We can enrich our knowledge of argumentation and debate if we draw on both value and policy paradigms and apply them as

---

1. Ken Broda-Bahm, "Community Concepts of Argumentative Legitimacy: Challenging Norms in National Circuit CEDA Debate," *Forensic of Pi Kappa Delta,* vol. 79, no. 3 (spring 1994), p. 30.

appropriate in our debates. In the real world of applied debate as well, we do not have the luxury of saying, "I do only value debate" or "I do only policy debate." As value debate tended to incorporate policy argumentation in the early 1990s, current policy debate practice relies heavily on critical and philosophical considerations of value.

In applied debate, we must be prepared to debate both value and policy or more likely to debate propositions in which both are interwoven. An understanding of both types of debate empowers us to play an effective role in the complex world of applied debate, where arbitrary distinctions between value and policy are not usually made.

We cannot intelligently and effectively debate the great issues of domestic or foreign policy without considering both value and policy. Nor can we use critical thinking to arrive at an individual decision (see Chapter 1) without considering both value and policy. Outside academic debate, of course, all of us will have occasion to debate both value and policy propositions as we apply the process of critical thinking to the problems of reasoned decision making.

I. OBJECTIVES OF THE AFFIRMATIVE CASE

Both value and policy debate are usually in the area of probability, not certainty, and time limitations—not only in academic debate but in informal debate as well—do not make it possible to introduce all the relevant evidence and arguments. The affirmative, therefore, is not required to establish its case as a matter of certainty. Such a degree of cogency is rarely attainable in life. Instead the affirmative has to establish a prima facie case that provides the highest possible degree of probability, giving those who render the decision good reasons to accept the resolution. For example, in debating the proposition "Resolved: That the American judicial system has overemphasized freedom of the press," the affirmative does not have to prove its position absolutely; it merely has to establish sufficient good reasons to justify the judges' accepting its position. In the same way, in debating the proposition "Resolved: That the United States should reduce substantially its military commitments to NATO member states," the affirmative is not required to establish its position as a certainty; it merely has to provide sufficient good reasons to justify the judges' accepting its position.

II. PROPOSITION OF VALUE AFFIRMATIVE CASES

As we saw in Chapter 3, in a debate on a proposition of value, the affirmative maintains that a certain belief, value, or fact is justified and that it conforms to the definition or criteria appropriate to evaluate the matter at hand. In developing the affirmative case on a proposition of value, the advocate needs to present a prima facie case, made up of argumentation in support of the stock issues.

Stock Issues: Proposition of Value

1. Definitive issues
   a. What are the definitions of the key terms?
   b. What are the criteria for the values?
2. Designative issues
   a. Do the facts correspond to the definitions?
   b. What are the applications of the values?

A. Requirement to Provide a Satisfactory Definition

As we saw in Chapter 4, advocacy of a proposition of value requires a reasonable definition of terms. In debating value propositions, definition is a stock issue essential to proving a prima facie case and is considered in that context here. Definition, however, involves more than providing definitions of the terms in the resolution. Definition provides the affirmative's interpretation of the meaning of the propositional statement.

In debating the proposition "Resolved: That federal government censorship is justified to defend the national interest of the United States," it was essential to define *censorship*. The Persian Gulf War (Operation Desert Storm) provided an interesting variety of definitions. American correspondents, for the most part, voluntarily cooperated with the U.S. government's *requests* not to report certain matters. British correspondents were *prohibited* from mentioning anything their government did not want mentioned, and this ban was enforced by harsh penalties. Other coalition governments had *even more stringent control* over their media. Clearly there is a vast difference between these interpretations of censorship.

In debating the proposition "Resolved: That individual rights of privacy are more important than any other constitutional right," it was clearly necessary to define *rights of privacy*. Actually there is no explicitly identified constitutional right to privacy, yet in many cases the courts act as if there were. What is the best definition in these circumstances? For many years the sex life of a political figure was considered to be a private matter. Times change, however, and President Clinton's sexual activities were extensively reported in the media before and during the impeachment proceedings. Almost everyone is in favor of privacy. Yet we recognize that the public interest requires some exceptions. What exceptions can you justify as part of your definition?

B. Requirement to Provide a Satisfactory Criterion

In debates on value propositions, the affirmative must provide a reasonable criterion for each of the value terms in the proposition and for the primary value defended. **Criteria** offer a measure of the values and a method of comparing competing values. The negative must also carefully consider the criterion offered by the affirmative and be ready either to offer a better criterion or to take advantage of any error of the affirmative.

In debating the proposition "Resolved: That American television has sacrificed quality for entertainment," it is essential for the affirmative to provide carefully considered criteria for the value term *quality*. How would one measure this term? If the criteria are properly chosen, they create a sound basis for the affirmative's case and greatly increase the affirmative's chances of winning the debate. But if the criteria are not well chosen, they open up opportunities for the negative to defeat the affirmative by providing better criteria or to turn the criteria against the affirmative by providing value objections.

C. Requirement to Provide Application

Here the affirmative must address the question "What is the application of this value?" **Application** is the measure of effect in accepting the value, or concrete implication of the value. If the value set out in the proposition is accepted, what will happen? In debating the proposition "Resolved: That increased restrictions on the civilian possession of handguns in the United States would be justified," the affirmative had to be prepared to demonstrate that increased restrictions would indeed be justified—that they would, for example, reduce crime. Reducing crime is a highly desirable value application. But would increased restrictions on handguns actually contribute to this goal? The negative would certainly argue that restrictions would have little impact on crime—most crimes don't involve guns (for example, white-collar crimes), and criminals could always get guns if they wanted them. The negative would no doubt also argue that, on balance, other values were more important than reducing crime—for instance, the constitutional right to bear arms. The affirmative in value debates has to develop and defend its application issue in a way very similar to the development and defense of the advantage issue in policy debate, in that both must establish a compelling impact. As in policy debates, the impact may be qualitative and thus philosophically based. Application of the value should be demonstrated as having a significant impact through qualitative and/or quantitative means.

D. Requirement to Prove the Intrinsic

In value debates the advocates must sometimes prove that certain factors are **intrinsic** to various elements of the case or to the relationship between certain elements of the case. A factor is intrinsic if it is embedded within the essential nature of a thing or is an inherent characteristic or consequence of the thing. In debating the "right to privacy" proposition considered previously, debaters often had to establish just what was intrinsic, or essential, to the right to privacy and why that was more important than other constitutional rights. In debating the censorship proposition also considered previously, debaters tried to establish that certain factors intrinsic to censorship were critical to the defense of the national interests of the United States.

E. Requirements of Significance

As in policy debate, the advocates in value debate have to prove that the essentials of their case are significant. The values they advocate must be proved to be significant values, and the application of those values must be significant. In the gun control example, reducing crime would certainly seem to be a significant application, but *how much* would crime be reduced? Enough to offset the negative's claim of lost constitutional rights? Thus, as in policy debate, significance is often established by weighing the application *on balance* against the value objections. Significance is also an important issue in policy debate and will be considered in more detail later in the chapter.

F. Putting the Case Together

Typically the debate case is the product of several debaters working together. Once the outline of the case is satisfactory, the next step is to prepare a manuscript of the first affirmative speech. The final draft of the manuscript should be the product of extensive rewriting and editing and should reflect the maximum skill of the advocate (or advocates, if the manuscript is a group effort) in speech composition. It must be so written that, when the speech is presented, the advocate can achieve maximum effectiveness in delivery. (You may find it helpful to review Chapters 15 and 16 when building and presenting an affirmative or negative case.)

Once the manuscript for the affirmative speech is completed, the advocates have to prepare *briefs*—short speech segments—that they will use to refute negative attacks and to extend affirmative arguments. Because these briefs must be adapted to the specific negative case met, they cannot simply be read from a manuscript; rather, they have to serve as carefully planned outlines for an extemporaneous presentation. Successful debaters also will be able to produce well-executed extensions. *Extensions* consist of new evidence and analysis to carry forward arguments introduced earlier; they are not simply repetitions of previously introduced evidence and argument.

III. PROPOSITION OF POLICY AFFIRMATIVE CASES

As we saw in Chapter 3, in a debate on a proposition of policy, the affirmative maintains that a certain policy or course of action should be adopted. In developing the affirmative case on a proposition of policy, the advocate is responsible for presenting a prima facie case.

The prima facie case is made up of a number of issues just as issues are made up of a number of arguments. In deciding whether or not to adopt a new policy, any reasonable person is likely to ask three questions:

1. Do I perceive a need for a change? Is there some harm or evil in the world that needs to be eliminated?

2. Is this problem likely to go away by itself or does some action really need to be taken? Is it inherent to the world as it is?

3. If this policy is adopted, will it really help? Will it solve the problem and not cause too many new problems?

These three questions make up the *stock issues* of policy debate. In order to establish a prima facie case for a policy resolution, an affirmative team must provide convincing arguments that answer each of these questions in the affirmative. In debate, these questions or issues are referred to as **harm,** *inherency,* and **solvency**. The affirmative must address all three in order for debate to begin and most of the clash in the debate will revolve around them.

A. Requirement to Prove the Harm

The first stock issue is harm. If there is no harm in the world, there is no reason to change things. Harm may be absence of a greater good (for example, things are OK now, but they could be a whole lot better) or a real, observable, existing evil. Existence of harm helps establish the need for change. To be persuasive, the harm identified by the affirmative should be *significant, compelling,* and *widespread.* It is important to remember that harm alone does not warrant an affirmative ballot, but without harm, there is no justification for a resolution change.

Significance asks the question, "How much harm is there?" Advocates strive to demonstrate quantitative significance, a numerical, observable, and concrete measure of the harm. This may be established by observing a numerical measure of the harm: by identifying the number of people affected negatively by the harm and/or by measuring the statistical probability of risk (how likely is it that the harm will actually occur?). Although big numbers are certainly impressive and serve an important persuasive function, it must be remembered that statistics can prove that a harm is significant without providing a head count. We do not know exactly how many homeless people there are in the United States or how many individuals have contacted AIDS, but there is little doubt that these are both significant problems. Affirmatives are wise to provide some realistic estimates of the extent of the harm and present evidence that such estimates are likely to be understated.

Harm must above all be *compelling.* As with all arguments, the key to a compelling harm is **impact**. If a reasonable person can be aware of the harm and ask, "so what?" the harm is probably not very compelling. The problem of male pattern baldness is quantitatively significant, but not compelling to all bald men. Baldness may not be thought to substantially reduce an individual's quality of life or violate any important human value (except perhaps vanity). In order to establish a compelling harm, the affirmative must establish a qualitative harm, one that points to diminished quality of life or denial of some important value.

Qualitative significance is important by definition and significant by implication. The United States Supreme Court establishes policy based on the denial of a single individual's rights because important values are at stake, that is, qualitative harm is established. **Quantitative significance**, on the other hand, is not compelling if it is not tied to a qualitative harm. That thousands of people are dying of AIDS warrants action not just because of the numbers of people affected, but more importantly because we place a great value on human life and avoidance of suffering. It is generally accepted that human life is valuable and thus death is a per se harm, and that avoidance of pain is valuable, and thus suffering is harmful. That a condition is harmful should not be taken for granted. The degree of harm must be examined with utmost scrutiny. Economic harm, for example, is not persuasive unless it is shown to diminish the quality of life for a number of individuals in a substantial way or lead to an increased risk of death. Qualitative harm establishes the impact of the harm and to have impact is to be compelling.

Finally, it is generally accepted that a harm should be demonstrated to be *widespread*. This depends somewhat on the nature of the resolution. Most policy resolutions call for national or international action. If a problem is local or regional, national or international action may not be called for. It is up to the advocates of change to prove the widespread and pervasive nature of the harm.

Although advocates are usually in a stronger position if they can provide both quantitative and qualitative needs, and indicate the widespread nature of the harms, it is not always possible to do this. In debating the proposition "Resolved: That the federal government should significantly strengthen the regulation of mass media communication in the United States," some affirmatives called for greater governmental control of the mass media's reporting of criminal trials on the grounds that sometimes mass media coverage led to unfair trials. Debaters using this case found that they could document few instances in which media coverage had influenced juries. But they argued that the Sixth Amendment right to an impartial jury was qualitatively so important that this right should be protected even if it was violated in only one out of thousands of trials.

B. Requirement to Prove the Inherency

Inherency may be thought of as a *propensity for future harm*. Once it has been established that there is a harm that needs to be corrected, a decision maker considers alternatives. If the problem is likely to go away without a major overhaul of the status quo, then substantial change is unwarranted. Inherency looks to the causes of a problem. Unfortunately, causes are seldom simple. Most problems have many interrelated causes, some of them unidentifiable. If the causes of a problem are relatively permanent fixtures within the status quo and a major reform on the level of resolutional change is need to alter them or overcome them, then inherency is established. Inherency is tricky, however, as systems are in a constant state of change. Description of the status quo, then, must predict the direction of change and indicate that the problems identified in the harm are not likely to disappear without resolutional action. Thus inherency asks, "Will the problem go away by itself, or do we need to do something major about it?"

The strongest form of inherency is **structural inherency**. Structural inherency demonstrates that the harm is permanently built into the status quo and that major revisions of the status quo are needed to in order to eliminate the harm. Structural inherency consists of law, court decisions that have the force of law, and societal structures. Prison construction is inherently difficult because it requires public approval and public funding by law. Public funded abortions may be banned because the Supreme Court allows the states to do so; the American flag can be burned as symbolic speech because the Court has so ruled. Marijuana smokers go to jail because there are law against illicit drug use and possession. In some states, labor unions have created closed shops through legal and social structures. If the affirmative can prove that laws, court decisions, or societal structures prevent the solution of its harm, then it has demonstrated structural inherency.

Inherency may also be based on the attitudes of people who have authority that affects decisions bearing on the harm. **Attitudinal inherency** suggests that attitudes prevent solution of the identified problem within the status quo. Racist and sexist attitudes in our society work to prevent equal rights and opportunities for women and minorities. Fear of crime prevents extensive use of prison work-release and furlough programs; ironically, even the construction of new penal institutions is feared because few communities welcome such facilities. It is useful to examine the core motives behind such attitudes. For instance, problems with drug distribution and crime are generally tied to profit or power. Once the core motive behind the harmful action is revealed, the attitudes can be clearly examined.

It is sometimes argued that because a harm exists and there is no sign of it going away, it is inherent. This analysis, referred to as *existential inherency,* is usually based on inadequate research. If it is true that the problem will not easily go away, then it is probable that there is a reason. This reason is either a structural or attitudinal barrier to solving the problem within the status quo. Existential inherency is "pseudo" inherency. It is a way of copping out and saying, "We know there is a harm, we just don't know why." If you cannot identify the reasons behind the harm, you cannot hope to solve that harm. In order to be prima facie, the affirmative must present either a structural or attitudinal barrier to solving the harm within the status quo. When it has done so, it has met the burden of inherency.

In the example involving mass media reporting of jury trials, affirmative advocates had an easy time establishing structural inherency. The First Amendment provides a formidable barrier to any government regulation of the press. The affirmative's plan could be put into effect only by amending the Constitution and giving the federal government powers specifically denied it by the First Amendment.

In this same case the affirmative was often able to prove attitudinal inherency as well. It argued that sensationalism increased newspaper circulation and increased TV ratings. For this reason, it maintained, newspapers and television stations were predisposed to seek out and present lurid and often unproven or inadmissible (in court) news that might prejudice jurors.

Existential inherency is not real inherency

C. Requirement to Prove the Solvency

Once the affirmative has established that there is a significant, compelling, and widespread harm and that the harm is not likely to go away without some radical change in the present system, it must provide a plan of action for solving that harm. This *plan* must meet the burden of solvency: It must solve the harm better than the status quo does. It is not expected that the affirmative will eliminate the harm, only that it can demonstrate a **comparative advantage**. In other words, the plan compared to the status quo is a superior system; it is comparatively advantageous. In order to do this, the affirmative must address the issue of solvency by proving that its plan would work, that it would solve the problem better than the status quo would, and that it would avoid side effects that would be worse than the harm itself.

The first requirement of solvency is workability. The affirmative is allowed to employ *fiat* in assuming implementation of its plan. Fiat is not magic; it only allows the affirmative to assume for the sake of argument that if its plan were shown to be desirable, it would be adopted through a normal legal procedure. Debate thus centers on whether or not it would be adopted. If debaters had to prove that their plan would be adopted, they would have to spend all their time arguing about the political feasibility of getting votes for the plan. This would prevent the policy analysis that is the core of the debate. Thus, fiat assumes hypothetical implementation, but not workability. The affirmative must prove that its plan could eliminate or overcome the structural and attitudinal barriers identified in inherency and that it could reasonably be expected to work in the real world. It may not invent magical technologies or create funding out of thin air, nor may the affirmative assume that it has demonstrated a feasible plan. Only then has it met the burden of workability.

The plan is the focal point of a policy debate, providing the connecting link between the needs and the advantages. The **plan** must solve the problems claimed in the justification as needs or harms, and it must produce the advantages claimed by the affirmative. The affirmative's plan has to be developed in sufficient detail to demonstrate that it can meet the alleged needs and that it can produce the claimed advantages. But it must be simple enough to be presented and defended within the time limits of academic debate.

Even though the plan should be tailored to fit the resolution and the specific case of the affirmative, it should be a reasonable policy with real-world advocates. In searching for plan ideas, debaters should look to experts who have produced relevant public statements, literature, and, in some cases, studies, to support the efficacy of plan adoption.

Beginning debaters should master a basic format; advanced advocates can make reasonable variations in this basic format that they feel are desirable and defensible. The major parts of a plan are, in common usage, designated as *planks*. The following inset shows the basic plan format.

The essential components of the plan, or plan planks, should be "topical." It is considered an illegitimate strategy to insert "extratopical" plan planks. These are parts of the plan from which advantages may be claimed but that are not

Basic Plan Format

PLANK 1—AGENCY

In this plank the affirmative specifies who will be responsible for administering its plan. This may include identifying who will enact the plan and/or who will do the work of the plan. Does the affirmative require an existing agency of the federal government to administer its plan? Does it create a new agency? Here's where the affirmative must provide the essential details of the agency that will put its plan into effect.

PLANK 2—MANDATES

In most debates this is the essence of the plan. In this plank the affirmative specifies the mandates given to the agency that administers the plan. The affirmative must specify exactly what it requires the agency to do. If new legislation is needed to carry out the affirmative's plan, this plank is the place to provide for it.

PLANK 3—ENFORCEMENT

In this plank the affirmative specifies how the plan will be enforced. In the need and inherency issues, the affirmative has provided many reasons people will resist its plan. Now it must provide a means of making people behave the way it wants them to. The affirmative may find it necessary to provide fines, prison terms, or other forms of coercion or incentives to make people act in the way necessary for its plan to work. In some circumstances the affirmative may be able to demonstrate that under the new conditions created by its plan people will act in the desired way because it is now in their self-interest to do so. Most often enforcement will be through "normal means," meaning it is not specified by the plan.

PLANK 4—FUNDING AND STAFFING

In this plank the affirmative specifies how it will get the funds and staff to permit the agency to carry out its mandates. Some cases on the proposition "Resolved: That the United States federal government should significantly increase exploration and/or development of space beyond the earth's mesosphere" required billions of dollars in increased taxes. By contrast, some cases on the "regulation of mass media communication" proposition required only a nominal increase in staff and funding to allow an existing agency to carry out the mandates. Again, these actions usually occur through "normal means."

PLANK 5—ADDENDUM

In this concluding plank the affirmative adds such further provisions as may be necessary to complete the implementation of its plan. For example, it might provide for the repeal of any conflicting legislation, indicate the intent of the plan, and provide other details that could help make the plan comprehensive and readily understandable.

essential to the policy action embedded within the resolution. For example, in debating the employment opportunities proposition, most affirmative cases necessarily caused an increase in income for the people who gained employment. This argument opened the way for the negative to run a "grain-fed beef" disadvantage. The argument indicated that with increased income people had a propensity to consume more grain-fed beef; and grain-fed beef, the negative argued, caused an increase in cardiovascular disease, thus killing off the very people the affirmative wanted to help. (This generic disadvantage applied to many affirmative plans. It was sometimes called the "meatballs" disadvantage; later all big-impact generic disadvantages were termed "meatballs.") Some affirmatives, anticipating this attack, stated that their plan would be partly financed by a tax on grain-fed beef. This tactic either discouraged the negative from running the disadvantage or allowed the affirmative to answer it by claiming that the increased cost of the now-taxed grain-fed beef would hold consumption of it to present levels, thus incurring no new disadvantage. Such a plan plank would likely be considered extratopical, and thus an unfair strategy. The affirmative action may only implement or enable the policy action essential to the resolution.

The affirmative is not required to demonstrate that its plan will be adopted, but it does have to demonstrate that its plan, if adopted, would be workable. As we saw in the Chapter 4 section "The Meaning of *Should* and the Convention of *Fiat*," the affirmative may fiat the enactment of its plan over the inherency it identifies. It may not, however, fiat the workability of its plan. If the plan calls for an increase in personal income taxes and a reduction in property taxes, it does not make sense for the negative to raise the workability issue; the status quo has effective means of enforcing tax collections. In some cases, however, workability may become an all-important issue. In debates on comprehensive medical care for all citizens, one affirmative plan called for annual physical examinations of all citizens. The affirmative sought to evade its responsibility by claiming that this provision of its plan would be "enforced by all necessary means." The negative established that millions of citizens—through fear, ignorance, or apathy—would not volunteer for the physical examinations and argued that the affirmative must provide an effective enforcement mechanism or lose its claimed advantage. The inexperienced affirmative debater, in a moment of excess, responded that this provision of the plan would be enforced by "drawing and quartering." The next negative speaker argued that the method of enforcement provided by the affirmative—drawing and quartering—was not only counterproductive to health but so repugnant to contemporary standards of law enforcement that it constituted grounds for rejecting the proposition. The judge agreed; drawing and quartering may have been accepted practice in the Middle Ages, but it was an unacceptable and unworkable plan provision for contemporary America.

Fiat assumes that the plan is adopted through "normal means"—typically the usual policymaking procedure of the relevant decision-making body, most often the U.S. federal government. Occasionally teams may have to debate just what constitutes *normal means* for a given situation. However, affirmatives may not fiat past the implications of the decision-making process. For example, they may not fiat that there would not be political costs of plan implementation (although they may be able to turn to their plan advocates to prove that there would not be such costs).

Affirmatives also may not fiat unreasonable provisions for their plan. For example, in a debate on consumer protection, the affirmatives may not fiat that their administrative body will be headed by Ralph Nader; in a debate on crime control, they may not fiat that the members of their administrative body will be incorruptible;[2] if they designate a congressional committee to investigate the CIA, they may not fiat that all of the committee members will be liberal Democrats. In short, the affirmative plan is subject to normal political processes, and its members are subject to normal human frailties. Thus the affirmative may not appoint Gandalf the White and Harry Potter to its administrative body and stipulate that magic will be enacted to overcome attitudinal inherency and any other problems that prevent the status quo from functioning perfectly.

In addition, the plan need only provide sufficient information as to the workings of the policy as advocated. In debating the proposition "Resolved: That the federal government should annually grant a specific percentage of its income tax revenue to the state governments," the affirmative was not obliged to specify how much money would be given to each state. But it was obliged to present a policy by means of which such amounts could be determined.

The second requirement of solvency is that the plan solve the harm to a greater extent than the status quo. This component is known as the "plan meet need" or "plan meet advantage." The affirmative, to meet its prime facie burdens, must guarantee some advantage, and if possible, provide some measure of probable success. It should be able to indicate how much of the harm the plan can reasonably be expected to eliminate.

In building the plan, the advocate should keep solvency in mind. In the research process it is a good idea to begin with the solvency advocates—those experts who support the particular policy. It is important to provide the appropriate agency to administer the plan. In debates on the development of outer space, for example, some affirmatives chose to have their plan administered by NASA, because NASA had the expertise to work in space. These affirmatives were prepared to defend NASA as the best agency to solve the problem.

The mandates should be carefully drafted to achieve the desired objective. In debates on the "guaranteed employment opportunities" proposition, the affirmative could not say, "The government will increase employment by 3 percent." Instead it had to specifically indicate what the government must do to achieve a 3 percent increase in employment. Some affirmatives mandated a reduction of the standard work week under the Fair Labor Standards Act and found that they had to spell out their mandate in great detail to demonstrate that the plan would solve the problem.

---

2. Of course, one may attempt to provide for desirable qualities in appointees. The mayor of Cleveland once appointed a special committee of clergy—promptly dubbed "The God Squad" by the media—to investigate crime. The mayor's supporters hailed the appointments on the ground that clergy would be incorruptible; his opponents scoffed that clergy led sheltered lives and did not know enough about crime to investigate it.

The enforcement plank has to provide incentives or coercive measures to make people behave in the desired way, and it must be realistic and supported by expert advocacy. The enactment of legislation to increase the drinking age to 21 provides an interesting example of plan building to provide for enforcement. The minimum drinking age is determined on a state-by-state basis. The proponents of the 21-year-old minimum recognized that it would take years of lobbying to get all 50 states to enact the legislation they desired, so they chose to lobby the federal government. They succeeded in getting the federal government to enact legislation requiring the states to raise the minimum drinking age to 21 or lose a substantial percentage of federal highway construction funds. This mixture of coercion and incentive provided the enforcement necessary to make the states pass the desired legislation. The proponents of the legislation felt that the states were doing a satisfactory job of enforcing drinking laws; what they wanted to change was the age at which the laws were enforced.

Funding and staffing must be balanced. That is, they must be sufficient to achieve the affirmative's objectives, yet not so great that they can easily be turned into disadvantages. In debates on the "development of space" proposition, many affirmatives found it necessary to provide for multibillion-dollar tax increases to fund their program and multibillion-dollar tax incentives to encourage private corporations' participation in their program. In these cases they had to be ready to prove that these vast sums could be raised. The age-21 drinking law, of course, required no funding plank; to enforce states' compliance, the federal government merely threatened not to distribute funds already appropriated. The addendum plank has to supply any provisions needed to make the plan operate effectively. Sometimes an affirmative plan is against existing laws or constitutional provisions. Remember, as we saw in Chapter 4, constitutionality is never an issue in academic debate. However, the plan must take appropriate action to make its provisions legal. People who wanted to lower the voting age to 18 clearly were proposing an unconstitutional action. The solution came in the form of the Twenty-sixth Amendment. Thus, if the affirmative's plan is unconstitutional, illegal, or extralegal (not regulated by existing law), the addendum plank should include the necessary provisions to legalize its proposal, consistent with normal means. If the negative can successfully argue that the plan is either illegal or so unclear that lengthy court battles will result, the affirmative will lose solvency.

Solvency must be unique to the plan. In developing this portion of the case, the affirmative must demonstrate that only this plan can solve the problem in the most advantageous way. If the needs can be solved by some means other than the plan, there is little reason to adopt the plan. In debates on the mass media proposition, some affirmatives built cases claiming that violence on television was harmful and called for a plan whereby the federal government would regulate television to ban violence. Some negatives meeting this case claimed that the National Association of Broadcasters (NAB) (a voluntary agency) could solve the problem without federal intervention. The affirmative responded by arguing that not all television stations belonged to the NAB and that not all NAB members followed all provisions of the NAB code. Thus the affirmative claimed that only its plan could guarantee full solvency of the needs by mandating that all television stations adhere to its regulations governing violence on television.

Ideally, the affirmative is able to rely on expert solvency advocates, real-world supporters of the affirmative plan. The affirmative is on far safer ground if it can refer to these experts who have designed the proposal and published their advocacy of it as opposed to being creative and designing its own plan. In many cases, the plan may also have been implemented in other areas or smaller jurisdictions as a pilot project or other policy, providing empirical evidence of its desirability.

Finally, the advocates must be prepared to compare the benefits of their proposal to any possible negative consequences or disadvantages. Any change has costs. The affirmative need not point these out, but it must be prepared to answer the negative's arguments that the cost of the plan is greater than its benefits. This third component of solvency is not a prima facie issue, as it need not be discussed until the negative raises the question of disadvantages.

D. Requirement to Prove the Advantages

The advantage portion of the affirmative case must be developed in sufficient detail to demonstrate that the plan meets the need and corrects the deficiencies and weaknesses that the affirmative has found in the status quo. **Advantage** refers to the benefits or gains that the affirmative claims will result from adopting its plan, which must be shown to outweigh the disadvantages. The affirmative also must be careful to link the advantages to the plan and demonstrate that the advantages are caused by the plan, are unique to the plan, and cannot be obtained by other factors outside the scope of the plan.

The advantage(s) should have a clearly identified impact or a substantial measure of importance so that they can be weighed positively against disadvantages. In fact, all arguments should be measured by their impact, both strategically in terms of their importance vis-à-vis all other arguments in the debate, and with regard to measurement of importance. The impact of an affirmative case is the importance and measured value of its advantages.

The advantages should be integrated with the needs. In a debate on the "guaranteed employment opportunities" proposition, if an affirmative argues that millions are unemployed and that these unemployed people suffer from poor health, have high rates of suicide, and commit many crimes, the affirmative must prove as its first advantage that it will provide employment opportunities for millions, that their health will improve, and that suicides and crime will be reduced as a result. The affirmative is most compelling if it is able to prove that increased employment, improved health, and reduction in suicide are a direct result of the plan action, and that the same benefits are *not* available through other programs.

Every policy action has costs. The affirmative's plan will almost invariably create some significant problems. Thus, it is in the negative's interest to discover and present the strongest possible set of disadvantages it can find and to prove that these disadvantages are inherent in the plan. The affirmative must, of course, be prepared to refute or minimize these disadvantages. Realistically, however, some disadvantages cannot be refuted. The affirmative must be able to prove a net gain; that is, it must prove that the advantages outweigh the disadvantages.

An everyday example of the need to prove that the advantages outweigh the disadvantages involves contact lenses. If you or some of your friends wear them, you are aware of a disadvantage—there is the risk of losing them. But those who wear contact lenses have decided that this disadvantage is outweighed by the advantages of convenience and appearance. They have chosen on balance to opt for contact lenses. The idea of balancing advantages against disadvantages is important to the debater. The affirmative seeks to show that on balance the advantages outweigh the disadvantages; the negative seeks to show that the disadvantages outweigh the advantages.

In debating the "guaranteed employment opportunities" proposition, some negatives argued that employment causes more health problems than unemployment does. They cited the number of injuries caused by industrial accidents and the number of illnesses caused by working with hazardous materials, and they claimed that on balance the affirmatives' plan caused more ill health than unemployment did. Affirmatives meeting this disadvantage often responded that they were providing employment opportunities for the unemployed, not forcing them to take jobs. Thus, they argued, on balance it is better for a person to have the opportunity for a job and to have the freedom to choose whether to accept the potential hazards of the job.

Another method of demonstrating that the advantages outweigh the disadvantages is risk analysis. This involves estimating the probability (likelihood) of occurrence of some negatively evaluated state of affairs. The impact of the negatively evaluated state of affairs also has to be determined. We are all familiar with the evidence showing that wearing seat belts saves lives. Death certainly is a high impact disadvantage to not wearing a seat belt. However, the evidence also shows that millions of drivers and passengers have decided that the likelihood of being involved in an accident in which a seat belt might save their lives is remote, so they don't wear seat belts.

In debating the "guaranteed employment opportunities" proposition, some affirmatives presented a plan that mandated a cutback on imported oil and the conversion of all possible industries to fossil fuel. (They argued that the high cost of imported oil caused unemployment and that the development of domestic fossil fuel would increase employment. Development of domestic fossil fuel production would necessarily rely on growth of the labor-intensive coal industry. Coal emissions, however, have an even greater impact on the environment than do oil emissions.) In response some negatives developed the disadvantage that the affirmative's plan would melt the polar ice caps by increasing coal emissions into the upper atmosphere and cause flooding of all the world's coastal cities, which, in turn, would cause trillions of dollars of damage. Certainly the negative had high impact—trillions of dollars of damage is an awesome disadvantage. Some affirmatives meeting this disadvantage, however, were able to demonstrate that these events had a very low likelihood of occurring. Melting of the polar ice caps would require a quantum increase of coal-based fossil fuel emissions on a worldwide scale, whereas the affirmative proposed only that the United States increase its use of fossil fuel. Because the negative was usually unable to establish any threshold—the point at which burning a million more tons of coal would actually melt the polar ice caps—the affirmative was usually able to demonstrate that the likelihood of the disadvantages occurring was remote and thus that the advantage outweighed the disadvantage.

A particularly effective way for an affirmative to answer a disadvantage argument against its plan is the turnaround. In common usage a **turnaround argument** is any statement that one turns against the originator. In debate usage the term is usually applied to the affirmative's turning around a negative's disadvantage and converting it into an advantage or to the negative's turning around an affirmative's advantage and converting it into a disadvantage. Thus both teams in a debate must seek to develop their arguments so as to avoid turnarounds of their own position. At the same time they must be alert for opportunities to provide turnarounds for their opponent's arguments. (We will consider the negative's use of turnarounds in Chapter 13.) Turnaround arguments may be "link turns" based on the links to the negative disadvantage arguments (that is, the plan not only does not cause the disadvantage, it actually prevents it!) or "impact turns" based on the impacts (the consequence of the disadvantage is not really a bad thing; in fact, it is a very good thing). Of course, the affirmative should be careful to avoid making both sorts of "turn" arguments at the same time, or it may fall into the trap of a "double turn" (if it argues that its plan better avoids the disadvantage impact, and that the disadvantage impact is actually good, it is offering a reason why the plan is bad).

In debates on the guaranteed employment proposition, some affirmatives claimed as an advantage that their plan would "raise millions out of poverty." Some negatives meeting this case countered with the disadvantage that the affirmative plan would "increase cardiovascular disease" (arguing that with increased income people would drink more alcoholic beverages, which would lead to more cardiovascular disease). Some affirmatives meeting this disadvantage were able to turn around the argument and claim the additional advantage of "improved health" (arguing that a moderate increase in consumption of alcohol actually reduced the risk of cardiovascular disease—the negative had merely shown that more people would drink alcohol, not that anyone would drink to excess).

The disadvantages just cited were used frequently by negative constructive speakers. But did they represent a hard-nosed assessment of the real world, or were they merely strategic ploys of little merit? Such arguments are made in real-world policy debates, and all of the evidence comes from reputable sources. The "real world" is a mixture of insightful and farfetched arguments, and the advocate must be prepared to respond to both. Only careful risk analysis will allow us to assess the merits of the argument and to demonstrate to those who render the decision whether the grounds, and the supporting arguments or intermediate conclusions, constitute good reasons for accepting the conclusion.

A familiar example of a turnaround is the pre-law student who considered taking an accounting course as an undergraduate because she felt she would need knowledge of accounting in law school. A friend advised her, "Don't take accounting now—it will take too much time from your other courses." The pre-law student decided that this argument was a turnaround. She chose to take the accounting course as an undergraduate on the grounds that she could better afford the time it would take as an undergraduate than as a law student.

E. Requirement to Defend Topicality

Topicality is sometimes mistaken for a prima facie issue. It is not. Topicality is certainly a critical issue, often the single most important issue in the debate, but it is considered independently of the stock issues. Topicality is an *a priori* issue. This means it must be decided first. After the debate, the judge first considers topicality. If the plan is topical, the judge will then evaluate the stock issues. If the plan is not topical, the judge need not examine the stock issues. Hence, it is a priori. Although presumption on the stock issues is generally negative because the negative opposes change, presumption on the issue of topicality is generally affirmative: Judges consider the plan to be topical unless and until the negative makes persuasive arguments that it is not. The affirmative need not prove that its plan is topical in order to be prima facie.

F. Preparation

Once the manuscript for the affirmative speech is completed, the advocates have to prepare *briefs*—short speech segments—that they will use to refute negative attacks and to extend affirmative arguments. Because these briefs must be adapted to the specific negative case met, they cannot simply be read from a manuscript; rather, they have to serve as carefully planned outlines for an extemporaneous presentation. Successful debaters also will be able to produce well-executed extensions. *Extensions* consist of new evidence and analysis to carry forward arguments introduced earlier; they are not simply repetitions of previously introduced evidence and argument analysis.

IV. BUILDING FOR OPTIMUM CAPABILITY

Affirmative advocates of both value and policy propositions have the burden of proof; they must take the offensive and mount a strong attack to advance their case. Much of what we have considered so far has to do with the affirmative's offensive position. Remember, though, that debate does not take place in a vacuum and that an able negative will mount strong attacks against the affirmative. The affirmative has to build its case and deploy its evidence so as to achieve the optimum balance of offensive and defensive capabilities.

In building their case, advocates have to anticipate the probable areas of negative attack. They frequently can adjust their case to avoid or blunt many negative attacks before they can be made. In developing cases on the "comprehensive medical care for all citizens" proposition, many affirmative advocates, foreshadowing the Clinton proposal, called for "universal coverage." As they studied possible negative attacks, they discovered that the enormous cost and complexity of universal coverage provided the negative with myriad plan attacks. After considering the difficulty of answering the potential attacks, many affirmative teams rejected universal coverage and opted for plans that provided for incremental increases in the number of people covered. The incremental plans, of course, covered only 80 or 90 percent of the population after five years rather than 100 percent immediately. The same negative attacks applied, but because an incremental plan would cost billions of dollars less than a universal plan, it was much easier to defend.

On the same proposition some affirmative advocates thought it would be a good idea to provide annual physical examinations for all citizens as a plank in their plan. Initially they discovered a good deal of evidence supporting the idea. But later they discovered evidence—which they were sure their opponents would also find—indicating that these examinations for the whole population were counterproductive when subjected to cost-benefit analysis. (The argument went that it would take so much time to give over 250 million physical examinations a year that physicians would not have time to do anything else.) Thus some affirmatives eliminated what had initially seemed a desirable plank for their plan and provided instead for multiphasic testing for the population. This method would check for many, but not all, diseases. Because the tests would be administered by physicians' aides and analyzed by computers, their cost would be much lower, in terms of both dollars and physicians' time.

Although it is defensively sound to choose a plan that avoids the strongest negative attacks, advocates are cautioned that they still must provide a plan that will produce significant advantages. Obviously it is easier to answer the cost attacks on a $1 billion plan than on a $70 billion plan. Given the context of the proposition, however, does the $1 billion plan produce significant advantages? The task of the affirmative advocates is to build a plan that achieves the optimum balance of offensive and defensive capabilities.

President Reagan once called his speechwriting staff together to plan a series of campaign speeches. He summed up his objective by saying, "Anyway, what I want is the kind of speech there ain't no rebuttal to."[3] Reagan's request is every debater's dream. And his graceful eulogy of the *Challenger* astronauts certainly evoked no rebuttal. But no team of speechwriters, no matter how talented, could produce a campaign speech that would face no rebuttal. Indeed, no speech on a debatable subject can be presumed to be safe from rebuttal.

Prudent affirmatives will consider the most likely and effective attacks against their case and build in reasonable defensive provisions. An axiom of debate is that a good case defends itself, and the well-planned case is built to provide for the maximally effective self-defense.

---

3. Peggy Noonan, *What I Saw at the Revolution* (New York: Random House, 1990), p. 146. Used by permission of Elizabeth Jones.

V. ALTERNATIVE DEBATE APPROACHES

As has been discussed earlier in this book (Chapters 2, 4, and 6), one thing intrinsic to debate is self-examination and change. Although what you have read thus far in this chapter will provide a sound traditional framework for policy and value debate, the traditions are slowly evolving. An unbounded creativity in practice has evolved, with new conceptions of fiat as the reflexive authority of those participating in the debate round itself, and with critical examination of the battle to give rhetorical space to marginalized voices and open the debate experience to more viewpoints, standpoints, and cultures. Debate approaches may disregard the traditional frameworks in favor of storytelling, hip-hop, music and film, poetry, and other novel challenges to the conventional approaches. In more subtle structures, debaters can build their comparative advantage cases with philosophical foundations. More radical challenges to tradition may offer argumentation (sometimes in aesthetic forms) to defend the resolution and/or to challenge the framework of policy debate. Critical approaches focus on philosophical and value-based interpretations of propositional terms, and performance-based approaches find clash in music, visual communication, role playing, and other creative forms of self expression. Elizabeth Jones of Louisville University presented the following rap as a part of her affirmative case in favor of U.S. withdrawal from NATO:

> Roma people feel just like me, tired of being deprived of their liberty.
> Relegated to ghettos, held as slaves, poor health care leading to early graves.
> Prison scars, from prison bars, walking round the prison yard.
> No running water, no heat, no jobs, and everything you've seemed to love, you've lost.
> While the rich get richer, who's paying the cost?
> George Soros, Bill Clinton, to Dick Cheney, the so-called bearers of democracy.
> NATO represents the military wing, of the all-powerful capitalist regime.
> While you think gangsters listen to rap and sag,
> They really wear suits and carry leather bags.
> Politicians with the power to pick, define, and choose who will win and who will lose.
> Not hearing the Roma or Palestine,
> I guess it depends how genocide is defined.

SOURCE: USED BY PERMISSION OF ELIZABETH JONES.

EXERCISES

1. Prepare the full manuscript for a first affirmative speech on a value proposition. Include all the evidence and reasoning necessary to establish a prima facie case.

2. Prepare the full manuscript for a first affirmative speech on a policy proposition. Include all the evidence and reasoning necessary to establish a prima facie case.

3. Write a rap in support of a proposition of value or policy.

13

Building the Negative Case

The negative case requires flexibility in planning. A careful analysis of the proposition will probably enable the negative to determine the issues the affirmative is most likely to advance. But until the debate is actually under way, the negative team may not know what type of case the affirmative is advocating; it will not know what weight the affirmative attaches to each issue or what evidence and argument it uses in developing its issues. This uncertainty places a high premium on the negative's ability to adapt to the affirmative's case as it is presented.

I. OBJECTIVES OF THE NEGATIVE CASE

As indicated earlier, the burden of proof rests on the affirmative. In theory the negative does not even have to speak until the affirmative has presented a prima facie case. The prudent advocate will recognize, however, that audiences sometimes equate silence with consent and may accept a proposition on the basis of less than a prima facie case. Therefore, the advocate has to be prepared to reply to any affirmative case, even though it does not meet all the logical requirements of a prima facie case. In the courtroom the defense may move that a case be dismissed on the ground that the prosecution or plaintiff has not presented a prima facie case. But this option is not generally available outside the courtroom.

While the burden of proof rests on the affirmative, the negative has the **burden of rebuttal**; that is, the negative has the obligation to refute at least one of the issues of the affirmative, or the affirmative will prevail. The negative may choose simply to point to holes in the affirmative case, hoping to damage the affirmative's ability to defend all issues. However, the negative will be much more effective if it constructs a coherent position, integrating its arguments into a policy advocacy that competes with the affirmative's advocacy. We will discuss first the proposition of value negative case and then the proposition of policy

Miniglossary

Burden of rebuttal   The obligation of the negative to refute at least one of the issues of the affirmative. Otherwise the affirmative will prevail.

Conditional counterplan   Argument by the negative that it may abandon advocacy of the counterplan if certain conditions prevail.

Case turn   Offensive negative strategy designed to demonstrate that the needs identified by the affirmative are not needs but, in fact, benefits to the status quo.

Counterplan   A plan presented by the negative that is competitive with the affirmative's plan and is a superior policy alternative.

Disadvantages   The undesirable consequences that the negative claims will flow from the affirmative's plan. These must be shown to outweigh the advantages.

Generic disadvantages   Disadvantages that may be applied to a number of possible affirmative plans.

Kritic   An argument which challenges the philosophical foundations, or applies ethical constructs to the opponent's advocacy and its implications.

Permutation   A test of competition of a counterplan offered by the affirmative.

Shells   Brief versions of arguments to be expanded upon later in the debate.

Slippery slope argument   The argument that a seemingly harmless proposal in the affirmative's plan would be an irreversible first step leading inevitably to the most deleterious disadvantages.

Topical counterplan   A counterplan that might be used as an affirmative plan under some definitions of the resolution but is nontopical with regard to the operational definition the affirmative has chosen to use. Once the affirmative has parametrically defined the resolution, almost any mutually exclusive plan may constitute grounds for a counterplan.

Topicality   The state of conformity to the intent of the debate resolution. A plan is topical if it justifies the full intent of the resolution, the needs are solved, or the comparative advantages are gained as a direct result of the planks in the plan that implement the resolution.

Utopian counterplan   A counterplan proposed by the negative that mandates that the nation or the world will be arranged in a manner consistent with anarchy, world government, socialism, authoritarianism, or some other future strategy and claims that this strategy will better solve the problem than the federal government or whatever agency of change is provided in the proposition.

Value objections   In value debate, the negative argument that undesirable consequences will flow from adoption of the affirmative's case. Similar to a disadvantage in policy debate.

negative case. The discussion of the policy negative case will include a consideration of many issues critical to both value and policy negative cases.

II. PROPOSITION OF VALUE NEGATIVE CASES

The negative has the burden of rebuttal and has to attack the case that the affirmative presents. The negative knows that the affirmative will present definitive and designative issues. The negative has to refute at least one of the affirmative issues, or else carry one of the issues the negative introduces, to win. Again, negatives will be much more persuasive if their arguments are integrated into a coherent, comprehensive negative position. In developing the negative case, the value debaters select the most appropriate combination of the various available options.

A. Attack Topicality

Topicality refers to the state of conformity to the intent of the debate resolution. When advocates argue that a matter is not topical, they maintain that it is not related to or does not directly stem from the proposition being debated. In a debate on a proposition of value, topicality is an attack on the affirmative's definitions as they come together to provide an interpretation of the proposition. For example, in a debate on the proposition that increasing foreign investment in the United States is detrimental to this nation, one negative debater argued that the affirmative's definition of terms must be consistent with its grammatical use in the proposition. The debater noted that whether a word is used as a noun, a verb, or an adverb will substantially alter the meaning of the proposition. Thus the negative concluded that the affirmative's was not topical, because its definition of the word *increasing* did not stem from the term as used in the proposition.

Topicality is an "a priori" issue—that is, it is considered separate from and prior to other issues. If the negative can convince the judges that the affirmative's case is not topical, it may win regardless of the strength of the case—the implication being that the affirmative case does not support the resolution being debated. If the affirmative can convince the judges that its case is topical, it will have won that issue but not the debate.

Definitions were discussed in some detail in Chapter 4. As noted there, in value debate the affirmative is required to present at least a reasonable interpretation of the proposition. If the affirmative's definition is perceived to be unreasonable, the negative may choose to attack the definition. The likely implication of a successful negative attack on the definitions of the affirmative is that the case is nontopical, which means the negative wins the debate.

B. Attack Criteria

To successfully attack the affirmative criteria, the negative should offer reasons the criteria initially presented are flawed or dangerous and also offer a *countercriterion.* In a debate on the proposition "Resolved: That significantly stronger third-party participation in United States presidential elections would benefit the political process," one affirmative argued that "survival" was the ultimate value—that is, the most important criterion. A negative meeting this case argued that "democracy" was the ultimate value. As the debate developed, the negative was able to sustain its position that democracy was the most important criterion and so won the decision. Accepting the countercriterion as superior will force the judge to measure the competing values and applications by the negative standard. If the negative can establish that other criteria are more important than those advanced by the affirmative and show that the affirmative does not meet these criteria, the negative will usually prevail.

C. Attack Significance

The negative's objective in attacking significance is to prove that at least some of the essential elements of the affirmative's case are not significant enough to justify adopting the resolution. If the affirmative can establish the significance of its case, it is in a strong position to counter other negative attacks. Thus the negative must find ways to minimize the significance of at least some of the essential elements of the affirmative's case.

D. Attack Uniqueness

The negative's objective in attacking uniqueness is to prove that at least some of the essential elements of the affirmative's case are not unique to the resolutional terms, and thus do not warrant accepting the resolution. In a debate on the third-party proposition mentioned previously, one affirmative argued that significantly stronger third parties would intrinsically lead to beneficial applications in the American political system. The affirmative cited the income tax, direct election of senators, women's suffrage, labor legislation, and social security as examples of desirable legislation originating with third parties. The negative meeting this case pointed out that these laws were enacted under the status quo and thus were not unique to strengthened third parties. If the negative can prove that some elements of the affirmative case are not unique to the case or could be obtained without adopting the resolution, it has successfully attacked the uniqueness claim of the affirmative.

E. Attack Application

In attacking application the negative tries to prove that the value or quasi-policy advocated by the affirmative will not be applied to the problem, that the implication of the value is not positive, or that the application offered is not a legitimate application of the values being upheld. In a debate on the third-party proposition, one affirmative claimed that the application of the resolution would result in strengthened third parties able to enact important legislation perceived as extreme by complacent majorities. A negative meeting this case attacked the application by arguing it would not function as the affirmative claimed it would. The negative maintained that a third party could not enact any legislation until it grew to major-party size, and to attract enough voters to do that, it would have to drop its extreme position.

F. Attack Solvency

Of course, in a debate over a proposition of value, the affirmative is not required to present a plan (although at times they may offer a plan or something like it to represent the implications of their value position.) However, it is often effective for the negative to point to the concrete implications of affirmative advocacy in order to challenge the benefits or reasons to accept the value(s) promoted by the affirmative. In attacking solvency the negative argues that, even if the application functions as the affirmative wants it to, it will not solve the problem, or achieve the good things implied by value advocacy. This is really a policy argument applied to the value or quasi-policy context. In debates on the proposition on foreign investment in the United States mentioned previously, some affirmative teams argued as follows:

1. Foreign investors would build coal-burning factories in the United States that would substantially increase the amount of carbon dioxide released into the atmosphere.
2. This increase of carbon dioxide would cause a greenhouse effect.
3. The greenhouse effect would warm the earth's atmosphere.
4. This would cause disastrous changes in the earth's climate, which would threaten life on earth.

Negative teams meeting this type of case often responded by arguing in this way:

1. If all U.S. coal-burning plants were shut down, the greenhouse effect would be delayed for only three or four years.
2. China, with 50 percent of global coal reserves, intends to increase coal consumption substantially in the near future.
3. Other countries are eager to increase industrialization and will use more coal.

The negative team then concluded that the affirmative's plan would not solve the greenhouse problem, which it gave as the justification for accepting the resolution. If the negative wins the solvency argument, there is no reason to adopt the resolution.

G. Provide Value Objections

Value objections are the negative arguments that undesirable consequences will flow from adoption of the affirmative's case. In other words, they are reasons the criteria and/or values upon which the affirmative case relies are philosophically or pragmatically bad. In providing value objections the negative argues that the affirmative's proposal or advocacy will produce something so objectionable—in effect, a disadvantage—that we should reject the affirmative's case. In a debate on the third-party proposition, one negative argued that multiple parties rather than a lone third party would result. Multiple parties, she claimed, inherently lead to unstable governments and domestic chaos, which in turn would lead to a totalitarian regime. Note that value objections are introduced by the negative. When the negative introduces them, the affirmative must be prepared to demonstrate that they are not significant and that they are outweighed by other issues.

III. PROPOSITION OF POLICY
NEGATIVE APPROACHES

As in value negative cases, in policy debates the negative has the burden of rebuttal and must attack the case that the affirmative presents. The negative knows that the affirmative will present harm, inherency, plan, solvency, and advantage issues. The negative must refute at least one of the affirmative issues, or else carry one of the issues the negative introduces, to win. Of course the negative will be in a much stronger and more persuasive position if it can create a consistent and coherent advocacy to compete with the affirmative's advocacy. The specific development of the case and the particular issues the negative uses in any given situation obviously will depend on the resolution under debate, the available evidence and arguments, the actual case of the opposition, the dynamics of the occasion, and the attitudes, interests, and intellectual capabilities of the audience.

Each negative strategy should be custom built and adapted to the specific affirmative case it must oppose. The negative selects among its arsenal of potential issues and develops those best suited to a particular situation. Although carrying one issue—workability, for instance—could win for the negative, advocates should remember that a competent affirmative will have anticipated and prepared for all possible attacks. Thus, because the negative can rarely be sure of winning an issue until the debate is over, its best strategy generally is to attack all vulnerable areas of the affirmative case. It should concentrate its major attacks on the most vulnerable areas—for example, not only attacking workability but also providing minor repairs or a counterplan and proving that disadvantages outweigh advantages.

A. Attack Topicality

All other arguments in a debate are weighed together, relative to one another, but topicality is a stand-alone issue. Because topicality is considered a priori, if the judge determines that the plan is not topical, he or she will usually not consider the other issues in the debate. In debate over policy propositions, the question of topicality is strictly a question of the plan and whether it represents the action called for in the language of the proposition. If the negative wins the topicality issue, it generally wins the debate. It is the one issue that if won by the negative is usually means the debate is won by the negative. Other issues are measured in relation to each other, but topicality stands alone.

When advocates argue that a plan is not topical, they maintain that it is not a legitimate or appropriate embodiment of the action called for in the proposition being debated. In the courts an attorney may object to a piece of evidence, a question, or an argument on the ground that it is not relevant to the case before the court. If the judge sustains the objection, the matter is excluded. In parliamentary debate the chair can rule as "out of order" any remarks or proposed amendments that are not germane to the business before the house. (The stringency with which this rule is enforced varies; for example, the U.S. Senate does not require that a senator's remarks be germane.) In academic debate the topicality issue usually becomes an absolute voting issue, and the judge awards the decision to the negative if it wins the issue. In less formal situations reasonable individuals tend to dismiss irrelevant arguments.

1. Topicality of the Plan.   Recall that topicality refers to whether the plan is a legitimate and fair interpretation of the policy action called for in the resolution. The primary test for topicality is the *plan in a vacuum*. The plan, absent arguments about justification, solvency, and advantages, must be topical.

The proposition "Resolved: That the federal government should grant annually a specific percentage of its income tax revenue to the state governments" provides an interesting example. This proposition mandated four specific things for the affirmative's plan: (1) an annual grant, (2) a specific percentage of the revenue, (3) funds coming from federal income tax revenue, and (4) funds distributed by the federal government to state governments. If any one of these items had been missing, the negative would have had grounds for arguing "not topical." The affirmative may add some nontopical provisions to its plan to provide for a reasonable implementation of its proposal. For example, in debating the revenue-sharing proposition, some teams provided that the funds could not be used for (1) matching federal funds for federal categorical grant programs or (2) highway construction. The negative is well advised to argue that portions of the plan are nontopical; thus any advantage gained by them is extratopical and should not be considered. An effective structure for negative topicality arguments is as follows:

2. Extratopicality of the Advantages.   The advantages must be a direct result of implementation of a topical plan. If the negative can prove an advantage is extratopical, that advantage should be rejected as a reason for adopting the resolution.

If the advantages come from a nontopical provision of the plan, the affirmative is in trouble. On the revenue-sharing proposition some affirmative teams argued that the states should be required to give the funds to the public schools and claimed the advantage of better education. Negatives meeting this case were usually able to prove that the provision was nontopical and that the advantage of

---

Topicality

---

1. *Definition(s):* The negative presents its definition(s) of terms or phrases in the resolution.
2. *Violation(s):* The negative argues that the affirmative plan violates or fails to meet the negatives definition(s).
3. *Reasons to prefer:* The negative offers standards or criteria by which definitions should be judged and argues that its definitions more completely meet these criteria than do the affirmatives definitions; therefore, its interpretation is superior and should be preferred.
4. *Impact (voting issue):* The negative explains why the affirmatives failure to present a topical plan means the judge should vote for the negative.

---

better education came from giving the money to the schools and not from any of the four items mandated in the resolution. They also demonstrated that the advantage was "not unique" to the resolution. The same advantage could be achieved by having the federal government give money (and not necessarily income tax revenue) directly to the schools.

As we have just seen, the advantage of "better education" was nontopical. As we have also noted, reasonable nontopical planks may be added to the plan to provide for its reasonable implementation. Any advantage that comes from a nontopical plank of the plan is itself nontopical. For example, the provision that no revenue-sharing funds be used for highway construction was a reasonable nontopical constraint. If, however, the affirmative claimed as an advantage that it would reduce waste in highway construction, such an advantage would clearly be nontopical; it would stem from adoption of a nontopical plank of the plan. Of course it would also be "not unique" in that any waste in highway construction could be eliminated by legislation other than revenue sharing.

B. Attack the Harm

The objective of the negative here is either to challenge the harm issue by demonstrating that the affirmative has not proved the existence of a harm, by proving that there is no harm, by minimizing the harm, or by arguing that the harm is, in fact, a benefit.

1. No Harm.   In rare circumstances, the negative may be able to argue successfully that there is no harm to the conditions identified by the affirmative. In debating the proposition "Resolved: That the federal government should control the supply and utilization of energy in the United States," some affirmatives called for the federal government to ban any further construction of nuclear energy plants to generate electricity. They pointed out that the status quo was committed to the construction of such plants and argued, as their harm issue, the claim that, when we had 100 or more such plants, there would be an unacceptable risk of radiation leakage or explosion. Many negatives argued that no harm existed or would exist. They maintained that nuclear power plants were perfectly safe and that any leakage or explosion was impossible. They cited evidence that no fatality had ever been caused by a civilian nuclear power plant and extended their argument by citing the elaborate safety precautions already in existence. The disaster at Chernobyl was irrelevant, the affirmative maintained, because the plant had been built to a design inferior to U.S. standards. Debates on this issue provided excellent examples of the clash of evidence. Solid evidence was available to both sides, and the debate inevitably was won by the team that could provide the most recent evidence from the best qualified authorities, who could be quoted most directly in support of the point under dispute.

2. Harm Not Significant. The negative objective in attacking significance is to prove that the harms or advantages of the affirmative (when weighed against the disadvantages of plan adoption and the advantages of a counterplan or modified status quo) are not sufficiently significant to warrant adopting the resolution. In many debates, this is synonymous with arguing existence of the harm issue, as discussed above. However, when the measure of importance of the harm is in question, the significance of the harm is the appropriate target of the negative.

The negative will usually find it advisable to examine the affirmative's harm for both quantitative and qualitative significance and attack the affirmative if either or both are not proved. In debates on the proposition "Resolved: That the federal government should significantly strengthen the regulation of mass media communication in the United States," some affirmatives argued that television commercials for sugar-laden food products caused cavities in children. Negatives meeting this case readily proved that an unknown number of cavities were not sufficient justification for government regulation of the mass media. On the same proposition some affirmatives argued that violence on television "affected children adversely." Again, negatives quickly refuted the significance of the harm—no significant numbers of children were proved to have been adversely affected, and no qualification was provided for "adversely affected."

In debates on the "guarantee employment opportunities" proposition, affirmatives could usually readily show that millions were unemployed, thus establishing quantitative significance. Negative advocates often granted this argument quickly and went on to argue that the affirmative had not proved any qualitative harm from unemployment. They continued this argument by introducing evidence to show that many unemployed persons received unemployment compensation, food stamps, and other welfare benefits. Thus, they maintained, the affirmative had not proved that the unemployed persons were harmed by their unemployment.

The negative may attack the affirmative for failing to prove quantitative significance, qualitative significance, or, in some circumstances, both quantitative and qualitative significance. Most often, of course, the affirmative will successfully establish some significance. The task of the negative then is to prove that the significance established by the affirmative is not sufficient on balance to outweigh the disadvantages the negative will try to prove.

3. Harm Overstated.   A well-prepared affirmative is usually able to identify an important harm area and to find expert evidence that portrays the harm in the most compelling way possible. It is the job of the negative to argue that the affirmative's estimation of the harm is overstated and to offer evidence to prove that point. Successfully done, this mitigates the magnitude of the impact won by the affirmative.

4. Case Turns.   The most effective way to argue against the affirmative's harms is to use the classic turnaround argument, or *case turn*. This is an offensive negative strategy designed to demonstrate that the harms identified by the affirmative are not harms but, in fact, benefits to the status quo. For example, during debates on the proposition "Resolved: That the United States federal government should amend Title VII of the Civil Rights Act of 1964, through legislation, to create additional protections against racial and/or gender discrimination," many affirmatives identified broad cases of discrimination occurring within the status quo. Negatives turned this issue by claiming that, although discrimination is evil, its existence motivated repressed people to organize movements and mobilize grassroots action, which would be far more effective in creating meaningful social change than the top-down solution mandated by the plan.

C. Attack Inherency

Negative teams often use two types of inherency arguments: (1) The status quo has no inherent barrier blocking the achievement of the advantage, and (2) the status quo has no inherent gap preventing the attainment of the advantage. Remember that if the affirmative inherency is very strong, it may swamp solvency; that is, no plan may be able to overcome the inherency. Fiat will allow implementation, but not workability. In addition, fiating affirmative action over strong attitudinal biases or disrupting existing governmental structures may result in substantial disadvantages. Finally, if the affirmative has not clearly identified the reasons the plan has not been implemented or the root causes of the problem, it may be missing the hidden disadvantages that are the real reasons the harm continues to exist.

1. Inherency of the Status Quo Barrier.   The negative tries to prove that no justification exists for adopting the resolution, because the advantages claimed by the affirmative can be achieved without the plan. In debating the energy proposition, some affirmatives proposed a plan whereby the government would require all electric generating plants to use coal as their only fuel and to generate electricity by the magnetohydrodynamic (MHD) process. They argued that this method used cheap and plentiful coal and was far more efficient than the status quo methods of producing electricity. As an advantage they claimed that the oil now used by the electric plants—which was in critically short supply—would be made available to industries that could not substitute coal as a source of energy. Some negatives meeting this type of case responded by pointing out that the affirmative had cited no reason that the electric industry would not adopt the

MHD process of its own volition. Using a conditional argument, they main-tained—because coal was both abundant and cheap—that, if the process really was more efficient, then it would obviously be more profitable for the electric companies to adopt the MHD process and that they would do so quickly; hence there was no justification for the plan. Some affirmatives had difficulty respond-ing to this argument until they found evidence allowing them to argue that the high initial cost of MHD equipment was an inherent barrier to the process being adopted by electric companies. The cost was so high that it would take many years for the companies to realize any profit from the changeover. Thus, they argued, the only way to obtain the advantages of MHD was to adopt the resolu-tion and use federal control to require the electric companies to use this process.

2. Inherency of the Status Quo Gap.   In debating the mass media proposition, some affirmatives maintained that television violence was harmful and argued that a gap in existing laws permitted the broadcast of violent programs. Some negatives meeting this argument held that the legal gap was irrelevant and that other status quo means existed to control violence. They agreed that television networks and stations were responsive to public pressure, and they cited various examples of programs that had been taken off the air because of public opposi-tion. If the affirmative's harms were valid, the negatives maintained, public pres-sure would be sufficient to cause the networks and stations to change their pro-gramming. Many negatives extended this argument by offering a minor repair—use voluntary means to keep violence off television—and claimed that this repair would achieve the affirmative's advantage of reducing television violence with-out the disadvantage of increased governmental control.

3. Repairs and Modifications.   Repairs and modifications reflect an affirma-tive's failure to accurately identify an inherent harm. They may also offer strate-gic ways that the negative may defend the status quo but not accept its flaws. Finally they can help to mitigate the need or advantage the affirmative can claim at the end of the debate.

The negative can use two types of repair or modification arguments: (1) to solve harms and (2) to provide advantages. The repairs or modifications should be relatively few and relatively minor; they have to be consistent with the status quo; there should be ample precedent for such actions; and they must be capable of being put into effect without any structural change in the status quo. Generally it is a superior strategy for the negative to consider repairs in the form of a counterplan, as this may provide a more consistent advocacy position (counterplans are discussed in detail later in the chapter).

a. To Solve Harm.   This type of argument is used when the negative is forced to admit certain shortcomings in the status quo but believes they can be repaired by status quo mechanisms. Usually the negative first seeks to minimize the harm issues and then presents its repairs. For example, in debates on the law enforce-ment proposition mentioned previously, some negative teams argued that the laws already on the books were adequate to deal with crime; all that was needed were more funds to provide for better enforcement. They maintained that more funds would (1) provide more "hardware," such as computers and mobile communication centers; (2) enable police forces to upgrade by paying higher salaries to attract and retain more able officers and to provide in-service training; (3) provide more prosecutors and more judges, ensuring prompt trials; (4) provide more effective rehabilitation programs in prisons; and (5) provide more parole officers to supervise the prisoners after they were released. This combination of repairs—although maintaining the status quo laws—would significantly reduce crime, they argued.

In debates on the "comprehensive medical care" proposition, many negative teams made effective use of repairs. If the affirmative limited its need analysis to the claim that "poor people can't afford medical care," the negative quickly offered repairs to extend Medicare, Medicaid, free clinics, the free care provisions of the Hill-Burton Act, and many other programs. The negative noted that all of these programs existed in the status quo, that they provided ample precedent for the government to provide free medical care for poor people, and that no structural change in any program was required.

In both of these examples, if the negative can show that the amount of money needed is relatively small and can be obtained without dislocating other government programs, they are true minor repairs. But if the amount of money needed is massive and would require serious tax increases or the curtailment of other government spending, the negative will be arguing "major" repairs that might provide the affirmative with the opportunity to claim that the negative's proposal will produce significant disadvantages.

The distinction between minor and major repairs is situational. *Minor* repairs utilize the status quo mechanisms in a way that does not significantly alter the status quo or change its structure. *Major* repairs significantly alter the status quo and may require a change in its structure. A plan that provided for the federal government to spend $1 billion more in grants to the nation's police forces would probably qualify as a minor repair. A senator once commented on the scale of federal expenditures by observing wryly, "A billion here, a billion there, and pretty soon it adds up to real money." A $1 billion increase for police by even the largest of cities would, of course, require massive structural changes in the status quo.

b. To Achieve Advantages.   This type of argument is used when the negative believes that the advantage claimed by the affirmative can be achieved without adopting the resolution but merely by making some modifications in the status quo that the advantage is "not unique" to the proposition. The debater might choose to make a conditional argument and show that the advantage could be provided by modifications without advocating that the advantage actually be achieved. If the advantage could be achieved without adopting the resolution, it would not be a justification for adopting the resolution.

In debating the energy proposition, some affirmatives introduced a plan to ban the use of coal in producing electricity and mandated the use of nuclear power plants. One of the advantages they claimed was "cleaner air." A negative team meeting this case argued that the status quo was already working to provide cleaner air and that, if we wanted even cleaner air, all we had to do was modify the standards of the Air Quality Act, because ample technology existed to make this cleanup practical. By merely making a minor modification in the status quo, we could achieve the advantage of cleaner air without adopting the affirmative's plan and suffering all the inherent disadvantages of nuclear power plants that the negative would try to prove in the "disadvantages" portion of its case.

The negative, of course, has to exercise discretion in making modifications or repairs. A multiplicity of repairs or modifications might open the way for the affirmative to argue that the negative has admitted the harm or advantage of so many repairs or modifications that we should "go all the way" and adopt the resolution.

D. Attack Solvency

Typically the negative will seek to minimize the affirmative advantage by arguing issues of harm and inherency, and then prove that the plan will not achieve the benefits claimed by the affirmative.

In developing solvency arguments, the negative attempts to prove that the plan will not work, that even if it works exactly as the affirmative wants it to, it will not solve the harm or achieve the advantages claimed, and that the advantages are not significant or compelling. For example, in debates on the "guaranteed annual wage for nonagricultural workers" proposition, some affirmatives argued as their harm issue that the purchasing power of unemployed persons must be maintained. They cited evidence that millions of persons were unemployed annually and then presented a plan that would provide a guaranteed annual wage for employees with one year's seniority. Negatives argued that the plan did not provide solvency because millions of the unemployed cited in the affirmative's harm were agricultural workers, who were not covered in the plan (they were excluded by the resolution). Negatives then introduced evidence to show that most unemployed persons had less than one year's seniority in their last job and so would not receive the guaranteed annual wage provided for in the plan. The plan would work for the relatively few unemployed persons with one year's seniority, but not for the millions cited by the affirmative in its need issue.

In debates on the "guaranteed employment opportunities for all U.S. citizens" proposition, some affirmatives proposed a plan to rebuild the inner cities and claimed as their advantage that this plan would provide jobs for all. Negatives meeting this case were quick to point out that the jobs created by this plan did not "guarantee employment opportunities" for workers unskilled in the building trades or for people who could not handle the physical demands of unskilled construction work.

1. Workability.   The negative's objective here is to block adoption of the resolution by proving that the plan proposed by the affirmative is unworkable. Those advocating a ban on personal ownership of handguns would have to prove that such a law would be enforceable given the likely inherency, that many gun owners would elect to keep their guns, and that in order to apply the ban, law enforcement agencies would have to violate privacy rights beyond their ability to do so. Advocates of nuclear fission as a method of energy production or manned space travel beyond the solar system would have a hard time proving the efficacy of the technologies. To argue workability, the negative should present a series of concisely stated, closely reasoned arguments. In preparing for this, as with other negative issues, advocates often develop a series of briefs against potential affirmative plans. When they hear the plan the affirmative is actually presenting, they pull the appropriate briefs from their file and adapt them to the specific plan presented by the affirmative.

Debating the energy proposition, one affirmative team cited the energy shortage as its harm and proposed to solve the harm by a plan that called for the federal government to require electric plants to phase out the use of oil and coal and to build solar, geothermal, and nuclear plants to produce electricity. Well-prepared negatives usually had briefs of arguments prepared for each of these energy sources. One negative argued against this plan by introducing evidence to establish the following:

> First, solar energy is unworkable because (1) it has never been proven in commercial use; (2) its potential is geographically limited by cloud cover; (3) the fuel cell method is prohibitively expensive—it would increase the cost of electricity one thousand times; and (4) the reflector method is prohibitive in land cost—it would require an area equal to the size of 21 states to solve the affirmative's needs.

> Second, nuclear energy is unworkable because (1) there will be a long time lag before reactors can be built—all present nuclear plants are two to seven years behind schedule, and future plants will be delayed even more because of lengthy lawsuits and hearings where the dangers to life and environment will be argued; and (2) there is now a shortage of uranium necessary to operate the present plants—there just will not be enough uranium to operate the number of plants proposed by the affirmative.

> Third, geothermal is unworkable because (1) there are very few potential sources of commercially useful size; (2) these are located in earthquake-prone areas, where drilling for the hot water might in itself cause earthquakes, or in areas remote from any population to use the electricity they might produce; and (3) there is a shortage of copper, which makes it commercially impractical to transmit electric power over great distances.

The negative concluded its workability argument by demonstrating that all three of the energy sources proposed by the affirmative could not solve its harm.

2. Plan Will Not Accrue Claimed Advantages.   In developing this argument, advocates concentrate on attempting to prove that the plan—even if it works exactly as the affirmative wants it to—will not accrue the advantages claimed by the affirmative. Often reasons why the case is inherent also provide reasons why the plan cannot succeed. Negative debaters seek to identify the reasons and mechanisms that will allow plans to be circumvented.

In debating the law enforcement proposition, some affirmatives proposed as their plan that wiretapping be legalized for state and local police forces and claimed as their advantage that there would be more convictions of criminals because wiretaps would produce direct evidence of crimes. Negatives meeting this case argued that the plan would not accrue the advantage, because criminals would assume their phones were tapped and take countermeasures to circumvent the plan. They argued that criminals would (1) reduce the use of the phone, (2) use scrambler phones, (3) use electronic devices to discover untapped phones and use those phones, (4) use randomly chosen public phones, (5) use frequently changed codes, (6) use frequently changed slang or code, and (7) use fragmentary references and identification.

In debating the "comprehensive medical care" proposition, one affirmative provided in its plan for free medical care for all citizens and claimed as one of its advantages "better medical care for the poor." The negative argued that the plan could not accrue this advantage because (1) few physicians practice in the rural and urban areas where most poor people live; (2) the poor lack the money to pay for transportation to travel to the areas where the physicians practice; (3) many poor people are not aware of the value of early medical care and will not seek it; (4) many poor people are afraid of medical care and will not seek it until their condition is critical; and (5) many of the working poor cannot afford to take time off to obtain medical care and do so only when their condition is critical.

3. Significance of Advantage.   Negative teams may also wish to argue that even if an advantage is achieved, it is not a compelling or significant advantage. In debates on the energy proposition, some affirmatives presented a plan providing for a ban of offshore drilling for oil and claimed the advantage of protecting the environment by (1) preventing unsightly oil rigs, (2) protecting fish life, and (3) preventing ecological damage from possible oil leakage. Some negative teams meeting this plan argued that the advantages were not significant, because (1) the oil rigs would be miles offshore so no one could see them from the shore; (2) oil rigs provided a feeding ground for fish, so the fish population actually increased in this area (note this negative case turn, in which the affirmative claimed that banning oil rigs protected fish life, and the negative turned this argument around, claiming that oil rigs increased the fish population); and (3) oil leakage was rare, and even in those few cases in which it occurred, the wildlife population returned to normal in two years. They concluded their argument by maintaining that the affirmative had provided neither quantitative nor qualitative significance for its advantage; that is, offshore wells did no harm to the environment, and, in any event, the need for oil clearly outweighed the insignificant environmental considerations the affirmative presented.

Recall the asbestos example mentioned in Chapter 7. Many people argued that asbestos in school buildings posed a life-threatening danger to schoolchildren. The negative might argue that only 1 in 11 million children were at risk. As economist Robert Samuelson notes, "The standard retort is: a rich country like ours can afford absolute safety. No we can't. Regulatory costs raise prices or taxes. Our incomes are lower than they might be. That's OK if we receive a lot of benefits—much cleaner air or healthier food. But it's not OK if the benefit is trivial or nonexistent."[1]

Saving even one child's life could hardly be called trivial. Is one life a significant advantage for a multibillion-dollar expenditure? Could that sum be used in other ways that might save or improve thousands or millions of lives?

E. Prove Disadvantages

Unless topicality is being argued, disadvantage arguments are the most important negative arguments in most policy debates. This is because they are the negative's offense: They offer reasons that adoption of the affirmative plan would be bad. The negative's objective here is to block the adoption of the resolution by proving that the plan proposed by the affirmative will produce disadvantages and that these disadvantages outweigh any possible advantage the plan may achieve. To do so, the negative should present a series of concisely stated, closely reasoned arguments. In preparing for this argument, as with workability and other negative attacks, the advocate develops a series of briefs against potential affirmative plans and adapts them to the specific plan presented by the affirmative.

In debating the energy proposition, one affirmative, having established as its need that strip mining damaged the environment, provided a plan that banned all strip mining and claimed the advantage of a better environment. A negative meeting this case argued that banning strip mining (which it called surface mining) would produce the following disadvantages: It would (1) cause a shortage of copper (most copper comes from surface mines, and copper wire is essential for the transmission of electricity from generators to users); (2) cause a shortage of iron (most iron comes from surface mines); (3) exacerbate the oil shortage (because oil would be used as a partial replacement for surface-mined coal); (4) increase the cost of electricity (because scarce oil and more expensive deep-mined coal would be used to replace surface-mined coal); (5) increase inflation (as a result of 1–4); (6) increase unemployment (as a result of disadvantages 1–5); (7) increase black-lung disease (because more people would work in deep mines under the affirmative's plan); (8) increase the number of mine accidents (because working in deep mines is inherently more dangerous than working in surface mines); (9) cause dependence on unreliable foreign sources for coal (because present domestic deep mines could not meet the demand for coal and foreign sources might embargo coal, as the Arabs embargoed oil); and (10) exacerbate the balance-of-payments problem (because dollars would flow out of the country to buy coal). The negative then concluded this portion of its case by arguing that these disadvantages far outweighed whatever aesthetic advantages might be

---

1. Robert J. Samuelson, "The Triumph of the Psycho-Fact," *Newsweek,* May 9, 1994, p. 73.

gained by viewing a landscape untouched by surface mining as contrasted with a landscape reclaimed after surface mining.

In debates on U.S. trade policies with China, some affirmative plans called for ending China's "most favored nation" status to force it to improve its human rights record. Some negatives meeting this plan argued the disadvantage: Increased Human Rights Violations. They maintained that China could easily shift its trade to nations that did not link trade and human rights, and with no incentive to improve, conditions would become worse.

Of course the negative must prove the disadvantage. As we saw in Chapter 3, whoever introduces an issue or contention into the debate has *a* burden of proof.

1. Prove the Slippery Slope.   When the affirmative's plan is not bad per se, the negative may try to prove that the plan includes a seemingly harmless proposal that would be an irreversible first step down a **slippery slope** to the most deleterious consequences. In debates on the mass media proposition, an affirmative plan to ban advertising of sugar-laden food products would probably have the advantages of reducing children's cavities and improving their general health. Certainly these are desirable things in themselves. Negatives meeting such cases argued that this seemingly benign plan would lead us down a slippery slope to abridgement of the First Amendment; that is, if we banned advertising for foods with a high sugar content, what would be next? It would set a dangerous precedent that could lead to the banning of advertising for books and for political candidates and would create unacceptable barriers to free speech. In short, the negative said, we should avoid taking the first step down the slippery slope that could lead to clearly disadvantageous consequences. The affirmative then had the burden of demonstrating that its proposal was a limited step and that its plan included safeguards to avoid the slippery slope.

Note that the slippery slope argument is not unique to the negative, nor is it limited to policy debate. In debates on the proposition "U.S. colleges and universities have inappropriately altered educational practices to address issues of race or gender," some affirmatives noted that many campuses had adopted rules to enforce "politically correct speech." Such rules were intended to reduce racist or sexist slurs. However, some affirmatives argued that rules enforcing "politically correct speech" would lead us down the slippery slope to abridgement of the First Amendment; that is, if we banned slurs, what would be next? It would set a dangerous precedent that could lead to all of the harms cited in the mass media example. The affirmative argued that, although we might deplore racist or sexist slurs, the far greater (more significant) value was the preservation of the First Amendment.

2. Provide Generic Disadvantages.   The disadvantages we have just considered were specific to the cases being attacked. Often, as we have noted, the negative will not know the affirmative's case until the debate is actually under way—and then it is too late to conduct specific research to refute the opponent's case. To provide for this situation, experienced negative advocates develop **generic**

disadvantages that may be applied to a number of possible affirmative plans; that is, after careful analysis of the proposition, they discover certain provisions that an affirmative must almost certainly include in its plan. Although they cannot be certain in advance exactly what form these provisions will take, they can make realistic estimates. For example, in debating the "guaranteed employment opportunities" proposition, some negative teams developed a series of generic disadvantages to any affirmative plan that would increase income. (By providing jobs for unemployed people, of course, the affirmative's plan usually did increase their income.) These negative teams argued: (1) When Americans' income went up, they ate more beef; (2) eating more beef would increase cardiovascular disease, causing millions of deaths; (3) because farmers would find it more profitable to feed cattle grain to produce more beef, there would be less grain for export to the less developed countries (LDCs); (4) millions of people in the LDCs would die, because they would be unable to get grain; (5) this would cause the LDCs to start World War III in order to obtain needed grain; and (6) World War III would cause the end of life on Earth—a truly Brobdingnagian disadvantage Would an increase in employment in the United States really cause the end of life on Earth? This issue was actually argued in many debates on this proposition. As we saw in Chapter 9, the advocate must be prepared to demonstrate that the cause is capable of producing the effect under consideration.

As we noted in discussing the slippery slope, the negative debating the mass media proposition could develop effective arguments against banning advertising for sugar-laden foods. Negatives found that arguments used against this specific case could be adapted as generic disadvantages for use against many affirmative cases that imposed limitations on free speech. The negative could not know in advance what the affirmative would argue in favor of banning—saccharin ads, pornography, violence on TV, or any of the other myriad variations available to the affirmative. Against many of these bans, however, the negative could run a slippery slope First Amendment disadvantage and claim that the affirmative's seemingly benign ban would result in the disadvantage of violating First Amendment rights—the point being that the disadvantage of violating free speech outweighed any advantage claimed by the affirmative. The ability to convert a specific disadvantage, with appropriate adaptation, into a generic disadvantage is an important weapon in the negative's arsenal.

3. Watch for Turnarounds.   As we noted in Chapter 12, the experienced affirmative will be alert for opportunities to "turn around" disadvantages and convert them into advantages. Negative advocates, as they build disadvantages, should be aware of this affirmative strategy and consider whether a disadvantage can be turned against them—in which case they should not use it. A successful turnaround means not only that the negative loses the disadvantage but also that the affirmative gains an advantage. As we saw in Chapter 12, the negative should also be alert to the possibility of providing turnarounds for the affirmative's advantages.

In Chapter 8, we considered an argument made by a second negative constructive speaker that work sharing would cause strikes. These strikes, the negative argued, were a disadvantage of the affirmative plan. The first affirmative rebuttalist sought to turn around the disadvantage by citing evidence that unions had gone on strike to obtain work sharing. This evidence proved, the rebuttalist argued, that the disadvantage of strikes would not occur. The rebuttalist went on to claim an additional advantage: Labor relations would be more peaceful under the affirmative plan, because unions would not have to go on strike to obtain work sharing. Of course new issues may not be introduced in rebuttal. But because the second negative had introduced the issue of strikes, it was perfectly proper for the first affirmative rebuttalist to turn around that issue.

In debates on increasing taxes on oil imports, some affirmative teams claimed the advantage of reducing dependence on foreign oil sources. Some negative teams, meeting this type of case, argued a turnaround. They claimed that if oil was more expensive, more nuclear energy plants would be built. This, they argued, would create a disadvantage—increased risk of a nuclear disaster.

4. Prepare Disadvantage Shells. To allow more time to develop and extend their arguments, negative advocates should present the entirety of their argumentation in some form at their first opportunity: the first negative constructive. **Shells** are brief versions of arguments to be expanded upon later in the debate.

F. Develop the Counterplan

The counterplan is a strong negative strategy because it releases the negative from the need to defend the status quo and it shifts some of the argumentative ground in the debate to the negative. The **counterplan** is a plan presented by the negative—one that is competitive with the affirmative's plan and is a superior policy alternative. Acceptance of the counterplan mandates rejection of the plan, and thus a negative decision. Negatives may offer a counterplan as a superior way to solve the affirmative need or as a superior policy that would be blocked by affirmative plan

---

The essential components of a prima facie disadvantage argument are as follows:

1. *Threshold:* This is the brink, or the point at which the disadvantage begins to happen. The negative argues that affirmatives plan action will push us over that threshold.

2. *Uniqueness:* The disadvantage, if a reason to reject the plan, must be uniquely caused by the plan. If it would occur absent the plan, it is not a reason to reject the plan.

3. *Link:* The disadvantage must link to the plan and be caused by the specific plan action called for. Even generic disadvantages should have links specific to the affirmatives plan.

4. *Impact:* The disadvantage must have a quantitative and/or qualitative impact to be weighed against the affirmatives advantage.

5. *Probability:* Many disadvantages have a huge impact (global nuclear war, for example) but a small probability of occurring. To be a reason to reject the affirmative, the disadvantage must have a genuine chance of happening.

adoption. A benefit of the counterplan is that it may offer a way to solve the affirmative problem that uniquely avoids the disadvantages offered by the negative.

1. Competition.   The counterplan must compete with the affirmative plan or it is not a reason to reject the plan. Competition may be demonstrated in several ways.

a. The Affirmative Plan and the Counterplan Are Mutually Exclusive.   This means that the plan and the counterplan cannot simultaneously coexist.

Here's an example: Following the collapse of communism in Eastern Europe, some argued that the United States should withdraw its troops from Eastern Europe. They maintained that, because the Cold War was over, the troops were no longer needed, and the money saved could be used to reduce the national debt. The negative team disagreed with the affirmative's justification and offered a redefined justification. It noted that the Cold War may be over but claimed that the threat of war was greater than ever. As a counterplan against this case, it argued that America should increase its troops in Europe. It held that the collapse of communism created a volatile situation and that wars might break out in the newly liberated nations. The presence of increased U.S. military forces in Europe, it maintained, would be a deterrent to such wars. It argued that, when the advantages and disadvantages of the plan and counterplan were weighed, there was a net benefit in favor of the counterplan. Obviously the United States cannot simultaneously withdraw its troops from Europe and increase its troops in Europe. The plan and counterplan are mutually exclusive.

The affirmative may seek to illustrate noncompetition of the counterplan by permuting its plan to adapt to the counterplan and argue that adoption of both the plan and the counterplan is feasible. A **permutation** is a test of competitiveness; it is the illustration (not the advocacy) that the plan and counterplan can be combined. The affirmative will win if it can establish that the plan and counterplan are not mutually exclusive and that adopting both is superior to adopting the counterplan alone.

b. The Counterplan Alone Is Superior to Simultaneous Adoption of the Affirmative Plan and the Counterplan.   It is often impossible to construct a counterplan that cannot simultaneously exist with the affirmative plan. Another measure of competition is the net benefits standard. Here the negative seeks to demonstrate that it would be better to adopt only the counterplan than it would be to adopt the combination of counterplan and plan. This might be the case if the counterplan better solves the affirmative need. In addition, the counterplan alone may be superior if it uniquely avoids disadvantages presented by the negative.

Formula for Net Benefit

CP > CP + P (the counterplan alone is better than the counterplan plus the plan)

For example, the affirmative might argue that heart disease is the nation's leading killer and so we should appropriate $1 billion for research on heart disease. The negative might argue that the government has already spent billions on heart disease, but with only modest results. AIDS, it might maintain, is a more urgent problem and so we should spend the $1 billion on AIDS research. An affirmative meeting this counterplan might agree that both diseases are terrible and permute its case by proposing the appropriation of $2 billion for research: $1 billion for heart disease, and $1 billion for AIDS. If the affirmative can show that simultaneously adopting its plan and the counterplan is possible (they are not mutually exclusive) and more desirable (they provide a greater net benefit) than adopting the counterplan alone, it will win. Given the size of the federal budget, it probably would be possible to add $2 billion without making disastrous cuts in other desirable programs or raising taxes to a level that would damage the economy. For the negative to win, it must establish that funding AIDS research alone would provide a greater net benefit. It could do so if it could demonstrate that funding in excess of $1 billion would be uniquely disadvantageous. In meeting affirmative permutations of this sort, the negative must be able to argue permutation standards and present good reasons that the affirmative cannot permute its case to include the counterplan or prove that the counterplan alone is superior.

The negative may establish that its counterplan is nontopical and mutually exclusive in a number of ways. It may argue that the counterplan should be carried out by a different level of government than the resolution calls for (for example, the states rather than the federal government), or that a different agency should carry out the counterplan (for instance, it should be voluntary rather than mandated by law), or that finite funds should be used in a different way (for example, the funds available for space research should be used to send a probe to Mars rather than to Venus). In debates on the mass media proposition, negative counterplans often called for a voluntary agency such as the National Association of Broadcasters (NAB), rather than an agency of the federal government, to regulate television. Similarly, in debates on the "consumer product safety" proposition, some negative counterplans called for action by the states rather than the federal government. A wide range of mechanisms is available to the negative for developing a nontopical counterplan; these will be discussed in the section "Topical Counterplans." In fact, once the affirmative has operationally defined the resolution, almost any mutually exclusive plan can constitute grounds for a counterplan. Careful examination of the problem area of the proposition and its context will help the negative choose the most effective one.

The negative has to demonstrate that its counterplan provides the best balance of risks and advantages when compared to the plan of the affirmative. In debates on the mass media proposition, negatives calling for the NAB to regulate television violence often argued that the risk of loss of First Amendment freedoms would be reduced if a voluntary agency, and not the federal government, regulated television violence. On the "consumer product safety" proposition, negatives using a "states" counterplan argued that the states rather than the federal government should regulate a particular consumer product. If a plan turned out to be undesirable, less harm would be done than if the plan were nation-wide. And if the plan turned out to be desirable, other states would adopt it.

2. Integration of the Counterplan.   Advocates using the counterplan negative case must carefully integrate their positions. Although the counterplan should be planned in advance, the decision to use it in an actual debate usually should be made only after the first affirmative presentation. Because the counterplan has to be perfectly adapted to the specific affirmative case under attack, this adaptation frequently requires a good deal of during-the-debate coordination by the negative speakers. Not only must they integrate their counterplan with the needs or goals as they have redefined them, they also must carefully integrate their indictment of the affirmative plan to make sure one speaker's plan attacks on the affirmative cannot be applied with equal force to the counterplan.

3. Conditional and Dispositional Counterplans.   The **conditional counterplan** is a counterplan offered as part of an if-then statement by the negative: If the status quo cannot solve the problem, then the counterplan can; or, if the counterplan fails, we will rely on the status quo. In developing this type of case, the negative argues that (1) the status quo can solve the problem, and (2) if the status quo can't solve the problem, it will advocate the negative counterplan. Such a strategy allows the negative to discard advocacy of the counterplan or the status quo depending on how the argumentation plays out in the debate.

Student debaters should consider two important constraints before selecting this approach. First, the time constraints of academic debate may make it extremely difficult to adequately develop both the defense of the status quo and the counterplan. Second, conditional arguments have to be presented with great clarity. This requirement for clarity, when combined with the difficult-in-itself counterplan, makes for a doubly complex problem for the debater.

The negative may also offer its counterplan as a *dispositional* counterplan. This is a special type of conditional argument in which the conditions for advocacy are predetermined. If a counterplan is dispositional, the negative may abandon advocacy of it unless it is turned—that is, unless it is compelled to answer disadvantages to the counterplan.

4. Utopian Counterplan.   In developing the **utopian counterplan**, the negative typically mandates in a single plank that the nation or world will be arranged in a manner consistent with anarchy, world government, socialism, authoritarianism, or some other future strategy and claims that this strategy will better solve the problem than the federal government or whatever agency of change is provided in the proposition under debate.[2] In debating the "guarantee employment opportunities" proposition, some negative teams using a utopian counterplan argued that a Socialist government rather than the federal government could better

---

2. For a more detailed discussion of utopian counterplans, see the *Journal of the American Forensic Association*, vol. 24 (fall 1987), pp. 95–136, which presents four essays under the heading "Point-Counterpoint: Essays on Utopian Fiat."

provide such a guarantee. In debating the "federal government should increase exploration and/or development of space" proposition, some negatives used a world government utopian counterplan.

For the negative the attraction of utopian counterplans is twofold: (1) *Utopia* is defined as "a place of ideal perfection, especially in laws, government, and social conditions"—certainly a desirable locale for one's plan—and (2) the utopian counterplan may be the ultimate generic argument in that it can be applied to an almost unlimited variety of affirmative cases.

Note that some judges object to utopian counterplans and are easily convinced to vote against them. They hold that such counterplans are topic-limitless; that is, they may be used against any affirmative policy and so are of dubious educational value, because debaters using them no longer have the incentive or need to research new topic-specificarguments.

5. Topical Counterplans.   Once the affirmative has operationally defined the resolution, almost any mutually exclusive plan may constitute grounds for a counterplan. Thus a **topical counterplan** is one that might be used as an affirmative plan under some definitions of the resolution but is nontopical with regard to the operational definition the affirmative has chosen to use. Put another way, the affirmative, by offering its plan, sets the parameters for the debate, defining the resolution as its plan; thus anything that is not the plan is nontopical. The negative may use a topical counterplan if the affirmative operationally defines the resolution as its plan.

In debating the proposition "Resolved: That the United States should significantly increase exploration and/or development of space beyond the earth's mesosphere," the affirmative had a wide range of possible plans. One affirmative said, "We define 'increased exploration and development' to mean that the United States should establish a manned colony on the moon." The affirmative went on to provide a detailed statement of the plan and cited the advantages that would flow from the plan.

A negative team meeting this case eagerly accepted the affirmative's definition and claimed that, because the affirmative had operationally defined the resolution as "establish a moon colony," anything other than a moon colony was inconsistent with the now-defined resolution and available to the negative as a counterplan. The negative then presented as a counterplan the plan it used when it debated as an affirmative team. Specifically it called for the United States to establish a number of manned and unmanned space stations to detect and provide early warning of approaching extraterrestrial aliens. It also provided a detailed statement of its counterplan and advantages.

The counterplan was, when presented as an affirmative case, clearly topical. The negative argued that the counterplan was clearly nontopical with regard to the resolution as defined by opponent's affirmative plan.

The negative went on to argue that the plan and counterplan were mutually exclusive because each would cost over a trillion dollars, and it would be impossible to fund both simultaneously. The negative maintained as well that its counterplan provided net benefits. The affirmative claimed economic advantages from the moon colony. The negative claimed that early-warning space stations would save humankind from destruction by hostile aliens.

Wise debaters find it desirable to become familiar with such counterplans, because even if they do not decide to use them, they may encounter their like.

6. Other Counterplans.   Other forms of counterplans include (1) the delay counterplan, (2) the exceptions counterplan, and (3) the plan-inclusive counter-plan. The *delay* counterplan advocates waiting some period of time before adopt-ing the affirmative plan. The rationale for delay is based on avoiding a disadvan-tage that would uniquely occur from immediate plan adoption. The *exceptions* counterplan advocates that the plan be adopted but that some jurisdiction or group of people be excluded from the plan mandates. For example, during the civil rights debates negatives advocated that affirmative plans be adopted but ex-clude regulations that would apply to Puerto Rico, Japan, or Native American jurisdictions. These counterplans claimed to avoid disadvantages unique to those groups or states so regulated. Both of these counterplans were types of *plan-inclusive* counterplans, which incorporate the good portions of the plan into a competitive counterplan.

7. Counterplans and Fiat.   It is generally (but not universally) accepted that negatives have some ability to assume fiat for implementation of their counter-plans. One approach to negative fiat is to assume that it is reciprocal: If the affir-mative can fiat federal government action, so can the negative. Another is to assume that the negative's fiat ground is based in alternative agents: If the affir-mative uses the federal government, the negative can use the states or the United Nations. Remember that fiat is not a magic wand, that fiat must assume some normal means of implementation, and that one cannot fiat workability.

8. Counterplans and Presumption.   There are also several ways to view the convention of presumption as it applies to counterplan debates. In a debate in which the negative defends the status quo, it is generally accepted that presump-tion favors the negative. But what happens if the negative defends a counterplan? One well-accepted theory holds that presumption lies with the policy incurring the least risk or the lesser change. Another is that presumption always opposes the resolution. Some traditional theorists would argue that, when the negative chooses to counterplan, it abandons presumption, which then ceases to exist or shifts to the affirmative. All of this is debatable, but it is worthwhile for the neg-ative to develop an argument for why it retains presumption with a counterplan.

G. Developing the Kritic (Critique)

The **kritic** (sometimes abbreviated to "K") is a popular form of argument usually (but not always) initiated by the negative team in a debate. It is an argument that challenges the philosophical foundations, or applies ethical constructs to the op-ponent's advocacy and its implications. In essence the kritic is a value objection used in a policy debate. The argument is structured much like a disadvantage and is argued as an absolute voting issue. Kritics may be based on attacks on some aspect of the opposing advocates' performance, such as language use or on the underlying presuppositions of the resolution or their proposal.

In general, when argumentation is considered "critical" it challenges the traditional power structures. Marx offered critical analysis based on economic elites. Some postmodern critics suggest that the paradigm or worldview with which one considers their world (including reflection on activities such as debate, as well as examination of larger social problems) colors what one sees. Thus, existing paradigms, or ways of arguing and understanding, serve to reinforce institutional frameworks and thus reinforce existing power hierarchies. Because they favor inclusion over exclusion, and seek ways to break down repressive regimes, critical scholars often advocate deconstruction of those traditional paradigms in favor of new ways of knowing and thinking. Such arguments tend to be very compelling in their criticism of existing approaches, but less persuasive in their offering of alternatives to the conventions.

One form of kritic argument begins with the recognition that fiat is only a debate convention and that, even when the affirmative wins a debate, the plan is not implemented. Hence, it is important and more immediate to consider the in-round impact of debater behavior and language use on the participants and observers than hypothetical policy implementation. For example, a negative might pick up on the affirmative's use of the generic *he* and suggest that the judge reject the affirmative for furthering the sexist thinking of those present in the debate. Similar arguments may be based on the tendency of the opponents' language, evidence, and/or argumentative positions to "otherize" peoples or groups by isolating them based on their victimization or characteristics, their use of "nukespeak" (talk about the impact of nuclear war) or other language-based approaches to discussion of public policy that might numb listeners to the importance of various issues. Criticism of fast or technical talk in a debate, linear modes of thinking, simplistic cause-effect analysis, and many other objections might be offered based on such a critical approach.

Another form of kritic argument questions the premises upon which the resolution, and therefore the affirmative plan, is based. For example, the negative might argue that the resolution (and the affirmative) relies on governmental solutions to social problems. It could then argue that it is governments that cause most of the world's problems and that reliance on the state to solve social problems is philosophically wrong. It then follows that the affirmative should be rejected, because it relies on the state.

Negatives advocating the kritic strategy must be careful to be consistent. To attack the philosophical notion of the state and to offer a world government counterplan, or to criticize use of the generic male pronoun while reading evidence using the term *mankind,* would be inconsistent and would likely result in a negative loss. Negatives should avoid the implied contradiction or hypocrisy of presenting arguments or positions of advocacy that are inconsistent with their kritic. In addition, as with all generic negative strategies, it is important to explain the application of the kritic to the particular round and affirmative (that is, the link). The negative offering a kritic argument should clearly identify its "alternative." The alternative may be a counterplan that embodies the philosophical commitment. However, a more likely critical alternative is a clear explanation of the new ethical foundation or premise(s) advocated by the negative. It is important for the negative to provide an competing mode of thinking, framework, or approach to debating the issues involved if the kritic is to offer a choice that justifies rejection of the affirmative advocacy. So, negatives offering a kritic must explain clearly why acceptance of their kritic philosophy results in affirmative rejection (that is, impact).

EXERCISES

1. Work in pairs of teams. Exchange your affirmative cases (prepared for Chapter 12). For your opponent's case, prepare briefs. If you are debating a value proposition, prepare briefs on Topicality, Criteria, Value Objection, and case-specific arguments. If you are debating a policy proposition, prepare briefs on Topicality, Harm, Circumvention, and Disadvantage.

2. Continue Exercise 1 by preparing a counterplan argument, including all necessary support.

3. Have a debate. Divide the class in half. Assume that you all normally eat at the cafeteria. The first debater should offer a plan to eat somewhere else (specify the plan). The first negative debater should offer a counterplan (eat at yet another location). Continue back and forth until everyone has participated.

14

Refutation

Debate takes place not in a vacuum but in the face of opposition. The debater is always confronted with the necessity of overcoming objections raised by his or her opponent. The process of overcoming these objections is known as **refutation**. Strictly interpreted, *refute* means "to overcome opposing evidence and reasoning by proving it to be false or erroneous." The **rebuttal**, strictly interpreted, refers to argumentation meant "to overcome opposing evidence and reasoning by introducing other evidence and reasoning that will destroy its effect." In practice the terms *refutation* and *rebuttal* are used interchangeably, except that the second speech by each advocate in an academic debate is designated as the rebuttal speech.

In academic debate advocates are required to refute only the specific arguments advanced by their opponents. In applied debate advocates must refute any evidence and reasoning that may influence the decision renderers.

I. SHIFTING THE BURDEN OF REBUTTAL

As the preceding chapters on cases indicated, the burden of proof always remains with the affirmative, whereas the burden of rebuttal initially belongs to the negative. This burden of rebuttal shifts back and forth between the opponents in the course of the debate and is finally placed on one side or the other. The side that bears the burden of rebuttal at the conclusion of the debate is the loser. In the typical academic debate the first affirmative speaker usually establishes his or her case sufficiently well to place the burden of refutation on the negative. The first negative speaker then attempts to shift that burden back to the affirmative. The second affirmative speaker, by rebuilding and extending the case, seeks to shift the burden to the negative again. At this point in the debate, the negative presents its second constructive speech and its first rebuttal. In these two speeches the negative tries to shift the burden of rebuttal back to the affirmative. Obviously these consecutive presentations provide the negative with its best chance of shifting the burden decisively. In each of the remaining rebuttal

---

Miniglossary

Flow sheet   An outline of a debate, with the arguments presented in each speech recorded in vertical columns and arranged so that a person can follow horizontally the flow of each argument as it evolves progressively through all the speeches in a debate.

Rebuttal   Argumentation meant to overcome opposing evidence and reasoning by introducing other evidence and reasoning that will destroy its effect. Also, the second speech by each advocate in an academic debate.

Refutation   Argumentation meant to overcome opposing evidence and reasoning by proving that it is false or erroneous.

---

speeches, the advocates try to carry their share of rebuttal and to shift the burden to their opponents. The affirmative's last opportunity comes in the final speech of the debate, in which the second affirmative speaker has the opportunity to review the entire debate and to demonstrate that the negative has not carried its burden of rebuttal.[1]

II. PURPOSE AND PLACE OF REFUTATION

The process of refutation has to be included in every speech of the debate. Obviously the first affirmative speech, which opens the debate, cannot include direct refutation because no opposition has preceded it. But even this speech may include a certain amount of anticipatory refutation. However, this anticipatory refutation should be directed to issues that the negative must inevitably support and not against "straw arguments" that the affirmative hopes the negative will advance. (See the box on page 263 for a summary of processes of refutation.)

In general advocates should refute an important issue early on rather than allow it to stand unchallenged for any length of time. But an advocate might ignore an issue temporarily while waiting for the opposition to commit itself further on the issue. Or advocates might advance a limited refutation, encouraging the opponents to pursue a given line of argument that will commit them to a position the advocates will refute later. Thus the advocates are able to bring into the debate arguments their opponents might prefer to avoid.

For example, in debates on the proposition "Resolved: That the nonagricultural industries of the United States should guarantee their employees an annual wage," some affirmative advocates argued that significant numbers of persons

---

1. See Chapter 18 for an outline of the speaking sequence and time allotments used in intercollegiate debating.

The Process of Refutation

1. Overthrow the opposition's evidence by demonstrating that it is invalid, erroneous, or irrelevant.
2. Overthrow the opposition's evidence by introducing other evidence that contradicts it, casts doubt on it, minimizes its effect, or shows that it fails to meet the tests of evidence.
3. Overthrow the opposition's reasoning by demonstrating that it is faulty.
4. Overthrow the opposition's reasoning by introducing other reasoning that turns it to the opposition's disadvantage, contradicts it, casts doubt on it, minimizes its effect, or shows that it fails to meet the tests of reasoning.
5. Rebuild evidence by introducing new and additional evidence to further substantiate it.
6. Rebuild reasoning by introducing new and additional reasoning to further substantiate it.
7. Present exploratory refutation—preliminary refutation offered for the purpose of probing the opponent's position and designed to clarify the opponent's position or to force the opponent to take a more definite position.
8. Present counterargumentation that competes with the opposition's.

---

were unemployed at the time this proposition was being debated. In using exploratory refutation, some negative advocates advanced a deliberately weak refutation—introducing evidence that some unemployed persons had built up substantial savings during the years they had worked—and drew the conclusion that some workers did not need a guarantee of annual wages. Some affirmative advocates responded to this refutation by claiming that the vast majority of unemployed persons did not have substantial savings, because low-seniority workers were the first to be laid off and many had worked for only a few months prior to their unemployment. Once the negative advocates had obtained such an admission from the affirmative as a result of its exploratory refutation, they were able, later in the debate, to focus on their main line of refutation. They then argued that, because the wage guarantees proposed by the affirmative required at least a year's seniority before becoming effective, the proposed plan did not meet the needs of the low-seniority workers, who, according to the affirmative, made up the largest group of unemployed.

III. PREPARING FOR REFUTATION

As advocates we should prepare our refutation with the same care that we prepare other portions of our case. Effective refutation is rarely the result of improvisation, but rather results from careful analysis and preparation.

We must be thoroughly familiar with all evidence and reasoning related to the proposition under debate. Our knowledge of the subject should never be confined to our own case or to the case we expect the opponent to use; instead it should include all possible aspects of the resolution. We should make certain that our research on the subject has been sufficiently detailed that we will not be taken by surprise by new evidence or reasoning introduced by the opposition. We should recognize that on most propositions the evidence is seldom complete; new evidence, or new interpretations of evidence, may appear frequently. In other words, we should never assume that our research is complete but should continue it until the very moment of the debate.

For example, one college debating team won a major tournament, in part, because it used more recent evidence than the opposition. During the tournament the president sent his budget message to Congress. This message contained some new information relating to the economic proposition debated in the tournament. One team redrafted its case overnight to include the new information. When this team met other teams that had not studied the president's message, the advocates found that the opposing speakers were at a serious disadvantage when they attempted to refute new evidence with which they were not familiar. In fact, most tournament debaters spend some time each evening of a tournament online, updating their research, and check the morning paper for anything they missed the night before.

Advocates should have a broad perspective in preparing their refutation. They should never limit themselves to one point of view or to one philosophy. They should try to analyze both sides carefully and should consider all possible positions that may be taken on the proposition. Student debaters will find that one of the best means of improving their refutations is to debate both sides of a proposition. This approach allows them to gain a broader perspective and avoid the danger of seeing only one side. Advocates in nonacademic debates draft the strongest possible cases their opponents might use and prepare refutations for each of these cases. Advocates should consider not only the evidence their opponents may use but also the lines of argument that may be introduced and the philosophical position that may form the basis of the opposition's case.

In planning answers to the possible cases advanced by an opponent, advocates should give careful consideration to the phrasing of any refutation. If an advocate's thinking has proceeded merely to the stage of "If the opposition quotes expert A, I will quote expert B," the refutation is likely to be verbose, uncertain, and lacking in specificity. Rather, the advocate should plan the phrasing of the refutation, making sure that the words are sharp and specific and that the reasoning is cogent.

After an appropriate signpost (for example, "argument number 1 ...") arguments should be presented with the claim first, in the form of a *tag line* or *slug*. This is the point of the argument phrased positively in seven words or less. Keeping the tag line brief increases the control the debater has over what the judge writes down on their flow sheets. The **flow sheet** is an outline of the debate, with the arguments presented in each speech recorded in vertical columns and arranged so that a person can follow horizontally the flow of each argument as it evolves progressively through all the speeches in a debate. Longer tags require the judge to paraphrase or interpret the debater's words. It is important to use powerful and compelling language in framing the tag line. It is much like the *sound bite* political candidates strive for in campaigns. These are the words most likely to be remembered by the judge.

After the tag line debaters should present their evidence or support. This is the data for the argument. Next the debater offers a summary of the warrant, or the reasoning that links the data to the claim. In other words the *warrant* is an explanation of why the evidence supports the claim. Finally the debater should summarize the impact of the argument in the debate. All of this is done quickly with no wasted words. Word economy is a key to effective debating.

IV. ARRANGING MATERIAL FOR REFUTATION

Until the debate is actually under way, the advocates cannot be certain what position their opponents will take. Thus they have to have a broad store of materials from which to draw refutation. These materials should be arranged in such a way that they are readily available.

It is essential to prepare refutation briefs in the form of *front lines,* or initial answers to an opponent's argumentation, and *extensions,* or defenses of the front-line answers and probable responses in subsequent speeches. These briefs are filed in folders or accordion files for ready access.

Conscientious student debaters make a habit of constructing detailed briefs and files. As advocates we should prepare refutation with the same thoroughness, using any method of recording material that is convenient and accessible. As we become knowledgeable and experienced, our dependence on mechanics will be reduced. Initially, however, specific, detailed preparation is essential.

V. SELECTING EVIDENCE AND REASONING

Just as our refutation file should contain more material than can be used in any one debate, our opponents' speeches will probably contain more evidence and reasoning than we can possibly refute in the allotted time. The problem before us, then, is one of *selection.* The fundamental concept underlying refutation is that we have to try to refute the case of our opponent. To do so, we must have an accurate picture of that case as it is presented. Let's look first at a sample debate case (see the inset on pages 266–267). This is a straightforward case that will be easy to follow. After you have studied the sample debate case, turn to the representation of the flow sheets shown on pages 268–269.

Charting the debate is one of the most important and also one of the most difficult skills the student must master. As discussed previously, the flow sheet is a detailed record of the debate created by systematic note taking. An accurate flow sheet will reflect every argument as it progresses through the eight speeches in

---

A Sample Debate Case*

Resolved: That the federal government should significantly strengthen the regulation of mass media communication in the United States.

Significance

I.   Terrorism is a major threat to American society.
    A.   Terrorism is significant.
        1.   Many terrorist incidents occur.
            UN Report evidence
            NY Times evidence

        Quantitative Significance
        2.   Terrorism is increasing.
            Wall Street Journal evidence
            U. of Mich. Law Rev. evidence
    B.   Terrorism is harmful.
        1.   Terrorism costs lives and money.
           a.   Thousands of lives are lost.
              Amnesty Int'l Report evidence
              House Hearings evidence
           b.   Billions of dollars worth of property damage occurs.
              Bus. Wk. evidence
              Senate Hearings evidence
           c.   Billions are paid in ransoms.
              Fortune evidence
              Forbes evidence
        Qualitative Significance
        2.   Terrorism threatens the basic liberties.
           a.   Liberties are lost.
              CLU Report evidence
              Wm. & Mary Law Rev. evidence
              U. of Penn. Law Rev. evidence
           b.   Loss of liberties will snowball.
              Time evidence
              Senate Hearings evidence
              U.S. News evidence
    C.   The harms of terrorism will increase.
        1.   Terrorists can use nuclear devices.
            NY Times evidence
            Senate Hearings evidence
            Science evidence
         2.   Terrorists can use chemical-biological agents.
            Wash. Post evidence
            Hudson Study evidence

Inherency

II. Present policies perpetuate terrorism.
    A.   Terrorists commit their crimes for publicity.
        FBI Report evidence
        Amnesty Int'l Study evidence
        Brookings Inst. Report evidence

    B.   Sensationalism causes a lack of media restraint.
        NY Times evidence
        Editor & Publisher evidence
        Senate Hearings evidence

Plan:

Agency

Plank 1. The plan will be administered by the Criminal *Agency* Justice Division of the Department of Justice.

Mandates

Plank 2. The federal government will enact legislation *Mandates* limiting all media coverage of terrorist events to reporting the event. Names and causes of terrorists may not be reported.

Enforcement

Plank 3. Violations of this law will, upon conviction, *Enforcement* result in fines of not less than 25% nor more than 50% of the gross annual income of the media company found guilty.

Funding and Staffing

Plank 4. Any and all necessary funding will be derived *Funding* from an optimal mix of general revenues and a 10% *and staffing* sales tax on all copies of *Argumentation and Debate.***

Addendum

Plank 5.

A. The Internal Revenue Service will be required to make available to the D.O.J. any and all records required for prosecutions under this law.
B. Any laws or regulations in conflict with Plank 2 are hereby repealed.
C. The Constitution will, if necessary, be amended to permit the effective enforcement of Plank 2.

Advantage

III.   The affirmative significantly reduces terrorism.
    A.   Media coverage motivates terrorist actions.
        Bochin Study evidence
        NY Times Mag. evidence
        Hornung Report evidence

Solvency
    B.   Removal of media coverage will cause terrorism to atrophy.
        Newsweek evidence
        Barron's evidence
        Senate Hearings evidence

---

* Adapted from a case prepared by Julia Davis, Lisa Garono, Timothy Ita, and Anthony Smith, John Carroll University debaters.

** Debate is not always somber and serious. Debaters delight in slipping jokes into their presentation—such as this provision for a 10 percent sales tax on this textbook. If the joke can be made at near-zero cost in time and does not open up any opportunity for the opponents to attack, the debater hopes to be rewarded by a chuckle from the judge or audience. Jokes, of course, must be adapted to the audience.

1AC	1NC	2AC	1NR	1AR	2NR	2AR
I. Terrorism major threat to Am. society	I. T— not a major threat	I. T— is sig major threat				
A. T— significant	A. Not sig.	A. T— sig				
1. many incidents	1. most incidents abroad	1. against U.S. nationals	→ 1. (drop)			
2. T— increasing	2. only statistically	2. sig Trend	→ state funded	→ recent	→ not accurate	
B. T— harmful	B. Not sig harm	B. T— harmful				
I. T— costs lives and $	I. most incidents abroad	1. against U.S. nationals	→ I. no U.S. jurisdiction	(drop)		
a. thousands of lives lost	a. not in U.S.	a. U.S. nationals				
b. billions in damage	b. not in U.S.	b. U.S.-owned property				
c. billions in ransom	c. not in U.S.	c. ransom for U.S. citizens				
2. T— threatens basic liberties	2. Not sig. threat	2. T— threatens liberties				
a. liberties lost	a. not unique - wire taps, etc. used for all crimes	A. massive increase in wire taps, etc needed against T—	→ a. foreign govts can wiretap	→ not all co-op w/ U.S.	→ (drop)	not all co-op w/ U.S.
b. loss will snowball	b. a prediction - not proof	b. 3 well-qualified experts. Best evidence	→ b. other experts disagree	→ best evidence	→ neg. source is better	→ aff. evidence more recent
C. Harms of T— will increase	C. Harms exaggerated	C.				
1. nuclear	1. T— can't get nuclear	1. may already have nuclear	1.} not on	→ can steal	→ real facilities	→ crude facilities enough
2. chemical-biological	2. chem - bio too sophisticated for T—	2. any chem-bio grad student could make chem-bio agents	2.} scale needed			
II. SQ perpetuates T—	II. (grant)					
A. T— seek publicity						
B. Sensational media						
IV. Plan reduces T—	IV. Plan won't reduce T—	IV. Plan will reduce T—				
A. Publicity is motive	A. Publicity not only motive	A. Seek publicity in U.S. by actions against U.S. nationals abroad				
B. Remove media coverage — T— atrophy	1. T— want money for their cause	1. media coverage increases tech-helps T— get $	→ events reported	→ not cause		
	2. T— want to free imprisoned colleagues	2. few in U.S.				
	3. T— not rational	3. Leaders are rational	→ fanatical	→ rational	→ eager to die for cause	→ leaders rational

III. Plan	2NC	1AR	2NR	2AR
1. Adm. by Criminal Justice Div. ± DOJ	I. Plan won't work	I. Plan will work; media fears fines → (Drop)		
	A. In-hurry proves motive to circumvent			
2. Fed. Legislation to limit media coverage of T- to events; no names or causes	B. Media has resources: will litigate for years		B. will litigate	
	C. Courts overloaded: will take years to reach S.C.	C. Not unique. Courts overcrowded now	C. propos Plan not work	C. not unique
3. Fines - 25% to 50% of gross annual income	D. SC sensitive to liberties: will dismantle off plan	D. SC conservative; will uphold plan	D. SC pro free press	D. SC more conservative now
4. Funding - gen. rev.	II. Disadvantages	II. Plan does not prevent public's knowing		
5. A. IRS give records to DOJ	1. If Plan works, it destroys public's right to know names and causes of T-	1. Legitimate causes can get publicity w/o T- off inherently proves media loves sensational		
B. conflicting laws repealed	A. Some causes may be legitimate			
C. Const. amend	B. Gov't is covering up illegal or unwise activities abroad	2. Evidence comes from Congressional committees, not T-		
	2. If Plan works, it destroys free media	III. Not destroy media	III	
	A. Becomes precedent	A. Plan strictly limited	A. Precedent slippery slope	A. Plan strictly limited
	B. Gov't wants to restrain media	B. Courts will check Gov't		
	C. Destruction of free media greater threat to am. society than T-	C. Not destroyed because of A & B	C. Destroy free media	
	3. If Plan works, it escalates	IV. T- won't escalate	IV.	
	A. T- escalates to force media coverage	A. Plan blocks	A. Incentive to escalate	→ Plan blocks
	B. Lack of news about T- means no public support for anti-T- measures	B. Full news of events only no names of causes		
		C. With full news of events public will support anti-T- measures		

the debate. It will record evidence and will show which arguments were answered and which ones were dropped, or not answered. The flow sheet is an indispensable tool for the debaters during a debate. More debates are decided because a debater capitalizes on an opponent's drop (or missed argument) than for any other reason. Learning to keep a complete and accurate flow sheet will also help students learn to be more effective critical listeners.

Our sample debate is on a policy proposition, and so the arguments are recorded in two parts—case side and plan (off-case) side. In this debate the speakers followed the basic speaker responsibilities considered in Chapters 12 and 13. Typically debaters and judges record the flow of argument on multiple sheets of legal-sized paper. The case arguments are usually recorded in seven columns on one side of a set of sheets of paper; this represents the case debate. (The heading *1AC* indicates the first affirmative constructive speech; *1AR,* the first affirmative rebuttal; *1NC,* the first negative constructive speech; and so on.) The plan and plan arguments are usually recorded on another group of sheets—thus the name "plan side"—in five columns. If counterplans or topicality arguments are used, they are also recorded on separate sheets. (Once students have mastered the basic concept of a flow sheet, they will find it easy to provide additional sheets to record these arguments.) Typically the 2AC speaker does not chart the 1AC speech; rather, the 2AC speaker will have prepared an outline of the 1AC speech in advance and will attach it to the flow sheet and then record the 1NC responses. This is called a *preflow.*

Debaters and judges often use arrows and other symbols to record the flow of the argument. Different-colored pens may be used to record cross-examination data or to identify other items. To save time, debaters and judges usually develop a system of abbreviations as well. On the sample flow sheet *T* is used to represent topicality, *SQ* stands for the status quo or present policies, *s* for significance, and *SC* for the Supreme Court. A granted argument (an opponent's argument that the speaker admits is valid; see item II in 1NC) is noted and circled; a dropped argument (an opponent's argument to which the speaker fails to respond; see item IA1 in the 1NR column in the case-side flow sheet and item 1B in the 1AR column in the plan-side flow sheet) is also circled.

Each column on the flow sheet should be the most accurate and detailed outline possible of that speech. An outline of this type helps debaters detect dropped arguments or weak links in the structure. It takes time and practice to learn how to keep an effective flow sheet, but debaters find it worthwhile to develop this essential skill. With appropriate adjustments the flow sheet can be adapted to any type of argumentative situation. For instance, a college senior confronted with the happy problem of weighing two job offers might find it helpful to prepare a flow sheet weighing the merits of the two offers. A corporate purchasing agent charged with the responsibility of making a major purchase for the company might prepare a flow sheet to help evaluate the advantages and disadvantages of competing products or services.

Tips for Keeping Flow Sheets

1. Concentrate! The key to creating useful flow sheets is listening and understanding.
2. Practice! Create flow sheets every chance you get—for the evening news, your classroom lectures, even movies.
3. Use plenty of paper. Record a limited number of arguments on each sheet.
4. Use two colors, one for the affirmative and another for the negative.
5. Be efficient. Use shorthand and symbols, and record only tag lines (the short claim statements) and evidence.
6. Use preflows. Preflow every brief and case you have on sticky note or similar gummed paper. Save the paper by sticking it to the inside of the folder holding the relevant argument, and place it in the appropriate spot on your flow sheet when you present the argument.
7. Use cross-examination and preparation time to fill in the gaps on your flow sheet.
8. Write small, keep columns narrow, and leave plenty of vertical white space. More and more debaters and judges have begun keeping their flow sheet with the help of a laptop computer. To learn more about this technique, visit http://www.wcdebate.com/1policy/9-edebate.htm.
9. Use arrows to indicate the relationships among arguments and answers.
10. When you miss something, indicate that by leaving a blank space or using some other symbol to remind you to fill in the missing material later.

VI. THE STRUCTURE OF REFUTATION

A. Basic Structure

The basic structure of refutation involves five distinct stages:

Basic Structure of Refutation

1. *Reference:* Identify clearly and concisely the argument you are attacking or defending.
2. *Response:* State your position succinctly.
3. *Support:* Introduce evidence and argument to support your position.
4. *Explanation:* Summarize your evidence and argument.
5. *Impact:* Demonstrate the impact of this refutation in weakening your opponent's case or in strengthening your own case.

This final stage is perhaps the most critical and is the stage beginning advocates most often overlook. Refutation loses its effectiveness unless we tie it in with the case of the opposition or our own case.

B. General Considerations

In addition to the basic structure of refutation, we should be aware of the following general considerations of refutation.

1. Begin Refutation Early. It is usually to our advantage to begin refutation early—both early in our speech and early in the debate. The purpose of beginning refutation early in the speech is to immediately offset the effect of some of the opponents' arguments. This does not mean, however, that the first portion of the speech should be reserved for refutation and the balance devoted to a constructive presentation. The skilled debater will interweave refutation and constructive materials throughout the entire speech. It is usually not desirable to allow a major contention to go unrefuted for too long in the debate. Generally an argument should be refuted in the next available speech. Thus a plan attack made in the first negative speech must be answered in the second affirmative speech. If the affirmative waits until the final rebuttal to answer this argument, the judge will weigh the answer lightly or even dismiss it, thinking, "Well, yes, they did finally get around to it, but it was so late that the negative had no chance to reply."

2. Conclude with Constructive Material. Usually we want to conclude a speech with constructive material designed to advance our own case. After giving the listeners reasons for rejecting the opponents' position, we give them positive reasons for concurring with our position.

3. Incorporate Refutation into the Case. Although it is usually a good idea to open a speech with refutation, refutation is by no means confined to the first part of the speech. Because the well-planned case meets many of the objections of the opposition, we will often find it advisable to incorporate refutation into our case. For example, in debating the proposition "Resolved: That the federal government should grant annually a specific percentage of its income tax revenue to the state governments," some negative teams objected to the adoption of the resolution on the grounds that it would place an additional burden on taxpayers. In refuting this objection, some affirmative teams made use of built-in refutation by pointing out that the gross domestic product was rising (as, indeed, it was at the time this proposition was debated); thus incomes would rise and more revenue would be derived from the same tax rate.

4. Evaluate the Amount of Refutation. Advocates often ask, "How much refutation is necessary?" Unfortunately no definitive answer is available; the amount varies from one occasion to another and depends on the judge, audience, and situation. When presenting refutation, in order to adapt to the audience more effectively, be sure to watch the judge or audience closely, looking for both overt and subtle signs of agreement or disagreement. At a minimum the refutation should progress through the five basic stages discussed previously. The goal is to introduce enough refutation to satisfy a reasonable person. Advocates should avoid the too-brief statement of refutation, such as "The recent Brookings Institution study disproves this contention." Such a statement may suggest a line of refutation, but until this line of refutation is actually developed within the context of the debate, it has little value.

5. Use Organized Refutation.   Advocates must use a clear, concise, carefully organized pattern of refutation that enables those who render the decision to follow the refutation readily. The objective is to make it easy for judges to "flow" the argument. Skilled advocates clearly identify the specific arguments of their opponents that they are refuting, so that the judge will know exactly where they want their arguments to apply. The basic speaker responsibilities considered in Chapters 12 and 13 indicate an organized pattern of refutation and a clear division of speaker responsibilities. Once debaters master this basic pattern, by prearrangement with their colleagues they may develop variations.

In informal situations in which we may not have a colleague and there is no judge with a flow sheet, it is still important to have a clear and precise pattern of refutation. We want to make it easy for those who render the decision to follow our arguments.

6. Make Use of Contingency Plans.   Advocates should prepare contingency plans; that is, they should compile briefs of evidence and arguments in advance to raise against issues they believe will be fundamental in meeting the opposing case. In fact, advocates should have a number of contingency plans available. In the course of the debate, they will determine which contingency plans are applicable to the case presented by the opponents; then, of course, they have to adapt the contingency plan to the specific argument used by the opposition.

For example, in debates on a national program of public work for the unemployed, the negative could have safely assumed that the affirmative would have to argue that unemployment is harmful. A negative team prepared contingency plans to meet affirmative arguments on "frictional unemployment," "cyclical unemployment," "long-term unemployment," and so on. In its contingency plan on "long-term unemployment" (unemployment of 15 weeks or more), it assembled evidence to establish that (1) a large percentage were elderly people with retirement incomes, (2) a large percentage were teenagers seeking part-time jobs, and (3) only a small percentage were heads of families. Recently one good college team preparing for the National Debate Tournament learned that the 71 other teams participating in the tournament had a total of 127 different affirmative cases available—and the team had to assume that there were other cases it had not found out about. Thus, before this team arrived at the NDT, it prepared more than 127 contingency plans. (CEDA Nationals often involves over 200 teams!) This, of course, is the burden of advocates who hope to win: They must have available sufficient contingency plans to overcome the probable opposition.

T A B L E 14.1 Responsibilities of the Speakers: Value Debate

1AC	1NC	2AC	2NC/1NR
It is the responsibility of the first affirmative constructive speaker (1AC) to present the affirmative's prima facie case for the resolution, usually read from a manuscript. It should include all the elements of the affirmative case. Here is an example:	It is the responsibility of the first negative constructive speaker (1NC) to present the negative arguments to be developed throughout the debate. This includes off-case (topicality, value objections) and on-case attacks on the affirmative's case. On-case attacks are presented on-point in exactly the same order as the issues are presented by the first affirmative constructive, with clear references to the affirmative claims. The actual order has to be adapted to the affirmative case. This speaker should do the following:	The basic responsibilities of the second affirmative constructive speaker (2AC) are to refute the negative off-case and on-case attacks, to reestablish the initial affirmative claims, and to extend affirmative case arguments.	It is important in the second negative constructive (2NC) and the first negative rebuttal (1NR) to efficiently divide labor. The second negative constructive speaker should "pick up" or extend an appropriate number of the negative arguments presented in the first negative constructive. The negative may elect not to extend all of their arguments at this point. For each position or argument, the speaker should do the following:
I. Definitions	1. Give an overview of the negative position or philosophy for the debate.	1. Address the negative's off-case attacks (which may include topicality, countercriteria, and value objections or, in the case of a quasi-policy debate, may include counterplan and disadvantages).	1. Respond to the second affirmative's answers to the argument.
II. Criteria	2. Present the negative topicality argument, if vulnerable.	2. Answer the negative's on-case attacks in first affirmative constructive order, and defend and extend the case proper: a. Refute the first negative constructive's attacks on each point.	2. Reestablish the initial first negative claims.
III. Value	3. Present shells of off-case arguments (value objections, disadvantages, counterplan arguments, kritics).	b. Reestablish the first affirmative constructive's claims and evidence on each point. c. Extend or magnify the initial claims with additional evidence and arguments.	3. Add to or magnify, if possible, the negative argument.
IV. Significance and V. Uniqueness	4. Attack vulnerable portions of the case, on-point, in affirmative order.		
VI. Application			
VII. Solvency (if a quasi-policy proposition)			

1AR	2NR	2AR
The basic responsibilities of the first affirmative rebuttal (1AR) speaker are to answer off-case and on-case attacks extended through the negative block (the second negative constructive and first negative rebuttal) and to extend the case arguments.	The second negative rebuttalist should be selective in extending those arguments the negative has the best opportunity to win. This speaker should leave out some arguments so as to maximize the time spent on the most promising ones. Specifically, this speaker should do the following:	The basic responsibility of the second affirmative rebuttal speaker is to reestablish and clinch the affirmative's case arguments.
1. Refute the negative's off-case arguments.	1. Begin with an overview previewing the reasons to vote for the negative.	1. Begin with an overview that encapsulates the reasons the affirmative should win the debate and previews the key issues.
2. Refute the negative's on-case attacks and case arguments, and extend case arguments from the second affirmative constructive.	2. Reestablish and clinch the few most important arguments in the negative's case.	2. Refute the off-case attacks extended by the second negative rebuttalist.
Note that this speech requires careful budgeting of time. The first affirmative rebuttalist has to efficiently answer the previous two negative speeches and will not have time to expand on constructive arguments.	3. Conclude by presenting the best reasons to justify a decision for the negative and recounting the negative.	3. Extend the affirmative case.
		4. Refute the second negative rebuttalist's attack on the case and extend case arguments.
		5. Conclude by presenting the best reasons for justifying a decision for the affirmative by telling the affirmative "story."

T A B L E   14.2   Responsibilities of the Speakers: Policy Debate

1AC	1NC	2AC	2NC/1NR
It is the responsibility of the 1st affirmative constructive (1AC) speaker to present the affirmative's prima facie case for the proposition, usually read from a manuscript. It should include all the elements of the affirmative case. For example:	It is the responsibility of the first negative constructive (1NC) speaker to present the negative arguments to be developed throughout the debate. This includes off-case (topicality, value objections) and on-case attacks on the affirmative's case. On-case attacks are presented on-point in exactly the same order as the issues are presented by the first affirmative constructive, with clear references to the affirmative claims. The actual order has to be adapted to the affirmative case. This speaker should do the following:	It is the job of the second affirmative constructive speaker (2AC) to answer all of the 1NC arguments, reestablish the initial claims of the affirmative (extend), and magnify the impact or importance of the affirmative arguments by adding onto them.	It is important in the second negative constructive (2NC) and the first negative rebuttal (1NR) to efficiently divide labor. The second negative constructive speaker should "pick up" or extend an appropriate number of the negative arguments presented in the first negative constructive, and the the first negative rebuttalist should extend those arguments presented in the first negative constructive not extended by the second negative constructive. The negative may elect not to extend all of their arguments at this point. For each position or argument chosen, the speaker should do the following:
1. Harm	1. Overview of the negative position	1. Answer topicality	1. Respond to the second affirmative's answers to the argument
2. Inherency	2. Topicality	2. Answer all off case arguments	
[Plan]	3. Shells of off-case arguments (value objections, disadvantages, counterplan arguments, kritics)	3. Answer on-point case attacks and extend 1AC claims	2. Reestablish the initial first negative claims.
3. Solvency	4. On-point case attacks	4. Add new impacts or arguments as time allows	3. Add to or magnify, if possible, the negative argument.

1AR	2NR	2AR
The basic responsibilities of the first affirmative rebuttal speaker (1AR) are to answer off-case and on-case attacks extended through the negative block (the second negative constructive and first negative rebuttal) and to extend the case arguments.	The second negative rebuttalist should be selective in extending those arguments the negative has the best opportunity to win. This speaker should leave out some arguments so as to maximize the time spent on the most promising ones. Specifically, this speaker should do the following:	The basic responsibility of the second affirmative rebuttal speaker is to reestablish and clinch the affirmative's case arguments.
1. Refute the negative's off-case arguments.	1. Begin with an overview previewing the reasons to vote for the negative.	1. Begin with an overview that encapsulates the reasons the affirmative should win the debate and previews the key issues. 2. Refute the off-case attacks extended by the second negative rebuttalist. 3. Extend the affirmative case.
2. Refute the negative's on-case arguments. 3. Extend case claims from the 2AC.	2. Reestablish and clinch the few most important arguments in the negative's case. 3. Conclude by presenting the best reasons to justify a decision for the negative and recounting the negative.	4. Refute the second negative rebuttalist's attack on the case and extend case arguments. 5. Conclude by presenting the best reasons for justifying a decision for the affirmative by telling the affirmative "story."

VII. METHODS OF REFUTATION

Toulmin's model offers a good method for providing answers to an opponent's arguments (see Chapter 8). First, consider offering a counterclaim to answer your opponent's claim. Generally, if you make a counterclaim, you must provide evidence to support it. Next, consider your opponent's data. Can any of the tests of evidence discussed in Chapter 7 be applied so as to discredit or reduce the strength of the evidence? Finally take a look at the warrant, or the logical reasoning that links the data to the claim. Can any of the tests of reasoning discussed in Chapters 8 and 9 be effectively applied to diminish the strength of the argument? Further refutation techniques involve evidence, reasoning, and fallacies.

A. Evidence

Evidence is refuted by applying the tests of evidence and demonstrating that the evidence advanced by the opposition fails to meet these tests. (See the tests of evidence considered in Chapter 7.) Counterrefutation against attacks on one's own evidence consists of demonstrating that the opposition has applied the tests of evidence incorrectly.

B. Reasoning

Reasoning is refuted by applying the tests of reasoning and demonstrating that the reasoning advanced by the opposition fails to meet these tests. (See the tests of reasoning considered in Chapters 8 and 9.) Counterrefutation against attacks on one's own reasoning consists of demonstrating that the opposition has applied the tests of reasoning incorrectly.

C. Fallacies

Fallacies are refuted by exposing the arguments of the opposition as fallacious. (Fallacies and methods of refuting fallacies are considered in Chapter 10.) Counterrefutation against attacks on one's own arguments as fallacies consists of demonstrating that the arguments are in fact valid.

D. Affirmative and Negative Refutation

In general, the affirmative side in the debate must answer all or most all of the negative's arguments and defend its entire case to win. The negative has the strategic advantage of being able to choose which arguments to extend, or keep alive, until the last rebuttal speech. All advocates are well advised to be strategic: Present evidence and argumentation early in the debate, which will serve you well later. This is to make your evidence work for you. If an argument made by your opponents may be answered by an argument you made earlier in the debate, you should not spend time reading new evidence or explaining a new argument. Instead, apply the earlier argument as your answer.

If the negative argues Topicality, the affirmative can defend the topicality of its plan by arguing that it meet the definitions offered by the negative and/or that its definition is superior to the negative one. It will be important for the affirmative to convince the judge that the negative's definitions are overly restrictive or inappropriate. If the negative offers a counterplan, the affirmative should argue that the counterplan is not competitive, that it fails to solve the harm identified by the affirmative, and/or that there are unique disadvantages to the counterplan, and thus the plan is a superior option to the counterplan.

E. Responsibilities of the Speakers

There are eight speeches in the two-person policy debate format (excluding the four cross-examination periods), and each has a fairly standard set of expectations and responsibilities (see Tables 14.1 and 14.2).

EXERCISES

1. Practice flowing by flowing the evening news, sports center, or any talk show.
2. Revisit the Spar Debates, this time debating a policy proposition with a plan, and following the standard responsibilities of the speakers.
3. Each student should make an argument (support with cards or briefs if available). An assigned respondent should refute the argument following the basic structure of refutation. A third student should use the same method to beat back the attack and defend the original point.
4. Organize one-issue debates on Topicality, Disadvantages, Harm, or any other single issue.
5. Refutation drills. Divide the class in half. The first student will begin a debate on any issue in the news. Continue back and forth, pro/con as long as you can keep going.

15

Presenting the Case: Composition

The case, as indicated in previous chapters, is the operational plan drafted by the advocates on one side of a proposition for the purpose of coordinating their reasoning and evidence and presenting their position as effectively as possible. The case outline incorporates some elements of speech composition and is an important starting point. But it is not a speech, nor is it an editorial or a book. Rather, it is the blueprint from which advocates develop their actual debate speeches. Although the case can be equally effective as the basis for a written document, our concern here is with the presentation of the case. In presenting their case orally, advocates are concerned with composing speeches that will get the audience's attention, convey their arguments, and make it easy to agree with their case.

The debate speech places utmost value on economy and power of language. The speech (and the brief) should be prepared to avoid repetition, reveal the outline structure through very clear **signposting**, and include verbatim presentation of all quoted or referenced materials with explicit "verbal footnotes" (clear references to the source citations). Unlike most other contexts for public speaking, the academic debate encourages a substantial amount of reading. Particularly in the early speeches of the debate, reading is preferred to maximize presentation of evidence and efficient use of the limited time allotted to each speaker.

I. ANALYSIS OF THE AUDIENCE

A. The Importance of Audience Analysis

As defined previously, argumentation is reason giving in communicative situations by people whose purpose is the justification of acts, beliefs, attitudes, and values. The first critical question in composing arguments, then, becomes, "Who are the people to whom these arguments are directed?" To answer this question advocates

---

Miniglossary

Headlining   The use of concise, precisely chosen words or short sentences to identify key points in the debater's speech; also know as tagging, or taglining.

Signposting   In academic debate the speakers often use numbers and letters to make their organization clear.

Spin control   Presentation of material from one's own perspective; putting a matter in the most favorable light. Should be done before the opponent plants a different spin in the minds of the decision makers.

---

must analyze the audience. The questions in the inset on pages 283–284 suggest information that speakers need to know about an audience. Most of these questions are relevant for most advocates on most propositions. Experienced debaters know that the type of composition suited to the final round of an NDT event simply will not work before a campus audience in a debate with a visiting team from Japan or Russia. Each audience requires analysis, and each case has to be adapted in the way best suited to the audience. If we will be speaking before a familiar campus group, we should have a good idea of who will be in the audience, and the answers to the questions in the inset on pages 283–284 will come quickly. But if, as is often the case, we will be speaking before an unfamiliar audience, we have to do the necessary research to be able to answer the questions.

For example, if the answers to the questions reveal that the audience traditionally opens its programs by singing "Solidarity Forever" or "We Shall Overcome," such songs might have a powerful emotional impact on the audience. If you find the audience is primarily from one cultural or ethnic group, you may wish to adapt to that fact. (*Caution:* Do not use regional or ethnic dialects or language or a foreign language, unless you come by it naturally. An African American speaking urban cool might win nods of approval from an African American audience; someone else attempting ebonics would be offensive.)

A dramatic example of the importance of audience analysis occurred in the second Bush–Dukakis presidential debate. The first question was: "Governor, if Kitty Dukakis were raped and murdered, would you favor an irrevocable death penalty for the killer?" Dukakis replied, "No, I don't … and I think you know that I've opposed the death penalty during all my life." Any debater who opposes the death penalty knows, or certainly should know, that this is the very first question that would be asked in cross-examination. (Of course the questioner would substitute girlfriend, sister, or mother for Kitty Dukakis.) The answer Dukakis gave was well suited for a tournament debate. The judge would nod with approval and note that the respondent had kept his cool and calmly and dispassionately addressed the issue. But the debate did not take place in a tournament round; it took place before a national TV audience of 62 million viewers, most of whom were not aware of the requirements of tournament debate. An entirely different response was called for.

The moderator's question and hypothetical scenario is likely to have engendered an emotional response on the part of the audience. Dukakis could have appealed to that pathos had he demonstrated anger and sensitivity through a more fitting response. Instead, his response was analytical and cool, appropriate for an appellate court judge but not for a general audience.

In 2004, Democratic presidential candidate Howard Dean of Vermont faced the opposite problem. When he yelled and screamed to motivate his volunteers after he had failed to win the Iowa Caucus as had been anticipated, he was perceived by some to be too emotional. He subsequently dropped out of the Democratic primaries with only one win: Vermont.

Again, we need to emphasize the importance of audience analysis. The correct answer in a tournament round is not necessarily the correct answer for a public debate.

B. Audience Analysis During the Speech

In addition to doing an audience analysis before a speech, we should also analyze our audience during the presentation, because audience members will react in various ways to the speech—and these reactions will give us useful clues. Such obvious demonstrations as applause, cheers and boos, and cries of approval or disapproval are easy to interpret. But the audience will also give the speaker important clues through the more subtle signs of body language. The most successful advocates are highly skilled at picking up the "vibes" provided by the audience, interpreting them, and adapting their case to establish rapport with the audience. Debaters should keep an eagle eye on the judge during a debate: They are likely to learn what issues that judge considers important and which way she is leaning on those issues.

C. Analysis of the Key Individual

In many situations we do not have to give reasons to all the members of an audience; instead we are concerned with winning a decision from a key individual or from a small group of individuals who have the decision-making power. College students quickly learn that within various clubs, and even in the official business of the college, key individuals often have the final say on various matters.

Intercollegiate debaters may occasionally address large audiences, but the decision is usually rendered by a single judge or by a panel of three or five judges. One of the great advantages of intercollegiate debating is that students usually have many opportunities to speak in small-audience situations and thus to adapt arguments to a key individual. By analyzing the judge in an academic debate and adapting the case to that individual, students can gain experience in an argumentative situation closely paralleling situations they will face in the future when directing arguments to a key individual. In fact, as we will see in Chapter 17, most

What the Advocate Needs to Know About the Audience

Audience Attitude Toward the Speaker

1. What is the probable audience attitude toward the speaker as a person?
2. What is the probable audience attitude toward the organization the speaker represents or is identified with?
3. What is the probable audience attitude toward the point of view the speaker represents?
4. What is the probable audience attitude toward the proposition the speaker is supporting (or opposing)?

The Occasion

1. Why have these people come together as an audience?
2. What will precede the advocate's speech?
3. What will follow the advocate's speech?
4. Are there any customs, ceremonies, or traditions that relate to the occasion?
5. Who else will speak on this occasion?
6. What will the other speakers probably say?
7. What leaders of the group or distinguished guests will be present?
8. How will their presence influence the audience's decision?
9. How much time is available?
10. What is the physical condition of the room in which the advocate will speak?

The Audience

1. Is the audience homogeneous or heterogeneous?
2. Does one age group predominate in the audience?
3. What is the probable size of the audience?
4. Does the audience consist predominantly or exclusively of members of one gender?
5. What is the educational attainment level of the majority of the audience?
6. Are there significant numbers of any one occupational group in the audience?
7. Are there significant numbers of any one ethnic group in the audience?
8. Are there significant numbers of any one cultural group in the audience?
9. What common interests do members of the audience share?
10. To what groups or organizations do significant numbers of audience members belong?

The Audience and the Advocate's Purpose

1. Will the audience know the speaker's purpose in advance?
2. What does the audience know about the subject area relating to the speaker's purpose?
3. What experience has the audience had with proposals similar to those of the advocate?

> What the Advocate Needs to Know About the Audience (Continued)
> 4. How would the audience be affected by the advocate's proposal?
> 5. What beliefs, prejudices, or predispositions does the audience have that relate to the speaker's purpose?

tournaments specifically provide for the debaters to adapt to the judge. Booklets describing judges' predispositions and biases are frequently compiled for individual tournaments and compilations are maintained online to assist debaters in their jobs of adaptation to judges (see http://www.planetdebate.com/). Debaters may also ask other advocates for information about their judge, and they can even direct questions about judging philosophy to the judge prior to the debate.

An interesting example of judge adaptation in applied debate can be found in courtroom debates. Although judges are supposed to apply the law impartially, they vary tremendously in the way they react to different types of motions and arguments and interpret many other factors critical to the outcome of the trial. Some, for example, run a "tight ship," whereas others allow attorneys considerable leeway. Many law firms require each attorney, after trying a case, to file a comprehensive evaluation of the judge for the benefit of other firm members who may argue before this judge. Although "judge shopping" is officially discouraged, attorneys will look for ways to avoid a judge who might make their case more difficult and to find a judge who is likely to be receptive to the kind of case they will present.

Student speakers will address most of their future arguments to small audiences or to key individuals. Even the president, who usually can command a larger audience than anyone else, more frequently argues with small groups of key congressional leaders who can decide the fate of legislation.

Many of the questions we have to answer about these key individuals are similar to those we need to answer about the audience. In preparing a list of questions about the key individual, advocates may begin by reviewing the inset "What the Advocate Needs to Know About the Audience" and substituting the term *key individual* where applicable.

D. Analysis of the Key Individual During the Speech

The analysis of the key individual is paradoxically both easier and more difficult than the audience analysis. It is more difficult in that it is usually inappropriate for the key individual to give overt signs like applause or cheers. Often the key individual, such as the judge in the courtroom or at an academic debate, will try to conceal any sign of approval or disapproval as the arguments are developed. But it is also easier because we do not have to pay attention to many individuals but can focus on one person or a small group. For example, when directing our presentation to the president of the bank, to the credit manager of the corporation, to the judge in the jury-waived trial, or to the judge in the academic debate, we can be more attentive to the subtle signs of agreement or disagreement and of attention or inattention. Thus we have a better opportunity to adapt our argument than we do when we have to consider the whole audience.

Evidence shows that skilled debaters can "read" nonverbal stimuli and interpret them correctly. James Sayer found in one research study that debaters in general evaluated the judges' nonverbal stimuli and predicted their decisions with 66.5 percent accuracy, whereas "better" debaters (defined as those with 5–3 or better records) were 80.7 percent accurate.[1] We do not know precisely what the nonverbal stimuli were—Sayer postulates that they may have been eye contact, facial expression, body movements, and posture—or how the debaters interpreted them. But debaters operating on an intuitive basis apparently can be very successful in analyzing the key individual during the debate. (Nonverbal communication is examined in Chapter 16.)

The problem becomes more complex when an audience is present along with the key individual, such as the spectators at a court trial. In such a situation, we have to give priority to those who render the decision—but we should never neglect the nondeciding audience. We should actually make a specific effort to win favor from it, because it may exert a positive influence on those who render the decision.

II. WRITTEN AND ORAL STYLES

Written and oral presentation styles differ significantly. In a now-classic quote Herb Wichelns pointed this out when he said:

> All the literary critics unite in the attempt to interpret the permanent value that they find in the work under consideration. That permanent value is not precisely indicated by the term *beauty,* but the two strands of aesthetic excellence and permanence are clearly found …
>
> If now we turn to rhetorical criticism … we find that its point of view is patently single. It is not concerned with permanence, not yet with beauty. It is concerned with effect. It regards the speech as a communication to a specific audience, and holds its business to be the analysis and appreciation of the orator's methods of imparting his ideas to his hearers.[2]

Writers can usually work at a more leisurely pace than speakers. They may write and rewrite their arguments; they may polish and re-polish style. They must consider enduring aesthetic standards and think of an audience that will read their arguments months or years afterward. A writer's audience may also

---

1. See James Edward Sayer, "Debaters' Perception of Nonverbal Stimuli," *Western Speech,* vol. 38 (winter 1974), pp. 2–6.
2. Herbert A. Wichelns, "The Literary Criticism of Oratory," in *Studies in Rhetoric and Public Speaking in Honor of James Albert Winans,* by Pupils and Colleagues (New York: Century, 1925), pp. 95–208 ff.

proceed at a leisurely pace, stopping to ponder a point, consult a reference work, or reread a passage.

Speakers, by contrast, usually work under stricter time limits. If they do not reply promptly to their opponents' argument, they may not have another chance. Writers can hope that readers will reread their words; speakers have only one opportunity to reach their listeners. Thus their arguments must be instantly intelligible to the audience. If listeners miss an argument, its value is lost unless the speaker repeats it. Most importantly, the speaker is concerned with a specific audience on a specific occasion. Famous trial attorney Louis Nizer makes this point:

> I have never made a speech from a script. A speech or argument in a court is made for the ear, not the eye. It demands instantaneous comprehension. Unlike a written work, it does not provide the opportunity for digestive deliberation. A reader sets his own pace and can call a recess at his own pleasure …
>
> The rule is reversed when one writes a book or essay. I believe it should not be dictated to a stenographer; the rhythm tends to be wrong; it will too much resemble a conversation in which the sentences may not end and the eyes punctuate. The grace and balance of well-written sentences can't be achieved orally.[3]

Writers should strive for a style that will have permanence; speakers should strive for a style appropriate to the moment.

III. A PHILOSOPHY OF STYLE

No one style of speech is suitable to all speakers and to all time. The style of the great nineteenth-century orator Daniel Webster was magnificent for his times, but today it would be considered too formal, too florid. Style also bears the mark of the individual. Students will readily recognize the differences in the styles of Bill Clinton and George Bush, David Letterman and Jay Leno, John Madden and Bob Costas, and Connie Chung and Jane Pauley.

Debaters should carefully study the styles of successful speakers on the contemporary scene. Rather than trying to imitate the style of a favorite politician or TV personality or the winner of last week's big tournament, debaters should develop the style best suited for them, adapting it to particular occasions. An attorney, for instance, would use one style when addressing a rural jury and a different style when pleading before the Supreme Court. Yet in both cases he or she would have the same purpose: to win an acquittal for the client. As another example, an advocate trying to win support for intercollegiate athletics would use one style in addressing a football rally and a totally different style in addressing a chapter of the American Association of University Professors. Even similar audiences will expect different styles on different occasions. The style of speech ap-

---

3. Louis Nizer, *Catspaw* (New York: Fine, 1992), pp. 103–104.

propriate for an informal banquet of the senior class would be different from the style appropriate to a commencement address.

IV. FACTORS OF STYLE IN SPEECH COMPOSITION

The factors of style considered here reflect the tastes of contemporary audiences, but these general principles should be modified when special considerations arise. A speech at a football rally, for example, would probably require short sentences, informal (even flamboyant) vocabulary, extreme partisanship, and brevity. A speech before a group of educators would probably require longer sentences, more dignified vocabulary, more formal structure, more restrained partisanship, and greater length.

A. Conciseness

Contemporary audiences prefer short sentences and succinct phrases rather than the full-blown, flowery prose popular in the nineteenth century. Today speakers should try to be concise. Some debaters may take this too far, however. A speech should be more than a string of evidence cards. Powerful and concise language offers the debater more control over the judge's flow sheet. If the judge is able to write down the exact wording of the debater's headlines (or tags), the debater has managed to control what is on the judge's flow. If the debater's phrases are too long and complicated to write down in a timely fashion, the judge will have to shorten and interpret, putting the control in the judge's hand (or pen). Numbers, tag lines, explanations, and transitions can only help the debater to convey their argumentative positions. Conciseness involves not only the succinct expression of ideas but also the overall length of the speech. One- or two-hour speeches were the usual thing in the days of Webster, Henry Clay, and John C. Calhoun. Perhaps the popularity of first radio and then television programs has helped to set the modern pattern of a half hour as the usual maximum for a speaker; indeed, the average speech today is often shorter.

Time is precious to us as advocates. Those portions of our speeches that are under our complete control (for example, the first affirmative, sometimes the plan attacks or value objections, and so on) should be the product of extensive rewriting and editing until each issue is stated with maximum conciseness and clarity and phrased for maximum impact on the judge or audience. Each piece of evidence should be presented with a cogent lead-in and edited to eliminate extraneous words (while preserving with scrupulous honesty the author's intent). This editing process must be done with extreme care, as negligent omission is an ethical violation just as is plagiarism.

B. Clarity

Clarity is of overwhelming importance to us as advocates. A perfectly sound case, a case superior to the opposing case, may be defeated if the audience cannot see the connections among our arguments or if the listeners do not get the point of our evidence. Our objective is to present our case so clearly that it is impossible for the average member of the audience not to understand it. Careful organization, well-chosen examples, and precise language will help us achieve clarity.

A lack of clarity and gross negligence in editing resulted in the following statement on a safety card that a United Airlines passenger found in her seat-back pocket. She was taken aback to read:

IF YOU ARE SITTING IN AN EXIT ROW AND CANNOT READ THIS CARD, PLEASE TELL A CREW MEMBER.

If a lack of clarity makes it possible to misunderstand your arguments, you can be sure that your opponents will misunderstand your arguments. And they may persuade others to do likewise.

C. Appropriate Vocabulary

Our vocabulary must be appropriate to the audience and the occasion. Attorney William Kunstler—an experienced lecturer—reports his method of adapting his vocabulary to his audience:

> … if I speak to an undergraduate audience I use a far different approach than when I am talking to the Junior Chamber of Commerce in Minnetonka, Minnesota, or a bar association, or a group of older people.
>
> The difference, I think, is that in talking to the young people I consciously try to use language that, while not being condescending, is at least in the genre to which they are accustomed. And I try to bring into the talk some relationship to the language of an undergraduate without sacrificing any content and without sacrificing any rhetorical artistry that you can utilize and without, I hope, condescension, because I think that condescension is probably the worst sin any speaker can commit.[4]

The task of the advocate is to present complex messages in comprehensible language geared to the genre of the decision renderers and with rhetorical artistry that will create a favorable impression. Student debaters should note that their approach is often the exact opposite of Kunstler's. They should consciously try to use the language and genre to which their often-older audiences are accustomed.

---

4. Nizer, *Catspaw*, p. 37.

D. Simple Structure

The overall structure of the speech should be simple. Our objective is to make it easy for those who render the decision to follow our case. We should emphasize simplicity, too, in the structure of our sentences and passages. The complex or compound sentence, full of subordinate clauses and studded with commas and semicolons, may, on careful reading, express an idea with great precision. But our listeners cannot see the punctuation in our notes, nor do they have a chance to reread a difficult sentence. Simple sentences are more desirable for speakers.

E. Concreteness

Specific rather than vague or general words or phrases will increase the impact of our ideas. We should use words and phrases that convey the exact shade of meaning we intend. The use of specific detail will often heighten interest and add an air of authenticity to the speaker's words. For example, when a first affirmative constructive speaker tried to show the harms of unemployment, he avoided a pointless generalization such as "unemployment is deleterious" and provided specific, concrete examples:

> Unemployment causes massive human suffering. The grim toll of even marginal increases in unemployment was documented by the painstaking study of Dr. Harvey Brenner of Johns Hopkins University, undertaken for the Joint Economic Committee.
>
> … That controlled epidemiological study revealed that for each 1 percent increase in unemployment, the nation suffered a 4.1 percent increase in suicides; a 1.9 percent increase in cardiovascular, renal, and cirrhosis mortality; and a 1.9 percent increase in overall mortality—that is, each 1 percent of unemployment results in 36,000 needless deaths.

Of course the negative argued about this evidence—but it was concrete.

Sometimes the speaker has to use unfamiliar words or phrases. These can be made more specific by careful definition. (Chapter 4 discusses various methods of defining terms.)

F. Imagery

If we can paint a vivid picture in the minds of audience members, we increase our chances of persuading them. A deftly phrased image will have an immediate impact on listeners and may linger in their memory to influence future as well as immediate decisions. In a debate on the proposition: "Resolved: That executive control of U.S. foreign policy should be significantly curtailed," a first affirmative speaker began by saying:

> "All the people who lined the streets began to cry, 'Just look at the Emperor's new clothes. How beautiful they are!' Then suddenly a little child piped up, 'But the Emperor has no clothes on. He has no clothes

on at all.'" In 1947 the United States created the Central Intelligence Agency and donned the cloak of secrecy to pursue communism. Experience has proven the cloak we donned was nothing more than the Emperor's new clothes, hiding far less than we long pretended and exposing America to peril.

A new term—*iron curtain*—entered the world's vocabulary when Winston Churchill proclaimed, "From Stettin in the Baltic to Trieste in the Adriatic an iron curtain has descended across the Continent."[5] An American government official seated behind Churchill at the time thought, "For this man, words are battalions, doing battle for his ideas."[6]

G. Connotation

Our concern with the selection of words and phrases is not limited to the choice of terms within the vocabulary of our audience. We are also concerned with the problem of choosing words and phrases with an awareness of their emotional connotations. Consider the following examples of phrases that present a concept in a "good" and a "bad" light:

Are certain aliens in the United States *illegal* or *undocumented?*

Is it *affirmative action* or *anti-white male bias?*

When interest groups give money to political candidates is it a *campaign contribution,* an *investment,* or a *bribe?*

Is it a *tax increase* or *revenue enhancement?*

Were the Friends of Bill (Clinton) *concerned citizens* or *lobbyists?*

Does a candidate have *advisors* or *handlers?*

Does a speaker have *researchers* or *ghostwriters?*

The change we propose is *reform;* the change they propose is *reckless.*

In all cases, of course, we retain *public relations counselors* to conduct an *educational campaign* while they hire *spin doctors* to operate their *propaganda machine.* (Recall the discussion of propaganda point in Chapter 1.)

Each of these designations involves an element of slanting, but decisions are often influenced by just such slanted phrases. As Joseph Conrad said, "Give me the right word and the right accent and I will move the world."[7]

---

5. A considerable literature has been built up around the term *iron curtain.* In 1918 Vasiliy Rozanov wrote in his book *Apocalypse of Our Time,* "An iron curtain is descending on Russian history." In *Through Bolshevik Russia* (1920), Ethel Snowden described that country as being behind an "iron curtain." In the last days of Hitler's Third Reich, Propaganda Minister Joseph Goebbels spoke of "an iron curtain." See Martin Gilbert, *Winston S. Churchill,* vol. 8 (Boston: Houghton Mifflin, 1988), p. 7. Although he was not the originator of the phrase, it is Churchill's usage that the world remembers.
6. Clark Clifford, *Counsel to the President* (New York: Random House, 1991), pp. 95–105.
7. Joseph Conrad, *A Personal Record* (Garden City, N.Y.: Doubleday, 1923), p. xvi.

H. Climax

The development of climax is an important consideration in speech composition. An advocate's speech typically contains a series of issues. Each of these should be built up to a climax, and the speech as a whole should build toward a final, major climax. We will often find it advantageous to place a strong climax early in our speech to capture audience attention. Our final climax may be in the form of an effective summary of our major arguments combined with a strong persuasive appeal. If we use an anticlimactic order, beginning with our strongest arguments and tapering off with our least effective arguments, we will diminish the force of our case and leave a weak impression with those who render the decision. We have three key tasks relating to climax: (1) We need to open with an attention-getting climax; (2) we need to end on a high note, leaving a strong, lasting impression with our audience; and (3) we need to offset the climax of a previous speech by our opponents.

V. RHETORICAL FACTORS IN SPEECH COMPOSITION

The rhetorical factors of coherence, unity, and emphasis aid advocates in composing effective, well-organized speeches. You may find it helpful to review the speaker responsibilities considered in Chapters 12 and 13 as you compose your speeches. This way you will have not only a well-written speech or brief but one that fulfills your speaker responsibilities as well.

Factors of Style in Speech Composition

- Conciseness

- Clarity

- Appropriate

- Simple Structure

- Concreteness

- Imagery

- Connotation

- Climax

A. Coherence

The speech should be arranged so effectively that it will be instantly intelligible to those who render the decision. The intelligibility of a speech depends to a great extent on coherent organization. Beginning advocates often have a cluster of evidence and reasoning that seems convincing to them but has no effect on those who render the decision. The same evidence and reasoning rearranged by skilled advocates may win a decision. The difference is that the skilled advocates have learned to arrange or order their materials properly and to blend them together with effective transitions into a coherent whole.

1. Order.   The materials of the speech must be presented in a carefully determined order designed to have maximum effect on those who render the decision. The issues of the proposition should be presented in an effective sequence. The supporting materials for each issue should be arranged to lend maximum support to the issues. Often, as advocates, we may first think of presenting our arguments in logical order—and in many situations logical order is the most effective arrangement. In other situations, however, we may want to arrange our arguments in a psychological order adapted to our audience. Other arrangements that are effective in certain situations include (1) the problem–solution order, (2) the "this-or-nothing" order, (3) the topical order, and (4) the chronological order. Sometimes the use of one arrangement for the overall speech and another for the development of certain supporting arguments is effective. In debating the proposition "Resolved: That the federal government should control the supply and utilization of energy in the United States," one debater used a combination of methods in his first affirmative speech. The organization of the debate case was problem–solution: The problem was identified, and a solution was proposed. Other types of organization were used in the development of the issues. Following is an excerpt from the outline of his speech:

> I. Today's energy crisis is not a matter of just a few years but of decades. (Under this heading the debater used chronological order to show how the crisis had come about and why it would project into the future.)

> II. Alternative sources of energy were impractical. (Under this heading the debater used the this-or-nothing order, as he considered and dismissed various alternative sources, concluding that coal was not an alternative because both coal and uranium were needed.)

> III. Nuclear power is safe. (Under this heading the debater used chronological order, reviewing the history of civilian nuclear power from its start to the present and claiming an unparalleled safety record.)

> IV. There is no reasonable alternative to nuclear power. (Under this heading the debater again used the this-or-nothing order to argue that an energy famine would result unless the affirmative plan was adopted.)

Though we may use a variety of methods, our objective is always to arrange our materials to achieve coherence.

2. Transition.   Transitions can be regarded as bridges between the various parts of the speech. A well-ordered series of arguments is not enough to ensure coherence. We also have to connect the parts of our argument in a way that makes it easy to follow the development of the total case. In many cases a transition may be only a word or a phrase. In a closely reasoned argument, however, an effective transition often includes three parts: (1) a terse summary of the preceding arguments, (2) a brief forecast of the next argument, and (3) a concise demonstration of the relationship between the two arguments.

The debater whose outline was just presented used the following transition in developing his fourth issue:

> Remember our analysis: One, the energy crisis will last for decades. Two, alternative sources are impractical. And three, nuclear power is safe. With this in mind consider the statement signed by 31 scientists— including 10 Nobel Prize winners—appearing in the *New York Times* on the 16th of this month: "On any scale the benefits of a clean, inexpensive, and inexhaustible domestic fuel far outweigh the possible risks. We can see no reasonable alternative to an increased use of nuclear power to satisfy our energy needs." And that's our fourth issue: There is no reasonable alternative to nuclear power.

Well-planned transitions make it easier for the audience to see the relationship of various parts of the argument and to link the parts of the speech together into an effective whole.

B. Unity

We should have one clear, definite, and specific objective for a speech. Once we have clearly formulated this objective, we can compose a speech aimed at attaining the objective. Effective speeches have unity of purpose and mood.

1. Unity of Purpose.   Unity of purpose requires that the speaker have one and only one specific purpose for a speech. The rhetorical purpose of the advocate is to prove, or to disprove, the proposition of debate. Anything that does not contribute to that goal—no matter how interesting, amusing, or informative it may be—must be ruthlessly excluded from the speech.

An example from academic debating will illustrate this point. One student, who had many of the qualities of an excellent debater, consistently lost debates on the energy proposition. A senior physics major, he was particularly well informed on nuclear power reactors. His response to negative workability attacks was brilliantly informative speeches on nuclear reactors. In fact, one judge commented that the student had delivered one of the best informative speeches the judge had ever heard on the operation of nuclear reactors. The student's problem was that he presented so much information on workability that—although he obviously carried that issue—he failed to respond to the disadvantages attacks. When he restructured his response-to-workability briefs—deleting the fascinating and informative but irrelevant material and retaining only the critical refutation—he suddenly had time to devote to other major arguments and began to win decisions.

2. Unity of Mood.   Unity of mood requires that we sustain a certain mood, emotional feeling, or "tone" appropriate to our purpose, audience, and occasion. Our materials should be in perfect unity with the mood we have chosen for our speech. Evidence and reasoning that may meet the logical requirements of the proposition but not the mood requirements should be replaced by materials that will meet both requirements.

A debater favoring a program of national compulsory health insurance de-cided she would try to establish a mood of pity. To support her argument about the high cost of medical care, she offered a series of examples of long-term ill-ness. But one poorly chosen example shattered the mood she sought to sustain:

> One young girl, just the age of many in this audience, spent seven long, lonely, tragically wasted years in the cold isolation of a TB hospital. One man in the prime of life, the age of many of your parents, spent five years in the living hell of bone cancer suffering the most terrible pain known to man. One dear old lady, the age of some of your grandpar-ents, spent 15 years in a mental institution knitting a 27-foot-long scarf.

The audience of high school students was still chuckling about the old lady and her 27-foot-long scarf as the debater completed her arguments showing the high cost of long-term hospitalization.

C. Emphasis

Not all parts of a speech are of equal importance—some are indispensable to the case whereas others are less important. Our goal is to emphasize the more im-portant parts of our speech. Emphasis makes it easier for the audience to grasp and retain the ideas we need to get across. Emphasis may be achieved by posi-tion, by time, by repetition, by headlining, and by perspective (spin control).

1. Position.   We can create emphasis by where we place an idea in our speech. The beginning and the ending provide greater emphasis than the middle does. This principle applies to the speech as a whole, to an argument within the speech, and even to a sentence. Consider the following excerpts, taken from speeches in debates on right-to-work laws. The speeches come from two differ-ent debates, but the same issue is involved. Note the difference in emphasis:

> They just don't work. That's the simple fundamental fact about right-to-work laws—they just don't work. Let's look at the record. Let's go right down the list of states with right-to-work laws. In every case we'll see they just don't work.

> Let us consider the feasibility of the proposal advanced by the affirma-tive. Let us examine the facts in those states where this plan has been

tried. We will find that such legislation does not work effectively to produce any significant change in labor–management relationships. There are now 17 states that have legislation of this type. As we review the evidence from these states, we find …

Both speakers maintained that right-to-work laws do not work. The first speaker emphasized this claim by giving it both first and last position; the second speaker buried it in the middle of his passage.

2. Time. Time is of the essence in argument—and we must spend our time wisely. Most of our time should be devoted to the important arguments. We never have enough time to cover all possible arguments or to fully refute all the contentions of our opponent. Thus we have to single out the important matters and emphasize them by devoting time to them.

3. Repetition. Repetition and redundancy are often frowned on in writing, and authors are urged to steer clear of them. For the speaker, however, judicious repetition is essential to both clarity and emphasis. If listeners miss a critical word or phrase that is uttered only once, the speaker's case may never be clear to them. Listeners cannot turn back the page to reread something they missed the first time. We have to compensate for inattention among some members of our audience by reiterating critical material. The old slogan "Tell them what you're going to tell them, tell them, then tell them what you've told them" has great merit. As speakers we cannot use italics, capital letters, or boldface type for emphasis, but we can use repetition. Repetition may be achieved by repeating the same idea in the same words or by restating an idea several times in slightly different ways.

The *echo effect* is often an effective technique. Here the speaker states a key sentence—usually a headline (considered next)—and then the speaker immediately echoes the sentence by repeating its critical words. Echoing in a written essay would undoubtedly be criticized as poor style, and rightly so. However, it is a valuable stylistic device in oral presentations—just one more example of the differences between oral and written style. For instance, in arguing the proposition "Resolved: That the federal government should implement a program which guarantees employment opportunities for all United States citizens in the labor force," a first affirmative speaker repeated his major claims, saying: "Our first issue: Unemployment will persist. Unemployment will persist.… Our second issue: Unemployment is a major social problem. Unemployment—a major social problem." The repetition was intended to lodge the argument firmly in the minds of the judge and audience and to ensure that the judge would record the speaker's exact phrasing of this argument on a flow sheet. This type of overt repetition is accepted by many judges, who recognize the pressure a speaker is under in a tournament. A more subtle method of repetition is required in other situations.

4. Headlining (Taglining).   Headlining is an essential technique in composing debate cases and, for that matter, in composing a speech on any relatively complex matter. **Headlining** involves the use of concise, precisely chosen words or short sentences to identify key points in the debater's speech. Tag lines should ideally be seven words or less.

The headlines, which are the first sentences of the major portions of the speech, should be short and succinct and should emphasize the major point you want to make. They are a specialized form of tag line (see Chapter 14). Recall the examples just cited:

Unemployment will persist.

Unemployment is a major social problem.

With these headlines the debater set out the need issues in short, succinct, and emphatic form.

All major portions of the case should be headlined in a similar way. Here's an example:

Inherency: Present economic policies can't reduce unemployment.

In the plan each plank should be clearly headlined. Here's an example:

Plank 1—Agency: NASA will administer the plan.

Plank 2—Mandate: By 2010 NASA will …

The headlines must concisely and precisely express the key ideas the debaters wish to lodge in the minds of the decision makers. Imprecision and ambiguity in phrasing headlines are counterproductive. A Miami newspaper headlined a story, "Developer Agrees to Restore Damage to Wetlands." A Birmingham newspaper headlined an editorial, "The Region Is Doing a Poor Job in Raising Its Illiteracy Rate." Another newspaper unabashedly proclaimed, "Teen Pregnancies Caused by Sex, Utah Study Says." If the headline leaves the audience puzzled, angry, or amused by inept word choice, the headline is a failure. Experienced debaters find it worthwhile to write and rewrite their headlines until they are honed to perfection.

Intercollegiate debaters often continue the headlining down through the substructure of the case using numbers and letters to make their organization clear. Note that in the debate in Appendix B, the debaters not only headline their arguments but also use numbers and letters to label their own arguments and to identify the points in their opponents' arguments that they are trying to refute. In nonformal debate, too, headlining is essential to add clarity and impact to the arguments. The phrasing will be more informal—"Now wait a minute, let's look at the second point Art made, about the fees for the MBA. You really can't compare …"—but it still helps listeners follow your argument. In any situation carefully developed headlining will make it easy for those who render the decision to follow your arguments.

5. Perspective (Spin Control).   As we saw in Chapter 7, data are often sus-
ceptible to more than one reasonable interpretation. This, of course, is not limited to statistical data. With **spin control** advocates present material from the
most favorable rhetorical perspective (see the Chapter 18 section "Respondent
Considerations") and, for that matter, to all aspects of speech composition. This
perspective or spin control should be applied to both the headline (see the preceding section) and the development of the statement.

Spin control became a major priority during the health care debate. The
New York Times reported:

> Tired of watching its members portrayed as patient-gouging money
> machines, the American Medical Association is changing the way it
> calculates doctors' median incomes. The association ... decided ... that
> ... it would lump the salaries of private practitioners with those of
> Federal Government doctors and young doctors in training, who make
> considerably less.
>
>   The mean income of American doctors in private practice (was)
> $177,400 a year ... In contrast, doctors in training earn(ed) only $22,000
> to $30,000 a year ... Government doctors ... are known to earn much
> less than doctors in private practice ... Dr. Sidney Wolfe, director of
> Public Citizen's Health Research Group in Washington, called the
> accounting change "unabashed deception." "It wounds like the kind
> of snake oil that the A.M.A. is very fond of criticizing others for,"
> Dr. Wolfe said.[8]

Clearly both sides are trying to put their spin on the matter of physicians' income. Is it showing the whole picture, or is it an unabashed deception? By the
way, did you detect the reporter's spin?

The lesson for the advocate is clear: Present the material from your perspective—put your spin on it—and if at all possible get your perspective on record
before your opponent plants a different perspective (or spin) in the minds of the
decision makers.

When President Clinton sent his budget proposal to Congress, he put
his spin on it, calling it "A Deficit Reduction Package." That had a nice ring
to it—reducing an enormous deficit sounds like a sensible thing to do. Had his
Republican opponents been quicker to put their spin on the legislation they
called "The Greatest Tax Increase in History," the result might have been different—tax increases are always unpopular. Clinton's early spin may have made the
difference. His budget passed the House by one vote and would have died in the
Senate on a tie if Vice President Gore had not cast the tie-breaking vote.

---

8. "New Math Used to Clean Up Doctors' Image," Associated Press, June 17, 1994.
Reprinted by permission.

Rhetorical Factors in Speech Composition

A. Coherence
1.   Order
2.   Transition

B. Unity
1.   Unity of purpose
2.   Unity of mood

C. Emphasis
1.   Position
2.   Time
3.   Repetition
4.   Headlining
5.   Perspective (spin control)

D. Ethical and inclusive use of language
1.   Gender-inclusive language
2.   Race-inclusive language

D. Ethical and Inclusive Use of Language

One of the basic premises of debate is that language has power. The power of words to repress is as compelling as the power of words to liberate. It is essential that debaters use—to the best of their ability—language that is inclusive, nonoffensive, and culturally appropriate. Insensitive reference to people based on their victimization, difference, or foreign cultural ethnicity or group identification may cause you to think of them as "others" and therefore less important or less understandable than you or groups you belong to. (For more about sexist language and how to avoid it, visit http://www.apa.udel.edu/apa/publications/texts/nonsexist.html. For more about racist language, visit http://www.asante.net/articles/racist-language.html.)

VI. EDITING

Everything can be improved by editing. As noted in a previous section, those portions of our speeches that are under our complete control should be the product of extensive rewriting and editing and phrased for maximum impact on the judge or audience. When an idea first occurs to us, it is often fragmented, deficient, awkwardly phrased, and lacking in the grace, polish, and forcefulness of the adroit phrase that will make the newspaper headlines, be highlighted as a network news sound bite, or be lodged in the mind of a debate judge. Extensive rewriting and skillful editing will turn an embryonic idea into an effective persuasive message.

Consider how these unedited statements were counterproductive for their authors:

> After being hit in the head with a baseball, pitcher Dizzy Dean joyfully informed the anxious media, "The doctors X-rayed my head and found nothing!" He spent a lifetime trying to live down that faux pas.
>
> The producer of a highly successful TV series indignantly protested a network's renewal offer by firing off a fax insisting, "You say this deal will be 50–50. In fact, it will be the reverse."
>
> An Army bulletin announced, "The unit had an estimated strength of 2,000 men, of whom 300 were women."
>
> Frank Rizzo—former police chief and mayor of Philadelphia—stated, "The streets of this city are safe. It's only the people who make them unsafe."[9]

Good editing would have turned these bloopers from items in the book *The 776 Stupidest Things Ever Said* into coherent and effective statements.

EXERCISES

1. Read some famous speeches from the plays of Shakespeare. A good source can be found at http://www.monologuearchive.com/s/shakespeare_william .html.
2. Watch and read Dr. Martin Luther King's "I Have a Dream" speech and identify the literary devices he uses to give power to the speech. (You can find it at http://www.americanrhetoric.com/speeches/Ihaveadream.htm.)
3. Select an evidence card developed earlier in the course. Write 10 possible tag lines that might be supported by this bit of evidence.
4. Write a first affirmative constructive speech for a debate on a proposition of value, then for a proposition of policy.
5. Share with your classmates a favorite poem or song lyric.

---

9. *New York Times,* Apr. 25, 1993, p. H1.

16

Presenting the Case: Delivery

Once we have prepared our case, our next step is to deliver it. Although a well-composed case is essential, good composition is not enough to win a debate decision. For the speech to have a positive impact, we have to add effective delivery. The importance of delivery in oral communication has been stressed ever since Aristotle pointed out, "Success in delivery is of the utmost importance to the effect of the speech."[1] Modern students of communication theory confirm this classical dictum. For example, James McCroskey examined a number of experimental studies and concluded, "Good delivery allows the rhetorically strong message to have its normal effect. Poor delivery tends to inhibit the effect of a verbal message."[2] Once we have composed a rhetorically strong message, we have to deliver that message in a way that will obtain the desired decision from our audience. Of course, a strong delivery is necessary, but not sufficient to debate or speech success. Delivery is the means to the ultimate end of having an audience listen to and act upon your case. It ensures that the message is received, but does not impact the quality of the message itself. When one orders a pizza for delivery, if the pizza arrives hot and fresh to your door, it tastes no better if it is delivered in a beautiful and new sports car, or a beat-up, rusty pick-up truck. As long as the vehicle does not break down, you are simply happy to have your meal. In a like manner, as long as the speaker's delivery is able to help the audience follow and understand the content of the message, it has done its part.

I. METHODS OF DELIVERY

The four methods of delivery available to the speaker are impromptu, extemporaneous, manuscript, and memorization. In most situations and for most

1. Aristotle, *Rhetoric*, III, p. 1.
2. James C. McCroskey, *An Introduction to Rhetorical Communication* (Englewood Cliffs, N.J.: Prentice Hall, 1968), p. 208.

Miniglossary

Extemporaneous speech   A prepared speech in which the speaker may or may not use notes.

Impromptu method   A speech delivered without specific preparation.

Nonverbal communication   Vocal expression and body language that convey meaning to another person.

---

advocates, the best method is the extemporaneous method. With the extemporaneous method, it is frequently necessary to have evidence cards available that contain quotations or statements we want to use in a very specific form. Often we find it advantageous to memorize brief passages of our speech. For example, we might want to conclude a speech with a carefully phrased summary. If we felt that reading this summary from a card would lessen its effect and yet we wished to be very precise in that statement, we might memorize our concluding sentences. And when our opponent introduces important unexpected matters into the debate, we must meet them with impromptu refutation.

A. Impromptu

We use the **impromptu method** of delivery when we make little or no preparation for the presentation of our thoughts. In fact, because the impromptu speech is made without specific preparation, we have no organized case and do not compose the speech ahead of time. Suppose that at this very moment you were asked to defend your views on U.S. foreign policy; your response would be impromptu. You could draw on your general knowledge of the subject, on the information you had happened to gather in your reading, and on whatever ideas you may have formulated, but you would have to organize your ideas as you went along.

It's important to be familiar with the impromptu method simply because in some circumstances it is the only method available. When news of an important development is received in the Senate during the day's session, for example, a senator might find it desirable to speak on this matter at once. A sales representative might meet a prospective customer unexpectedly and find the occasion to be an opportune moment to attempt a sale. The business executive, while attending a board of directors meeting, might learn of a new problem and be called on immediately to participate in debate on it. In each situation the individual probably would have a good general background knowledge but would have had no opportunity to make specific preparations. Because the impromptu method is often the only available method, argumentation teachers sometimes require their students to present impromptu arguments, so they can gain experience in organizing and presenting a case "on the go."

The best preparation for meeting the impromptu situation when it arises is experience in delivering prepared speeches. Actually we may plan and organize the impromptu speech to a degree. We will have at least a few seconds in which to organize our thoughts, and if we are experienced speakers, we can do a lot in a short time. Some speakers have developed the faculty of thinking ahead and planning their future lines of argument while they are speaking on matters that do not require their full attention.

B. Extemporaneous

The **extemporaneous speech** is a prepared speech. In delivering the extemporaneous speech, we neither read from a manuscript nor memorize our entire speech. We may or may not use notes; we may or may not read short quotations as a part of our speech; and we may or may not memorize a few short passages of our speech.

The extemporaneous method provides almost all the advantages found in other methods of delivery and few disadvantages. Its greatest advantage lies in the fact that it is both prepared and flexible, allowing us to plan exactly what we want to say and how we want to say it. Thus all the advantages of case building and speech composition can be brought to bear in the extemporaneous speech. In addition, because the speech is planned but not "carved in stone," we can modify the presentation to adapt to the situation and to the statements of previous speakers. Because we can watch the audience closely during the speech, we can gauge the listeners' reaction and adapt the speech to their response.

The extemporaneous method has few disadvantages. It does have a greater possibility of error than do manuscript or memorized speeches, but careful preparation can minimize this risk. When the time element is critical, as in a radio or television speech, the extemporaneous method may pose some problems for the beginning speaker. It is more difficult to control the time with this method than with the manuscript or memorized speech. Experienced speakers, however, develop an excellent sense of time, and college debaters have little difficulty adjusting to the time limits in intercollegiate debate. The repeat guests on TV talk shows are those who, among other things, have learned to adapt to the strict time requirements while retaining the spontaneity of the extemporaneous method. Political candidates, who have to make numerous speeches every day at the height of a campaign, usually develop "The Speech"—a block of material in which they can present their views extemporaneously in as little as 5 minutes or extend them to as much as 20 minutes, as the occasion requires. After the first affirmative speech, almost all debaters, be they students or senators, use the extemporaneous method of delivery. Only extemporaneous delivery provides for the carefully prepared on-the-spot adaptation and refutation so essential to effective debate.

The extemporaneous method most frequently makes use of note cards or legal pads, on which the speaker writes key words and phrases, making maximum use of abbreviations. Ronald Reagan used index cards in the mid-1950s when he was touring the country as a spokesman for General Electric. He continued to use the same method during his presidency.[3] A similar method is used for television shows, although the cards are much larger and usually are placed off camera.

C. Manuscript

In using the manuscript method, we prepare our speech carefully, write it out in full, and read it to our audience. The advantage of the manuscript is that it provides us with the opportunity, even under pressure of the debate, to say exactly what we want to say in exactly the way we want to say it. When minimizing the possibility of error is the prime consideration, the manuscript speech is generally used. In delivering a State of the Union message or other major state addresses, all U.S. presidents, even those who were brilliant extemporaneous speakers, have used the manuscript method. A slip of the tongue in such a situation would be too dangerous; it might lead to a domestic or international crisis. The first affirmative constructive is a manuscript speech.

The disadvantages of the manuscript method include the lack of flexibility and the difficulty of reading the manuscript effectively. Because the manuscript is prepared in advance, it does not provide for adjustments to the situation, to previous speeches, or to audience reaction. Furthermore, the manuscript often becomes a barrier between the speaker and the audience when the speaker's objective is to establish rapport with the audience. Audiences would rather have the speaker talk *with* them than read *at* them. Ronald Reagan, the "Great Communicator," made the same point when he wrote, "I've always believed that you can't hold an audience by reading a speech."[4] Skilled speakers, when they find it necessary to use a manuscript, often plan their delivery in such a way as to create the impression that they are frequently departing from the manuscript.

Experienced debaters have found it worthwhile to master the art of effective delivery from a manuscript. As we practice the delivery of our speech, we should give careful consideration to the "Steps to Good Delivery" considered later in this chapter.

Portions of the speech under the advocate's complete control—that is, when there is little or no need or opportunity for adaptation—should reflect the maximum skill in speech composition. The first affirmative speech, for example, provides the greatest opportunity for advocates to say precisely what they want to say in precisely the way they want to say it and to deliver their carefully chosen words with maximum effectiveness. The well-planned first affirmative speech is a masterpiece of composition and delivery. The issues, the contentions, the transitions, the analysis, the evidence,[5] and the summaries—all should be polished to

---

3. Ronald Reagan, *An American Life* (New York: Simon & Schuster, 1990), p. 130.
4. Reagan, *An American Life,* p. 130.
5. Again the admonition: Evidence may be edited to eliminate extraneous material, but the advocate must scrupulously preserve the author's intent.

perfection so that they will be recorded on the judge's flow sheet or lodged in the minds of the audience precisely as the speaker wants them to be. The well-written and well-delivered first affirmative speech is a graceful, forceful, highly literate, lucid, cogent statement that should be a powerful factor in advancing the affirmative's case.

A well-planned manuscript may be adapted to the situation at many points in a debate. Experienced debaters prepare briefs in anticipation of these situations —that is, short manuscripts that may be blended into their speech by use of extemporaneous methods. Negative debaters prepare briefs of plan attacks. The plan attacks, of course, must be adapted to the specific case of the affirmative. Frequently, however, it is possible to anticipate a considerable part of this portion of the negative's case. The negative speaker may select from a number of previously prepared briefs, choosing the one directly relating to the particular affirmative plan of the moment and carefully adapting it to the specifics of that plan. Judges and audiences do not like "canned arguments." The scripted plan attack will work effectively only if it is adapted to the exact plan used by the affirmative with specific linking evidence and explanation and only if it is presented so that it appears spontaneous.

The reading copy of the manuscript should be a carefully prepared document of professional quality. The rough draft will be covered with corrections, and reading from a manuscript in that condition is too difficult. (Of course, if you prepare your manuscript on a computer, the task becomes much simpler.) A professional quality manuscript is easier to read, and its appearance adds to the speaker's credibility. It can help the speaker achieve more effective delivery and increase the impact on the arguments. The manuscript should be typed on 8½ × 11-inch paper with 1½-inch margins on both sides. Double spacing makes it easier to read and allows space for last-minute changes. Underlining, capitalization, highlighting, phonetic spelling of difficult words, and dashes or slash marks to indicate pauses make it easier to deliver the speech effectively. Be sure to leave extra space at the bottom of a page rather than break a key sentence between two pages. Also be sure to begin a new argument at the top of a new page rather than near the bottom of a page. Where possible, have one argument per page; the act of turning to a new page can help indicate to the audience that you are making a transition to a new argument.

D. Memorization

Advocates rarely memorize an entire speech today. This method is still required in many college oratory contests, because it provides practice with certain aspects of speech composition and delivery. Outside the contest situation, however, most advocates do not feel they have time to memorize a speech—except, of course, when "The Speech" is used. The memorized speech is, in fact, a manuscript that has been committed to memory. It provides all the advantages of the manuscript method, as well as the additional advantage that the manuscript is not present. Memorization also provides the maximum opportunity for polished presentation. With this advantage, however, comes a potential disadvantage.

Methods of Delivery

- Impromptu
- Extemporaneous
- Manuscript
- Memorized

Inexperienced advocates who memorize their speeches often appear stilted, artificial, and lacking in spontaneity. Further disadvantages of the memorized speech include the time necessary for memorization, the lack of flexibility, and the possibility that the advocate may forget a portion of his or her speech. Many speakers, however, do find it beneficial to memorize speech segments. The answer to an obvious value objection may be rambling and ineffective the first time that debaters respond to it. After they have met the attack in essentially the same form several times, they may hone their answers to perfection and present them concisely and incisively. Competent advocates preplan answers to recurring problems—and to problems they anticipate may arise.

II. STEPS TO GOOD DELIVERY

A. Speech Outline

The speech outline is different from the case outline. Recall that the *case outline* is an operational plan that coordinates the evidence and reasoning of the speakers on a given side of the proposition. The *speech outline* is a detailed plan of exactly what we intend to say and how we intend to say it to a specific audience.

B. Speaker Notes

The speaker's notes in a debate typically take two forms. The first involves the debate situation itself. The debater will record notes on the flow sheet (see pages 266–267) as an opponent is speaking. These notes are designed to guide the debater's response to an opponent's arguments. The second involves briefs prepared in advance. These briefs are responses that will be adapted for use against the anticipated arguments of an opponent. In the course of the debate, the speaker would make a note on the flow sheet to use this particular brief. On the brief itself, the speaker would make additional notes adapting the brief to the specific arguments of the opponents or would attach a sticky note with a preflow of the brief on it.

C. Preparation

Just as we have to prepare by building our case and composing our speech, we also have to prepare the delivery of our speech. Experienced advocates do not deliver a speech for the first time to those who render the decision. They deliver it a number of times, preferably to colleagues who can make suggestions on how to improve the delivery. Our presentation will be far more effective if we have delivered our speech or brief a number of times, anticipated the potential problem in delivery, and worked out the most effective methods of communication. The requirement of flexibility, of course, means that we will revise our speech up to the very moment of delivery. We should also anticipate probable arguments of our opponents and practice the way we will answer them should they be used.

In rehearsing your delivery, you need to be aware of all the factors considered in the next section, "Nonverbal Communication." A good starting point is to have a friend tape you delivering your speech and briefs. Play them back, and invite one or two friends whose judgment you respect to critique your delivery. Next you might use the "tape and ape" technique recommended by Roger Ailes,[6] who advised three presidents, along with many other prominent figures, on how to prepare for public appearances. Get a tape of a famous actor or actress reading selections from literary works or speeches. Record yourself reading the same selections. Your goal is not to become a performer but to learn how professionals deliver a speech. Your goal is not to mimic but to learn from the professionals and to become proficient in your own delivery. Just as you would watch a tape of Tiger Woods swinging a golf club to help perfect your own swing or a tape of Steffi Graf swinging a tennis racquet to improve your backhand, you can utilize tapes of professional speakers to improve your spoken delivery. Continue studying the professionals and revising, critiquing, and improving your delivery until you can deliver your speech or briefs with maximum effectiveness.

III. NONVERBAL COMMUNICATION

We communicate with others not only through language (verbal behavior) but also by means of nonverbal behavior. When we address an audience, we use not only verbal language but also **nonverbal communication**—vocal expression and movement to convey meaning. The meaning the audience perceives from our message comes not from our words alone, nor solely from vocal expression or body language. The message is a function of all these factors working together. For example, a simple verbal message such as "Hi" can, with the addition of appropriate vocal expression and body language, be perceived to mean "I love you," "Don't interrupt me now, I'm too busy to talk," "Have I seen you somewhere before?" or a wide variety of other meanings. Thus our task as advocates is to use the techniques of nonverbal communication to clarify and enhance our messages. Nonverbal communications must be consistent with the verbal com-

---

6. Roger Ailes, *You Are the Message* (New York: Doubleday, 1988), p. 46.

munications—the smile or frown, for example, reinforcing rather than contradicting the verbal message.

The importance of nonverbal communication is stressed by modern students of communication theory. Kenneth Hance and his colleagues maintain that "the ideas and feelings that we want to express to our audience are determined as much by nonverbal behavior and vocal signals as they are by the words we use."[7] And Randall Harrison has estimated that "in face-to-face communication no more than 35 percent of the social meaning is carried in the verbal messages."[8] Much of the remaining 65 percent of social meaning comes from the delivery of nonverbal messages.

A. Vocal Expression

We communicate with our audience partly by means of vocal expression. The words we pronounce are intended to be heard by our listeners and to have meaning to them. A number of aspects of vocal expression are important to advocates.

1. Rate.   The rate at which we talk is important. We must speak slowly enough for the audience to follow us, but not so slowly that the audience will lose interest in our words. Beginning advocates sometimes try to pack too much evidence and reasoning into their speeches; consequently they are forced to deliver their speech so fast that the audience cannot follow them without difficulty. Those who render the decision are not always willing to make the effort necessary to follow these rapid-fire presentations. The solution is often found in careful speech composition. Rather than using three pieces of evidence and delivering them too quickly for easy comprehension, it is better to use one well-chosen piece of evidence, integrating it carefully into the case, and helping to drive it home by use of an effective rate. We can benefit from listening to good speakers, both in audience situations and on radio and television, noting the speech rate they use. We should also adapt our own speech rate to suit the needs of our audience.

Experienced intercollegiate debaters operating in tournament situations on the national circuit are under great pressure to pack as much evidence and argument as possible into the available time. Their delivery may often exceed 300 words per minute. Their opponents will strain to follow every word; the judge, usually an argumentation professor who may well have "been there," will understand the situation and often be willing to concentrate on the speech and record the arguments accurately on a flow sheet. The human mind is easily capable of absorbing far more than 300 words a minute, provided the listener is willing to concentrate and the delivery is intelligible. Be warned, however, that audiences made up of members of the general public usually are unwilling to provide the

7. Kenneth G. Hance, David C. Ralph, and Milton J. Wiksell, *Principles of Speaking,* 3rd ed. (Belmont, Calif.: Wadsworth, 1975), p. 250.
8. Randall Harrison, "Nonverbal Communication: Explorations into Time, Space, Action and Object," in *Dimensions in Communication,* 2nd ed., ed. James H. Campbell and Hal W. Hepler (Belmont, Calif.: Wadsworth, 1970), p. 285.

same degree of concentration that is available in the tournament situation. Because selecting and using the appropriate rate of speech for those who render the decision is often problematic for the beginning debater, it is well to remember the question posed early in Chapter 15: Who are the people to whom our arguments are directed? The judges at the NDT event will have one set of expectations about rate; an audience of, say, college students or business executives will have very different sets of expectations. In such circumstances a coach might well offer the "Coaches' Prayer":

> God, give my debaters the speed and logos to impress the intercollegiate debate judge,
> The ethos and pathos to impress the lay judge,
> And the audience analysis to distinguish the one from the other.
>
> [*with apologies to Reinhold Neibuhr*][9]

Successful advocates are able to adapt their rate of speech to the requirements of the judge and audience. Observe the delivery of television network anchors—their rate is usually ideally suited to general public audiences.

2. Pitch.   Pitch refers to the tone level of the voice. Men generally have a deeper pitch than women have, and adults a deeper pitch than children. A pitch appropriate to the advocate's age and gender is an important consideration. Whereas it is best to *vary* your pitch, in general, a lower pitch provides for a more compelling presentation. Speakers should occasionally raise their pitch to provide emphasis, but they should resist the tendency to speak in a continuously high-pitched voice as they increase their energy and excitement during a debate.

3. Intensity.   Intensity refers to the loudness or softness of the speaker's voice. At a minimum, our voice must be loud enough to be heard easily by everyone we want to reach. In some circumstances the use of a public address system may be necessary. In such cases we should address the microphone with normal conversational intensity and allow the electronic system to provide the amplification rather than shout into the microphone. At the same time, we should guard against too much intensity. Beginning debaters sometimes make the mistake of addressing a small audience in a classroom with an intensity that would be appropriate for a large gathering in an auditorium. Our intensity level should be such that it easy for those who render the decision to hear us.

4. Flexibility.   We should be able to adapt our voice, as well as our arguments, to the situation. One type of delivery is appropriate at a football rally; another is appropriate in a small committee meeting. We may use variation of rate, intensity, and pitch to make our delivery more effective. For example, when we come to a particularly important concept in a speech, we might use a much slower

---

9. Alan Cirlin, "Judging, Evaluation, and the Quality of CEDA Debate," *National Forensic Journal*, vol. 4 (1986), pp. 81–151.

rate, greater intensity, and a deeper pitch than we used previously. When we come to a minor transition, we might provide contrast by increasing the rate, lowering the intensity, and raising the pitch. These variations have to be subtle, however. If the variation is too obvious, it calls attention to itself rather than to the argument the speaker wants to emphasize. Listen to good speakers in audience situations or on radio or television. Their use of variation to increase effectiveness will not be immediately apparent; but if you look for it, you will see how they vary their delivery to achieve a desired effect.

5. Quality.   The quality of our voice is important; we want people to find our voice easy and pleasant to listen to. Good quality results from good resonance and from a lack of undesirable voice qualities resulting from the improper production of tone, such as breathiness, nasality, huskiness, and throatiness. Other voice qualities considered undesirable in most circumstances include tones that are guttural, falsetto, or shrill. We should try to cultivate well-modulated, resonant tones. Under certain conditions (considered in the section "Expressional Patterns"), we will deliberately use unpleasant voice qualities to convey special meaning to our audience. These exceptions notwithstanding, which are confined to isolated words or brief passages, our overall quality should produce a positive reaction in the audience.

6. Fluency.   We should cultivate verbal fluency. Because beginning speakers are sometimes at a loss for words, they may vocalize pauses while they grope for the next word and litter their speeches with "ers," "ahs," and "uhs." A good knowledge of the subject, a well-developed case outline, a well-composed speech plan, and rehearsal of the speech will help the advocate overcome these problems and acquire the necessary verbal fluency. Practice in impromptu speaking also aids in the development of verbal fluency.

7. Expressional Patterns.   Our concern with delivery is not limited to the production of clear, pleasant, readily intelligible speech. On many occasions we will use nuances of delivery to convey meaning. Skillful advocates use rate, pitch, intensity, quality, and inflection to create an expressional pattern giving special meaning and emphasis to certain words and phrases in their speeches. With a well-chosen expressional pattern we can do much to clarify and communicate our meaning. For example, foreign demonstrators chanting for the television cameras can often convey their meaning despite the language barrier. When there is no expressional pattern, as in a printed report of a speech, it is sometimes difficult, if not impossible, to know what the speaker meant.

B. Movement

We communicate with our audience partly with verbal language, partly with vocal expression, and partly with movement. Just as audience members are influenced by the speaker they hear, so too are they influenced by the speaker they see (radio speaking is, of course, an exception). Ray Birdwhistell believes that we do most of our "talking" with our body movements. He maintains that we pour

---

Nonverbal Communication

A. Vocal Expression
1. Rate
2. Pitch
3. Intensity
4. Flexibility
5. Quality
6. Fluency
7. Expressional Patterns

B. Movement
1. Eye Contact
2. Movement
3. Gestures
4. Facial Expression

---

out information with our shrugs, our hand and body movements, our eyes, and our facial expressions and that these signals often convey more reliable messages than do the words we utter.[10] Several considerations of body language are important to the advocate.

1. Eye Contact.   We should maintain direct eye contact with members of the audience throughout our speech. Of course we will have to refer to our notes or manuscript, but this checking should be done as briefly as possible. The vast majority of our time should be spent looking at and talking to our audience. If there is a key individual in the audience—such as a single judge for a debate— we may focus most of our attention on that key individual. We should, however, establish some eye contact with others in the audience. In a general audience situation we should make sure that we establish eye contact with persons in all parts of the audience, thereby getting vital feedback from the audience.

2. Movement.   When speaking, our movement should be purposeful—it should aid us in communicating with our audience. The way we approach the lectern, for example, is important. If we approach the lectern with a confident step and take possession of the rostrum with quiet authority, our ethos is enhanced. Our movements should be easy, economical, and purposeful, yet apparently spontaneous. We should not remain in a fixed position behind the lectern or rooted to one spot on the rostrum as if we were inanimate. We might move

10. Ray L. Birdwhistell, *Introduction to Kinesics: An Annotation System for Analysis of Body Motion and Gesture* (Washington, D.C.: Department of State, Foreign Service Institute, 1952).

away from the lectern and closer to our audience to emphasize a major issue; we might move from one side of the rostrum to the other as we make a transition from one issue to another. But our movement should never compete with our case for the attention of the audience. A story, which just might be true, is told of a young prosecuting attorney who lost his first case in a burglary trial, although he had ample evidence that the accused was guilty. The novice lawyer was so nervous that, in presenting his evidence, he continually paced to and fro before the judge. This pacing so attracted the attention of the jury that they concentrated on estimating how many steps he took in each direction and how many miles he walked in the course of the trial, rather than following the case he was attempting to present.

3. Gestures.   Our gestures should be purposeful, aiding our communication with the audience. A distinct preference is shown today for restrained gestures in contrast to the flamboyant breast-beating of other eras. As with movement, the gesture should be easy, economical, and purposeful, yet apparently spontaneous.

When we use a three-fingered gesture as we say, for example, "The three major issues are ...," it should appear natural and spontaneous rather than calculated.

4. Facial Expression.   Our facial expression should be consistent with the attitude we are trying to express. One novice debater was so pleased to be participating in his first intercollegiate debate that he smiled happily as he said, "The energy crisis is going to produce the worst depression this country has ever seen." The incongruity of the speaker's smile did much to minimize the effect of his argument on this issue.

Experienced communicators such as Dan Rather or Peter Jennings can convey a world of meaning by a tilt of an eyebrow, a toss of the head, a curl of the lip, or a slight change of expression. And, of course, others are constantly trying to "read" our facial expressions. After a news conference, for example, reporters often tell us that the president or the secretary of state looked "pleased" or "tense," "confident" or "worried."

IV. SPECIAL CONSIDERATIONS: TOURNAMENT DEBATE DELIVERY

The experienced intercollegiate debate judge is a specialized audience. Each individual has different biases, and it is worthwhile to consider the judge's philosophy statement and ask him or her about delivery preferences. But also remember as well that these judges are used to distinct styles of delivery. Intercollegiate tournament debate delivery requires some special considerations:

1. *Vary the rate.* As noted previously, college debaters may speak at a very rapid pace, in excess of 300 words per minute. Judges are accustomed to listening to and "flow sheeting" very fast delivery if it is clear. Developing the ability to speak, or read, at such a fast pace is not easy. It is critical to maintain clarity and to enunciate at any speed. It is also important to remember to pause, use effective emphasis, and vary nonverbal vocal qualities. Introductions, conclusions, and transitions offer good opportunities to slow the pace for effect.

2. *Make eye contact.* If the judge is keeping a flow sheet scrupulously, the debater may see little more than the top of his or her head. Although continuous eye contact is impossible for the debater reading briefs and referring to the flow sheet, it is important to make eye contact when possible. The best opportunities for this are in the opening and closing to a speech. Effective eye contact commands attention and demonstrates confidence. In addition, it is important for the debater speaking (and the debater sitting at a desk) to watch the judge closely for any reaction to arguments made.

3. *Show energy, sincerity, and enthusiasm.* Debaters are salespersons selling their advocacy. Effective debaters display passion for their advocacy and present themselves with confidence and competence. One of the most exciting aspects of debate is its high energy level. It is better to be a little too loud than too quiet, and nonverbal behaviors demonstrating sincerity and commitment to the advocate's positions will enhance the presentation. Many debaters make the mistake of sitting to speak, bending over their notes, or hiding behind mountains of boxes. Tournament debaters should use proper posture to influence the judge's perception of their confidence and authority. Straight posture also facilitates deeper breathing, allowing debaters to enhance the projection and resonance of their voice and even their rate.

4. *Behave with courtesy and professionalism.* Perceptions begin to form before the debate begins, when the judge first sees the debaters. Their behavior during their opponents' speeches, their partners' speeches, and the cross-examination, as well as after the debate, can have powerful subliminal effects on the judge's evaluation.

5. *Avoid distracting mannerisms.* Repetitive gestures, tapping of feet or pens, gasping for breath—all diminish the potential impact of the debater's presentation. Speech delivery and composition involve many considerations. As in many other contexts, the great art is to conceal the art. As advocates our purpose is to win a decision. We use the arts of speech communication to help attain this objective.

6. *Be confident and controlled during cross-examination periods.* Do not busy yourself with preparation for the next speech or arrangement of materials at your desk. Look the judge in the eye as much as possible and demonstrate confidence and mastery of the situation and the material. Shake hands at the end of the debate.

Special Considerations: Tournament Debate Delivery

- Vary the rate
- Make eye contact
- Show energy, sincerity, and enthusiasm
- Behave with courtesy and professionalism
- Avoid distracting mannerisms
- Be confident and controlled during cross-examination periods

---

When the debate is over, we are not interested in having the audience applaud our clever word choices, or comment on the quality of our voice, or note our graceful gestures; rather, we want it to make the decision we have argued for. The arts of speech communication should never attract attention to themselves, but should be blended into the total communicative effort to win over the audience.

EXERCISES

1. Breathing from the diaphram. Good breathing for all public speaking requires the speaker to stand up straight and breathe from the diaphragm: belly breathing. When speakers are nervous or in a hurry, they usually take quick breaths off the top of their lungs. To work to fix this, hold a chair chest high in front of you, arms straight out (no resting the chair on anything, against one's chest, etc.). Put a brief on the seat of the chair and read it: Breathe from your diaphragm as you read out loud. Now put down the chair and reread the brief. Continue alternating until you start to notice the physical difference in your breathing process.

2. Hold a pen or pencil in your teeth and read a brief out loud.

3. Read a brief aloud, adding the "a" sound between each word.

4. Read a long section of quoted material aloud, backwards.

5. As fast as you can, but with emphasis, read any book by Dr. Seuss. Suggestions for this exercise are *Oh Say Can You Say, The Butter Battle Book, Oh The Thinks You Can Think, There's A Wocket in my Pocket,* and *Fox in Socks,* but any book by Dr. Seuss is excellent.

6. Read a debate brief, but with exaggerated emotion and feeling.

17

Evaluating the Debate

We often ask, "What was the vote?" "What was the verdict?" "Who won?" Members of Congress put their voting cards into electronic slots, the electronic scoreboards on the gallery walls light up, and we learn the fate of legislation. The judge in the courtroom asks the jury to state the verdict, and we learn the outcome of the trial. In academic debate the judge announces the decision or writes it on a ballot available to the debaters at a later time. Everything we have considered thus far builds to this climactic moment—the decision.

How do we evaluate the debate? What is the basis for the decision? The decision should be based either on the proposition of debate or on the debate itself. In applied debate the decision should be rendered on the proposition itself; in academic debate the decision should be based on the debate itself—that is, on the comparative merits of the arguments and evidence presented by the opposing teams, not on the merits of the proposition. Here we consider the role of the judge in academic debates.

I. FUNCTIONS OF THE JUDGE

Judges in academic debates have three functions: to be (1) decision makers, (2) critics, and (3) educators. As decision makers they have to discern which team did the better debating, and therefore which team won the debate; as critics they have to report their decisions and the rationale for them in an educationally useful manner; and as educators they must consider the pedagogical implications of their work as debate judge.

Judge interaction with the debaters during the debate is relatively limited. Judges will usually keep time for the debaters, calling out by minute the time remaining in each speech and during preparation. Judges may occasionally call out "Clearer" if the debater is being unclear, or even more infrequently, "Explain" or "What was that?" if they wish to give the speaker an opportunity to clarify something. Parliamentary debate engages a higher level of judge–debater interaction during the debate. Some judges make it a point to give nonverbal feedback

---

Miniglossary

Activist judge   Judges in this approach see themselves as active participants in the debate process, and view the debate not as a game, but as an act.

Evaluator of argument   This judge recognizes the inevitability of intervention, but strives to determine the quality of logic, clash, and evidence presented by debaters in order to choose the superior case or argumentative advocacy.

Hypothesis-testing judge   A judge who focuses on testing the affirmative case and requires that the affirmative overcome any negative attack to win the decision.

Issues judge   A judge who focuses on the stock issues and requires the affirmative to win all the stock issues to win the decision.

Policymaker judge   A judge who contrasts the affirmative's and negative's policy systems and requires that the affirmative's policy system be viable and better than the negative's policy system in order to win the decision. This judge tends to evaluate competing policies on a basis of cost versus benefit.

Skills judge   A judge who focuses on the skills listed on the AFA ballot—analysis, reasoning, evidence, organization, refutation, and delivery—and awards the decision to the team that has done the best debating with regard to these skills.

Tabula rasa judge   A judge who takes no position and allows and expects the debaters to decide the theoretical framework for the decision. If no judging philosophy emerges in the debate, the judge may choose whatever judging philosophy seems most appropriate as a basis for the decision.

---

about the arguments as they are presented; others work just as hard not to provide visual reactions that could influence the debate or negatively affect the debaters.

A. Discerning Which Team Did the Better Debating

Judges of academic debates must answer the question "Which team did the better debating?" or "Which team won the debate?"[1] To answer these questions, they are guided by certain principles.

1. Judges Must Apply Their Total Knowledge of Argumentation and Debate as Well as Their Knowledge about the Proposition.   In debates an almost infinite range of possibilities may become factors in the decision-making

---

1. There are two penalty situations for which a team might be given an automatic loss.
One, considered later in this section, involves the use of evidence of doubtful credibility.
The second is a forfeit (usually for being late for the scheduled starting time of a debate)
as stipulated in the rules of a tournament.

process. Therefore judges must be able to bring to bear a comprehensive knowledge of the principles of argumentation and debate in order to evaluate the arguments advanced. Judges should do their best to make substantive decisions based upon the content and quality of the evidence and reasoning as presented during the actual debate. The First National Developmental Conference on Forensics stated:

> As decision maker the judge is called upon to make choices among alternatives emerging out of the proposition. The judge should value content above delivery and substance above technique. The stronger position on the issue should prevail, and the more credible evidence should prevail over a greater quantity of evidence having less probative force.[2]

2. Judges May Set Aside Biases Derived from Their Special Knowledge of the Subject for the Duration of the Debate.   The best prepared judges for academic debate have read about the proposition and heard many debates. They are familiar with the literature and in a position to fairly evaluate the quality of the debaters' analysis and use of expert information. This additional knowledge may generate certain attitudes, stereotypes, anticipations, or even distortions in their thinking on the proposition. Their responsibility as judges is to apply this knowledge and be informed by it, while setting aside for the duration of the debate their personal biases. In rendering the decision, most judges will work to consider only the evidence and reasoning actually introduced into the debate. For example, one team may introduce some evidence found in an article by source A. The judge may know that source A's position is superficial and that it could easily be refuted by evidence found in a scholarly book written by source B. However, the judge should not enter into the debate except to evaluate the relative merits of competing claims as supported by the evidence presented. Unless and until the opposing team refutes the weak evidence drawn from source A's article, that evidence should be accepted at its face value within the context of the debate. Subject-matter experts ordinarily do not make good judges for academic debates. Because of their expertise, they have usually formed judgments on the proposition after long and careful study, and find it difficult to set aside these judgments for the duration of the debate.

Judges should draw on their special knowledge of the subject in critiques to suggest ways the debaters can improve their arguments. Here judges assess the debaters' subject-matter knowledge and reflect their findings in the quality-rating points on the ballot. When judges discover a deliberate misuse of evidence, they may impose an appropriate penalty. The NDT has adopted a rule stipulating the following: "If a judge determines that distortion and/or falsification [of evidence] has occurred, the judge shall award the offending team a loss and award zero speaker points to the offending speaker(s)." The judge's

---

2. James H. McBath, ed., *Forensics as Communication* (Skokie, Ill.: National Textbook, 1975), p. 30.

knowledge of the subject may also produce preferences for certain types of cases. These too must be set aside for the duration of the debate. The First National Developmental Conference on Forensics stated:

> In the area of case forms, students may evolve new paradigms that are consistent with the issues under consideration. The appropriateness of such paradigms should be determined primarily by the process of argumentation. In choosing between different interpretations of a proposition, the judge should encourage methods of analysis and reasoning about meaning. Only in those instances where the students themselves have failed to agree upon the basis for a reasonable interpretation of the proposition should the judge exercise his or her individual and carefully considered judgment.[3]

3. Judges Must Base Their Decisions on the Debate as It Is Presented.

Because they are experts on argumentation and debate, judges could easily refute some of the arguments advanced in the debate. They might know that one team could have taken a much stronger position than it actually did. However, they should never require the students to debate them rather than the opposing team. They must never ask, "Could *I* refute a particular argument?" but rather, "Did the opposing team refute that argument?" They do not ask whether a team's position was weak or strong in relation to the ideal position, but whether the team's position was weaker or stronger than that of their opponents. For example, in debating the proposition "Resolved: That executive control of U.S. foreign policy should be significantly curtailed," an affirmative team took the position that the United States should adopt an isolationist foreign policy. In the opinion of one educator who was asked to judge this debate, such a foreign policy would be disastrous for the United States. His opinion, however, was irrelevant to his function as a judge. The issue was not whether isolation would be good or bad for the United States but whether the affirmative team, within the context of the debate, supported its case for curtailing executive control of U.S. foreign policy.

In fact, because a debate has to be judged within its own framework, almost any statement made or position taken by either team stands until refuted. The sole exception is the last affirmative speech, when the judge may take judicial notice of the validity of the evidence or of the introduction of a new concept. If a team fails to ask the judge to take judicial notice of an obvious error or contradiction in the opponent's case, the judge must assume that the team failed to detect the error; therefore it must stand against them.

Judges, of course, take note of the strengths and weaknesses in a debate case and refer to them in their critiques and reflect their findings in the quality-rating points on the ballot.

---

3. McBath, *Forensics as Communication,* p. 30.

4. Judges Take Comprehensive Notes during the Debate. Experienced judges are known for the care with which they take notes during a debate. (Note, some judges have abandoned the flow sheet and either do not take notes, or take limited notes in a nonlinear fashion. These judges choose to approach the debate experience in a nonlinear fashion in order to be more inclusive of those who may not have the skill, experience, training, or "privilege" to flow a debate.) The above caveat notwithstanding, all judges should develop a comprehensive note-taking system so that they can record all of the significant developments during the debate in order to evaluate the debate effectively.

Experienced educators judging academic debates find the flow sheet to be the most convenient method of taking comprehensive notes. Judges using the flow sheet method seek to record the development of each issue throughout the debate. This method is similar to the debater's flow sheet considered in Chapter 14 but with one difference: The debater may make notes on a flow sheet to aid in planning future speeches; the judge, of course, will record only the arguments actually presented by the debaters.

Although the methods suggested in Chapter 14 are designed specifically for use in judging the academic debate, they may be adapted for use in rendering a decision on an applied debate. Many trial judges and attorneys use a comparable method to follow courtroom debates, and many business executives use a comparable "balance sheet" to help them weigh arguments in debates on corporate policy. Whenever it is necessary to render a decision on an important debate, some system should be developed to facilitate the process of analyzing and weighing the arguments.

Because the flow sheet is never a verbatim record of the debate, many tournament debate judges will examine evidence, or even the text of arguments, plans, and counterplans, before making their decision. These judges must keep in mind that, although reading material after the debate may clarify their understanding of what was said during the debate, it is not a substitute for paying careful attention and keeping an effective flow sheet during the debate. In addition, most tournament situations demand that the judge make a decision in a timely manner to facilitate the tournament schedule.

B. Reporting the Decision in an Educationally Useful Manner

The decision, as part of the educational process of debate, should be reported in a way that will contribute to the students' educations. This reporting may be done either by means of an oral critique, a carefully prepared ballot, or, ideally, a combination of these two methods.

1. The Oral Critique. If an oral critique is used, the judge has a few minutes to review his or her notes before presenting the critique. The effective critique should do the following:

1. Review the progress of the debate.
2. Cite examples of effective application of the principles of argumentation and debate.

3. Offer suggestions for improvement.

4. Cite the factors most significant in determining the decision.

5. Announce the decision (this is optional and in some tournaments may even be prohibited by tournament or league rules; some judges prefer to offer suggestions and feedback to the debaters but to report the decision only on the ballot).

6. Offer an opportunity for questions and interaction with the debaters.

When the oral critique is used, adequate time should be allocated for its presentation.

2. The Ballot.   Whereas oral critiques and decision disclosures are the norm in tournament debating, a written ballot is generally required to facilitate tabulation. Even when decisions are orally discussed, it is desirable to have a written record of the decision. When a ballot is used, an oral critique may be presented as well. The judge will generally be asked to prepare a written critique on the ballots that will be handed to the participating teams. Samples of judges' written critiques follow the national championship debate transcript in Appendix B. An effectively designed ballot should facilitate the following:

1. Record the decision of the debate.

2. Record the name, team affiliation (if relevant), side, speaker position, rank and points for each debater.

3. Record the name (and affiliation if relevant) of the judge, and provide a signature line.

4. Provide a place for a written critique and reason for decision.

5. Provide a record of the debate for each team.

6. Provide a record of the debate for the tournament director.

Four ballots meeting these requirements are shown in insets. The AFA Form A ballot (shown on page 320), one of several ballots published by the American Forensic Association, was originally designed for use in CEDA or cross-examination debates; Form W (shown on page 321) was designed for use in NDT debates. Of course, the two are now interchangeable. The Form H ballot (shown on page 322) is meant for Lincoln–Douglas debates. All three ballot types come in convenient no-carbon form. The top sheet, recording the decision and points, can be sent to the tournament control room as soon as the judge reaches a decision. The judge may then complete the written critique at his or her leisure and send the completed ballot to the control room in timely fashion. Completed copies of the ballot containing the critique may then be distributed to the debaters. AFA Ballots (including parliamentary debate ballots) may be ordered directly from the American Forensic Association at AmForensicAssoc@uwrf.edu. Although the AFA form ballots are useful, they are not necessary. Most tournaments now utilize computer programs that print out simple ballots for use by judges. Of course, to provide the debaters copies of these ballots requires photocopying. A simple ballot

FORM A

CROSS EXAMINATION
DEBATE ASSOCIATION

DIVISION [   ] ROUND [   ] ROOM [   ] JUDGE [   ]

AFF. [   ] NEG. [   ]

INSTRUCTIONS: Fill out ALL shaded areas of the ballot (even if ballot label is attatched). RATE all speakers on a scale from **30** (superior) to **1** (poor). RANK each speaker in order of excellence (1-4; ties are not permitted). If you are awarding the decision to the team with fewer speaker points, check the appropriate box. The boxes should be checked according to the following scale (the boxes do NOT have numerical significance):

P - poor/needs improvement   F - fair   A - average   E - excellent   S - superior

1st Affirmative	2nd Affirmative		1st Negative	2nd Negative
P F A E S	P F A E S	Analysis/Definition	P F A E S	P F A E S
		Evidence		
		Refutation/Rebuttal		
		Cross-Examination		
		Organization		
		Delivery		
		Language/Style		

NAMES

Pts. (30 max) [   ] Rank [   ]   Pts. (30 max) [   ] Rank [   ]   Pts. (30 max) [   ] Rank [   ]   Pts. (30 max) [   ] Rank [   ]

I am persuaded to vote for team [   ] REPRESENTING: [   ] CODE: [   ]
(aff. or neg.)

Low point win? [   ]   AFFILIATION [   ]
JUDGES SIGNATURE

REASON FOR DECISION/COMMENTS:

that meets the necessary requirements can easily be fashioned, as exemplified by the ballot on page 323.

A ballot for shift-of-opinion debating, which may be prepared locally and distributed to the audience, is shown on page 324.

II. JUDGING PHILOSOPHIES

All qualified judges for academic debate agree that the decision must be based on the answer to the question "Which team did the better debating?" However, judges may use different philosophical approaches—or different decision-making paradigms—in answering this question.[4] Identifying judging paradigms is now somewhat historical, as tournament debate judges have evolved beyond the labels which identified their approach in the 1970s and 1980s. At that time, judges tended to fall into the following characterizations.

---

4. John D. Cross and Ronald J. Matlon, "An Analysis of Judging Philosophies in Academic Debate," *Journal of the American Forensics Association*, vol. 15, no. 2 (fall 1978), pp. 110–123.

A. Skills Judge

The **skills judge** focused on the skills listed on the AFA Form W ballot—analysis, reasoning, evidence, organization, refutation, and delivery—and carefully evaluates which team has performed better with regard to each of these skills. The judge in this case does not merely assign points and add up the score to "find out who won." The ballot is an instrument the judge uses to report decisions. Skills judges base their decisions on their total knowledge of argumentation and debate, and they recognize that, although the skills are given equal weight in the ballot in an actual debate, one or two skills might outweigh all the others and constitute the reason for the decision. For example, one team's use of evidence or its analytic skill in developing a particular critical issue might be decisive. Ultimately, the skills judge worked to evaluate the public-speaking qualities of the debate and identify the team that did a better job of blending form and content, style, and material.

B. Issues Judge

The **issues judge** focuses on the stock issues. To win the decision from such a judge, the affirmative has to win all the stock issues, whereas the negative needs to win only one stock issue. The affirmative is not required to win every argument and every contention in the debate, but it must win each stock issue. Note that issues are won or lost in comparison to the arguments of the opposing team. A negative team might establish that the affirmative's plan will cause substantial

---

American Forensic Association Debate Ballot   FORM **W**

Division _____ Round _____ Room _____ Judge _____

Affirmative _____ Negative _____

Check the column on each item which, on the following scale, best describes your evaluation of the debater's effectiveness:

1-poor	2-fair	3-average	4-excellent	5-superior

1st Affirmative	2nd Affirmative		1st Negative	2nd Negative

(Name) _____   (Name) _____   (Name) _____   (Name) _____

1 2 3 4 5	1 2 3 4 5		1 2 3 4 5	1 2 3 4 5
		Analysis		
		Reasoning		
		Evidence		
		Organization		
		Refutation		
		Delivery		

Total_____ Rank _____   Total _____ Rank _____   Total _____ Rank _____   Total _____ Rank _____

Rank each debater in order of excellence (1st for best, 2nd for next best, etc.)

In my opinion, this debate was won by_____ representing _____
                                      (Aff. or Neg.)   (School and/or #)

_____   _____
         (Judge's Name)   (School)

AMERICAN FORENSIC ASSOCIATION

FORM **H**

LINCOLN-DOUGLAS DEBATE BALLOT

Round _____ Room_____ Date _____ Judge_____

	Name-Code	Points		Name-Code	Points

Aff. _____ _____ Neg. _____ _____

Scale:	12-15	16-19	20-23	24-27	28-30
	Below Average	Average	Excellent	Outstanding	Exceptional

COMMENT/RECOMMENDATION (REGARDING ANALYSIS, SUPPORT, REFUTATION, DELIVERY):

AFF.   NEG.

REASONS FOR DECISION (MIGHT INCLUDE ISSUES, REASONABLENESS OF POSITION, PERSUASION):

IN MY OPINION, THE BETTER DEBATING WAS DONE BY _____ REPRESENTING _____

CODE   AFF./NEG.

_____   _____

SIGNATURE OF JUDGE   AFFILIATION

```
┌─────────────────────────────────────────────────────────────────────┐
│                        DEBATE BALLOT                                  │
│                                                                       │
│   Judges Name _____ │
│                                                                       │
│   Affirmative                        Negative                         │
│   _____                _____              │
│                                                                       │
│   ┌────┬──────────┬───────┬───────┐  ┌────┬──────────┬───────┬───────┐│
│   │Pos │ Speakers │Points │ Ranks │  │Pos │ Speakers │Points │ Ranks ││
│   │    │ Names    │       │       │  │    │ Names    │       │       ││
│   ├────┼──────────┼───────┼───────┤  ├────┼──────────┼───────┼───────┤│
│   │    │          │       │       │  │    │          │       │       ││
│   ├────┼──────────┼───────┼───────┤  ├────┼──────────┼───────┼───────┤│
│   │    │          │       │       │  │    │          │       │       ││
│   └────┴──────────┴───────┴───────┘  └────┴──────────┴───────┴───────┘│
│                                                                       │
│   In my opinion, the debate was won by the _____ side          │
│                                              (AFF or NEG)              │
│   ☐ Low point win intended                                            │
│                                                                       │
│   Judge's Signature: _____ │
│   ...................................................................│
│                                                                       │
│   Comments and Reasons for Decision:                                  │
│                                                                       │
└─────────────────────────────────────────────────────────────────────┘
```

disadvantages. To win this issue, however, the negative must demonstrate that the disadvantage has greater impact than the significance of the need itself. In debating the proposition "Resolved: That the federal government should significantly strengthen the guarantee of consumer product safety required of manufacturers," an affirmative argued that the lack of mandatory air bags in automobiles caused 14,000 deaths per year (thus establishing the significance of the need it claimed that the plan would solve), while the negative argued as a disadvantage that the accidental deployment of air bags would cause 500 deaths a year. The affirmative clearly won by saving 13,500 more lives than the negative; the advantage outweighs the disadvantage. In fact, anyone subscribing to the issues approach recognized that argumentation over each of the issues was rarely definitive, and so although it seemed absolutist, competing claims and evidence were considered in weighing consideration of each issue, and the proposition as a whole. The central tenet of the issues judge was the identification of the issues as a sort of checklist to be identified as necessary elements in their decision.

C. Policymaker Judge

Like a legislator evaluating competing pieces of legislation, the **policymaker judge** evaluates the affirmative's policy system (that is, its plan) as it represents a departure from the status quo, contrasts it with the negative's policy system (for example, a defense of the status quo, a repair, a counterplan, an attack on the affirmative's plan as unworkable, or any of the other options open to the negative), and then decides whether the affirmative has offered a viable plan. If the affirmative's plan is viable, the judge will also require that it be better than the

---

Shift-of-Opinion Ballot

UNIVERSITY DEBATING TEAMS
Audience Shift-of-Opinion Ballot

INSTRUCTIONS TO THE AUDIENCE:

The debaters will appreciate your interest and cooperation if you will, *both before and after the debate,* indicate on this ballot your *personal opinion* on the proposition of debate.

The proposition is: ''Resolved: That (the proposition of debate is stated here).''

BEFORE THE DEBATE
FILL OUT THIS SIDE
(Check one)

     I believe in the affirmative of the resolution.

     I am undecided.

     I believe in the negative of the resolution.

AFTER THE DEBATE
FILL OUT THIS SIDE
(Check one)

     I believe more strongly in the affirmative than I did.

     I believe in the affirmative of the resolution.

     I am undecided.

     I believe in the negative of the resolution.

     I believe more strongly in the negative than I did.

---

negative's policy system. The policymaker judge would agree with the issues judge cited previously: Saving 13,500 more lives is clearly the better policy (unless, of course, the negative introduced a new issue and argued that the 500 lives lost in the accidental deployment of air bags was an involuntary loss of life, whereas the 14,000 lives lost because of the lack of air bags represented a voluntary assumed risk, and that consumers should be free to choose whether they want air bags in their cars). If this argument were introduced, the judge then would have to weigh it in the policy decision. In order to compare policy systems, the policymaker judge would probably have to consider the stock issues, especially solvency, in making the relevant comparisons. The focus of this paradigm is the direct comparison of competing policies.

D. Hypothesis-Testing Judge

The **hypothesis–testing judge** takes the perspective of a scientist seeking to determine the probable truth of a hypothesis. Unlike the policymaker judge the hypothesis-testing judge does not seek to compare two policy systems. He or she is testing the hypothesis—that is, the affirmative case—alone. Thus the negative is free to defend anything or everything that is nontopical. If the negative demonstrates that no need exists for the proposition, the hypothesis-testing judge will conclude that the hypothesis is not true and should not be affirmed. The hypothesis-testing judge tends to be receptive to conditional or hypothetical counterplans. The main point of this paradigm is a primary focus on the statement that is the proposition. Debate occurred as a means of testing the probable truth of the proposition as embodied in the affirmative team's example.

E. Tabula Rasa Judge

The **tabula rasa** (or clean-slate) **judge** avoids the imposition of his or her own debate philosophy and allows and expects the debaters to decide the theoretical framework for the decision as the debate evolves. If the affirmative is using a stock issue case and argues successfully that the debate should be decided on stock issues, this judge will vote for the affirmative if it carries the stock issues. If the negative offers a conditional counterplan and argues successfully that the judge should function as a hypothesis tester, the judge will vote for the negative if it carries the conditional counterplan. If neither team chooses to argue the judging philosophy, the judge may decide that a certain type of judging philosophy is implicit in the way the debate evolves and choose that philosophy as the basis for decision. All judges work to be tabula rasa to some degree, striving to make their decisions based on the arguments offered by the debaters in the debate round, and not based on their predispositions about the topic and the materials presented.

F. The Evaluator of Argument

Somewhat like the tabula rasa judge; however, the **evaluator of argument** recognizes that he or she has an expertise and special knowledge in evaluating argumentation and that given the nature of debate, some degree of interpretation or "intervention" by the judge may be necessary. The evaluator of argument will apply standards of good argumentation to compare the relative quality of argumentation by each team in order to determine a winner. This judge tries to avoid imposing a framework for judging the debate but recognizes that it is his or her role as an expert on argumentation to evaluate the relative quality of competing arguments. For example, the evaluator of argument would compare the competing claims of debaters based on such criteria as quality of sources, logical support for claims, and sufficiency of data and warrant in support of claims. If no judging philosophy emerges as clearly implicit in the debate, this judge may decide to select any one of the philosophies to use as the basis for decision. The evaluator of argument is most comfortable recognizing their superior knowledge of debate and of the topic, and feel obliged to consider the quality of in round arguments based on both the arguments launched by the opponents in the debate and by their own evaluation of the quality of argumentation based on factors external to the debate.

G. Current Practice

As indicated earlier, the division of judges into paradigms is now archaic, as most judges have developed their own more individualized approaches combining some of the theoretical precedents. Although each debate judge has a unique approach, in general, they currently fall into one of two main camps.

The more traditional group of debate judges works to compare competing advocacy (whether policy or critical philosophical positions) based on the arguments, evidence, and clash as presented in the debate; works to remove itself from personal bias and involvement; and favors decisions based on the content of the argumentation over the delivery of the message. This group works to keep a complete and accurate flow sheet to record the debate and after the debate may examine evidence for precise wording. There is a preference among most of these judges for arguments about the concrete nature of the policies being debated, and an acceptance that the arguments are offered as hypothetical. They are comfortable with the notion of switch-sides debating, which debaters learn from the process of defending and opposing all sides of any issue. The judge is an observer of the educational game that is an academic debate, whose job is to promote the educational experience by fairly deciding the debate based on the content of argumentation.

A newer trend in debate judging could be characterized as more **activist** and interactive in nature. Judges in this approach see themselves as active participants in the debate process, and view the debate not as a game, but as an act. The performances of the debaters are extensions of themselves and their advocacy, which has importance in the lives of the participants in and out of the debate context. To some extent, this paradigm considers the unique skills expressed by the debaters, as well as their ability to engage their audience and exemplify ethical and right behavior. These judges are less likely to evaluate a text of the debate, but are more holistic in their evaluations. They are also more interested in form: The activist approach has incorporated music, rap, video, personal narrative, and dramatic performance. Activist judges are likely to consider themselves social critics, extending their critique of social structures and hierarchy to the activity of debate, which by its technical nature serves to exclude participation. A consistent measure for the activist approach to debate and debate judging is inclusion of repressed and underrepresented groups in the debate activity.

H. Significance to the Debater

We have considered six different historical judging philosophies and two general descriptions of contemporary judging practice, but these are hardly the limit. In fact, there may be as many ways to judge a debate as there are judges. Because the debaters usually will not know the philosophy of the judge, the question arises: How can debaters adapt to the situation? There are two considerations. First, the debater should know argumentation theory and be prepared to argue that the judge should serve, for example, as an issues judge for "this" debate if the debater intends to argue the case on issues. Second, although judges have their preferences for specific judging philosophies, most judges are willing to consider arguments about judging philosophies from the debaters and apply the model most appropriate to a specific debate. John Cross and Ronald Matlon have found that "the majority of judges in the academic debate community view debates with extraordinary consensus regardless of their stated judging philosophies."[5] Although this observation was made some time ago, it is still a fairly accurate statement.

It is the judges' responsibility to communicate their predispositions, preferences, and paradigms to debaters before the debate. Many tournaments, including the CEDA National Tournament and the NDT, require that each judge's philosophy statement be available. Most intercollegiate debate judges post their philosophies publicly at Debate Results (http://commweb.fullerton.edu/ jbruschke/web/home.aspxand/) or Planet Debate (http://www.planetdebate .com/). One judge at the 1999 CEDA National Tournament wrote his philosophy as a rap (a portion is presented here):

> I decided to rhyme this/so check this verse/It's as accurate/as one page can get/If I'm judging you/this is what I'll do/... and if you don't like/ consider me a strike ...
>
> In the round/I get down/and I flow every card/I listen hard/to your tags/extensions and cross-apps/If you'd like to win/then you better begin/with good analysis/and then evidence.
>
> Qualified warrants/for the claims you make/is where/most debaters make/the fatal mistake/Don't mistake my understanding/of the issues you bring/you better hustle/in rebuttals/so your arguments/mean something/I mean/tell me about the way it comes together/or your speaker points/will look like/Rochester weather.[6]

Another, more traditional example of a judging philosophy statement is provided in the inset on pages 328–329.

In addition, judges may voluntarily offer the debaters guidance by telling them their philosophy prior to the debate. Debaters are always free to ask judges to discuss their preferences. Debaters may also find it helpful to talk to people who know the judges about their judging habits.

We have considered the major decision-making paradigms used in academic debate. You should be aware that in other forums the decision renderers often will have formulated decision-making paradigms they deem appropriate to the subject or occasion. Although these paradigms may not be as clearly stated or as precisely articulated as the paradigms for academic debate, they are important and advocates must discover them. (See the Chapter 15 section "Analysis of the Audience.") When necessary, the advocate should be prepared to debate the paradigm for decision making, as well as the issues and evidence relating to the resolution.

---

5. Cross and Matlon, "An Analysis of Judging Philosophies," p. 123.
6. Myron King, "Judging Philosophy Rap Sheet," in CEDA National Judging Philosophy Booklet, Southern Illinois University, 1999. Reprinted with permission.

Veronica Barreto Judge Philosophy 2004

Number of YEARS Judging:
High School: 0
College: 2
Number of TOURNAMENTS Judged (This Year's Topic):
High School: 0
College: 2
Number of ROUNDS Judged (This Year's Topic):
High School: 0
College: 16
PHILOSOPHY
Veronica Barreto Tournaments this year: 9
California State University, Bakersfield Rounds: 70+
Years Coaching: 1

The role of the critic: "My job is just to regulate funkiness"—James Gandolfini

I don't determine what is true or what I believe to be true, only what is argued better in this particular instance. Some general comments that apply across the board: If you make a well-warranted argument of value on your own, you'll never hear me say "awww ... if you only had a card that said that" you, Spanos ... same difference. The right analits on a disad can do the job. A corollary to that is that I don't call for very much evidence ... at all ... don't count on it. You can save the laundry lists of authors. I'm more interested in how a debater uses evidence, than what evidence a debater reads. All the same, if there is a dispute over what a card says, I'll call for it to settle that. I'm not wed to any particular type of argumentation as long as it happens to make an argument. There will be more on that under performance.

Fiat is simply the ability to imagine a world where the plan/counterplan is enacted. Take from that what you will.

Topicality: I love to see topicality used strategically, perhaps to arrest link concessions on other portions of the debate. I tend to think that that is the best way to use T and I'm impressed when it's done effectively. Of course, topicality functions on its own. I come from the school of thought that T is a ground issue. That doesn't mean I haven't voted on other justifications for the argument, just that I'm disappointed when one team lets the other get away with it. Standards aren't there for decoration; they're critical in evaluating the debate, so use them.

Disads: You got 'em, bring 'em. I prefer deep, developed, intricate debates over a shallow spread. After a certain number, there's bound to be a double turn somewhere, but that's up to you to find.

Counterplans: I think they're quite effective in neutralizing some of the advantages dealt to the affirmative. I lend them a very willing ear. I tend to err in favor of PIC's and dispositionality, but don't take my predispositions as an invitation to take theory debates for granted. I will assume a perm is a test of competition unless otherwise instructed and that usually requires some justification.

Kritiks: I read the goo as a debater and I read even more of the goo as a grad student. I happen to be fluent in fru fru joo joo bee, that doesn't mean that you can string a bunch of catch phrases, do a boogey boogey, then sit back in the corner, cross your fingers and have me make an argument out of it. Seriously, I have an understanding of critical argumentation but often find myself most interested in questions of praxis in debates. The link seems fairly easy to establish, e.g., "you use the state," but the more complicated question has to deal with the implications of that.

Veronica Barreto Judge Philosophy 2004 (Continued)

It's funny how the most important part of the debate gets under covered because debaters get bogged down on the top level.

If the K is your deal, go ahead and "Do The [Goo]" just be aware. If you want to make your life infinitely simpler in front of me when engaging in critical argumentation, run a counterplan. You're totally welcome to forgo that option, but then you have to be prepared to discuss how the argument generates unique (yep, I said it ... UNIQUE) offense. Using the kritik as a solvency turn works. Please do not say the words "pre fiat" or "post fiat" in my presence ... gives me the hee bee jee bees and makes me make me cringe. Those words mean nothing to me. I can explain further upon request.

Performance: Most of the time I find myself at a loss. I don't see how performativity is any different from the debate I practiced when running my F-16's affirmative. If you've ever seen my blocks, you know they're a work of art. You're welcome to explore a plethora of formats, but choosing an innovative format alone does not warrant a ballot, only the arguments made using that format can do that. If you think that performativity gives you superpowers, the ability to leap tall buildings in a single bound, or create an ultrasonic force field that shields you from having to defend the implications of your advocacy, then it's unlikely that I'd be a good critic for you. If you've already got me ... well, there's always the 2–1. On the other hand, if you've got a cogent argument that happens to be articulated using an alternate format, I'm down.

III. FUNCTIONS OF THE BALLOT

A. Reporting the Decision

The ballot is, first and foremost, an instrument for reporting the judge's decision. The debaters and the tournament director in a tournament situation want to know who won. The ballot furnishes this information.

B. Reporting the Quality of the Debaters' Work

For educational purposes debaters should know not only the judges' decisions on debates but also the judges' evaluations of the quality of their debating. Reference to the quality points indicates how the judge evaluated debaters' work both in terms of its own merit and in comparison to that of the other participants in the debate. The quality points and rank may also be critical information to the tournament director as a means of determining speaker awards and as a device for breaking ties in a tournament. Generally, ballots offer a range of 0–30 speaker points to be awarded to each debater. Typically, only the top end of the range is used (roughly 25–30). This will vary by region and convention. In many tournaments, judges may award half points (for example, 27.5).

C. Serving as an Educational Tool

At the conclusion of the debate or tournament, the ballots are distributed to the participants. The ballots thus become available to the director of forensics as an important educational tool. After a tournament debate directors often arrange conferences in which they review the judges' evaluations with each student. The quality of a student's work will vary from one debate to another, and different judges may place a different emphasis on different aspects of argumentation. But student performance in a number of debates as recorded by a number of judges provides important insights into the student's ability, and further study and training can be planned accordingly. The critiques written by the judges for the 1995 CEDA Nationals final round are available in Appendix B, following the transcript of the debates.

Although forensic directors ordinarily do not judge intercollegiate debates involving teams from their own schools, they will judge many debates between their own students as they prepare for intercollegiate debates. The evaluations given at this time are often the most valuable part of the students' education. Usually time is available for a much more detailed critique than is possible in other circumstances. Because the directors have seen the students debate many times, often over a period of several years, they have considerable knowledge about their students' abilities and limitations and more insight into each student's problems than does a judge who sees the student only once.

IV. SPECIAL BALLOTS FOR SPECIAL PURPOSES

The traditional team policy debate ballot is pretty basic. It identifies the two teams by school name, each of the four debaters by speaker position, calls for a ranking (1–4) for each debater, a rating (on a scale to 30), and designation of a winner. It may be used for most types of debate (see Chapter 18). The exceptions are the town hall format, which uses a division of the house, and parliamentary debate, which may use any of the various methods of voting. In addition, audience-decision debating and Lincoln–Douglas debating require special ballots.

A. Ballots for Lincoln–Douglas Debating

Lincoln–Douglas debating requires a special ballot, because only two debaters participate in the debate. The AFA Form H ballot, shown on page 322, is designed for these debates.

B. Ballots for Shift-of-Opinion Debating

Because lay audiences are obviously not qualified to evaluate the debate as an educational process, their decision has value only when the merits of the proposition are being considered or when certain data are being collected for research purposes. An audience-decision ballot is sometimes used as a device to increase audience interest. In these cases a shift-of-opinion ballot may be used. The ballot shown on page 324, a modification of the Woodward ballot,[7] provides a means of compensating for the lack of understanding of the principles of argumentation and debate found among most audiences. Members of the audience are simply asked to state their beliefs about the proposition before and after hearing the debate, and the decision is based on the shift of audience opinion. At the conclusion of the debate, the ballots are collected and then tabulated as those recording a shift to the affirmative, those reporting no change, and those reporting a shift to the negative. The team that has produced the greater shift of opinion is determined by inspecting the tabulation. The results obtained by this method may be regarded as interesting but not necessarily significant. Carefully controlled tests of statistical reliability are necessary to guard against chance variables. These controls, or the use of other experimental methods, require more elaborate statistical procedures than are practical for the average academic debate.

In presenting debates before popular audiences, students gain valuable experience in addressing large groups and have an opportunity to analyze and adapt to popular audiences. Audience-judges challenge students to win a popular response, whereas educator-judges challenge students to win a critical response. It is educationally necessary that students have their work evaluated by persons who know more about argumentation and debate than they do—the educators—rather than by people who know less about argumentation and debate than they do—the popular audience. It is inherent in our tradition of liberal education that students should seek the highest rather than the lowest common denominator.

EXERCISES

1. Write your philosophy of judging.
2. View a debate (in class, online, at a tournament), and write a ballot for the debate.
3. Assign class members different philosophies of judging (skills, issues, policy, tabula rasa, hypothesis testing, activist). View a debate together, and staying true to your assigned philosophy, write a ballot explaining your decision, role playing the approach.
4. Read judging philosophies at Planet Debate or Debate Results.
5. Read the judges' ballots in Appendix B.

---

7. See Howard S. Woodward, "Measurement and Analysis of Audience Opinion," *Quarterly Journal of Speech,* vol. 14 (Feb. 1928), pp. 94–111.

18

Academic Debate Formats and Cross-Examination

Although debating is as old as civilization, the procedures of debating have evolved and changed considerably over the centuries. Academic debating today, while retaining the essential values of debating in ancient times, is an interesting example of the rapid pace of adaptation to contemporary interests. To gain the full benefit of academic debate, you should be aware of its various formats.

I. FORMATS OF DEBATE

The various formats of academic debate tend to have certain common elements: (1) Both sides must have an equal number of speakers; (2) both sides must have an equal amount of time; and (3) the affirmative generally speaks first and last. The First National Developmental Conference on Forensics has recommended that "more frequent use of alternative events and formats in forensics should be encouraged." One thing that all formats have in common is a limit on time. Most debate formats prescribe a precise length for all speeches (a nine-minute 1AC). Debaters are well advised to have their own timers to monitor the length of their speeches.

A. Cross-Examination Format

The most widely used format in intercollegiate team topic policy debating is cross–examination. The most popular organization of this format, as utilized in NDA/CEDA practice, is as follows:

Cross-Examination Debate Format	
First affirmative constructive	*9 minutes*
Cross-examination by second negative	*3 minutes*
First negative constructive	*9 minutes*
Cross-examination by first affirmative	*3 minutes*
Second affirmative constructive	*9 minutes*
Cross-examination by first negative	*3 minutes*
Second negative constructive	*9 minutes*
Cross-examination by second affirmative	*3 minutes*
First negative rebuttal	*6 minutes*
First affirmative rebuttal	*6 minutes*
Second negative rebuttal	*6 minutes*
Second affirmative rebuttal	*6 minutes*
Preparation time	*10 minutes per team per round*

The use of preparation time during the course of the debate should be carefully planned. Generally, no preparation time should be used before the cross-examination periods, and debaters not engaged in the cross-examination question/answer roles should use that time for their own preparation. The first negative speaker may wish to use a few minutes to help prepare their 1NC, especially to consult with their partner; however, as much of the argumentation presented by that speaker will be prepared in brief form prior to the debate, and because they can use the preceding cross-examination period to prepare, the 1NC should not require much time. Similarly, the 2AC should not require very much preparation time. The negative will need to coordinate their strategy prior to the negative block, and make sure that they carefully answer all 2AC arguments, so some time may be used prior to the 2NC. No preparation time should be used before the 1NR! The first affirmative rebuttalist must be certain to answer all arguments advanced by the negative team in the negative block, so some time may be helpful. A team is in good shape if they have at least half of their preparation time available to prepare for their last rebuttal speech.

Edward Bennett Williams, once called "the country's hottest criminal lawyer," gave this tough but practical advice on the most difficult of trial techniques, cross-examination:

> It is … the art of putting a bridle on a witness who has been called to do you harm, and of controlling him so well that he helps you. You must think of him as a man with a knife in his hand who is out to stab you, and you must feel your way with him as if you were in a dark room together. You must move with him, roll with him. You must never explore or experiment during cross-examination. *You must never ask a question if you do not already know the answer.* If you do know it and the witness refuses to say what you know, you can slaughter him. Otherwise he may slaughter you. Never attack a point that is unassailable.

And if you hit a telling point, try not to let the witness know it. Keep quiet and go on. The time to dramatize it to the jury is during your closing argument.[1]

1. Questioner Considerations.   All the considerations of argumentation and debate apply to cross-examination debate. In addition, certain considerations arise from the form of this debate. Let us examine some of the considerations of cross-examination, beginning with the questioner.

1.   Clarification. Some portions of your opponent's speech may have been unclear—either by accident or design. Cross-examination affords an opportunity to clarify them. Here's an example:

> Q: Your plan calls for placing a space station in orbit. What sort of an orbit will that be?
>
> A: Geosynchronous. That way we will be able to ...
>
> Q: Thank you. That's what I wanted to know.

This brief exchange clarified the affirmative's plan. The negative now knows that the affirmative is going to use a high orbit that will be far more costly than a low orbit and will present many technical difficulties. With the now-clarified plan before them, the negative can begin to develop plan attacks specific to the type of orbit the affirmative is now committed to using in its plan. Clarification may even include questions such as "I missed your third answer on the disadvantage, what was that again?" "Who was the source of your evidence about the dangers of long-term presence in space?" or "May I please see the text of your plan?" And, clarification may also be for the benefit of the judge. Even though you know the answer, you may wish to make sure the judge is aware of it.

2.   If you know of a defect in your opponent's evidence, cross-examination gives you an excellent opportunity to expose it. Consider this example:

> Q: You justify your plan for greater freedom for law enforcement agencies by claiming that crime increased 16 percent last year?
>
> A: Yes, and not only last year; it has been a steady trend.
>
> Q: And the source of your evidence was?
>
> A: The *Boston Globe*.
>
> Q: And where did the *Globe* get its figures?
>
> A: [Consulting card] From, err, let me see. From the FBI study. Yes, from an FBI report.
>
> Q: From the 2004 FBI report. Thank you; we'll come to that later. Now ...

---

1. *Life* magazine, June 22, 1959, p. 116. Used by permission of Edward Bennett Williams and *Life*. (Emphasis added.)

The questioner has now established the source of the affirmative's evidence. In the next speech the negative will certainly emphasize the flaw in that evidence. You may recall that the FBI had warned against using these statistics to make year-to-year comparisons.

Let's consider another example:

Q: You claim industry will move to escape environmental controls?

A: Right. They certainly will.

Q: Would you please read that card? I think it was the ...

A: *State Street Report.* "When faced with unreasonably high taxes and excessive regulation, industry will give serious consideration to their option to move to a location that offers a more favorable business climate."

Q: That specifically says a combination of high taxes and unreasonable regulations, doesn't it?

A: Well, err, yes, but I think the focus is ...

Q: Does the evidence say that any industry moved because of environmental regulations alone?

A: Err, no, I don't think so. Not in this report, but environmental controls are a part of it.

Q: Does the *State Street Report* specifically mention environmental controls?

A: It cites "unreasonable regulations" and many of the ...

Q: No mention of environmental controls. Thank you. And it said industry would consider moving, didn't it?

A: Yes, and they have moved.

Q: Does your evidence say so?

A: Well, no, not this evidence. We have other evidence that my partner will read ...

Q: We'll be looking for it in her speech. But so far there is no evidence of industry moving; no evidence about environmental controls. Thank you.

This cross-examination gave the questioner an opportunity to point out important flaws in the evidence. If the respondent's partner fails to provide the promised new evidence in her speech, the questioner's colleague should be prepared to point that out.

3. Cross-examination may be used to advance your position. Here's an example:

Q: What was your answer to our #4 argument that unemployment will persist in Iraq?

A: Uh, I guess I didn't get to that, but ...

Q: Thank you.

This brief exchange allowed the debater to emphasize that the other team had dropped an argument. The "development of space" resolution provides another example:

Q: Our evidence says that industry will make billions in the new space station, doesn't it?

A: Yes, but industry is reluctant to go into space.

Q: You mean industry is reluctant to make billions in profits?

A: No. They're reluctant because they're not certain that the station will be built.

Q: Our plan mandates that the space station will be built, doesn't it?

A: Yes, but ...

Q: And industry will certainly want those billions of dollars of profit, won't they?

A: Well, once it's built ...

Q: Thank you.

4. Cross-examination may be used to establish your response to an attack made on your position. Consider this example:

Q: In your workability attack you said our plan wouldn't work because the people in the new space station would get sick.

A: Right. The evidence shows they develop low blood pressure and lose bone marrow. Both Russians and Americans. And it takes three months ...

Q: They get low blood pressure. So what?

A: Low blood pressure isn't good for you.

Q: Does the evidence say that?

A: Well, no, but everybody knows that low blood pressure ...

Q: The evidence doesn't say it's low enough to do any harm, does it?

A: It says they develop low ...

Q: The evidence doesn't say it gets low enough to stop them from working, does it?

A: Well, no, but everyone knows low blood pressure ...

Q: No significance shown in low blood pressure. Now, about the bone marrow—so what?

A: They lose 5 percent of their bone marrow, and it takes three months to get it back to normal. Both Russians and Americans.

Q: Again, no significance. The evidence doesn't say that they can't work, does it?

A: It does say that it takes them three months to ...

Q: And they're back to normal. But the evidence doesn't attach any significance to a 5 percent loss, does it?

A: I certainly think it's significant.

Q: Do the physicians who made the report say it's significant?

A: Well, what they say is … they report … they report low blood pressure and loss of bone marrow.

Q: And in neither case do they say it's significant. Thank you.

Here the debater defended his case by establishing that the workability attack had no significance.

5. You should avoid "open-ended" questions that allow the respondent freedom to roam at will. Look at this example:

Q: Do you think your plan will reduce fuel consumption?

A: Absolutely. The Petroleum Study proves our carbon tax will effectively reduce consumption. The hearings prove we have the technology. The Berkeley Report says that this combination of increased taxes and already proved technology will reduce oil imports by at least 20 percent within …

The "do you think" opening gives respondents license to say anything they want to. Of course, they think their position is favorable and will use this opportunity to advance it.

Lawyer and best-selling author Scott Turow, echoing Edward Bennett Williams' sage counsel, admonishes, "A good trial lawyer never asks why, unless he knows the answer."[2] Like the "do you think" opening, a "why" question invites respondents to give the best possible reasons for their position.

Further considerations of the questioner include the following:

6. Questioners should try to elicit brief responses (although questioners may not require a "yes" or "no" answer). They may not cut off a reasonable qualification, but they may cut off a verbose response with a statement such as "Thank you, that gives us enough information" or "That's fine, thank you. That makes your position clear."

7. Questioners should not make arguments during cross-examination. Cross-examination is a time for asking questions and getting responses. The significance of the responses should be argued in the constructive speeches or in rebuttal.

8. Questions should be brief and easily understandable. Rambling, ambiguous questions may confuse the opponent, but they may also confuse those who render the decision. Respondents would certainly ask for a clarification of such questions, and the resultant waste of time would reduce the number of questions that could be asked.

9. Questioners may set the stage for a question—for example, "You know, of course, that President Bush has announced his support for …"

---

2. Scott Turow, *Presumed Innocent* (New York: Farrar, Straus & Giroux, 1987), p. 324.

10. Questioners should never ask a question unless they already know the answer. Remember the advice of Edward Bennett Williams.

11. Questioners should not attempt to attack unassailable points. Some of the arguments in the respondents' case will probably be so well established as to be irrefutable. An unsuccessful attack on them will merely make their strength more obvious to those who render the decision. Questioners should focus on the points they can carry.

12. Questioners should always remember that the primary purpose of asking questions in cross-examination is to obtain information that they can use to their advantage in their next speech. On the flow sheet questioners can make notes of their questions and the responses they receive—the judge will be doing this as well—so that they can refer to them directly. Rather than assume that the significance of an opponent's response is self-evident, questioners can drive the point home to the audience in their next speech. Here are some examples:

> In cross-examination, Gail admitted that their space station would be in geo-synchronous orbit. Let's see what that really means in terms of cost....

> Roger admitted in cross-examination that their figures on increased crime came from the FBI. Now I'm going to tell you what the FBI itself said about using those figures for year-to-year comparisons....

> Remember when I asked Mark about the significance of his claim that people get sick in space stations? He couldn't give you any significance of low blood pressure. None. Again, on the bone marrow, Mark couldn't give you any significance there either. There's no significance shown in their workability attack....

2. Respondent Considerations. Considerations for the respondent include the following:

1. Respondents must keep in mind that each question is designed to destroy their case or to advance the case of their opponents. Consequently they must constantly be on guard. Consider the motivation or strategy behind the question and try to diffuse it.

2. Respondents must answer any reasonable question in a cooperative fashion. Your attitude as well as the content of your answer are important in the audience and judge's evaluation of your credibility. As noted earlier, however, they can refuse to give a "yes" or "no" answer and can add reasonable qualifications. Here's an example:

> Q: The report adopted the recommendations of the chemical companies, didn't it? Yes or no.

> A: There were Democrats and Republicans on the committee, and the report was adopted by a unanimous vote.

Questioner Considerations

---

1. Clarification
2. Expose defects in opponent's evidence
3. Advance your positions
4. Respond to an attack
5. Avoid "open-ended" questions
6. Elicit brief responses
7. Ask questions, do not make arguments
8. Keep questions brief
9. Set the stage for the question
10. Ask questions to which you know the answer
11. Do not attack the unassailable
12. Use information gained in c-x in the next speech

---

3. Respondents may refuse to answer ambiguous or "loaded" questions. Consider this example:

    Q: Have you stopped cheating on examinations?

    A: I quit the same day you stopped snorting cocaine.

    Q: But, but, but I never snorted cocaine.

    A: Bingo!

4. Respondents may qualify their response. The "Yes, but" qualification is weak. It is better to give the qualification first and then give a direct response, as in this example:

    Q: Do you believe that all branches of government should be responsive to the will of the people?

    A: I believe that the Supreme Court is responsive to the will of the people by protecting their constitutional rights. With this important constitutional safeguard, I would say that government should be responsive to the will of the people.

5. Respondents must answer from their perspective (see Chapter 15). Former Governor Mario Cuomo of New York provided an example:[3]

    REPORTER: Aren't you pretty thin-skinned about that, Governor?

    CUOMO: If by thin-skinned you mean very, very quick to respond—that's what I've done for a lifetime. I'd been a lawyer for more than twenty years. You can't let the comment from the witness pass. If

---

3. William Safire, "On Language," *New York Times* Magazine, Dec. 22, 1991, p. 10.

[by thin-skinned] you're talking about being personally sensitive to criticism, that's a lot of [expletive].

Caution: Expletives, even mild ones, are out of order in academic debate, and the judge will penalize any debater who uses them.

6. Respondents should promptly admit not knowing the answer to a question, as in this example:

   Q: Do you know what methodology Kwarciany and Langer used in their study?

   A: They're reputable scholars. I'm sure they used an appropriate methodology. But, no, I don't know their exact methodology.

7. Respondents should not attempt to defend an indefensible point. It is better to yield a point immediately than to allow questioners to wring admissions from the respondents in a series of questions that will only fix the point more firmly in the minds of those who render the decision.

3. Considerations of Both Questioner and Respondent.   Next we will examine some considerations that apply to both questioners and respondents.

1. The questions should focus primarily on arguments developed in the speech of the respondent. However, questions about arguments in a previous speech by the respondent's colleague, or any matter relevant to the proposition, are admissible.

2. The questioner and the respondent should treat each other with courtesy. Sarcasm, "browbeating," or obvious evasion will boomerang to the discredit of the one using them.

   If your opponent comes on too strong and seeks to goad you into losing your temper, keep your cool. Counter this aggression by adopting a friendlier, quieter, slower style. You will appear more confident and competent by comparison. The judge will take note and award points accordingly.

3. Both the questioner and the respondent should bear in mind that they are not conducting a private conversation but are asking questions and giving

---

Respondent Considerations

1. Be on guard
2. Answer reasonable questions
3. Do not answer unreasonable questions
4. Qualify responses
5. Answer from your perspective
6. If you do not know the answer, admit it
7. Do not defend the indefensible

responses designed to have an effect on the judge and audience. To facilitate communication with the audience, both speakers should stand and face the audience during the question period.

4.   As a general rule, once the questioning has begun, neither the questioner nor the respondent may consult a colleague. In some cases, however, courteous and limited participation by both colleagues may be acceptable. It is wise to know the judge's predisposition on "tag team" cross-examination. Even when it is possible to do so, it is bad practice to conduct or participate in a chaotic group questioning period. Prefer the one questioner, one respondent format. If partners have questions or important information to offer as answers, they should provide courteous nonverbal cues to indicate that.

5.   Finally a special consideration for both questioners and respondents is to prepare and *practice*. Once you have prepared your affirmative case or your negative briefs, prepare sets of questions, anticipate opponents' questions, prepare possible answers, and practice for cross-examination. Consider the questions that a skilled opponent will ask. What are the points of your case that are most vulnerable to attack? What questions can hurt you most? What are the questions you will have the most difficulty answering? Plan your answers to such questions, and rephrase them until you have concise, convincing, and effective responses.

In the same manner plan in advance the questions you will ask of your opponent. What arguments is your opponent most likely to advance? What questions will you ask? How will your opponent most likely respond to those questions? How will you follow up on that response? Will a skilled opponent give a response that will help or hurt you? If it will help you, plan how you will follow up on it with further questions or with analysis and argument in your speech.

In summary, when cross-examination is used, it is an essential part of the debate, and advocates must prepare for it with the same care given to all other parts of the debate. This preparation should include careful planning for and actual phrasing of the questions and answers they anticipate using, as well as an analysis of those who will render the decision. In 1987, Governor Dukakis had apparently anticipated and planned for a question about capital punishment in his

---

Considerations of Both Questioner and Respondent

1.   Focus questions on previous speeches
2.   Be courteous
3.   Face the judge and audience, not each other
4.   One person asks, one person answers
5.   Prepare and practice

second debate with then–Vice President Bush. His preparation, however, apparently did not include an analysis of how the audience would react to his calm and dispassionate response.

Advocates preparing for cross-examination might find it helpful to arrange with friends to simulate the preparation that is used to prepare for congressional cross-examination. Presidential nominees to the U.S. Supreme Court are advised to prepare for the rigorous questioning they will receive from members of Congress by undergoing intensive practice sessions:

> Each day for a week, Ruth Bader Ginsburg sat at a table in Room 108 of the Executive Office Building, fielding questions from a panel of lawyers on legal questions....
>
> The question-and-answer sessions for Judge Ginsburg, President Clinton's nominee to the Supreme Court, are part of what the modern nomination process has become, a full-throttle effort, much like prepping a candidate for a presidential debate.
>
> A senior White House official involved in the process said, "If when she goes before the committee and every question they ask her is one we've already asked her in practice sessions, we'll have done our job well...."
>
> In 1987, Judge Robert H. Bork, President Reagan's choice for the Supreme Court, insisted that he had no need for practice sessions. Bork, a federal appeals judge and a former law professor, told the White House that such sessions would be a waste of time because he was fluent in constitutional give-and-take.
>
> After Bork's nomination was defeated by the Senate after a tumultuous set of hearings ... it has become fixed political law in Washington that no one should forgo practice sessions.[4]

As Bork's disastrous experience proved, it is folly to face determined opponents in cross-examination without intensive preparation. The debater's objective in preparing for cross-examination is to anticipate every question an opponent might ask and to develop an effective answer.

B. Lincoln–Douglas Format

The Lincoln–Douglas format is simply a two-person debate, named in honor of the two famous nineteenth-century debaters who used this form. Interest in this format is growing in high schools and colleges and in politics, where the tendency increasingly is for opposing candidates to meet in debate before the voters. The famous Kennedy–Nixon debates of 1960 marked the first time in American history that presidential candidates met in debate in the tradition of Lincoln and Douglas.

---

4. Neil A. Lewis, "Ginsburg Gets Set for Her Most Public Law Exam," *New York Times,* July 15, 1993, p. B9. © 1993 by the New York Times Co. Reprinted by permission.

The organization of this format as practiced by the National Forensics Association is as follows:

Lincoln–Douglas Format	
Affirmative constructive	*6 minutes*
Cross-examination by negative	*3 minutes*
Negative constructive	*7 minutes*
Cross-examination by affirmative	*3 minutes*
Affirmative rebuttal	*6 minutes*
Negative rebuttal	*6 minutes*
Affirmative rebuttal	*3 minutes*
Preparation time	*4 minutes*

The NFA style of Lincoln–Douglas debate is policy debate, with all the same sorts of arguments, evidence, and case construction as occurs in team topic policy debates in NDT/CEDA. Recent NFA L–D topics include:

2007–2008: Resolved: that the United States Federal Government should substantially increase assistance to the Greater Horn of Africa in one of the following areas: economic development, human rights protection, or public health.

2006–2007: Resolved: that the United States Federal Government should adopt a policy to significantly increase the production of energy from renewable sources.

2005–2006: Resolved: that the United States Federal Government should adopt a policy to increase the protection of human rights in one or more of the following nationals: Tibet, Bhutan, Afghanistan, Nepal, Myanmar, Thailand, East Timor, Indonesia, Philippines, and/or Pakistan.

2004–2005: Resolved: that the United States Federal Government should significantly reform the criminal justice system.

2003–2004: Resolved: that the United States Federal Government should substantially increase environmental regulations on industrial pollution.

2002–2003: Resolved: that the United States Federal Government should significantly increase assistance to United States residents living below the poverty line.

2001–2002: Resolved: that the United States Federal Government should significantly alter its policy for combating international terrorism.

2000–2001: Resolved: that the United States Federal Government should significantly increase restrictions on civil lawsuits.

1999–2000: Resolved: that the United States Federal Government should increase restrictions on the development, use, and/or sale of genetically modified organisms.

1998–1999: Resolved: that the United States Federal Government should significantly increase its regulation of electronically mediated communication.

1997–1998: Resolved: that the United States Federal Government should significantly change its foreign policy toward Taiwan.

1996–1997: Resolved: that the U.S. Department of Education should require the implementation of more rigorous methods of teacher and/or student performance evaluation in secondary school systems.

1995–1996: Resolved: that participation in one or more of the six principal bodies of the United Nations should be significantly restricted by altering the U.N. charter and/or rules of procedure.

1994–1995: Resolved: that the FG should significantly reform the U.S. public welfare system.

1993–1994: Resolved: that the USFG should significantly alter laws for immigration into the U.S.

1992–1993: Resolved: that the terms of federal legislators should be limited to a specific duration.[5]

To learn more about Lincoln–Douglas debate competition, visit http://cas.bethel.edu/dept/comm/nfa/nfa-ld.html.

C. Mock Trial Format

The mock trial format emulates trial court debating. In mock trial debate the emphasis is on debate and argumentation skills and on cross-examination. This differs from moot court debate, widely used in law schools, which is concerned with the sometimes highly technical rules of procedure and which may emulate the appellate court rather than the trial court.

Instead of a proposition, the mock trial debaters are provided with the facts of a legal case. If the case is a criminal one, the affirmative becomes the prosecution and the negative becomes the defense; if the case is a civil suit, the affirmative is the plaintiff and the negative is the defendant. For example, the 2006–2007 national case debated by the American Mock Trial Association:

Case Summary

On January 2nd, 2005, off-duty police officer Jamie Conmey heard a radio transmission came over dispatch saying that two suspects had just robbed Joe's Corner Store. The description said that the perpetrators were wearing white T-shirts and blue jeans, appeared to be teenagers, and had taken the cash in a brown paper bag. Officer Conmey put on the siren and started searching the neighborhood surrounding the store. Officer Conmey saw a teenager dressed in a white shirt and jeans

---

5. National Forensic Association, Lincoln–Douglas Debate, downloaded July 30, 2007, http://cas.bethel.edu/dept/comm/nfa/nfa-ld.html.

climbing a fence in an alleyway. Officer Conmey pulled over and told the teenager to come down. The teenager stopped climbing the fence but did not come down. Seconds later, Officer Conmey shot the teenager in the side. Officer Conmey claims to have seen a gun, however, no weapon was found at the scene. The teenager was rushed to the hospital as quickly as possible, where the teenager almost immediately fell into a coma—a state in which the teenager remains today.

The teenager was Max Jeffries. Max's parents, Sean and Leigh Jeffries, filed suit against the Polk County Police Department, alleging that the actions of Officer Conmey, who committed suicide shortly after the incident, and thus the Polk County Police Department, deprived Max Jeffries of Jeffries' constitutional rights to due process of law. In addition, the Jeffries allege that through its policy, custom, and practice, the Polk County Police Department deprived Max Jeffries of Jeffries' rights to due process of law. The Jeffries allege that as a result of the actions of Officer Conmey and the Polk County Police Department, their child experienced life-threatening injuries, and as such they are entitled to damages. This case has been bifurcated and as such, damages are not to be considered in this same proceeding.[6]

Students follow a format modeling a real trial. Teams in the AMTA teams consist of six to eight students. They are governed by a set of rules of procedure and rules of evidence for the fictional jurisdiction of Midland. Time is limited to the following format:

Mock Trial Format	
Opening	*5 minutes*
Case-in-chief	*25 minutes*
Cross-Exams	*25 minutes*
Closing	*9 minutes* total—max of 5 minutes may be reserved for Plaintiff's rebuttal

This format is a popular exercise in argumentation and debate classes. Members of the class are assigned the various roles, including attorneys, defendant, judges, juries, and witnesses. Both sides are limited to the information about the case provided by the instructor. No additional information may be introduced into the mock trial. In the format shown on page 346, suitable for classroom application, substitute plaintiff's attorney for prosecuting attorney if the case is a civil one.

For more information about mock trial debate, visit the American Mock Trial Association at http://www.collegemocktrial.org/welcome/welcome.php.

---

6. American Mock Trial Association, downloaded July 30, 2007,
http://www.collegemocktrial.org/welcome/welcome.php.

Classroom Mock Trial Format	
Judge gives background information and outlines the procedure.	*3 minutes*
Prosecuting attorney outlines the case.	*3 minutes*
Defense attorney outlines the defense.	*3 minutes*
Prosecuting attorney calls three witnesses and questions each one for four minutes.	*12 minutes*
Defense attorney may cross-examine witnesses, asking each a maximum of three questions.	*6 minutes*
Defense attorney calls three witnesses and questions each one for four minutes.	*12 minutes*
Prosecuting attorney may cross-examine witnesses, asking each a maximum of three questions.	*6 minutes*
Defense attorney sums up and makes final plea.	*3 minutes*
Prosecuting attorney sums up and makes final plea.	*3 minutes*
The judge instructs the jury.	
The jury votes.	

D. Town Hall Format

The town hall format has been used at a number of annual conventions of the National Communication Association, the Southern States Communication Association, and the Florida Communication Association to debate issues of professional interest. This format may be used for any matter of interest to the participants and audience. A popular variation for campus debates provides for a student and a faculty member to serve as "kickoff" speakers for the motion and another student–faculty team to serve as "kickoff" speakers against the motion. (See the following format items 3–6.)

The town hall format may be organized as follows:

1. The chair opens the debate by announcing the motion before the house and reviewing the rules of procedure.

2. The chair introduces each of the four kickoff speakers in order.

3. The first advocate gives a seven-minute speech moving the adoption of the motion.

4. The second advocate gives a seven-minute speech opposing the motion.

5. The third advocate gives a seven-minute speech moving the adoption of the motion.

6. The fourth advocate gives a seven-minute speech opposing the motion.

7. The floor is then open to audience members, who may speak for no more than three minutes. The chair recognizes speakers alternately for and against

the motion. Preference should be given to those who have not previously spoken.

8. The debate proceeds in this manner for usually not more than 60 minutes. The chair then permits each of the kickoff speakers to summarize the arguments, first against and then for the motion. The summary speeches last no more than three minutes each.

9. The chair calls for a division of the house (a vote) and announces the result.

The town hall format also has some special procedural guidelines:

1. All action on the floor is channeled through the chair. It is the prerogative of the chair to exercise his or her judgment in any action not explicitly covered in these regulations.

2. Any speaker except the maker of the motion may be interrupted at any time if a member wishes to call attention to a violation of the rules by "rising to a point of order" or wishes to question the speaker "on a point of information." The speaker may refuse to answer the question or even to give the member a chance to ask it. But he or she cannot refuse to yield for points of order. The time involved in stating the point of information is not charged against the speaker; the time consumed in giving the information is.

3. Only these points of order will be considered: Objections to the behavior of an audience member and objections that the speaker's remarks are irrelevant.

4. The timekeeper will give each speaker a one-minute warning and a termination signal. Members must conclude their remarks on receiving the second signal.

5. Unused time may not be passed to a speaker on the same side.

6. The resolution before the house may not be amended.

The town hall format also has some special seating arrangements. Those favoring the motion at the beginning of the debate seat themselves to the chair's right; those opposed, to the chair's left. A section is provided for the undecided. If, as a result of the debating, at any time the sentiment of a member changes, the member then moves from undecided to decided or across the aisle and sits with the side he or she now favors.

E. Academic Parliamentary Format

1. Academic Parliamentary Debate.   Intercollegiate tournament competition in parliamentary debate has grown exponentially in recent years. Parliamentary debate tournaments and activities are held under the auspices of the National Parliamentary Debate Association (NPDA) and the American Parliamentary Debate Association (APDA). National championships and even a world championship of parliamentary debate are held.

In the British (and Worlds) format, The debate consists of four teams of two speakers, called *factions*, with two factions on either side of the case. The format is:

Worlds Debate Format

1. Prime Minister
2. Opposition Leader
3. Deputy Prime Minister
4. Deputy Opposition Leader
5. Member for the Government
6. Member for the Opposition
7. Government Whip
8. Opposition Whip

Each debater is allowed to speak for seven minutes, and the others may offer points of information during the speeches.

Academic parliamentary debate as practiced in the APDA and NPDA involves two, two-person teams. They receive their topics 15 minutes before the debate round is to begin. The emphasis is on logic, reasoning, general knowledge, and presentation skills rather than evidence use and debate technique. Use of preprinted materials and evidence is not allowed.

The topics for the 2006 NPDA National Championship tournament were[7]:

Round	Resolution
1	One or more of the extended provisions of the U.S. Patriot Act should be revoked.
2	The U.S. Federal Government should offer amnesty to illegal immigrants in the United States.
3	Israel should recognize Hamas as the legitimate government of the Palestinian National Authority.
4	The U.S. should significantly decrease its military presence in Europe.
5	Oust the elephant.
6	TH would retire.
7	U.S. food aid programs do more harm than good.
8	The expansion of eminent domain by the U.S. Supreme Court inappropriately privileges public use.
Quad Octas	Censure President George W. Bush.
Triple Octas	United Nations peacekeeping missions in Africa do more harm than good.

---

7. National Parliamentary Debate Association, downloaded July 30, 2007, http://cas.bethel.edu/dept/comm/npda/index.html.

Double Octas	The United States Federal Government should promote the domestic use of nuclear energy.
Octas	Roll back George W. Bush's tax cuts.
Quarters	Three Iraqs are better than one.
Semis	The United States should adopt a policy to substantially protect private pensions.
Finals	Public schools in the United States place insufficient value on fine arts education.

In parliamentary tournament debate, debaters may request points of information, points of order, and points of personal privilege (see Chapter 19). The standardized format is as follows:

Parliamentary Tournament Format	
Prime minister constructive	*7 minutes*
Leader of the opposition constructive	*8 minutes*
Member of the government constructive	*8 minutes*
Member of the opposition constructive	*8 minutes*
Leader of the opposition rebuttal	*4 minutes*
Prime minister rebuttal	*5 minutes*

Debaters in NPDA parliamentary debate receive their proposition and are allowed 15 minutes to prepare before the debate begins, but no preparation time during the debate. The government presents a case. The debaters first define the terms of the proposition and set their framework for the debate. They may choose to offer a policy interpretation measured by cost–benefit analysis or a value interpretation measured by designated criteria. In outline form, the prime minister (the first speaker) offers the government case. The leader of the opposition then offers refutation, which may include a challenge to the definitions and framework offered by the government. The debate continues much as a team topic policy debate, but without formal cross-examination periods.

While a debater is speaking (except during the first and last minute of their speech), an opponent may rise to a point of information, similar to a cross-examination question. The speaker may choose to recognize the questioner and answer the question or not.

For more information about parliamentary tournament debate, visit the National Parliamentary Debate Association website at http://cas.bethel.edu/dept/comm/npda/index.html.

2. Applied Parliamentary Debate.   Applied parliamentary debate is a specialized format involving the use of special procedures. This format is considered separately in Chapter 19.

Customary Debate Arrangements

Formats A through C are conducted in approximately the same manner. Formats D through E require certain special arrangements (see the discussion of each type).

- This diagram shows the simplest form of physical arrangements for a debate, suitable for classroom or tournament use. (AFF represents the affirmative team; NEG, the negative team; L, the lectern or table; T, the time- keeper; J, the judges; and A, the audience.) Judges may sit anywhere in the audience, facing the debaters.

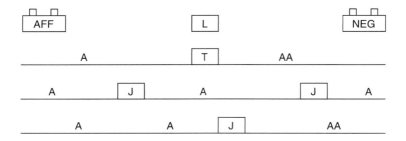

- The teams sit facing the audience. Customarily the affirmative is on the audience's left. As we saw in Chapter 17, on all ballots except the audience shift-of-opinion ballot, the affirmative's evaluation is recorded on the left side of the page. By sitting in these positions, the teams avoid needless confusion.
- A lectern is placed between the two teams.
- A timekeeper, if available, sits in the center of the first row of the audience facing the debaters. If no timekeeper is available, the debaters generally use countdown digital stopwatches to show their time remaining, and to monitor the progress of other speakers. The judge uses a stopwatch to check elapsed time and "prep time." In many tournaments, though never in public debates, each team is allowed an equal number of minutes of preparation time to use at its discretion. (For example, after the first affirmative speech the first negative speaker may, in agreement with his or her partner, take a few minutes to prepare before beginning the first negative speech; the same might apply for the interval between each of the remaining speeches. If a team exceeds its prep time, any excess is deducted from the speaking time.)
- The judge sits at any convenient place in the audience. If there are multiple judges, they make a point of sitting apart from one another. In most tournaments decisions in preliminary rounds are not announced after each debate but are published at the conclusion of that portion of the tournament. Results of elimination rounds—usually determined by a panel of judges—are often announced after each of those rounds in the room in which the debate was held.

II. THE AUDIENCE

The First National Developmental Conference on Forensics recommended: "Audience debating should be promoted through public appearances on the national proposition and on issues of local concern, as well as through tournaments, or rounds within tournaments, based on the audience vote model." CEDA has promoted public debate with a national award for the debate program making the greatest effort to sponsor public debating, and it experimented in 1997–1998 with a public debate division at many of its tournaments.

Directors of forensics provide opportunities for their students to speak before a variety of audiences. Because a number of debates are conducted simultaneously in a tournament, the audience for any one debate is usually small. The debaters thus have an opportunity to adjust to a limited audience and can gain experience in directing arguments to the key individual (in this case the judge) in that audience. In the final round of a tournament, which is usually well attended, the debaters have an opportunity to address an audience well versed in argumentation. Here they seek to influence several key individuals, because three or more experts usually serve as the panel of judges for the final round.

In addition to the audiences found in tournaments, general public audiences may be found on the campus and in the community. Sizable campus audiences are usually obtained for debates with traditional rival institutions. However, because audiences that may be obtained on any one campus are usually limited in size, debates are sometimes presented before various community audiences. Schools, church groups, and civic and social organizations are often interested in securing debates for their programs. Community audiences may be used for both tournament and individual debates. Local commercial radio and television stations, as well as educational radio and television stations, may be interested in carrying well-planned debates adapted to their special needs, thus offering debaters further opportunities to obtain experience in various types of communication situations. Online debates are also increasingly offering access to interested students.

The tournament situation makes provision for both the novice and the experienced debater. In fairness to both students and audience, the director of forensics usually assigns only the more proficient debaters to appear before campus and community audiences. Debates conducted before these groups require that the debaters undertake a careful audience analysis and make specific preparation in terms of the audience. (Audience analysis and adaptation are considered in Chapter 15.)

Although it is hoped that debates presented before public audiences will be both interesting and profitable for the audience, they should never be regarded as entertainment. Debates presented before public audiences should be regarded as an opportunity to educate students about audience analysis and to educate the audience about debate. The listeners, of course, may attend a debate for a variety of reasons. Some may want to gain more information about the subject of the debate; others may hope to use the debate process to help them arrive at a decision on the proposition. These reasons, however, are subordinate to the educational reasons for presenting the debate.

When critic-judges are used in the public audience debate situation, they can make a significant contribution to the audience's knowledge about debate by explaining the factors leading to a decision, in a manner that will be interesting and informative to the audience and profitable for the debaters.

III. ADAPTING THE DEBATE TO
COMMUNICATIONS MEDIA

The use of public address systems, radio, television, and computer streaming enables debaters to reach larger audiences, but it also poses the problem of adapting the debate to the specific media. The public address system requires only a simple adjustment; radio and television require a more complex adjustment and afford the opportunity to develop a type of debate specifically designed for the medium and for the specific broadcast situation (see the inset on pages 353–354). The audience for a debate streamed over the Internet is self-selected and similar to the live audience in a tournament debate, so little adjustment tends to be made (aside from accommodation to cameras and audio equipment).

Speakers sometimes must use radio or television at the same time that they are addressing an audience assembled before them. Adapting a style of debate or a style of speaking to two such different audience situations is difficult. Although superior speakers are able to reach both audiences effectively, it is usually preferable to concentrate on one audience. For debaters, the problem is simple: They must direct their principal attention to the audience that will render the decision. Most political speakers consider radio or television audiences more important, because these audiences include a greater number of voters who will render the decision with their ballots. After the first presidential debate between George Bush and Michael Dukakis, Peter Jennings, who had been on the panel of questioners, rushed from the stage to the ABC booth to participate in the post-debate broadcast. David Brinkley asked him what he thought of the debate. "I don't know," Jennings replied. "I haven't seen it on television."[8] Jennings, of course, recognized that the debate as seen by the millions who watched on television was far more important than, and in some ways different from, the debate he had seen in person at a distance of a few feet.

Today's audiences have a strong preference for a conversational style of delivery in contrast to the oratorical style so popular in the days of Daniel Webster. When former President Reagan was starting out as a young radio sports announcer in Des Moines, he used a conversational style of delivery. He got mail from people all over the Midwest telling him he sounded as if he was talking directly and personally to them. "The Great Communicator" remembered that response and always made a point of addressing crowds or television audiences as if he were speaking to a few friends sitting in a living room.[9]

In both radio and television debates, time is of great importance. Online debates may offer more freedom. This factor places a premium on extemporaneous speeches, which allow speakers to condense or extend remarks as the situation may demand. In television debates two cameras are usually used; often one camera is turned on a participant other than the speaker to allow the audience to see various reactions to the speech. Speakers should direct their remarks to the

8. Roger Simon, *Road Show* (New York: Farrar, Straus & Giroux, 1990), p. 120.
9. Ronald Reagan, *An American Life* (New York: Simon & Schuster, 1990), p. 247.

Suggestions for Adapting to Media

Public Address System

1. Avoid the use of a public address system unless you clearly need it to be heard in the auditorium.
2. If possible, test the public address system before the audience arrives.
3. Before beginning a speech, adjust the microphone to a convenient height, and place it in a convenient location—so that it is sufficiently close to you but does not obstruct your access to the lectern or your view of the audience.
4. Allow the public address system to amplify your voice; do not shout into the microphone.
5. Remain close to the microphone during your talk, adjusting your movements and gestures to the microphone; avoid moving "off mike."

Radio

1. Speak as though you were addressing two, three, or four persons seated in their living room.
2. Because you cannot ordinarily use visual aids in a radio speech, depend on vivid and precise words to paint the desired pictures in the minds of your audience.
3. If you use a manuscript (for plan or negative briefs), be sure to simplify complex arguments and present them in a conversational manner.
4. Adjust your presentation to the time available. Sometimes only half-hour or 15-minute time segments are allotted for the debate. In such situations the speeches should be short, with a frequent change of speakers. Sometimes a program format may evolve wherein the moderator addresses questions, based on the principal issues of the debate, to members of each team alternately, and they give a one- or two-minute answer. In other cases a modification of cross-examination debate may be used. The best format for radio debate is usually worked out in consultation between a director of forensics who knows the details of debate and a radio producer who knows the details of radio.

Television and Internet

1. Keep in mind the same considerations of style that apply to radio.
2. Use visual aids if appropriate. Visual aids must be prepared in consultation with the program director so that they meet the special requirements of television and so that they get "on camera" at the proper time.
3. Remember that movements, gestures, and facial expressions can be seen by the audience and have communicative value. Movement must be within previously defined limits—you must not move "off camera." Gestures, facial expression, and movements should be restrained, because the camera will frequently take a tight head "shot" of the speaker.
4. Dress appropriately. Avoid large, bright pieces of jewelry and noisy bracelets, as well as clothing with sharply contrasting colors or "busy" patterns. Debaters may need makeup for color television; this special makeup is usually applied by a studio makeup artist. If you wear glasses only occasionally, remove them to reduce the chance of light reflection. If you wear glasses constantly, however, wear them during the show, because you will probably feel more comfortable and be less likely to squint.

5. Keep the use of a manuscript to an absolute minimum. Most program directors strongly prefer that presenters speak extemporaneously, with a minimum of notes.

6. Adjust your presentation to the time available and to the special problems of the medium. The sketches below indicate floor plans used in various television debates. (M designates moderator; L, lectern; D, debater; J, judge; and A, audience members who appear on camera.)

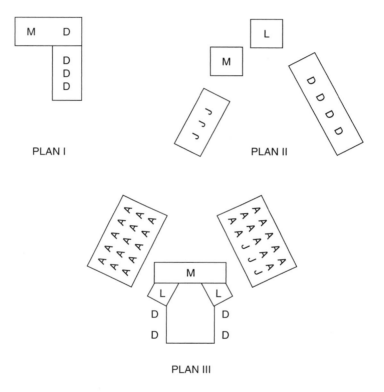

Plan I: The moderator and debaters are seated at an L-shaped table.

Plan II: The moderator is seated apart from the debaters' table, and the debaters speak from the lectern.

Plan III: The judges and a number of audience members are seated on raised chairs in "jury box" style. (Two lecterns are provided so that the debaters may stand facing each other during cross-examination.)

"live" camera—the one with a small red glowing light near the lens—unless the program format calls for addressing remarks to the moderator or to some other participant. If a monitor—a television set showing the program going out over the air—is in sight, the speakers should ignore it.

Television and online debates generally require more planning than radio debates do, because the medium is more complex, and the special problems of camera placement, sets, and lighting and the need for rehearsal time influence the format to be used. In planning the format of television and online debates, debaters should remember that television is a *visual* medium. The debate format should be selected and its presentation planned with this factor in mind.

For a television debate speakers should plan to arrive at the studio well ahead of broadcast or recording time to allow the producer or director to make the necessary arrangements: Check for voice balance, adjust lighting, plan camera arrangements, and so on. For a radio debate speakers should make a point of getting acquainted with the various signals that will be given from the control room as cues at different points during the program. For the television debate speakers should make a point of acquainting themselves with the various signals the floor person will give from time to time during the debate. They should also prepare themselves to present their speeches in a conversational manner amid the apparent chaos of the movement of cameras and technicians during the broadcast.

EXERCISES

1. Practice cross-examination. After one side reads their 1AC, conduct untimed cross-examination until you run out of questions. Variations are to form a circle, and go around the circle having each person ask a question. Or have each individual write down their secret goal for cross-examination on an index card, pass it to their neighbor, and have that person ask a series of questions designed to achieve the goal (for example, "I want to reveal that their link card disproves the brink.")

2. Organize a debate using each of the formats identified but on the same proposition. Compare the strengths and weaknesses of each. This is obviously a long-term project.

19

Applied Parliamentary Debate

Whenever a group finds it necessary or desirable to hold a formal debate, some rules for that debate must be provided to ensure order, efficiency, and impartiality. The law courts have special rules for debates conducted in the courtroom; the governing body of each city, town, or village conducts its debates under a special set of rules, as do the state legislatures and Congress; civic, social, and business organizations have special sets of rules governing debate. Parliamentary debate permits a large number of persons to participate and provides a means for a large group to reach a decision.

Parliamentary debate derives its name from the parliaments of Britain, but the details of parliamentary debate, however, vary from one group to another. The rules of debate for the British Parliament are different in many ways from the rules of debate in the U.S. Congress. The rules of debate in the Senate, for example, are far too complicated and specialized for general use by other organizations. In fact, they are different in important respects from the rules of debate in the House of Representatives. The NPDA and APDA offer special rules for academic parliamentary debating (see Chapter 18). All well-conceived rules of parliamentary debate, however, have a common nature and certain common purposes, including the following:

1. *Parliamentary debate provides for the orderly and efficient conduct of business.* It does so by considering one matter at a time and by disposing of each matter before going on to another.

2. *Parliamentary debate assures a decision.* It does so by requiring that every motion be acted on in some way. Once a motion has been introduced, it must be passed, defeated, or postponed. A postponement, of course, is a decision not to pass a motion at the present time.

3. *Parliamentary debate protects the rights of the majority.* It does so by providing that the decisions of a sufficient number of members must prevail.

4. *Parliamentary debate protects the rights of the minority.* It does so by giving the minority many important privileges. For example, any member, without the necessity of securing a second, has the right to be heard on many important matters; only two members are required to introduce any motion; and one-third of the members plus one can exercise important restraints.

5. *Parliamentary debate is impartial.* Because the rules of procedure apply equally to all members, each member has an equal right to be heard and has equal voting power.

I. SOURCES OF PARLIAMENTARY DEBATE RULES

Parliamentary debate has no one set of rules, although a body of commonly accepted practices and some legal requirements are recognized. As has been indicated, the two branches of Congress do not debate under the same rules. The faculty and student governments of a university undoubtedly operate under different rules of parliamentary debate; and even two different clubs probably conduct their debates under somewhat different rules. Where, then, do the rules of parliamentary debate come from? Members of each group must adopt or create their own rules. If the decisions made by the group are of particular importance—for example, the decisions of a legislative body or a corporation—prudence dictates that those conducting the meeting have on hand expert parliamentarians familiar with general usage and attorneys familiar with the special laws applicable to the particular organization. For example, state laws, which differ considerably from one state to another, often dictate the methods of voting that have to be used by corporations. For the average group, however, the problem is simpler. It is usually enough that its members follow one set of commonly accepted practices and make provision for their special needs. The rules of parliamentary debate for the average group come from five sources: (1) the constitution of the organization, (2) the bylaws of the organization, (3) the standing rules of the organization (which are recorded in the minutes of the organization), (4) the agenda of the meeting (although not necessary, an agenda is often convenient), or (5) another stipulated source.

With the exception of national and state legislative bodies, few organizations attempt to write their rules of parliamentary debate in full. Rather, most organizations provide a set of rules to take care of their most obvious needs and special requirements and then stipulate some source as the basis for rules not otherwise provided. Small groups, for instance, could stipulate the rules presented in the table on pages 362–363 as the source of their rules. Larger groups, or groups likely to be confronted with complicated problems, would select one of the various books devoted entirely to parliamentary procedure as the stipulated source of their rules.

Sometimes the special requirements of an organization make it desirable to set aside common usage in parliamentary practice. Groups that meet annually or infrequently might take from the motion to adjourn its customary privileged status and give it the lowest possible priority. This provision is usually unnecessary for groups that meet weekly, but it is often advisable for groups that meet only at infrequent intervals or in situations in which a hastily passed motion to adjourn might seriously inconvenience the organization. Although deviations from common practice are sometimes desirable or necessary, they should be made rarely and only after careful consideration of all their implications.

II. THE ORDER OF BUSINESS

The usual order of business for an organization using parliamentary procedure follows a clear, logical pattern.

1. *Call to order:* The call to order is usually a simple announcement by the chair: "The meeting will be in order" or "The National Convention of the Democratic [or Republican] party is now in session."

2. *Roll call:* A roll call is taken only if one is required by the rules or customs of the organization. A roll call is a useful device in a larger organization; most smaller organizations find it unnecessary.

3. *Reading of the minutes of the previous meeting:* The minutes are usually read by the secretary in smaller organizations, although this reading may be omitted by unanimous consent. Larger organizations and many smaller organizations find it convenient to have the minutes printed or duplicated and distributed to the membership. Once the minutes have been presented, they may be corrected, amended, or accepted.

4. *Reports of standing committees:* Most organizations have various committees that are established by the constitution or whose duties continue for a long period of time, such as the executive committee or the finance committee. These committees report at this time.

5. *Reports of special committees:* Most organizations also have various committees that are appointed to serve for a shorter period of time or to deal with a specific issue, such as a special fund-raising committee or the committee to recommend a site for next year's convention. These committees report at this time.

6. *Unfinished business:* Unfinished business is that business not completed at the previous meeting. For example, if a motion was on the floor at the time the previous meeting adjourned, that motion now comes before the assembly as unfinished business. A motion that was postponed at a previous meeting, by a motion to postpone temporarily or "lay on the table," may be brought before the assembly at this time by a motion to resume consideration to "take from the table." The motion to postpone to a particular time often specifies that the motion shall come before the assembly as unfinished business at the next meeting.

7. *New business:* Once the unfinished business has been disposed of, the floor is open to new business.

8. *Miscellaneous:* The last matter of business includes announcements and other miscellaneous items that may come before the group, such as "The executive committee will meet at eight o'clock" or "Members wishing to obtain tickets for the annual outing should see Debbie Jones after this meeting."

9. *Adjournment:* Once the business of the meeting is completed, the chair may ask for a motion to adjourn. Such a motion may, however, be introduced earlier.

Larger organizations, or organizations that have many items of business to consider, find it convenient to prepare an agenda. An *agenda* is a special order of business, drawn up in advance of the meeting, that takes precedence over the usual order of business. The agenda may be changed by passage of a motion setting a special order of business. The agenda often includes a detailed statement of the order in which reports will be presented and motions considered. When an organization's meetings extend over more than one day, it is desirable to indicate ahead of time which matters will be considered on each day.

III. PRESENTATION OF MOTIONS

When motions are in order, a member who wishes to make a motion must first obtain recognition from the chair. To gain recognition, the member rises and addresses the presiding officer: "Mr. Chairman" or "Madam Chairwoman." (If the constitution of the organization provides for a chairperson, the form of address is then "Mr. Chairperson" or "Ms. Chairperson.") The chair grants recognition by addressing the member; "Tina" would suffice in an informal group, and "Ms. Smith" or "The delegate from Massachusetts" in a more formal group. If the member's name is not known, the chair may ask, "Will the member state her name?" The member replies, "Tina Smith, delegate from Massachusetts." In granting recognition, the chair replies, "The chair recognizes Ms. Smith from Massachusetts" (the chair always speaks in the third person and never says, "I recognize …").

When several members seek recognition at the same time, the chair must decide which one to recognize. In granting recognition, the chair should consider the following factors:

1. Priority should be given first to the maker of the motion.

2. Priority should be given alternately to speakers favoring and opposing the motion if they are known to the chair. If the chair does not know which speakers favor or oppose the motion, he or she may state, "The chair will recognize a speaker favoring [or opposing] the motion."

3. Priority should be given to a member who has not spoken previously.

4. If none of the other considerations apply, the chair should, when possible, recognize the member who first sought recognition.

Once a member has gained recognition, he or she states the motion by saying, "I move that ..." In many organizations a member is required to give the secretary a written copy of the motion at the time it is introduced. The secretary has the privilege, should it be necessary, of interrupting a member to request a restatement of the motion so that it may be entered into the minutes accurately.

Before a main motion may be debated, it must be seconded by another member. Any other member, without the necessity of being recognized, may state, "I second the motion." If the motion is not seconded immediately, the chair may ask, "Is there a second?" If there is no second, the chair announces, "The motion is lost for lack of a second." The motion is then no longer before the assembly, and a new motion is in order. If the motion is seconded, the chair announces, "It has been moved and seconded that ..." and then recognizes the proposer of the motion to speak on that motion.

IV. PRECEDENCE OF MOTIONS

In the interests of order and efficiency, a definite order of precedence of motions is followed. As shown in the table on pages 362–363, the main motion has zero, or lowest, precedence, because it may be introduced only when no other business is before the house. Once a main motion is before the house, any of the other motions, when appropriate, may be applied to it. The highest precedence —1—is given to a motion to fix the time of the next meeting, and the other privileged motions follow this motion in precedence. The incidental motions rank after the privileged motions in precedence but have no precedence among themselves; they are considered in the order in which they arise. The subsidiary motions follow the incidental motions in precedence and have a definite order of precedence among themselves. The table of precedence lists the motions most often used in parliamentary debate and the preferred rules applying to these motions. Some of the rules may be modified by special circumstances.

V. PURPOSES OF MOTIONS

The four types of motions—main, subsidiary, incidental, and privileged—have different purposes, as outlined in detail here.

A. Main Motions

Main motions bring substantive proposals before the assembly for consideration and decision. Main motions are the core of the conduct of business; they are the most important and most frequently used motions. Main motions are the plan by which the maker of the motion seeks to attain an objective. This may be very simple, such as a motion directing the treasurer to pay a small sum to the Scholarship Fund, or very complex. If the motion is other than very simple, you will find it helpful to review the "Basic Plan Format" in Chapter 12. The author of the plan illustrated in Exercise 6(g) at the end of this chapter had an easy task. This plan merely calls for an increase in an existing tax, and the author had only to specify when the tax increases were to go into effect and to provide certain exemptions (the mandates). The agency to administer the excise tax and penalties to enforce it and the other elements of the plan are already in existence. Main motions include the following:

General main motion: To bring new business before the meeting.

Reconsider: To stop all action on a motion previously voted until the motion has been reconsidered. This motion may be made by any member (unless the rules of the organization specifically establish some limitation), but it may be made only on the same day as the original motion was passed or on the next business day of a convention—not at the next weekly or monthly meeting or at the next convention. A motion to reconsider cannot be applied to a matter that has left the assembly. For example, if a motion has been passed directing the treasurer to pay $50 to the Scholarship Fund and if the treasurer has already paid that money, the motion cannot be reconsidered. If carried, the motion to reconsider places the motion previously voted on in the exact status it had before it was voted on. If defeated, the motion to reconsider may not be renewed.

Rescind: To cancel an action taken at some previous meeting. This motion may be made at any time when other business is not before the meeting; it cannot be applied to a matter that has left the assembly.

Resume consideration (take from the table): To bring a temporarily postponed motion (a motion that had been laid on the table) before the meeting in the same state that the motion held before it was postponed temporarily.

Set special order of business: To set a date or time at which a certain matter will be considered.

B. Subsidiary Motions

Subsidiary motions are alternative aids for changing, considering, and disposing of the main motion. Consequently they are subsidiary to the main motion. Examples of subsidiary motions include the following:

Postpone temporarily (lay on the table): To postpone consideration of a matter. This device may be used to allow more urgent business to come before the assembly or to allow time for some members to gather additional information before voting. It is also a way of "sidetracking" a matter in the hope that it will not be taken up again.

Vote immediately (previous question): To close debate and bring the matter before the meeting to an immediate vote.

Table of Precedence of Parliamentary Motions

Once a main motion is before the meeting, any of the following motions, when appropriate, maybe made. In the following table the motions are arranged from the strongest—1—to the weakest—0. A stronger motion takes precedence over any weaker motion and becomes the business before the meeting.

Precedence Number	Interrupt Speaker?	Require a Second?	Debatable?	Vote Required?	Amendable?	Subject to Referral to Committee?	Subject to Post- ponement?	Subject to Reconsideration?
Privileged Motions								
1. Fix time of next meeting	No	Yes	No	Maj.	Yes[1]	No	No	No
2. Adjourn	No	Yes	No	Maj.	No	No	No	No
3. Recess	No	Yes	No	Maj.	Yes	No	No	No
4. Question of privilege	Yes	No	No	Chr.	No	No	No	No
Incidental Motions								
Incidental motions are of equal rank among themselves; they are considered in the order they are moved.								
5. Appeal decision of the chair	Yes	Yes	Yes	Maj.	No	No	Yes	Yes
5. Close nominations	No	Yes	No	2/3	Yes	No	No	No
5. Division of the house	Yes	No	No	None	No	No	No	No
5. Object to consideration	Yes	No	No	2/3	No	No	No	No
5. Parliamentary inquiry	Yes	No	No	None	No	No	No	No
5. Point of order	Yes	No	No	Chr.	No	No	No	No
5. Suspension of rules	No	Yes	No	2/3	No	No	No	No
5. Request for information (Will the speaker yield for a question?)	Yes	No	No	Chr. or speaker	No	No	No	No
5. Withdraw a motion	No	No	No	Maj.	No	No	No	No

Subsidiary Motions

Motion								
6. Postpone temporarily (lay on the table)	No	No	No	No	Maj.	No	Yes	No
7. Vote immediately (previous question)	No	No	No	No	$2/3$	No	Yes	No
8. Limit or extend debate	No[2]	No	No	Yes	$2/3$	No	Yes	No
9. Postpone to a specified time	No	No	No	Yes	Maj.	Yes	Yes	No
10. Refer to committee	No	No	No	Yes	Maj.	Yes	Yes	No
11. Refer to the committee of the whole	No	No	No	Yes	Maj.	Yes	Yes	No
12. Amend an amendment	Yes	Yes	Yes	No	Maj.	No	Yes	No
13. Amend	Yes	Yes	Yes	Yes	Maj.	Yes	Yes	No
14. Postpone indefinitely	No	No	No	No	Maj.	No	Yes	No

Main Motions

Main motions are of equal rank among themselves. They have zero precedence since they may not be considered when any other motion is before the house.

Motion								
0. General main motion	Yes	Yes	Yes	Yes	Maj.	Yes	Yes	No
0. Reconsider	No	Yes[3]	No	No	Maj.	No	Yes	Yes
0. Rescind	Yes	Yes	Yes	Yes	$2/3$[4]	Yes	Yes	No
0. Resume consideration (take from table)	No	No	No	No	Maj.	No	Yes	No
0. Set special order of business	Yes	No	Yes	Yes	$2/3$	Yes	Yes	Yes

1. Although the motion is not debatable, the amendment may be debated.
2. Motion may be renewed after a change in the parliamentary situation.
3. May be postponed to a specified time only.
4. Only a majority is required if previous notice has been given.

Limit or extend debate: To set or extend a limit on debate on a matter before the meeting.

Postpone to a specified time: To delay action on a matter before the meeting until a specified time.

Refer to committee: To refer a matter before the meeting to a committee. If applied to an amendment, this motion also takes the main motion with it. It may be used to secure the advantage of having the matter studied more carefully by a small group or to delay action on the matter.

Refer to the committee of the whole: To refer a matter to the committee of the whole, in order to debate the matter "off the record" and in the greater informality of the committee of the whole.

Amend an amendment: To amend an amendment to a motion before the meeting. Most organizations find it advisable to prohibit an amendment to an amendment to an amendment.

Amend: To change a motion. A motion to amend may take any of four forms: (1) amend by striking out, (2) amend by substitution, (3) amend by addition, or (4) amend by dividing the motion into two or more parts.

Postpone indefinitely: To suppress the main motion to which it is applied without the risk of adopting the main motion. This device is sometimes used to identify, without the risk of adopting the motion, who favors and who opposes it.

C. Incidental Motions

Incidental motions arise only incidentally out of the business before the assembly. They do not relate directly to the main motion but usually relate to matters that are incidental to the conduct of the meeting. Types of incidental motions include the following:

Appeal decision of the chair: To secure a reversal of a ruling by the chair.

Close nominations: To prevent nomination of other candidates. Voting is not limited to those candidates who have been nominated.

Division of the house: To require a standing vote.

Object to consideration: To prevent consideration of a matter.

Parliamentary inquiry: To allow a member to ascertain the parliamentary status of a matter or to seek parliamentary information.

Point of order: To demand that the chair rule on an alleged error, mistake, or violation of parliamentary procedure.

Suspension of rules: To suspend rules to allow procedure contrary to certain rules of the organization.

Request for information: To allow a member to ask the chair—or, through the chair, the speaker who has the floor—for information on a matter before the meeting.

Withdraw a motion: To prevent action on a motion before the meeting.

D. Privileged Motions

Privileged motions have no direct connection with the main motion before the assembly. They relate to the members and to the organization rather than to substantive proposals. They deal with matters so urgent that they are entitled to immediate consideration. Privileged motions would be main motions except for their urgency. Because of their urgency, they are given the privilege of being considered ahead of other motions that are before the house. Privileged motions include motions to do the following:

Fix time of next meeting: To fix a time at which the group will meet next.

Adjourn: To close the meeting. This motion is also used to prevent further consideration of a matter before the meeting.

Recess: To suspend the meeting temporarily.

Question of privilege: To request the chair to rule on a matter relating to the privileges of the assembly or the privileges of an individual member.

VI. UNANIMOUS CONSENT

To expedite business on a routine or obviously desirable matter, any member may ask that approval for a certain course of action be given by unanimous consent. The chair will ask, "Is there any objection?" and then, if no objection is made, will announce, "Hearing none, it is so ordered." If any member objects, the required parliamentary procedure must be followed.

EXERCISES

1. List the organizations to which you belong that conduct their business through parliamentary debate. Evaluate the effectiveness of each group in parliamentary debate.

2. From your experiences in groups that conduct their business through parliamentary debate, can you recall an instance when the will of the majority was defeated by a minority better versed in parliamentary procedure? Prepare a brief report of this instance.

3. Select a proposition for parliamentary debate, and hold a debate on this proposition in class.

4. Conduct a debate using the same arrangement suggested in Exercise 3. This time, by prearrangement with your instructor, select a small group of students who will seek to secure passage of the proposition; select a second small group of students who will seek to defeat the proposition. The majority of the class will be uncommitted on the proposition at the start of the debate.

5. Conduct a debate using the same arrangement suggested in Exercise 4. This time, the supporters of the proposition will be instructed to use every possible parliamentary motion in order to "railroad" the passage of the proposition. The opponents of the proposition will be instructed to use every possible parliamentary motion in order to obstruct or defeat passage of the proposition. The class will probably encounter some difficult problems in this exercise. In working your way out of these problems—with some help from the instructor, who will serve as parliamentarian when needed—you will gain practical experience in parliamentary procedure.

6. Arrange to conduct a model congress in class. Elect a speaker and a clerk. Your instructor will serve as parliamentarian. Before the class meets, each student will prepare a bill on a subject that would be suitable for consideration by the Congress of the United States at the present time. Prepare enough copies of your bill for each member of the class and for your instructor. Distribute copies of your bill at the first meeting of the class as a model congress. Prepare bills in the following form:

    a. They must be typewritten, duplicated, and double-spaced on a single sheet of white, 8½ × 11-inch paper.

    b. The first line will consist of these words: "Congress Bill Number."

    c. The second line will consist of these words: "by [your name]."

    d. Commencing with the third line, the title of the bill must be stated, beginning with the words "AN ACT" and containing a statement of the purpose of the bill.

    e. The text of the bill proper must begin with the words "BE IT ENACTED BY THE MODEL CONGRESS." The material following must begin with the word "That." Each line of the material that follows must be numbered on the left margin of the page, beginning with "1."

    f. Every section will be numbered commencing at "1." No figures will be used in the bill except for the numbers of sections and lines. No abbreviations will be used.

    g. The following form is an illustration of the prescribed form for drafting bills.

Congress Bill Number _____
by Rick Rogers
AN ACT to make the United States energy independent by the year 2012.
BE IT ENACTED BY THE MODEL CONGRESS

1. Section 1. That the federal excise tax on gasoline be
2. increased by twenty-five cents a gallon effective thirty days
3. after this bill becomes law.
4. Section 2. That the federal excise tax on gasoline be
5. increased by an additional twenty-five cents a gallon
6. effective one year from the date this bill becomes law.
7. Section 3. That gasoline purchased for agricultural and
8. fishery purposes be exempt from this tax.
9. Section 4. That the ...

Appendix A

A Presidential Debate

Presidential debates are the paramount example of applied debate. They become the focal point of presidential campaigns and have sometimes been the decisive factor in determining the winner of the election. For days in advance of each presidential debate, the media feature the coming event. The debates usually are carried on all major networks in the United States and are widely broadcast around the world; they are viewed by more people than any other debates in history. For days afterward the media continue to feature news about the debate, first trying to determine who won and then assessing the impact of the debate on the campaign.

Presidential debates are a relatively new tradition in American history. In 1959, a group of speech professors began to organize the Committee on Presidential Campaign Debates to call on the candidates for the presidency to meet in debate in the tradition of Abraham Lincoln and Stephen Douglas. Initially the committee consisted of all the past presidents of the American Forensic Association. The movement quickly gained momentum and was endorsed by the American Forensic Association, Delta Sigma Rho–Tau Kappa Alpha, and the Ohio Association of College Teachers of Speech. These organizations named additional members to the committee. Senator John F. Kennedy promptly endorsed the proposal, as did all the potential candidates in 1960 except for Vice President Richard Nixon. The idea of presidential debates quickly captured the public's imagination. Soon editorials, columns, and articles appeared in support of the idea. Television networks indicated their willingness to cooperate.

September 26, 1960, brought the first presidential debate between Kennedy and Nixon. Four debates were held during the campaign; the first, which Kennedy "won," was judged to be the most important. The *New York Times* called the debates "the really decisive factor" in the election.

The presidential debates have an interesting, tangled background of law and legal fiction. Under Federal Communication Commission rules it was illegal for the networks to sponsor such debates. The "equal-time" rule required the networks to give equal time to all presidential candidates. In 1960, for example, 16 legally qualified candidates ran (including one who campaigned in an Uncle Sam suit on the platform "Drop the Bomb"). Naturally the networks would not consider giving equal time to 16 candidates, nor would the major candidates consider sharing a platform with unknown candidates who had no chance of winning. The problem was solved when Congress passed legislation suspending the equal-time requirement for 60 days in 1960. The debates won widespread public approval, and the public demanded more presidential debates in 1964, 1968, and 1972. But the candidates in those years (including Nixon, who once remarked that he had flunked debating in the Electoral College) didn't want to debate, and their allies in Congress found a convenient way to avoid the pressures for debate. Both the House and the Senate passed bills suspending the equal-time law during the campaign, which allowed the senators and representatives to report to their constituents that they had voted in favor of presidential debates. However, because the House bill and the Senate bill differed in the number of days for which the law was suspended, the bills were referred to a Joint Conference Committee, where they quietly died.

In 1976 the League of Women Voters found a way to have presidential debates without the need to suspend the equal-time law. The league invited the major candidates to debate. The league, of course, was not subject to the equal-time law, and the networks maintained that the debates were a news event—not something sponsored by the networks—and thus not subject to the equal-time law. President Gerald Ford and Governor Jimmy Carter accepted the invitation to debate. Members of the Committee on Presidential Debates generally regarded the debates as "eminently forgettable."

During the 1980 presidential campaign president Carter declined to meet with Ronald Reagan and third-party candidate John Anderson in a three-way debate. Reagan agreed to debate Anderson and won points for being a "good sport"; Carter, conversely, lost points for being a "bad sport." Later in the campaign Carter, apparently reluctantly, agreed to meet Reagan in one debate.

After the election both Reagan and Carter supporters and many independent commentators cited the debate as the "turning point" in the election and the major factor in Reagan's landslide victory.

After the 1984 conventions the League of Women Voters invited Reagan and Walter Mondale for a series of debates. Mondale, sorely needing the visibility the debates would give him, eagerly accepted. Reagan, enjoying a 20-point lead in the polls, was advised not to give Mondale the visibility and status the debates would bring. However, apparently remembering the "poor sport" charge that had hurt Carter in 1980, Reagan agreed to two presidential debates and one vice-presidential debate. (The first vice-presidential debate was between Senator Bob Dole and Mondale in 1976.) Mondale was generally credited with winning the first debate, in which Reagan was perceived as being tired and unsure of himself. In the second debate Mondale was credited with winning the issues, but Reagan, returning to his customary style that had won him the title of "the Great Communicator," clearly carried the burden of communication and won the decision of the voters.

Since 1988 presidential debates have been under the sponsorship of the Commission on Presidential Debates. (The commission, organized in 1987 by the Democratic and Republican National Committees, had taken over the sponsorship of the debates.) The format might be described as a highly specialized type of joint press conference. However, the presidential debates did have some important elements of real applied debates. Each candidate was allotted equal time, each had an opportunity for rebuttal, and each made a closing statement. Although the format fell short of a real debate, it did provide the American voters with their only opportunity to see and hear the candidates on the same platform at the same time as they responded to the journalists and to one another.

Presidential debates are now a firmly established part of the American political scene. In 1992 there were three presidential debates and one vice-presidential debate. That year marked the first three-way presidential campaign debates. Although Ross Perot was not expected to win the election, he commanded far larger public support than Anderson did in 1980, and both major-party candidates treated him as if he were an 800-pound bantam rooster, nodding at his arguments, smiling at his country homilies, and laughing at his jokes. Neither George Bush nor Bill Clinton came close to challenging him on a single point, obviously hoping that his supporters might switch to them on election day. This debate was noteworthy as well for its format. Clinton had, in the Democratic primary debates, been successful utilizing a "town hall format," in which audience members provided questions to be addressed by the debaters.

In 1996 two presidential debates and one vice-presidential debate were held. The second presidential debate in 1996 was held using the town hall format. While respondents did not proclaim a clear winner, it was generally thought that Clinton won by not losing: Dole would have needed to score a knockout to catch up in the polls. He did not.

In 2000, George W. Bush was reluctant to agree to participate in the debates, then agreed to one debate, and finally to three (along with a vice-presidential debate). The debates were all too close to call, according to media and post-debate polls. Whether such a conclusion was reflective of the closeness of the campaign or the actual debates was unclear. In the first debate, October 3, 2000, at the University of Massachusetts, Amherst, Vice President Gore was criticized for being too aggressive, although generally perceived to be more knowledgeable and competent. In the second debate, October 11 at Wake Forest, Gore seemed strained to appear nicer, and the debate was close but cordial. In the third debate, October 17 at Washington University in St. Louis, the debaters seemed to agree more than disagree. All three debates were moderated by Jim Lehrer with the same format: single moderator; candidates questioned in turn with two minutes to answer; 60-second rebuttal; two-minute closing statements. Approximately 46.6 million people watched the first debate, with about 37.5 million watching the second and third debates. As with the election itself, the debates were too close to call.

In 2004, President Bush and Senator John Kerry participated in three debates. The first was limited to questions of foreign policy, and was moderated by Jim Lehrer of PBS News. The candidates stood at podiums and answered the moderator's questions. The second debate involved domestic and foreign policy questions and was moderated by Charlie Gibson of ABC News in a town hall format, engaging audience questions. The third and final debate (which follows), intended to focus on domestic policy, was moderated by Bob Schieffer of CBS News, and returned the candidates to podiums as in the first debate. Sixty-two point four million viewers watched the first debate, 46.7 million the second, and 51.1 million watched the third debate. Vice-presidential candidates Dick Cheney and John Edwards also participated in a nationally televised debate, moderated by Gwen Ifill of PBS News, with both candidates seated at a table. Forty-three point five million viewed the vice-presidential debate. Most observers felt that Senator Kerry did the better job of debating during the first debate, the second debate was considered fairly even, and post-debate polls indicated a majority of viewers considered Kerry the winner of the third debate.

Presidential debates have come to dominate the landscape of the Democrat and Republican Parties' campaigns prior to their primaries. Beginning in April 2007 through January 2008 as many as 8 Democratic contenders for their party's nomination and 11 Republican candidates participated in 39 planned debates. Although many of the debates offered traditional opportunities for candidates to answer moderators' questions, new formats have included the YouTube debates, engaging online contributors in a sort of cyber–town hall debate, and debates translated into Spanish language and moderated by Spanish-language news anchors. Sponsors of debates included Logo, a TV network targeted to lesbian, gay, bisexual, and transgender communities. The YouTube debates presented candidates with video questions contributed through the Internet service YouTube in a wide range of creative presentations, personalizing the questions in unique ways.

THE THIRD 2004 BUSH–KERRY PRESIDENTIAL DEBATE: OCTOBER 13, 2004[*]

SPEAKERS:
GEORGE W. BUSH, PRESIDENT OF THE UNITED STATES
U.S. SENATOR JOHN F. KERRY (MA), DEMOCRATIC
PRESIDENTIAL NOMINEE BOB SCHIEFFER, CBS ANCHOR

SCHIEFFER: Good evening from Arizona State University in Tempe, Arizona. I'm Bob Schieffer of CBS News. I want to welcome you to the third and last of the 2004 debates between President George Bush and Senator John Kerry.

As Jim Lehrer told you before the first one, these debates are sponsored by the Commission on Presidential Debates.

---

[*] Republished with permission of Janet Brown of the Commission on Presidential Debates. Some minor, inconsequential inaccuracies may appear in the text.

Tonight the topic will be domestic affairs, but the format will be the same as that first debate. I'll moderate our discussion under detailed rules agreed to by the candidates, but the questions and the areas to be covered were chosen by me. I have not told the candidates or anyone else what they are.

To refresh your memory on the rules, I will ask a question. The candidate is allowed two minutes to answer. His opponent then has a minute and a half to offer a rebuttal.

At my discretion, I can extend the discussion by offering each candidate an additional 30 seconds.

A green light will come on to signal the candidate has 30 seconds left. A yellow light signals 15 seconds left. A red light means five seconds left.

There is also a buzzer, if it is needed.

The candidates may not question each other directly. There are no opening statements, but there will be two-minute closing statements.

There is an audience here tonight, but they have agreed to remain silent, except for right now, when they join me in welcoming President George Bush and Senator John Kerry.

(APPLAUSE)

Gentlemen, welcome to you both.

By coin toss, the first question goes to Senator Kerry.

Senator, I want to set the stage for this discussion by asking the question that I think hangs over all of our politics today and is probably on the minds of many people watching this debate tonight.

And that is, will our children and grandchildren ever live in a world as safe and secure as the world in which we grew up?

KERRY: Well, first of all, Bob, thank you for moderating tonight.

Thank you, Arizona State, for welcoming us.

And thank you to the Presidential Commission for undertaking this enormous task. We're proud to be here.

Mr. President, I'm glad to be here with you again to share similarities and differences with the American people.

Will we ever be safe and secure again? Yes. We absolutely must be. That's the goal.

Now, how do we achieve it is the most critical component of it.

I believe that this president, regrettably, rushed us into a war, made decisions about foreign policy, pushed alliances away. And, as a result, America is now bearing this extraordinary burden where we are not as safe as we ought to be.

The measurement is not: Are we safer? The measurement is: Are we as safe as we ought to be? And there are a host of options that this president had available to him, like making sure that at all our ports in America containers are inspected. Only 95 percent of them—95 percent come in today uninspected. That's not good enough.

People who fly on airplanes today, the cargo hold is not X-rayed, but the baggage is. That's not good enough. Firehouses don't have enough firefighters in them. Police officers are being cut from the streets of America because the president decided to cut the COPS program.

So we can do a better job of homeland security. I can do a better job of waging a smarter, more effective war on terror and guarantee that we will go after the terrorists.

I will hunt them down, and we'll kill them, we'll capture them. We'll do whatever is necessary to be safe.

But I pledge this to you, America: I will do it in the way that Franklin Roosevelt and Ronald Reagan and John Kennedy and others did, where we build the strongest alliances, where the world joins together, where we have the best intelligence and where we are able, ultimately, to be more safe and secure.

SCHIEFFER: Mr. President, you have 90 seconds.

BUSH: Thank you very much.
I want to thank Arizona State as well.

Yes, we can be safe and secure, if we stay on the offense against the terrorists and if we spread freedom and liberty around the world.

I have got a comprehensive strategy to not only chase down the Al Qaeda, wherever it exists—and we're making progress; three-quarters of Al Qaeda leaders have been brought to justice—but to make sure that countries that harbor terrorists are held to account.

As a result of securing ourselves and ridding the Taliban out of Afghanistan, the Afghan people had elections this weekend. And the first voter was a 19-year-old woman. Think about that. Freedom is on the march.

We held to account a terrorist regime in Saddam Hussein.

In other words, in order to make sure we're secure, there must be a comprehensive plan. My opponent just this weekend talked about how terrorism could be reduced to a nuisance, comparing it to prostitution, illegal gambling. I think that attitude and that point of view is dangerous. I don't think you can secure America for the long run if you don't have a comprehensive view as to how to defeat these people.

At home, we'll do everything we can to protect the homeland. I signed the homeland security bill to better align our assets and resources. My opponent voted against it.

We're doing everything we can to protect our borders and ports.

But absolutely we can be secure in the long run. It just takes good, strong leadership.

SCHIEFFER: Anything to add, Senator Kerry?

KERRY: Yes. When the president had an opportunity to capture or kill Osama bin Laden, he took his focus off of them, outsourced the job to Afghan warlords, and Osama bin Laden escaped.

Six months after he said Osama bin Laden must be caught dead or alive, this president was asked, "Where is Osama bin Laden?" He said, "I don't know. I don't really think about him very much. I'm not that concerned."

We need a president who stays deadly focused on the real war on terror.

SCHIEFFER: Mr. President?

BUSH: Gosh, I just don't think I ever said I'm not worried about Osama bin Laden. It's kind of one of those exaggerations.

Of course we're worried about Osama bin Laden. We're on the hunt after Osama bin Laden. We're using every asset at our disposal to get Osama bin Laden.

My opponent said this war is a matter of intelligence and law enforcement. No, this war is a matter of using every asset at our disposal to keep the American people protected.

SCHIEFFER: New question, Mr. President, to you.

We are talking about protecting ourselves from the unexpected, but the flu season is suddenly upon us. Flu kills thousands of people every year.

Suddenly we find ourselves with a severe shortage of flu vaccine. How did that happen?

BUSH: Bob, we relied upon a company out of England to provide about half of the flu vaccines for the United States citizen, and it turned out that the vaccine they were producing was contaminated. And so we took the right action and didn't allow contaminated medicine into our country. We're working with Canada to hopefully—that they'll produce a—help us realize the vaccine necessary to make sure our citizens have got flu vaccinations during this upcoming season.

My call to our fellow Americans is if you're healthy, if you're younger, don't get a flu shot this year. Help us prioritize those who need to get the flu shot, the elderly and the young.

The CDC, responsible for health in the United States, is setting those priorities and is allocating the flu vaccine accordingly.

I haven't gotten a flu shot, and I don't intend to because I want to make sure those who are most vulnerable get treated.

We have a problem with litigation in the United States of America. Vaccine manufacturers are worried about getting sued, and therefore they have backed off from providing this kind of vaccine.

One of the reasons I'm such a strong believer in legal reform is so that people aren't afraid of producing a product that is necessary for the health of our citizens and then end up getting sued in a court of law.

But the best thing we can do now, Bob, given the circumstances with the company in England is for those of us who are younger and healthy, don't get a flu shot.

SCHIEFFER: Senator Kerry?

KERRY: This really underscores the problem with the American health-care system. It's not working for the American family. And it's gotten worse under President Bush over the course of the last years.

Five million Americans have lost their health insurance in this country. You've got about a million right here in Arizona, just shy, 950,000, who have no health insurance at all. 82,000 Arizonians lost their health insurance under President Bush's watch. 223,000 kids in Arizona have no health insurance at all.

All across our country—go to Ohio, 1. 4 million Ohioans have no health insurance, 114,000 of them lost it under President Bush; Wisconsin, 82,000 Wisconsinites lost it under President Bush.

This president has turned his back on the wellness of America. And there is no system. In fact, it's starting to fall apart not because of lawsuits—though they are a problem, and John Edwards and I are committed to fixing them—but because of the larger issue that we don't cover Americans.

Children across our country don't have health care. We're the richest country on the face of the planet, the only industrialized nation in the world not to do it.

I have a plan to cover all Americans. We're going to make it affordable and accessible. We're going to let everybody buy into the same health-care plan senators and congressmen give themselves.

SCHIEFFER: Mr. President, would you like to add something?

BUSH: I would. Thank you.

I want to remind people listening tonight that a plan is not a litany of complaints, and a plan is not to lay out programs that you can't pay for.

He just said he wants everybody to be able to buy in to the same plan that senators and congressmen get. That costs the government $7,700 per family. If every family in America signed up, like the senator suggested, if would cost us $5 trillion over 10 years.

It's an empty promise. It's called bait and switch.

SCHIEFFER: Time's up.

BUSH: Thank you.

KERRY: Actually, it's not an empty promise.

It's really interesting, because the president used that very plan as a reason for seniors to accept his prescription drug plan. He said, if it's good enough for the congressmen and senators to have choice, seniors ought to have choice.

What we do is we have choice. I choose Blue Cross/Blue Shield. Other senators, other congressmen choose other programs.

But the fact is, we're going to help Americans be able to buy into it. Those that can afford it are going to buy in themselves. We're not giving this away for nothing.

SCHIEFFER: All right.

Senator Kerry, a new question. Let's talk about economic security. You pledged during the last debate that you would not raise taxes on those making less than $200,000 a year. But the price of everything is going up, and we all know it. Health-care costs, as you are talking about, is skyrocketing, the cost of the war.

My question is, how can you or any president, whoever is elected next time, keep that pledge without running this country deeper into debt and passing on more of the bills that we're running up to our children?

KERRY: I'll tell you exactly how I can do it: by reinstating what President Bush took away, which is called pay as you go.

During the 1990s, we had pay-as-you-go rules. If you were going to pass something in the Congress, you had to show where you are going to pay for it and how.

President Bush has taken—he's the only president in history to do this. He's also the only president in 72 years to lose jobs—1.6 million jobs lost. He's the only president to have incomes of families go down for the last three years; the only president to see exports go down; the only president to see the lowest level of business investment in our country as it is today.

Now, I'm going to reverse that. I'm going to change that. We're going to restore the fiscal discipline we had in the 1990s.

Every plan that I have laid out—my health-care plan, my plan for education, my plan for kids to be able to get better college loans—I've shown exactly how I'm going to pay for those.

And we start—we don't do it exclusively—but we start by rolling back George Bush's unaffordable tax cut for the wealthiest people, people earning more than $200,000 a year, and we pass, hopefully, the McCain-Kerry Commission which identified some $60 billion that we can get.

We shut the loophole which has American workers actually subsidizing the loss of their own job. They just passed an expansion of that loophole in the last few days: $43 billion of giveaways, including favors to the oil and gas industry and the people importing ceiling fans from China.

I'm going to stand up and fight for the American worker. And I am going to do it in a way that's fiscally sound. I show how I pay for the health care, how we pay for the education.

I have a manufacturing jobs credit. We pay for it by shutting that loophole overseas. We raise the student loans. I pay for it by changing the relationship with the banks.

This president has never once vetoed one bill; the first president in a hundred years not to do that.

SCHIEFFER: Mr. President?

BUSH: Well, his rhetoric doesn't match his record.

He's been a senator for 20 years. He voted to increase taxes 98 times. When they tried to reduce taxes, he voted against that 127 times. He talks about being a fiscal conservative, or fiscally sound, but he voted over—he voted 277 times to waive the budget caps, which would have cost the taxpayers $4.2 trillion.

He talks about PAYGO. I'll tell you what PAYGO means, when you're a senator from Massachusetts, when you're a colleague of Ted Kennedy, pay go means: You pay, and he goes ahead and spends.

He's proposed $2.2 trillion of new spending, and yet the so-called tax on the rich, which is also a tax on many small-business owners in America, raises $600 million by our account—billion, $800 billion by his account.

There is a tax gap. And guess who usually ends up filling the tax gap? The middle class.

I propose a detailed budget, Bob. I sent up my budget man to the Congress, and he says, here's how we're going to reduce the deficit in half by five years. It requires pro-growth policies that grow our economy and fiscal sanity in the halls of Congress.

SCHIEFFER: Let's go to a new question, Mr. President. Two minutes. And let's continue on jobs.

You know, there are all kinds of statistics out there, but I want to bring it down to an individual.

Mr. President, what do you say to someone in this country who has lost his job to someone overseas who's being paid a fraction of what that job paid here in the United States?

BUSH: I'd say, Bob, I've got policies to continue to grow our economy and create the jobs of the 21st century. And here's some help for you to go get an education. Here's some help for you to go to a community college.

We've expanded trade adjustment assistance. We want to help pay for you to gain the skills necessary to fill the jobs of the 21st century.

You know, there's a lot of talk about how to keep the economy growing. We talk about fiscal matters. But perhaps the best way to keep jobs here in America and to keep this economy growing is to make sure our education system works.

I went to Washington to solve problems. And I saw a problem in the public education system in America. They were just shuffling too many kids through the system, year after year, grade after grade, without learning the basics.

And so we said: Let's raise the standards. We're spending more money, but let's raise the standards and measure early and solve problems now, before it's too late.

No, education is how to help the person who's lost a job. Education is how to make sure we've got a workforce that's productive and competitive.

Got four more years, I've got more to do to continue to raise standards, to continue to reward teachers and school districts that are working, to emphasize math and science in the classrooms, to continue to expand Pell Grants to make sure that people have an opportunity to start their career with a college diploma.

And so the person you talked to, I say, here's some help, here's some trade adjustment assistance money for you to go a community college in your neighborhood, a community college which is providing the skills necessary to fill the jobs of the 21st century. And that's what I would say to that person.

SCHIEFFER: Senator Kerry?

KERRY: I want you to notice how the president switched away from jobs and started talking about education principally.

Let me come back in one moment to that, but I want to speak for a second, if I can, to what the president said about fiscal responsibility.

Being lectured by the president on fiscal responsibility is a little bit like Tony Soprano talking to me about law and order in this country.

(LAUGHTER)

This president has taken a $5.6 trillion surplus and turned it into deficits as far as the eye can see. Health-care costs for the average American have gone up 64 percent; tuitions have gone up 35 percent; gasoline prices up 30 percent; Medicare premiums went up 17 percent a few days ago; prescription drugs are up 12 percent a year.

But guess what, America? The wages of Americans have gone down. The jobs that are being created in Arizona right now are paying about $13,700 less than the jobs that we're losing.

And the president just walks on by this problem. The fact is that he's cut job-training money. $1 billion was cut. They only added a little bit back this year because it's an election year.

They've cut the Pell Grants and the Perkins loans to help kids be able to go to college.

They've cut the training money. They've wound up not even extending unemployment benefits and not even extending health care to those people who are unemployed.

I'm going to do those things, because that's what's right in America: Help workers to transition in every respect.

SCHIEFFER: New question to you, Senator Kerry, two minutes. And it's still on jobs. You know, many experts say that a president really doesn't have much control over jobs. For example, if someone invents a machine that does the work of five people, that's progress. That's not the president's fault.

So I ask you, is it fair to blame the administration entirely for this loss of jobs?

KERRY: I don't blame them entirely for it. I blame the president for the things the president could do that has an impact on it.

Outsourcing is going to happen. I've acknowledged that in union halls across the country. I've had shop stewards stand up and say, "Will you promise me you're going to stop all this outsourcing?" And I've looked them in the eye and I've said, "No, I can't do that."

What I can promise you is that I will make the playing field as fair as possible, that I will, for instance, make certain that with respect to the tax system that you as a worker in America are not subsidizing the loss of your job.

Today, if you're an American business, you actually get a benefit for going overseas. You get to defer your taxes.

So if you're looking at a competitive world, you say to yourself, "Hey, I do better overseas than I do here in America."

That's not smart. I don't want American workers subsidizing the loss of their own job. And when I'm president, we're going to shut that loophole in a nano-second and we're going to use that money to lower corporate tax rates in America for all corporations, 5 percent. And we're going to have a manufacturing jobs credit and a job hiring credit so we actually help people be able to hire here.

The second thing that we can do is provide a fair trade playing field. This president didn't stand up for Boeing when Airbus was violating international rules and subsidies. He discovered Boeing during the course of this campaign after I'd been talking about it for months.

The fact is that the president had an opportunity to stand up and take on China for currency manipulation. There are companies that wanted to petition the administration. They were told: Don't even bother; we're not going to listen to it.

The fact is that there have been markets shut to us that we haven't stood up and fought for. I'm going to fight for a fair trade playing field for the American worker. And I will fight for the American worker just as hard as I fight for my own job. That's what the American worker wants. And if we do that, we can have an impact.

Plus, we need fiscal discipline. Restore fiscal discipline, we'll do a lot better.

SCHIEFFER: Mr. President?

BUSH: Whew!

Let me start with the Pell Grants. In his last litany of misstatements. He said we cut Pell Grants. We've increased Pell Grants by a million students. That's a fact.

You know, he talks to the workers. Let me talk to the workers.

You've got more money in your pocket as a result of the tax relief we passed and he opposed.

If you have a child, you got a $1,000 child credit. That's money in your pocket.

If you're married, we reduced the marriage penalty. The code ought to encourage marriage, not discourage marriage.

We created a 10 percent bracket to help lower-income Americans. A family of four making $40,000 received about $1,700 in tax relief.

It's your money. The way my opponent talks, he said, "We're going to spend the government's money." No, we're spending your money. And when you have more money in your pocket, you're able to better afford things you want.

I believe the role of government is to stand side by side with our citizens to help them realize their dreams, not tell citizens how to live their lives.

My opponent talks about fiscal sanity. His record in the United States Senate does not match his rhetoric.

He voted to increase taxes 98 times and to bust the budget 277 times.

SCHIEFFER: Senator Kerry?

KERRY: Bob, anybody can play with these votes. Everybody knows that.

I have supported or voted for tax cuts over 600 times. I broke with my party in order to balance the budget, and Ronald Reagan signed into law the tax cut that we voted for. I voted for IRA tax cuts. I voted for small-business tax cuts.

But you know why the Pell Grants have gone up in their numbers? Because more people qualify for them because they don't have money.

But they're not getting the $5,100 the president promised them. They're getting less money.

We have more people who qualify. That's not what we want.

BUSH: Senator, no one's playing with your votes. You voted to increase taxes 98 times. When they voted—when they proposed reducing taxes, you voted against it 126 times.

He voted to violate the budget cap 277 times. You know, there's a main stream in American politics and you sit right on the far left bank. As a matter of fact, your record is such that Ted Kennedy, your colleague, is the conservative senator from Massachusetts.

SCHIEFFER: Mr. President, let's get back to economic issues. But let's shift to some other questions here.

Both of you are opposed to gay marriage. But to understand how you have come to that conclusion, I want to ask you a more basic question. Do you believe homosexuality is a choice?

BUSH: You know, Bob, I don't know. I just don't know. I do know that we have a choice to make in America and that is to treat people with tolerance and respect and dignity. It's important that we do that.

And I also know in a free society people, consenting adults can live the way they want to live.

And that's to be honored.

But as we respect someone's rights, and as we profess tolerance, we shouldn't change—or have to change—our basic views on the sanctity of marriage. I believe in the sanctity of marriage. I think it's very important that we protect marriage as an institution, between a man and a woman.

I proposed a constitutional amendment. The reason I did so was because I was worried that activist judges are actually defining the definition of marriage, and the surest way to protect marriage between a man and woman is to amend the Constitution.

It has also the benefit of allowing citizens to participate in the process. After all, when you amend the Constitution, state legislatures must participate in the ratification of the Constitution.

I'm deeply concerned that judges are making those decisions and not the citizenry of the United States. You know, Congress passed a law called DOMA, the Defense of Marriage Act.

My opponent was against it. It basically protected states from the action of one state to another. It also defined marriage as between a man and woman.

But I'm concerned that that will get overturned. And if it gets overturned, then we'll end up with marriage being defined by courts, and I don't think that's in our nation's interests.

SCHIEFFER: Senator Kerry?

KERRY: We're all God's children, Bob. And I think if you were to talk to Dick Cheney's daughter, who is a lesbian, she would tell you that she's being who she was, she's being who she was born as.

I think if you talk to anybody, it's not choice. I've met people who struggled with this for years, people who were in a marriage because they were living a sort of convention, and they struggled with it.

And I've met wives who are supportive of their husbands or vice versa when they finally sort of broke out and allowed themselves to live who they were, who they felt God had made them.

I think we have to respect that.

The president and I share the belief that marriage is between a man and a woman. I believe that. I believe marriage is between a man and a woman.

But I also believe that because we are the United States of America, we're a country with a great, unbelievable Constitution, with rights that we afford people, that you can't discriminate in the workplace. You can't discriminate in the rights that you afford people.

You can't disallow someone the right to visit their partner in a hospital. You have to allow people to transfer property, which is why I'm for partnership rights and so forth.

Now, with respect to DOMA and the marriage laws, the states have always been able to manage those laws. And they're proving today, every state, that they can manage them adequately.

SCHIEFFER: Senator Kerry, a new question for you.

The *New York Times* reports that some Catholic archbishops are telling their church members that it would be a sin to vote for a candidate like you because you support a woman's right to choose an abortion and unlimited stem-cell research.

What is your reaction to that?

KERRY: I respect their views. I completely respect their views. I am a Catholic. And I grew up learning how to respect those views. But I disagree with them, as do many.

I believe that I can't legislate or transfer to another American citizen my article of faith. What is an article of faith for me is not something that I can legislate on somebody who doesn't share that article of faith.

I believe that choice is a woman's choice. It's between a woman, God and her doctor. And that's why I support that.

Now, I will not allow somebody to come in and change *Roe v. Wade*.

The president has never said whether or not he would do that. But we know from the people he's tried to appoint to the court he wants to.

I will not. I will defend the right of *Roe v. Wade*.

Now, with respect to religion, you know, as I said, I grew up a Catholic. I was an altar boy. I know that throughout my life this has made a difference to me.

And as President Kennedy said when he ran for president, he said, "I'm not running to be a Catholic president. I'm running to be a president who happens to be Catholic."

My faith affects everything that I do, in truth. There's a great passage of the Bible that says, "What does it mean, my brother, to say you have faith if there are no deeds? Faith without works is dead."

And I think that everything you do in public life has to be guided by your faith, affected by your faith, but without transferring it in any official way to other people.

That's why I fight against poverty. That's why I fight to clean up the environment and protect this earth.

That's why I fight for equality and justice. All of those things come out of that fundamental teaching and belief of faith.

But I know this, that President Kennedy in his inaugural address told all of us that here on Earth, God's work must truly be our own. And that's what we have to—I think that's the test of public service.

SCHIEFFER: Mr. President?

BUSH: I think it's important to promote a culture of life. I think a hospitable society is a society where every being counts and every person matters. I believe the ideal world is one in which every child is protected in law and welcomed to life. I understand there's great differences on this issue of abortion, but I believe reasonable people can come together and put good law in place that will help reduce the number of abortions.

Take, for example, the ban on partial birth abortion. It's a brutal practice. People from both political parties came together in the halls of Congress and voted overwhelmingly to ban that practice. It made a lot of sense. My opponent, in that he's out of the mainstream, voted against that law.

What I'm saying is, is that as we promote life and promote a culture of life, surely there are ways we can work together to reduce the number of abortions: continue to promote adoption laws—it's a great alternative to abortion—continue to fund and promote maternity group homes; I will continue to promote abstinence programs.

The last debate, my opponent said his wife was involved with those programs. That's great. I appreciate that very much. All of us ought to be involved with programs that provide a viable alternative to abortion.

SCHIEFFER: Mr. President, let's have a new question. It goes to you. And let's get back to economic issues.

Health insurance costs have risen over 36 percent over the last four years according to The Washington Post. We're paying more. We're getting less.

I would like to ask you: Who bears responsibility for this? Is it the government? Is it the insurance companies? Is it the lawyers? Is it the doctors? Is it the administration?

BUSH: Gosh, I sure hope it's not the administration.

There's a—no, look, there's a systemic problem. Health-care costs are on the rise because the consumers are not involved in the decision-making process. Most health-care costs are covered by third parties. And therefore, the actual user of health care is not the purchaser of health care. And there's no market forces involved with health care.

It's one of the reasons I'm a strong believer in what they call health savings accounts. These are accounts that allow somebody to buy a low-premium, high-deductible catastrophic plan and couple it with tax-free savings. Businesses can contribute, employees can contribute on a contractual basis. But this is a way to make sure people are actually involved with the decision-making process on health care.

Secondly, I do believe the lawsuits—I don't believe, I know—that the lawsuits are causing health-care costs to rise in America. That's why I'm such a strong believer in medical liability reform.

In the last debate, my opponent said those lawsuits only caused the cost to go up by 1 percent. Well, he didn't include the defensive practice of medicine that costs the federal government some $28 billion a year and costs our society between $60 billion and $100 billion a year.

Thirdly, one of the reasons why there's still high cost in medicine is because this is—they don't use any information technology. It's like if you looked at the—it's the equivalent of the buggy and horse days, compared to other industries here in America.

And so, we've got to introduce high technology into health care. We're beginning to do it. We're changing the language. We want there to be electronic medical records to cut down on error, as well as reduce cost.

People tell me that when the health-care field is fully integrated with information technology, it'll wring some 20 percent of the cost out of the system.

And finally, moving generic drugs to the market quicker.

And so, those are four ways to help control the costs in health care.

SCHIEFFER: Senator Kerry?

KERRY: The reason health-care costs are getting higher, one of the principal reasons is that this administration has stood in the way of common-sense efforts that would have reduced the costs. Let me give you a prime example.

In the Senate we passed the right of Americans to import drugs from Canada. But the president and his friends took it out in the House, and now you don't have that right. The president blocked you from the right to have less expensive drugs from Canada.

We also wanted Medicare to be able to negotiate bulk purchasing. The VA does that. The VA provides lower-cost drugs to our veterans. We could have done that in Medicare.

Medicare is paid for by the American taxpayer. Medicare belongs to you. Medicare is for seniors, who many of them are on fixed income, to lift them out of poverty.

But rather than help you, the taxpayer, have lower cost, rather than help seniors have less expensive drugs, the president made it illegal—illegal—for Medicare to actually go out and bargain for lower prices.

Result: $139 billion windfall profit to the drug companies coming out of your pockets. That's a large part of your 17 percent increase in Medicare premiums.

When I'm president, I'm sending that back to Congress and we're going to get a real prescription drug benefit.

Now, we also have people sicker because they don't have health insurance. So whether it's diabetes or cancer, they come to hospitals later and it costs America more.

We got to have health care for all Americans.

SCHIEFFER: Go ahead, Mr. President.

BUSH: I think it's important, since he talked about the Medicare plan, has he been in the United States Senate for 20 years? He has no record on reforming of health care. No record at all.

He introduced some 300 bills and he's passed five.

No record of leadership.

I came to Washington to solve problems. I was deeply concerned about seniors having to choose between prescription drugs and food. And so I led. And in 2006, our seniors will get a prescription drug coverage in Medicare.

SCHIEFFER: Senator Kerry? Thirty seconds.

KERRY: Once again, the president is misleading America. I've actually passed 56 individual bills that I've personally written and, in addition to that, and not always under my name, there is amendments on certain bills.

But more importantly, with respect to the question of no record, I helped write—I did write, I was one of the original authors of the early childhood health care and the expansion of health care that we did in the middle of the 1990s. And I'm very proud of that.

So the president's wrong.

SCHIEFFER: Let me direct the next question to you, Senator Kerry, and again, let's stay on health care.

You have, as you have proposed and as the president has commented on tonight, proposed a massive plan to extend health-care coverage to children. You're also talking about the government picking up a big part of the catastrophic bills that people get at the hospital.

And you have said that you can pay for this by rolling back the president's tax cut on the upper 2 percent.

You heard the president say earlier tonight that it's going to cost a whole lot more money than that.

I'd just ask you, where are you going to get the money?

KERRY: Well, two leading national news networks have both said the president's characterization of my health-care plan is incorrect. One called it fiction. The other called it untrue.

The fact is that my health-care plan, America, is very simple. It gives you the choice. I don't force you to do anything. It's not a government plan. The government doesn't require you to do anything. You choose your doctor. You choose your plan.

If you don't want to take the offer of the plan that I want to put forward, you don't have do. You can keep what you have today, keep a high deductible, keep high premiums, keep a high co-pay, keep low benefits.

But I got a better plan. And I don't think a lot of people are going to want to keep what they have today.

Here's what I do: We take over Medicaid children from the states so that every child in America is covered. And in exchange, if the states want to—

they're not forced to, they can choose to—they cover individuals up to 300 per-cent of poverty. It's their choice.

I think they'll choose it, because it's a net plus of $5 billion to them.

We allow you—if you choose to, you don't have to—but we give you broader competition to allow you to buy into the same health care plan that senators and congressmen give themselves. If it's good enough for us, it's good enough for every American. I believe that your health care is just as important as any politician in Washington, D.C.

You want to buy into it, you can. We give you broader competition. That helps lower prices.

In addition to that, we're going to allow people 55 to 64 to buy into Medicare early. And most importantly, we give small business a 50 percent tax credit so that after we lower the costs of health care, they also get, whether they're self-employed or a small business, a lower cost to be able to cover their employees.

Now, what happens is when you begin to get people covered like that—for instance in diabetes, if you diagnose diabetes early, you could save $50 billion in the health care system of America by avoiding surgery and dialysis. It works. And I'm going to offer it to America.

SCHIEFFER: Mr. President?

BUSH: In all due respect, I'm not so sure it's credible to quote leading news organizations about—oh, never mind. Anyway, let me quote the Lewin report. The Lewin report is a group of folks who are not politically affiliated. They ana-lyzed the senator's plan. It cost $1.2 trillion.

The Lewin report accurately noted that there are going to be 20 million people, over 20 million people added to government-controlled health care. It would be the largest increase in government health care ever.

If you raise the Medicaid to 300 percent, it provides an incentive for small businesses not to provide private insurance to their employees. Why should they insure somebody when the government's going to insure it for them?

It's estimated that 8 million people will go from private insurance to govern-ment insurance.

We have a fundamental difference of opinion. I think government-run health will lead to poor-quality health, will lead to rationing, will lead to less choice.

Once a health-care program ends up in a line item in the federal govern-ment budget, it leads to more controls.

And just look at other countries that have tried to have federally controlled health care. They have poor-quality health care.

Our health-care system is the envy of the world because we believe in mak-ing sure that the decisions are made by doctors and patients, not by officials in the nation's capital.

SCHIEFFER: Senator?

KERRY: The president just said that government-run health care results in poor quality.

Now, maybe that explains why he hasn't fully funded the VA and the VA hospital is having trouble and veterans are complaining. Maybe that explains why Medicare patients are complaining about being pushed off of Medicare. He doesn't adequately fund it.

But let me just say to America: I am not proposing a government-run program. That's not what I have. I have Blue Cross/Blue Shield. Senators and congressmen have a wide choice. Americans ought to have it too.

SCHIEFFER: Mr. President?

BUSH: Talk about the VA: We've increased VA funding by $22 billion in the four years since I've been president. That's twice the amount that my predecessor increased VA funding.

Of course we're meeting our obligation to our veterans, and the veterans know that.

We're expanding veterans' health care throughout the country. We're aligning facilities where the veterans live now. Veterans are getting very good health care under my administration, and they will continue to do so during the next four years.

SCHIEFFER: Mr. President, the next question is to you. We all know that Social Security is running out of money, and it has to be fixed. You have proposed to fix it by letting people put some of the money collected to pay benefits into private savings accounts. But the critics are saying that's going to mean finding $1 trillion over the next 10 years to continue paying benefits as those accounts are being set up.

So where do you get the money? Are you going to have to increase the deficit by that much over 10 years?

BUSH: First, let me make sure that every senior listening today understands that when we're talking about reforming Social Security, that they'll still get their checks.

I remember the 2000 campaign, people said if George W. gets elected, your check will be taken away. Well, people got their checks, and they'll continue to get their checks.

There is a problem for our youngsters, a real problem. And if we don't act today, the problem will be valued in the trillions. And so I think we need to think differently. We'll honor our commitment to our seniors. But for our children and our grandchildren, we need to have a different strategy.

And recognizing that, I called together a group of our fellow citizens to study the issue. It was a committee chaired by the late Senator Daniel Patrick Moynihan of New York, a Democrat. And they came up with a variety of ideas for people to look at.

I believe that younger workers ought to be allowed to take some of their own money and put it in a personal savings account, because I understand that they need to get better rates of return than the rates of return being given in the current Social Security trust.

And the compounding rate of interest effect will make it more likely that the Social Security system is solvent for our children and our grandchildren. I will work with Republicans and Democrats. It'll be a vital issue in my second term. It is an issue that I am willing to take on, and so I'll bring Republicans and Democrats together.

And we're of course going to have to consider the costs. But I want to warn my fellow citizens: The cost of doing nothing, the cost of saying the current system is OK, far exceeds the costs of trying to make sure we save the system for our children.

SCHIEFFER: Senator Kerry?

KERRY: You just heard the president say that young people ought to be able to take money out of Social Security and put it in their own accounts.

Now, my fellow Americans, that's an invitation to disaster.

The CBO said very clearly that if you were to adopt the president's plan, there would be a $2 trillion hole in Social Security, because today's workers pay in to the system for today's retirees. And the CBO said—that's the Congressional Budget Office; it's bipartisan—they said that there would have to be a cut in benefits of 25 percent to 40 percent.

Now, the president has never explained to America, ever, hasn't done it tonight, where does the transitional money, that $2 trillion, come from?

He's already got $3 trillion, according to the *Washington Post,* of expenses that he's put on the line from his convention and the promises of this campaign, none of which are paid for. Not one of them are paid for.

The fact is that the president is driving the largest deficits in American history. He's broken the pay-as-you-go rules.

I have a record of fighting for fiscal responsibility. In 1985, I was one of the first Democrats—broke with my party. We balanced the budget in the '90s. We paid down the debt for two years.

And that's what we're going to do. We're going to protect Social Security. I will not privatize it. I will not cut the benefits. And we're going to be fiscally responsible. And we will take care of Social Security.

SCHIEFFER: Let me just stay on Social Security with a new question for Senator Kerry, because, Senator Kerry, you have just said you will not cut benefits.

Alan Greenspan, the chairman of the Federal Reserve, says there's no way that Social Security can pay retirees what we have promised them unless we recalibrate.

What he's suggesting, we're going to cut benefits or we're going to have to raise the retirement age. We may have to take some other reform. But if you've just said, you've promised no changes, does that mean you're just going to leave this as a problem, another problem for our children to solve?

KERRY: Not at all. Absolutely not, Bob. This is the same thing we heard —remember, I appeared on "Meet the Press" with Tim Russert in 1990-something. We heard the same thing. We fixed it.

In fact, we put together a $5.6 trillion surplus in the '90s that was for the purpose of saving Social Security. If you take the tax cut that the president of the United States has given—President Bush gave to Americans in the top 1 percent of America—just that tax cut that went to the top 1 percent of America would have saved Social Security until the year 2075.

The president decided to give it to the wealthiest Americans in a tax cut. Now, Alan Greenspan, who I think has done a terrific job in monetary policy, supports the president's tax cut. I don't. I support it for the middle class, not that part of it that goes to people earning more than $200,000 a year.

And when I roll it back and we invest in the things that I have talked about to move our economy, we're going to grow sufficiently, it would begin to cut the deficit in half, and we get back to where we were at the end of the 1990s when we balanced the budget and paid down the debt of this country.

Now, we can do that.

Now, if later on after a period of time we find that Social Security is in trouble, we'll pull together the top experts of the country. We'll do exactly what we did in the 1990s. And we'll make whatever adjustment is necessary.

But the first and most important thing is to start creating jobs in America. The jobs the president is creating pay $9,000 less than the jobs that we're losing. And this is the first president in 72 years to preside over an economy in America that has lost jobs, 1.6 million jobs.

Eleven other presidents—six Democrats and five Republicans—had wars, had recessions, had great difficulties; none of them lost jobs the way this president has.

I have a plan to put America back to work. And if we're fiscally responsible and put America back to work, we're going to fix Social Security.

SCHIEFFER: Mr. President?

BUSH: He forgot to tell you he voted to tax Social Security benefits more than one time. I didn't hear any plan to fix Social Security. I heard more of the same.

He talks about middle-class tax cuts. That's exactly where the tax cuts went. Most of the tax cuts went to low- and middle-income Americans. And now the tax code is more fair. Twenty percent of the upper-income people pay about 80 percent of the taxes in America today because of how we structured the tax cuts. People listening out there know the benefits of the tax cuts we passed. If you have a child, you got tax relief. If you're married, you got tax relief. If you pay any tax at all, you got tax relief. All of which was opposed by my opponent.

And the tax relief was important to spur consumption and investment to get us out of this recession.

People need to remember: Six months prior to my arrival, the stock market started to go down. And it was one of the largest declines in our history. And then we had a recession and we got attacked, which cost us 1 million jobs.

But we acted. I led the Congress. We passed tax relief. And now this economy is growing. We added 1.9 million new jobs over the last 13 months.

Sure, there's more work to do. But the way to make sure our economy grows is not to raise taxes on small-business owners. It's not to increase the scope of the federal government. It's to make sure we have fiscal sanity and keep taxes low.

SCHIEFFER: Let's go to a new question, Mr. President.

I got more e-mail this week on this question than any other question. And it is about immigration.

I'm told that at least 8,000 people cross our borders illegally every day. Some people believe this is a security issue, as you know. Some believe it's an economic issue. Some see it as a human-rights issue.

How do you see it? And what do we need to do about it?

BUSH: I see it as a serious problem. I see it as a security issue, I see it as an economic issue, and I see it as a human-rights issue.

We're increasing the border security of the United States. We've got 1,000 more Border Patrol agents on the southern border.

We're using new equipment. We're using unmanned vehicles to spot people coming across.

And we'll continue to do so over the next four years. It's a subject I'm very familiar with. After all, I was a border governor for a while.

Many people are coming to this country for economic reasons. They're coming here to work. If you can make 50 cents in the heart of Mexico, for example, or make $5 here in America, $5.15, you're going to come here if you're worth your salt, if you want to put food on the table for your families. And that's what's happening.

And so in order to take pressure off the borders, in order to make the borders more secure, I believe there ought to be a temporary worker card that allows a willing worker and a willing employer to mate up, so long as there's not an American willing to do that job, to join up in order to be able to fulfill the employers' needs.

That has the benefit of making sure our employers aren't breaking the law as they try to fill their workforce needs. It makes sure that the people coming across the border are humanely treated, that they're not kept in the shadows of our society, that they're able to go back and forth to see their families. See, the card, it'll have a period of time attached to it.

It also means it takes pressure off the border. If somebody is coming here to work with a card, it means they're not going to have to sneak across the border. It means our border patrol will be more likely to be able to focus on doing their job.

Now, it's very important for our citizens to also know that I don't believe we ought to have amnesty. I don't think we ought to reward illegal behavior. There are plenty of people standing in line to become a citizen. And we ought not to crowd these people ahead of them in line.

If they want to become a citizen, they can stand in line, too.

And here is where my opponent and I differ. In September 2003, he supported amnesty for illegal aliens.

SCHIEFFER: Time's up.
Senator?

KERRY: Let me just answer one part of the last question quickly, and then I'll come to immigration.

The American middle-class family isn't making it right now, Bob. And what the president said about the tax cuts has been wiped out by the increase in health care, the increase in gasoline, the increase in tuitions, the increase in prescription drugs.

The fact is, the take-home pay of a typical American family as a share of national income is lower than it's been since 1929. And the take-home pay of the richest .1 percent of Americans is the highest it's been since 1928.

Under President Bush, the middle class has seen their tax burden go up and the wealthiest's tax burden has gone down. Now that's wrong.

Now, with respect to immigration reform, the president broke his promise on immigration reform. He said he would reform it. Four years later he is now promising another plan.

Here's what I'll do: Number one, the borders are more leaking today than they were before 9/11. The fact is, we haven't done what we need to do to toughen up our borders, and I will.

Secondly, we need a guest-worker program, but if it's all we have, it's not going to solve the problem.

The second thing we need is to crack down on illegal hiring. It's against the law in the United States to hire people illegally, and we ought to be enforcing that law properly.

And thirdly, we need an earned-legalization program for people who have been here for a long time, stayed out of trouble, got a job, paid their taxes, and their kids are American. We got to start moving them toward full citizenship, out of the shadows.

SCHIEFFER: Do you want to respond, Mr. President?

BUSH: Well, to say that the borders are not as protected as they were prior to September the 11th shows he doesn't know the borders. They're much better protected today than they were when I was the governor of Texas.

We have much more manpower and much more equipment there.

He just doesn't understand how the borders work, evidently, to say that. That is an outrageous claim.

And we'll continue to protect our borders. We're continuing to increase manpower and equipment.

SCHIEFFER: Senator?

KERRY: Four thousand people a day are coming across the border.

The fact is that we now have people from the Middle East, allegedly, coming across the border.

And we're not doing what we ought to do in terms of the technology. We have iris-identification technology. We have thumbprint, fingerprint technology today. We can know who the people are, that they're really the people they say they are when they cross the border.

We could speed it up. There are huge delays.

The fact is our borders are not as secure as they ought to be, and I'll make them secure.

SCHIEFFER: Next question to you, Senator Kerry.

The gap between rich and poor is growing wider. More people are dropping into poverty. Yet the minimum wage has been stuck at, what, $5.15 an hour now for about seven years. Is it time to raise it?

KERRY: Well, I'm glad you raised that question.

It's long overdue time to raise the minimum wage.

And, America, this is one of those issues that separates the president and myself.

We have fought to try to raise the minimum wage in the last years. But the Republican leadership of the House and Senate won't even let us have a vote on it. We're not allowed to vote on it. They don't want to raise the minimum wage. The minimum wage is the lowest minimum wage value it has been in our nation in 50 years.

If we raise the minimum wage, which I will do over several years to $7 an hour, 9.2 million women who are trying to raise their families would earn another $3,800 a year.

The president has denied 9.2 million women $3,800 a year, but he doesn't hesitate to fight for $136,000 to a millionaire.

One percent of America got $89 billion last year in a tax cut, but people working hard, playing by the rules, trying to take care of their kids, family values, that we're supposed to value so much in America—I'm tired of politicians who talk about family values and don't value families.

What we need to do is raise the minimum wage. We also need to hold on to equal pay. Women work for 76 cents on the dollar for the same work that men do. That's not right in America.

And we had an initiative that we were working on to raise women's pay. They've cut it off. They've stopped it. They don't enforce these kinds of things.

Now, I think that it's a matter of fundamental right that if we raise the minimum wage, 15 million Americans would be positively affected. We'd put money into the hands of people who work hard, who obey the rules, who play for the American dream.

And if we did that, we'd have more consumption ability in America, which is what we need right now in order to kick our economy into gear. I will fight tooth and nail to pass the minimum wage.

BUSH: Actually, Mitch McConnell had a minimum-wage plan that I supported that would have increased the minimum wage.

But let me talk about what's really important for the worker you're referring to. And that's to make sure the education system works. It's to make sure we raise standards.

Listen, the No Child Left Behind Act is really a jobs act when you think about it. The No Child Left Behind Act says, "We'll raise standards. We'll increase federal spending. But in return for extra spending, we now want people to measure—states and local jurisdictions to measure to show us whether or not a child can read or write or add and subtract."

You cannot solve a problem unless you diagnose the problem. And we weren't diagnosing problems. And therefore just kids were being shuffled through the school.

And guess who would get shuffled through? Children whose parents wouldn't speak English as a first language just move through.

Many inner-city kids just move through. We've stopped that practice now by measuring early. And when we find a problem, we spend extra money to correct it.

I remember a lady in Houston, Texas, told me, "Reading is the new civil right," and she's right. In order to make sure people have jobs for the 21st century, we've got to get it right in the education system, and we're beginning to close a minority achievement gap now.

You see, we'll never be able to compete in the 21st century unless we have an education system that doesn't quit on children, an education system that raises standards, an education that makes sure there's excellence in every classroom.

SCHIEFFER: Mr. President, I want to go back to something Senator Kerry said earlier tonight and ask a follow-up of my own. He said—and this will be a new question to you—he said that you had never said whether you would like to overturn *Roe v. Wade*. So I'd ask you directly, would you like to?

BUSH: What he's asking me is, will I have a litmus test for my judges? And the answer is, no, I will not have a litmus test. I will pick judges who will interpret the Constitution, but I'll have no litmus test.

SCHIEFFER: Senator Kerry, you'd like to respond?

KERRY: Is that a new question or a 30-second question?

SCHIEFFER: That's a new question for Senator—for President Bush.

KERRY: Which time limit ...

SCHIEFFER: You have 90 seconds.

KERRY: Thank you very much.
Well, again, the president didn't answer the question.
I'll answer it straight to America. I'm not going to appoint a judge to the Court who's going to undo a constitutional right, whether it's the First Amendment, or the Fifth Amendment, or some other right that's given under our courts today—under the Constitution. And I believe that the right of choice is a constitutional right.

So I don't intend to see it undone.

Clearly, the president wants to leave in ambivalence or intends to undo it.

But let me go a step further. We have a long distance yet to travel in terms of fairness in America. I don't know how you can govern in this country when you look at New York City and you see that 50 percent of the black males there are unemployed, when you see 40 percent of Hispanic children—of black children in some cities—dropping out of high school.

And yet the president who talks about No Child Left Behind refused to fully fund—by $28 billion—that particular program so you can make a difference in the lives of those young people.

Now right here in Arizona, that difference would have been $131 million to the state of Arizona to help its kids be able to have better education and to lift the property tax burden from its citizens. The president reneged on his promise to fund No Child Left Behind.

He'll tell you he's raised the money, and he has. But he didn't put in what he promised, and that makes a difference in the lives of our children.

SCHIEFFER: Yes, sir?

BUSH: Two things. One, he clearly has a litmus test for his judges, which I disagree with.

And secondly, only a liberal senator from Massachusetts would say that a 49 percent increase in funding for education was not enough.

We've increased funds. But more importantly, we've reformed the system to make sure that we solve problems early, before they're too late.

He talked about the unemployed. Absolutely we've got to make sure they get educated.

He talked about children whose parents don't speak English as a first language? Absolutely we've got to make sure they get educated.

And that's what the No Child Left Behind Act does.

SCHIEFFER: Senator?

KERRY: You don't measure it by a percentage increase. Mr. President, you measure it by whether you're getting the job done.

Five hundred thousand kids lost after-school programs because of your budget.

Now, that's not in my gut. That's not in my value system, and certainly not so that the wealthiest people in America can walk away with another tax cut.

$89 billion last year to the top 1 percent of Americans, but kids lost their after-school programs. You be the judge.

SCHIEFFER: All right, let's go to another question. And it is to Senator Kerry.

You have two minutes, sir.

Senator, the last debate, President Bush said he did not favor a draft. You agreed with him. But our National Guard and Reserve forces are being severely strained because many of them are being held beyond their enlistments. Some of them say that it's a back-door draft.

Is there any relief that could be offered to these brave Americans and their families?

If you became president, Senator Kerry, what would you do about this situation of holding National Guard and Reservists for these extended periods of time and these repeated call-ups that they're now facing?

KERRY: Well, I think the fact that they're facing these repeated call-ups, some of them two and three deployments, and there's a stop- loss policy that prevents people from being able to get out when their time was up, is a reflection of the bad judgment this president exercised in how he has engaged in the world and deployed our forces.

Our military is overextended. Nine out of 10 active-duty Army divisions are either in Iraq, going to Iraq or have come back from Iraq. One way or the other, they're wrapped up in it.

Now, I've proposed adding two active-duty divisions to the armed forces of the United States—one combat, one support.

In addition, I'm going to double the number of Special Forces so that we can fight a more effective war on terror, with less pressure on the National Guard and Reserve. And what I would like to do is see the National Guard and Reserve be deployed differently here in our own country. There's much we can do with them with respect to homeland security. We ought to be doing that. And that would relieve an enormous amount of pressure.

But the most important thing to relieve the pressure on all of the armed forces is frankly to run a foreign policy that recognizes that America is strongest when we are working with real alliances, when we are sharing the burdens of the world by working through our statesmanship at the highest levels and our diplomacy to bring other nations to our side.

I've said it before, I say it again: I believe the president broke faith to the American people in the way that he took this nation to war. He said he would work through a real alliance. He said in Cincinnati we would plan carefully, we would take every precaution. Well, we didn't. And the result is our forces today are overextended.

The fact is that he did not choose to go to war as a last result. And America now is paying, already $120 billion, up to $200 billion before we're finished and much more probably. And that is the result of this president taking his eye off of Osama bin Laden.

SCHIEFFER: Mr. President?

BUSH: The best way to take the pressure off our troops is to succeed in Iraq, is to train Iraqis so they can do the hard work of democracy, is to give them a chance to defend their country, which is precisely what we're doing. We'll have 125,000 troops trained by the end of this year.

I remember going on an airplane in Bangor, Maine, to say thanks to the reservists and Guard that were headed overseas from Tennessee and North Carolina, Georgia. Some of them had been there before.

The people I talked to their spirits were high. They didn't view their service as a back-door draft. They viewed their service as an opportunity to serve their country.

My opponent, the senator, talks about foreign policy.

In our first debate he proposed America pass a global test. In order to defend ourselves, we'd have to get international approval. That's one of the major differences we have about defending our country.

I'll work with allies. I'll work with friends. We'll continue to build strong coalitions. But I will never turn over our national- security decisions to leaders of other countries.

We'll be resolute, we'll be strong, and we'll wage a comprehensive war against the terrorists.

SCHIEFFER: Senator?

KERRY: I have never suggested a test where we turn over our security to any nation. In fact, I've said the opposite: I will never turn the security of the United States over to any nation. No nation will ever have a veto over us.

But I think it makes sense, I think most Americans in their guts know, that we ought to pass a sort of truth standard. That's how you gain legitimacy with your own country people, and that's how you gain legitimacy in the world.

But I'll never fail to protect the United States of America.

BUSH: In 1990, there was a vast coalition put together to run Saddam Hussein out of Kuwait. The international community, the international world said this is the right thing to do, but when it came time to authorize the use of force on the Senate floor, my opponent voted against the use of force.

Apparently you can't pass any test under his vision of the world.

SCHIEFFER: Mr. President, new question, two minutes.

You said that if Congress would vote to extend the ban on assault weapons, that you'd sign the legislation, but you did nothing to encourage the Congress to extend it. Why not?

BUSH: Actually, I made my intentions—made my views clear. I did think we ought to extend the assault weapons ban, and was told the fact that the bill was never going to move, because Republicans and Democrats were against the assault weapon ban, people of both parties. I believe law-abiding citizens ought to be able to own a gun. I believe in background checks at gun shows or anywhere to make sure that guns don't get in the hands of people that shouldn't have them.

But the best way to protect our citizens from guns is to prosecute those who commit crimes with guns. And that's why early in my administration I called the attorney general and the U.S. attorneys and said: Put together a task force all around the country to prosecute those who commit crimes with guns. And the prosecutions are up by about 68 percent—I believe—is the number.

Neighborhoods are safer when we crack down on people who commit crimes with guns.

To me, that's the best way to secure America.

SCHIEFFER: Senator?

KERRY: I believe it was a failure of presidential leadership not to reauthorize the assault weapons ban.

I am a hunter. I'm a gun owner. I've been a hunter since I was a kid, 12, 13 years old. And I respect the Second Amendment and I will not tamper with the Second Amendment.

But I'll tell you this. I'm also a former law enforcement officer. I ran one of the largest district attorney's offices in America, one of the ten largest. I put people behind bars for the rest of their life. I've broken up organized crime. I know something about prosecuting.

And most of the law enforcement agencies in America wanted that assault weapons ban. They don't want to go into a drug bust and be facing an AK-47.

I was hunting in Iowa last year with a sheriff from one of the counties there, and he pointed to a house in back of us, and said, "See the house over? We just did a drug bust a week earlier, and the guy we arrested had an AK-47 lying on the bed right beside him."

Because of the president's decision today, law enforcement officers will walk into a place that will be more dangerous. Terrorists can now come into America and go to a gun show and, without even a background check, buy an assault weapon today.

And that's what Osama bin Laden's handbook said, because we captured it in Afghanistan. It encouraged them to do it.

So I believe America's less safe.

If Tom DeLay or someone in the House said to me, "Sorry, we don't have the votes," I'd have said, "Then we're going to have a fight."

And I'd have taken it out to the country and I'd have had every law enforcement officer in the country visit those congressmen. We'd have won what Bill Clinton won.

SCHIEFFER: Let's go to a new question. For you, Senator Kerry, two minutes.

Affirmative action: Do you see a need for affirmative action programs, or have we moved far enough along that we no longer need to use race and gender as a factor in school admissions and federal and state contracts and so on?

KERRY: No, Bob, regrettably, we have not moved far enough along.

And I regret to say that this administration has even blocked steps that could help us move further along. I'll give you an example.

I served on the Small Business Committee for a long time. I was chairman of it once. Now I'm the senior Democrat on it. We used to—you know, we have a goal there for minority set-aside programs, to try to encourage ownership in the country. They don't reach those goals. They don't even fight to reach those goals. They've tried to undo them.

The fact is that in too many parts of our country, we still have discrimination. And affirmative action is not just something that applies to people of color. Some people have a mistaken view of it in America. It also is with respect to women, it's with respect to other efforts to try to reach out and be inclusive in our country.

I think that we have a long way to go, regrettably. If you look at what's happened—we've made progress, I want to say that at the same time.

During the Clinton years, as you may recall, there was a fight over affirmative action. And there were many people, like myself, who opposed quotas, who felt there were places where it was overreaching. So we had a policy called "Mend it, don't end it." We fixed it.

And we fixed it for a reason: because there are too many people still in this country who feel the stark resistance of racism, and so we have a distance to travel. As president, I will make certain we travel it.

Now, let me just share something. This president is the first president ever, I think, not to meet with the NAACP. This is a president who hasn't met with the Black Congressional Caucus. This is a president who has not met with the civil rights leadership of our country.

If a president doesn't reach out and bring people in and be inclusive, then how are we going to get over those barriers? I see that as part of my job as president, and I'll make my best effort to do it.

SCHIEFFER: Mr. President?

BUSH: Well, first of all, it is just not true that I haven't met with the Black Congressional Caucus. I met with the Black Congressional Caucus at the White House.

And secondly, like my opponent, I don't agree we ought to have quotas. I agree, we shouldn't have quotas.

But we ought to have an aggressive effort to make sure people are educated, to make sure when they get out of high school there's Pell Grants available for them, which is what we've done. We've expanded Pell Grants by a million students.

Do you realize today in America, we spend $73 billion to help 10 million low- and middle-income families better afford college?

That's the access I believe is necessary, is to make sure every child learns to read, write, add and subtract early, to be able to build on that education by going to college so they can start their careers with a college diploma.

I believe the best way to help our small businesses is not only through small-business loans, which we have increased since I've been the president of the United States, but to unbundle government contracts so people have a chance to be able to bid and receive a contract to help get their business going.

Minority ownership of businesses are up, because we created an environment for the entrepreneurial spirit to be strong.

I believe part of a hopeful society is one in which somebody owns something. Today in America more minorities own a home than ever before. And that's hopeful, and that's positive.

SCHIEFFER: Mr. President, let's go to a new question.

You were asked before the invasion, or after the invasion, of Iraq if you'd checked with your dad. And I believe, I don't remember the quote exactly, but I believe you said you had checked with a higher authority.

I would like to ask you, what part does your faith play on your policy decisions?

BUSH: First, my faith plays a lot—a big part in my life. And that's, when I was answering that question, what I was really saying to the person was that I pray a lot. And I do.

And my faith is a very—it's very personal. I pray for strength. I pray for wisdom. I pray for our troops in harm's way. I pray for my family. I pray for my little girls.

But I'm mindful in a free society that people can worship if they want to or not. You're equally an American if you choose to worship an almighty and if you choose not to.

If you're a Christian, Jew, or Muslim, you're equally an American. That's the great thing about America, is the right to worship the way you see fit.

Prayer and religion sustain me. I receive calmness in the storms of the presidency.

I love the fact that people pray for me and my family all around the country. Somebody asked me one time, "Well, how do you know?" I said, "I just feel it."

Religion is an important part. I never want to impose my religion on anybody else.

But when I make decisions, I stand on principle, and the principles are derived from who I am.

I believe we ought to love our neighbor like we love ourself, as manifested in public policy through the faith-based initiative where we've unleashed the armies of compassion to help heal people who hurt.

I believe that God wants everybody to be free. That's what I believe.

And that's been part of my foreign policy. In Afghanistan, I believe that the freedom there is a gift from the Almighty. And I can't tell you how encouraged I am to see freedom on the march.

And so my principles that I make decisions on are a part of me, and religion is a part of me.

SCHIEFFER: Senator Kerry?

KERRY: Well, I respect everything that the president has said and certainly respect his faith. I think it's important and I share it. I think that he just said that freedom is a gift from the Almighty.

Everything is a gift from the Almighty. And as I measure the words of the Bible—and we all do; different people measure different things—the Koran, the Torah, or, you know, Native Americans who gave me a blessing the other day had their own special sense of connectedness to a higher being. And people all find their ways to express it.

I was taught—I went to a church school and I was taught that the two greatest commandments are: Love the Lord, your God, with all your mind, your body and your soul, and love your neighbor as yourself. And frankly, I think we have a lot more loving of our neighbor to do in this country and on this planet.

We have a separate and unequal school system in the United States of America. There's one for the people who have, and there's one for the people who don't have. And we're struggling with that today.

And the president and I have a difference of opinion about how we live out our sense of our faith.

I talked about it earlier when I talked about the works and faith without works being dead.

I think we've got a lot more work to do. And as president, I will always respect everybody's right to practice religion as they choose—or not to practice—because that's part of America.

SCHIEFFER: Senator Kerry, after 9/11—and this is a new question for you—it seemed to me that the country came together as I've never seen it come together since World War II. But some of that seems to have melted away. I think it's fair to say we've become pretty polarized, perhaps because of the political season.

But if you were elected president, or whoever is elected president, will you set a priority in trying to bring the nation back together? Or what would be your attitude on that?

KERRY: Very much so.

Let me pay a compliment to the president, if I may. I think in those days after 9/11, I thought the president did a terrific job. And I really was moved, as well as impressed, by the speech that he gave to the Congress.

And I think the hug Tom Daschle gave him at that moment was about as genuine a sense of there being no Democrats, no Republicans, we were all just Americans. That's where we were.

That's not where we are today. I regret to say that the president who called himself a uniter, not a divider, is now presiding over the most divided America in the recent memory of our country. I've never seen such ideological squabbles in the Congress of the United States. I've never seen members of a party locked out of meetings the way they're locked out today.

We have to change that. And as president, I am committed to changing that. I don't care if the idea comes from the other side or this side. I think we have to come together and work to change it.

And I've done that. Over 20 years in the United States Senate, I've worked with John McCain, who's sitting here, I've worked with other colleagues. I've reached across the aisle. I've tried to find the common ground, because that's what makes us strong as Americans.

And if Americans trust me with the presidency, I can pledge to you, we will have the most significant effort, openly—not secret meetings in the White House with special interests, not ideologically driven efforts to push people aside—but a genuine effort to try to restore America's hope and possibilities by bringing people together.

And one of the ways we're going to do it is, I'm going to work with my friend, John McCain, to further campaign finance reform so we get these incredible amounts of money out of the system and open it up to average people, so America is really represented by the people who make up America.

SCHIEFFER: Mr. President?

BUSH: My biggest disappointment in Washington is how partisan the town is. I had a record of working with Republicans and Democrats as the governor of Texas, and I was hopeful I'd be able to do the same thing.

And we made good progress early on. The No Child Left Behind Act, incredibly enough, was good work between me and my administration and people like Senator Ted Kennedy.

And we worked together with Democrats to relieve the tax burden on the middle class and all who pay taxes in order to make sure this economy continues to grow.

But Washington is a tough town. And the way I view it is there's a lot of entrenched special interests there, people who are, you know, on one side of the issue or another and they spend enormous sums of money and they convince different senators to taut their way or different congressmen to talk about their issue, and they dig in.

I'll continue, in the four years, to continue to try to work to do so.

My opponent said this is a bitterly divided time. Pretty divided in the 2000 election. So in other words, it's pretty divided during the 1990s as well.

We're just in a period—we've got to work to bring it—my opponent keeps mentioning John McCain, and I'm glad he did. John McCain is for me for president because he understands I have the right view in winning the war on terror and that my plan will succeed in Iraq. And my opponent has got a plan of retreat and defeat in Iraq.

SCHIEFFER: We've come, gentlemen, to our last question. And it occurred to me as I came to this debate tonight that the three of us share something. All three of us are surrounded by very strong women. We're all married to strong women. Each of us have two daughters that make us very proud.

I'd like to ask each of you, what is the most important thing you've learned from these strong women?

BUSH: To listen to them.
(LAUGHTER)
To stand up straight and not scowl.
(LAUGHTER)
I love the strong women around me. I can't tell you how much I love my wife and our daughters.

I am—you know it's really interesting. I tell the people on the campaign trail, when I asked Laura to marry me, she said, "Fine, just so long as I never have to give a speech." I said, "OK, you've got a deal." Fortunately, she didn't hold me to that deal. And she's out campaigning along with our girls. And she speaks English a lot better than I do. I think people understand what she's saying.

But they see a compassionate, strong, great first lady in Laura Bush. I can't tell you how lucky I am. When I met her in the backyard at Joe and Jan O'Neill's in Midland, Texas, it was the classic backyard barbecue. O'Neill said, "Come on over. I think you'll find somebody who might interest you." So I said all right. Bopped over there. There was only four of us there. And not only did she interest me, I guess you would say it was love at first sight.

SCHIEFFER: Senator Kerry?

KERRY: Well, I guess the president and you and I are three examples of lucky people who married up.
(LAUGHTER)
And some would say maybe me more so than others.

(LAUGHTER)

But I can take it.

(LAUGHTER)

Can I say, if I could just say a word about a woman that you didn't ask about, but my mom passed away a couple years ago, just before I was deciding to run. And she was in the hospital, and I went in to talk to her and tell her what I was thinking of doing.

And she looked at me from her hospital bed and she just looked at me and she said, "Remember: integrity, integrity, integrity." Those are the three words that she left me with.

And my daughters and my wife are people who just are filled with that sense of what's right, what's wrong.

They also kick me around. They keep me honest. They don't let me get away with anything. I can sometimes take myself too seriously. They surely don't let me do that.

And I'm blessed, as I think the president is blessed, as I said last time. I've watched him with the first lady, who I admire a great deal, and his daughters. He's a great father. And I think we're both very lucky.

SCHIEFFER: Well, gentlemen, that brings us to the closing statements. Senator Kerry, I believe you're first.

KERRY: My fellow Americans, as you heard from Bob Schieffer a moment ago, America is being tested by division. More than ever, we need to be united as a country.

And, like Franklin Roosevelt, I don't care whether an idea is a Republican idea or a Democrat idea. I just care whether it works for America and whether it's going to make us stronger.

These are dangerous times. I believe I offer tested, strong leadership that can calm the waters of the troubled world. And I believe that we can together do things that are within the grasp of Americans.

We can lift our schools up. We can create jobs that pay more than the jobs we're losing overseas. We can have health care for all Americans. We can further the cause of equality in our nation.

Let me just make it clear: I will never allow any country to have a veto over our security. Just as I fought for our country as a young man, with the same passion I will fight to defend this nation that I love.

And, with faith in God and with conviction in the mission of America, I believe that we can reach higher. I believe we can do better.

I think the greatest possibilities of our country, our dreams and our hopes, are out there just waiting for us to grab onto them. And I ask you to embark on that journey with me.

I ask you for your trust. I ask you for your help. I ask you to allow me the privilege of leading this great nation of ours, of helping us to be stronger here at home and to be respected again in the world and, most of all, to be safer forever.

Thank you. Goodnight. And God bless the United States of America.

SCHIEFFER: Mr. President?

BUSH: In the Oval Office, there's a painting by a friend of Laura and mine named—by Tom Lee. And it's a West Texas painting, a painting of a mountain scene.

And he said this about it.

He said, "Sarah and I live on the east side of the mountain. It's the sunrise side, not the sunset side. It's the side to see the day that is coming, not to see the day that is gone."

I love the optimism in that painting, because that's how I feel about America. And we've been through a lot together during the last 33/4 years. We've come through a recession, a stock market decline, an attack on our country.

And yet, because of the hard work of the American people and good policies, this economy is growing. Over the next four years, we'll make sure the economy continues to grow.

We reformed our school system, and now there's an achievement gap in America that's beginning to close. Over the next four years, we'll continue to insist on excellence in every classroom in America so that our children have a chance to realize the great promise of America.

Over the next four years, we'll continue to work to make sure health care is available and affordable.

Over the next four years, we'll continue to rally the armies of compassion, to help heal the hurt that exists in some of our country's neighborhoods.

I'm optimistic that we'll win the war on terror, but I understand it requires firm resolve and clear purpose. We must never waver in the face of this enemy that—these ideologues of hate.

And as we pursue the enemy wherever it exists, we'll also spread freedom and liberty. We got great faith in the ability of liberty to transform societies, to convert a hostile world to a peaceful world.

My hope for America is a prosperous America, a hopeful America and a safer world.

I want to thank you for listening tonight.

I'm asking for your vote.

God bless you.

SCHIEFFER: Thank you, Mr. President.

Thank you, Senator Kerry.

Well, that brings these debates to a close, but the campaign goes on.

I want to wish both of you the very best of luck between now and Election Day.

That's it for us from Arizona State University in Tempe, Arizona. I'm Bob Schieffer at CBS News.

Goodnight, everyone.

(APPLAUSE)

EXERCISES

1. Prepare a flow sheet of the presidential debate between Senator John Kerry and President George W. Bush. On what issues did the most substantive clash occur? What arguments were "dropped" by either debater? You may wish to listen to the debate by visiting www.c-span.org.

2. Identify the most important issues addressed by the candidates. Which candidate won the debates on each (be sure to justify your evaluations)?

3. Which debater made the best opening statement? Which made the best closing statement? Justify your evaluation.

4. Based on your analysis of the arguments as presented, which candidate won the whole debate? Why?

5. If available in your library, view the following videotape: *Debating Our Destiny: 40 Years of Presidential Debate,* MacNeil/Lehrer Productions in association with the Commission on Presidential Debates, WETA, and Thirteen/WNET. Washington, D.C.: MacNeil/Lehrer Productions, Alexandria, VA: Distributed by PBS Video, © 2000. Or read the transcript of the program at http://www.pbs.org/newshour/debatingourdestiny/dod_full_transcript.html.

6. In what ways did Bush and Gore seem to have learned from their predecessors? Did Vice President Gore seem to have learned from his previous debates (as the vice-presidential candidate)?

7. In what ways was the third 2004 Presidential Debate between Bush and Kerry like an academic debate? In what ways was it different? Would a different format have created a better debate? In what ways? Why?

8. Visit the following websites:

    The History of Televised Presidential Debates
    http://www.museum.tv/debateweb/html/index.htm

    Commission on Presidential Debates
    http://www.debates.org/

    Create a time line tracing the history of presidential campaign debates. Note significant occurrences on the time line.

9. In 2000, Ralph Nader, the Green Party candidate for president, was not invited by the Commission on Presidential Debates to participate in the presidential debates. Should the standard for participation in presidential debates be reconsidered to include third-party candidates? Write an essay defending your answer. You may wish to visit: Open Debates: http://opendebates.org/

10. If you had been able to coach Senator Kerry or President Bush prior to their third presidential debate in 2004, how would you have advised them to change their argumentation on any of the issues raised? Prepare a briefing book to guide the candidate debaters (for an example, visit http://www.heritage.org/research/features/issues/).

11. Create a debate at Generation Engage, www.generationengage.org.

12. Prepare a question for a YouTube debate.

Appendix B

National Championship
Debate

The debate presented here is an example of contemporary intercollegiate debate. The debaters, at the time they participated in this debate, were about the age of the average college student. The composition and delivery of the speeches in these debates and the exchanges in cross-examination are characteristics of intercollegiate tournament debate. Citations of evidence and authorities are, of course, subject to the usual omissions and errors of the extemporaneous methods. Even presidential candidates—as may be seen in Appendix A—make occasional errors under the pressure of debate. In studying these debates, it should be remembered that many of the classical models of the great argumentative "speeches" are not verbatim transcripts of the speech. The "text" of Patrick Henry's famous "Liberty or Death" speech, for example, was actually written by Henry's biographer, Wirt, some 50 years after Henry gave the speech.

As you read the text of this debate, you may wonder whether the documentation of much of the evidence is so minimal that it falls below the desideratum for the argumentation speech. The level of documentation is below the acceptable level for general argumentation. Yet, as we saw in our consideration of judicial notice in Chapter 6, this type of documentation is often acceptable in the final round of an academic tournament debate, as it was to the panel of judges for this debate.

The explanation is simple: The students were adapting to the highly specialized audience found in the final round of a national tournament. The four debaters, the panel of judges, and the debaters in the audience who had participated in the previous rounds of the tournament were all knowledgeable about the available evidence. All of them had researched the subject for months; a considerable body of evidence was common knowledge in the forensics community. To this specialized audience, a brief reference was enough to establish much of the evidence.

Time is precious in a debate. Given the choice between citing four pieces of evidence incompletely or two pieces of evidence completely, the experienced debater in this situation would take the risk of incomplete citation. The "in-group," the experienced judges and debaters, would understand why the choice was made and, for better or worse, would accept it in this situation.

This premium on time, as may be seen in this verbatim transcript, sometimes causes the debater to use fractured language or to fail to provide the audience with referents for the points being made. Note, however, that the debaters are aware of these problems and do provide headlining for both their main arguments and their substructure (see Chapter 15).

The following debate was presented in the final round of the Tenth National CEDA debate tournament.* The proposition for debate was, "Resolved: That the United States should significantly increase the development of the earth's ocean resources." The decision was 5–2 for the affirmative.

1995 CEDA FINAL ROUND TRANSCRIPT

First Affirmative Constructive
Jason Trice, Michigan State University

I am very honored to be here today. There are several people I'd like to thank. The first is I'd like to thank Mr. Duke, Mr. Larson, and Mr. Miller and the rest of the CEDA organization and the co—and the tab room staff. They ran an excellent tournament. The 2nd person I'd like to thank is Biza. She—all I can say is she rocks. Without her I probably wouldn't be here. We probably wouldn't have any cards and she has a lot of foresight in rounds. The next person I'd like to thank is ah Sean Lemoine. I was on the squad with him for three years and now he's my coach for all that's worth. And more importantly than that, he's one of my best friends he ah even though he's a redneck from Louisiana. [Laughter] The next person I'd like to thank is Dave Devereaux. I hated him because he was such a jerk in rounds when I debated him, but I've gotten to know him a little bit better this year and I really like him. He's —his coaching advice is wonderful. I'd like to thank Jim Roper. He's only got our interests at heart, that's what he's concerned with, and besides, he likes Metallica. He rocks. [Laughter] Next person, I'd like to thank the rest of our squad, John, Viking, Corn Dog, Will, and Marla. They all sacrificed a lot of sleep and probably their health to help us be prepared to get to this final round. I'd like to thank my former assistant coaches including Jon Dean and John Johnston. They—they're wonderful. I'd like to thank Martin Glendenning. I've known him forever. He's always been one of my best friends and he's been very supportive of me. And finally, I'd like to thank Todd Graham. Even though we don't speak very much and he probably hates my guts, a lot of his coaching advice I still use today as he will readily tell you. [Laughter]

Human excess has pushed the Earth's ocean resources to the brink of extinction; immediate action is necessary to save the bounty left on our seas.

Observation One: Fish stocks are nearly exhausted.

First, due to overfishing, stocks are on the brink and will collapse soon if action is not taken. Greenwire in '95:

> Global overfishing has reached the crisis point and many stocks will collapse unless countries cut back on fishing, according to the new UN Food and Agriculture Organization study. To maintain current per capita consumption levels as population increases, global production will have to rise over the next

*Republished with permission of Dr. Patrick Jablonski.

10 years. But officials warn this target will be difficult to meet. Over 70% of fish stocks are fully exploited, overexploited or rebuilding from the past. **(1AC#1)**

Moreover, the current system of open access fishing is not sustainable and will inevitably cause a fishery collapse. Weber explains in '94:

> Fisheries, regulators, and coastal communities are at a crossroads. If they continue on their current path, marine fisheries will continue to decline, millions of fisheries will lose their jobs, and coastal communities and low-income consumers will suffer disproportionately. If instead these groups combine forces to improve fishery management, the oceans can continue to yield fish—and economic and social benefits—for centuries to come. **(1AC#2)**

In order to correct the problems of the status quo, we present our plan. The US government, acting through the National Marine Fisheries Services, will change the current open access fishing to be replaced by a system of ITQs or Individual Transferable Quotas for fish research to determine a maximum sustainable yield or MSI—Y along with a total allowable catch or TAC will take place to determine the areas in which ITQs are economically and ecologically sound. Funding will be through normal means, which includes auction fees to purchase quotas. Enforcement will be through normal means. Our speeches will clarify our intent.

Our plan has two advantages. The first advantage is starvation.

Initially, fish are a primary source of protein for many southern nations; as their stocks deplete the risk of starvation for these nations rises. First, fish provide fully half of the protein consumed around the world and are at risk of disappearing. The *Houston Chronicle* in 1994:

> Fish and other food sources from the sea make up more than 50 percent of the animal protein consumed worldwide. Yet, once the plentiful oceans seem to be yielding less and less, posing a threat to the future. Stocks of some fish have dwindled, dwindled greatly in the past 20 years. **(1AC#3)**

The next argument is depletion of fish stocks will coincide with massive increases in population and decreases in food production; a food crisis is more imminent. The *Sunday Telegraph* on January 29th of 1995:

> The world's fish stocks, some of the most important food resources, are being overfished at an alarming rate, raising the specter of increased food shortages. Falling catches are likely to coincide with increased strains on grain production, bringing higher prices, food crises, and potential social tensions. Some of the gloomiest findings come on the reporter's finding on the world's fish stocks. Once considered the poor person's protein, fish, is becoming expensive for consumers in industrialized countries, and some species that were once common in supermarkets are no longer readily available. **(1AC#4)**

As fish stocks increase—decrease globally, industrial countries are shifting to the southern nations to take their fishing, resulting in more starvation. Nickerson explains in 1994:

> Fish ranks one of the most important food resources of the Third World. But as fish stocks reach dangerous levels of depletion in nearly every sea and ocean in the world, fleets from the West and prosperous nations of Asia are hitting the

coastal waters of Africa, the Indian subcontinent and other poor regions as never before. The result is an increasing diversion of all the vital sources of protein from countries where it is desperately needed to nations to fish just one of the many available choices of food. Commercially harvested fisheries are increasingly moving away from people who need it the most. **(1AC#5)**

The impact of the loss of protein risks the lives of billions of people because of food scarcity. Wacker explains in 1994:

> Even the salt water laps the shore hundreds of millions **[FIVE]** of humans—a billion in Asia alone—rely on fish as their principal source of protein. What are we going to do when it all runs out? Not if but—Not if but when, unless the great fishing powers of the world abandon present practices that find, trap, suck up, and slaughter every fish within the reach of their technology. We must be remembered that we are dealing with fish that naturally ignore jurisdictional limits and, consequently, the competing rights and duties of coastal states and states that take these fish on the high seas. It is a delicate balance. Hanging in that balance are the lives and well-being of a large part of the earth's population. Just how serious it is underscored by a recent issue of the *New Scientist*: Virtually every fisher in the world has been criminally over-fished for years. You can run out of them. The world is doing just that. **(1AC#6)**

Scenario two is marine biodiversity.

Overfishing reduces the biodiversity of fish stocks which in turn threatens marine bio—biodiversity, risking human life. First, overfishing threatens fish stocks with extinction in two ways: First is it crushes genetic diversity and secondly it selectively removes certain species. Bohnsack explains eloquently in '93:

> Fishing can also reduce genetic diversity within a species, especially when a stock has the size greatly reduced from natural levels. Fishing depends on harvesting as a wild stock. Unlike animal husbandry, which protects animals with desirable characteristics from slaughter in order to breed future generations, fishing operates by removing the most desirable individuals from the breeding populations. Excessive mortality can alter genetics by selecting the individuals most that mature early and have a shorter life span, smaller adult sizes, and wary behavior. Although the species continue to exist, it may be less desirable and differ greatly from its original condition. Sustained fishing can also lead to the loss of diversity between species by selectively removing vulnerable species. Loss of certain species could cause unforeseen disruptions or permanent alterations to the ecosystem. Many species targeted by fishing are the top predators that can be critically important in regulating the marine ecosystem. **(1AC#7)**

The loss of marine biodiversity risks ocean health and the health of humanity along with it since the oceans are our primary support system. Gianni argues in '93:

> The oceans are a vulnerable and complex environment. Fish as well as many other unique and important species live or depend upon the ocean. The oceans are the plan—planet's primary life support system. They provide most of our oxygen, moisture and weather patterns. We count on the seas for food, recreation and commerce. Without healthy oceans, life as we know it would end. The long term health consequences of the ocean and the diverse forms of marine plant and animal life is critical to the life support of this planet. Of urgent concern **[THREE]** is the viability of living marine ecosystems and global food

security is the impact and the management in fishing in all areas of the world's ocean. **(1AC#8)**

Observation Two is solvency. ITQs or Individual Transferable Quotas solve overfishing by providing an economic incentive not to fish. First, ITQs are better than open access fishing since they give an incentive not to fish. Litz in '94:

> In the late 1970s, fishery economists began suggesting an alternative to the rigid regulatory approach embodied in the Magnuson Act. They suggested a system of quasi-property rights in the fishery. Allocating shares of the total availability catch in the fishery. Much of the tragedy of the fishery of the commons is eliminated. This solves the conservation problem. Such systems eliminate competition between fishermen because fishermen can only catch the fish which belong to them. Thus, a property rights system removes the problem of declining fish populations, since fish bring in collectively only those fish to which they are given rights. In addition, since property rights systems take the race out of fishing harvest, many of the economic problems are solved. Facing no competition for their allocated share of the fishery stock, fishermen are able to allocate their fishing efforts in the most cost-effective way. **(1AC#9)**

Second, ITQs cause sustainability, ending the race for fish. All empirical evidence proves this. Fujati and Hopkins explains in '94:

> There is very strong evidence that **[TWO]** ITQs reduce or eliminate the race for fish that has destroyed, and continues to destroy, fish populations and fishing profits all around the country. This syndrome has resulted in the absurdity of a forty-eight se—fishing season for halibut, with an intolerable cost in human lives, bycatch, ghost fishing from lost gear, and market gluts. By guaranteeing fishers a certain proportion of the TAC, ITQs eliminate the incentive to race and overcapitalize. ITQs have ended the race in most fisheries in which they have been used. In some cases, racing persisted to exploit the fish densities and market conditions, but it soon ended if fisheries were not penalized for leaving their part of their quotas unfished. The end of the race for fish should save lives, increase profits, reduce pressure on managers to set unsustainable TACs, reduce ghost fishing, and perhaps increase the survival rate for discarded fish by allowing fishers time to handle bycatch more carefully. **(1AC#10)**

Third, ITQs reduce the need for costly enforcement through market-based solutions. Litz explains in '94:

> Fourth, under an ITQ market system, proponents argue there is less need for government enforcement mechanism, a costly component of the fishery management. This assertion rests on the belief that ITQ system provides a sufficient economic **[ONE]** incentive for self-enforcement. Each ITQ holder has an incentive to report incidence of poaching, since poachers in some cases may endanger the ITQ holder's property. In the cases of allocation made in the percentages of TACs, ITQ holders stand to gain by protection of the long term growth of the fishery stocks from poachers. **(1AC#11)**

Actions by the United States are critical to securing the UN conference which comes for a vote this spring. The US mu—must adopt a strong conservation standard, compliance with international rules, and exercise leadership. Speer concludes in 1994:

> The UN negotiations **[FORTY]** began last year and will nego—and will with the goal of reaching in the Spring of 1995. The agreement that emerges from this process has had significant potential to improve the fisheries are managed around the world and to help ensure the integrity of ocean systems. For this goal to be realized however, major obstacles to reaching a strong, legal binding agreement must be overcome and the role of the US in both efforts will be key. If we urge the United States to take the following initiatives: Advocate the adoption of a strong conservation measure. Strong minimum conservation **[QUARTER]** standards are necessary to effectively address over-fishing, depletion, and the impacts on non-targeted species in their ecosystems. US leadership is required. Unresolved conflicts between nations over key issues continue to stand in the path of reaching an agreement. **[TIME]** Overcoming these hurdles will require vision and leadership on the part of the US and a clear signal that the US is serious about achieving a strong, binding global fishing regime that will considerable U—US leverage in the governments to come to an agreement will be essential. **(1AC#12)**

Cross Examination of the First Affirmative
Jason Trice, Michigan State University
Blake Dias, Gonzaga University

Dias: Okay. In the status quo, I'm sorry, the government doesn't want to do ITQs.

Trice: They're not doing them.

Dias: They're not doing them.

Trice: Right.

Dias: Okay. Your evidence, Speer card says that we need to have strong leadership at the conference.

Trice: Right.

Dias: ... the role of the US at the vote is key.

Trice: Right.

Dias: Right. Okay, what's the internal link between the plan, which you just have to fiat ...

Trice: Yes.

Dias: ... right now ITQs haven't and our ah people at the co—at the meeting have ...

Trice: We're taking, taking a leadership role.

Dias: ... a solid leadership role in trying to convince other nations.

Trice: We're taking the first step towards trying to solve the fishery problem I think that would select us for a leadership role ...

Dias: I understand ...

Trice: ... in fisheries.

Dias: ... I understand that we take our own role, but your evidence says that our role at the vote is key.

Trice: Yes.

Dias: I'm wondering, just because you fiat your plan ...

Trice: Well, the United States ...

Dias: ... how does that affect the delegates, the delegates ...

Trice: ... the United States is going to the vote regardless and we are going in and saying, "look we've already made these strong steps and we are taking a leadership position."

Dias: Okay, here's my next question, are delegates to this vote, are they in favor of the world, ah, this new world fishing regime now?

Trice: No—well, the evidence says the US is key to getting that passed.

Dias: That's not my question. Are the delegates at this vote in favor of the, of this new world fishing regime in the Status Quo.

Trice: I don't think so, my evidence says that ...

Dias: Okay ...

Trice: ... absent US leadership it wouldn't be passed.

Dias: If that is not the case, what about your plan is gonna change those delegates' mind? You just fiat the plan happens ...

Trice: We have US—we have US leadership, the biggest, most important country in the world goes ...

Dias: Not my question, not my question.

Trice: Okay, what's your question?

Dias: What changes the delegates' mind? Because your, the Speer evidence says that's ...

Trice: US leadership—that's what it says. It says US leadership is key to the passage of this conference and the reason is because we're taking the first step, we're showing ...

Dias: Okay, because the US just happened to pass a law which the delegates may or may not, in fact, you say, didn't, agree with. You're suddenly saying that means that ...

Trice: Well, no, they—I'm not saying that. I—they, they do ...

Dias: Well ...

Trice: —they would agree with the ITQs, we've got evidence to support that, there's no reason why the ...

Dias: Okay, so now the delegates do want the ...

Trice: ... the delegates would not agree with ITQs.

Dias: ... world fishing regime. So you've reversed course now.

Trice: No ...

Dias: The delegates.

Trice: No, they don't want it now ...

Dias: Right.

Trice: ... but there's no evidence that says they wouldn't support ITQs.

Dias: Okay, your evidence on Observation One says that the population is greatly increasing.

Trice: Yes.

Dias: Okay, now you don't do anything to solve the population problem ...

Trice: No, the card says that population is increasing. Our supplies of other ...

Dias: Given the ever-expanding need for food supplies, right.

Trice: ... food are decreasing which will cause a crisis without fish.

Dias: I know. And you also don't do anything to do solve the problems, with like, who gets the food and distribution, that kind of thing, those kind of questions, right?

Trice: Well, we allow for sustainable use ...

Dias: Okay ...

Trice: ... though we would increase the overall food supplies ...

Dias: Okay ...

Trice: ... which would feed that increasing population ...

Dias: Okay, let's say for some reason you didn't get the international solvency.

Trice: Okay.

Dias: Okay. You are left with the ... how much are we importing fish from other nations?

Trice: I don't know. That's not, that's not a claim that we make in the 1AC.

Dias: You said shifts to southern nations, Advantage One, third card.

Trice: Well, it says that we're—**[HALF]** I mean it doesn't quantify it.

Dias: You said our own fishing causes us to shift to—ah, importing it from other nations. That is a claim you make.

Trice: Yes ...

Dias: I see.

Trice: But it doesn't quantify it, which is what I'm saying.

Dias: Okay, okay. Now the lives of billions are at stake? That assumes world-wide overfishing, right? Not just the United States **[FIFTEEN]** overfishing ...

Trice: Right.

Dias: ... not the US's importation of other nations' overfishing.

Trice: Right, but there are certainly people stronger than the United States.

Dias: So, in order to claim billions of lives, you have to prove the plan gets worldwide solvency.

Trice: Well, I mean for the billions ...

Dias: And in fact, in order to get your advantage ...

Trice: ... I mean for the billions of lives ...

Dias: ... period. **[FIVE]**

Trice: It says that there are billions in China alone but we would still get a significant ...

Dias: Okay.

Trice: ... solvency in the US. **[TIME]**

First Negative Constructive
Ian McLaughlin, Gonzaga University

Blake and I are also very happy to be here. Ah, we have a few people that we would like to thank. First of all, we'd like to thank everybody at SDSU and every-one on the CEDA organization for running a great tournament. We've had a lot of fun here. It's great. We'd also like to thank the Gonzaga administration and all the support that we get at the school for our debate program. It really helps out. Also, we'd like to thank our own squad, especially W and Chad and Fred who put most of our positions together. We really appreciate all their efforts. And, ah, lastly Blake and I together would like to thank the entire Northwest region. They've really supported us and helped us out a lot, especially here. Thanks a lot everybody.

Ah, specifically, I'd like to thank, um, some of my past coaches. Ah, Bill De—Joe Sullivan. He helped us out a lot last year and he was my lab leader when I was at camp when I was a sophomore. He taught me a lot about debate. Also, my current coach, Bill DeForrest. He's really supported Blake and I and it's been great. As far as coaches, I'd really like to thank Mark West. He pretty much taught me what debate was. I thank him a lot for that. And I'd also like to thank my past partner, Jason Menzes who's here. Who's a great partner, a great friend, my best friend. I'd also thanks—like to thank Jared Holland, who was the first person to introduce me to some of the concepts in debate. We all went to high school together, Jared, Jason and I. And ah I'd like to thank my family, who isn't—who's not here. And last of all, and most importantly, I'd like to thank Blake. He's the best.

I'll have ah four off-case arguments and then I'll go to the case.

There's no impact to waiting a month and we will prove that doing the plan now will disrupt the non-proliferation treaty. The first off-case argument is topically on increased development of ocean resources. A. Definition. First, decrease. *Webster*'s,

> To become greater in size, amount, number, value, degree, etcetera. **(1NC#1)**

Second, development. The *Oxford English Dictionary*,

> The process of developing which in turn means to bring forth from latent or alimentary condition. **(1NC#2)**

Third, this is contrasted with conservation. From *Webster*'s,

> Act of keeping free from depletion, decay, or injury. Wise management maintains and conserves natural resources. **(1NC#3)**

Fourth, contextually, development and conservation are competing concerns. Coal development laws prove. *PR Newswire* on December 28th:

> The Interior Department's Bureau of Land Management today proposed new regulations for LMUs which are designed to help better ensure the efficient, economic, and orderly development of coal on federal lands. The proposed mandated lease production requirements concern LMUs, which are areas of land in which the coal resource can be developed in an efficient, economic, and orderly manner as a unit with due regard to conservation of coal and other resources. **(1NC#4)**

Their own evidence on case says that they are conservation not development. C is the st—B is the standards. First is that the conservation case makes the topic bidirectional. This vastly expands the topic. We are forced to research cases that exploit and stop exploitation of the environment. Second, effects topically **[SEVEN]** destroys ground, the plan causes an increase in utilization, but that is only after they conserve it. First, the plan mandates alone don't cause development. If they can do the opposite of the topic to get to topical action, the plan could mandate anything to achieve topical action, like stopping ozone depletion to save phytoplankton. Third, ban development counterplan test. If we can ban development as a counterplan, you can still do the plan which you can in this case. It's an illegitimate plan. D is a voting issue. The reason is ground, and also jurisdiction.

The next off-case argument is spending.

A is the dollar is surging after the German rate cut. Marshall & Petruno, March 31st:

> In a surprise turnabout, Germany on Thursday cut short-term interest rates, a move that could halt the U.S. dollar's slide. The unexpected half-point rate cut was immediately followed by similar cuts across Europe and sent the beleaguered dollar surging in value against the German mark. **(1NC#5)**

B is the links. First, ITQs require two to three times the current enforcement funds. From Zuckerman in '94:

Given the conservation concerns with an ITQ system, there is an associated problem with enforcement and monitoring of such a program. NMFS admits that with ITQs, especially in high volume fisheries like those of the North Pacific, the cost of enforcement and monitoring would be two to three times the current level. Moreover, since no legal mechanism exists to collect rents, royalties or other compensation from the fishing industry, that costs of implementing the necessary enforcement program will have to be borne by US taxpayers. **[SIX]** **(1NC#6)**

Second, is fiscal restraint now is key to halting dollar decline. BNA's banking report on March 13th from the——:

Indeed, given the recent weakness in the foreign exchange value of the dollar, world capital markets may be sending us just that message. This suggests that a key element in dealing with the dollar's weakness is to address our underlying fiscal imbalance convincingly. **(1NC#7)**

C is a weak US dollar hurts the world economy. *Investor's Business Daily* on July 22nd:

Treasury Undersecretary Summers said a stronger dollar would buoy the US economy, stabilize financial markets and take the heat off inflation, while a weaker dollar could hurt the world economy. We believe—and this view is shared by other G-7 countries—that a renewed decline of the dollar would be counterproductive to the global recovery. **(1NC#8)**

D is a bad global economy equals war. Ming '92:

What if the global economy stagnates—or even shrinks? In that case, we will face a new period of international conflict: South against North, rich against poor. Russia, China, India—these countries with their billions of people and their nuclear weapons will pose a greater danger to world order than Germany and Japan did in the '30s. **(1NC#9)**

The next off-case argument is bipartisanship.

A subpoint is that Clinton is seeking compromise over confrontation with Congress now. Thomas on March 1st:

Like Harry Truman, President Clinton is dealing with a Republican-controlled Congress. Unlike Truman, Clinton tends to seek compromise rather than confrontation—and the question whether his efforts will succeed or fail. Since the devastating Republican landslide at the polls last November, Clinton has had to decide **[FIVE]** on a course of action. As president, he still retains a lot of power, much as the opposition would like to dismiss him as irrelevant. During his recent state visit to Ottawa, a newspaper referred to Clinton as the titular head of the United States. However, at a news conference he pointed out that he still had many powers, telling a reporter he did not consider himself irrelevant and you shouldn't either. While most of the action and attention has shifted to Capitol Hill, Clinton pointed out that so far, Congress has sent him only one bill, "and I signed that." **(1NC#10)**

B is the links. The first one is that executive and legislative branch are at odds over the environment there is a difference of view. O'Hanlon on December 24th:

Leaders of the incoming GOP majority have vowed to reduce environmental regulations, saying they hurt the economy and put unnecessary burdens on business and local governments. Gore met with leaders of the major environmental groups Thursday to assure them the White House would fight attempts in Congress to dismantle environmental laws. **(1NC#11)**

Also, a failure to compromise ends in a stalemate. From Pastor in '91:

Tension is built into the system. Conflict or stalemate occur when there is a difference of views on policy, both branches reject the democratic injunction to compromise, or one branch judges that the other has overstepped the constitutional boundary in pursuit of its policy preference. **(1NC#12)**

Third is that bipartisanship is key to CTB and NPT regimes. Now is key. Furse on January 17th:

1995 is a very important year for the NPT, which is a vital check on the spread of nuclear weapons throughout the world. The new Congress must provide the strong bipartisan political **[FOUR]** support necessary to expand efforts to halt nuclear proliferation and achieve a CTB. **(1NC#13)**

C is the impacts. First, ending '95 agreement could eliminate the NPT. Simpson, po—political science professor '94:

Conference will be convened from April 17th to May 12th 1995 to decide on the further duration of the NPT, as well as to review its implementation. The significance of this event is that the NPT is the keystone of the non-proliferation regime. It is within the competence of this confer—conference, even if such a result is highly unlikely, to terminate the treaty's existence a short, fixed period of time after the end of the meeting. In 1996 there could be no NPT in existence. **(1NC#14)**

Second, NPT is the sole obstacle to proliferation. Simpson again:

States are guided and constrained in their international behavior by norms that they have accepted voluntarily or that have been imposed upon them. Nuclear non-proliferation can now be regarded as such a norm, voluntarily accepted by over 150 non-nuclear weapon states that have ratified or acceded to the NPT. This treaty is the sole global standard-setting instrument to contain a commitment by nuclear—non-nuclear weapon states not to acquire nuclear explosive devices. **(1NC#15)**

The last offcase is the delay counterplan.

The counterplan text is that on May 15th the plan mandates will be enacted. Observation One. Topical counterplans are legitimate. First of all, they parametricize and defend only one example of the topic; we get all the ground outside of the topic. Second, competition checks abuse. If we prove a net benefit, counterplan alone is better than a combination **[THREE]** of the two, they should be prepared to debate us. Third, the counterplan is different than the plan, the plan implies action now. Counterplan acts later. It's like an exclusion counterplan, they have to defend all of their plan. Observation Two, competition. Net benefits. We solve all of the affirmative harms delaying only a few months with no risk of disrupting an NPT conference. Combination of the two still risks now upsetting bipartisanship and disrupting the NPT and we get the spending impacts later.

Now, on Advantage One.

The first argument is that they have no internal link to the Webber card. This assumes international overfishing would still—which would still happen even if you did the plan because I'll take out their international solvency below. The second argument is that I'll argue that there's no impact to delay—delaying the collapse of one month—either the ecosystems will collapse or they won't. If you wait one month, there's no risk that there will be increased starvation. Off of Advantage Two, I'll just—I'll handle this on solvency proving that the plan doesn't solve and there's no impact to delay.

Now on solvency.

The first argument is that the plan doesn't cause international leadership at the conference. The fourth card just says that US leadership at the conference is important for them to make other countries cooperate with overfishing but the plan doesn't do that. All it does is change the US's domestic regulations. The second argument is the first card **[TWO]** proves our topicality story. It says that they are doing conservation; they do the opposite of the topic to get to topical action. The third argument is that ITQs equal overfishing, habitat destruction and waste. Zuckerman in '94:

> ITQs will not improve the status of marine fisheries. In fact, problems such as overfishing habitat destruction, bycatch and waste will most likely intensify. In New Zealand, where ITQs have already been implemented, bycatch and waste have increased due to the practice of highgrading. Only fish of marketable size are retained, while the remainder are thrown overboard dead and never re—reported. An ITQ system—because quotas are worth more money—creates a strong impetus to highgrade and under-log, so that the fishing company can stretch the life of its quota share. **(1NC#16)**

Also, ITQs increase capitalization and destruction of the ocean. From Duncan in '94:

> So even in the orange roughy and hoki fisheries which have had such a high percentage of the research budget, the ITQ system has not prevented overfishing. Clearly, at a practice level the ITQ system does not amount to a conservative, precautionary, approach that engenders cooperation. Nor, for that matter, are its procedures transparent, publicly accountable, or contestable. In reality, ITQs are far more than just a component of a system for management of levels of fishing effort. Though supposedly a means for achieving economic efficiency while respecting long-term sustainability criteria, in practice the ITQs become an instrument for the increased **[ONE]** capitalization of nature and society. **(1NC#17)**

Also, the fish are not fished to extinction because it costs too much. From Anderson and Leeds in '91:

> Whether the population of fish ends up becoming extinct ultimately depends on the cost of capturing the last fish in the stock. Because these costs tend to rise exponentially, declining fisheries have historically reached commercial extinction before biological extinction; that is, the additional costs of capturing the few remaining fish exceed the returns, so that it has become unprofitable to continue fishing. **(1NC#18)**

Also, exp—exploitation is inevitable. There are four reasons. From Ludwig and ah—and others in 1993:

We suggest that such consistency is due to the following common features: Wealth or prospect of wealth generates political and social power **[HALF]** that is used to promote unlimited exploitation of resources. Scientific understanding and consensus is hampered by the lack of controls and replicates, so that each new problem involves learning about a new system. The complexity of the underlying biological and physical systems precludes a reductionist approach to management. Optimum levels **[FIFTEEN]** of exploitation must be determined by trial and error. Fourth, large levels of natural variability mask the effects of overexploitation. Initial overexploitation is not detectable until it is severe and often irreversible. **(1NC#19)**

Cross Examination of the First Negative
Ian McLaughlin, Gonzaga University
Jason Trice, Michigan State University

Trice: The spending disad.

McLaughlin: Uh-huh.

Trice: The dollar collapsed last month. It's at the lowest level since World War II. Why is this unique?

McLaughlin: OK, in the status quo there's been a slow decline of the dollar.

Trice: It's still at the lowest point since World War II.

McLaughlin: No, the March 31st evidence says that the German banks and what they've done is increasing the amount of the dollar ...

Trice: Right, but the ...

McLaughlin: ... the value of the dollar now.

Trice: The dollar collapsed in March. Three days ago, the German bank made some interest rate adjustment that slightly helped the dollar. But even with those adjustments, it's still at the lowest point since World War II and it was lower three days ago before they made their mark, so why is your disad unique?

McLaughlin: The perception of the investors is that the dollar is gonna gain value in the status quo. And the, the argument is that the plan causes a rapid decline in the dollar because you spend so much money immediately. Right now we have a slow decline which they can handle but if there's new spending ...

Trice: OK, how—so much money, how much money do we have to spend to cause the dollar to collapse more than it already is?

McLaughlin: Well as much as—I'm not sure exactly how much ...

Trice: I mean I wouldn't, I wouldn't think we'd get ...

McLaughlin: ... money. Your plan spends a lot of money. Costs two to three times as much as the current enforcement system.

Trice: Where—where's that evidence?

McLaughlin: It's not out in—that's the link card.

Trice: May I see that?

McLaughlin: Yeah.

Trice: The NPT disad. What's your link?

McLaughlin: The link is that you cause interbranch conflict.

Trice: Why do we do that?

McLaughlin: When you have a plan that—OK, the executive branch and the legislative branch are at odds over the environment.

Trice: OK.

McLaughlin: And when the executive branch just passes a policy just like that, Congress isn't gonna like it. An environmental policy. That causes infighting among …

Trice: Can I see that?

McLaughlin: Yeah. **[ONE AND A HALF]**

Trice: Now why would the executive branch passing a policy cause infighting? I mean, the executive branch has done lots of things, they've provided relief to the California floods, they've helped out the Mexican peso, all through executive order. I think that's a little bit more executive branch than national marine fishe—fishery service. Why wouldn't those things cause your disad?

McLaughlin: It's—those aren't environmental regulations. That's what the Republicans don't like.

Trice: OK, so it's only **[ONE]** the environment? Why isn't the flood an environment—I mean, that's certainly an environmental thing.

McLaughlin: It's not an environmental regulation. You're changing the whole nature of the way that fishing regulations is …

Trice: We're trying to solve a crisis of fishing, just like the flood relief, we're trying …

McLaughlin: That's another, that's a disaster.

Trice: … to solve a crisis of food.

McLaughlin: The government is …

Trice: It's still an environment …

McLaughlin: … has to react to that …

Trice: … It's a natural disaster …

McLaughlin: The Congress is gonna get mad if they try to …

Trice: … It's a disaster, but it's a natural disaster, an environmental disaster, it's an environmental policy, right?

McLaughlin: No. No, that's not right.

Trice: Why?

McLaughlin: The link is off of environmental regulations. That's not what you said—it's not helping people out with the flood. It's not … **[HALF]**

Trice: It doesn't say the regulations, it says …

McLaughlin: Yeah it does. Environmental regulations, right there. Check it out. [Laughter]

Trice: OK. You're right. It says it hurts the economy. Now why would ours hurt the economy? I mean this is generic …

McLaughlin: That's the link …

Trice: This is generic environmental regulation. Our claim on case is that the **[FIFTEEN]** industry will inevitably collapse because they're overexploiting their foodstock.

McLaughlin: It won't matter then, because then the NPT conference will have been convened and that's the only impact to bipartisanship.

Trice: OK.

Second Affirmative Constructive
Biza Repko, Michigan State University

Alright. I told myself if I ever got back here, I was gonna thank the right people 'cause when you're up here you always forget everybody that you're supposed to thank. The first thing I want to do is to thank Jason for, ah, getting the 1AC in on time.

[Laughter] I want to thank all of CEDA. I want to thank President Papa Doug Duke. Last night he talked about respecting our history and remembering the people that are important to history and he is really an important facet of CEDA, an important bed-rock, and he's always supported me. I—I think he rocks. I want to thank our coaches, Dave Devereaux, our van driver slash coach. Actually doesn't even drive the van, so I don't know why I'm saying that. Sean and ah, by the way, Skull, called for you. They're out there, talk to 'em. My brother, Marla, Professor Roper, who rocks and does everything, buys us paper, does everything for us. There's a couple people that I want to thank. People who, through my experience, have truly represented superior debate and commitment to this activity. Those people are, Terry Richardson, Nick, Brent, Brad Thompson, Greg Hopper, Kieran Ringgenberg, (and I know there's peo-ple out there going, "She's thanking Kieran!"), Paul Hayes, Jarvis—Jason Jarvis, Will Rogers, Des and ET, Geoff and Larry and Jared Holland. I also want to thank a couple people who've allowed me to believe in myself before I did. Those are Josh Hoe, Jim Haefele, and Doug Hennessy. I want to thank my brother who makes me what I am, not just as a debater, but he's always made me what I am as a person. And ah, I want to say in front of everybody, yeah, Devon Reese, I will marry you.

Same order. [Laughter]

Anonymous judge: I don't have the order.

OK. Topicality. The dollar disad.

Bipartisanship. The counterplan. Observation One. The advantages, and then Observation Two.

The counterplan is unfair. They become the affirmative by running the counter-plan. The only thing they test is the time when you can run the counterplan. That is unfair. It means that the negative would always win. They wouldn't have to research anything except for NPT.

Start on the T debate.

Group the A subpoint, the one through three together. The first is that we meet. We definitely are a process. Their definition only says you have to become a process by doing something. We would certainly necessitate we meet that. We be-come a process. The second is their evidence does not assume the ocean. It assumes the context of coal. Remember that's what he says in the coal context. You don't think that conversation and development are the same thing but it's not in the con-text of ocean. The third argument is the third argument is a counterdefinition. Ocean development means research and food production. Lipp in 1964:

> I should like to subdivide the field of ocean development into half a dozen parts. These are: naval weapons, underwater transportation and communica-tions, freshwater conversion, mining or chemical extraction of minerals, food production, and finally research activities. **(2AC#1)**

The next argument is definition is superior for three reasons, Little A, it is field contextual. Jay Lipp is a member of National Academy of Sciences Panel on Ocean Exploration and Development. The B, it assumes resolutional context. Our definition assumes the resolutional context of oceans which is superior to the definition which is talking about coal. The C subpoint is resolutional limits. The Lipp definition provides six examples of cases that can be run in a few different ways and it's a fair interpreta-tion of the resolution. The next is development activities include conservation.

Pivo in 1993:

> Even though the GMA defines forest land and **[SEVEN]** agricultural land in terms of commercial production, that definition should not be seen to

imply permission to allow unbridled deterioration of other uses being provided by these lands, such as their recreational or habitat values. The planning goals in the GMA encourage the retention of open spaces, the development of recreational opportunities, the conservation of fish and wildlife.
These goals therefore indicate that development regulations should conserve
more than commercial uses. **(2AC#2)**

Our definition is superior, it gives a normative reason why you would want to
vote for conservation over development because conservation is more superior. The
C subpoint, the standards they make is bidirectionality. The first, is we pick one side
of the resolution and we defend it. We will pick the conservation side. Why is it
more important to pick the exploration side? They don't—they don't explain. The
second is they say it is effects topical. The first is we are not effects topical. The evidence that we read above proves that we dir—directly develop through research. The
second is development is a step-by-step process. *Webster's New World Dictionary* 1993:

Development is a step-by-step process. **(2AC#3)**

Which means it must be effectual. The last is they say you could just ban development. The first is that's not our interpretation. We don't ban development. Our
interpretation is conservation which is the other half of the topic. Why is that abusive? The C subpoint they say it's a voting issue, decreases ground, but first, is we are
fishing which is huge ground on the topic. There's no reason why we decrease the
ground, the second is literature tracks abuse. Literature tracks—against case is the reason why you wouldn't vote on topicality.
Dollar Surge.
There's no link perceptually. We don't spend any money. I don't understand this
position. The first is no link. We don't spend any money. Why would we have to
spend any money to be ITQs and why would **[SIX]** we perceive. The second is that
there's no link. The evidence that they read—the evidence that we read on the case
from Lintz in 1993 says we don't cost any more money to enforce. Remember, their
link relies on enforcement. Our evidence says that it becomes a market system. People
enforce themselves. We don't have to spend any money on it. Third, is it's longer-
term spending. Remember the cross-examination, he says that the link would have
to be perceptual, but the only time we'd have to spend to enforce an ITQ is a long
time away. After we'd have the ITQ, would not have a policy—it would not be immediate. The fourth is cross apply the spending mechanism in the plan. It allows us to
spend through an auctioning off of the quotas. It's not answered by the 1NC. The fifth
is the internal link evidence is awful it doesn't say that we would get a recession. It
merely says that the economy stagnates. The economy has stagnated since 1992, which
is the evidence that they read. The next argument is the dollar's at the lowest point in,
since World War II. He says in the cross examination this is true. Even if it has increased the per—the perception should be that the dollar is low. The next is ITQs
generate enough money without any federal allocation. Lundsten in 1994:

As with any management system, the Councils are responsible for management aimed at sustainable use of the resource. As long as they do that, the
harvest of fish under ITQs provides economic benefits to a productive fishing industry while depriving the public of nothing further, not requiring
any special aid or buy-back programs. **(2AC#4)**

The last argument is not unique, the dollar has already crashed, from Shilling in 1995:

> According to popular wisdom, the Fed has effected what it has already pulled off before—a soft landing. **[FIVE]** Don't bet on things happening that way. I look for further interest rate hikes, with the usual results, a recession, starting as early as midyear. The interest rate increases, the Mexican crisis, and the collapse of the dollar only exacerbate these domestic problems. **(2AC#5)**

Now, to Clinton.

The first is there's no impact. We are—there's no there's no impact comparison. It doesn't explain why you would want, why you'd wa—why you'd want to, want to, to do the impacts of the case over the c—over the effects of the case. Remember, the impacts to the case are all of humanity. This is just a risk—their risk of nuclear war which they don't explain the type of war. The second is there's no link specific. The link evidence they read is just co-op—it's just—inter co—inter, interbran, branch crippling, but it's not specific to the NMFS or fishing or anything. The third is no internal link to the impact. Their evidence just says that they get angry at things, not that they cut the NPT. They have to read that piece of evidence, but they don't. I don't have to debate the rest of the disad. The fourth is the internal link evidence is awful. It says they need bipartisanship to get the NPT. It just says it's a—it necessitates, not that a loss of bipartisanship would mean that we lose the NPT. The next is bipartisanship is dead in the status quo. *Dayton Daily News,* March 23rd, 1995:

> Despite the appeal for more bipartisanship, the administration officials acknowledged the unfunded mandates measure should be viewed as a symbol of the limited control in which Clinton intends to work with the Republican Congress. White House officials were quick to note Wednesday that the president still opposes most of the legislative goals outlined in the GOP contract and has threatened to veto such Republican measures as changes **[FOUR]** in the 1994 anti-crime law. Clinton, nonetheless, still stresses cooperation. **(2AC#6)**

The next argument is that NPT does not solve for enforcement. The technical development of former Soviet Union arsenals will outstrip any solvency we get. Mandelbaum in 1995:

> The different parts of the supply-side regime share a common weakness: Including none of the power of enforcement. If a sovereign state violates any of its norms, no international mechanism can compel compliance or mete out punishment. Many of them portable, scattered throughout the Soviet Union, thousands of scientists and engineers and hundreds of tons of missile material from laboratories, reactors, submarines, and weapons to be dismantled under the terms of the laboratory of one or another international agreement. **(2AC#7)**

Now, the next argument is that evidence also says that proliferation is inevitable. It will happen no matter what in the status quo. The last argument is focus on prevention is bad. It trades off with the preparation for nuclear wars and increases the risk. From Millot in 1994:

> There is little evidence that the United States takes this new threat seriously. The Clinton Administration has largely denied emerging reality of nuclear adversary and the norm of nonproliferation. The outcome of refusal to face the

emerging reality of nuclear adversaries is that the United States is not preparing seriously for the possibility of having to fight another war. If we cannot assure that the security of its allies against this threat, the result is likely to be further proliferation among these allies. **(2AC#8)**

Now the counterplan. Wait a little while.

The first is permutation. Do both. There's no reason why we couldn't. We can act now and act later. The second is there's no time element in the plan. The plan doesn't say when it's adopted. In fact, it only says normal means, which would take out the link to **[THREE]** the disad and the reason why I can't permute it. The next argument they make is parametricizing the resolution. First is, is an unfair—argument about parametricizing. It would say that I would get out of the links to all the disads because I would just say they don't read a specific ITQ link. If they continue to go for this argument, I'll win because they don't have an ITQ disad. The next two arguments they make on the counterplan abuse and you can act later. The first is it discourages research. It just would say that—you would just—you would discourage research. You would just always run the same generic negative strategy. The second is every part of the plan must be topical. The opposing part of the counterplan which competes with the affirmative plan is, "do my plan." But that is not one part of the counterplan. I can perm out of it by saying do my plan and do my plan. There's no reason why they should be able to suck up our solvency. The last arguments they make is the net benefits. First, they must 100% win their net benefit. If they don't 100% win their net benefit, you vote for MSU. But the second is you won't be able to solve case. The Speer evidence we read on case says you have to be able to solve by Spring 1995 to set a strong conservation signal. They would not be able to suck up that solvency. It wouldn't happen.

The Observation One.

He says there's no way they can solve internationally. The first is US is overfishing now, that's what the evidence assumes. Assumes we're doing it in America. It's the—sm—the Webber evidence. The second argument he makes is we will be able to solve in one month. But first, extend across the Greenwire evidence says we're on the brink now as of a couple weeks ago, which means that the fish stocks are about to collapse. The second is that they **[TWO]** wouldn't be able to solve for the UN—the UN council. Remember, the UN council is going to meet in Spring of 1995. They wouldn't be able to solve that through the counterplan.

The solvency debate.

The first argument he makes is that we wouldn't be able to solve because the evidence doesn't say it, but first is the evidence does say it. What it says it we have to have leadership when we get to the conference. That's the only way we'll get—will be able to solve if we have a strong conservation measure. We won't have that in the status quo, we only have that under the affirmative. The conference will end in Spring of 1995. We have to have a strong conservation measure. The next argument he makes is this proves topicality. But first is no it doesn't. All the evidence on topicality would take this away. Also—it also proves that we fish, which would decrease—which would get rid of his argument which is we only have to conserve. The next argument he makes is that ITQs equal habitat waste. The first is extend all of the evidence in the 1AC. The Lintz evidence in 1994 says that we decrease overfishing. The Hop—the Fujita & Hopkins which says it solves all empirically and the Lintz evidence also which says that we will get enforcement. The next is ITQs solve for the bycatch problem. Fujita & Hopkins '94:

In addition to increasing compliance with TACs and creating incentives to conserve fish populations, ITQs decrease the bycatch by reducing total fishing effort. ITQ management are more ecologically sound than fishing practices in the US wreckfish fishery, where bans, limited entry, and other conservative measures have all failed previously. **(2AC#9)**

The next answer he makes is they will increase waste but first, it's only specific to certain parts. Remember, the plan does research **[ONE]** about where to put the ITQ, which means that we are putting in the right place. The second is the evidence I read above also answers this argument. It says it won't increase waste. They will solve all the bycatch problems. Also all the evidence in the 1AC solvency says it gives them an economic incentive not to fish because they get paid not to do it. It's a reason why they would just sit at home. It wouldn't increase the problems. His next argument he makes is you will not fish—fish to extinction. But the first is they don't need to go to extinction. None of our evidence says they have to go all the way to extinction. It just says there has to be a decrease in the amount of biodiversity. The worst fish are left. That's how we get the impact where there aren't enough fish for people to eat. The second is the evidence that we, that we read **[HALF]** from Greenwire in 1995 the first card on the case says that we are on the brink and close to losing all the stocks. The last argument he makes is that resource depletion is inevitable. First, it's not specific to fish. It's only talking about other types of resource depletion are inevitable. The second is it's a warrant to vote affirmative, it says, in the status quo, all the fish problems are inevitable. The last argument is ITQs solve **[FIFTEEN]** overfishing empirically. Lundsten in 1994:

> The problems we face today are the result of an expanding population of a finite annual resource. In two fisheries, the essential ingredient of our open access system and the tragedy of that commons, is a waste. The only way, the only way to end this in a ludicrously short timeframe is to have something are a fraction of ours but are almost worth to their nation because they are these, the ITQs. **(2AC#10)**

Cross Examination of the Second Affirmative
Biza Repko, Michigan State University
Ian McLaughlin, Gonzaga University

McLaughlin: OK, what's the internal link between doing the plan and US leadership at the conference?

Repko: What, what it says is the way that we can have leadership at the conference—it's right here, is that we send a strong conservation measure. That's the only way that we will have leadership at the conference. Once we have leadership at the conference, our delegates, y'know, will be able to be leaders and push the—

McLaughlin: No, this says that. Whoa, OK.

Repko: Yes.

McLaughlin: It is.

Repko: Yeah.

McLaughlin: Whatever. Alright. On the NPT turns, that focus on the NPT is bad or focus on non-proliferation. What's the alternative? Like—it might be bad to focus on non-proliferation but if we don't at all, proliferation will decrease. That's your own thing, right …

Repko: Well …

McLaughlin: ... it's inevitable.

Repko: ... the argument is proliferation is inevitable. So you should not focus on trying to get weapons out of people's hands but trying to set up a policy to stop the use of nuclear weapons. That's what the Millot evidence says.

McLaughlin: OK, what—is that going to happen in the status quo? Is there any uniqueness for your flip?

Repko: Yes, the ah—the first—the only piece of evidence I read from Millot said that it will.

McLaughlin: Ah, what does that say? Is there going to be a new regime or ...?

Repko: It's not a new regime. It's not that the United States signs another regime or tries to control people from getting nuclear weapons. The evidence says if they want nuclear weapons—if a country wants nuclear weapons and well—has enough money, they're gonna to get them no matter what.

McLaughlin: OK.

Repko: We need to focus on how we will react if someone uses a nuclear weapon against us or threatens to ...

McLaughlin: OK, so ...

Repko: ... use a weapon.

McLaughlin: ... what steps do we take?

Repko: What steps have we taken?

McLaughlin: What—what would we do?

Repko: What would we do?

McLaughlin: If all these countries have nuclear weapons ...

Repko: Well, I mean there's there's **[TWO]** many ...

McLaughlin: ... how could we stop them from using them?

Repko: How could we stop them from using ...

McLaughlin: Yes.

Repko: ... nuclear weapons? Well, there's many different ways we could try to stop the use of a nuclear weapon. Like, instead of trying to stop, um, for example, let's say North Korea, from getting it or acquiring a nuclear weapon, we could do something like, I mean, we could do something like just negotiate with North Korea to try to stop their use. We could do something radical.

McLaughlin: Just let them have it and say "please ...

Repko: No, no, well, I mean ...

McLaughlin: ... don't use it"?

Repko: We could do something radical like have, um, have a defense system which would able to stop a nuclear weapon from ...

McLaughlin: OK, does your evidence say ...

Repko: ... coming towards us.

McLaughlin: ... that anything like that is gonna happen in the status quo?

Repko: It says we're making moves to do things which are more ...

McLaughlin: So, we should just let as many countries have nuclear weapons as they want.

Repko: No. That's not our argument, that we should let ...

McLaughlin: OK.

Repko: ... as many countries have nuclear weapons as they want. Our argument is, in this type of world, in the post-cold war world, they're going to get a nuclear weapon if they want it. You could do something to try to stop their acquisition of it—not try to stop their acquisition, but deal with the use of it.

McLaughlin: OK. Now the spending link, um, ...

Repko: OK.

McLaughlin: ... you say there's no link. Now, how do you get out of the enforcement part? The card says that you cost **[ONE]** ...

Repko: OK, the Lintz in 199—

McLaughlin: How do you get out of that?

Repko: There's two ways. The Lintz in 1994 evidence that we read on the case debate says that it won't cost any money to enforce. The reason why is it says that market functions will take over the enforcement.

McLaughlin: OK.

Repko: It says that the reason why you would have to enforce an ITQ is you'd be afraid that, um, ...

McLaughlin: OK.

Repko: ... I give somebody ... oh.

McLaughlin: What is somebody violates that?

Repko: The evidence says, OK, this is the evidence says that, you know, the reason why you'd be, you'd have to spend money to enforce it is if somebody starts to violate the ITQ.

McLaughlin: Uh-huh.

Repko: But our Lintz evidence says that if somebody starts to violate your ITQ and you've sold out to **[HALF]** like a, a big fisher and you gave—given them their money to take your ITQ, you will become the enforcement mechanism. You'll get angry if they start to over-fish ...

McLaughlin: So what are you going to do, kill them?

Repko: ... money you could have had. They don't kill 'em!

McLaughlin: They gonna take legal action against them and it's ...

Repko: You report that.

McLaughlin: ... gonna cost money for that. I mean ...

Repko: Well, I mean if you were to sue a person individually **[FIFTEEN]** the government doesn't have to allocate money ...

McLaughlin: OK ...

Repko: ... if I were to ...

McLaughlin: ... you're right.

Repko: ... sue you.

McLaughlin: You're right. OK.

Second Negative Constructive
Blake Dias, Gonzaga University

Well, I'd be lying if I said I haven't dreamt about this moment and, ah, I want to take the time myself to thank the people who are in large part responsible for me being here. First of all, the coaches, my former coaches and people who have influenced my debate career both in my high school days and in my college days. Some one or the other and some both and many hopefully into the future. David Brownell, Jeff Hepper, Mark West, Ken Bahm, Dave Devereaux, Dave Hanson, Bob Gilmore, and Bill DeForrest are all people who in different ways have shaped my debate career and in their own ways are responsible for my successes. Secondly, my partners and teammates. Everyone on the squad has been great. Not only are they my teammates, they're my best friends. Um especially Ben Stuckert, Will Brewer, Chad Rigsby, Joe Sullivan, who not only was my partner, but my mentor, kinda showed me the ropes when I was just a little pup. Ian McLaughlin, I literally could not be here without him. He's great. And, ah, Greg Peterson. And if I forgot anybody, I'm sorry.

The order is spending and bipartisanship.

Michigan State's policy is extremely controversial. Not only do they fiat a plan that the Congresspeople expressly do not like, they have the executive branch do it without a care or regard to what Congress thinks. The third argument in 2AC on spending is that it's long-term spending. That's true. So are their savings which means there's no link to any type of a turn. Off the seventh argument, they say that ITQs will save enough money to pay for itself. The first argument, this is not labeled a turn, it just says it would pay for itself, not that it would cause increased savings. The second argument, it's irrelevant. It's not a turn even if they caused increased savings in the status quo, there's no scenario to the impact to that. Also it's irrelevant because it's not unique. The dollar has already crashed.

Bipartisanship. Their first answer is that there's no impact comparison. The first argument is that that will, the, the plan does not solve and there's no impact to delaying if we win the counterplan. So a small impact is all that's necessary. Also, the proliferation impacts will happen below. She says that there's no link to the plan. The first argument is that's not true, look at the B-1 subpoint, the O'Hanlon in '94 evidence. It says explicitly that the executive and legislative branches are **[SEVEN]** at odds over the environment. They've told each other not to mess with each other. The plan has the executive branch through the NMFS which is part of the Department of Interior take a great environmental regulation action. That is not answered. The Congress doesn't like that. The Pastor evidence says that when they disagree or when they have a failure to compromise or change the agenda, that will cause a stalemate and ruin bi—bipartisanship. Their next argument is that there's no internal link. That's not true. They'd get a stalemate. That's the Pastor evidence. The next argument is, that empirically, executive action ignites a backlash. The environment is a touchy subject. Percival in '91:

> The distrust generated by the politicization of the review process has stimulated a congressional backlash. As a result, Executive Office intervention has largely been unsuccessful, unsuccessful in providing relief to the regulated community. Rather, it has inspired Congress to intensify its own oversight activities and to produce increasingly explicit legislation narrowing EPA's discretion. **(2NC#1)**

The next argument is that the White House action destabilizes the system, they escalate interbranch rivalry. From Shapiro in '94:

> The fact that constitutional arrangements and political realities give the White House more power to influence regulatory policy produces an unstable equilibrium. When the White House escalates its oversight efforts, **[SIX]** Congress responds in a futile attempt to catch up, producing additional oversight by the White House. This cycle of competition has led both branches into activities that have harmed regulatory policy; namely the use of secrecy and micromanagement. As a result, congressional and White House conduct has not been politically accountable and neither branch has taken sufficient account of agency expertise and experience. **(2NC#2)**

The next argument is I think there's a good link story on this case. For instance, the Magnuson Act is up for—up for reauthorization within Congress. It's probably something that the Re—Republicans think that they can do something about whereas the fed—the plan has the federal government or the president do something about it now. It beats them to the punch. The next argument is that executive branch rule-making is currently under attack—or is under attack by Republicans. From Chen in '95, March 30th:

> Moving to assert new authority over the executive branch, the Senate unanimously approved legislation Wednesday that would give Congress power to block all rules issued by federal agencies aimed at protecting the environment and public health and safety. **(2NC#3)**

The next argument is executive branch rule-making bills at crossroads—chances for compromise are unclear. From Chen in the *LA Times* again:

> The Republican-initiated drive to curtail administrative rule-making began earlier this year in the House, which has adopted a year-long moratorium. The Senate bill takes a different approach. It gives Congress—on a permanent basis —**[FIVE]** forty-five days to block any new rule from taking effect that has a projected economic impact of 100 million dollars or more. The differences between the House and Senate bills must be resolved in a conference committee and the prospects for a compromise were not clear Wednesday. **(2NC#4)**

In other words, they are debating the specific type of thing that the affirmative is doing right now within Congress.

The next argument is it's unique because Clinton supports current environmental regulation compromise. The fate of the bill is still uncertain. The affirmative would push us over the brink. From Lee, *Washington Post,* March 24th:

> Even Clinton administration officials, who have flatly opposed other risk statutes, tentatively lauded the bill. We think it is quite promising. But a few aspects of the bill still trouble the administration. We're encouraged. We're very pleased with the movement we see. The fate of the Roth bill is nonetheless uncertain. Although likely to receive broad support in the Senate, it would have to be reconciled with the House bill, which imposes far greater restrictions on the regulatory power of federal agencies. The White House, which is conducting an administrative review of the federal regulatory process, in the past has hinted that risk—risk legislation would be voted. **(2NC#5)**

The next argument is Senate gave bipartisan support to regulation limits. The new bill will avoid conflict with Clinton over the environment. Greenwire March 24th:

> Ah, in a surprising show, show of bipartisanship, the Senate Governmental Affairs Committee yesterday gave unanimous approval to a bill requiring more cost-benefit analyses before new federal rules are issued. The measure, introduced by Senator Roth, directs agencies **[FOUR]** to do risk assessments and cost-benefit analyses for all rules costing more than 100 million dollars. It only suggests that the regulation include an explanation of why the benefits justify the costs. **(2NC#6)**

The next argument is that the plan doesn't say that they have any of the cost-benefit analysis etcet—etcetera. It only has the executive agency pass the ITQs without regard to cost, etcetera which means they link to the disad. Her next argument. Says that the—there's bad evidence on the—or she says that there's bad evidence on the internal link. The first argument that's not true. The evidence is excellent. It's the B-

3 sub-point. It says that without bipartisanship, we can't persuade other states to joint the NPT. The next argument is domestic and foreign policy, ah—partisan policy intertwined. From Collier in '91:

> A final issue is whether bipartisanship can exist in foreign policy when partisanship is intense in other areas. Can and should politics stop at the water's edge? To some extent it appears impossible to keep domestic politics out of foreign policy. Political parties are a basic part of the U.S. governmental system. Each party searches for issues and methods to promote its own interests and diminish the election prospects of the other party. Both political parties have large permanent offices and each party has policy and study committees in Congress that consider foreign policy as well as domestic issues. **(2NC#7)**

[THREE] Her next argument it says that bipartisanship is dead. The first answer, that's a mistag. It just says that he has considered vetoing certain policies but not that he has in the status quo or that he has changed the agenda. In addition, the above evidence that I read is more recent from March 23rd. That says they've come to an agreement over environment—ah, executive branch rulemaking. The next argument, if anything this proves the brink. They're currently on the brink of being contentious with anothe—one another. The next argument is even if I've lost this card, we would still win the round. It just says that in the future there might be a problem, but we only need bipartisanship through May. That's all we need, whereas the plan acts now. In addition, Clinton won't clash with Congress on important issue—no. New regulatory legislation receives strong bipartisan support. *Washington Post,* March 24th:

> A compromise version of controversial regulatory legislation received strong bipartisan support from a key Senate panel yesterday and tentative praise from the Clinton administration and some environmentalists. **(2NC#8)**

The next argument is that Clinton's urging more bipartisanship. *Chicago Sun-Times,* March 23rd:

> President Clinton signed the unfunded manstate—mandates bill and said he hopes there will be more bipartisanship in Washington. **(2NC#9)**

The next argument is that this card's irrelevant, it's just Clinton's rhetoric saying that he wants to veto the stuff, but the A-subpoint evidence in **[TWO]** the shell takes out the assumption of this. It says he's seeking compromise. He may be politically—his political rhetoric might be different, but in point of fact he will not veto the bills. The sixth argument they make is that the NPT will not solve because of enforcement. The first answer, this is not an absolute takeout. The NPT is still comparative—comparatively advantageous over a world without the NPT. The second argument is this is irrelevant. It assumes they get the weapons in the first place but the evidence that I'm going to read says that we prevent their acquisition from ever occurring—ah, ah, also that groups, that groups her seventh argument that says prolif inevitable. The next argument is NPT's necessary to have disarm and stop global proliferation. Holum in '94:

> The NPT is an important stimulus to disarmament. Pressure to disarm will be kept on the nuclear weapons states by reaffirming article six of the treaty and keeping the treaty in force indefinitely. Anything less will have the perverse result of easing the pressure to disarm. **(2NC#10)**

The next argument is no NPT equals weapons proliferation. Holum in '94:

> The Japanese have a saying: The nail that stands out will be hammered down. Today, proliferant countries know how that feels, because they are exposed to the global hammer against nuclear weapons—the NPT. **(2NC#11)**

The NPT's empirically been successful. MacGwire in '94:

> Given these powerful drives, the Nuclear Non-Proliferation Treaty has been unexp—unexpectedly successful. The small number of industrialized states that refused to sign in 1968 **[ONE]** has been progressively reduced, despite there now being twenty to thirty states with the technological capacity to produce nuclear weapons. **(2NC#12)**

Her eighth argument says that focusing on prevention is bad. The first answer, this assumes counterproliferation, not just—the non—non-proliferation treaty. It doesn't say the NPT. The second argument is the status quo disproves. We've had the NPT and the world is safe. That's the comparisons that my evidence makes. The next argument is this is not unique. In order to win the turn, Michigan State must either prove that we will stop u—using, ah, we will stop our nonproliferation efforts or that we will do efforts to stop proliferation in a more proactive way in the world **[HALF]** without the NPT. That's not proven. Extend the impact on proliferation. One more card says decreased proliferation equals decreased risk of accidental launch. Kaysen and Rathjens in '91:

> First is the simple calculation that reducing the number and variety of weapons and the geographical breadth of their deployment reduces the probability of their accidental or unauthorized use. **(2NC#13)**

We can't accept any risk, from Fox in '87:

> The degree of risk we are willing to take should be inversely proportional to the magnitude of the disaster that could result from the act being evaluated. Since the consequences **[TEN]** of an all-out nuclear exchange could very possibly be the most extreme, we should tolerate no such risk, and likewise no policy or plan of action that creates this risk. **(2NC#14)**

Cross Examination of the Second Affirmative
Blake Dias, Gonzaga University
Biza Repko, Michigan State University

Repko: Alright. Now, how many countries have signed the NPT?
Dias: Something like a hundred and fifty.
Repko: OK, so how could the NPT necess …
Dias: A hundred and eighty or something …
Repko: … necessarily solve for …
Dias: One hundred fifty.
Repko: … proliferation if not everybody has signed the NPT? It only solves for proliferation of the members of the NPT, right?
Dias: That's true. That's true.
Repko: Alright, now let's look at the cards you read that says that NPT solves proliferation.

Dias: OK.

Repko: OK. Do you know where I am?

Dias: Ah …

Repko: On the flow?

Dias: Yes, I …

Repko: OK, the third card—the third card you read that says NPT equals disarmament and no NPT equals proliferation. I want to see both those cards.

Dias: OK. Go ahead and ask me a different question.

Repko: I'll have questions when I have the card.

Dias: OK … No NPT equals proliferation.

Repko: OK, this is the card. The Japanese have a saying: "The nail that stands out will be hammered down." Today, proliferant countries know how that feels, because they are exposed to the global hammer against nuclear weapons—the NPT. Now why does that say no NPT equals no nuclear weapons? It says NPT right now might work 'cause the Japanese have some saying. It doesn't say the lack of **[TWO]** NPT means that proliferation increases …

Dias: OK, OK. Even if it were true that a world without the NPT didn't mean I mean a world with the NPT means there are no nuclear weapons, that doesn't disprove the claim of the evidence that a world with the NPT is better off than a world without one.

Repko: OK, what claim in what evidence makes that comparison for you?

Dias: Well, the Holum card. That I read. The other one.

Repko: The other one you read that says that NPT …

Dias: There's the MacGwire card …

Repko: This one.

Dias: … says that it's been successful.

Repko: Which one? This one? Given the power drives, the Nuclear Non-Proliferation Treaty has been unexpectedly successful. The small number of industrialized states that refused to sign in 1968 has been **[ONE AND A HALF]** progressively reduced, despite there now being twenty to thirty states with the technological capacity to produce nuclear weapons. That makes a comparison between a world with NPT and a world without NPT?

Dias: Yeah, it says that it's been successful …

Repko: Yeah? Where? It says the NPT has worked. That's not a comparison between no NPT and, NPT. It just …

Dias: Well, in order to say that it's worked it assumes some kind of comparison.

Repko: Right. But your argument and the reason why …

Dias: Also …

Repko: … your evidence is better is 'cause it's comparative with the world without NPT and a world with NPT. There's no sentence in this that says that.

Dias: Yeah, I also …

Repko: It just says NPT …

Dias: … read another Holum card **[ONE]** which is what I'm looking for now. Here it is.

Repko: Which card?

Dias: That. The top.

Repko: The top card? The NPT is important stimulus for disarmament. Pressure to disarm will be kept on the nuclear we—weapons states by reaffirming Article 6—or 7, I mean …

Dias: MmHmm.

Repko: ... of the treaty keeping the treaty in force indefinitely. Anything less will have the perverse result of easing the pressure to disarm.

Dias: You can't say that something has worked unless you're comparing it to something ...

Repko: Yeah, but you have to have reversibility in your evidence. If your claim is a world with NPT is safer than a world without NPT, it'd be nice if you read a piece of evidence that supported that and I've read all three that you said did and none of them do.

Dias: OK, OK. **[HALF]** But they say the NPT has worked.

Repko: OK, so the fact that the NPT has worked is a comparison to a world without an NPT?

Dias: Ah, also, the 1NC card said it's the sole obstacle to proliferation.

Repko: Alright ...

Dias: I don't ...

Repko: ... so I wanna see the 1NC shell.

Dias: Do you already have that?

Repko: No. **[TEN]**

Dias: There's nothing saying that, in a world without the NPT, we would have **[FIVE]** counterproliferation efforts that your turn talks about.

Repko: OK.

Repko: So this is all academic anyway. **[TIME]**

First Negative Rebuttal
Ian McLaughlin, Gonzaga University

OK. I'm gonna go to the counterplan and then the case.

Anonymous judge: Hold on just a second.

The counterplan solves for all of the case impacts and even without that we are winning the case turns on the case. Now the c—on the counterplan. Their first argument is permutation but that's not net beneficial if we win the bipartisanship disad because if you act now and later, acting now risks upsetting bipartisanship. Ah, their second argument is that there's no time frame in the plan. The first argument is we assume that the plan acts now and that her argument below proves that. Her last argument on the counterplan is that we can't solve because we don't do the case in the Spring of 1995, assuming that the plan is acting now. The second argument is they're a moving target. Otherwise if they don't act now, they could just shift and say that, that they acted at any time. There's no way that we could ever **[FOUR AND A HALF]** link a disadvantage.

Off of Observation One that topical counterplan's legitimate. She talks about parametrics and how we could outlink, she could outlink all the da's. That's not true. That's not what our argument is. Our argument is just that they parametricize the topic so we get all of the ground outside of that. If we can prove a competitive alternative, we still link all our disadvantages because if you do the plan that's an executive action now which upsets bipartisanship. She can't outlink this dis—the disads. Off of competition checks abuse. She talks about how we'd decrease research. The first argument is that she still has all kinds of ground. She could run impacts **[FOUR]** to delay or she could impact turn the disads. There are all kinds of arguments she could make. The second argument we still have to link the disads to the plan which means that we have to research all the plans to find the disads to them. The third argument is that there's there's a couple of reasons in the shell why it's legitimate. They have to justify all their plan and part of their plan is acting now. It's the same as any other type of exclusion counterplan. The fourth argument is that it's a huge topic. Topicality demonstrates how it can be bidirectional. It's been interpreted that way. You give us leeway on the counterplan. Her next argument off of the third standard is that every part of the plan has to be topical. The first argument, this doesn't make any sense. The counterplan **[THREE AND A HALF]** is different than the plan. They're not the same thing. The plan acts now and the counterplan only acts later which means that you would vote for just the counterplan. There's no reason. This is illegitimate.

Now off Observation Two she says it has to be 100% net beneficial, but she gives no reason. There's no reason. It's just like any other issue. If it's more likely that the pl—that the plan or permutation would accrue the disadvantage and solve all the case impact than the, than the counterplan alone you'd vote for the counterplan. Her second argument is that we don't solve because of the Spring 1995. The first answer, her evidence just her last card on case, all it says is that the US needs to do two things **[THREE]** in order to ah make the negotiations successful. It says one of them is domestic regulations and the other one is US leadership at the conference, but there's no proof that there will be US leadership at the conference and there's another thing—another part of the card that's not highlighted and there's no proof that the US will do any of those other things so even if we have domestic regulation there's no proof there will be international cooperation. The second argument is May is still the Spring.

On Advantage One [Laughter]

She says she, ah, just group it. Remember I've taken out the international solvency **[TWO AND A HALF]** solvency, I've explained that above on Observation Two. It's the first argument, 1NC one. I just explained on the counterplan.

Drop down to 1NC three. She extends some of her case evidence but the first answer is her empirics argument is disproven because our evidence is also empirical, talking about New Zealand and other states where they tried ITQs and in practice they don't work. The second argument is that the fourth card out of the 1NC is comparative. It says that despite the projections that the ITQs will do this and it will be a good idea, in practice they don't work. That proves our evidence is better. The next argument is that the only—they only, they only ration fish that are of a marketable size. That's what the **[TWO]** ITQs cause. They only want to make more money, so the ones that won't make money, they still throw them over the side of the boat, which causes bycatch which is exactly their impacts. The next argument is—off her next answer she says that ITQs solve, but that's the same reasons as above. I've answered it. Also, ITQs are not a safe investment. From Townsend in '90:

> Under virtually all limited entry programs, no fisherman can invest in—fisherperson can invest in future catches by delaying current catches. The destructive effects of this inherent competition are constrained by the limits on effort, but the fundamental incentives for individual fisherpeople are unchanged. Even under ITQs, the fisher-people **[ONE AND A HALF]** cannot reduce today's catch in return for higher catches tomorrow. **(1NR#1)**

Now off 1NC four, she, ah, she says that it's, ah, off her first two answers, the first argument is that our evidence is comparative. It says in practice it's supposed to be this way, but in actuality it's not. Her third argument is that the 1AC economic incentive takes out but that exactly proves why they kill the fish because they only want fish that are good for their economies. The ones that are smaller and not good for their economy they won't take.

The next—off her next answer, 1NC five, which is that, um—that we'll never —they'll never go extinct, she says they don't need to go extinct to get the impact, but that's not true, the **[ONE]** biodiversity will alw—always recover so if—as long as the species persis—persist there will still be biodiversity. Unless the species die, there's no biodiversity impact and it greatly minimizes the impact to starvation 'cause it says that they will always recover. She extends her Greenwire card, but this card answers that.

Now off of 1NC six, she says that it's not specific to the fish, but it's inclusive of fish. It's talking about all resources including fish. She says it's a warrant to vote affirmative, that's not true. She simply doesn't understand this. It says there are scientific reasons why exploitation is inevitable. Even if you do the plan, even if you do things like the plan, the fish will still inevitably **[HALF]** be exploited which means the impacts are inevitable. Any risk of the disad outweighs. She says ITQs empirically solve, but I've answered that above. More evidence. Is that there's too many obstacles to solve. Ludwig in '93:

> There are great obstacles to any sort of experimental approach to management. The impossibility of estimating the sustained yield without reducing fishing **[FIFTEEN]** effort can be demonstrated from statistical arguments. These results suggest that sustainable exploitation cannot be achieved without first overexploiting the resource. **(1NR#2)**

First Affirmative Rebuttal
Jason Trice, Michigan State University

OK. The counterplan, disad and case in order.

The counterplan is completely abusive. If we win that it is abusive, it goes away which means that we would outweigh because the case impact is bigger. Extend the first argument which is a permutation. He says that it doesn't get the net benefits. However, it proves that it's not competitive and also the arguments that I'm making below will prove the abuse of it. The permutation proves that it is not competitive. Extend the second argument, which says plan goes through normal means, he says we act now and we're a moving target. Group it, normal means is in the 1AC we're not a moving target. Moreover, the card that he reads on the disad that I will point out later says normal means makes—means that it will be on the docket for forty-five days which would be after the link to the disad. Extend the fil—fourth argument it says that it discourages research.

Group his answers. First is he's not answering our argument. He **[FOUR AND A HALF]** says that we have ground, however, that is irrelevant. He is not researching, he is not learning anything about the topic. You would try to help them and tell them that they should learn next year because he's—he run—he could run this against any topic. Extend the fifth argument it says all things must be competitive. He says it doesn't make sense, but it certainly does. Remember, all things must be competitive. If he is doing the exact same thing as us, there's nothing to compete off of. Moreover, it hurts our ground. We would normal turn alternative solvency mechanism, but when he uses our own solvency mechanism and our own agent, we can't turn the counterplan which makes—it hurts our ground. Now you would extend the sixth argument it says that it's 100% **[FOUR]** net beneficial. He says that we solve for the case. Any risk of this proves the abuse. Remember, it has to be 100% certain of the net benefit because he is abusing us. His any risk—destroy—

hurts the abuse. Extend the seventh argument that says the Spring of 1995. He says it doesn't prove US leadership and other things. The other things argument is new, but my evidence says we would get US leadership. That is conceded and remember he is conceding that he would delay after the Spring of 1995 so he wouldn't get the solvency. The conference happens before him.

Now, bipartisanship.

Extend the first argument it says is risk of all humanity. He says we—there's no impact to delaying, however, I think the—our impact to delay argument is the last argument I'm **[THREE AND A HALF]** going for on the counterplan. The case impact says extinction, we would outweigh. Extend the second argument. It says it's just the IBC it's not case specific. The—he says, he says that the branches are at odds. However, this assumes President Clinton's action that is the only reason why it would get done. There—why they would perceive this why they would fight with Clinton. The marine fisheries is not perceived as Clinton.

Extend the fifth argument. It says that bipartisan is false. He says it's only in the future and that we have strong bipartisan support. This is only one policy with some policies everyone supports. Our evidence says they are opposed to each other. That he hates the Republican agenda, the Contract With America, that they have been working on. Now, extend **[THREE]** the sixth and the seventh arguments which say that prolif is inevitable. He says that it assumes that they get the weapons. Exactly. Our cards say that they will. He reads four cards—three cards that say the NPT solves, however, it assumes that they don't get the weapons. The next argument is prolif is inevitable. Focus on prevention denies the reality. Millot in '94:

> Efforts to deny even minor, isolated countries nuclear weapons capabilities are becoming problematic as the world catches up to the level of technological sophistication achieved by the United States, the sources of nuclear weapons-related supplies dual-use technologies become an ambiguous feature of the global economy. Similarly, there is little reason to believe in the efficacy of forcible nonproliferation. For military and political reasons, the prospects of all the nuclear weapons before it yields a nuclear arsenal are not **[TWO AND A HALF]** good. A small survivable arsenal of nuclear weapons in the hands of regional adversaries are likely to become more important than US military operations in the post-cold war world. **(1AR#1)**

Now he—off the eighth argument which is the turn and prevention denies. He says that it assumes counterproliferation. Yes, exactly. It assumes that prevention trades off with that. Now group his next argument. His next argument is that the status quo proves we have the NPT. Yes, we have the NPT and lots of countries are getting weapons. It's inevitable, that's my argument above. Now group his next two arguments. It says that we should stop prolif and decrease the risk of accidental launch. First it—assumes they don't get the weapons. My evidence says that they, that they will and any—anyway. Also extend the card it says that the deter focus it trades off with counterpro **[TWO]** counterproliferation which is the only way that we can solve a nuclear war. Our allies would proliferate. It is a turn. He doesn't understand it. Now he says that we cannot risk a nuclear war. First, it's 1987, it assumes—it even says an all-out launch. It assumes a cold war with the Soviet Union. The next argument is nuclear war will remain local, it doesn't threaten human extinction. Rauschenbach in '93:

> Even if a normal sequence of events leads to a nuclear war is ruled out, a nuclear conflict can be provoked by international terrorists or some other group. Its consequences will likely be horrific, it would not end the human

race; for that matter, the major nuclear powers with the mind-boggling "overkill" capacity would have to get involved. None of them seem risk precipitating a nuclear conflict endangering the earth, essentially only **[ONE AND A HALF]** accident remains all the conflict. **(1AR#2)**

Now, Observation One.

You would extend it. There's no—there's the, the, the, it is inevitable. The fishery collapse is inevitable. Any risk of a turn they get means that you would still vote for me.

Now, the Observation Two, which is solvency.

He says the counterplan solves and he—but however, I'm arguing that on the counterplan. It's completely abusive. He says it's still springtime but the plan man—mandate of the text says at the end of May. Remember, Spring ends in May and the conference card indicates that it is before that. Now he says—he extends his card. His first argument, he says that over—it's empirically tried and failed. However, our evidence answers this. It says the two places that his card isolates it didn't work initially but it soon **[ONE]** did. The long-term results are that we solve.

Now his next two cards—he, he extends his next 1NC argument. He says it's only rational and that it's not a safe investment. However, the cards, the cards—my evidence says that it makes them a more—they have more time to handle, they are limited in what fish they can catch, so each fish they can handle more. So when they return it to the ocean it's more likely to live. His no safe investment argument. There's no explanation of this argument. I don't understand it. You would protect me here and not let him vote for it. Now he says it doesn't equal extinction. He says biodiversity would recover. However, you take genes out of the pool. It decreases genetic diversity and causes a risk of a collapse. **[HALF]** Also, it is a selective—you selectively take the species out, which weakens them. He says our evidence answers, however the Greenwire evidence says a collapse is inevitable. It postdates all of his evidence. You know that the collapse is coming. Now he says exploitation is **[TWENTY]** inevitable. You will extend Biza's first argument that says not fish. He says others but it's irrelevant. The only thing that case talks about **[QUARTER]**. You will also extend her solvency evidence. It says we solve empirically. He says there are too many obstacles. The card does not talk about ITQs. The next argument is benefits of ITQs outweigh the costs. Schmidt in '94: **[FIVE]**

> In conclusion, ITQ programs can be a very useful tool to conserve and manage the nation's marine resources. Although they're not a panacea, they do not represent the approach the ITQ systems as applied to fisheries where the shoe fits will lead to increased industry support. **(1AR#3)**

Second Negative Rebuttal
Blake Dias, Gonzaga University

Delay counterplan. Bipartisanship.

Anonymous judge: One more time?

The counterplan and then, ah, the disad.

A two-minute link story is ignored by the 1AR. The plan is a gross violation of a status quo compromise. In the status quo, Congress and the executive branch have come to agreement about executive rule-making, especially on the environment. The plan acts without their consultation. It doesn't even tell them about that. In fact, it expressively—acts expressly, acts against their wishes. It will destroy the

NPT. The internal link to that isn't answered. Also, on the counterplan, he's just extending tag lines from the 2AC. He's not answering of the—any of the 1NR analysis which preempted that stuff. I'm the 2NR, don't let the 2AR talk about this and give new reasons. It's my last round. I'm the 2NR. Protect me now.

The first argument they say. He extends the permutation and says it proves it's not competitive. That begs the question: Why does it prove it's not competitive? The 1NR answered this. It's competitive for reasons of net benefits. If you vote for the permutation, you would be both doing the plan now and later which would get the disadvantage, but if you voted for the negative you would be voting for the counterplan alone which solves for the case turn with no impact of delaying until May 15th while avoiding the **[FOUR]** NPT disad. They say there's abuse, but I will answer that below. They say—they extend the second argument in 2AC that says normal means and that means it would happen forty-five days later. The first argument is he doesn't answer the 1NR argument that says they must act now, they can't be a moving target. The assumption both within the 1AC and the 2AC arguments and their whole story about how the del—the counterplans worse 'cause it delays is an assumption they act now. If they say they act later makes them a moving target, which is a more gross violation of ground than their own reasons **[THREE AND A HALF]** for abuse below.

The second argument is that the forty-five days card is just a bill that they're currently considering. It's not what the normal means would include. In addition, I answered this in the 2NC. Remember, part of my link story was that the plan doesn't mandate acting within the status quo compromise on rule-making. It doesn't expressly say that. That was my independent link story which he neglects to answer. They don't do anything like a cost-benefit analysis, etcetera. That was my link answer. It's not helped. It's not answered.

Now, on the ground stuff. He says ground, research, must be competitive, and it hurts their ground. Group this. The first answer is that's false. **[THREE]** The ground claim is false in two ways. The first is that they still have to—they could do two things to still have ground. They could prove that the case impact of delay is out —outweighs the disad link—or the disad link and the impact. They could also impact turn the disad. They could prove the NPT's a bad thing. Those are two things that they're trying to do and it proves that they have ground. Secondly, it's not true. The 1NR says that we still had to link their case to the disad which means we still have to do the research. In addition, he's not answering any of the evidence given in the shell which is extended in the 1NR that says that since **[TWO AND A HALF]** the plan is a different document than the counterplan and since they parametricize the topic, they still have to defend acting now which gives us the ground to act later. In addition, he drops the fourth argument in 1NR which says that since this topic especially is huge it gives us leeway on the ground issue. So even if we hurt a little bit of their ground that's OK because they had so much to begin with. He says it must be 100% net beneficial. That's wrong. Why? You're a policy maker. It's still the best policy. They say the Spring of '95, US leadership. The first argument, he's not answering the 1NR analysis of how the **[TWO]** US delegates wouldn't change their mind and also May is still within the Spring. Look at the card, it just says that sometime in '95 we have to get this going. Nothing says that if we wait until May 15th, we wouldn't get the case solvency. I'd also like to note that there's absolutely no impact to waiting for 'til May 15th in order to solve the case harm.

Bipartisanship.

He says risk impacts delay, etcetera, but delay—waiting until May solves the case turn with no risk. He says there's no link because it assumes Clinton. That's not true.

The NMFS is part of the executive branch and I read the specific link evidence in the 2NC that says that executive **[ONE AND A HALF]** branch rule-making empirically has angered Congress. He doesn't answer this. Also, the whole story about the current compromise on executive rule-making is dropped. Conceded. The 2AR can't talk about it. Right now we have a compromise. The plan acts without consulting Congress. This is conceded. You know that they will upset the NPT. He says that the bipartisanship is dead because he hates Contract With America, etcetera.

The first argument is that my evidence takes this into account and that's my answer in the 2NC. The A-subpoint takes out the assumption despite his rhetoric and things like they're talking about in the card, he **[ONE]** will not change the agenda. They have—would have to prove an agenda change before May 15th in order to make the disad not unique. He says prolif's inevitable. First answer—and it prevents —prevention denies reality, I will get to the prevention denies reality stuff below but off the inevitability, remember the status quo disproves, and the evidence **[FORTY-FIVE]** that I read from Holum disproves the solv—the solvency is empirically true and we stop them from getting the weapons in the first place. Now he extends the turn on focus on prevention's bad. There's no uniqueness for the turn. They don't prove that in a world without the NPT we would have the good system of anti-proliferation **[HALF]** that's the argument in the 2NC. It's never offered in the 1AR which makes this all irrelevant. Also, the evidence from the 2NC makes the comparison. It says that the NPT is the sole obstacle to proliferation. That's the Simpson evidence. Extend the accidental use stuff. It gives me a scenario for a nuclear war. He says that the Fox **[FIFTEEN]** evidence is from 1987 and it would not kill everything but the evidence still says it would be a horrific impact and the evidence says that it's, ah, the most, most likely wouldn't kill everything but Fox takes **[FIVE]** that into account the risk of omnicide means it's intolerable. Look, they definitely anger the Congress, **[TIME]** they definitely destroy bipartisanship. That outweighs the case.

Second Affirmative Rebuttal
Biza Repko, Michigan State University

I'm going to Observation Two first on the case. The counterplan. And bipartisanship. The mike in the wrong place? Mike OK? Everybody set?

You vote for MSU for one simple reason: The counterplan is unfair to run. When I win this argument I will win the debate. The impacts to case are larger and they are more certain than the risk of a shaky risk of a limited nuclear war with shaky internal links and bad uniqueness. Think about the counterplan Blake is asking you to vote on. He's saying—you, when you, when you vote on this counterplan in the final round, the signal you send is this: Hey, don't research this topic. Don't research anything about oceans. Just research links to the NPT. Their argument is, well, we still have to research links to the NPT. Yeah, that's our argument. It makes the research of the topic not ma—matter. It makes the research of the topic ungermane. It's a reason why you don't vote on the counterplan.

Now, the counterplan. Oh, I'm sorry. The Observation Two.

I want you to extend across Jason's second answer on the Observation Two which says that we will have to vote on it at the end of Spring. They mandate that we wait 'til the end of Spring. That's when the conference is over. They can't solve for the case if they wait until the end of Spring. This argument is conceded by Blake. There's not an answer, which concedes all of the solvency. MSU will win the solvency debate, we will win the case debate and our impacts are bigger.

The counterplan.

Extend the second answer. That says—that says, says—our second—it's the first answer off the top of the counterplan which says it discourages research. He says **[FOUR]** it's irrelevant. We still have to research about, about the impacts to links to our disads. The first is it puts us behind the eight ball before the research ever starts. They are allowed to counterplan all—out of all the cases and they don't have to research anything about the topic. The second is the topic germa—germanity should be important. The topic is an important thing, not just a link to the Congress. All they have to research is a link to Clinton or a link to the Congress. That's only two things they have to research. They can counterplan out all the cases. The reason why it wouldn't be important. The third is why would you make affirmative strategy have to be that they impact turn the disad. That gives all the ground to the negative. The only thing that we could do is impact, turn the disad **[THREE AND A HALF]** that's their argument. It's really unfair.

Now the next answer they make is the document causes parametricizing and the topic is huge. The first is, oh, a mention of the topic! That's kind of important, you should probably research about it. [Laughter] The second answer is the doc—we don't parametricize the resolution down to just one thing. If we did, we'd get out of all the disads, but we don't, we still want there to be some debate about the topic which is the reason why it's important.

Now he concedes the next argument that says all parts of plan must be competitive. Not answered. He's trying to group it, but there's no specific answer to it. Extend across that all parts of the plan must be competitive. The reason why is because if they aren't it becomes unfair to the affirmative. We can just perm out of the part of the plan which is not to do it through, which is not to do it through—not to wait. We could say just do the plan and do the plan. It proves our argument true. That's conceded by Blake. No answer. It'd be really pretty tough to drop us on the counterplan now.

The last answer I want you to extend across is they would not be able to solve the case. He says that, he says 1995, 1995, but first is the argument Jason makes on case is conceded. Remember, the conference ends at the end of Spring of 1995. They don't even start thinking about overfishing until May 15th, 1995 which just **[TWO AND A HALF]** means that they are able to solve for all the case debate. Remember, the case impacts are bigger. Once we win that they can't run the counterplan, you vote for MSU.

The disad.

Blakes's big argument is that he has a link. That's interesting, but you don't have uniqueness, nor do you have a specific link. That's the reason why you vote for MSU. Extend across the second answer that says the links not rec—specific. He says that Clinton is fighting but first is our argument, is why would this be perceived as a policy that Clinton does. That's not the argument that he answers. He merely says that the Republicans and Clinton hate each other. Yeah. But we pass our policy through the NMFS. Why is that perceived as something that Clinton would hegemonically do? It's in the executive council, but it has to be something that Clinton does to make the Republicans dislike them. It decreases **[TWO]** the credibility of the link.

Now extend across the sixth answer which is bipartisanship is dead. He says our A point evidence answers this, but first is the A point evidence in the shell is awful. All it says is Clinton is like Harry Truman. It doesn't say anything about our arguments. The second is our argument takes theirs into account. It says, even though Clinton has made some attempts and pushes to be bipartisan—ship bipartisan, it's not true. The reason why is he will veto the things in the crime bill and he hates, personally, all of the Republicans. [Laughter] It means that there is no uniqueness to this position. You don't vote on this disad if there's no uniqueness. They can't just run **[ONE AND A HALF]** [unintelligible] all of the uniqueness to this position.

Now, the turn. On the turn, he says that I will an—this is the original number seven and eight which is prolif is inevitable. He says he will answer it below but he never does. Extend across the evidence that Jason reads in the 1AR, conceded by Blake in the 2NR which is proliferation is inevitable. Even if I don't win the turn below it makes the disadvantage impact not unique. It will always happen. When we win the counterplan, the impacts to the disad are inevitable. They'll always happen. Nothing below answers that. Now, the turn. His only good argument to the turn **[ONE]** is that there's no uniqueness to the turn. We don't prove it's happening now, but the argument makes no sense. The first answer is the evidence proves that there's a tradeoff. It says there's a tradeoff between counterproliferation measures and other measures that we do in the status quo to try to stop the acquisition of nuclear weapons. The second is their argument in the shell is that we're focused on the NPT now, which means we're focused on non-proliferation measures. We are not focused on the other measures. There's a tradeoff which means that we would be focusing on use. If we're not going to get the NPT in the status quo because it is threatened, then that means we must be focusing on the other parts because there is a tradeoff. The third is even **[HALF]** if he wins this argument and decreases the uniqueness on the turn, the uniqueness on the disadvantage is so bad that at least it gives you some risk to vote for MSU. Now, the last answer he says is he'll extend across the Fox card. It says—it's horrific. The first is, so would be starvation of a billion people. When I win the case I think that that would be horrific. The second is the accidental launch **[QUARTER]** is not proved that he would get to his impact. Remember, our argument is that proliferation is inevitable. It will always happen. You **[TEN]** vote for MSU for one simple reason: They can't run the counterplan. It is unfair. **[FIVE]** When they lose the solvency to the case, they lose the debate. Our impact is bigger, it happens **[TIME]** faster, and it's bigger than the Fox evidence.

REASONS FOR DECISIONS

Michigan State University (Affirmative) won the debate on a 5–2 decision.

Each judge was required to submit a written critique of the debate by May 1, 1995. Critiques were only altered for some stylistic reasons. Any typographical errors, for the most part, appear in the original critique.

Will Baker
Queens College & IMPACT Coalition
Voted: Affirmative

Congratulations to Biza, Jason, Blake and Ian for a fine round. Both the Michigan State and Gonzaga programs have a great deal to be proud of based upon this year's final round. Thank you to those in the region, especially Dr. Tuna Snider, responsible for my having the opportunity to judge. Here is how the round boils down for me. Spending and topicality are punted so they are not factors in my decision.

On Obs II: SOLVENCY—2NR concedes the solvency time frame for case argued in 1AR (that the counterplan would start at the conference's conclusion). The case solvency (absent competition from the counterplan) gets 1 billion risk from the starvation scenario as well. 2NR is correct that the Speer evidence does not totally exclude the Delay c-plan so the debate will be settled elsewhere.

DELAY C-PLAN—Blake asks for protection and I provide it. Biz's answers in 2AR on the abuse questions regarding options are new. Nowhere in 1AR are explanations given for why it's enough to have (1) impact turns or (2) disads to delay so I don't evaluate the topic germanity discussion beyond the line by line on 100% Net Benefits standard and the every part of c-plan must be competitive.

The latter is conceded, which leads us to BIPART DA—Blake says to look to Simpson evidence and extend the launch evidence with comparison that even mitigated this would still be horrific. He concedes 1AR card (Millot) which says proliferation is inevitable and denies the reality of the situation. This nonuniques the DA, at least, and turns it at most. Blake is right that the Executive rule link story is conceded but that fails to make the impacts unique and answers only marginally why the NMFS acting would create tension. It's kind of tough to meet a NB standard with a non-unique disadvantage which leaves me with an affirmative ballot.

Russell T. Church
Middle Tennessee State University
Voted: Affirmative

I would like to congratulate both teams for their success and proven excellence by reaching the final round of the 1995 CEDA National Debate Tournament. The coaching staffs of both Michigan State University and Gonzaga University should be very proud of their accomplishments and the excellent debating so evident in this round. In particular, I would like to congratulate the Directors of both programs. My long time colleague and friend, Jim Roper, has worked very hard for many years to secure funding, an excellent coaching staff and the support of the Administration at Michigan State University. Bill DeForrest has directed and coached a program in the finest tradition of debate, the finest tradition of Jesuit education and with the clear view debate should be humane and intellectual dialogue among all the participants. I salute both fine Directors.

I considered these issues this debate. First, the delay counterplan occupied legitimate non-topical ground in this debate. As the negative argued when the affirmative claims parametrics, the affirmative gives up any non-affirmative case and plan as legitimate for the negative to argue. I should note that there was no clear claim of parametrics by the affirmative on my flow. However, a parametrical stance was evident in the assumptions behind the affirmative responses to the topicality position. In addition, the affirmative did not deny the claim that they were parametricizing the case. I also agreed that there was no reason why every part of the counterplan must be non-topical. This did not make sense to me and would be abusive to the negative ground. Perhaps the failure of the affirmative to give a clear warrant for this argument was the reason I find this difficult to accept. There was also no reason given for the affirmative demand for the 100 percent net benefits analysis demanded by the affirmative. The affirmative was asked why by the negative and the affirmative fails to respond.

Although I agreed with the negative on much, there were several very persuasive responses given to the counterplan by the affirmative. While this topic was huge and the negative would have been both justified and wise in carving out a clean and narrow ground for argument, I was troubled by the narrow ground that remains for debate given this counterplan. The final rebuttal was quite persuasive in arguing that the counterplan seriously diminishes the learning and education that takes place in this kind of narrowly defined ground. Clearly, research burdens for the negative would be very minimal. Also the responses that the affirmative might theoretically be able to make would be greatly restricted.

Furthermore, the time frame debate on counterplan would suggest that there would be a risk of counterplan solvency not coming in time since the affirmative says spring is the time when action is necessary and the counterplan comes in the later part of the spring. Given the above arguments, I decided not to consider the counterplan as a reason to reject the affirmative.

I also considered the bipartisanship disadvantage. As the final negative speaker argued, the executive rule making analysis critical to this argument was ignored by the affirmative. I also agree that there was a sufficient internal link story in the second negative rebuttal in terms of the "angering Congress" analysis. Moreover, the second negative effectively extended that the Administration's rhetoric would not change the agenda. On the uniqueness debate the affirmative argued that there was movement ("pushes to bipartisanship") to bipartisanship occurring. Upon examination of the evidence from the affirmative, it seemed to be speculating about possible bipartisanship. Anyhow, the evidence was not clear enough to take out the negative position. The affirmative also argued that proliferation is inevitable. On this affirmative evidence was specific to nuclear non-proliferation mechanisms, but it was not specific to the Non-Proliferation Treaty in particular that the negative demanded. Furthermore, the negative extends that the Non-Proliferation Treaty empirically has reduced the number of weapons. I believe there was a good reason to believe that the Non-Proliferation Treaty has some value in reducing proliferation. The negative also extended in the last rebuttal that impact will be "horrific" and the risk is intolerable. I believe that at the end of this last negative speech there was certainly reason to consider voting negative based on the negative disadvantage on bipartisanship.

The second affirmative rebuttal, however, was able to capitalize on some dropped arguments by the negative. The last speaker extended that there is no impact comparison by the negative. The affirmative also noted that the second negative dropped the case debate. This allows the affirmative to extend the impact of starving billions and to compare the risk accidental launch argued by the negative. The negative had earlier argued a comparison of the world with and world without the Non-Proliferation Treaty. However, this was not the impact comparison that was more relevant since the affirmative scenario and specific impacts were not included. Finally, in weighing the case impacts against the disadvantage impacts, I chose the more specific and more extensive harms documented by the affirmative case as the more compelling rationale for my decision.

Thus, at the end of the debate, I did not consider the counterplan. I granted the negative their disadvantage, but the impact comparison by the second affirmative speaker meant the affirmative case outweighed the negative disadvantage. Therefore, I voted for the affirmative in a very close round.

John Fritch
Southwest Missouri State University
Voted: Affirmative

Congratulations are obviously in order to the two teams and their coaching staffs. Both teams have had excellent seasons and it is only fitting that their year should end in the final round of the national tournament. I think that it is also exciting for the debate community to have teams representing two entirely different institutions and two entirely different programs in terms of institutional support reach the final round.

The 1995 final round is an excellent example of how quickly CEDA debate has changed and, I would say, progressed. The development of counterplan theory in CEDA has been rapid and the analysis on the disadvantage debate occurs on the link level as much as on the impact level. The use of counterplans and the analysis of links to disadvantages provides for increased quality of debates.

The negative position in the debate is the counterplan that does the plan on May 15 in order to avoid disrupting the Non-Proliferation Treaty negotiations. The CP obviously avoids the bipartisanship disadvantage and claims to solve the case entirely. There are three main issues involved in adjudicating this debate: first, the legitimacy of the counterplan; second, the solvency of the counterplan for the case; third, the bipartisanship disadvantage.

The first issue is the legitimacy of the counterplan. While this issue has a large effect on the rest of the debate, I will do here as I did while making my decision and save this issue until the other issues are resolved.

The second issue is the solvency of the counterplan for the case. I decide that the counterplan achieves little solvency. The international solvency for the case rests on the US leadership which will accompany the passage of the plan. The affirmative argues that the counterplan will not solve because spring is over in May and that the conference could be completed by May 15. I find the first argument less than persuasive since May is part of spring. However, the second argument does significant damage to the solvency claims for the counterplan for two reasons. First, the conference could be completed by May 15. The Speer evidence in the 1AC does not indicate when the conference will be completed, only that there is a "goal of reaching agreement" in the spring of 1995. There is substantial chance that the negotiations could be completed by the time the counterplan is enacted. Second, the reason the case solves is the use of US leadership at the negotiations. The Speer evidence states that US leadership is required and that this will require vision by the United States. In addition, the evidence indicates that the negotiations are an ongoing affair. The result is that even if the negotiations are not concluded by the May 15 counterplan date, the affirmative solves better by providing the crucial US leadership and vision during the negotiation period. The impacts to the case are conceded. The negative solves for very little of the case and must win the disadvantage outright to compete with the affirmative impacts of starvation and marine biodiversity.

The final issue is the bipartisanship disadvantage. I decide that the disadvantage is not unique since nuclear proliferation is inevitable and that there may be some minimal impact turn. The affirmative arguments as to the inevitability of proliferation hinge on technical development and nuclear materials being transported from the former Soviet Union in the 2AC evidence and on the military and political reasons why nonproliferation will fail in the 1AR Millot evidence. The 2NR argues that the status quo disproves the uniqueness argument and extends the Hallof evidence claiming that it is empirically true that nonproliferation has stopped the expansion of weapons. I find these arguments to be less than compelling given the reasons why proliferation is inevitable in the future. Nonproliferation may have worked before, but with the end of the Soviet Union and the military and political problems identified by Millot, there are new proliferation threats which the nonproliferation regime will not be able to prevent. The lack of uniqueness becomes problematic for the negative given the lack of a rate of proliferation debate. The only argument advanced by the negative which begins to get at the rate of proliferation is the 2NC evidence which claims that decreased proliferation decreases the risk of arguments. However, the impact of this evidence is greatly mitigated by the 1AR and 2AR indicts of the 2NC Fox evidence which argues that an "all out nuclear war" should be avoided at all costs. The 1AR and 2AR argue that a nuclear war will be local and that the evidence assumes an all out nuclear war in the Cold War.

In addition, the affirmative may get some minimal amount of a turn to the disadvantage. The 2AC evidence indicates that if the US cannot guarantee the security of its allies against the threat of proliferated states, "the result is likely to be further proliferation among these allies, highly unstable regional military situations, a sure reduction of the United States' international influence, and a growing probability of regional nuclear wars involving US forces." As the negative argues, there is little hint of a tradeoff in the 2AC evidence. (A more important implication of the evidence could have been that absent the tradeoff in evidence, the allied proliferation becomes another uniqueness argument.)

The first, and final, issue is the legitimacy of the counterplan. Even if the counterplan is legitimate I had decided that the plan is superior to the counterplan for the reasons discussed above. Typically, I would not resolve this issue, but for purposes of the critique I will discuss it here. The debate on the legitimacy of the counterplan is plagued by a lack of clash. The negative offers reasons why the counterplan is legitimate and the affirmative offers reasons why the counterplan is illegitimate, but the reasons seldom explicitly address each other. While this is not a necessity in theory debates, it is typically the manner in which these debates happen. Unfortunately for debaters, this makes the issue difficult to resolve and forces the judge to evaluate the debate based primarily on personal beliefs as to which claims are more acceptable and more important. I find the affirmative arguments on this issue more compelling. I believe the research of the topic is minimized by the counterplan and that the topic is an "important thing" as described by the 2AR. In addition, I find the affirmative's argument that every part of the counterplan needs to be competitive compelling, and the part of the counterplan which does the affirmative plan is not competitive with the affirmative plan. As the 2AC eloquently explains, "Do the plan and the plan." Unfortunately, the implications of these arguments are not well developed. I think they are important claims, but the importance is not well identified in the debate.

This was a close debate. The issues were not easily resolvable due to the quality of argumentation, and all debaters performed well in a uniquely pressured situation. My suspicion is that the 5–2 decision is at least partially reflective of the nature of the negative strategy employed in this debate. By employing this particular counterplan, the negative isolated three key arguments: legitimacy of the counterplan, the ability of the counterplan to solve for the case, and the bipartisanship disadvantage. The negative must win all three of these three issues to win this debate. Such a situation is very different from more traditional negative strategies which give the negative a variety of ways in which to win the debate. My hunch is that the judges on the final round panel who voted for the affirmative will have done so for a variety of reasons, which only furthers my belief that this was a close debate.

Jeffrey Dale Hobbs
Abilene Christian University
Voted: Negative

First, let me offer my sincerest congratulations to both teams. I was impressed with your talents and with your dedication to the activity, and I thoroughly enjoyed the debate. My vote was cast for the negative. Let me explain my decision.

The debate came down to the answers to three questions: (1) Should the counterplan be accepted? (2) If the counterplan is accepted, will it meet the affirmative's advantage? And, (3) if the affirmative plan is accepted, is there an increased risk to nuclear proliferation?

Should the counterplan be accepted? If it was left up to my own personal preference, my answer would probably be no. I can't say that I am particularly fond of counterplans. Especially, those counterplans which are essentially the affirmative plan. However, the arguments in this debate led me to another conclusion. Let me work backwards from the 2AR to explain my decision. The 2AR gives two basic reasons to reject the counterplan. First, the 2AR argues that the negative counterplan should be rejected because allowing this strategy would mean the negative would not have to research the topic. I thought the 2NR response that research would have to be done to find links was sufficient to answer this position. There weren't any clear standards given as to how much research should be done for a strategy to be considered legitimate. Additionally, the importance of research on the topic seemed to balloon in the 2AR. It just didn't seem to be that big of an issue before the last speech. Second, the 2AR argued that all parts of the counterplan must be competitive. The 2AR claimed that the negative had conceded this point to the affirmative. However, I believe the 2NR had responded to this position by arguing that the counterplan and plan are different documents. This isn't a great answer, but it is far from conceding the point. Thus, absent a clear reason to disallow the counterplan, it becomes an "alternative" policy to consider. After accepting the counterplan, the debate becomes one of timing. When should the "affirmative" action be taken—now or one month later?

If the counterplan is accepted, will it meet the affirmative's advantage? After waiting a month, would the counterplan still be able to achieve the affirmative case advantages? I think the answer is yes. The affirmative claims that the counterplan would not get the advantages because agreement has to be reached by the end of the spring. They read a card from Speer (94) which says "... with the goal of reaching agreement in the spring of 95." The negative satisfactorily answers this position by pointing out that May is this spring. So, the affirmative plan and the negative counterplan can claim the same advantages. Is there a reason to vote for the counterplan?

If the affirmative plan is accepted, is there an increased risk to nuclear proliferation? This question was the most difficult one to resolve. Ultimately, the risk to this disadvantage is minuscule, but it is a risk that one would not have to take with the counterplan.

I'm not convinced that taking action now would definitely lead to a break in bipartisanship, nor am I convinced that it wouldn't. I am convinced that there is a slim possibility of acting now hurting bipartisanship, thus interfering with the NPT conference.

Does the NPT do any good or is nuclear proliferation inevitable? To answer this question, both teams read mass quantities of evidence. However, the victor of this "card war" is not clearly decided in the debate. Why should one accept one card over another? Is there a story that would take into account the issues presented in both teams' cards? Unfortunately, those questions are never addressed in the debate. My view of the debate led me to believe that the NPT has done some good in the world. While it can't stop all proliferation, it has and can continue to stop some.

Is there a turn provided by the affirmative's position that there is a tradeoff between nonproliferation measures and preparation for nuclear attacks (the Millot 94 card)? I bought the negative's answer that there is no uniqueness for this turn. That is, the affirmative did not demonstrate that, absent the NPT, our focus would be any different than it is now. Reverse causality is not proven, and this seemed to be an implicit standard accepted by both teams due to questions asked by the 2AC during cross-x.

In summary, the negative counterplan was an acceptable strategy in this debate, the counterplan was able to accrue the affirmative advantages, and there is ever so slight a risk that acting now could increase the risk of nuclear war. Thus, I voted negative. Again, congratulations to both teams and thanks for a most enjoyable debate.

Matt Taylor
California State University Long Beach
Voted: Affirmative

Let me begin by congratulating both teams and both universities for their outstanding accomplishments. Although this debate lacked a tremendous amount of sophistication it was enjoyable to watch.

At the end of this debate I am left with the following stories. The negative argues that I should delay implementing the affirmative plan until May 15 to ensure that Congress and the President maintain an amicable bipartisan relationship. This relationship, the negative argues, is essential to passing the Non-Proliferation Treaty (NPT) which is vital to slowing the spread of nuclear weapons and reducing nuclear accidents. The negative concludes their story arguing that the risks associated with not passing the NPT are larger than the risks associated with species exploitation for two reasons. First, they argue on case that status quo species depletion will not lead to species extinction. Second, they argue that delaying implementation of the affirmative plan until May 15 does not pose any additional significant risk to species extinction. Thus, they conclude that the risks associated with increased proliferation from not passing the NPT outweigh the risk of not implementing ITQs for 45 days.

The affirmative argues that I should implement their plan (ITQs) immediately to prevent the extinction of fish which are a vital source of protein to millions of people and to prevent a decrease in biodiversity which is necessary to ocean and human life. They argue that delaying implementation of their plan is unfair, unnecessary, and counterproductive. They argue that the counterplan is unfair because the competition is, for lack of a better term, artificial and because delay counterplans discourage research on the topic. They argue that the delay is unnecessary because the bipartisan climate, so necessary to the passage of the NPT, is already dwindling. They argue that it would be counterproductive to vote for the counterplan because the NPT may actually make war more likely. Thus, they conclude that the only prudent action is to immediately implement ITQs to save the starving masses.

From these stories several points of controversy seem to emerge. The first question I must resolve is: Is the delay counterplan legitimate? I have to admit that I am not a fan of delay counterplans. I generally believe that the affirmative arguments are correct—the counterplan competition is artificial and it discourages topic specific research. However, I accept the legitimacy of the counterplan in this round for three reasons. First, the affirmative strategy to cry foul is not developed with sound arguments in rebuttals. If the affirmative really wanted me to reject the legitimacy of the counterplan I would have expected and required the 1AR to spend much more time answering the 1NR arguments supporting the legitimacy of the counterplan. Second, the affirmative argument that delay counterplans decrease research is adequately answered on two levels. First, I am persuaded that negative teams must be allowed to argue generics on large topics. The 1NR argues that broad topics can be unfair to negatives if judges require specific evidence on every possible case area.

Second, I am persuaded that the negative, at least in this round, is researching topic specific evidence. The 1NR points out that they are reading case specific solvency cards and they are reading topic specific links to their disadvantages. Third, the negative justification for the counterplan, that the affirmative case suggests we must act now, is never answered. As a policy maker I am left with the policy option of acting now to stop overfishing or waiting 45 days. Because the affirmative case is predicated on the urgency of action the option to delay is theoretically legitimate.

The second question I must resolve is: Will implementation of the affirmative plan undermine the bipartisan climate necessary to the passage of the NPT? I am convinced that passing the affirmative plan through executive order will risk undermining bipartisanship for two reasons. First, the negative's story and evidence on bipartisanship is better and more specific to environmental issues than the affirmative's. Second, the best affirmative evidence states that bipartisanship exists now but will need constant nurturing. They use this evidence to argue that bipartisanship is weak and declining, but I think the evidence feeds the negative story that bipartisanship exists but it is fragile. Thus, I do not want to risk passing a plan that might disrupt the fragile balance that will ensure passage of the NPT.

The third question I must resolve is: What is the impact of not passing the NPT? I believe that not passing the NPT risks increased proliferation and increased nuclear accidents which is something the decision rule read in the 2NC tells me I should never risk. The affirmative has three answers. First, the affirmative argues that proliferation is inevitable and thus the impact to the disadvantage is not unique. The negative, however, reads very good evidence that the NPT has and will slow the spread of weapons. Thus, I am not persuaded that proliferation is inevitable. Even if the affirmative is right I am not sure why I should not try to slow the spread when I can. Second, they argue that the NPT may actually make war more likely. The 2NC argues that the turn is not unique and the 1AR does not respond. Thus, for me, the turn goes away. Third, the affirmative argues that millions of starving children outweighs the risk of increased proliferation and nuclear accidents. This argument does not deny the impact of the disadvantage—it only compares the risk of inaction on our overfishing problem with inaction on the NPT. Thus, I am persuaded that the NPT is vital to reducing proliferation and the risk of nuclear accidents.

The final question I must resolve is: Are the risks associated with not passing the NPT greater than waiting 45 days to implement ITQs. The only evidence that suggests an urgent action on overfishing says that I must act in the Spring of 1995. O.S.C.1061 Thus, both the affirmative plan and the counterplan act quickly enough to save millions of people from starving. If I vote for the affirmative plan I may help reduce overfishing but I risk losing the NPT, increased proliferation, and increased nuclear accidents. If I vote for the counterplan I provide the best chance for passing the NPT and, in 45 days, help reduce overfishing.

In the end, the decision in this round is clear. I vote for Gonzaga to ensure passage of the NPT, reduce proliferation, reduce the chance of nuclear accidents, and to help reduce overfishing.

Joe Tuman
San Francisco State University
Voted: Negative

No critique submitted. (Each judge provided their critiques directly to the debaters: Independently they were asked to submit written critiques for publication.)

Steve Whitson
DePaul University
Voted: Affirmative

Reason for Decision

Topicality—The negative violation itself, in theory, is a logical argument, as conservation, the prevention of a future decrease in fish stocks, is not directly an increase in my mind. But the 2AC answers were very persuasive: The violation evidence did not assume the context of oceans, and the evidence equating the development of fish with conservation (2AC#5) was excellent. Smart for the negative to kick it.

Spending—This should never have been run in the first place, considering that, as of 1NC, the Negative did not bother to answer the third solvency card, that ITQs decrease the need for government enforcement because of self-regulation by fishermen. Not a wise choice when the link is "increased cost of enforcement." The link card was not bad, but the solvency card should have been argued, to prevent the Affirmative pulling it as undenied. Thank you for not extending the DA.

The substantive issues that were left by the last two rebuttals were not as clear as Biza made them sound, largely because of a number of new responses and explanations of things the 1AR did not say. But the necessary answers *were* there, and given *those,* the decision was solidly Affirmative—it simply could have been more concrete. Observation 1, Advantage 1, and Advantage 2 are conceded, so there is certainly a justification for change; the question is between Affirmative solvency and the Delay Counterplan.

Observation 2, Solvency, is somewhat problematic. The 2NR drops it, so there is no longer any question that ITQs will solve. (Personally, I think the last Negative card that was read here, "Too many obstacles to solvency—impossible to set a maximum sustainable yield," should have been pursued, because it directly cuts against ITQs, and it was not answered specifically in 1AR, except with a generic "Benefits of conservation outweigh" card.) So they solve. But the response Biza pulls from 1AR in her 2AR, that "the UN action must be voted on by the end of Spring in order to create an international fishing regime" is simply not in the 1AR on Solvency. The 1AR argued the presses against specific cards, but this timeframe argument was *not* on solvency, and the Negatives *did* answer it on the counterplan.

On the delay counterplan, Biza pursues three major issues in 2AR, none of which take out the counterplan. The entire block on the discouraging of research as a result of this counterplan is new in 2AR. The negative block gives five answers off the original 2AC argument (even if they are only "lots of ground to argue DA impacts," "must research DA links," "point of plan is immediate action," etc.), and the 1AR's only argument is "irrelevant, they are not researching the topic." I completely agree with the reasons Biza articulates in 2AR on why the research is important and that the counterplan excludes some Affirmative ground, but *all* of the explanation is brand new. The second issue, that all parts of plan must be competitive with the counterplan was not argued as an absolute take-out. The third issue, that the UN conference ends in Spring '95 and only the affirmative meets the deadline, is the cross-application of the 1AR solvency response that was not made. In fact, the section of the counterplan where the 1AR did argue the conference date, 1AR#1 & #2 off the three negative answers to 2AC#2, was argued by 2NR. He says that "the 45 day docket is generic, not assuming immediate adoption by normal means" and that "it does not assume current (bipartisan) compromise in Congress," which the 2AR does not touch. The negative wins the Counterplan itself, but the only net benefit to it requires the Bipartisanship DA.

The DA goes away for two reasons. The second 2AC answer, "no specific link to ITQs or evidence that ITQs will be a policy perceived as 'Clinton's Environmental Policy'" is never adequately refuted. The 2NC gives generic environmental policy evidence, and argues that there is a compromise now, but never proves a concrete link that an ITQ policy will break that compromise. It is pulled by the 1AR, the 2NR only repeats 2NC, and Biza hammers the analysis home. I cannot see any reason why this would be perceived as Clinton's environmental policy (if anything, it's a trade policy with environmental impacts). That answer is enough. However, I also believe that proliferation is inevitable. The 2AC#6 and #7 are good, especially #6 that the NPT will not prevent Russian arms sales, and eventually that will outstrip any international enforcement mechanism. The 2NR collapses to arguing that the NPT empirically works, but this does not answer the affirmative position that even if it is effective now, the NPT will inevitably fail, making proliferation not-unique. Biza pulls this also in 2AR, and this would also independently eliminate the DA. Absent the DA, there is no advantage to voting for the counterplan over the affirmative plan, so the decision is clearly for Michigan State University.

FLOW SHEET OF THE 1995 FINAL ROUND

On the following pages is a flow sheet of the 1995 CEDA final round. Some notes should be made about the composition of this flow sheet. First and foremost, evidence, when read for the first time in the debate, is symbolized by an "❡". We also include the source and date next to the ❡. Second, in the interest of clarity, the major sections of argumentation are split into multiple pages. For example, the entire debate focusing on Observation Two on case does not readily fit onto one word-processed page. Hence, the flow sheet runs across two pages.

Several abbreviations are used. We have tried to keep these to a minimum in order to maximize the educational value of the flow sheet. However, some could not be avoided. In addition, the use of abbreviations probably serve an educational capacity anyway.

The order of the flow is fairly logical. The first affirmative is first; the off-case arguments follow in the order in which they were presented.

EXERCISES

1   What type of case did the affirmative use?
2.   Write a ballot indicating and justifying your decision of who won the debate. Specifically answer these questions:
   a.   Who won the harm issue?
   b.   Who won the inherency issue?
   c.   Who won the solvency issue?
   d.   Who won the disadvantage issue?
   e.   Who won the counterplan?
   f.   Who won topicality?
3.   Examine the judges' critiques. What, if any, judging philosophy do they reveal?
4.   Carefully read and flow the debate up until the first affirmative rebuttal. Give your own second negative rebuttal speech.
5.   Carefully read and flow the debate up until the second negative rebuttal. Give your own second affirmative rebuttal speech.

Flow Sheet of Final Round—Page 1

1AC	1NC	2AC	2NC / 1NR	1AR	2NR	2AR
Case Observation One: Fish Stocks Nearly Gone 🍎 Greenwire '95 Fish stocks on brink of collapse SQ = inevitable collapse. 🍎 Weber '94 Must improve fishery management	1. No internal link to Weber 2. No impact to delay	1. US overfishing now, can solve for it. 1. Extend Greenwire. On brink of collapse CP won't be able to solve for the UN meeting		**Case** Fishery collapse is inevitable Any risk of the turn means vote Affirmative		
Plan: NMFS replaces open access fishing with ITQs. Research done to determine MSY & TAC.						
Advantage One **Starvation** Decreased fish = increased starvation 🍎 Houston Chronicle '94 Oceans = 1/2 the animal protein consumed globally Pop. growth and fewer fish = ↓ food crisis. 🍎 Sunday Telegraph 1/29/95 Fish disappearing: could = social tensions						

Flow Sheet of Final Round—Page 2

1AC	1NC	2AC	2NC / 1NR	1AR	2NR	2AR
Industrialized nations now fishing the Southern oceans ☞ Nickerson '94 = more starvation Impact = billions of lives at risk ☞ Wacker '94 World is running out of fish **Scenario Two:** **Marine Biodiversity** ☞ Bohnsack '93 Overfishing crushes genetic diversity and removes most desirable fish ☞ Gianni '93 Ocean health key to life on the planet **Observation Two:** **Solvency** ☞ Litz '94 ITQs superior to SQ b/c provide economic incentive not to fish Empirically, ITQs end the race for fish. ☞ Fujita & Hopkins '94 = 's sustainability	1. Plan = US leadership at the conference. Plan only changes US reg's 2. First card proves Topicality Says are doing conservation.	1. Ev says can do it w/strong conservation measure. 1. No it doesn't. T evidence takes this away. 2. Proves we fish, t/o T arg.	1. Explained on the CP	Is answered on the CP. Spring ends in May, conference ends before that.		Extend. Dropped in 2NR. Conference ends before the CP. Means CP can't solve

Flow Sheet of Final Round–Page 3

1AC	1NC	2AC	2NC / 1NR	1AR	2NR	2AR
ITQs reduce cost of enforcement via market forces. ♣ Litz '94 ='s self-enforcement	3. ITQs = overfishing ♣ Zuckerman '94 New Zealand shows more waste and destruction w/ITQs	1. Extend all 1AC evidence 2. ITQs solve for bycatch ♣ Fujita & Hopkins '94 Reduces total fishing effort	1. New Zealand denies her evidence 2. 1NC #4 is comparative. ITQs fail in practice. 3. Still get bycatch by only rationing marketable fish. 4. ITQ solvency answered above. 5. ITQs = a safe investment ♣ Townsend '90	Our evidence says it didn't work at first but soon did. My evidence says that they have more time to eliminate bycatch. No safe investment argument makes no sense.		
US action key to international compliance ♣ Speer '94 US must adopt strong conservation measure	4. ITQs = more destruction ♣ Duncan '94 Not conservative approach. In practice, ITQs increase ocean capitalization 5. No extinction b/c costs too much ♣ Anderson & Leeds '91 Cost of catching final fish too high 6. Exploitation inevitable ♣ Ludwig, et al. '93 4 reasons	1. Plan does research to prevent this. 2. Ev. above answers this 3. Economic incentive denies 1. Don't need total extinction 2. Greenwire card says on brink now 1. Not specific to fish 2. Is a warrant to vote aff. since all fish problems inev. 3. ITQs solve overfishing empirically ♣ Lundsten '94 Need ITQs	(Group 1 & 2) 1. Our ev is comparative. 1. Proves bycatch argument above 1. Biodiversity always recovers. 1. Ev answers Greenwire card 1. Is inclusive of fish. Is all resources. 1. Not true. Is inevitable. Will still exploit fish. Any risk of disad outweighs. 1. Above 2. Too many obstacles to solve ♣ Ludwig '93 Cannot solve w/o overexploiting the resource.	Taking genes out of the pool means that causes a risk of collapse. Is also selectively taking out strong members of the species. Greenwire card says collapse inev. Extend 2AC not specific to fish argument. His answer is irrelevant. Extend 2AC solvency evidence. Says we solve empirically. Too many obstacles card doesn't talk about ITQs Benefits of ITQs outweigh costs. ♣ Schmidt '94 ITQs useful		

Flow Sheet of Final Round—Page 4

1NC	2AC	2NC / 1NR	1AR	2NR	2AR
Topicality A. Definitions 1. Decrease 🍎 Webster's become greater in size 2. Development 🍎 Oxford English Dict. Process of dev'ing. 3. Contrasts w/ conservation 🍎 Webster's Act of keeping free from depletion, decay, etc. 4. Development and conservation are competing concerns 🍎 PRNewswire 12/28/94 Coal development not conservation B. Standards 1. Case makes topic bidirectional. 2. Effects T destroys ground Must conserve to develop. Unfair	1. We meet. Are a process 2. Neg evidence ≠ oceans 3. Counterdefinition: ocean develop. means research & food production 🍎 Lipp '64 Six things, including food & research 4. Defn. superior a. is field contextual b. assumes resolutional context c. resolutional limits 5. Development includes conservation 🍎 Pivo '93 Forest production includes conservation 1. We pick one side. No explanation of why this is bad. 1. Not effects topical. Directly develop thru research. 2. Development = step by step process 🍎 Webster's Development is a step by step process				

Flow Sheet of Final Round—Page 5

1NC	2AC	2NC 1NR	1AR	2NR	2AR
3. Ban development CP test. Can still do the plan.	1. Not aff interpretation. Don't ban development				
C. Voting issue Ground jurisdiction	1. They have huge ground. 2. Literature stops abuse				
Spending					
A. Dollar surging after German rate cut	1. No link. Don't spend any money.				
♣ Marshall & Petruno 3/31/95	2. No link. Litz in '93 sez no $ to enfoce				
Dollar soars after rate cut	3. Is longer-term spending.	1. True. Savings also long term. Therefore, no turn.			
	4. C/A spending mechanism in plan. Auctioning off quotas will save $				
	5. Internal link evidence stinks. Global economy stagnated since 1992				
	6. Non-unique. Dollar at lowest point since WWII now				
	7. ITQs generate $ w/o Federal spending	1. Only pay for itself. Not a turn. No savings.			
	♣ Lundsten '94 Requires no aid or buy-back programs	2. Irrelevant. No scenario for a turn w/savings.			
	8. Non-unique. Dollar already crashed	3. Irrelevant b/c non-unique. Dollar has crashed.			
	♣ Shilling '95 Will = a recession				
B. Links 1. ITQs require 2–3X enforcement $					
♣ Zuckerman '94 NMFS says would be much more expensive					

Flow Sheet of Final Round—Page 6

1NC	2AC	2NC / 1NR	1AR	2NR	2AR
2. Fiscal restraint now key to halting dollar decline ♣ BNA 3/13/95 Must address fiscal imbalance C. Weak dollar hurts world economy ♣ Investor's Bus. Daily '94 Strong dollar cool; weak one not cool D. Bad global econ = war ♣ Ming '92 Stagnation could mean war	1. No impact comparison. Case outweighs.	1. Plan not solve. No impact to delay if win the CP. Only need a small impact. Prolif. impacts will happen below.	Extend 2AC 1, case outweighs impact to delay is extinction. Extend 2AC #2. Not specific. No reason perceive NMFS as Clinton	Waiting until May solves case w/no risk	
Bipartisanship A. Clinton seeking compromise w/Congress now ♣ Thomas 3/1/95 Clinton seeks compromise, just like Harry Truman. B. Links 1. Exec. & legis. branches at odds over environment ♣ O'Hanlon 12/24/94 GOP will reduce env. reg; Clinton will fight	2. No specific link. Not specific to NMFS 3. No internal link to the impact. Just says they get mad, not that they cut the NPT	2. Not true. B-1 explains the interbranch conflict. Pastor evidence denies as well. 1. Not true. = stalemate via the Pastor evidence 2. Empirically, executive environmental action = 's backlash. ♣ Percival '91 3. White House action escalates interbranch rivalry ♣ Shapiro '94 Cycle of competition	MNFS is executive branch, po's Cong. 1AR drops entire story on executive rule-making. No new 2AR answers. Plan acts w/o compromise.	Link not specific. Dropped. Why perceive NMFS as Clinton. Very little credibility for the link	

Flow Sheet of Final Round—Page 7

1NC	2AC	2NC / 1NR	1AR	2NR	2AR
		4. God link story for this case. Magnuson Act renewal.			
		5. Executive branch rule making attacked by GOP ☙ Chen 3/30/95 Administrative rule-making not liked.			
		6. Is unique b/c Clinton supp's current enviro. compromise Aff pushes over brink ☙ Lee 3/24/95			
		7. Senate gave bipart supp't to regulation limits. ☙ Grenwire 3/24/95 CBA legislation = bipart cooperation			
		8. Plan not use CBA as in the legislation.			
2. No compromise = stalemate ☙ Pastor '91 No compromise = stalemate	4. Internal link ev is awful. Just says need bipart for NPT, not lose some bipart kills NPT	1. Not true. Is excellent. B-3 subpoint. 2 Domestic & foreign policy intertwined ☙ Collier '91			
	5. Bipartisanship dead in status quo. ☙ Dayton Daily News 3/23/95 Opposes many GOP bills, still stresses cooperation, though.	1. Is a mistag. Only says has considered vetoing. 2. Above evidence from 3/23/95 postdates, have an agreement now 3. Proves the brink true. Only need bipart to exist thru May. 4. New regulatory legis. receives bipart support ☙ Washington Post 3/24/95			
3. Bipart key to NPT ☙ Furse 1/17/95 Now is key for NPT; Congress must provide bipart supp't for it.			Extend 2AC #5 Agreement is only 1 policy that Clinton likes. Hates the GOP.	A-sub ev denies bipart dead Must prove an agenda change b/4 May 15th to make DA non-unique	A-sub evidence stinks. Merely says Clinton = Truman Clinton has made some attempts, but still hates GOP Means the DA is non-unique.

Flow Sheet of Final Round—Page 8

1NC	2AC	2NC / 1NR	1AR	2NR	2AR
		5. Clinton's urging more bipartisanship ◖ Chicato Sun/Times 3/23/95 6. Card irrelevant, just Clinton's rhetoric. A-subpoint evidence denies this			2NR says will answer below, but never does.
	6. NPT not solve for enforcement ◖ Mandelbaum '95 Former Soviet tech all over the place, outstrips NPT 7. Above card says prolif inevitable	(Group 6 & 7) 1. Not an absolute take out. NPT still comparatively adv. 2. Is irrelevant. Assumes they get the weapons.	Extend 6 and 7. Exactly, assumes they get weapons. Cards 2NC reads assumes that they don't get weapons.		
	8. Focus on prevention is bad, trades off with preparation for nuke war; increases risk ◖ Millot '94 Allies will prolif b/c US is not preparing		Prolif is inevitable ◖ Millot '94 Focus on prevention denies reality.	SQ disproves Holum card shows SQ works Will get below	Extend Millot '94. conceded Win CP, impacts inevitable on DA
		1. Assumes counter-proliferation. Not say the NPT. 2. Status Quo disproves. NPT = world is safe. My ev makes the comparisons, theirs doesn't.	(Off of 2AC #8) Exactly right. It trades off. We have the NPT and countries are getting weapons. Is inevitable.	Turn is non-unique 2NC ev makes comparison to NPT & no NPT–NPT = sole obstacle to profit	Makes no sense. Ev proves tradeoff, shell says focused on NPT now. Even if T/A N/U, DA uniqueness so bad, can't vote on it.
C. Impacts 1. Ending '95 agreement could kill NPT ◖ Simpson '94 Meeting could kill NPT 2. NPT = sole obstacle to proliferation ◖ Simpson '94 Nonprolif = norm. NPT is the sole instrument to save this norm		Extend the impact on prolif. Decreased prolif = less chance of accidental nuke war ◖ Kaysen & Rathjens '91 Fewer weapons statistically means less chance of war	Will get the weapons anyway. Extend the evidence that says focus on counterprolif only way to solve.	Extend accidental use stuff ⇒ scenario	Not prove will get to the all-out war in Fox card.

Flow Sheet of Final Round–Page 9

1NC	2AC	2NC / 1NR	1AR	2NR	2AR
Enact plan on May 15th		Can't accept any risk ● Fox 87 All-out exchange risk should not be tolerated	Fox card is '87 even says all-out nukes Nuclear war remains local, won't spread ● Rauschenbach '93	Will still be bad # of deaths Risk of omnicide intolerable	Case impact = starvation of a billion people. Bigger impact to case.
Delay Counterplan					
1. Topical CPs legit 1. Aff parametricizes, neg gets all the ground	1. Permutation. Do both 2. No time element in plan.	1. Not net-beneficial b/c of bipart. disad. 1. We assume plan acts now. Her arg below proves that. The last 2AC argument. 2. Makes aff a moving target.	1. Extend permutation, proves CP ≠ compete 2. Extend 2AC 2nd, plan =normal means (Group 1 & 2) 1. Normal means in 1AC = no moving target. Disad card says 45 days.	1. Is competitive b/c of net ben's; plan gets the disad 1. Doesn't answer 1NR argument, must act now. 2. Normal means not mean 45 days 3. Answered this in 2NC; plan doesn't act within rule-making compromise.	Extend discourages research. Exactly our argument, neg not research the topic Why make aff strategy be impact turns? Unfair 1. Should research the topic! 2. We don't parametricize down to just 1 thing; wouldn't be fair.
2. Competition checks abuse. Competing plans.	1. Unfair, they have no ITQ disad (Group 2 & 3) 1. Discourages research.	1. Not our argument. We say we get all the ground if complete. 1. She has tons of ground. Can impact flip, for instance. 2. Still have to link disads to plan, = have to research the links 3. Shell of CP justifies—they have to defend all of plan, part of plan is acting now. 4. Is a huge topic. T proves on bidirectionality.	Extend 2AC 4th, discourages research (Group 1NR's 4 answers) 1. Not answering 2AC argument. 2. Our ground irrel. you are not researching the topic.	1. False. Aff can do a variety of things 2. Still have to research NPT links 3. CP is a different document. 4. Drops 1NR#4 topic is huge; give neg leeway	1. Concedes all parts of CP must compete. Unfair No answer, can't lose the CP b/c doesn't compete Cross-apply Obs. II argument in 1AR, conference happens b/4 CP
3. CP not the plan. Plan is action now. CP is later	2. Plan can't compete w/itself	1. CP & Plan not same thing.	Extend the 2AC 5th. All things must compete. Hurts our ground, too. Extend 2AC 6th. Any risk of CP solvency Must be 100% certain of the net benefit.	Wrong policy-maker choose best one Drops 1NR analysis. US not change other delegates' minds. May is the Spring. No impact to waiting until May 15th.	

Flow Sheet of Final Round—Page 10

1NC	2AC	2NC / 1NR	1AR	2NR	2AR
II. Competition I. Net benefits Not disrupt the NPT; get spending impacts later	1. Must 100% win net benefit. 2. Won't be able to solve case b/c Speer evidence says must solve by Spring '95 to send strong conservation signal.	1. Gives no reason. 1. Is no proof that the US will do all that is necessary at the conference. No proof of international cooperation. 2. May is still the Spring of 1995.	Extend 2AC 7th. Other things argument is new. Aff ev says US will lead, world will follow. Neg conceding delay after Spring '95. =s no solvency for the negative. Conference happens before him.		

Appendix C

National Intercollegiate Debate Propositions (NDT)

Following is a list of the national intercollegiate debate propositions from the academic year 1920–1921 to the present.[1] Initially these propositions were used by virtually all colleges and universities. With the emergence of CEDA debating these propositions were identified as NDT propositions. A list of CEDA propositions appears in Appendix D. Propositions beginning in 1996–1997 are shared by NDT and CEDA.

1920–1921

(Men) Resolved: That a progressive tax on land should be adopted in the United States. (Men) Resolved: That the League of Nations should be adopted. (Women) Resolved: That intercollegiate athletics should be abolished.

1921–1922

Resolved: That the principle of the "closed shop" is unjustifiable.

1922–1923

Resolved: That the United States should adopt the cabinet-parliamentary form of government.

1923–1924

Resolved: That the United States should enter the World Court of the League of Nations as proposed by President Harding.

1924–1925

Resolved: That Congress should be empowered to override, by a two-thirds vote, decisions of the Supreme Court which declare acts of Congress unconstitutional.

1925–1926

(Men) Resolved: That the Constitution of the United States should be amended to give Congress power to regulate child labor. (Women) Resolved: That the United States should adopt a uniform marriage and divorce law.

1926–1927

(Men) Resolved: That the essential features of the McNary-Haugen bill be enacted into law.[2] (Women) Resolved: That trial by jury should be abolished.[3] Resolved: That the Volstead Act should be modified to permit the manufacture and sale of light wines and beer.[4]

1927–1928

Resolved: That the United States should cease to protect, by force of arms, capital invested in foreign lands, except after formal declaration of war.

1928–1929

Resolved: That a substitute for trial by jury should be adopted.

1929–1930

Resolved: That the nations should adopt a plan of complete disarmament, excepting such forces as are needed for police purposes.

1930–1931

Resolved: That the nations should adopt a policy of free trade.

1931–1932

Resolved: That the Congress should enact legislation providing for the centralized control of industry.

1932–1933

Resolved: That the United States should agree to the cancellation of the interallied debts.

1933–1934

Resolved: That the powers of the President of the United States should be substantially increased as a settled policy.

1934–1935

Resolved: That the nations should agree to prevent the international shipment of arms and munitions.

1935–1936

Resolved: That the Congress should have the power to override, by a two-thirds majority vote, decisions of the Supreme Court declaring laws passed by Congress unconstitutional.

1936–1937

Resolved: That Congress should be empowered to fix minimum wages and maximum hours for industry.

1937–1938

Resolved: That the National Labor Relations Board should be empowered to enforce arbitration of all industrial disputes.

1938–1939

Resolved: That the United States should cease the use of public funds (including credits) for the purpose of stimulating business.

1939–1940

Resolved: That the United States should follow a policy of strict economic and military isolation toward all nations outside the Western Hemisphere engaged in armed international or civil conflict.

1940–1941

Resolved: That the nations of the Western Hemisphere should form a permanent union.

1941–1942

Resolved: That the federal government should regulate by law all labor unions in the United States.

1942–1943

Resolved: That the United States should take the initiative in establishing a permanent federal union with power to tax and regulate commerce, to settle international disputes and to enforce such settlements, to maintain a police force, and to provide for the admission of other nations which accept the principles of the union.

1943–1944

Resolved: That the United States should cooperate in establishing and maintaining an international police force upon the defeat of the Axis.

1944–1945

Resolved: That the federal government should enact legislation requiring the settlement of all labor disputes by compulsory arbitration when voluntary means of settlement have failed.

1945–1946

Resolved: That the policy of the United States should be directed toward the establishment of free trade among the nations of the world.

1946–1947

Resolved: That labor should be given a direct share in the management of industry.

1947–1948

Resolved: That a federal world government should be established.

1948–1949

Resolved: That the federal government should adopt a policy of equalizing educational opportunity in tax-supported schools by means of annual grants.

1949–1950

Resolved: That the United States should nationalize the basic nonagricultural industries.

1950–1951

Resolved: That the noncommunist nations should form a new international organization.

1951–1952

Resolved: That the federal government should adopt a permanent program of wage and price controls.

1952–1953

Resolved: That the Congress of the United States should enact a compulsory fair employment practices law.

1953–1954

Resolved: That the United States should adopt a policy of free trade.

1954–1955

Resolved: That the United States should extend diplomatic recognition to the communist government of China.

1955–1956

Resolved: That the nonagricultural industries should guarantee their employees an annual wage.

1956–1957

Resolved: That the United States should discontinue direct economic aid to foreign countries.

1957–1958

Resolved: That the requirement of membership in a labor organization as a condition of employment should be illegal.

1958–1959

Resolved: That the further development of nuclear weapons should be prohibited by international agreement.

1959–1960

Resolved: That Congress should be given the power to reverse decisions of the Supreme Court.

1960–1961

Resolved: That the United States should adopt a program of compulsory health insurance for all citizens.

1961–1962

Resolved: That labor organizations should be under the jurisdiction of antitrust legislation.

1962–1963

Resolved: That the noncommunist nations of the world should establish an economic community.

1963–1964

Resolved: That the federal government should guarantee an opportunity for higher education to all qualified high school graduates.

1964–1965

Resolved: That the federal government should establish a national program of public work for the unemployed.

1965–1966

Resolved: That law enforcement agencies in the United States should be given greater freedom in the investigation and prosecution of crime.

1966–1967

Resolved: That the United States should substantially reduce its foreign policy commitments.

1967–1968

Resolved: That the federal government should guarantee a minimum annual cash income to all citizens.

1968–1969

Resolved: That executive control of United States foreign policy should be significantly curtailed.

1969–1970

Resolved: That the federal government should grant annually a specific percentage of its income tax revenue to the state governments.

1970–1971

Resolved: That the federal government should adopt a program of compulsory wage and price controls.

1971–1972

Resolved: That greater controls should be imposed on the gathering and utilization of information about United States citizens by government agencies.

1972–1973

Resolved: That the federal government should provide a program of comprehensive medical care for all citizens.

1973–1974

Resolved: That the federal government should control the supply and utilization of energy in the United States.

1974–1975

Resolved: That the power of the Presidency should be significantly curtailed.

1975–1976

Resolved: That the federal government should adopt a comprehensive program to control land use in the United States.

1976–1977

Resolved: That the federal government should significantly strengthen the guarantee of consumer product safety required of manufacturers.

1977–1978

Resolved: That United States law enforcement agencies should be given significantly greater freedom in the investigation and/or prosecution of felony crime.

1978–1979

Resolved: That the federal government should implement a program which guarantees employment opportunities for all United States citizens in the labor force.

1979–1980

Resolved: That the federal government should significantly strengthen the regulation of mass media communication in the United States.

1980–1981

Resolved: That the United States should significantly increase its foreign military commitments.

1981–1982

Resolved: That the federal government should significantly curtail the powers of labor unions in the United States.

1982–1983

Resolved: That all United States military intervention into the internal affairs of any foreign nation or nations in the Western Hemisphere should be prohibited.

1983–1984

Resolved: That any and all injury resulting from the disposal of hazardous waste in the United States should be the legal responsibility of the producer of that waste.

1984–1985

Resolved: That the United States federal government should significantly increase exploration and/or development of space beyond the earth's mesosphere.

1985–1986

Resolved: That more rigorous academic standards should be established for all public elementary and/or secondary schools in the United States in one or more of the following areas: language arts, mathematics, natural sciences. (Narrow) Resolved: That more rigorous academic standards should be established for all public elementary and/or secondary schools in the United States in the subject of mathematics.

1986–1987

Resolved: That one or more presently existing restrictions on First Amendment freedoms of press and/or speech established in one or more federal court decisions should be curtailed or prohibited. (Narrow) Resolved: That one or more presently existing national security restrictions on First Amendment freedoms of press and/or speech established in one or more federal court decisions should be curtailed or prohibited.

1987–1988

Resolved: That the United States should reduce substantially its military commitments to NATO member states. (Narrow) Resolved: That the United States should reduce substantially its nuclear military commitments to NATO member states.

1988–1989

Resolved: That United States foreign policy toward one or more African nations should be substantially changed. (Narrow) Resolved: That United States foreign policy toward South Africa should be substantially changed.

1989–1990

Resolved: That the federal government should adopt an energy policy that substantially reduces nonmilitary consumption of fossil fuels in the United States. (Narrow) Resolved: That the federal government should reduce nonmilitary consumption of fossil fuels in the United States by expanding the use of nuclear power.

1990–1991

Resolved: That the United States should substantially change its trade policy toward one or more of the following: China, Hong Kong, Japan, South Korea, Taiwan.

1991–1992

Resolved: That one or more United States Supreme Court decisions recognizing a federal Constitutional right to privacy should be overruled.

1992–1993

Resolved: That the United States should substantially change its development assistance policies toward one or more of the following nations: Afghanistan, Bangladesh, Burma, Bhutan, India, Nepal, Pakistan, Sri Lanka.

1993–1994

Resolved: That the Commander-in-Chief power of the United States President should be substantially curtailed.

1994–1995

Resolved: That the federal government should substantially change rules and/ or statutes governing criminal procedure in federal courts in one or more of the following areas: pretrial detention, sentencing.

1995–1996

Resolved: That the United States government should substantially increase its security assistance to one or more of the following: Egypt, Israel, Jordan, Palestinian National Authority, Syria.

1996–1997

Resolved: That the United States federal government should increase regulations requiring industries to decrease substantially the domestic production and/or emission of environmental pollutants.

1997–1998

Resolved: That the United States federal government should substantially increase its security assistance to one or more of the following Southeast Asian nations: Brunei Darussalam, Myanmar (Burma), Cambodia, Indonesia, Laos, Malaysia, Phillipines, Singapore, Thailand, Vietnam.

1998–1999

Resolved: That the United States federal government should amend Title Seven of the Civil Rights Act of 1964, through legislation, to create additional protections against racial and/or gender discrimination.

1999–2000

Resolved: That the United States federal government should adopt a policy of constructive engagement, including the removal of all or nearly all economic sanctions, with the government(s) of one or more of the following nation-states: Cuba, Iran, Iraq, Syria, North Korea.

2000–2001

Resolved: That the United States federal government should substantially increase its development assistance, including increasing government-to-government assistance, within the Greater Horn of Africa.

2001–2002

Resolved: That the United States federal government should substantially increase federal control throughout Indian Country in one or more of the following areas: child welfare, criminal justice, employment, environmental protection, gaming, resource management, taxation.

2002–2003

Resolved: That the United States federal government should ratify or accede to, and implement, one or more of the following: The Comprehensive Nuclear Test Ban Treaty; The Kyoto Protocol; The Rome Statute of the International Criminal Court; The Second Optional Protocol to the International Covenant on Civil and Political Rights aiming at the Abolition of the Death Penalty; The Treaty between the United States of America and the Russian Federation on Strategic Offensive Reductions, if not ratified by the United States.

2003–2004

Resolved: That the United States federal government should enact one or more of the following: Withdrawal of its World Trade Organization complaint against the European Union's restrictions on genetically modified foods; A substantial increase in its government-to-government economic and/or conflict prevention assistance to Turkey and/or Greece; Full withdrawal from the North Atlantic Treaty Organization; Removal of its barriers to and encouragement of substantial European Union and/or North Atlantic Treaty Organization participation in peacekeeping in Iraq and reconstruction in Iraq; Removal of its tactical nuclear weapons from Europe; Harmonization of its intellectual property law with the European Union in the area of human DNA sequences; Rescission of all or nearly all agriculture subsidy increases in the 2002 Farm Bill.

2004-2005

Resolved: the United States federal government should establish an energy policy requiring a substantial reduction in the total non-governmental consumption of fossil fuels in the United States.

2005-2006

Resolved: The United States Federal Government should substantially increase diplomatic and economic pressure on the People's Republic of China in one or more of the following areas: trade, human rights, weapons nonproliferation, Taiwan.

2006-2007

Resolved: The United States Supreme Court should overrule one or more of the following decisions: Planned Parenthood v. Casey, 505 U.S. 833 (1992); Ex parte Quirin, 317 U.S. 1 (1942); U.S. v. Morrison, 529 U.S. 598 (2000); Milliken v. Bradley, 418 U.S. 717 (1974).

2007-2008

Resolved: that the United States Federal Government should increase its constructive engagement with the government of one or more of: Afghanistan, Iran, Lebanon, the Palestinian Authority, and Syria, and it should include offering them a security guarantee(s) and/or a substantial increase in foreign assistance.

NOTES
1. See George McCoy Musgrave, *Competitive Debate: Rules and Techniques,* 3rd ed. (New York: Wilson, 1957), pp. 143–145, for a list of intercollegiate debate propositions from 1920–1921 through 1956–1957; and E. R. Nichols, "The Annual College Question," *Debater's Magazine* (Dec. 1947), pp. 206–207, for a list of intercollegiate debate propositions from 1922–1923 through 1947–1948. Announcements issued by the Committee on Intercollegiate Debate and Discussion give the current NDT debate proposition.
2. Listed in Musgrave, *Competitive Debate,* pp. 143–145.
3. Musgrave, *Competitive Debate,* pp. 143–145.
4. Listed in Nichols, "The Annual College Question," pp. 206–207.

Appendix D

National Intercollegiate Debate Propositions (CEDA)

Following is a list of the national intercollegiate debate propositions (CEDA) for the academic years 1971–1972 to the present.[1]

1971–1972

Resolved: That the United States should withdraw all its ground combat forces from bases located outside the Western Hemisphere.

1972–1973

(1st Semester) Resolved: That the penal system in the United States should be significantly improved. (2nd Semester) Resolved: That the United States should seek to restore normal diplomatic and economic relations with the present government of Cuba.

1973–1974

(1st Semester) Resolved: That "victimless crimes" should be legalized. (2nd Semester) Resolved: That the United States should reduce its commitment to Israel.

1974–1975

(1st Semester) Resolved: That the federal government should grant amnesty to all those who evaded the draft during the Viet Nam war. (2nd Semester) Resolved: That American television has sacrificed quality for entertainment.

1975–1976

Resolved: That education has failed its mission in the United States.

1976–1977

Resolved: That legal protection of accused persons in the United States unnecessarily hinders law enforcement agencies.

1977–1978

Resolved: That Affirmative Action promotes deleterious hiring practices.

1978–1979

Resolved: That a United States foreign policy significantly directed toward the furtherance of human rights is desirable.

1979–1980

Resolved: That compulsory national service for all qualified United States citizens is desirable.

1980–1981

(1st Topic) Resolved: That protection of the national environment is a more important goal than the satisfaction of American energy demands. (2nd Topic) Resolved: That activism in politics by religious groups harms the American political process.

1981–1982

(1st Topic) Resolved: That unauthorized immigration into the United States is seriously detrimental to the United States. (2nd Topic) Resolved: That the American judicial system has overemphasized the rights of the accused.

1982–1983

(1st Topic) Resolved: That a unilateral freeze by the United States on the production and development of nuclear weapons would be desirable. (2nd Topic) Resolved: That individual rights of privacy are more important than any other Constitutional right.

1983–1984

(1st Topic) Resolved: That United States higher education has sacrificed quality for institutional survival. (2nd Topic) Resolved: That federal government censorship is justified to defend the national security of the United States.

1984–1985

(1st Topic) Resolved: That the method of conducting Presidential elections in the United States is detrimental to democracy. (2nd Topic) Resolved: That the

United States is justified in providing military support to nondemocratic governments.

1985–1986

(1st Topic) Resolved: That significant government restrictions on coverage by United States media of terrorist activity are justified. (2nd Topic) Resolved: That membership in the United Nations is no longer beneficial to the United States.

1986–1987

(1st Topic) Resolved: That improved relations with the Soviet Union are a more important objective for the United States than increased military preparedness. (2nd Topic) Resolved: That regulations in the United States requiring employees to be tested for controlled substances are an unwarranted invasion of privacy.

1987–1988

(1st Topic) Resolved: That continued United States covert involvement in Central America would be undesirable. (2nd Topic) Resolved: That the American judicial system has overemphasized freedom of the press.

1988–1989

(1st Topic) Resolved: That significantly stronger third-party participation in the United States Presidential elections would benefit the political process. (2nd Topic) Resolved: That increased restrictions on the civilian possession of handguns in the United States would be justified.

1989–1990

(1st Topic) Resolved: That violence is a justified response to political oppression. (2nd Topic) Resolved: That the trend toward increasing foreign investment in the United States is detrimental to this nation.

1990–1991

(1st Topic) Resolved: That government censorship of public artistic expression in the United States is an undesirable infringement of individual rights. (2nd Topic) Resolved: That the United States Supreme Court, on balance, has granted excessive power to law enforcement agencies.

1991–1992

(1st Topic) Resolved: That United States colleges and universities have inappropriately altered educational practices to address issues of race or gender. (2nd Topic) Resolved: That advertising degrades the quality of life in the United States.

1992–1993

(1st Topic) Resolved: That the welfare system exacerbates the problems of the urban poor in the United States.

(2nd Topic) Resolved: That United Nations implementation of its Universal Declaration of Human Rights is more important than preserving state sovereignty.

1993–1994

(1st Topic) Resolved: That United States military intervention to support democratic governments is appropriate in a post–cold war world. (2nd Topic) Resolved: That the national news media in the United States impair public understanding of political issues.

1994–1995

(1st Topic) Resolved: That throughout the United States, more severe punishment for individuals convicted of violent crime would be desirable. (2nd Topic) Resolved: That the United States should significantly increase the development of the earth's ocean resources.

1995–1996

(1st Topic) Resolved: That the United States should substantially change its foreign policy toward Mexico. (2nd Topic) Resolved: That the United States should substantially change its foreign policy toward Mexico.[2]

1996–1997

Resolved: That the United States federal government should increase regulations requiring industries to decrease substantially the domestic production and/or emission of environmental pollutants.

1997–1998

Resolved: That the United States federal government should substantially increase its security assistance to one or more of the following Southeast Asian nations: Brunei Darussalam, Myanmar (Burma), Cambodia, Indonesia, Laos, Malaysia, Phillipines, Singapore, Thailand,Vietnam.

1998–1999

Resolved: That the United States federal government should amend Title Seven of the Civil Rights Act of 1964, through legislation, to create additional protections against racial and/or gender discrimination.

1999–2000

(Policy) Resolved: That the United States federal government should adopt a policy of constructive engagement, including the removal of all or nearly all economic sanctions, with the government(s) of one or more of the following nation-states: Cuba, Iran, Iraq, Syria, North Korea. (Non-policy) Resolved: That economic embargoes, on balance, are a justified tool of United States foreign policy.

2000–2001

(Policy) Resolved: that the United States federal government should substantially increase its development assistance, including increasing government-to-government assistance, within the Greater Horn of Africa. (Non-policy) Resolved: that United States intervention in armed conflict involving Sub-Saharan African nation-states is desirable.

2001–2002

(Policy) Resolved: That the United States federal government should substantially increase federal control throughout Indian Country in one or more of the following areas: child welfare, criminal justice, employment, environmental protection, gaming, resource management, taxation. (Non-policy) Resolved: That decreased Federal jurisdiction throughout Indian Country would be desirable.

2002–2003

Resolved: That the United States federal government should ratify or accede to, and implement, one or more of the following: The Comprehensive Nuclear Test Ban Treaty; The Kyoto Protocol; The Rome Statute of the International Criminal Court; The Second Optional Protocol to the International Covenant on Civil and Political Rights aiming at the Abolition of the Death Penalty; The Treaty between the United States of America and the Russian Federation on Strategic Offensive Reductions, if not ratified by the United States.

2003–2004

Resolved: That the United States federal government should enact one or more of the following: Withdrawal of its World Trade Organization complaint against the European Union's restrictions on genetically modified foods; A substantial increase in its government-to-government economic and/or conflict prevention assistance to Turkey and/or Greece; Full withdrawal from the North Atlantic Treaty Organization; Removal of its barriers to and encouragement of substantial European Union and/or North Atlantic Treaty Organization participation in peacekeeping in Iraq and reconstruction in Iraq; Removal of its tactical nuclear weapons from Europe; Harmonization of its intellectual property law with the European Union in the area of human DNA sequences; Rescission of all or nearly all agriculture subsidy increases in the 2002 Farm Bill.

2004–2005

Resolved: the United States federal government should establish an energy policy requiring a substantial reduction in the total non-governmental consumption of fossil fuels in the United States.

2005–2006

Resolved: The United States Federal Government should substantially increase diplomatic and economic pressure on the People's Republic of China in one or more of the following areas: trade, human rights, weapons nonproliferation, Taiwan.

2006–2007

The United States Supreme Court should overrule one or more of the following decisions
* Planned Parenthood v. Casey, 505 U.S. 833 (1992)
* Ex parte Quirin, 317 U.S. 1 (1942)
* U.S. v. Morrison, 529 U.S. 598 (2000)
* Milliken v. Bradley, 418 U.S. 717 (1974)

2007–2008

Resolved: that the United States Federal Government should increase its constructive engagement with the government of one or more of: Afghanistan, Iran, Lebanon, the Palestinian Authority, and Syria, and it should include offering them a security guarantee(s) and/or a substantial increase in foreign assistance.

NOTES

1. The list of CEDA propositions from 1971 through 1985 was furnished by Jack H. Howe, executive secretary of CEDA. Announcements by CEDA give the current CEDA propositions.
2. In December 1995 the CEDA topic ballot included a number of new topics *and* the fall topic. The membership elected to repeat the fall topic.

Appendix E

Debate Bibliography

The following bibliography for the debate student and the debate educator is adapted from the excellent bibliography prepared by Steven Hunt. In addition, you may wish to visit the following websites:

American Debate Association
http://www.umw.edu/cas/debate/ada/default.php

American Parliamentary Debate Association (APDA)
http://www.apdaweb.org/

Cross Examination Debate Association (CEDA)
http://www.cedadebate.org/

Canadian University Society for Intercollegiate Debate
http://www.cusid.ca/

Debate Central
http://debate.uvm.edu

The English-Speaking Union
http://www.esu.org/

Forensic Friend (from Whitman College)
http://www.wcdebate.com/forensicfriend.htm

How to Debate Effectively and Rationally
http://www.truthtree.com/debates.shtml

International Debate Education Association (IDEA)
http://www.idebate.org/

International Public Debate Association (IPDA)
http://www.ipdadebate.org/

National Debate Tournament (NDT) home page
http://www.wfu.edu/NDT/

National Educational Debate Association (NEDA)
http://neda.us/

National Forensic Association Lincoln–Douglas home page
http://www.bethel.edu/college/dept/comm/nfa/nfa-ld.html

National Parliamentary Debate Association (NPDA)
http://www.bethel.edu/college/dept/comm/npda/

Rich Edwards Home Page (tab room software)
http://www.baylor.edu/~Richard_Edwards/Software.html

DebateScoop
http://www.debatescoop.org/

The National Debate Project
http://www.nationaldebateproject.org/

Open Debates
http://www.opendebates.org/theissue/

Teaching Debate
http://www.teachingdebate.com/

National Association of Urban Debate Leagues
http://www.urbandebate.org/index

A SELECT BIBLIOGRAPHY ON DEBATE THEORY

I. Overview of Key Debate Theory Resources

Top Eight Sources for Debate Theory

It is very difficult to get a comprehensive vision of debate theory because the sources are difficult to find. There are a wide variety of forensics organizations separately publishing debate materials. Most debate materials are not well indexed or indexed at all.

1. *Argumentation and Advocacy,* formerly *Journal of the American Forensic Association* (referred to as *JAFA*)
2. Books on argumentation and debate
3. *Contemporary Argumentation & Debate: The Journal of the Cross Examination Debate Association,* formerly *CEDA Yearbook*
4. Thomas, David A., and Jack Hart, eds. *Advanced Debate: Readings in Theory, Practice, and Teaching,* 4th ed. Lincolnwood, IL: National Textbook, 1992
5. *The Forensic* of PKD
6. *Speaker and Gavel* of DSR-TKA
7. SCA/AFA Conferences on Argumentation (There have been nine biannual conferences since 1979.)
8. *National Forensic Journal* of NFA

Other Important Sources

Griffin Research, Berkeley, CA. Used to publish debate theory booklets.

James W. Pratt, Executive Secretary, American Forensic Association, P.O. Box 256, River Falls, WI 54033.

Championship Debates and Speeches, annual national final transcripts of final rounds of NDT, CEDA, etc.

Philosophy and Rhetoric.

The Southern Journal of Forensics, ed. Jack E. Rogers, The University of Texas at Tyler.

II. Bibliographies

Bartanen, Michael. "Works Cited." *Teaching and Directing Forensics.* Scottsdale, AZ: Gorsuch Scarisbrick, 1994. Pp. 179–184.

——, and David Frank. "Select Bibliography: Scholarly Materials on Value Theory and Value Argument." In *Non-policy Debate,* 2nd ed. Scottsdale, AZ: Gorsuch Scarisbrick, 1994. Pp. 51–53.

Berube, David. *Non-Policy Debating.* Lanham, MD: University Press of America, 1994. Pp. 351–370.

Brownlee, Don, Julia Johnson, and Mike Buckley. "A Bibliometric Analysis of the CEDA Yearbook." *CEDA Yearbook* (1991): 108–120.

Brownlee, Don. *Coaching Debate and Forensics (annotated bibliography).* Annandale, VA: SCA, 1988.

Church, Russell T. A bibliography for argumentation and debate for 1975–76, 1977–78, and 1979. In various editions of *JAFA.*

———, and David C. Buckley. "Argumentation and Debating Propositions of Value: A Bibliography." *JAFA* 19 (Spring 1983): 239–250.

Conklin, Forrest. A bibliography for argumentation and debate. Published annually in *JAFA,* 1968–73.

Cureton, Robert D. A bibliography for argumentation and debate. Published annually in *JAFA,* 1972–74.

Hansen, Hans V. "An Informal Logic Bibliography." *Informal Logic* 12(3) (Fall 1990): 155–183.

Hunt, Steven B. "A Select Partially Annotated Bibliography for Directing Forensics: Teaching, Coaching, and Judging Debate and Individual Events." *The Forensic* 81(2) (Winter 1996): 1–40.

Jensen, J. Vernon. "Bibliography on Argumentation." *Rhetoric Society Quarterly* 19 (1989): 71–81.

Johnson, Ralph H., and J. Anthony Blair. "A Bibliography of Recent Work in Informal Logic." In *Informal Logic: The First International Symposium,* ed. J. Anthony Blair and Ralph H. Johnson. Inverness, CA: Edgepress, 1980. Pp. 163–172.

Pfau, Michael, David Thomas, and Walter Ulrich. *Debate and Argument: A Systems Approach to Advocacy.* Glenview, IL: Scott, Foresman, 1987. Pp. 313–323.

Sproule, J. Michael. "The Roots of American Argumentation Theory: A Review of Landmark Works, 1878–1932." *JAFA* 23 (Fall 1986): 110–115.

Steadman, Clarence. "An Index to *The Forensic* 1915–1990." *The Forensic* 75(4) (Summer 1990): 1–30.

Towne, Ralph, Robert M. Smith, and Thomas Harris. "Recommended Debate Texts and Handbooks: A Survey." *Speaker and Gavel* 11(3) (Jan. 1974): 52–54.

Trapp, Robert, and Janice Schuetz, eds. "Bibliography." In *Perspectives on Argumentation: Essays in Honor of Wayne Brockriede.* Prospect Heights, IL: Waveland Press, 1990. Pp. 315–338.

III. Values of Debate

Aden, Roger. "Reconsidering the Laboratory Metaphor: Forensics as a Liberal Art." *National Forensic Journal* 9 (Fall 1991): 97–108.

Bartanen, Michael. "The Educational Benefits of Forensics." In *Teaching and Directing Forensics.* Scottsdale, AZ: Gorsuch Scarisbrick, 1994. Pp. 3–5.

Bennett, William H. "The Role of Debate in Speech Communication." *Communication Education* (Nov. 1972): 281–288.

Bradley, Bert E., Jr. "Debate: A Practical Training for Gifted Students." *The Speech Teacher* 7 (Mar. 1959): 134–138.

Brockriede, Wayne. "College Debate and the Reality Gap." *Speaker and Gavel* 7(3) (Mar. 1970): 71–76.

———. "The Contemporary Renaissance in the Study of Argument." In *Argument in Transition: Proceedings of the Third Summer Conference on Argumentation,* ed. David Zarefsky, Malcolm O. Sillars, and Jack Rhodes. Annandale, VA: SCA, 1983. Pp. 17–26.

Chandler, Robert C., and Jeffrey Hobbs. "The Benefits of Intercollegiate Policy Debate Training to Various Professions." In *Argument in Controversy: Proceedings of the Seventh SCA/AFA Conference on Argumentation,* ed. Donn Parson. Annandale, VA: SCA, 1991. Pp. 388–390.

Clark, Ruth Anne, and Jesse G. Delia. " 'Topoi' and Rhetorical Competence." *Quarterly Journal of Speech* 65(2) (Apr. 1979): 187–206.

Clevenger, Theodore. "Toward a Point of View for Contest Debate." *Central States Speech Journal* (Autumn 1960): 21–26.

Colbert, Kent. "The Effects of Debate Participation on Argumentativeness and Verbal Aggression." *Communication Education* 42(3) (July 1993): 206–214.

———. "Replicating the Effects of Debate Participation on Argumentativeness and Verbal Aggression." *The Forensic* 79(3) (Spring 1994): 1–13.

———, and Thompson Biggers. "Why Should We Support Debate?" *JAFA* 21(3) (Spring 1985): 237–240.

DeLancey, Charles A. "The Values of Forensics Activities to Speech Communication Programs in Liberal Arts Colleges." *Association for Communication Administration Bulletin* (Jan. 1984): 56–57.

Douglas, Donald. "Toward a Philosophy of Forensic Education." *JAFA* 8 (Summer 1971): 36–41.

Dowling, Ralph. "Arguers as Lovers: Implications for Forensics." *Communication Education* 32 (Apr. 1983): 237–241.

Farrell, Thomas B. "The Tradition of Rhetoric and the Philosophy of Communication." *Communication* 7(2) (1983): 151–180.

Freeley, Austin J. "An Anthology of Commentary on Debate." *The Speech Teacher* 10 (Jan. 1961): 44–47.

Goodnight, G. Thomas. "The Re-Union of Argumentation and Debate Theory." In *Dimensions of Argument: Proceedings of the Second Summer Conference on Argumentation,* ed. George Ziegelmueller and Jack Rhodes. Annandale, VA: SCA, 1981. Pp. 415–432.

Heymann, Philip, and Jody Heymann. "The Fate of Public Debate in the U.S." *Harvard Journal of Legislation* 33 (Summer 1996): 511–526.

Hill, Bill. "Intercollegiate Debate: Why Do Students Bother?" *Southern Speech Communication Journal* 48 (Fall 1982): 77–88.

Hobbs, Jeffrey Dale, and Robert C. Chandler. "The Perceived Benefits of Policy Debate Training in Various Professions." *Speaker and Gavel* 28 (1991): 4–6.

Hollihan, Thomas, and Patricia Riley. "Academic Debate and Democracy: A Clash of Ideologies." In *Argument and Critical Practices: Proceedings of the Fifth SCA/AFA Conference on Argumentation,* ed. J. W. Wenzel. Annandale, VA: SCA, 1987. Pp. 399–404.

Hunt, Steven B. "The Values of Forensics Participation." In *Intercollegiate Forensics,* ed. T. C. Winebrenner. Dubuque, IA: Kendall Hunt, 1994. Pp. 1–19.

Jones, Kevin T. "Cerebral Gymnastics 10l: Why Do Debaters Debate?" *CEDA Yearbook* 15 (1994): 65–75.

Kay, Jack. "Rapprochement of World 1 and World 2: Discovering the Ties Between Practical Discourse and Forensics." In *Argument in Transition: Proceedings of the Third Summer Conference on Argumentation,* ed. David Zarefsky, Malcolm O. Sillars, and Jack Rhodes. Annandale, VA: SCA, 1983. Pp. 927–937.

Kruger, Arthur. "Debate and Speech Communication." *Southern Communication Journal* (Spring 1974): 233–240.

Kully, Robert D. "Forensics and the Speech Communication Discipline: Analysis of an Estrangement." *JAFA* 8 (Spring 1972): 192–199.

Leeper, Karla, and Dale Herbeck. "Policy Debate as a Laboratory for Teaching Argument Skills." *Forensic Educator* 6 (1991–92): 23–28.

Littlefield, Robert S. "An Assessment of University Administrators: Do They Value Competitive Debate and I.E. Programs." *National Forensic Journal* 9(2) (Fall 1991): 87–96.

Matlon, Ron, and Lucy M. Keele. "A Survey of Participants in the National Debate Tournament, 1947–1980." *JAFA* 20 (Spring 1984): 194–205.

McBath, James. "Rationale for Forensics." In *American Forensics in Perspective: Papers from the Second National Conference on Forensics,* ed. Donn Parson. Annandale, VA: SCA, 1984. Pp. 5–11.

McGlone, Edward L. "The Behavioral Effects of Forensics Participation." *JAFA* 10 (Winter 1974): 140–146.

McGough, M. "Pull It Across Your Flow." *The New Republic* (Oct. 10, 1988): 17–19.

McGuckin, Henry E., Jr. "Forensics in the Liberal Education." *Western Journal of Speech Communication* (Spring 1970): 133–138.

Morello, John T. "Intercollegiate Debate: Proposals for a Struggling Activity." *Speaker and Gavel* 17(2) (Winter 1980): 103–107.

Nobles, W. Scott. "Tournament Debating and Rhetoric." *Western Journal of Speech Communication* 22 (Fall 1958): 206–210.

Norton, Larry. "Nature and Benefits of Academic Debate." In *Introduction to Debate,* ed. Carolyn Keefe, Thomas B. Harte, and Larry E. Norton. New York: Macmillan, 1982. Pp. 24–40.

Pearce,W. Barnett. "Forensics and Speech Communication." *Association for Communication Administration Bulletin* (Apr. 1974): 26–32.

Ritter, Kurt. "Debate and a Liberal Arts Education: The Forensics Program at the U. of Illinois." *Speaker and Gavel* 14(4) (Summer 1977): 72–84.

———. "Debate as an Instrument for Democracy." *Speaker and Gavel* 8(3) (Spring 1976): 41–43.

Rohrer, Dan M. "Debate as a Liberal Art." In *Advanced Debate: Readings in Theory, Practice, and Teaching,* 3rd ed., ed. David A. Thomas and Jack Hart. Lincolnwood, IL: National Textbook, 1987. Pp. 7–14.

Rowland, Robert, and Scott Deatherage. "The Crisis in Policy Debate." *JAFA* 24 (Spring 1988): 246–250.

———. "A Defense of Rational Argument." *Philosophy and Rhetoric* 28(4) (1995): 350–364.

———. "The Practical Pedagogical Function of Academic Debate." *Contemporary Argumentation and Debate* 16 (1995): 98–108.

———, and John E. Fritch. "The Relationship Between Debate and Argumentation Theory." In *Spheres of Argument: Proceedings of the Sixth SCA/AFA Conference on Argumentation,* ed. Bruce E Gronbeck. Annandale, VA: SCA, 1989. Pp. 457–463.

Sellnow, Deanna. "Justifying Forensics Programs to Administrators." *National Forensic Journal* 11 (Winter 1994): 1–14.

Thomas, David A. "Forensics Shock: Making Forensics Relevant to Tomorrow's Higher Education." *Speech Teacher* 13 (Sept. 1974): 235–241.

Trapp, Robert. "The Need for an Argumentative Perspective in Academic Debate." *CEDA Yearbook* 14 (1993): 23–33.

Treadaway, Glenda. "A Pedagogical Rationale for Re-Establishing Complementary Debate and Individual Events Programs." In *Proceedings from the Pi Kappa Delta Development Conference: Re-Formulating Forensics for the New Century,* ed. Scott Jensen. Lake Charles, LA: McNeese State University, 1995. Pp. 17–24.

Windes, R. R., Jr. "Competitive Debating, the Speech Program, the Individual, and Society." *Speech Teacher* 9 (Mar. 1960): 99–108.

Winebrenner, T. C. "Reaffirming the Role of Argumentation Theory in Academic Debate." *The Forensic* 79(2) (Winter 1994): 1–9.

Zarefsky, David. "Keynote Address." In *Dialogue in the Forensic Community: Proceedings of the Conference on Forensic Education,* ed. Jack Kay and Julie Lee. Kansas City, MO: National Federation of State High School Associations, 1990.

IV. Debate and Critical Thinking

Beckman, V. "An Investigation of Their Contributions to Critical Thinking Made by Courses in Argumentation and Discussion in Selected Colleges." Unpublished Ph.D. dissertation, University of Minnesota, 1955.

Blair, J. Anthony. "Teaching Argument in Critical Thinking." *The Community College Humanities Review* 5 (1984): 19–30.

Brembeck, W. "The Effects of a Course in Argumentation on Critical Thinking." *Speech Monographs* 16 (1949): 172–189.

Colbert, Kent. "Enhancing Critical Thinking Ability Through Academic Debate." *Contemporary Argumentation and Debate* 16 (1995): 52–72.

———. "The Effects of CEDA and NDT Debate Training on Critical Thinking Ability." *JAFA* 23(4) (Spring 1987): 194–201.

———. "The Debate–Critical Thinking Relationship: Isolating the Effects of Self-Selection." Paper presented at the SCA Convention, San Antonio, TX, 1995.

Cross, G. "The Effects of Belief Systems and the Amount of Debate Experience on the Acquisition of Critical Thinking." Unpublished Ph.D. dissertation, University of Utah, 1971.

Follert, V., and Kent Colbert. "An Analysis of the Research Concerning Debate Training and Critical Thinking Improvements." ERIC Document Reproduction Service #ED 238 058, 1983.

Frank, D. "Teaching High School Speech to Improve Critical Thinking." *The Speech Teacher* 18 (1969): 296–302.

Greenstreet, Robert. "Academic Debating and Critical Thinking: A Look at the Evidence." *National Forensic Journal* 11 (1993): 13–28.

Gruner, Charles, Richard Huseman, and James Luck. "Debating Ability, Critical Thinking Ability, and Authoritarianism." *Speaker and Gavel* 8(3) (Mar. 1971): 63–65.

Hill, Bill. "The Value of Competitive Debate as a Vehicle for Promoting Development of Critical Thinking Ability." *CEDA Yearbook* 14 (1993): 1–22.

Huseman, Richard, Glenn Ware, and Charles Gruner. "Critical Thinking, Reflective Thinking, and the Ability to Organize Ideas: A Multi-Variate Approach." *JAFA* 9 (Summer 1972): 261–265.

Jackson, Ted. "The Effects of Intercollegiate Debating on Critical Thinking." Unpublished Ph.D. dissertation, University of Wisconsin, 1961.

Katula, R., and C. Martin. "Teaching Critical Thinking in the Speech Communication Classroom." *Communication Education* 33 (1984): 160–167.

Perella, Jack. *The Debate Method of Critical Thinking.* Dubuque, IA: Kendall Hunt, 1983.

Powell, Robert G. "Critical Thinking and Speech Communication: Our Critical Strategies Are Warranted NOT!" *Journal of Applied Communication Research* 20(3) (Aug. 1992): 342–347.

Sanders, Judith, Richard Wiseman, and Robert Gass. "Does Teaching Argumentation Facilitate Students' Critical Thinking?" *Communication Reports* 7(1) (Winter 1994): 27–35.

Whalen, Shawn. "Intercollegiate Debate as a Co-Curricular Activity: Effects on Critical Thinking Skills." In *Arguments in Controversy: Proceedings of the Seventh SCA/ AFA Conference on Argumentation,* ed. Donn Parson. Annandale, VA: SCA, 1991. Pp. 391–397.

V. Books on Argumentation and Debate

Adler, Mortimer. *Dialectic.* New York: Harcourt, Brace, 1929.

Anderson, Jerry M., and Paul J. Dovre, eds. *Readings in Argumentation.* Boston: Allyn & Bacon, 1968.

Bartanen, Michael, and David Frank. *Non-policy Debate,* 2nd ed. Scottsdale, AZ: Gorsuch Scarisbrick, 1994.

———. *Teaching and Directing Forensics.* Scottsdale, AZ: Gorsuch Scarisbrick, 1994.

Benoit, William, Dale Hample, and Pam Benoit, eds. *Readings in Argumentation.* New York: Foris, 1992.

Berube, David. *Nonpolicy Debating.* New York: University Press of America, 1993.

Branham, Robert James. *Debate and Critical Analysis: The Harmony of Conflict.* Hillsdale, NJ: Lawrence Erlbaum, 1991.

Campbell, Cole. *Competitive Debate.* Chapel Hill, NC: Information Research Associates, 1974.

Capp, Glenn R., and Thelma Capp. *Principles of Argumentation and Debate.* Englewood Cliffs, NJ: Prentice Hall, 1965.

Corcoran, Joseph. *An Introduction to Non-Policy Debating.* Dubuque, IA: Kendall Hunt, 1988.

Cox, J. Robert, Malcolm O. Sillars, and Gregg B. Walkers, eds. *Argument and Social Practice: Proceedings of the Fourth SCA/AFA Conference on Argumentation.* Annandale, VA: SCA, 1985.

Ehninger, Douglas, and Wayne Brockriede. *Decision by Debate,* 2nd ed. New York: Harper & Row, 1978.

Ericson, J. M., and J. J. Murphy, with Bud Zeuschner. *The Debater's Guide,* rev. ed. Carbondale: Southern Illinois University Press, 1987.

Fadely, Dean. *Advocacy: The Essentials of Argumentation and Debate.* Dubuque, IA: Kendall Hunt, 1994.

Foster, William T. *Argumentation and Debating.* Boston: Houghton Mifflin, 1932 [1908]. A classic.

Freeley, Austin J. *Argumentation and Debate: Critical Thinking for Reasoned Decision Making,* 9th ed. Belmont, CA: Wadsworth, 1996. Probably used in more college debate classes than any other text from the 1960s to today.

Gronbeck, Bruce E., ed. *Spheres of Argument: Proceedings of the Sixth SCA/AFA Conference on Argumentation.* Annandale, VA: SCA, 1989.

Hollihan, Thomas A., and Kevin Baaske. *Arguments and Arguing: The Products and Process of Human Decision Making.* New York: St. Martin's Press, 1994.

Jackson, Sally, ed. *Argumentation and Values: Proceedings of the Ninth SCA/AFA Conference on Argumentation.* Annandale, VA: SCA, 1995.

Kahane, Howard. *Logic and Contemporary Rhetoric,* 5th ed. Belmont, CA: Wadsworth, 1988.

Makau, Josina M. *Reasoning and Communication: Thinking Critically About Arguments.* Belmont, CA: Wadsworth, 1990.

McBath, James., ed. *Forensics as Communication: The Argumentative Perspective.* Skokie, IL: National Textbook, 1975. Critical to developing a sound debate coaching philosophy.

McKerrow, Ramie, ed. *Argument and the Postmodern Challenge: Proceedings of the Eighth SCA/AFA Conference on Argumentation.* Annandale, VA: SCA, 1993.

McPeak, J. *Teaching Critical Thinking: Dialogue and Dialectic.* New York: Routledge, 1990.

MacRae, Duncan. *Policy Indicators: Links Between Social Science and Public Debate.* Winston-Salem: University of North Carolina Press, 1985.

Parella, Jack. *The Debate Method of Critical Thinking.* Dubuque, IA: Kendall Hunt, 1986.

Parson, Donn, ed. *American Forensics in Perspective: Papers from the Second National Conference on Forensics.* Annandale, VA: SCA, 1984.

———, ed. *Argument in Controversy: Proceedings of the Seventh SCA/AFA Conference on Argumentation.* Annandale, VA: SCA, 1991.

Patterson, J. W., and David Zarefsky. *Contemporary Debate.* Boston: Houghton Mifflin, 1981.

Perelman, Chaim, and Lucie Olbrechts-Tyteca. *The New Rhetoric: A Treatise on Argumentation.* Trans. John Wilkinson and Purcell Weaver. Notre Dame, IN: University of Notre Dame Press, 1969. Along with Toulmin's *Uses of Argument,* should be familiar to all serious students of argumentation and debate.

Pfau, Michael, David A.Thomas, and Walter Ulrich. *Debate and Argument: A Systems Approach to Advocacy.* Glenview, IL: Scott, Foresman, 1987.

Reinard, John. *Foundations of Argument: Effective Communication for Critical Thinking.* Dubuque, IA: Brown & Benchmark, 1991.

Rhodes, Jack, and Sara Newell, eds. *Proceedings of the Summer Conference on Argumentation.* Annandale, VA: SCA, 1980.

Rieke, Richard D., and Malcolm O. Sillars. *Argumentation and the Decision Making Process,* 4th ed. Reading, MA: Addison-Wesley, 1996.

Roden, Sally, ed. *Commitment to Forensic Education: The Challenge to the Twenty-First Century: Proceedings of the 1991 PKD Professional Development Conference.* Conway: University of Central Arkansas, 1991.

Thomas, David, and John Hart. *Advanced Debate: Readings in Theory, Practice, and Teaching,* 4th ed. Lincolnwood, IL: National Textbook, 1992.

————, and Stephen Wood, eds. *CEDA Twentieth Anniversary Assessment Conference Proceedings.* Dubuque, IA: Kendall Hunt, 1993.

Thompson, Wayne. *Modern Argumentation and Debate: Principles and Practices.* New York: Harper & Row, 1971.

Toulmin, Stephen. *The Uses of Argument.* Cambridge: Cambridge University Press, 1958.

Ulrich, Walter. *Judging Academic Debate.* Lincolnwood, IL: National Textbook, 1986.

Warnick, Barbara, and Edward S. Inch. *Critical Thinking and Communication: The Use of Reason in Argument,* 2nd ed. New York: Macmillan, 1994.

Weiss, Robert O. *Public Argument.* New York: University Press of America, 1994.

Wenzel, Joseph, ed. *Argument and Critical Practices: Proceedings of the Fifth SCA/AFA Conference on Argumentation.* Annandale, VA: SCA, 1987.

Williams, David, and Michael Hazen, eds. *Argumentation Theory and the Rhetoric of Assent.* Tuscaloosa: University of Alabama Press, 1990.

Winebrenner, T. C., ed. *Intercollegiate Forensics.* Dubuque, IA: Kendall Hunt, 1994.

Winkler, Carol, William Newman, and David Birdsell. *Lines of Argument: Core Volume, Lines of Argument: Policy Argument, and Lines of Argument: Values Argument.* Dubuque, IA: Brown & Benchmark, 1993.

Zarefsky, David, Malcolm O. Sillars, and Jack Rhodes, eds. *Argument in Transition: Proceedings of the Third Summer Conference on Argumentation.* Annandale, VA: SCA, 1983.

Ziegelmueller, George, and Jack Rhodes, eds. *Dimensions of Argument: Proceedings of the Second Summer Conference on Argumentation.* Annandale, VA: SCA, 1981.

————, and Jack Kay. *Argumentation: Inquiry and Advocacy,* 3rd ed. Boston: Allyn & Bacon, 1997.

VI. Prima Facie Cases and Stock Issues

Giffin, Kim, and Kenneth Magill. "Stock Issues in Tournament Debates." *Central States Speech Journal* (Autumn 1960): 27–32.

Herlitz, Georg Nils. "The Meaning of the Term 'Prima Facie'." *Louisiana Law Review* 55(2) (Nov. 1994): 391–408.

McCroskey, James, and Leon R. Camp. "A Study of Stock Issues Judging Criteria and Decisions in Debate." *Southern States Communication Journal* (Winter 1964): 158–168.

Scott, Robert. "On the Meaning of the Term 'Prima Facie'" in Argumentation." *Central States Speech Journal* (Autumn 1960): 33–37.

Tuman, Joseph S. "Getting to First Base: Prima Facie Arguments for Propositions of Value." *JAFA* 24(2) (Fall 1987): 84–94.

Young, Gregory, and Paul Gaske. "On Prima Facie Value Argumentation: The Policy Implications Affirmative." *CEDA Yearbook* (1984): 24–30.

VII. Presumption and the Burden of Proof

Brydon, Steven R. "Presumption in Non-Policy Debate: In Search of a Paradigm." *JAFA* 23(2) (Summer 1986): 15–22.

Burnett, Nicholas. "Archbishop Whately and the Concept of Presumption: Lessons for Non-Policy Debate." *CEDA Yearbook* 12 (1992): 37–43.

Cronkhite, Gary. "The Locus of Presumption." *Central States Speech Journal* 17 (Nov. 1966): 270–276.

Hill, Bill. "An Evolving Model of Presumption for Non-Policy Debate." *CEDA Yearbook* 15 (1994): 43–64.

———. "Toward a Holistic Model of Presumption in Non-Policy Debate." *CEDA Yearbook* 10 (1990): 22–32.

Lichtman, Allan, and Daniel Rohrer. "Critique of Zarefsky on Presumption." In *Proceedings of the National Conference on Argumentation,* ed. James Luck. Fort Worth: Texas Christian University, 1973. Pp. 38–45.

Podgurski, Dwight. "Presumption in the Value Proposition Realm." *CEDA Yearbook* (1983): 34–39.

Rowland, Robert C. "The Function of Presumption in Academic Debate." *CEDA Yearbook* 13 (1992): 20–24.

Sproule, J. Michael. "The Psychological Burden of Proof: On the Evolutionary Development of Richard Whately's Theory of Presumption." *Speech Monographs* 43(2) (June 1976): 115–129.

Thomas, David. "Presumption in Nonpolicy Debate: A Case for Natural Presumption Based on Current Nonpolicy Paradigms." In *Advanced Debate: Readings in Theory, Practice, and Teaching,* 4th ed., ed. David Thomas and John Hart. Lincolnwood, IL: National Textbook, 1992. Pp. 220–242.

Vasilius, Jan. "Presumption, Presumption, Wherefore Art Thou Presumption." *CEDA Yearbook* (1980): 33–42.

VIII. Research

Adams, Tyrone, and Andrew Wood. "The Emerging Role of the World Wide Web in Forensics: On Computer-Mediated Research and Community Development." *The Forensic* 81(4) (Summer 1996): 21–35.

Bart, John. "Is There an Exit from the Information Superhighway? The Dangers of Electronic Research." *Forensic Educator* 9(1) (1994–95): 28–31.

Harris, Scott. "Databases in the Marketplace of Academic Debate: A Response to Tucker." *Argument and Advocacy* 32(1) (Summer 1995): 41–45.

Herbeck, Dale, ed. "Computer Mediated Research." *Forensic Educator* 9(1) (1994–95).

Pitt, Carl Allen. "Upgrading the Debater's Research Methods." *Speaker and Gavel* 7(2) (Jan. 1970): 44–46.

Rhodes, Jack, and Glenda Rhodes. "Guidelines for Library Services to College and High School Debaters." *Reference Quarterly* (Fall 1987): 87–94.

Scheckles, T. F. "Applications of Computer Technology in Intercollegiate Debate." *Speaker and Gavel* 23 (1986): 52–61.

Stafford, Shane, and Brian Lain. "Hitchhiking on the Information Superhighway: Research on the Net." *Debaters' Research Guide.* Winston-Salem, NC: Wake Forest University, 1994. Pp. A10–A15.

Tucker, Robert. "Argument, Ideology, and Databases: On the Corporatization of Academic Debate." *Argumentation and Advocacy* 32(1) (Summer 1995): 30–40.

Wood, Stephen C. "Threads: An Introduction to Forensic E-Mail." *The Forensic* 80(2) (Winter 1995): 18–29.

IX. Argumentation Theory, Dialectics, Logic and Reasoning, and Proof Standards as Applied to Debate

Aden, Roger. "The Enthymeme as Postmodern Argument Form: Condensed, Mediated Argument Then and Now." *Argument and Advocacy* 31(2) (Fall 1994): 54–63.

Adler, Mortimer. *Dialectic.* New York: Harcourt, Brace, 1929.

Anderson, Ray Lynn, and C. David Mortenson. "The Limits of Logic." *JAFA* 7 (Spring 1970): 71–78.

———. "Logic and Marketplace Argumentation." *Quarterly Journal of Speech* 53 (Apr. 1967): 143–151.

Aristotle. *The Rhetoric of Aristotle.* Trans. Lane Cooper. New York: Appleton-Century-Crofts, 1932.

Bator, Paul G. "The Good Reasons Movement: A Confounding of Dialectic and Rhetoric." *Philosophy and Rhetoric* 21(1) (1988): 38–47.

Benoit, William. "Aristotle's Example: The Rhetorical Induction." *Quarterly Journal of Speech* 66 (Apr. 1980): 182–192.

———. "On Aristotle's Example." *Philosophy and Rhetoric* 20(4) (1987): 261–267.

Billig, Michael. *Arguing and Thinking: A Rhetorical Approach to Social Psychology.* Cambridge: Cambridge University Press, 1987.

Blair, J. Anthony, and Ralph H. Johnson. "Argument as Dialectical." *Argumentation* 1 (1987): 41–56.

Brockriede, Wayne. "A Standard for Judging Applied Logic in Debate." *The AFA Register* (Spring 1962): 10–14.

———. "Arguers as Lovers." *Philosophy and Rhetoric* 5 (Winter 1972): 1–11.

———. "The Contemporary Renaissance in the Study of Argument." In *Argument in Transition: Proceedings of the Third Summer Conference on Argumentation,* ed. David Zarefsky, Malcolm O. Sillars, and Jack Rhodes. Annandale, VA: SCA, 1983. Pp. 17–26.

———, and Douglas Ehninger. "Toulmin on Argument: An Examination and Application." *Quarterly Journal of Speech* 46 (Feb. 1960): 44–53.

Brooks, Richard O. "Legal Studies and Liberal Arts: Outline of Curriculum Based upon the Practical Syllogism." *The Legal Studies Forum* 10(1) (Winter 1986): 97–120.

Clarke, Ruth Anne, and Jesse G. Delia. "'Topoi' and Rhetorical Competence." *Quarterly Journal of Speech* 65(2) (Apr. 1979): 187–206.

Conley, Thomas M. "The Enthymeme in Perspective." *Quarterly Journal of Speech* 70 (May 1984): 168–187.

Consigny, Scott. "Dialectical, Rhetorical, and Aristotelian Rhetoric." *Philosophy and Rhetoric* 22(4) (1989): 281–287.

Copi, Irving. *Informal Logic.* New York: Macmillan, 1986.

Delia, Jesse G. "The Logic Fallacy, Cognitive Theory, and the Enthymeme: A Search for the Foundations of Reasoned Discourse." *Quarterly Journal of Speech* 56 (Apr. 1970): 140–148.

Douglas, Rodney B., and Carroll Arnold. "On Analysis of Logos: A Methodological Inquiry." *Quarterly Journal of Speech* 55 (Feb. 1970): 22–32.

Ehninger, Douglas. "Argument as Method: Its Nature, Its Limitations, and Its Uses." *Communication Studies* 37 (1970): 101–110.

Epstein, William. "The Classical Tradition of Dialectics and American Legal Education." *Journal of Legal Education* 31(3–5) (Summer/Fall 1982): 399–423.

Fisher, Walter R. "Rationality and the Logic of Good Reasons." *Philosophy and Rhetoric* 13(2) (Spring 1980): 121–130.

Golden, J. L., and J. J. Pillotta, eds. *Practical Reasoning in Human Affairs.* Dordrecht, Holland: D. Reidel, 1986.

Goodnight, G. Thomas. "The Re-Union of Argumentation and Debate Theory." In *Dimensions of Argument: Proceedings of the Second Summer Conference on Argumentation,* ed. George Ziegelmueller and Jack Rhodes. Annandale, VA: SCA, 1981. Pp. 415–432.

Gottlieb, Gordon. *The Logic of Choice.* New York: Macmillan, 1968.

Hamer, David. "The Civil Standard of Proof Uncertainty: Probability, Belief, and Justice." *Sydney Law Review* 16(4) (Dec. 1994): 506–536.

Hample, Dale. "Argument: Public, Private, Social and Cognitive." *JAFA* 25 (Summer 1988): 13–19.

———. "Teaching the Cognitive Context of Argument." *Communication Education* 34 (July 1985): 196–204.

Hollihan, Thomas A., and Pat Riley. "Academic Debate and Democracy: A Clash of Ideologies." In *Argument and Critical Practices: Proceedings of the Fifth SCA/AFA Conference on Argumentation,* ed. J. W. Wenzel. Annandale, VA: SCA, 1987. Pp. 399–404.

Hunt, Everett. "Dialectics: A Neglected Method of Argument." *Quarterly Journal of Speech* (June 1921): 221–232.

Iseminger, Gary. "Successful Argument and Rational Belief." *Philosophy and Rhetoric* 7 (1974): 47–57.

Jamieson, Kathleen Hall. *Eloquence in an Electronic Age.* New York: Oxford University Press, 1988.

Kennedy, George, ed. and trans. *Aristotle on Rhetoric: A Theory of Civic Discourse.* New York: Oxford University Press, 1991.

Klumpp, James. "Keeping Our Traditions Straight: Working with the Intellectual Modes of Argumentative Studies." In *Argument in Controversy: Proceedings of the Seventh SCA/AFA Conference on Argumentation,* ed. Donn Parson. Annandale, VA: SCA, 1991. Pp. 33–38.

Lakoff, George, and Mark Johnson. *Metaphors We Live By.* Chicago: University of Chicago Press, 1980.

Lichtman, Allan J., and Daniel M. Rohrer. "The Logic of Policy Dispute." *JAFA* 16 (Spring 1980): 236–247.

Miller, Gerald R. "Some Factors Influencing Judgments of the Logical Validity of Arguments: A Research Review." *Quarterly Journal of Speech* 55 (Oct. 1969): 276–286.

Mills, Glen E., and Hugh Petrie. "The Role of Logic in Rhetoric." *Quarterly Journal of Speech* 54 (Oct. 1968): 260–267.

Mortenson, C. David, and Ray L. Anderson. "The Limits of Logic." *JAFA* 7 (Spring 1970): 71–78.

Nelson, William F. "Topoi: Evidence of Human Conceptual Behavior." *Philosophy and Rhetoric* 2 (Winter 1969): 1–11.

Newman, Robert P. "Analysis and Issues—A Study of Doctrine." In *Readings in Argumentation,* ed. Jerry M. Anderson and Paul J. Dovre. Boston: Allyn & Bacon, 1968. Pp. 166–180.

Nothstine, William L. "Topics as Ontological Metaphor in Contemporary Rhetorical Theory and Criticism." *Quarterly Journal of Speech* 74 (May 1988): 151–163.

Perelman, Chaim, and Lucie Olbrechts-Tyteca. *The New Rhetoric: A Treatise on Argumentation.* Trans. by John Wilkinson and Purcell Weaver. Notre Dame, IN: University of Notre Dame Press, 1969.

Petrie, Hugh. "Does Logic Have Any Relevance to Argumentation?" *JAFA* 6 (Spring 1969): 55–60.

Pierce, Donald C. "The History of the Concept of Stasis." *The Forensic* 72 (1987): 75–81.

Pinto, Robert C., and John Anthony Blair. *Reasoning: A Practical Guide.* Englewood Cliffs, NJ: Prentice Hall, 1993.

Powers, John M. "On the Intellectual Structure of the Human Communication Discipline." *Communication Education* 44(3) (July 1995): 191–222.

Pruett, Robert. "Dialectic: A Starting Point for Argument." *Ohio Speech Journal* (1970): 42–47.

Rescher, Nicholas. *Dialectics: A Controversy Oriented Approach to the Theory of Knowledge.* Albany: State University of New York Press, 1977.

———. *Rationality: A Philosophical Inquiry into the Nature and the Rationale of Reason.* New York: Oxford University Press, 1988.

Rowland, Robert C. "Argument Fields." In *Dimensions of Argument: Proceedings of the Second Summer Conference on Argumentation,* ed. George Ziegelmueller and Jack Rhodes. Annandale, VA: SCA, 1981. Pp. 56–79.

———. "On Defining Argument." *Philosophy and Rhetoric* 20 (1987): 140–159.

———, and John E. Fritch. "The Relationship Between Debate and Argumentation Theory." In *Spheres of Argument: Proceedings of the Sixth SCA/AFA Conference on Argumentation,* ed. Bruce E. Gronbeck. Annandale, VA: SCA, 1989. Pp. 457–463.

Self, Lois. "Rhetoric and Phronesis: The Aristotelian Ideal." *Philosophy and Rhetoric* 12 (Spring 1979): 130–145.

Sunstein, Cass. "On Analogical Reasoning." *Harvard Law Review* 106(3) (Jan. 1993): 741–793.

Shiffrin, Steven. "Forensics, Dialectic, and Speech Communication." *JAFA* 8 (Spring 1972): 189–191.

Toulmin, Stephen. *The Uses of Argument.* Cambridge: Cambridge University Press, 1958.

———, Richard Rieke, and Allan Janik. *An Introduction to Reasoning.* New York: Macmillan, 1979.

Trapp, Robert. "The Need for an Argumentative Perspective for Academic Debate." *CEDA Yearbook* 14 (1993): 23–33.

Warnick, Barbara. "Judgment, Probability and Aristotle's Rhetoric." *Quarterly Journal of Speech* 85 (Aug. 1989): 299–311.

Zarefsky, David. "The Role of Causal Argument in Policy Controversies." *JAFA* 8 (Spring 1977): 179–191.

X. Evidence

Benson, James A. "The Use of Evidence in Intercollegiate Debate." *JAFA* 7 (Spring 1971): 260–270.

Dresser, William R. "The Impact of Evidence on Decision Making." *JAFA* 3(2) (May 1966): 43–47.

———. "Studies of the Effects of Evidence: Implications for Forensics." *The AFA Register* (Fall 1962): 14–19.

Gregg, R. B. "The Rhetoric of Evidence." *Western Speech* 31 (Summer 1967): 180–189.

Hobbs, Jeffrey. "Surrendering Decision Authority from the Public to the Technical Sphere of Argument: The Use of Evidence in Contemporary Intercollegiate Debate." *The Forensic* 80(1) (Fall 1994): 1–6.

Huff, Darrell. "How to Lie with Statistics." *Harper's Magazine* (Aug. 1950) 97–101.

Insalata, S. John. "The Persuasive Use of Evidence in Formal Argument." *The Forensic* (Mar. 1960): 9–11.

Kazoleas, Dean C. "A Comparison of the Persuasive Effectiveness of Qualitative Versus Quantitative Evidence." *Communication Quarterly* 41(1) (Winter 1993): 40–51.

Kellermann, Kathy, and Allan Louden. "Coping with Statistics in Debate." In *Debaters' Research Guide.* Winston-Salem, NC: Wake Forest University, 1979. Pp. 12–21.

———. "The Concept of Evidence: A Critical Review." *JAFA* 16 (Winter 1980): 159–172.

Luchok, Joseph, and James C. McCroskey. "The Effect of Quality of Evidence on Attitude Change and Source Credibility." *Southern Speech Communication Journal* 43(4) (Summer 1978): 371–383.

McCroskey, James. "A Summary of Experimental Research on the Effects of Evidence on Persuasive Communication." *Quarterly Journal of Speech* 55 (Apr. 1969): 169–176.

Newman, Robert P., and Dale R. Newman. *Evidence.* New York: Houghton Mifflin, 1969.

———, and Keith R. Sanders. "A Study in the Integrity of Evidence." *JAFA* 2(1) (Jan. 1965): 7–13.

Reinard, John C. "The Empirical Study of the Persuasive Effects of Evidence: The Status After Fifty Years of Research." *Human Communication Research* 15(1) (Fall 1988): 3–59.

Sanders, Keith. "Toward a Solution to the Misuse of Evidence." *JAFA* 3(1) (Jan. 1966): 6–10.

Sanders, Gerald H. "Misuse of Evidence in Academic Debate." In *Advanced Debate,* ed. David A. Thomas. Skokie, IL: National Textbook, 1975. Pp. 220–227.

Scott, Robert L. "Evidence in Communication: We Are Such Stuff." *Western Journal of Speech Communication* 42(1) (Winter 1978): 29–36.

Spiker, Barry K., Tom Daniels, and Lawrence Bernabo. "The Quantitative Quandry in Forensics: The Use and Misuse of Statistical Evidence." *JAFA* 19 (Fall 1982): 87–96.

Winebrenner, T. C. "Authority as Argument in Academic Debate." *Contemporary Argumentation and Debate* 16 (1995): 14–29.

XI. The Affirmative, Comparative Advantage, and Criteria Cases

Brock, Bernard. "The Comparative Advantages Case." *Speech Teacher* (Mar. 1967): 118–123.

Chesebro, James W. "The Comparative Advantage Case." *JAFA* 5(2) (Spring 1968): 57–63.

———. "Beyond the Orthodox: The Criteria Case." *JAFA* 7 (Winter 1971): 208–215.

Fadely, L. Dean. "The Validity of the Comparative Advantage Case." *JAFA* 4(1) (Winter 1967): 28–35.

Flaningam, Carl D. "Concomitant vs. Comparative Advantages: Sufficient vs. Necessary Conditions." *JAFA* 18(1) (Summer 1981): 1–8.

Lewinski, John, Bruce Metzler, and Peter L. Settle. "The Goal Case Affirmative: An Alternative Approach to Academic Debate." *JAFA* 9 (Spring 1973): 458–463.

Lichtman, Alan, Charles Garvin, and Jerry Corsi. "The Alternative Justification Affirmative: A New Case Form." *JAFA* 10 (Fall 1973): 59–69.

Ware, B. L., Jr., and William B. English. "A Comparison of the Need Plan and the Comparative Advantage Approach: There Is a Difference." *Kansas Speech Journal* (Spring 1973): 4–11.

Zarefsky, David. "The Traditional Case Comparative Advantage Case Dichotomy: Another Look." *JAFA* 6(1) (Winter 1969): 12–20.

XII. Negative Approaches to Debate

Brewster, B. "Analysis of Disadvantages: Scenarios and Intrinsicness." *Debaters' Research Guide.* Winston-Salem, NC: Wake Forest University, 1984. Pp. 14–16.

Cragan, John, and Donald Shields. "The Comparative Advantage Negative." *JAFA* 7(2) (Spring 1970): 85–91.

Hemmer, Joseph J., Jr. "The Comparative Advantage Negative: An Integrated Approach." *Speaker and Gavel* 13 (Winter 1976): 27–30.

Hemphill, Dwaine R. "First Negative Strategies: A Reevaluation of Negative Division of Duties." In *Argument in Transition: Proceedings of the Third Summer Conference on Argumentation,* ed. David Zarefsky, Malcolm O. Sillars, and Jack Rhodes. Annandale, VA: SCA, 1983. Pp. 883–892.

Patterson, J. W. "The Obligations of the Negative in a Policy Debate." *The Speech Teacher* (Sept. 1962): 208–213.

Solt, Roger. "Negative Fiat: Resolving the Ambiguities of Should." *Argumentation and Advocacy* 25 (Winter 1989): 121–139.

Thomas, David, and Jerry M. Anderson. "Negative Approaches to the Comparative Advantages Case." *Speaker and Gavel* (May 1968): 148–157.

———. "Response to Cragan and Shields: Alternative Formats for Negative Approaches to Comparative Advantage Cases." *JAFA* 8 (Spring 1972): 200–206.

XIII. Criteria

Berube, David. "Parameters for Criteria Debating." *CEDA Yearbook* 11 (1990): 9–25.

Broda-Bahm, Ken. "Community Concepts of Argumentative Legitimacy: Challenging Norms in National-Circuit CEDA Debate." *The Forensic* 79(3) (Spring 1994): 26–35.

Brownlee, Don. "Approaches to Support and Refutation of Criteria." *CEDA Yearbook* 8 (1987): 59–63.

Cole, Mark, Ronald Boggs, and Kevin Twohy. "The Functions of Criteria in Nonpolicy Argumentation: Burdens and Approaches." *CEDA Yearbook* 7 (1986).

XIV. Kritiks/Critiques

Broda-Bahm, Ken. "Meaning as Language Use: The Case of the Language-Linked Value Objection." *CEDA Yearbook* 12 (1991): 67–78.

———, and Thomas L. Murphy. "A Defense of Critique Arguments: Beyond the Resolutional Question." *CEDA Yearbook* 15 (1994): 20–32.

Moris, Eric, and John Katsulas. "Pro and Con: The Relevance Irrelevance of the Critique to Policy Debate." *Forensic Educator* 11(1) (1996–97).

Roskoski, Matt, and Joe Peabody. "A Linguistic and Philosophic Critique of Language Arguments." Paper presented at the SCA Convention, Chicago, Nov. 1, 1992.

Shanahan, William. "Kritik of Thinking." *Debaters' Research Guide.* Winston-Salem, NC: Wake Forest University, 1993. Pp. A3–A8.

Shors, Matthew, and Steve Mancuso. "The Critique: Skreaming Without Raising Its Voice." *Debaters' Research Guide.* Winston-Salem, NC: Wake Forest University, 1993. Pp. A14–A18.

Solt, Roger. *The Anti-Kritik Handbook.* Denton, TX: Paradigm Research, 1995.

———. "Demystifying the Critique." *Debaters' Research Guide.* Winston-Salem, NC: Wake Forest University, 1993. Pp. A8–A12.

XV. Topicality

Adams, N., and T. Wilkins. "The Role of Justification in Topic Analysis." *CEDA Yearbook* 8 (1987): 21–26.

Allen, Mike, and Nancy Burrell. "A Pragmatic Theory of Topicality." In *Argument and Social Practice: Proceedings of the Fourth Conference on Argumentation,* ed. Robert J. Cox, Malcolm O. Sillars, and Gregg Walker. Annandale, VA: SCA, 1985. Pp. 854–861.

Berube, David. "Debating Hasty Generalization." In *Advanced Debate: Readings in Theory, Practice and Teaching,* 3rd ed., David Thomas and Jack Hart. Lincolnwood, IL: National Textbook, 1987. Pp. 483–489.

———. "Parametric Topicality: An Analysis and a Rebuttal." *CEDA Yearbook* 12 (1991): 12–26.

———. "Parametrical Interpretation: Issues and Answers." *Contemporary Argumentation and Debate* 16 (1995): 30–51.

———. "What Killed Schrodinger's Cat?: Parametric Topicality, That's What." *CEDA Yearbook* 12 (1991): 12–26.

Bile, Jeffrey. "When the Whole Is Greater Than the Sum of the Parts: The Implications of Holistic Resolutional Focus." *CEDA Yearbook* 8 (1987): 8–15.

———. "Propositional Justification: Another View." *CEDA Yearbook* 9 (1988): 54–62.

Cross, Frank. *Debating Topicality.* San Francisco: Griffin Research, 1987.

Dudczak, Craig. "Topicality: An Equal Ground Standard." *CEDA Yearbook* 10 (1989): 12–21.

Hastings, Arthur. "On the Meaning of Should." *Speaker and Gavel* 4(1) (Nov. 1966): 8–10.

Herbeck, Dale A., and John P. Katsulas. "The Affirmative Topicality Burden: Any Reasonable Example of the Resolution." *JAFA* 21 (Winter 1985): 133–145.

————. "The Case Against the Problem Area: A Response to Ulrich." *Forensic Educator* 4 (1989–90): 8–11.

Hingstman, David. "Topicality and Division of Ground." In *Framing Policy Dialectic in Argument and Social Practice: Proceedings of the Fourth SCA/AFA Conference on Argumentation,* ed. J. Robert Cox, Malcolm O. Sillars, and Gregg Walker. Annandale, VA: SCA, 1985. Pp. 841–853.

Hynes, Thomas J., and Walter Ulrich. "The Role of Propositions in Forensic Argument." In *Argument and Social Practice: Proceedings of the Fourth SCA/AFA Conference on Argumentation,* ed. J. Robert Cox, Malcolm O. Sillars, and Gregg Walker. Annandale, VA: SCA, 1985. Pp. 827–840.

Madsen, Arnie, and Al Louden. "Jurisdiction and the Evaluation of Topicality." *JAFA* 24(2) (Fall 1987): 73–83.

————. "The Jurisdiction/Topicality Analogy." *Argumentation and Advocacy* 26(4) (Spring 1990): 141–154.

————, and Robert C. Chandler. "Further Examination of Resolutional Focus." In *Spheres of Argument: Proceedings of the Sixth SCA/AFA Conference on Argumentation,* ed. Bruce Gronbeck. Annandale, VA: SCA, 1989. Pp. 411–416.

————. "When the Whole Becomes a Black Hole: Implications of the Holistic Perspective." *CEDA Yearbook* 9 (1988): 30–37.

McBath, James, and Joseph Aurbach. "Origins of the National Debate Resolution." *JAFA* 4(3) (Fall 1967): 96–103.

Murphy, Thomas L. "Assessing the Jurisdictional Model of Topicality." *Argumentation and Advocacy* 26 (Spring 1990): 145–150.

Parson, Donn W. "On Being Reasonable: The Last Refuge of Scoundrels." In *Dimensions of Argument: Proceedings of the Second Summer Conference on Argumentation,* ed. George Ziegelmueller and Jack Rhodes. Annandale, VA: SCA, 1981. Pp. 532–543.

————, and John Bart. "On Being Reasonable: The Last Refuge of Scoundrels Part II: The Scoundrels Strike Back." In *Advanced Debate: Readings in Theory, Practice, and Teaching,* ed. David Thomas and Jack Hart. Lincolnwood, IL: National Textbook, 1989. Pp. 130–138.

Rhodes, Jack, and Michael Pfau. "Resolution of Example: A Reply to Herbeck and Katsulas." *JAFA* 21 (Winter 1985): 146–149.

Sherwood, Ken. "Claim Without Warrant: The Lack of Logical Support for Parametric Topicality." *CEDA Yearbook* 15 (1994): 10–19.

Ulrich, Walter. "The Nature of the Problem Area." *Forensic Educator* 4 (1989–90): 5–7.

————. "The Nature of the Topic in Value Debate." *CEDA Yearbook* 5 (1984): 1–6.

XVI. Counterplans

Branham, Robert J. "Roads Not Taken: Counterplans and Opportunity Costs." *Argumentation and Advocacy* 25 (Spring 1989): 246–255.

————, ed. "The State of the Counterplan." *JAFA* 25 (special issue) (Winter 1989): 117–191. A key to modern counterplan theory.

Dempsey, Richard H., and David N. Hartmann. "Mirror State Counterplans: Illegitimate, Topical, or Magical?" *JAFA* 21 (Winter 1985): 161–166.

Fadley, Dean. "Fiat Power and the Mirror State Counterplan." *Speaker and Gavel* 24 (Winter 1987): 69–76.

Gossett, John. "Counterplan Competitiveness in the Stock Issues Paradigm." In *Dimensions of Argument: Proceedings of the Second Summer Conference on Argumentation,* ed. George Ziegelmueller and Jack Rhodes. Annandale, VA: SCA, 1981. Pp. 568–578.

Herbeck, Dale, John Katsulas, and Karla Leeper. "The Locus of Debate Controversy Re-Examined: Implications for Counterplan Theory." *Argumentation and Advocacy* 25 (Winter 1989): 150–164.

————. "A Permutation Standard of Competitiveness." *JAFA* 22 (Summer 1985): 12–19.

————, and John Katsulas. "Point of Theory: Counterplan Competitiveness." *The Forensic Quarterly* (Fall 1985): 46–48.

Hill, Bill. "Counterplans: Requirements, Presumption and Study." *Debaters' Research Guide*. Winston-Salem, NC: Wake Forest University, 1980. Pp. 2–7.

Hynes, Thomas J., Jr. "The Counterplan: An Historical and Descriptive Study." Unpublished M.A. thesis, University of North Carolina at Chapel Hill, 1972.

————. *Debating Counterplans*. San Francisco: Griffin Research, 1987.

————. "The Studies Counterplan: Still Hoping—A Reply to Shelton." *JAFA* (Winter 1985): 156–160.

Kaplow, Louis. "Rethinking Counterplans: A Reconciliation with Debate Theory." *JAFA* 17(4) (Spring 1981): 215–226.

Katsulas, John, Dale Herbeck, and Edward M. Panetta. "Fiating Utopia: A Negative View of the Emergence of World Order Counterplans and Futures Gaming in Policy Debate." *Argumentation and Advocacy* 24 (Fall 1987): 95–111.

————. "Fiating Utopia, Part Two: A Rejoinder to Edwards and Snider." *Argumentation and Advocacy* 24 (Fall 1987): 130–136.

Lane, Gina. "The Justification of Counterplans in Nonpolicy Debate: A Skeptical View." *CEDA Yearbook* 15 (1994): 33–42.

Lichtman, Allan, and Daniel M. Rohrer. "A General Theory of the Counterplan." *JAFA* 12 (Fall 1975): 70–79. A classic early article on counterplan theory.

Madsen, Arnie. "General Systems Theory and Counterplan Competition." *Argumentation and Advocacy* 26 (Fall 1989): 71–82.

Mayer, Michael. "Epistemological Considerations of the Studies Counterplan." *JAFA* 19 (Spring 1983): 261–266.

————, and J. Hale. "Evaluating the Studies Counterplan: Topicality and Competitiveness." *Speaker and Gavel* 16 (Summer 1979): 67–72.

Nebergall, Roger E. "The Negative Counterplan." *Speech Teacher* 6 (Sept. 1957): 217–220.

Panetta, Edward M., and Steven Dolley. "The Topical Counterplan: A Competitive Policy Option." *Argumentation and Advocacy* 25 (Winter 1989): 165–177.

Perkins, Dallas. "Counterplans and Paradigms." *Argumentation and Advocacy* 25(3) (Winter 1989): 140–149.

Shelton, Michael W. "In Defense of the Study Counterplan." *JAFA* 21 (Winter 1985): 150–155.

Solt, Roger. "Counterplan Competition: Permutations and Beyond." *Debaters' Research Guide*. Winston-Salem, NC: Wake Forest University, 1985. Pp. 18–23.

Thompson, Wayne N. "The Effect of the Counterplan upon the Burden of Proof." *Central States Speech Journal* 13 (Fall 1962): 247–252.

Ulrich, Walter. "The Legitimacy of the Counter Procedure Counterplan." *JAFA* 23 (Winter 1987): 166–169.

Unger, James. "Investigating the Investigators: A Study of the Study Counterplan." *Debate Issues* 12 (Feb. 1979): 1–8.

Walker, Gregg B. "The Counterplan as Argument in Non-Policy Debate." *Argumentation and Advocacy* 25 (Winter 1989): 178–191.

XVII. Counterwarrants

Ganer, Patricia. "Counterwarrants: An Idea Whose Time Has Not Come." In *Dimensions of Argument: Proceedings of the Second Summer Conference on Argumentation,* ed. George Ziegelmueller and Jack Rhodes. Annandale, VA: SCA, 1981. Pp. 478–484.

Hunt, Steven B., and Greg Tolbert. "Counter-Warrants: A Method for Testing Topical Justification in CEDA Debate." *CEDA Yearbook* 6 (1985): 21–28.

Keeshan, Marjorie, and Walter Ulrich. "Critique of the Counter-Warrant as a Negative Strategy." *JAFA* 16(3) (Winter 1980): 199–203.

Mayer, Michael. "Extending Counter-Warrants: The Counter Resolutional Counterplan." *JAFA* 19 (Fall 1982): 122–127.

Paulsen, James W., and Jack Rhodes. "The Counter-Warrant as a Negative Strategy: A Modest Proposal." *JAFA* 15 (Spring 1979): 205–210. The article that started counter-warrant theory.

Rhodes, Jack. "A Defense of the Counter-Warrant as Negative Argument." In *Dimensions of Argument: Proceedings of the Second Summer Conference on Argumentation,* ed. George Ziegelmueller and Jack Rhodes. Annandale, VA: SCA, 1981. Pp. 485–493.

———. "Counter-Warrants After Ten Years." In *Spheres of Argument: Proceedings of the Sixth SCA/AFA Conference on Argumentation,* ed. Bruce Gronbeck. Annandale, VA: SCA, 1989. Pp. 406–410.

XVIII. Inherency

Benoit, William L. "The Nature and Function of Inherency in Policy Argumentation." *Speaker and Gavel* 19 (Spring 1982): 55–63.

Cherwitz, Richard A., and James W. Hikins. "Inherency as a Multidimensional Construct: A Rhetorical Approach to the Proof of Causation." *JAFA* 14(2) (Fall 1977): 82–90.

Cox, J. Robert. "Attitudinal Inherency: Implications for Policy Debate." *Southern Speech Communication Journal* 40 (Winter 1975): 158–168.

Dudczak, Craig. "Inherency in Non-Policy Propositions: Rediscovering the Lost Issue." In *Argument and Critical Practices: Proceedings of the Fifth SCA/AFA Conference on Argumentation,* ed. Joseph Wenzel. Annandale, VA: SCA, 1987. Pp. 371–378.

———. "Inherency as a Stock Issue in Non-Policy Propositions." *CEDA Yearbook* 9 (1988): 15–22.

Flaningam, Carl D. "Inherency and Incremental Change: A Response to Morello." *JAFA* 20 (Spring 1984): 231–236.

Goodnight, Tom, Bill Balthrop, and Donn W. Parson. "The Problem of Inherency: Strategy and Substance." *JAFA* 10 (Spring 1974): 229–240.

Ling, David, and Robert V. Seltzer. "The Role of Attitudinal Inherency in Contemporary Debate." *JAFA* 7 (Spring 1971): 278–283.

Morello, John T. "Defending the Present System's Capacity for Incremental Changes." *JAFA* 19 (Fall 1982): 115–121.

Parson, Donn W. "Response to a Critique of the Problem of Inherency." *JAFA* 12(1) (Summer 1975): 46–58.

Pfau, Michael. "The Present System Revisited. Part One: Incremental Change." *JAFA* 17 (Fall 1980): 80–84.

———. "The Present System Revisited. Part Two: Policy Interrelationships." *JAFA* 17 (Winter 1981): 146–154.

Schunk, John. "Affirmative Fiat, Plan Circumvention, and the Process Disadvantage: The Further Ramifications of Psuedo-Inherency." *Speaker and Gavel* 18(3) (Spring 1981): 83–87.

———. "Farewell to Structural Change: The Cure for Psuedo-Inherency." *JAFA* 14(3) (Winter 1978): 144–149.

XIX. Cross-Examination

Beard, Raymond S. "Legal Cross-Examination and Academic Debate." *JAFA* 6 (Spring 1969): 61–66.

Cirlin, Alan. "Evaluating Cross Examination in CEDA Debate: On Getting Our Act Together." *CEDA Yearbook* 7 (1986): 43–50.

Clevenger, Kenneth. "Cross-Examination for Trial Defense Counsel." *Army Lawyer* (Jan. 1992): 9–10.

Coverstone, Alan. "Rediscovering the Lost Art of Cross-Examination." *Debaters' Research Guide.* Winston-Salem, NC: Wake Forest University, 1992. Pp. A3–A6.

Durst, John E., Jr. "Cross-Examination." *Trial Lawyers Quarterly* 19(3) (Fall 1988): 29–42.

Fuge, Lloyd, and Robert P. Newman. "Cross Examination in Academic Debating." *The Speech Teacher* 5 (Jan. 1956): 66–70.

Hartje, Jeffrey H. "Cross-Examination: A Primer for Trial Advocates." *American Journal of Trial Advocacy Annual* 10 (1987): 135–179.

Henderson, Bill. "A System of Teaching Cross-Examination Techniques." *Communication Education* 27 (Mar. 1978): 112–118.

Larson, Suzanne. "Cross-Examination in CEDA Debate: A Survey of Coaches." *CEDA Yearbook* 8 (1987): 33–41.

Lewis, David L. "Cross-Examination." *Mercer Law Review* 42(2) (Winter 1991): 627–642.

Lisnek, Paul. "Direct and Cross-Examination: The Keys to Success." *Trial Diplomacy Journal* 18(5) (Sept.–Oct. 1995): 263–269.

Miller, Thomas, and E. Caminker. "The Art of Cross-Examination." *CEDA Yearbook* 3 (1982): 4–15.

Ulrich, Walter. "Vitalizing Cross-Examination Debate: A Proposal." *JAFA* 18 (Spring 1982): 265–266.

Younger, Irving. "A Letter in Which Cicero Lays Down the Ten Commandments of Cross-Examination." *Law Institute Journal* 61(8) (Aug. 1987): 804–806. See also Younger's excellent videotape on the ten commandments of cross-examination.

Ziegelmueller, George. "Cross Examination Reexamined." In *Advanced Debate: Readings in Theory, Practice and Teaching,* ed. David Thomas and Jack Hart. Lincolnwood, IL: National Textbook, 1987. Pp. 66–74. Also in *Argument in Transition: Proceedings of the Third Summer Conference on Argument,* ed. David Zarefsky, Malcolm O. Sillars, and Jack Rhodes. Annandale, VA: SCA, 1983. Pp. 904–917.

XX. Rhetoric and Persuasion in Debate: Public Debates, Style, and Speaking Rates

Bartanen, Kristine, and Jim Hanson. "Advocating Humane Discourse." *The Forensic* 80(1) (Fall 1994): 16–21.

Carpenter, Ronald H. "Style and Emphasis in Debate." *JAFA* 6(1) (Winter 1969): 27–31.

Cathcart, Robert. "Adopting Debate to an Audience." *Speech Teacher* (Mar. 1956): 113–116.

Christopherson, Merrill G. "The Necessity for Style in Argument." *Speech Teacher* (Mar. 1960): 116–120.

Colbert, Kent. "A Study of CEDA and NDT Finalists' Speaking Rates." *CEDA Yearbook* 12 (1991): 88–94.

———. "A Quantitative Analysis of CEDA Speaking Rates." *National Forensic Journal* 6 (Fall 1988): 113–120.

———. "Speaking Rates of NDT Finalists from 1968–1980." *JAFA* 18 (Summer 1981): 73–76.

Cox, E. Sam, and W. Clifton Adams. "Valuing of Tournament Debate: Factors from Practitioners and Administrators." *The Forensic* 80(4) (Summer 1995): 7–12.

Friedman, Robert P. "Why Not Debate Persuasively?" *Today's Speech* 5 (1957): 32–34.

Giffin, Kim, and D. A. Warner. "A Study of the Influence of an Audience on the Rate of Speech in Tournament Debates." *The Speaker* (1962).

Hill, Bill. "Improving the Quality of CEDA Debate." *National Forensic Journal* 4 (Fall 1986): 105–121.

McBath, James H., and Nicholas M. Cripe. "Delivery: Rhetoric's Rusty Canon." *JAFA* 2(1) (Jan. 1965): 1–6.

McGough, M. "Pull It Across Your Flow." *The New Republic* (Oct. 10, 1988): 17–19.

Murrish, Walter. "Training the Debate in Persuasion." *JAFA* 1(1) (Jan. 1964): 7–12.

Olson, Donald O. "A Survey of Attitudes on the Spread." *Speaker and Gavel* 8(3) (Mar. 1971): 66–69.

Peterson, Owen. "Forum Debating: 150 Debates Later." *Southern Speech Communication Journal* 47(4) (Summer 1982): 435–443.

Stelzner, Hermann G. "Tournament Debate: Emasculated Rhetoric." *Southern Speech Communication Journal* 27 (Fall 1961): 34–42.

Swinney, James P. "The Relative Comprehension of Contemporary Tournament Debate Speeches." *JAFA* 5(1) (Winter 1968): 16–20.

Vasilius, Janet M., and Dan DeStephen. "An Investigation of the Relationship Between Debate Tournament Success and Rate, Evidence, and Jargon." *JAFA* 15 (Spring 1979): 197–204.

Voor, John B., and Joseph M. Miller. "The Effect of Practice upon the Comprehension of Time-Compressed Speech." *Speech Monographs* 32 (1965): 452–454.

Weiss, Robert O. "The Public Presence of Forensics." *Speaker and Gavel* 23(1) (Fall 1985): 23–28.

XXI. Debating Judging and Debate Paradigms

Allen, Mike, and Kathy Kellermann. "Using the Subjective Probability Model to Evaluate Academic Debate Arguments." *Argumentation and Advocacy* 25 (Fall 1988): 93–107.

Balthrop, William V. "Argumentation and the Critical Stance: A Methodological Approach." In *Advances in Argumentation Research,* ed. J. Robert Cox and Charles Willard. Carbondale: Southern Illinois University Press, 1982. Pp. 238–258.

———. "Citizen, Legislator, and Bureaucrat as Evaluators of Competing Policy Systems." In *Advanced Debate: Readings in Theory, Practice, and Teaching,* 2nd ed., ed. David Thomas. Skokie, IL: National Textbook, 1979. Pp. 402–418.

———. "The Debate Judge as Critic of Argument." *JAFA* 20 (Summer 1983): 1–15.

Bartanen, Michael. "The Case for Using Nontraditional Judges in Forensics Contests." *Argumentation and Advocacy* 30(4) (Spring 1994): 248–254.

Benoit, William, S. R. Wilson, and V. F. Follert. "Decision Rules for the Policy Metaphor." *JAFA* 22 (Winter 1986): 135–146.

Boileau, Don M., Jon Fitzgerald, David Ling, and Dan P. Millar. "A Debate Judge Certification Test: Development and Operation on a State-Wide Scale." *Communication Education* 30(4) (Oct. 1981): 414–420.

Branham, Robert J., and Thomas Isaacson. "The Ascent of Policy Making: Academic Debate from 1970 to 1980." *Speaker and Gavel* 17 (Fall 1979): 5–10.

Brey, James. "A Descriptive Analysis of CEDA Judging Philosophies, Part I: Definitive Acceptance or Rejection of Certain Tactics and Arguments." *CEDA Yearbook* 10 (1989): 67–77.

———. "An Analysis of CEDA Judging Philosophies, Part II: Accepting Certain Tactics and Arguments with Reservations." *CEDA Yearbook* 11 (1990): 72–79.

Brydon, Steven. "Judging CEDA Debate: A Systems Perspective." *CEDA Yearbook* 5 (1984): 85–88.

Buckley, David C. "A Comparison of Judging Paradigms." In *Argument in Transition: Proceedings of the Third Summer Conference on Argumentation,* ed. David Zarefsky, Malcolm O. Sillars, and Jack Rhodes. Annandale, VA: SCA, 1983. Pp. 858–870.

Cirlin, Alan. "Judging, Evaluation, and the Quality of CEDA Debate." *National Forensic Journal* (Fall 1986): 81–90.

Clevenger, Theodore, Jr. "Toward a Point of View for Contest Debate." *Central States Speech Journal* 12 (Fall 1960): 21–26.

Corsi, Jerome R. "Zarefsky's Theory of Debate as Hypothesis Testing: A Critical Re-Examination." *JAFA* 19 (Winter 1983): 158–170.

Cox, J. Robert. "A Study of Judging Philosophies of the Participants of the National Debate Tournament." *JAFA* 11 (Fall 1974): 61–71.

————, and Julia T. Wood. "The Effects of Consultation on Judges/Decisions." *The Speech Teacher* 24 (Mar. 1975): 118–126.

Crawford, C. B., and Willis M. Watt. "Argument Supporting the Requirement for Debate Judging Philosophy Statements at the PKD National Tournament." *The Forensic* 80(2) (Winter 1995): 1–10.

Cross, John D., and Ronald J. Matlon. "An Analysis of Judging Philosophies in Academic Debate." *JAFA* 15 (Fall 1978): 110–123.

"Debate Paradigms." *JAFA* 18 (special forum) (Winter 1982): Pp. 133–160.

Dempsey, Richard H., and David J. Hartmann. "Emergent Voting Criteria and the Judicial Impotence of Critics." *Argumentation and Advocacy* 22(3) (Winter 1986): 167–175.

Fisher, Walter R. "The Narrative Paradigm: In the Beginning." *Journal of Communication* 35(4) (Fall 1985): 74–89.

Freeley, Austin J. "Judging Paradigms: The Impact of the Critic on Argument." In *Dimensions of Argument: Proceedings of the Second Summer Conference on Argumentation,* ed. George Ziegelmueller and Jack Rhodes. Annandale, VA: SCA, 1981. Pp. 433–447.

Gass, Robert H., Jr. "The Narrative Perspective in Academic Debate: A Critique." *Argumentation and Advocacy* 25 (Fall 1988): 78–92.

Giffin, Kim. "A Study of the Criteria Employed by Tournament Debate Judges." *Speech Monographs* (Mar. 1959): 69–71.

Gill, Mary. "Knowing the Judge: The Key to Successful Debate." *CEDA Yearbook* 9 (1988): 96–101.

Hanson, C. T. "What Are the Options? The Philosophy of Using Ballots." *The Forensic* 73(3) (May 1988): 1–5.

Henderson, Bill, and David L. Boman. "A Study to Determine If Debate Judges' Judging Philosophy Statements Are Consistent with Their Later Related Ballot Statements." *JAFA* 19 (Winter 1983): 191–198.

Hollihan, Thomas A. "Conditional Arguments and the Hypothesis Testing Paradigm: A Negative View." *JAFA* 19 (Winter 1983): 171–178.

————, Kevin T. Baaske, and Patricia Riley. "Debaters as Storytellers: The Narrative Perspective in Academic Debate." *JAFA* 23 (Spring 1987): 184–193.

Hufford, Roger. "Toward Improved Tournament Judging." *JAFA* 2(3) (Sept. 1965): 120–125.

"Hypothesis Testing." *JAFA* 19 (Winter 1983): 158–190.

Klump, James F., Bernard L. Brock, James W. Chesebro, and John F. Cragan. "Implications of a Systems Model of Analysis on Argumentation Theory." *JAFA* 11 (Summer 1974): 1–7.

Lichtman, Alan, Daniel M. Rohrer, and Jack Hart. "Policy Systems Revisited." In *Advanced Debate: Readings in Practice and Teaching.* Lincolnwood, IL: National Textbook, 1987. Pp. 231–240.

McAdoo, Joe, ed. *Judging Debates.* Springfield, MO: Mid-America Research, 1975.

Miller, Gregory R. "The Forensics Critic as an Ideologue Critic: An Argument for Ideology as a New Paradigm for Academic Debate." *CEDA Yearbook* 10 (1989): 71–80.

———, John Gates, and Paul Gaske. "Resolving Paradigmatic Disputes as a Pre-Debate Issue: A Modest Proposal." *Speaker and Gavel* 26 (1988): 37–43.

Parson, Donn W. "Root Metaphors and Terministic Screens: Another Look at Paradigms." In *Argument in Transition: Proceedings of the Third Summer Conference on Argumentation,* ed. David Zarefsky, Malcolm O. Sillars, and Jack Rhodes. Annandale, VA: SCA, 1983. Pp. 792–799.

Rowland, Robert C. "The Debate Judge as Debate Judge: A Functional Paradigm for Evaluating Debates." *JAFA* 20 (Spring 1984): 183–193.

———. "Debate Paradigms: A Critical Examination." In *Dimensions of Argument: Proceedings of the Second Annual Conference on Argumentation,* ed. George Ziegelmueller and Jack Rhodes. Annandale, VA: SCA, 1981. Pp. 448–475.

———. "A Defense of Rational Argument." *Philosophy and Rhetoric* 28(4) (1995): 350–364.

———. "On Argument Evaluation." *JAFA* 21 (Winter 1985): 123–132.

———. "Standards for Paradigm Evaluation." *JAFA* 18 (Winter 1982): 133–140.

———. "Tabula Rasa: The Relevance of Debate to Argumentation Theory." *JAFA* 21 (Fall 1984): 76–88.

Smith, Mark. "To Disclose or Not to Disclose." *CEDA Yearbook* 11 (1990): 88–94.

Snider, Alfred C. "Games Without Frontiers: A Design for Communication Scholars and Forensics Educators." *JAFA* 20 (Winter 1984): 162–170.

Thomas, David A., ed. "Forum on Policy Systems Analysis." *JAFA* 22 (Winter 1986) 123–175.

Ulrich, Walter. "An Ad Hominem Examination of Hypothesis Testing as a Paradigm for Evaluation of Argument." *JAFA* 21 (Summer 1984): 1–8.

———. "Debate as Dialectic: A Defense of the Tabula Rasa Approach to Judging." *JAFA* 21(2) (Fall 1984): 89–93.

Wright, Tim, et al. "What Are the Characteristics of the Ideal Debate Judge?" *Speaker and Gavel* 7(4) (May 1970): 143–145.

Zarefsky, David, and Bill Henderson. "Hypothesis Testing in Theory and Practice." *JAFA* 19 (Winter 1983): 179–185.

———. "Reflections on Hypothesis Testing: A Response to Ulrich." *JAFA* 21 (Summer 1984): 9–13.

XXII. Ethics

Note: See AFA and CEDA ethics codes.

Church, Russell. "The AFA Code: Work Left Undone." *JAFA* 9 (Winter 1973): 378–379.

Day, Dennis. "The Ethics of Democratic Debate." *Central States Speech Journal* 17 (Feb. 1966): 5–14.

Duffy, Bernard. "The Ethics of Argumentation in Intercollegiate Debate: A Conservative Appraisal." *National Forensic Journal* 1 (Spring 1983): 65–71.

Fisher, Daryl. "Should a Coach Research and Develop Arguments for Debaters?" *Forensic Educator* 1 (1987): 15–16.

Inch, Edward S. "Forensics, Ethics, and the Need for Vision." In *PKD Proceedings of the 1991 Professional Development Conference: Commitment to Forensic Education: The*

Challenge to the Twenty-First Century, ed. Sally Roden. Conway: University of Central Arkansas, 1991. Pp. 47–57.

Klopf, Donald, and James McCroskey. "Ethical Practices in Debate." *JAFA* 1 (Jan. 1964): 13–16.

Muir, Star. "A Defense of the Ethics of Contemporary Debate." *Philosophy and Rhetoric* 26(4) (1993): 277–295.

Murphy, Richard. "The Ethics of Debating Both Sides." *Speech Teacher* (Jan. 1957): 1–9.

Newman, Robert P., and Keith R. Sanders. "A Study in the Integrity of Evidence." *JAFA* 2 (Jan. 1965): 7–13.

Rieke, Richard D., and David H. Smith. "The Dilemma of Ethics and Advocacy in the Use of Evidence." *Western Journal of Speech Communication* 32 (Fall 1968): 223–233.

Sanders, Keith R. "Toward a Solution to the Misuse of Evidence." *JAFA* 3 (Jan. 1966): 6–10.

Snider, Alfred C. "Ethics in Academic Debate: A Gaming Perspective." *National Forensic Journal* 2 (Fall 1984): 119–134.

Thomas, David A. "The Ethics of Proof in Speech Events: A Survey of Standards Used by Contestants and Judges." *National Forensic Journal* 1 (Spring 1983): 1–17.

Ulrich, Walter. "The Ethics of Forensics: An Overview." In *American Forensics in Perspective,* ed. Donn Parson. Annandale, VA: SCA, 1984. Pp. 13–22.

Watkins, Lloyd, ed. "Ethical Problems in Debating: A Symposium." *Speech Teacher* 8 (Mar. 1959): 150–156.

XXIII. Value Debate

See materials on value debating and CEDA. See especially CEDA yearbooks 1980 to present. See also materials on nonpolicy debate and L–D value debate, as well as Aristotle's enthymeme, Toulmin, Perelman, and informal logic.

Allen, Mike, and Lisa Dowdy. "An Analysis of CEDA and NDT Judging Philosophies." *CEDA Yearbook* 5 (1984): 74–79.

Bartanen, Michael. "Application of the Issues Agenda Paradigm to Speaker Duties in Value Debates." *CEDA Yearbook* 8 (1987): 42–51.

———. "The Role of Values in Policy Controversies." *CEDA Yearbook* 3 (1982): 19–24.

———, and David Frank. "Creating Procedural Distinctions Between Values and Policy Debate: The Issues Agenda Model." *The Forensic* (1983): 1–9.

———, and David Frank. *Debating Values.* Scottsdale, AZ: Gorsuch Scarisbrick, 1991.

Boggs, Ronald. "Comparing Values: A Review of Analytical Value Hierarchies." *CEDA Yearbook* 8 (1987): 27–32.

Church, Russell, and David Buckley. "Argumentation and Debating Propositions of Value: A Bibliography." *JAFA* 19 (Spring 1983): 239–250. An excellent values debate bibliography.

———, and Charles Wilbanks. *Values and Policies in Controversy: An Introduction to Argumentation and Debate.* Scottsdale, AZ: Gorsuch Scarisbrick, 1986.

Cirlin, Alan. "On Negative Strategy in Value Debate." *CEDA Yearbook* 5 (1984): 31–39.

Cole, Mark, Ronald Boggs, and Kevin Twohy. "The Function of Criteria in Non-Policy Argumentation: Burdens and Approaches." *CEDA Yearbook* 7 (1986): 36–42.

Corcoran, Joseph. *An Introduction to Non-Policy Debating.* Dubuque, IA: Kendall Hunt, 1988.

Dobkin, Milton. "Social Values and Public Address: Some Implications for Pedagogy." *Western Speech Communication Journal* (Summer 1962): 140–145.

Fisher, Walter. "Debating Value Propositions: A Game for Dialecticians." In *Dimensions of Argument: Proceedings of the Second Summer Conference on Argumentation,* ed. George Ziegelmueller and Jack Rhodes. Annandale, VA: SCA, 1981. Pp. 1014–1030.

———. "Rationality and the Logic of Good Reasons." *Philosophy and Rhetoric* (Spring 1980): 121–130.

————. "Toward a Logic of Good Reasons." *Quarterly Journal of Speech* (Dec. 1978): 376–384.

Flaningam, Carl. "Value-Centered Argument and the Development of Decision Rules." *JAFA* (Fall 1982): 107–115.

Gaske, Paul, Drew Kugler, and John Theobold. "Judging Attitudes and Paradigmatic Preferences in CEDA Debate: A Cumulative and Construct Validity Investigation." *CEDA Yearbook* 6 (1985): 57–66.

Gronbeck, Bruce. "From Is to Ought: Alternative Strategies." *Central States Speech Journal* (Spring 1968): 31–39.

Hample, Dale. "Testing a Model of Value Argument and Evidence." *Communication Monographs* 44(2) (June 1977): 106–120.

Henderson, Bill. "Theoretical Implications of Debating Non-Policy Propositions." *CEDA Yearbook* 1 (1980): 1–8.

Hill, Bill, and Richard W. Leeman. "Developing Fields Dependent Criteria in Non-Policy Debate." *The Forensic* 79(3) (Spring 1994): 14–25.

Hollihan, Thomas. "An Analysis of Value Argumentation in Contemporary Debate." *Debate Issues* 14 (Nov. 1980): 7–10.

————, Patricia Riley, and Curtis C. Austin. "A Content Analysis of Selected CEDA and NDT Judges' Ballots." In *Argument in Transition: Proceedings of the Third Summer Conference on Argumentation,* ed. David Zarefsky, Malcolm O. Sillars, and Jack Rhodes. Annandale, VA: SCA, 1983. Pp. 871–882.

Howe, Jack. "CEDA's Objectives: Lest We Forget." *CEDA Yearbook* 2 (1981): 1–3.

————, and Don Brownlee. "The Founding Principles of CEDA." In *Twentieth Anniversary Assessment Conference Proceedings, 1993,* ed. David Thomas and Stephen Wood. Dubuque, IA: Kendall Hunt, 1993. Pp. 249–262.

Kennedy, George. *Aristotle on Rhetoric: A Theory of Civic Discourse.* New York and Oxford: Oxford University Press, 1991.

Kluckhorn, Clyde. "The Evolution of Contemporary American Values." *Daedalus* (Spring 1958): 78–109.

Louden, Allan, and Curtis Austin. "CEDA vs. NDT: A Dysfunctional Myth." *CEDA Yearbook* 4 (1983): 6–12.

Matlon, Ronald J. "Analyzing and Debating Propositions of Value in Academic Forensics." *Journal of Communication Association of the Pacific* 6 (July 1977): 52–67.

————. "Debating Propositions of Value." *JAFA* 14 (Spring 1978): 194–204.

————. "Debating Propositions of Value: An Idea Revisited." *CEDA Yearbook* 9 (1988): 1–14.

————. "Propositions of Value: An Inquiry into Issue Analysis and Locus of Presumption." In *Dimensions of Argument: Proceedings of the Second Summer Conference on Argumentation,* ed. George Ziegelmueller and Jack Rhodes. Annandale, VA: SCA, 1981. Pp. 494–512.

Micken, Kathleen, and Patrick Micken. "Debating Values: An Idea Revitalized." *CEDA Yearbook* 14 (1993): 54–71.

Miller, Gerald. "Questions of Fact and Value: Another Look." *Southern States Speech Journal* (Winter 1962): 116–122.

Perelman, Chaim. "How Do We Apply Reason to Values?" *Journal of Philosophy* (Dec. 22, 1955): 797–802.

————. *The Idea of Justice and the Problem of Argument.* New York: Humanities Press, 1963.

————, and Lucie Olbrechts-Tyteca. *The New Rhetoric: A Treatise on Argumentation.* Notre Dame, IN: University of Notre Dame Press, 1969.

————. "Value Judgments, Justifications, and Argumentation." *Philosophy Today* (Spring 1962): 45–50.

Rescher, Nicholas. *Introduction to Value Inquiry*. Englewood Cliffs, NJ: Prentice Hall, 1969.

Rokeach, Milton. *Beliefs, Attitudes, and Values*. San Francisco: Jossey-Bass, 1976.

————. *Understanding Human Values*. London: Free Press, 1979.

Rowland, Robert C. "The Philosophical Presuppositions of Value Debate." In *Argument in Transition: Proceedings of the Third Summer Conference on Argumentation*, ed. David Zarefsky, Malcolm O. Sillars, and Jack Rhodes. Annandale, VA: SCA, 1983. Pp. 822–836.

Self, Lois. "Rhetoric and Phronesis: The Aristotelian Ideal." *Philosophy and Rhetoric* (1979): 130–136.

Sillars, Malcolm O. "Audiences, Social Values, and the Analysis of Argument." *Communication Education* (Nov. 1973): 291–303.

————, and Patricia Ganer. "Values and Beliefs: A Systematic Basis for Argumentation." In *Advances in Argumentation Theory and Research*, ed. J. Robert Cox and Charles A. Willard. Carbondale: Southern Illinois University Press, 1982.

Steele, Edward, and Charles Redding. "The American Values System: Premises for Persuasion." *Western Speech Communications Journal* 26 (Spring 1962): 83–91.

————. "Social Values in Public Address." *Western Journal Speech Communication* (Winter 1978): 37–42.

Stevenson, Charles L. *Facts and Values*. New Haven, CT: Yale University Press, 1963.

Sumner, L. W. "Value Judgments and Action." *Mind* (July 1968): 383–399.

Toulmin, Stephen. *An Examination of the Place of Reason in Ethics*. Cambridge: Cambridge University Press, 1950.

Tuman, Joseph. "Getting to First Base: Prima Facie Arguments for Propositions of Value." *JAFA* 24(2) (Fall 1987): 84–94.

Ulrich, Walter. *Debating Value Resolutions*. Berkeley, CA: Griffin Research, 1988.

Wallace, Karl. "Substance of Rhetoric: Good Reasons." *Quarterly Journal of Speech* (Oct. 1963): 239–249.

Warnick, Barbara. "Arguing Value Propositions." *JAFA* 18(2) (Fall 1981): 109–119.

Wentzel, Joseph. "Toward a Rationale for Value Centered Argument." *JAFA* 13 (Winter 1977): 150–158.

Werkmeister, W. H. *Historical Spectrum of Value Theories*. Lincoln, NE: Johnsen, 1973.

————. *Man and His Values*. Lincoln: University of Nebraska Press, 1967.

Williams, Robin M. "Values in American Society." In *American Society: A Sociological Interpretation*, 3rd ed. New York: Knopf, 1970. Pp. 438–504.

Wood, Stephen, and John Midgley. *Prima Facie: A Guide to Value Debate*. Dubuque, IA: Kendall Hunt, 1989.

Zarefsky, David. "Criteria for Evaluating Non-Policy Argument." *CEDA Yearbook* 1 (1980): 9–16.

XXIV. Lincoln–Douglas Debate

Grice, George L., and Edwin W. Knaak. *Lincoln–Douglas for Novices*. San Antonio, TX: Texas Group, 1985.

Kemp, Robert. *Lincoln–Douglas Debating*. Clayton, MO: Alan, 1984.

"Lincoln–Douglas Debate." *National Forensic Journal* 14(2) (special issue) (Fall 1996): 1–68. Concerns L–D at NFA tourneys.

Luong, Minh. "Defining the Role of Presumption in Lincoln–Douglas Debate." *NFL Journal* 2 (1992): 1–16.

Minch, Kevin, and Timothy Borchers. "A Philosophy for Judging NFA Lincoln–Douglas Debate." *National Forensic Journal* 14(2) (Fall 1996): 19–36.

Morris, Charles E., III, and Dale Herbeck. "Lincoln–Douglas: An Educational Exercise." *National Forensic Journal* 14(2) (Fall 1996): 1–17.

Pollard, Tom, and Diana Prentice, eds. *Lincoln–Douglas Debate: Theory and Practice.* Lawrence: University of Kansas Press, 1981.

Williams, David E. "Educational Criteria in Forensics: An Argument for Lincoln–Douglas Debate." *National Forensic Journal* 14(1) (Spring 1996): 60–70.

XXV. Parliamentary Debate

See the new annual *Parliamentary Debate* and articles on parliamentary debate by Robert Trapp and Steve Johnson.

Bailey, R. J. "Adding Communication to Debate: A Look at Parliamentary Debate as a Complement to Cross-Examination Debate in Intercollegiate Debate." *Parliamentary Debate* 1 (1992): 25–37.

Bingle, Donald. "Parliamentary Debate Is More Serious Than You Think: Forensics at the University of Chicago." *Speaker and Gavel* 15(2) (Winter 1978): 36–42.

———. "What About Research?: How to Be Well Read." *Parliamentary Debate* 4 (1996): 3–13.

Johnson, Tom. "Full of Sound and Fury? The Role of Speech in Parliamentary Debate." *Speaker and Gavel* 1(3) (Mar. 1964): 88–92.

O'Neill, Daniel. "Recollections of University Parliamentary Debater: Irish Style." *The Forensic* 71(3) (Spring 1986): 66–69.

Sheckels, Theodore, Jr., and Annette Warfield. "Parliamentary Debate: A Description and a Justification." *Argumentation and Advocacy* 27 (Fall 1990): 86–96.

Trapp, Robert. "Parliamentary Debate as Public Debate." *Argumentation and Advocacy* 32(2) (Fall 1996): 85.

Williams, David E., J. Brent Hagy, and Ali McLane-Hagy. "Introducing Parliamentary Debate in the Argumentation and Debate Course." *The Forensic* 82(1) (Fall 1996): 16–21.

XXVI. Research in Forensics

The following studies represent only a small sample of research in forensics. For more information, see M.A. theses and Ph.D. dissertations, ERIC, papers from NCA and regional speech communication conventions, and so on. Names in forensics associated with quantitative research are fairly few in number but would include Mike Allen, Kenneth Andersen, Kent Colbert, Paul Dovre, Don Faules, Kim Giffin, C. T. Hanson, Bill Hill, Ed Hinck, Brenda Logue, Mike Mayer, John Reinard, and Wayne Thompson.

Anderson, Kenneth. "A Critical Review of the Behavioral Research in Argumentation and Forensics" *JAFA* 10 (Winter 1974): 147–155.

Bennett, William B. *The How To's of Library Research.* Taos, NM: Championship Debate Enterprises.

Colbert, Kent. "The Effects of Debate Participation on Argumentativeness and Verbal Aggression." *Communication Education* 42(3) (July 1993): 206–214.

———. "The Effects of CEDA and NTA Debate Training on Critical Thinking Ability." *JAFA* 12 (Spring 1987): 194–201.

———. "Enhancing Critical Thinking Ability Through Academic Debate." *Contemporary Argumentation and Debate: The Journal of the Cross Examination Debate Association* 16 (1995): 52–72.

———. "A Quantitative Analysis of CEDA Speaking Rates." *National Forensic Journal* 6 (Fall 1988): 113–120.

———. "Replicating the Effects of Debate Participation on Argumentativeness and Verbal Aggression." *The Forensic* 79(3) (Spring 1994): 1–13.

———. "Speaking Rates of N.D.T. Finalists from 1968–1980." *JAFA* 18 (Summer 1981): 73–76.

Douglas, Donald G. "A Need for Review: Forensic Studies in Contemporary Speech Education." *JAFA* 8 (Spring 1972): 178–181.

————. "The Status of Historical Research in Argumentation." *JAFA* 10 (Winter 1974): 156–174.

Dovre, Paul, and John Wenburg. "Experimental Research in Forensics: New Resources." *JAFA* 8 (Summer 1971): 47–51.

————. "Historical-Critical Research in Debate." *JAFA* 2 (May 1965): 72–79.

————. "Measuring Refutation Skills: An Exploratory Study." *JAFA* 4 (Spring 1967): 47–52.

"Forensics as a Laboratory in Communication Studies." *National Forensic Journal* 10 (special issue) (Spring 1992): 49–82.

"Forensics Research." *National Forensic Journal* 8 (Spring 1990): 1–103. Probably the best recent whole journal dedicated to forensic research.

Giffin, Kim, and D. A. Warner. "A Study of the Influence of an Audience on the Rate of Speech in Tournament Debates." *The Speaker* (1962).

Gruner, Charles, Richard Huseman, and James L. Luck. "Debating Ability, Critical Thinking Ability, and Authoritarianism." *Speaker and Gavel* 8(3) (Mar. 1971): 63–65.

Harris, Edward, Richard Kropp, and Robert Rosenthal. "The Tournament as Laboratory: Implications for Forensic Research." *National Forensic Journal* (Spring 1986): 13–22.

Hunt, Steven B., and Edward S. Inch. "The Top Fifty Forensics Programs in the U.S.: A Twenty Year Retrospective." Paper presented at the Annual Meeting of the Western States Communication Association, Albuquerque, NM, Feb. 12–16, 1993. This study also listed on and available from ERIC.

Huseman, Richard, Glenn Ware, and Charles Gruner. "Critical Thinking, Reflective Thinking, and the Ability to Organize Ideas: A Multivariate Approach." *JAFA* 9 (Summer 1972): 261–265.

Jensen, Scott. "A Survey Analysis of Regional and National Programs and Competitive Trends in Collegiate Forensics." *The Forensic* 78(4) (Summer 1993): 1–10.

Klumpp, James F. "Wading into the Stream of Forensics Research: The View from the Editorial Office." *National Forensic Journal* 8 (Spring 1990): 77–86.

Logue, Brenda, and B. Christine Shea. "An Examination and Criticism of Forensic Research: The Last Five Years, 1984–1988." In *Spheres of Argument: Proceedings of the 6th SCA/AFA Conference on Argumentation,* ed. Bruce Gronbeck. Annandale, VA: SCA, 1989. Pp. 449–456.

Mayer, Mike, and Vince Meldrum. "The Effects of Various Time Limits on the Quality of Rebuttals." *JAFA* 23 (Winter 1987): 158–165.

McBath, James, Michael Bartanen, and John Gossett. "Research in Forensics." *ACA Bulletin* (Apr. 1979): 5–9.

McGlone, Edward L. "The Behavioral Effects of Forensics Participation." *JAFA* (Winter 1974): 140–146.

McKerrow, Raymie E. "Evaluating Research in Forensics: Considerations of the Tenure and Promotion Process." *National Forensic Journal* 8 (Spring 1990): 73–76.

Pitt, Carl Allen. "Upgrading the Debater's Research Methods." *Speaker and Gavel* 7(2) (Jan. 1970): 44–46.

Porter, Sharon. "Forensics Research: A Call for Action." *National Forensic Journal* 8 (Spring 1990): 95–103.

Semlack, William D., and Donald C. Shields. "The Effect of Debate Training on Students Participating in the Bicentennial Youth Debates." *JAFA* 13 (Spring 1977): 192–196.

Stepp, Pamela, and Ralph B. Thompson. "A Survey of Forensics Activity at Selected Colleges and Universities in the United States, 1987." *National Forensic Journal* 6 (Fall 1988): 121–136.

Walwik, Theodore J. "Research in Forensics: An Overview." *JAFA* 6 (Spring 1969): 43–48.

XXVII. Women and Minorities in Forensics

Bartanen, Kristine. "Developing Student Voices in Academic Debate Through a Feminist Perspective of Learning, Knowing, and Arguing." *Contemporary Argumentation and Debate* 16 (1995): 1–13.

Bruschke, Jon, and Ann Johnson. "An Analysis of Differences in Success Rates of Male and Female Debaters." *Argumentation and Advocacy* 30(3) (Winter 1994): 162–173.

Crenshaw, Carrie. "Dominant Form and Marginalized Voices: Argumentation about Feminism(s). *CEDA Yearbook* 14 (1993): 72–79.

Friedley, Sheryl, and Bruce Manchester. "An Analysis of Male/Female Participation at Select National Championships." *National Forensic Journal* 3 (1985): 3–12.

———. "An Examination of Male/Female Judging Decision in Individual Events." *National Forensic Journal* 5 (Spring 1987): 11–20.

Hayes, Michael T., and Joe McAdoo. "Debate Performance: Differences Between Male and Female Rankings." *JAFA* 8 (Winter 1972): 127–131.

Johnson, Ann, and Jon Bruschke. "A Research Agenda for the Study of Women in Debate: A Framework and Preliminary Analysis." In *Argument and the Postmodern Challenge: Proceedings of the 8th SCA/AFA Conference on Argumentation,* ed. Raymie McKerrow. Annandale, VA: SCA, 1993. Pp. 55–60.

Loge, Peter. "Black Participation in CEDA Debate: A Quantification and Analysis." *CEDA Yearbook* 12 (1991): 79–87.

Logue, Brenda. "CEDA Male/Female Participation Levels: A Research Report." *CEDA Yearbook* 7 (1986): 64–75.

Murphy, John M. "Separate and Unequal: Women in the Public Address Events." *National Forensic Journal* 7 (Fall 1989): 115–125.

Nadler, Marjorie Keeshan. "The Gender Factor in Selecting Extra-Curricular Activities." *National Forensic Journal* 3 (Spring 1985): 29–36.

Pettus, Ann Burnett, and Mary Ann Daniels. "Coaching Intercollegiate Debate and Raising a Family: An Analysis of Perspective from Women in the Trenches." *National Forensic Journal* 11 (Winter 1994): 47–53.

Rogers, Jack. "Interrogating the Myth of Multiculturalism: Toward Significant Membership and Participation of African Americans in Forensics." *The Forensic* 80(4) (Summer 1995): 21–30.

Simerly, Greg, Ro Bites, and L. Scott. "Strategies to Achieve Cultural Diversity in Intercollegiate Debate." *Speech and Theatre Association of Missouri Journal* 22 (1992): 28–34.

Stepp, Pam, Greg Simerly, and Brenda Logue. "Sexual Harassment in CEDA Debate." *Argumentation and Advocacy* 31 (1994): 36–40.

Szwapa, C. "Sexual Harassment and Gender Discrimination in NDT Debate." *Argumentation and Advocacy* 31 (1994): 41–44.

XXVIII. Evidence and Ethics in Forensics

Bart, John. "Is There an Exit from the Information Superhighway?: The Dangers of Electronic Research." *Forensic Educator* 9(1) (1994–95): 28–31.

Benson, James A. "The Use of Evidence in Intercollegiate Debate." *JAFA* 7 (Spring 1971): 260–270.

Church, Russell. "The AFA Code: Work Left Undone." *JAFA* 9 (Winter 1973): 378–379.

Duffy, Bernard K. "The Ethics of Argumentation in Intercollegiate Debate: A Conservative Appraisal." *National Forensic Journal* 1 (Spring 1983): 65–71.

Kellerman, Kathy. "The Concept of Evidence: A Critical Review." *JAFA* 16 (Winter 1980): 159–172.

Klopf, Donald, and James McCroskey. "Ethical Practices in Debate." *JAFA* 1 (Jan. 1964): 13–16.

Newman, Robert P., and Keith R. Sanders. "A Study in the Integrity of Evidence." *JAFA* 2 (Jan. 1965): 7–13.

———, and Dale R. Newman. *Evidence*. New York: Houghton Mifflin, 1969.

Reinard, John C. "The Empirical Study of the Persuasive Effects of Evidence: The Status After Fifty Years of Research." *Human Communication Research* 15(1) (Fall 1988): 3–59.

Rieke, Richard, and David H. Smith. "The Dilemma of Ethics and Advocacy in the Use of Evidence." *Western Journal of Speech Communication* 32 (Fall 1968): 223–233.

Sanders, Keith R. "Toward a Solution to the Misuse of Evidence." *JAFA* 3 (Jan. 1966): 6–10.

Snyder, Alfred C. "Ethics in Academic Debate: A Gaming Perspective." In *Advanced Debate: Readings in Theory, Practice, and Teachings,* ed. David A. Thomas and Jack P. Hart. Skokie, IL: National Textbook, 1992. Pp. 15–29.

Spiker, Barry K., Tom D. Daniels, and Lawrence M. Bernabo. "The Quantitive Quandry in Forensics: The Use and Abuse of Statistical Evidence." *JAFA* 19 (Fall 1982): 87–96.

XXIX. Some Contemporary Debate Issues

Bruschke, Jon. "Debate Factions and Affirmative Actions." *Contemporary Argumentation & Debate* 25 (2004): 78–88.

English, Eric, Stephen Llano, Gordon R. Mitchell, Catherine E. Morrison, John Rief, and Carly Woods. "Debate as a Weapon of Mass Destruction." *Communication & Critical/Cultural Studies* 4(2) (2007): 221–225.

Godden, David M., and Douglas Walton. "A Theory of Presumption for Everyday Argumentation." *Pragmatics & Cognition* 15(2) (2007): 313–346.

Louden, Allan. "Debating Dogma and Division." *Contemporary Argumentation & Debate* 25 (2004): 40–42.

McGee, Brian R., Michael Bartanen, David M. Berube, Dale A. Herbeck, John P. Katsulas, and Linda M. Collier. "Whatever Happened to 'Value Debate'?: Reflections on Non-Policy Debating in CEDA." *Contemporary Argumentation & Debate* 23 (2002): 72.

Parcher, Jeff. "Factions in Policy Debate: Some Observations." *Contemporary Argumentation & Debate* 25 (2004): 89–94.

Rogers, Jack E. "Graduate School, Professional, and Life Choices: An Outcome Assessment Confirmation Study Measuring Positive Student Outcomes Beyond Student Experiences for Participants in Competitive Intercollegiate Forensics." *Contemporary Argumentation & Debate* 26 (2005): 13–40.

———. "Longitudinal Outcome Assessment for Forensics: Does Participation in Intercollegiate, Competitive Forensics Contribute to Measurable Differences in Positive Student Outcomes?" *Contemporary Argumentation & Debate* 23 (2002): 1.

Shuster, Kate. "Games, Which From a Long Ways Off Looks Like Flies." *Contemporary Argumentation & Debate* 25 (2004): 95–100.

Solt, Roger E. "Debate's Culture of Narcissism." *Contemporary Argumentation & Debate* 25 (2004): 43–65.

Warner, Ede, and Jon Bruschke. "'Gone on Debating:' Competitive Academic Debate as a Tool of Empowerment." *Contemporary Argumentation & Debate* 22 (2001): 1.

Zompetti, Joseph P. "Personalizing Debating: Diversity and Tolerance in the Debate Community." *Contemporary Argumentation & Debate* 25 (2004): 26–39.

Appendix F

Glossary of Terms in Argumentation and Debate

Academic debate: Debate conducted under the direction of an educational institution for the purpose of providing educational opportunities for its students. The same as *educational debate*.

ADA: American Debate Association.

Add-on: When an affirmative speaker presents additional advantages after the initial presentation of a case.

Advantages: The benefits or gains that the affirmative claims will result from adopting its plan, which must be shown to outweigh the disadvantages.

Advocate: One who supports a position; to support a position.

AFA: American Forensic Association.

Affirmative: The side in a debate that argues for the resolution.

Ambiguity: Arises when the meaning of the word, phrase, or passage may reasonably be interpreted in two or more ways.

Analogy, figurative: A process of reasoning in which cases in different classifications are compared and inferred to be alike—for example, used car dealers are like sharks.

Analogy, literal: A process of reasoning in which cases in the same classification are compared and inferred to be alike—for example, New York is like Chicago.

Analogy, reasoning by: The process of making a comparison between two similar cases and inferring that what is true in one case is true in the other.

APDA: American Parliamentary Debate Association.

Applied debate: Debate presented before a judge or audience with the power to render a binding decision on the proposition. (Compare with *academic debate*.)

Arguing in a circle: Occurs when one assumes as a premise for the argument the very conclusion one intends to prove.

Argument, an: A potentially controversial statement, offering good reasons to believe it. Consists of a claim, supported by data and warrant.

Argumentation: Reason giving in communicative situations by people whose purpose is the justification of acts, beliefs, attitudes, and values.

Assertion: A claim offered without supporting evidence or reasoning.

Attitudinal inherency: A widely held belief, bias, or attitude that prevents the problem identified by the affirmative from being solved within the status quo.

Audience debate: A debate presented before and adapted to an audience. Usually the audience is not empowered to render a binding decision on the resolution.

Backing: Additional evidence and reasoning advanced to support a warrant.

Benefits: See *Advantages*.

Block: A prepared group of arguments designed to support or refute a single point. May also refer to the negative block: the second negative constructive speech and the first negative rebuttal speech.

Blurb: A one- or two-word argument, generally incoherent or incomplete, that lacks supporting evidence or analysis.

Brainstorming: A method of shared problem solving in which all members of a group spontaneously contribute ideas. Individuals may use brainstorming by rapidly generating a variety of possible solutions.

Brief: Used interchangeably with *block*. A prepared argumentative position or set of answers to an anticipated argument.

Burden of proof, a: The obligation to prove what one asserts. Applies to both the affirmative and the negative, as any advocate forwarding a claim must provide support sufficient to overcome the natural presumption against that claim.

Burden of proof, the: The risk of the proposition; the obligation of the affirmative, in order to overcome presumption, to give good and sufficient reasons for affirming a resolution.

Burden of rebuttal: The obligation of the negative to refute at least one of the issues of the affirmative. Otherwise the affirmative will prevail.

Burden of refutation: The obligation to refute, or respond to, opposing arguments. Applies to both the affirmative and the negative. Failure to fulfill the burden of refutation results in the acceptance of the unrefuted argument. May also be called the *burden of rejoinder*.

Burden of the negative: The burden of rebuttal that the negative has to try to shift to the affirmative.

Card: A piece of evidence or evidence card. From the historical practice of debaters recording evidence on index cards.

Case: The operational strategy drafted by the advocates on one side of a proposition for the purpose of coordinating their reasoning and evidence and presenting their position with maximum effectiveness.

Case turn: A negative turnaround argument, directed at the affirmative case claims.

Casual evidence: That which is created without an effort being made to create it and is not designed for possible future reference.

Categorical syllogism: A syllogism in which the major premise is an unqualified proposition. Such propositions are characterized by words like *all, every, each*, and *any*, either directly expressed or clearly implied.

Causal reasoning: The process whereby one infers that a certain factor (a cause) is a force that produces something else (an effect).

CEDA: Cross Examination Debate Association.

Circumvention argument: The negative argument that the affirmative's plan won't work because many have the incentive and ability to check, evade, or otherwise defeat that plan—for example, gas rationing won't work because a widespread black market will develop.

Claim: The conclusion we seek to establish by our arguments; the concise statement of the point we are making.

Clash: The obligation to respond to arguments that might harm one's position. (See *Burden of refutation.*)

Coercion: The threat or use of force.

Comparative advantages case: Situation in which the affirmative accepts the goals of the status quo and argues that its plan is a better way of attaining these goals and will produce greater advantages than the status quo.

Competitive: Usually refers to the negative counterplan and requires that accepting the counterplan be a reason to reject the affirmative plan, either because it is mutually exclusive or because there is a net benefit to the counterplan over the plan. May also refer to any argumentative position, including the kritic (critique).

Conclusive proof: Evidence that is incontrovertible, either because the law will not permit it to be contradicted or because it is strong and convincing enough to override all evidence to the contrary and to establish the proposition beyond reasonable doubt.

Conditional counterplan: Argument by the negative that it may abandon advocacy of the counterplan if certain conditions prevail.

Conditional syllogism: A syllogism in which the major premise deals with uncertain or hypothetical events. Usually identified by *if, assuming, supposing,* or similar terms, either expressly stated or clearly implied. Also known as the *hypothetical syllogism.*

Constructive speech: The first and longer of the two speeches presented by a debater, in which new evidence and new arguments for or against the proposition are presented. (See *Rebuttal speech.*)

Contention: Statement offered in support of an issue.

Corroborative proof: Strengthening or confirming evidence of a different character in support of the same fact or proposition.

Cost–benefit analysis: Comparing the advantages and disadvantages of a proposal and drawing a conclusion in favor of a position.

Counterintuitive rejection of evidence: Evidence the audience rejects in the first instance because they "know" it's wrong—for example, that employment causes harms.

Counterplan: A plan presented by the negative that is competitive with the affirmative's plan and is a superior policy alternative.

Counter value: A value claimed by the negative to be of greater importance than the principal value claimed by the affirmative.

Criteria: The standards on the basis of which a decision is made. A major issue in value debate; sometimes used in policy debate.

Critical thinking: The ability to analyze, criticize, and advocate ideas; to reason inductively and deductively; and to reach factual or judgmental conclusions based on sound inferences drawn from unambiguous statements of knowledge or belief.

Critique (kritic): A type of argument, usually initiated by the negative, which brings into question the language or behavior used in a debate or challenges the fundamental principles or premises upon which the affirmative case or proposition is built. Similar to a disadvantage argument.

Cross apply: A request by the debater to the judge to apply previously stated evidence or argument to another point.

Cross-examination: The three-minute period, in a debate using the standard cross-examination format, following each constructive speech, during which opponents may question the constructive speaker.

Data: The grounds for an argument. In academic debate, usually in the form of evidence.

Debate: The process of inquiry and advocacy; the seeking of a reasoned judgment on a proposition.

Decision rule: A criteria or measure to aide in impact comparisons.

Definition, satisfactory: One that meets the expectations of those who render the decision.

Definition of terms: The advocate's supported interpretation of the meaning of the words in a proposition.

Degree of cogency: The extent to which an argument is both sound and intellectually compelling because it is well founded in fact, logic, or rationality.

Direct evidence: That which tends to show the existence of a fact in question without the intervention of the proof of any other fact.

Disadvantages: The undesirable consequences that the negative claims will flow from the affirmative's plan. These must be shown to outweigh the advantages.

Disjunctive syllogism: A syllogism in which the major premise contains mutually exclusive alternatives. Usually indicated by such words as *either, or, neither, not, but,* and *although,* either expressly stated or clearly implied.

Educational debate: Used interchangeably with *academic debate.*

Enthymeme: (1) A *truncated* syllogism, in which one of the premises or the conclusion is not stated. (2) A syllogism based on probabilities, signs, and examples, whose function is rhetorical persuasion. Its successful construction is accomplished through the joint efforts of speaker and audience.

Ethical: Being in accordance with the accepted principles of right and wrong that govern the conduct of a profession.

Evidence: Consists of facts, opinions, and objects used to generate proof.

Evidence aliunde: Evidence that explains or clarifies other evidence.

Evidence brief: A prepared argument, or set of arguments, complete with evidence.

Example, reasoning by: The process of inferring conclusions from specific cases.

Existential inherency: The argument that because a problem exists it must be inherent in the status quo.

Extemporaneous speech: A prepared speech in which the speaker may or may not use notes.

Extension: The development of an argument presented in an earlier speech.

Extrajudicial evidence: Evidence that is not admissible in court; such evidence may be used outside the court.

Extratopicality: An advantage that is the result of a nontopical portion of the affirmative plan.

Fallacy: Any unsound mode of arguing, which appears to demand our conviction, and to be decisive of the question at hand, when in fairness it is not.

Fiat: The convention in academic policy debate that, for the sake of argument, participants may assume implementation of a reasonable policy. This allows debaters to focus on the question of whether a policy *should* be adopted and to avoid as irrelevant questions about whether the policy *would* be adopted.

Forensics: Rhetorical scholarship that takes various forms, including debate, public address, and the interpretation of literature. Usually organized as a competitive student activity.

Flow sheet: An outline of a debate, with the arguments presented in each speech recorded in vertical columns and arranged so that a person can follow horizontally the flow of each argument as it evolves progressively through all the speeches in a debate.

Generic disadvantages: Disadvantages that may be applied to a number of possible affirmative plans.

Goals: In a value debate the values expressed in the resolution or argued by the debaters. In a comparative advantages case the affirmative argues that it can reach the agreed-on objectives of the status quo in a better way than the status quo can.

Good reasons: Reasons that are psychologically compelling for a given audience, that make further inquiry both unnecessary and redundant—hence justifying a decision to affirm or to reject a proposition.

Grounds: Evidence and reasoning advanced to establish the foundation of a claim. Also called *data*.

Harm: The evil, or important problem, that the affirmative claims exists in the status quo and requires remedy. One of the stock issues in policy debate.

Headlining: The use of concise, precisely chosen words or short sentences to identify key points in the debater's speech. In academic debate the speakers often use numbers and letters to make their organization clear. Also called *tag lining*.

Hypothesis–testing judge: A judge who focuses on testing the affirmative case and requires that the affirmative overcome any negative attack to win the decision.

Hypothetical syllogism: See *Conditional syllogism*.

Impact: The importance or relevance of an argument in a debate. (See also *Significance*.)

Impromptu method: A speech delivered without specific preparation.

Indispensable proof: Evidence without which a particular issue cannot be proved.

Inherency: The probability of future harm. The affirmative must prove that the significant harm it identifies is built into the essential nature of the status quo through legal structures and/or societal attitudes.

Intuitive acceptance of evidence: Evidence the audience accepts in the first instance because they "know" it's right—for example, that unemployment causes harms.

Issues: Critical claims inherent in the proposition.

Issues judge: A judge who focuses on the stock issues and requires the affirmative to win all the stock issues to win the decision.

Judicial debate: Debate conducted in the courts or before quasi-judicial bodies.

Judicial evidence: Evidence that is admissible in court.

Judicial notice: Evidence introduced into an argument without the necessity of substantiation; it is assumed to be so well known that it does not require substantiation.

Justification: Arguments to establish the reason for changing the status quo.

Kritic: See *Critique*.

Link: An essential component of a disadvantage argument. The causal connection between the plan of action and the undesirable impact claimed.

Loaded language: Use of emotionally charged words in an effort to establish a conclusion without proof.

Mock trial debate: A form of academic debate that emulates trial court debating.

Modal qualification: The degree of cogency we attach to our claim.

Moot court debate: An academic form of judicial debate used by law schools to prepare students for courtroom debate.

Mutually exclusive: Means the negative's counterplan and the affirmative's plan cannot be adopted simultaneously. One measure of competitiveness.

NDT: National Debate Tournament.

NEDA: National Educational Debate Association.

Need: Refers to the evil or important problem existing in the status quo and requiring remedy. Used interchangeably with *harm*.

Negative: The side in a debate that argues against the resolution.

Negative evidence: The absence of evidence that might reasonably be expected to be found were the issue in question true.

Net benefit: The negative claim that, when the advantages and disadvantages of the plan and counterplan are weighed, there is a net benefit in favor of its counterplan. The formula is $CP > CP + P$ (adoption of the counterplan alone is superior to adoption of the counterplan plus the plan).

Nonformal debate: Debate that occurs in various contexts without formal or prearranged procedural rules.

Non sequitur: A conclusion that does not follow from the premises or evidence on which it is based.

Nonverbal communication: Vocal expression and body language that convey meaning to another person.

NPDA: National Parliamentary Debate Association.

Off-case: Negative arguments that, while not directly responding to the affirmative's case point by point, are offered as significant reasons for rejecting the case or plan—for example, countervalues, kritics, value objections, disadvantages, topicality and counterplans. They are organized and first presented by the negative.

On-case: Arguments that directly respond to the affirmative's case, on point, using the affirmative's organization.

Operational definition: A critical word or phrase (usually from the proposition) that is defined by its usage in the debate. In policy debate the affirmative's plan may be its definition of critical terms in the proposition.

Overview: A general argument offered at the beginning of a speech.

Parliamentary debate, academic: A form of competitive impromptu, off-topic tournament debate focusing on logic, reasoning, and presentation rather than evidence and technical debate strategy or jargon.

Parliamentary debate, applied: Debate conducted under the rules of parliamentary procedure.

Partial proof: Used to establish a detached fact in a series of facts tending to support the issue in dispute.

Permutation: A test of competition of a counterplan offered by the affirmative.

Permutation standards: The negative's arguments to forestall or refute an affirmative's permutations—for example, "The resolution mandates that the federal government [do something]; the affirmative cannot propose voluntary action."

Persuasion: Communication intended to influence the acts, beliefs, attitudes, and values of others.

Plan: The affirmative's method of solving the problem claimed in the justification as needs or harm. It must produce the advantages claimed by the affirmative.

Planks: The major parts of a plan: agency, mandates, enforcement, funding and staffing, addendum.

Policy implications: In value debate the negative argument that deleterious policies will result if the affirmative's value is accepted.

Policymaker judge: A judge who contrasts the affirmative's and negative's policy systems and requires that the affirmative's policy system be viable and better than the negative's policy system to win the decision.

Post hoc: Assuming a causal relationship where none has been proved.

Prearranged evidence: That which is created for the specific purpose of recording certain information for possible future reference.

Presumption: A predisposition favoring a given side in a dispute. From the judicial perspective the presumption favors the status quo. From the policy perspective the presumption favors the position that provides the greatest advantages while incurring the least disadvantages. In value debate the presumption favors the greater over the lesser value.

Presumptive evidence: Evidence that tends to show the existence of a fact by proving other, related facts.

Prima facie case: A case that in and of itself provides good and sufficient reason for adopting the proposition. It must provide effective issue statements to answer each of the stock issue questions.

Primary evidence: The best evidence that the circumstances admit; original or first-hand evidence that affords the greatest certainty of the matter in question.

Propaganda: The use of persuasion by a group (often a closely knit organization) in a sustained, organized campaign using multiple media for the purpose of influencing a mass audience.

Proposition: A statement of judgment that identifies the central issue in a debate. May be a proposition of fact, value, nonpolicy, or policy.

Pseudoargument: Fallacy created (by accident or design) by distortion, confusion, manipulation, or avoidance of the matters at issue or by substitution of matters not germane to the issue.

Public records: All documents compiled or issued by or with the approval of any governmental agency.

Public writing: A frequently used source of evidence that includes all written material, other than public records, made available to the general public.

Quasi-policy proposition: A proposition that expresses a value judgment about a policy.

Rebuttal: Argumentation meant to overcome opposing evidence and reasoning by introducing other evidence and reasoning that will destroy its effect. Also, the second speech by each advocate in an academic debate.

Rebuttal speech: The second and shorter of two speeches presented by a debater. New evidence and new argument may not be presented in such a speech. (See *Constructive speech*.)

Refutation: Argumentation meant to overcome opposing evidence and reasoning by proving that it is false or erroneous.

Resolution: See *Proposition*.

Road map: Introductory remarks in which the debater states the order in which arguments will be presented.

Secondary evidence: Evidence that by its nature suggests the availability of better evidence in the matter in question.

Should: As used in policy debate, means that intelligent self-interest, social welfare, or the national interest prompts an action that is both desirable and workable. (See also *Fiat, Would*.)

Significance: The degree of importance or impact attached to an issue. The advocate must prove that the essential elements of the case are quantitatively and/or qualitatively important. Also applies to the relative importance of an argument.

Signposting: See *Headlining*.

Sign, reasoning by: The process of inferring relationships or correlations between two variables.

Skills judge: A judge who focuses on the skills listed on the AFA ballot—analysis, reasoning, evidence, organization, refutation, and delivery—and awards the decision to the team that has done the better debating with regard to these skills.

Slippery slope argument: The argument that a seemingly harmless proposal in the affirmative's plan would be an irreversible first step leading inevitably to the most deleterious disadvantages.

Solvency: The ability of a plan to work and to reduce the harm identified by the affirmative.

Special debate: Debate conducted under special rules drafted for a specific occasion—for example, presidential debates.

Special pleading: Urging that an exception be made to an accepted line of reasoning.

Spin control: Presenting material from one's own perspective; putting a matter in the most favorable light. Should be done before the opponent plants a different spin in the minds of the decision makers.

Spread: A large number of arguments, presented independently with minimal supporting evidence or analysis. The debater using a spread hopes to overwhelm the opponent's ability to respond to each.

Squirrel: A traditional term for a very small case or a case that relies on an unusual or creative interpretation of the proposition.

Status quo: The existing state of things; the present system.

Stock issues: Those issues common to most debates on given types of propositions. In value debate they are definitive and designative; in policy debate they include harm, inherency, and solvency.

Straw argument: Setting up an issue merely so it can be knocked down.

Structural inherency: (1) A structural *barrier* that necessarily prevents something from being done, or (2) a structural *gap*, the absence of a structure necessary to permit something to be done.

Sufficient evidence: A fair preponderance of evidence.

Syllogism: A systematic arrangement of arguments consisting of a major premise, a minor premise, and a conclusion. (See also *Categorical syllogism, Conditional syllogism,* and *Disjunctive syllogism.*)

Tabula rasa judge: The judge who takes no position and allows and expects the debaters to decide the theoretical framework for the decision. If no judging philosophy emerges in the debate, the judge may choose whatever judging philosophy seems most appropriate as a basis for the decision.

Time suck: An argument presented in anticipation that it will take longer for the opposing team to respond than for the presenting team to initially offer the argument. Such arguments are often dropped later in the debate, suggesting that the initiating team never seriously intended to develop them.

Topical counterplan: A counterplan that might be used as an affirmative plan under some definitions of the resolution but is nontopical with regard to the operational definition the affirmative has chosen to use. Once the affirmative has operationally defined the resolution, almost any mutually exclusive plan may constitute grounds for a counterplan.

Topicality: The state of conformity to the intent of the debate resolution. A plan is topical if it justifies the full intent of the resolution, the needs are solved, or the comparative advantages are gained as a direct result of the planks in the plan that implement the resolution.

Topicality attack: An issue advanced by the negative that argues that the affirmative's case does not stem directly from the proposition being debated; it falls short of the resolution, or, conversely, goes beyond it. Referred to as "T."

Turnaround: Converting a negative's disadvantage into an affirmative advantage. In common usage any statement that one turns against the originator.

Underview: An argument presented at the end of the speech or at the conclusion of argument on a specific issue.

Uniqueness: A necessary component of a disadvantage argument; the argument that absent the affirmative plan, the disadvantage will not occur.

Utopian counterplan: A counterplan proposed by the negative that mandates that the nation or the world will be arranged in a manner consistent with anarchy, world government, socialism, authoritarianism, or some other future strategy and claims that this strategy will better solve the problem than the federal government or whatever agency of change is provided in the proposition.

Value applications: In value debate the negative argument that the values or quasi-policies advocated by the affirmative will not be applied to the problem.

Value objections: In value debate the negative argument that undesirable consequences will flow from adoption of the affirmative's case. Similar to a disadvantage in policy debate.

Verbalism: The abundant use of words without conveying much meaning.

Voting issue: An issue claimed to be so important that by itself it justifies the judge's vote.

Warrant: Evidence and reasoning advanced to justify the move from grounds to claim.

Workability: The issue, in policy debate, in which the negative argues that the affirmative plan is not feasible or practical, that it will not work. The affirmative argues the opposite.

Would: In policy debate the argument that a certain policy would not be adopted; made irrelevant by fiat power.

Index